The
DICTIONARY
of
GENEALOGY

TERRICK V H FITZHUGH

The
DICTIONARY
of
GENEALOGY

Fourth Edition

revised by Susan Lumas
on behalf of the Society of Genealogists

A & C Black · London

Fourth edition 1994
A & C Black (Publishers) Limited,
35 Bedford Row
London WC1R 4JH

ISBN 0-7136-4000-6

First edition 1985 published by Alphabooks
Second edition 1988 published by Alphabooks
Third edition 1991 published by
A & C Black (Publishers) Limited

Typeset in 8½ on 10pt Linotron Palatino by
Rowland Phototypesetting Ltd,
Bury St Edmunds, Suffolk

Printed in Great Britain by The Bath Press, Bath

Contents

Acknowledgements

During my practice as a professional genealogist I compiled, as I went along, a collection of notes on genealogical sources and related matter, which I kept, in alphabetical order, at my elbow, where it served me as a rapid-reference aide-mémoire. The compilation, growing through fifteen' years, was amplified from time to time with information from published material. In adding these latter jottings I kept no record of their sources, as I had no thought then of publication. I am therefore unable to acknowledge their authors' help as I should like. I cannot however, forget being indebted at various times, both in my researches and note-taking, to A.J. Camp's *Wills and Their Whereabouts*, D.E. Gardner and F. Smith's *Genealogical Research in England and Wales*, G. Hamilton-Edward's *In Search of Ancestry*, P. Litton's article on 'Foundlings' in the *North Cheshire Family Historian*, I. Mordy's article on 'Jewish Genealogy' in the *A.G.R.A. Newsletter*, L.M. Munby's *Short Guides to Records*, and D.J. Steel's *National Index of Parish Registers*, and also articles and news items too numerous to trace in *The Amateur* (and *Local*) *Historian*, *Archives, Family History News and Digest* and *The Genealogists' Magazine*.

To Jeremy Gibson, who read the finished work in typescript, I am grateful for a number of suggestions. Finally, I should especially like to express my thanks to Faith and Nick Russel for inducing me to expand my private genealogical encyclopedia into its present, more readable form for the benefit, I hope, of other genealogists.

T.V.H.F.

Acknowledgements to the Fourth Edition

Ten years have elapsed since the dictionary was first produced. Although it has been ably updated by Brian Christmas in its most recent edition, new information and easier access to records has meant that family historians need to master more skills than ever before. To come new to the subject and have to cope with the wealth of terminology and sources must be daunting. In revising the text, I have sought to add entries which were lacking and to clarify entries by separating items from the text in which they were buried in order that they should stand in their own right. I have tapped the expertise and advice of many friends and colleagues and would like to thank the following in particular for their enthusiasm and willingness to give of their time: Geraldine Beech, Amanda Bevan, Paul Blake, Anne Brommel, Anthony Camp, Jane Cox, Andrea Duncan, Michael Gandy, June and Dennis Hall, Paul Harvey, Richard Harvey, David Hawgood, Geoffrey Mawlam, Brenda Merriman, Marilyn Miller Morton, Brian Oldham, Sheila Rowlands, Peter Seaman, Mark Tapping, Charles Tucker, Jill Valentine, Christopher Watts, Jan Worthington and the Computer Committee of the Society of Genealogists.

S.B.L.

Foreword

Everyone has wondered at one time or another, 'Where did my family come from? What sort of people were they? Rich or poor? Merchants or labourers? Royalists or Roundheads? Do the skeletons of gibbeted sheep-stealers or smugglers rattle in our family cupboard? Do we really have any link with the great man, or family, whose surname we share?'

For people of English descent, the tracing of bygone generations is now so much easier than it was for our fathers, because the essential sources of information have been brought together, catalogued and made freely available to the public. Before the Second World War there were only six county record offices in England, but during the late 1940s and '50s record offices were established in every county, not only for offical county archives but also for the safe-keeping of a great variety of historical documents, many of which had previously been in private hands. Most of these county offices also became diocesan registries, thus bringing together under one roof thousands of parish registers and other church records alongside the civil archives of the area. This easy availability of the genealogically useful documents, in almost all cases free of charge, provided the initial impetus for the tremendous growth in the popularity of family history research.

Soon this growth of interest itself produced an important new development making genealogy even more popular. Until the mid 1960s there was only one family history society in England — The Society of Genealogists, in London. All over the country family researchers were treading solitary trails, but as their numbers grew the situation became transformed. First in Birmingham, then gradually all over the country, enthusiasts came together to form county or neighbourhood family history societies, and what had formerly been a lonely hobby became a sociable one. At regular monthly meetings, members are now able to hear talks by knowledgeable genealogists, to discuss problems they have encountered, and to share experiences.

From the development of the county societies came yet another stage in the genealogical 'revolution' — the mass indexing of Britain's basic genealogical source material. Where, twenty years ago, there were only two partial indexes to marriages recorded in parish registers, now nearly every society has an index in progress for its own county. This invaluable research aid has been matched by the Genealogical Society of Salt Lake City, Utah, with its INTERNATIONAL GENEALOGICAL INDEX containing millions of British baptismal entries and many thousands of marriages. Copies, on microfiche, are available at many of the county record offices, public libraries and family history societies.

All these developments are both cause and effect of the now widespread enthusiasm for researching our family past. But the interest has also deepened. All over England, university extra-mural departments and local Adult Education Institutes offer evening and day courses in genealogy that enable people to advance quickly from the hesitant gropings of the beginner to the real knowledge of how to go about their researches systematically and effectively.

The exceptional wealth of Britain's historical documentary material, now so readily accessible, can lead a genealogist on to discoveries he never dreamed possible. The compilation of a family tree is fascinating, and success a matter for pride; but the names that hang on its branches can provide, for the persistent researcher, a starting point for a quest, even more exciting, into the lives lived by those people, each in their generation and historical period. It may well be possible to discover the kinds of work by which they earned their living, the exact sites of their homes, the events that moulded their careers, and so place them in their historical, geographical and social context. It is astonishing how much can be found about ordinary private people. This final stage in the unfolding of our past can be the most rewarding, and should be crowned by the writing of a narrative history to pass the results of our researches on to future generations — incidentally immortalising the author as 'the family historian'.

Part One of this book, *The Guide to Ancestry Research*, outlines the various choices open to the researcher and describes, step by step, the main sources of information and the techniques to be used in tracing the family back through time. By concentrating on the basic principles and the logic behind them, and by reserving the indispensable, but initially overwhelming, detail for the dictionary section, the Guide spares the beginner the common difficulty of not being able to see the wood for the trees. Links between the Guide and between compatible entries in the Dictionary are provided by cross-references indicated by SMALL CAPITALS.

Part Two, the Dictionary section, contains more than 1000 entries, setting out the essential information on virtually everything the researcher will need to know about genealogically useful records – where to find them and what they can reveal. Armed with this knowledge, the researcher will understand what to expect from each document and will know how to extract the maximum advantage from it. Sometimes a seemingly unimportant word can provide a pointer to a new source of information, and such clues are the very essence of family history research.

Some old documents present difficulties because they contain words and phrases that have disappeared from common use; so those most often met with are explained in the Dictionary, to enable the searcher to assess correctly what the record tells him.

The major part of the Dictionary was originally compiled by the author as an aide-mémoire for his own use during years of professional genealogical work. As such it proved its worth, and so now, greatly extended, provides a tested research tool for beginner and experienced researcher alike.

A comment worth repeating is taken from the Society of Genealogists Exhibition catalogue of 1937: 'It is of importance that individuals should be encouraged to study the history of their own families: not in the boastful and snobbish spirit which produced such a spate of false pedigrees in the nineteenth century, but on the scientific lines of modern genealogical research which demands proof of every statement and the recording of every fact, whether pleasant or unpleasant, for whatever view may be held on the merits of such research, all will agree that unless it be conducted with accuracy it is entirely futile.'

Part One

The Guide to Ancestry Research

Several choices are available to the beginner in ancestry research. Many people set out to find all their ancestors on both their father's and mother's, grandfathers' and grandmothers' sides (their Ancestry Chart). Some like to trace just their own family with its surname (their Family Tree), perhaps later spreading their interest to take in all branches of it, often including distant cousins in America, Australia and elsewhere (their Extended Family Tree). People with a fairly uncommon surname may decide to look for traces of all people of the same name, just in case they may be distantly related (one-name studies). And finally, for those who have compiled a family tree there is the fascinating quest to find out what kind of lives their forebears lived, and to write a narrative account of them (a Family History). Let us take a closer look at these aims.

Ancestry Chart

For anyone ambitious to trace his descent as far back as possible this is the choice to make, because with every newly discovered generation the number of ancestors doubles (at least, it does in theory; in practice, the same ancestors crop up in different lines), so that when the scent on one trail dries up or is temporarily difficult to follow, there are plenty of others to turn to. As there has been a good deal of intermarriage between the social classes in England it is not uncommon to be able to trace one's ancestry back to William the Conqueror himself. An example of an Ancestry Chart is given under the entry of that title in the Dictionary.

Family Tree

This shows descent in the male line through one's father, his father, and so on, and includes not only ancestors and ancestresses but also the ancestors' brothers and sisters. As the husband-cum-father was always the breadwinner, male-line research traces not only a biological line but also the social continuity of the family. There is an example of a Family Tree under the entry of that title in the Dictionary.

Extended Family Tree

Having traced a family tree, it is interesting to find other members of one's family, distant cousins descended from ancestors' brothers, and thus of the same name and blood as oneself. The short example under FAMILY TREE could be extended by tracing the descendants of John's brother Nicholas.

One-name Studies

This type of interest, in all people of the same surname, has resulted in the formation of a number of one-name societies made up of namesake members, related or unrelated, engaged in joint research into every bygone person of their surname. This often leads to the discovery that some of the researchers are indeed distant cousins.

Family History

A development from the Family Tree. Knowing the names and dates of ancestors whets the curiosity to find out more about them, the things they did, the incidents that happened to them and the local backgrounds of their homes and places of work. This calls for searches into a wider range of records than those used to prove a descent. Nowadays the term 'family history' is applied to this type of research into biographical detail to distinguish it from the tracing of descents, for which the term 'genealogy' is reserved.

There are thus five avenues facing the newcomer to ancestry research. The following pages provide an outline guide to the basic principles and sources of information applicable to all of these.

Making a Start

First, it is best to check that no one has already researched your ancestors. The majority of existing family trees and histories are known only to their compilers and their close relations, but many have been printed and catalogued. Also, a large number in print, typescript and manuscript can be found in the library of the Society of Genealogists (*see* FAMILY TREES AND HISTORIES in the Dictionary section). If that does not lead you to the discovery, possibly disappointing, that all the work (or much of it) has been done already, you can start to blaze your own trail from the very beginning.

A tree of five generations can normally be made up right away from the living members of a family — grandparents, parents and children — and from the memories of the elderly. All relevant genealogical information should be entered on the chart, using the standard signs and abbreviations illustrated on page 109 and described in the FAMILY TREE entry in the Dictionary section. Dates and places of birth, marriage and death are needed to identify each person, and in constructing the chart ample space should be left at the top for the later addition of earlier generations.

Domestic Clues Stage two is to take a very careful look around the house, paying particular attention to old desks and chests, and of course attic and box-room storage areas, for articles that may throw light on the family's past. Other members of the family should also be asked to do the same in their own homes.

At the very beginning of research into the family past, much time and expense can sometimes be saved by making sure that no clues have been overlooked that may be lying about the house. The best known of these is the FAMILY BIBLE, in which births, marriages and deaths in the family may have been recorded by a Victorian paterfamilias. Lucky is the family in which such a volume has been handed down.

Other family relics provide useful clues rather than ready-made additions to the family tree. Old letters will show, either from their headings or from their postmarks, where people lived, which will be a pointer for future research; and they probably contain interesting information about the family, otherwise they would not have been kept. Old diaries can be a mine of information about the family's life-style, as can newspaper cuttings, although unfortunately in too many cases the name of the newspaper and its date will not have been preserved. Other indications of where members of the family lived can be found in visitors' books and address books. Certificates of qualification tend to be among the documents preserved after the death of a professional man.

Dates of birth and marriage are among the most important items of information to be discovered for every member of the family. Birthday Books, once a popular means of remembering people's anniversaries, usually show the day and month, but not the year of birth; but in a search of the indexes of the General Register of Births a birthday date can be useful in picking out the right person from a number of namesakes born in, or about, the same year.

Books received as prizes will have inscriptions showing the boy's or girl's school or college, the subject of study and the date. This can lead the researcher to school attendance records or printed registers, or, failing any of these, enable him to write to the present Head Teacher for further information about the former pupil, which may well include his parentage. Inscriptions in books given as Christmas or birthday presents may reveal unknown uncles and aunts, but it must be remembered that 'uncle' and 'auntie' are terms often loosely used. A bookplate often shows only a name, but if it is heraldic the clue of the arms can be followed up (*see* ARMS, COAT OF).

Cap badges and metal buttons bearing insignia are clues to members of the family in the army or navy, or other uniformed services. Service medals, often for individual campaigns and bearing clasps for battles, are helpful for narrowing down the field within which a man's regiment and battalion may be identified (*see* MEDALS). Decorations for bravery or distinguished service are also useful for this purpose, and some provide an indication of whether or not the recipient held commissioned rank. An old uniform would, of course, show the exact rank its owner held, probably at the end of his service career.

Among the family records most likely to be treasured and passed down are photographic portraits. Too often these bear no name and so in a generation or two become difficult to identify, but comparing several photographs can be a help. Nineteenth-century photographs will usually have been taken by a professional whose name and address will appear either below the picture or on the back. Reference to old local directories to find the period during which the practitioner was in business at that address may enable the photograph to be dated approximately (*see* DIRECTORIES, LOCAL). The photographer's address may also give some indication of the district in which the sitter lived, but photographers at holiday resorts tended to draw their customers from a wide catchment area. The clothes of the sitter are another clue. The *Handbook of English Costume in the 19th Century* by C.W. and P. Cunnington, lavishly illustrated, shows how the fashions changed from year to year for both men and women. The apparent age of the sitter acts as another check on the dates deduced from other evidence. See *An Introduction to Planning Research: Short Cuts in Family History*, by Michael Gandy FFHS (1993) and *Dating Old Photographs*, by Robert Pols FFHS (1992).

Memories The final stage before embarking on documentary research is the questioning of all elderly members of the family about their own parents and grandparents, uncles and aunts, and others among whom they grew up. This stage, described under ORAL FAMILY HISTORY can be enormously rewarding. Each person interviewed will add something to the record, no matter how good or bad the memory, or how willing or reticent he or she may be — and reticence itself is a clue not to be overlooked.

Basic Facts

It is a good idea to write yourself a checklist of facts you would like to discover about each ancestor.

Name	Forename(s)
When and Where of Birth	
Baptism	
Marriage	
Death	
Burial	

Monumental Inscription	Religion(s)	
Occupation(s)	Education	Apprenticeship
Abode(s)	Settlement	
Father	Mother (with maiden name)	Siblings (with year of birth)
Spouse(s)	Children	

Documents consulted where available (record their precise references)
Registration of Birth Marriage and Death
Census (six years)   Parish or Non-conformist registers
Marriage Bonds, Allegations or Licences
Will or Administration

Compiling the Record

All the information from these interviews, as well as that to be obtained later from records, must be meticulously transcribed for eventual use in compiling an ancestry chart or writing a history, and also as evidence for their accuracy. The proper method of doing this is described under TRANSCRIPT.

If the aim is eventually to write a narrative history, all family mentions found in records should be transcribed in generous extracts. For instance, an old local directory that supplies the address of an ancestor will also provide the names of his neighbours, and these should be noted because they may well crop up again in other connections, such as witnessing a wedding or a will. The odd names occurring around those of our ancestors are all part of the family background.

When the searching of historical records gets under way, the researcher will soon find a quantity of transcripts building up, so that orderly RECORD KEEPING becomes important. There are many systems of record keeping from index cards through notebooks and printed forms to computer programs. Everyone has their favourite method. What is important is that it is systematic and clear from the start. Every time you look at a published source or a document you need to record where you saw it and what it was. If a published work was consulted, state the title, author, publisher and edition, and the page on which you found the information. If a document was transcribed, cite its reference and where you consulted it. Keep a note even of those documents consulted, and why, that yielded no useful information. Then you will not repeat the fruitless search again when you have forgotten exactly what it was you looked at.

Beginning the Documentary Research

For the last four hundred years, nearly everyone living in England has left behind some trace of his or her existence. By law, certain records have been written down and preserved; for example, the entries of people's birth, baptism, marriage, death and burial, their tax assessments, the leases and title deeds of their houses, the census forms they filled out, and so on.

These records are the raw material of genealogical research, and the art and science lie in knowing what records to look for, where to find them, and — once found — how to understand them. This essential knowledge falls under four main headings, the four 'knowhows', of genealogy: Linkage Records, Location Records, The Records' Whereabouts, and Understanding the Records.

Linkage Records

To compile a family tree we need to know our ancestors' names and certain dates and places connected with them, and there is one more essential piece of information — clear proof of their relationship within the family. Just finding a person of the right name, in the right place, at the right time, is not enough. Their relationship to an already known member of the family has to be proved. What is needed, therefore, is a document bearing the names of two or more members of the family, at least one of which is already known, and which states the link between them. An example of such a Linkage Record might be a grandfather's birth certificate. It shows the names of three people: our grandfather (who is already known to us), plus two more, shown by the document to be his father and mother.

Linkage records and their whereabouts

Birth, Marriage & Death Certificates	*General Register Office*
Census Returns	*Public Record Office* *County record offices*
Parish Registers	*County record offices* *Parish churches*
Bishops' Transcripts	*County record offices or Diocesan* *Registry, if separate*
Non-parochial Registers	*Public Record Office (mostly)*
Memorial Inscriptions	*Burial grounds and churches* *Copies at family history societies*
Marriage Licence Records	*County record offices* *Lambeth Palace Library* *Borthwick Institute, York*
Wills and other probate records	*County record offices* *Public Record Office* *Somerset House, London*

Apprentice Bindings	*Public Record Office*
	Guildhall Library, London
	Some London guilds
	County and borough record offices
	Society of Genealogists
Manor Court Rolls	*County record offices*
	Public Record Office
	Lawyers' offices
	Family Estate Muniments
	University Colleges' Archives

Location Records

When tracing a descent back as far as the year 1837, we are fortunate in having one GENERAL REGISTER OF BIRTHS, DEATHS AND MARRIAGES for the whole of England and Wales, so in whatever town or village the family was living their essential records will be found at the GENERAL REGISTER OFFICE. However, once 1 July 1837, is passed on our backward journey through time, there is no longer one single source of information. Before that date the only comparable records were the local parish registers of baptism, marriage and burial, maintained by parish clergy and now to be found mostly in county record offices.

It follows, therefore, that before the right records can be consulted, the parish in which the family was then living must be identified. To do this without the wearying work of searching through one parish register after another, advantage can be taken of certain records that offer short cuts. These are the Location Records. They provide a thin coverage of a region — a county, an archdeaconry or a diocese — containing a large number of parishes, and thus enable a quick search to be made of the areas in which the ancestors are thought to have lived.

The eighteen types of Location Record are summarised in the list below, and, as with the Linkage Records, each is described in detail in the relevant Dictionary entry.

The importance of these Location Records must not be underestimated. Many beginners waste valuable time, and experience frustration, by searching through endless Linkage Records when they could be taking advantage of these valuable 'short cut' facilities.

Location records and their whereabouts

Census Returns	*Public Record Office*
	County record offices
	Guildhall Library, London
	Society of Genealogists
Local Directories	*County Record Offices*
	Guildhall Library, London
	Society of Genealogists
Electoral Registers	*County record offices*
	Public Record Office
County Marriage Indexes	*Family history societies*
	Society of Genealogists
	Institute of Heraldic & Genealogical Studies

International Genealogical Index	Family history societies County record offices Society of Genealogists Public Record Office Some libraries
Poll Books	County record offices Guildhall Library, London Society of Genealogists
Association Oath Rolls	Public Record Office
Juror's (Freeholders') Lists	County record offices
Marriage Licence Indexes	County record offices Lambeth Palace Library
Probate Indexes	County record offices Public Record Office Society of Genealogists
Land Tax Returns	County record offices Public Record Office
Lay Subsidies (Inc. Hearth Tax)	Public Record Office
Protestation Oath Returns	House of Lords Record Office
Collection for Distressed Protestants in Ireland	Public Record Office
Muster Rolls	County record offices Public Record Office
Society of Genealogists' Great Index	Society of Genealogists
Published Records with Indexes	Society of Genealogists County record offices Public libraries
Apprentice Bindings Index	Society of Genealogists

The Records' Whereabouts

Most linkage and Location Records are housed in record repositories, of which there are four main kinds: national, regional, local and private.

The General Register of Births, Deaths and Marriages falls into the first category: it is a national repository, as is the Public Record Office, which houses government archives and law court records, and the Principal Registry of the Family Division with its accumulation of all wills proved in England and Wales since 1858. These are all to be found in London, where the researcher may also refer to the extensive collection of genealogical record copies housed in the library of the Society of Genealogists.

The main regional repositories are the county record offices, situated usually in the county towns and often also housing the archives of the local diocesan registries.

The principal local repositories are the record offices of cities and boroughs, and some of the public libraries. Until recently the vestries of Anglican parish churches formed a large class of record repository, but now the records once housed there have largely found their way to the appropriate county record office.

The only private archives of any size are those of the great land-owning families. The researcher who finds an ancestor living or working on one of these ancient estates may well find, in the account books, rent books, surveys and maps, a useful amount of biographical material. Long-established solicitors' firms also hold a variety of old family records, and from time to time these get deposited in the local county record office. The whereabouts of the Linkage and Location Records are shown in the lists on pages 13–15.

Understanding the Records

Historical documents often say a great deal more — and occasionally a great deal less — than at first meets the eye, so some knowledge of what lies behind the wording is essential. The Dictionary aims to supply that information where necessary, but one example will illustrate the point: In the 'Age' column of the Census Returns of 1841, the figures appearing for people older than 14 are not intended to show their actual age, but only their five-year age group. For instance, the figure 15 stands for 15–19; 20 means 20–24; and so on. This does not apply in the later censuses.

Progress into the Past

All genealogical research must proceed backwards in time, working from the known to the unknown. In each period of history the law, for various purposes (but not for genealogy), has required certain official records to be kept; and today the genealogist consults these for the family evidence they contain. Given reasonable luck, he is carried along by them in his search from one generation to another. Assuming we have extracted all the oral evidence still available, let us now trace our steps further back, from period to period and from record to record.

The Victorian Era

The first year of Victoria's reign, 1837, saw the beginning of the General Register of Births, Deaths and Marriages, containing (at least in theory) a record of every one of these events in England and Wales since 1 July of that year. This Mecca for all genealogical researchers, formerly in Somerset House in central London, is now housed in the Office of Population Censuses and Surveys at St Catherine's House in nearby Aldwych.

Here the researcher studies the huge index volumes, and, having found the wanted name, applies for a copy certificate for the event: no information is issued by the office except by certificate. When the copy document is received, usually a few days later, it will be found to show not only the date and place of the event, but also information hitherto unknown: such as, the father and mother of a newly born child; the fathers of both a bride and bridegroom, and their occupations; the maiden name of a wife and mother.

The exact wording of the document should be carefully transcribed into the family records, and the document itself filed away separately. For original documents such as this, and for photocopies, it is best to keep a separate storage file for each category — the file being clearly labelled with the class of document.

The Early Nineteenth Century

Census Returns 1841–91

To see a family in its context, use must be made of the second of the linkage records as listed on page 13, the CENSUS RETURNS of 1851–1891. (The Return for 1841 is less informative.) The 1901 Census will become available in 2002.

If the family was living in a village in or near a census year, the search will usually be easy: the Returns for the whole place can be searched in a matter of minutes. But if the family was resident in a large town or city, the first requirement will be an exact address. This may be obtained from a birth certificate or death certificate, registered in a year close to census year. A certificate for a birth registered in 1862, for example, would provide a guide to a search of the 1861 Census Return. Alternatively, the family may be looked up in another Location Record — either a LOCAL DIRECTORY published in or near a census year, or an ELECTORAL REGISTER. Searches of census returns have been simplified in recent years by the publication of many surname indexes compiled by Family History Societies.

Once the census entry has been found, it will provide, among other useful information, an ancestor's age and place of birth: this will direct the search to the PARISH REGISTER in which his baptismal entry will be recorded, and from that entry the names of his parents will be discovered. Thus the Census Return will have done its job as a Location Record; and it will also have served as a Linkage Record because the Return shows all members of the family who were at home on census night, and some of these may not have been previously known.

International Genealogical Index

Another very valuable Location Record, and one which will be of particular use over the next three hundred years of the search, is the INTERNATIONAL GENEALOGICAL INDEX of English baptismal registers, compiled at Salt Lake City, Utah, by the Church of Latter-Day Saints (Mormons). This is an index of baptismal entries, plus a smaller number of marriages and burials taken from many English parish registers and all the non-conformist registers held by the Public Record Office. They are arranged in alphabetical order of surname, by county. Though its coverage of the country is far from complete, the index contains many millions of names. Copies are housed at many of the county record offices, the Public Record Office, at the Society of Genealogists, and also with many of the family history societies.

Marriage Indexes

The computerised index of baptismal entries (IGI) has its counterparts in a number of very useful marriage indexes. BOYD'S MARRIAGE INDEX, at the Society of Genealogists, gives partial coverage of sixteen counties with records going back to 1538; and PALLOT'S INDEX OF MARRIAGES, for the period 1780–1837 at the Institute of Heraldic and Genealogical Studies, Canterbury, covers mainly London and Middlesex. Individual county family history societies are now engaged in compiling indexes of their own counties, which are either published upon completion or in which searches can be made on your behalf. Their addresses may be found through the FEDERATION OF FAMILY HISTORY SOCIETIES.

Having discovered from an index the place and date of a baptism or marriage, the next step is to obtain a copy of the full original register entry, as this may contain valuable information not mentioned in the index. It will also act as a check on the accuracy of the index.

Parish Registers 1538 onward

The parish register containing a wanted entry for a baptism, marriage or burial may be found in a county record office, though a few are still housed in the local church vestry, in which case a search fee may be required. Alternatively there may be a modern copy in the library of the Society of Genealogists. In addition, there are a number of other copies elsewhere and the Society has a catalogue giving their location. (Non-members are allowed to use the library facilities of the Society on payment of a search fee.)

BISHOPS' TRANSCRIPTS provide yet another avenue. It was once the obligation of a parson to make a copy of his register at the end of each year and send it to his bishop. These valuable transcripts are now housed at the county record offices or Diocesan Registry, if separate.

Where a sought-after record is housed in some distant part of the country, it may prove economical to write to the county archivist and request a list of local professional record searchers. The fee charged, particularly for a simple search, is likely to be less than the cost of travelling to the source of the record.

Once an ancestor has been located in a baptismal register the search should immediately be extended, initially for about ten years either side of the ancestor's entry, in order to discover any brothers or sisters registered in the same parish, and then earlier still to see whether earlier generations are present. A family may have lived in the same parish for many generations. Any moves that were made were usually of twenty miles or less. The eldest son usually inherited his father's land, no matter how small the holding, while his younger brothers moved away in search of employment. The search of the baptismal register having been completed, the ancestors so far found should also be looked up in the marriage register and burial register of that same parish, so providing further material for the Family Tree, the Ancestral Chart and the Family History.

Memorial Inscriptions

Memorial inscriptions on the church walls and gravestones of an ancestral parish church should always be carefully inspected, as these often provide more information than the simple entry in the burial register. Several members of a family may be buried in the same churchyard, sometimes even in the same grave, and the inscription on the stone should be carefully examined: it may contain names not previously known. Memorial plaques may also reveal useful information about a man's former station in life, by referring, for example, to his regiment, coat of arms, or to government service in some overseas territory.

Many family history societies are engaged in transcribing these incriptions before the agencies of weathering and decay take their toll, and copies of these transcripts are usually presented to the Society of Genealogists.

Records of the Poor . . .

Even the poorest of our ancestors may not have gone unrecorded, thanks to the provisions of the Poor Laws of 1601 onward. Men and women who fell on hard times were entitled to parish relief: but from which parish?

A system of SETTLEMENT was laid down by law, and from 1697 parochial churchwardens were empowered to issue a parishioner with a Settlement Certificate acknowledging his right to their aid. Armed with this, a poor man could travel and take up residence elsewhere, and the wardens of his new parish would accept him because they had documentary evidence on which to return him, if necessary, to the parish that acknowledged responsibility for him.

More worrying for churchwardens were those who had neither Settlement in their parish, nor a certificate from any other. Such people were subjected to a verbal examination and details were recorded of their stated birth-place, apprenticeship, employment and so on, in an attempt to establish where they may last have gained Settlement — usually in order that they might be returned thither. The answers given in these Settlement Examinations were written down and many have survived, ironically providing life-stories that are often the envy of researchers whose forebears were more successful in making ends meet.

. . . and of the Prosperous

One more Location Record, and an associated Linkage Record, concerns mainly, though not entirely, the more prosperous section of the community. The former are the indexes to probate records, and the latter the records themselves. Only a minority of people made wills, but a very much larger number of people are mentioned in them, and in most cases their relationship to the testator is clearly stated.

Wills were required to be proved in ecclesiastical courts, which would also grant LETTERS OF ADMINISTRATION in cases of intestacy where the estate was considerable. Such matters were not taken out of church hands until 1858. Probate records before that date are now generally in the county record office, together with indexes. These indexes are useful Location Records, as they can be searched quickly and usually mention the testator's parish. The wills themselves are among the most useful of all Linkage Records, because they commonly mention most of the closer living adult relatives of the deceased, and sometimes also their children. Letters of Administration are less useful, because they specify only the relative appointed to administer the estate.

Non-parochial Registers and the Dissenters

The Church of England parish registers are not the only records of baptisms and burials. From the late seventeenth century onward, an increasing number of people belonged to churches of dissenting denominations, including the BAPTISTS, CONGREGATIONALISTS, METHODISTS, PRESBYTERIANS, QUAKERS, UNITARIANS and many smaller sects. Though their earliest records date from the 1600s, few survive from much earlier than 1780, but, fortunately for the modern researcher, from 1754 onward all marriages with the exception of those of QUAKERS and JEWS had to be performed in Church of England churches or chapels. It was not until 1837 that marriages by Roman Catholic and Protestant dissenting rites were made legal, providing they were registered in the civil register.

Most non-parochial registers prior to 1837 are now held at the Public Record Office and are indexed in the IGI: records of Roman Catholic marriages, baptisms and burials are less centralised, and reference should be made to the extensive Dictionary entry for details of their location (*see* ROMAN CATHOLICS).

The Hanoverian Period 1714–1837

For the greater part of this period the Linkage Records continue as for the later nineteenth century, except, of course, for the General Register and the Census Returns. Non-parochial registers, however, become few and far between. Location Records differ somewhat; electoral registers and census returns are left behind and few local directories show private residents.

Location Records

There are, however, others to take their place in indicating a family's movements from place to place. The Jurors' Lists (*see* FREEHOLDERS' LISTS) of each parish show every person owning a freehold of 40 shillings per year or more, and these will be found in the county record offices. There are also the POLL BOOKS, printed lists showing how people voted in county parliamentary elections before the introduction of the secret ballot, and the LAND TAX records, mainly from 1780 onward, housed in the county record offices. And we have, too, for this period the thousands of names in the Great (card) Index of the Society of Genealogists, compiled from many different kinds of records.

Records of Apprentices

From the year 1710, whenever a boy was apprenticed to a trade a stamp duty had to be paid, and these records of the binding of APPRENTICES survive to provide the name of the apprentice, that of his father or widowed mother, and his master, as well as his parents' abode. Apprentice Records serve, therefore, as both Linkage and Location Records, and are held at the Public Record Office, where they form a part of the Inland Revenue archives; at the Society of Genealogists; and, for the London LIVERY COMPANIES, at the Guildhall Library, London.

In addition to the trade apprentices there were also Poor Apprentices, whose destiny, in the main, was governed by the *Poor Law Act*. Churchwardens and Overseers of the Poor were empowered to apprentice to husbandry any child under the age of 16 whose parents they judged unable to maintain him. If a master could be found in a neighbouring parish, this form of apprenticeship was often a convenient way of getting rid of a pauper child, because the apprenticeship conferred Settlement after a period of forty days. 'Husbandry' for a boy, or 'housewifery' for a girl, simply meant being a servant on the land or in the house: later, in the Industrial Revolution, it might mean life in the mill, or even down a mine.

1752: a Date to Remember

In the middle of the eighteenth century, two changes were made in the English calendar. The first, and the only one of importance to genealogists, moved the official start of the year from 25 March (Lady Day) to 1 January, so changing January, February and March from being the last three months of the old year to the first three months of the new. The second, by 'losing' eleven days from September, was from the Julian calendar to the Gregorian, bringing England into line with the rest of Europe where the Gregorian system had been in use since 1582.

As the new system was adopted by some people *before* its official introduction, great care must be taken in transcribing extracts containing dates in January, February and March before 1752. The correct procedure is to transcribe the dates in both Old Style and New: 5 Feb. 1626 O.S., should therefore be shown as 5 Feb. 1626/7.

The Use of Latin

In the period before 1733, many legal documents were written in what is known as Medieval Latin, and this can naturally cause some difficulties for researchers. Nor is the knowledge of classical Latin a complete answer. The language is full of later, but now archaic, words and expressions, many of them abbreviated, but fortunately the vocabulary needed to deal with the more genealogically useful documents is not extensive, and, as the same words and phrases recur time and time again, any researcher armed with one of the useful aids described in the Dictionary (*see* LATIN, MEDIEVAL) will, with a little practice, become able to cope with most Latin records. Should an unfamiliar or unusually difficult document need to be deciphered or translated, the staff of the record office are usually ready to help.

The Stuart and Late Tudor Period 1600–1714

A more common difficulty in this period is the handwriting used in sixteenth- and seventeenth-century documents. It is known as SECRETARY HAND and differs considerably from that we use today. The Dictionary entry under HANDWRITING contains a specimen alphabet, and with a little practice most difficulties in transcribing such documents can be overcome.

Most of the Linkage Records remain the same as in the Hanoverian period, but one important set that runs through both periods comprises the estate records described in some detail in the Dictionary entry under MANOR. In addition to rent books, surveys and maps, these court rolls note the passing of copyhold properties from father to son on the thousands of manors that were once the unit of English local government. Until the Commonwealth in the mid seventeenth century these records were written in Latin, to which language most manors returned after the Restoration of the monarchy, and the researcher about to tackle any manorial records would be well advised first to acquire and study some of the aids and word-lists referred to above.

Among the Location Records, Jurors' Lists and Poll Books are no longer (on our backward journey) available, but in their place we have the taxation records known as the LAY SUBSIDY ROLLS for every parish in the country. These include the HEARTH TAX Returns of 1662 and 1689. Similarly useful are the PROTESTATION OATH RETURNS of 1641/2. By order of Parliament the Returns listed all who signed, and all who refused to sign, an oath to live and die for the true Protestant religion, the liberties and rights of subjects, and the privileges of Parliament. Many of the lists are housed in the House of Lords Record Office, but some survive only among local parish records. Other useful Location Records of the same year are the parochial lists of those who subscribed to a Collection for DISTRESSED PROTESTANTS IN IRELAND, mentioning many more women than the LAY SUBSIDY lists. For 1696 there are the ASSOCIATION OATH ROLLS. Lastly, through much of the period, there are the MUSTER CERTIFICATES that list, in each parish, men between the ages of 16 and 60 available for service in the militia.

For Apprentice Records in the period before 1710, it is necessary to turn to the archives of the London LIVERY COMPANIES and those of the Craft Guilds (*see* GUILD, CRAFT) of provincial boroughs. The former are often very detailed and of great value to the genealogist: the latter, although of undoubted historical interest, are less detailed.

Tudor, Plantagenet and Beyond

The parish registers which, until now, have provided by far the most valuable source of Linkage information, come to an end (or, more properly, their beginning) during this period. Most of those now surviving do not go back beyond 1558; the oldest of all date from 1538.

In these oldest parish registers the entries tend to be very brief, and information sparse. Parents are usually omitted from baptismal records, and sometimes even the wife's name does not appear in a marriage entry. Only a very fortunate few will find it possible to trace their descent beyond this period. There are mentions of many people (most, but not all, of the upper classes) in the early sixteenth-century records that have been summarised and printed under the title *Letters and Papers of the Reign of Henry VIII*. Also, descents can sometimes be traced well back into the Middle Ages for those families whose ancestors were tenants-in-chief of the king in feudal times, or were the lords or tenants of manors of which the medieval court rolls have survived.

Of the handful of families for which records go right back to the Norman Conquest, the male-line descents have been well researched.

The Oldest Documentary Records

The study of very old documents naturally presents a great many difficulties. Latin and Court Hand scripts are two; the physical ageing of the materials causes others. Inks fade, the parchment becomes brittle and discoloured. Special facilities may be required for handling and reading them.

Fortunately for the researcher, however, many of the most useful of the medieval records have been calendared (i.e. their gist has been briefly rendered into English, with all names of people and places mentioned), and they are usually indexed. These published CALENDARS can be found on the open shelves of the British Library at the British Museum, and at the Public Record Office. They include the CLOSE ROLLS and PATENT ROLLS (the two forms in which records were kept of the King's Letters issued by the Court of Chancery; the INQUISITIONS POST MORTEM and their associated documents, introduced by Henry III to control the handing-on of lands held by tenants-in-chief; the FEET OF FINES (final agreements establishing titles to land); and a number of others.

This Guide has outlined the trails along which the researcher may travel in tracing the history of his family: detailed guidance will be found in the Dictionary that follows. But there are still a couple of useful hints to be given.

When visiting any repository of manuscript records, take a pencil, because you will not be allowed to use ink or a ball-point pen, an eraser or pencil sharpener in the Search Rooms. Go with a clear idea, gleaned from this Dictionary, about what records you wish to consult, and ask for them to be brought to you. You will find the archivists very helpful, and you will feel an urge to tell them your family history, but this is a temptation to be resisted. Two-thirds of all their visitors are on a similar quest. In the case of county or borough record offices, it is as well to check in advance on the opening days and times, that they have the records you wish to see, and that they have room for you. Some of the smaller offices can only accommodate visitors by prior appointment.

Genealogy is a fascinating kind of detective work. We find clues, often in little bits of seemingly irrelevant information; we make guesses from them and follow them up. Every piece of evidence we find we must interpret critically, never letting the wish be father to the thought. A pedigree based solely on a string of names from parish registers is hypothetical and needs confirmation by other evidence e.g. wills. *See* EVIDENCE. Each new generation we discover gives us a greater sense of achievement.

Luck will play its part, both good and bad. Some records on which we could expect to depend will turn out to be damaged or lost, or never written at all. But there are often ways around these checks, and every now and then strokes of luck occur that take the search forward in leaps. Somehow, the more experienced we become the better luck we get! As the great bio-chemist, Pasteur, once said: 'Chance favours the prepared mind.' An Englishman put it another way: 'The winds and waves are on the side of the ablest navigators.' The purpose of this Dictionary is to prepare your minds, and so bring you luck.

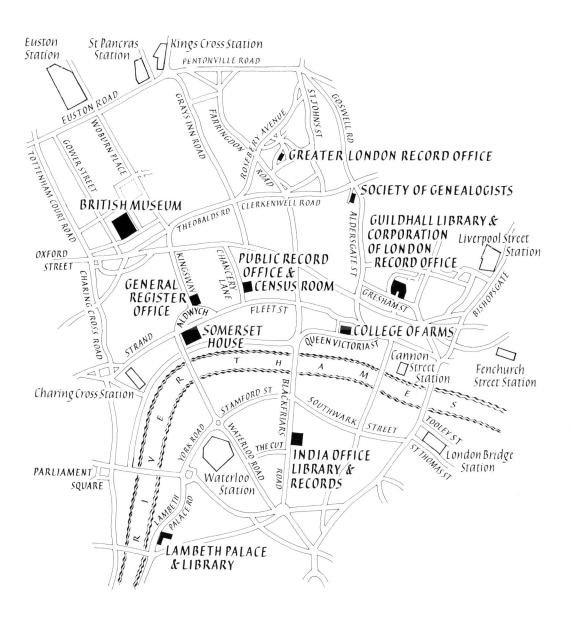

Major record repositories are located within a small area of central London. The above map by Charmian Mocatta shows where they are.

Abbreviations

The following are abbreviations commonly found in English records (although some are Latin) or used by genealogists.

Admon.   Letters of Administration
Ag. Lab.   Agricultural Labourer
AGRA.   Association of Genealogists and Record Agents
B   Burial Register
b.   born
BL   British Library
bp or *bpt.*   baptized
BRA   British Record Association
BRS   British Record Society
BT   Bishop's Transcript
bur.   buried
C   Christening Register
c. or *ca.*   *circa*
Cal.   Calendar
Chan. Proc.   Chancery Proceedings
Cit.   Citizen
CLRO   Corporation of London Record Office
CMB   All 3 types of parish register
Co.   County
CRO   County Record Office
d.   died, also *denarius* (penny)
dau.   daughter
d.b.n.   *de bonis non administratis*
DNB   Dictonary of National Biography
d.s.p.   *decessit sine prole* (died without issue)
d.s.p.leg.   died without legitimate issue
d.v.p.   *decessit vita patris* (died within his father's lifetime)
Exch.   Exchequer, Court of
FHG   Fellow of the Institute of Heraldic and Genealogical Studies
FHND   Family History News and Digest
FHS   Family History Society
FFHS   Federation of Family History Societies
fo.   folio
F. of F.   Feet of Fines
f.p.   foreign parts
F.R. Hist. S.   Fellow of the Royal Historical Society
F.S.   Female servant
F.S.A.   Fellow of the Society of Antiquaries
F.S.G.   Fellow of the Society of Genealogists
FWK   Framework knitter
gent.   gentleman
GLAN   Greater London Archives Network

GLRO   Greater London Record Office
GOONS   Guild of One-Name Studies
GRO   General Register Office
GSU   Genealogical Society of Utah
HEIC   Honourable East India Company
Hist MSS Comm   Royal Commission on Historical Manuscripts
IGI   International Genealogical Index
IHGR   Institute of Heraldic and Genealogical Research
Ind.   of independent means
IOLR   India Office Library and Records
IPM   Inquisition Post Mortem
ISBG   International Society for British Genealogy and Family History
J   Journeyman
k.   killed
LAUF   London Archives Users Forum
M   Marriage Register
m.   married
mem.   membrane
MI   Monumental Inscriptions
M.L.   Marriage Licence records
M.S.   Male servant
MS   Manuscript
NIWM   National Inventory of War Memorials
N.K.   Not known
NLW   National Library of Wales
N.R.A.   National Register of Archives
ob.   *obit* (died)
OPCS   Office of Population Censuses & Surveys
o.t.p.   of this parish
p.   page
PCC   Prerogative Court of Canterbury
PCY   Prerogative Court of York
Pec.   Peculiar Court
PLU   Poor Law Union
pr.   proved
PRO   Public Record Office
PRONI   Public Record Office of Northern Ireland
RD   Registration District
R.O.   Record Office
s. & h.   son and heir
SOG   Society of Genealogists
SP   State Papers
TS   Typescript
unm.   unmarried
VCH   Victoria History of the Counties of England

Part Two

The Dictionary

A

Abbey In the Catholic England of the Middle Ages, the term 'abbey' described a community of monks and also the building in which they lived and prayed. The community might also have several subordinate monasteries, called priories. The abbot, who was the head of the community, was usually elected by his brethren but subject to confirmation by the bishop of the diocese within which the abbey lay; but some abbeys were exempt from episcopal jurisdiction, in which case the new abbot would go to Rome for confirmation.

In the course of time many abbeys came to own extensive lands, granted by benefactors, and their abbots became men of secular and political influence, at the same time tending to lose much of their religious character. At the Dissolution of the Monasteries by Henry VIII, abbots against whom no offences were alleged were pensioned off. Many manorial families held their lands of abbeys and priories.

Records of monastic estates are to be found at the Public Record Office and in the British Library MSS Department.

Abeyance A peerage falls into abeyance when more than one heir is equally entitled to inherit. This occurs in baronies (*see* BARON) created by writ of summons when, for want of a male heir, the right of succession is divided equally between sisters who are all co-heiresses — the law of primogeniture not applying in such cases. The peerage can be brought out of abeyance only after all but one of the sisters' lines of descent have become extinct.

Abjuration of the Realm *see* **Sanctuary**

Abstract When there is no need, or no time, to transcribe a document in full, an abstract can be made, containing all the necessary genealogical and family history information. An abstract should include, in addition to the document's title, reference number and location and a note of what it is about (e.g. a conveyance, obligation, or whatever), all names of persons and places, all dates, names of any offices or courts involved, all occupations and sums of money. 'All' includes details of persons outside the family who may seem unimportant or irrelevant at the time. You never know whether further searches may reveal them to be relations by marriage or persons who influenced the family in some way. If you are planning an eventual narrative history of the family, then mentions of household possessions, statements quoted and other human details should be noted, also the wording of sentences or phrases that convey atmosphere or character. *See also* RECORD KEEPING; TRANSCRIPT.

Acceptor *see* **Bill of Exchange**

Account, Action of An action at law to oblige a bailiff to submit an account of moneys administered by him. In more recent times it has been used of a similar action against a partner.

Achievement A complete representation of a family's heraldic insignia, including the coat of arms, crest, helmet, mantling, torse and motto; plus, in the case of peers, chapeau, coronet, supporters and compartment.

Acre The word sometimes meant nothing more than a piece of arable land without reference to size. It is never safe to assume that it corresponded to our present statute acre. In Lancashire there were three different acres in use well into the nineteenth century.

Act Book A register in which the minutes of a court were written. Some entries are very cramped and difficult to read, because the same page space was allowed under each heading.

Act of Renunciation *see* **Renunciation**

Actors Information about the careers of actors can best be found in the advertisement and review columns of national and local news-papers, and in the journals devoted to the pro-fession, namely *The Era* (from 1838), *Theatrical Journal* (1839–73), *Theatre* (1877–97), *The Stage* (from 1879). All these can be found at the British Newspaper Library at Colindale, and the special-ist journals can also be consulted at the West-minster Central Library, St Martin's Street, Leicester Square, London WC2 7HP. Two useful reference books are *Who's Who in the Theatre* and *Spotlight*.

The Enthoven Theatre Collection at the Vic-toria and Albert Musuem has photographs, press-cuttings, programmes and playbills. Most theatrical companies deposit copies of their pro-grammes there and the collection is card-indexed. The British Library also has a collection of programmes and playbills.

The British Theatre Association library is at the Theatre Museum, 1e Tavistock Street, Covent Garden, London WC2E 7PA, (tel: 071 836 7891) as is that of the Society for Theatre Research. You need to make an appointment if you want to consult their holdings. The collection of the British Music Hall Society is at the Passmore Edwards Museum, Romford Road, Stratford, London E15 4LZ; they accept written enquiries only. For further reading on records, see *London Theatres and Music Halls 1850–1950* by D. Howard (Library Association, 1970).

Acts of Parliament

All Acts of Parliament since 1500 are contained in the Statute Rolls housed in the Victoria Tower at the House of Lords. Public Acts are those intended to alter the general law. Private Acts, of which there are 34 categories, alter the law relating to a particular locality or confer rights on, or relieve from liabil-ity, a particular person or body of persons. From 1797 Local, Personal and Private Acts are also to be found among the Parliament Rolls at the Public Record Office.

Public Acts from 1485 to 1702 have been printed under the title *Statutes of the Realm* together with the titles, but not the texts, of Pri-vate Acts for the same period. From 1702, Public Acts are printed as *Statutes at Large*. Private, Per-sonal and Local Acts not printed can be inspected at the House of Lords Record Office in the Victoria Tower on payment of a search fee for each Act. Application should be made to The Clerk of the Records, Parliament Office, House of Lords, London SW1A OPW. Most of the House of Commons records were destroyed by fire in 1834.

For the period before 1800 there is no complete index of Personal or Local Acts, but there is a privately produced index, called *Analytical Table of the Private Statutes from 1727 to 1812*. It does not contain Local Acts, because at that time they were classified as semi-public Acts. In the eigh-teenth century, annual lists of Private and Per-sonal Acts were published and these can sometimes be found at the front of the Statute volume for the year.

There are printed sets, perhaps not complete, of Local and Personal Acts at the British Library. Some printed eighteenth-century Acts are really Bills. *See also* PARLIAMENTARY PAPERS.

Administration, Letters of

When a person died intestate, i.e. leaving no will, the next-of-kin or a close friend or creditor was supposed to apply to a probate court for Letters of Adminis-tration of the estate. Unfortunately, in the major-ity of cases where the estate was small and there was no doubt as to who should inherit, no appli-cation was made and so no record remains. Where letters were sought, the applicant had to swear that there was no will, that he would pay all funeral expenses and debts, administer truly, and submit a true inventory and account of his stewardship. The court granted the Letters and entered the Administration Act, in Latin until 1733, into a register, sometimes in the same book as its Probate Acts. The court might require the administrator to enter into a bond to administer the estate faithfully, in which case a copy of the Act was endorsed on the bond document before it was filed.

The court's annual index of Administration Acts (popularly called Admons.) may be com-bined with that of its wills, or it may be listed separately. Sometimes the index shows an 'Admon. With Will Annexed'. This usually means that a will had been made but that the executors named in it were unavailable, through death or otherwise, so Admon. was granted to someone else, usually the next of kin. Admon. records are kept with those of wills. For their location, *see* the section on wills under the rel-evant county heading.

A typical Latin Administration Act can be translated word by word, as follows:

Vicesimo sexto die mensis Martii
On the twenty-sixth day of the month of March

1596 Venerabilis Vir Magister Egidius
1596 the Worshipful [man] Master Giles

Richardson legum doctor surrogatus etc.
Richardson of laws doctor surrogate etc.

commisit administrationem bonorum etc.
committed the administration of the goods etc.

Johannis Mercer nuper de Farnham defuncti
of John Mercer formerly of Farnham deceased

Jacobo Mercer filio naturale et legitimo ejus
to James Mercer son natural and lawful of him

de bene et fideliter administrando, etc, jurato
to well and truly administer, etc, being sworn

etc, salvo, etc, Maria
etc, saving (the rights of others), Mary

relicta dicti defuncti renunciante.
the relict of the said deceased renouncing

Adoption The first mechanism for regulating adoption was set up in 1926. Before that year, adoption was often covered by a deed drawn up between parents and adopter, or simply by unrecorded verbal agreement. However, from the year 1927 onward a register of adoption exists at the General Register of Births, Deaths and Marriages. Birth certificates can be applied for from the Adopted Children's Register there. These show the dates of birth and adoption and the names of the adopting parents. The child's original surname and the names of its natural parents are not shown. Even its Christian name may be changed. Adoptive parents know the original names of the child and natural mother (and sometimes father), but natural parents do not usually know the adopters' identity.

By the *Children Act*, which came into force on 12 November 1975, an adopted person over the age of 18 may apply for his original birth certificate at the General Register Office (on Form CA8), or by writing to the Adopted Children Register, Smedley Hydro, Trafalgar Road, Birkdale, Southport PR8 2HH.

If the Adoption Order was made before the date of the *Children Act*, the applicant will be interviewed by an experienced social worker before the certificate is issued; if adopted after that date he or she can decide whether or not to be interviewed, and can also choose whether to be interviewed at the General Register Office in St Catherine's House, London WC2B 6JP, at the office of his or her own local authority, at the office of the authority of the area where the adoption was made, or at the office of the approved adoption society.

An organisation known as NORCAP (National Organisation for the Re-unification of Children and Parents) can be a help. Their address is: 3 New High Street, Headington, Oxford OX3 7AJ.

Finding aid: *Where to Find Adoption Records*, by Georgina Stafford.

Advowson The right to appoint a cleric to an ecclesiastical office in a living which was patronised by an institution or an individual. The candidate had to be presented to the bishop for approval and induction.

Affeerer The officer of a manorial court whose responsibility it was to assess the amount of the monetary penalties which offenders were sentenced to pay. To affeer means to assess.

Affidavit A written statement, made on oath or by affirmation. It was, among many other occasions, required in the case of burial in woollens. For that purpose some clergy kept Affidavit Books of record.

Affinity (i) A relationship other than one of blood, e.g. a spouse, in-law, step relative. Such a relative is an 'affine'. A Table of Affinities, to be found in the *Book of Common Prayer*, lists degrees of relationship within which marriage is forbidden. At one time 'Deceased Wife's Sister' and 'Deceased Husband's Brother' were on this list, but they have now been removed. Earlier still a 'spiritual affinity', such as the relationship between godparent and godchild or between baptizer and baptized, constituted an impediment to marriage. This could be removed by papal or episcopal dispensation.

(ii) The followers of a magnate in the system of MAINTENANCE were known as his 'affinity'.

Affirmation An affirmation is a statement made without an oath, such as was used by dissenters, as opposed to an affidavit which is a sworn statement.

Agnate A relative descended in the male line from a common male ancestor, related on the father's side. An agnatic line of descent is one entirely through males.
See also COGNATE.

Agricultural Labourers Before the Industrial Revolution, workers on the land constituted the largest single class of the community, but also one that left few records in virtue of their occupation. However, that does not necessarily mean that their lives cannot be successfully researched. As members of religious denominations their baptisms, marriages and burials can be found in either parish or nonconformist registers. As occupants of cottages they are to be found named in land tax and manorial records and in the estate accounts of landowning families, which may also mention the type of work they did. When moving from one place to another, they were liable to give rise to settlement documents. In times of misfortune they will have received parochial assistance and so be mentioned in the accounts of Overseers of the Poor and churchwardens. They may well at some time have been involved, perhaps only as witnesses, in parochial troubles brought to the attention of ecclesiastical courts or ecclesiastical visitations. In lawsuits tried in the courts of Chancery, Exchequer, Star Chamber, and Requests they may have been called upon to make depositions. The indexes of Quarter Sessions records, where they exist, are also worth consulting. As children they are likely to have been either trade or parochial apprentices.

After 1837, as members of the population, they appear in the General Register of Births, Deaths and Marriages, and (as Ag. Labs.) in the census returns. If the poet Thomas Gray could return to life today, he would be surprised to find how modern genealogy had outdated much of his *Elegy in a Country Churchyard*.

Brunel University, London has a collection of working-class autobiographies.

In the Census of 1851, 1,200,000 men and 143,000 women were earning their living on the land. By 1901 these figures had been halved.

Further reading: *The Village Labourer 1760–1832* by J.L. and B. Hammond (1911, reprinted 1987) and *Labouring Life in the Victorian Countryside* by Pamela Horn (1987).

Aid A feudal due payable by a tenant to his lord, either to ransom him after capture or on the occasions of the lord's eldest son being knighted and his eldest daughter being married. Feudal Aids were abolished in 1660.

Ale (i) A country festival at which ale was the usual drink; often one held to raise funds for a particular purpose, e.g. a Church Ale for the maintenance of the building. Ale Plays were sometimes performed at such events.

(ii) An Assize of Ale was the inspecting of ale, by tasting and other means, by assessors appointed by the Quarter Sessions. These officials called from time to time to ensure that ale and beer were being sold by the correct measures, and at the price and quality laid down. The manorial or parochial official responsible to the assessors was the Aleconner, also called Aletaster and Alefounder.

Alias Latin for 'otherwise'. When a person changed his surname, or was known by more than one name, he might sometimes be described in records as 'Smith alias Jones'. The term had no disreputable connotation. In a few cases both names joined by 'alias' were retained for several generations and so became the equivalent of our hyphen in a modern 'double-barrelled' name. Once hereditary surnames became established, a change of name might be caused by the inheritance of a property from a maternal relative, by a young person's being adopted, by becoming known by a stepfather's surname, or by a number of other causes. In legal papers a married woman often had her maiden name added as an alias to show her connection with the matter in hand.

Alienation The transfer of a property, holding or lease, from one person to another by sale, inheritance or any other means whatsoever.

Aliens, Return of From 1792 a foreigner arriving in England had to register with a Justice of the Peace. Householders accommodating aliens were obliged to inform the parish constable, who passed the information to the Clerk of the Peace of his county.
See also DENIZATION; IMMIGRANTS.

Allegation A solemn statement, usually made on oath, most commonly met with by genealogists when made to obtain a marriage licence. The word has much the same meaning as affidavit.

Allegiance Rolls With the accession of George I, an Act was passed compelling all persons over the age of 18 to take an Oath of Allegiance, in the wording of which they renounced the Catholic Church. The Rolls recording these oaths are in the Public Record Office in class CP 37 *Court of Common Pleas: Rolls of Oaths of Allegiance*.

Almshouses These are homes for the poor and elderly erected by institutions, guilds, individuals etc. In the middle ages they also catered for the infirm and wayfarers by providing halls and chapels where food and nursing could be provided. The chapels attached to them were dissolved in 1547 but the old hospitals were revived as almshouses in the Elizabethan period. In the seventeenth and eighteenth centuries wealthy patrons established charitable foundations to care for virtuous but needy inmates. Further reading: *Almshouses*, by B. Bailey (R. Hale 1988).

Alnager An Alnager was a person appointed to test the quality of woollen goods. The office was discontinued in the early eighteenth century.

Alumni Lists of students of schools and universities (alumni) can provide useful genealogical background information. There is a collection of such published lists in the library of the Society of Genealogists. *See also* SCHOOLS; UNIVERSITIES.

Amateur Historian, The *see* **Local Historian, The**

Amen The words 'In the Name of God Amen' appear at the commencement of almost all early wills and of some other documents. They are a short prayer that the provisions about to be described may be carried out, the word 'Amen' in that context meaning 'So be it'. In other contexts it can mean 'Verily'.

Amerce To levy a money penalty for an offence at a manorial court, the culprit being said to be 'in mercy'. The penalty itself was called an amercement.

Anabaptist Properly used, this term denotes a member of a German Protestant sect that repudiated the interference of any secular authority in religious affairs and promoted adult baptism. However, as found in the records of the English church, it is usually a loose derogatory term for a Baptist or a Quaker. They were precursors of the Mennonites.

Ancestor A person from whom others are descended. A person's ancestry includes all lines of ascent through male and female lines, as distinct from his/her family, which includes only those in the male line. See FAMILY. In English the only way of identifying an ancestor three or more generations removed is by prefacing the word 'grandfather' with the word 'great' one or more times. The Latin usage is more economical:

Grandfather	=	Avus
Great-grandfather	=	Proavus
Great-great-grandfather	=	Abavus
Great-great-great-grandfather	=	Attavus

Ancestral File A large database of pedigrees maintained by the Genealogical Society of Utah and available at their Family History Centres on CD-ROM as part of FAMILYSEARCH.

Ancestry Chart A term denoting a chart that shows all ancestral lines of ascent, male and female. Also called a Blood Descent, or Birth Brief. The chart is similar to that used for pure-bred dogs and racehorses, in which cases it is called a pedigree; but for human beings a pedigree means something different (*see* FAMILY TREE).

In an ancestry chart, the arrangement of the ancestral generations may be either vertical or horizontal, only ancestors and ancestresses are shown, with their dates of birth/baptism, marriage and death/burial. In theory, the number of ancestors doubles at each generation, so it is usual for an ancestry sheet to have room to show no more than five generations, leaving continuation sheets to show the ancestors of each of the sixteen great-great-grandparents at the head of the first sheet, and so on. In practice, the number of ancestors does not keep doubling, because two separate lines of descent will sooner or later converge to people who are cousins, then to siblings, and then to a parental couple common to both lines.

For many families, the number of generations from 1975 to the Conquest is twenty-seven, so the number of theoretical ancestors in the generation of 1066 would be 41,508,864; but the whole population of England at that time is reckoned to have been about 1,500,000, made up of three generations — grandparents, parents and children. The middle, parental, generation will then have been about 600,000 persons, or 300,000 couples. It is reasonable to assume that the descent of at least half of those will have died out at various times during the last 900 years, so surviving lines will lead back to about 150,000 couples. If these pairs have to embrace all the 41,508,864 theoretical ancestors of each of us who is of English descent, it seems statistically inevitable that all the 150,000 couples are our ancestors, and that includes, William the Conqueror himself and his queen. Admittedly Scottish ancestors and foreigners will affect the figures to some extent, but the extent of compression of a constantly doubling number of theoretical ancestors into the constantly 'contracting' population, seems more than great enough to outweigh the effect of 'alien' lines. The above conclusion has been objected to on the grounds of exclusive class divisions and the static position of families in remote valleys, but this alleged difficulty seems to overlook the facts that class divisions have never been absolute in England, and that family immobility is largely irrelevant when all female descents are included, since only a minority of brides and bridegrooms have been 'both of this parish', and only one bride from outside the valley is needed to break any segregation of descent.

Ancestry charts can be conveniently displayed in book form On the page devoted to the male-line descent, the spaces for the ancestresses' names can be cut out, so that their names show through from where they are written on other pages, on which their own male-line descents are charted.

Ancient *see* Ensign

Ancient Demesne   Land that had belonged to the Crown in 1066. By the thirteenth century

the law afforded special privileges to the tenants of such manors, even in cases where they were no longer held 'in chief'.

See also DEMESNE.

Angel   A gold coin introduced in the reign of Edward IV. It bore the image of St Michael and varied in value from six shillings and eightpence to ten shillings.

In the sixteenth century it was the coin given to those touched for the King's Evil (scrofula). It was withdrawn as legal tender under Charles I, but small copies were struck for the later Stuarts to present at the traditional touching ceremonies.

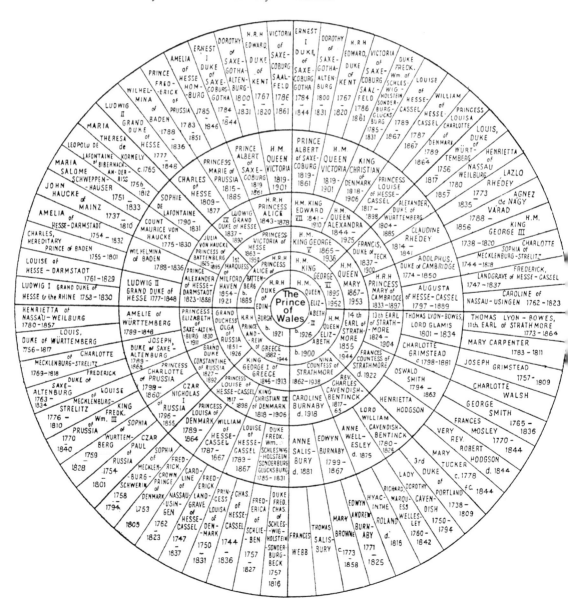

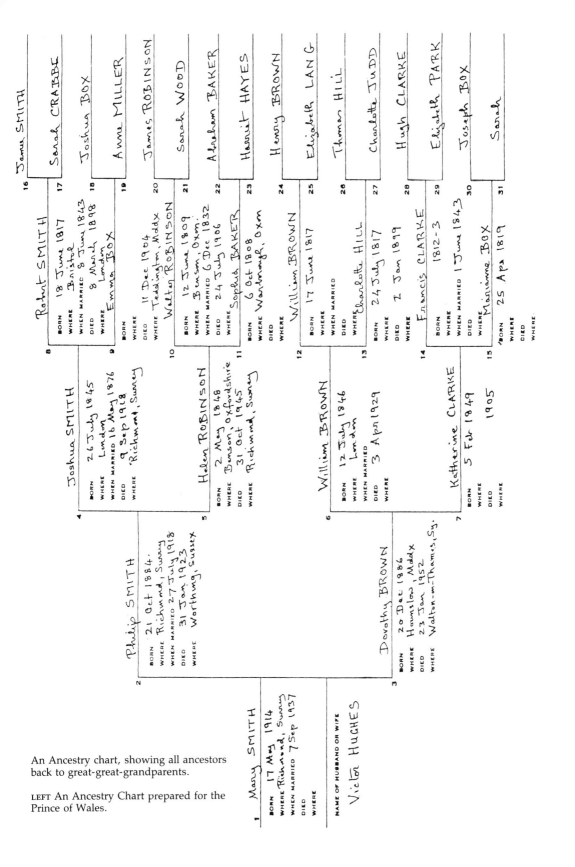

An Ancestry chart, showing all ancestors back to great-great-grandparents.

LEFT An Ancestry Chart prepared for the Prince of Wales.

Anglican Church   Established by Henry VIII when he declared himself head of the church in England and divorced himself from Rome. Also called the Church of England. The records of the clergy of the Established Church are contained in the bishops' registers of the various dioceses. Those concerning ordination may, according to their parish, include a testimonial of character, a certificate of baptism, a nomination by the incumbent whose curate the ordinand was to be, a certificate that his intention to enter the church had been published in his own parish church, and covering letters. Later career information in the register is revealed by his institution to benefices. From 1556 such information can be found at the Public Record Office (PRO) in the Institution Books (E331). Appointments during the period 1800–40 have been published in J. Foster's *Index Ecclesiasticus*. Thereafter *Clergy Lists* began publication, and Crockford's *Clerical Directory* has appeared regularly since 1858. It covers Anglican clergy anywhere in the world. Until quite recently it gave no information about date of birth, but the normal minimum age for ordination was 23½. Incumbents are mentioned in ecclesiastical visitations, at which they were obliged to exhibit their written credentials and those of their curates and lecturers. Many clergy were university graduates, so details of their parentage can be found in the university registers; but from the mid nineteenth century, theological colleges were founded, and these accepted non-graduates. Such students often commenced their careers as curates in the colonies. An Ecclesiastical Census was taken in 1851 and is available at the PRO, Kew (HO 129).

Royalty, noblemen, and their sons, Knights of the Garter and high officials of state were entitled to employ chaplains — in the case of dukes, as many as six. From 1660 until well into the nineteenth century, a record of their appointments and deaths or dismissals is contained in the Faculty Office's Books of Chaplains' Appointments held at LAMBETH PALACE LIBRARY. They are only partly indexed.

The official term for a clergyman is 'clerk in holy orders'; and until the mid nineteenth century that is what is meant by the simple term 'clerk'; a commercial clerk was called a 'writer'. Until the eighteenth century a graduate clergyman will be found in Latin records entitled *Magister* (Master); and a non-graduate, *Dominus* (Sir). Many churches display a tablet showing a chronological list of their incumbents from the Middle Ages until today (*see* INCUMBENT).

In the mid seventeenth century many clergy were ejected from their livings for failing to adapt to the changes introduced by a Presbyterian parliament and, later, to the Anglican restoration of 1662. Details of these, including in many cases the parentage of the parson, can be found in two volumes by A.G. Matthews, *Walker Revised* and *Calamy Revised*.

The Church Missionary Society has a register of Anglican missionaries at its HQ, 157 Waterloo Road, London SE1 8XN.

For further reading: The PRO issues a free leaflet, Number 51, *The Ecclesiastical Census of 1851*.

See also CLERGY, ANGLICAN (chart).

Anglo-French Family History Society

Recently established, this society specialises in helping those who need to research ancestry in France. Many French emigreés arrived in England over the centuries and many of us may need to seek ancestors across the Channel. A directory of members interests is being started and a regular newsletter circulated. The society can give advice on French archival systems and how to access them. It will affiliate itself with French national associations so that it can keep up to date with the current news and record agents in France. No translation work is undertaken but eventually a register of translators will be maintained. Write to The Secretary, Anglo-French Family History Society, 31 Collingwood Walk, Admiral's Way, Andover, Hampshire SP10 1PU.

Anglo-German Family History Society

This society specialises in the German genealogy of immigrants to the United Kingdom. It produces a quarterly journal and holds regular meetings. It is creating and maintaining indexes of those with German ancestry. Write to The Secretary, Anglo-German Family History Society, 162 Marlow Bottom Road, Marlow, Bucks. SL7 3PP.

Anglo-Indian Family History Society   This

society holds no meetings and has no committee but keeps in touch with its membership by the publication of a newsletter produced by Miss G. L. Charles, 68 Greenway Close, Friern Barnet, London N11 3NT.

Anglo-Norman language *see* Norman-French language

Anglo-Scottish Family History Society

This society promotes research into families who have crossed the border in either direction. At present it operates under the umbrella of the Manchester and Lancashire Family History Society. *See* FAMILY HISTORY SOCIETIES

Angwite A fine paid to compound, i.e. to settle out of court, for bloodshed. Also called Blodwite.

Anilepman A smallholding tenant of a manor.

Annates These were dues paid by the new appointee to a see or a benefice of the Roman Catholic Church. They had to pay the whole of their first year's revenue to the Pope. Their alternative name is First Fruits.

Annual Feast This event is frequently referred to in the footnotes of the population tables of the 1841 and 1851 censuses. It accounts for a significant fluctuation in the population of rural townships as 'owing to x number of persons being absent (or who have come into town) for the Annual Feast'. It refers most probably to the annual village festival held in honour of the saint to whom the parish church is dedicated. Annual feasts were also held by friendly societies.

Annual Register A publication first produced in 1758 which contains much of interest to family historians. It is still published today but its content now is more of a review of literature, politics and the events of the year.

Annuitants An annuitant is a person in receipt of an annual pension, grant or income.

Annuities The first state life annuity was launched in the 1690s and was not followed by others until 1745, but between that date and 1789, ten were available. The records at the Public Record Office in Kew (NDO 1–3), show the participants' names, addresses, ages at entry, and the dates of the last payments made, also some marriages, deaths and wills. There were over 15,000 of these nominees. An account is given in F.L. Leeson's *A Guide to the Records of British State Tontines and Life Annuities of the 17th and 18th Centuries.*
See also TONTINE.

Answer An answer is a reply to an interrogatory which states a defendant's case, sometimes in the form of an affidavit.

Antiquaries of London, Society of The oldest historical and archaeological society in the country. Originally founded in 1572, it was banned in 1604 by James I on political grounds. Meetings were resumed in 1707, and the Society was formally re-established in 1717. Its papers were printed in 1720, but regular publication started in 1747 with *Vetusta Monumenta*. In 1751 the Society obtained a Charter from George II, and its *Archaelogia* began publication in 1770.

The Society has a fine library, open to members only, at Burlington House, Piccadilly, London W1V OHS.

Apothecaries In the sixteenth century apothecaries dispensed drugs and generally acted as family doctors. In London they were incorporated in 1606 in conjunction with the Grocers' Company, but became a separate body in 1617. Their right to prescribe medicines was hotly resisted by the Physicians (incorporated in 1518) as an encroachment on their proper sphere. In 1722 the Company gained the right to inspect all druggists' shops in London and destroy any drugs found unfit for use. In 1815 the Apothecaries' Company was empowered to license apothecaries throughout England and Wales, and all candidates for licences were obliged to have served a five-year apprenticeship.

The early records of the Worshipful Society of Apothecaries (from 1670) are at the Guildhall Library, London. The apprenticeship details usually include the date of the lad's baptism, the name and abode of his father, the date of his binding, and the name of his master. A list of all apothecaries 1715–1840 has been published on microfiche by the Society of Genealogists.
See also APPRENTICES: LIVERY COMPANIES.

Apparitor The official messenger of an ecclesiastical court, responsible for summoning people to appear. Also called a Summoner.

Apprentices Apprentices were of two kinds: Trade Apprentices, bound by their parents voluntarily to a master to learn a town trade, and Poor Apprentices — pauper children put out by the parish churchwardens and Overseers of the Poor to service with householders or their wives.

Trade Apprentices

By the *Statute of Labourers and Apprentices* of 1563 it was enacted that no person should exercise any of the crafts or mysteries at that time exercised in England, unless he had served an apprenticeship of at least seven years. Previously, a similar arrangement had been laid down in some towns in corporation by-laws, but even when it became law, the Statute applied only to market towns. It required that the boy must be over 10 and under 18 years of age, and that his apprenticeship must last until he was at least 21. He must be the son of a freeman, not 'occupying husbandry', and not a labourer. The master must be a householder, at least 24 years of age, and exercising an 'art, mystery or manual occupation'.

In corporate towns, special conditions applied to merchants, mercers, drapers, goldsmiths, ironmongers, embroiderers and clothiers. They could only be masters of either their own sons or the sons of a parent (father or widowed mother) who had an estate of inheritance or freehold of forty shillings per year or more. This qualification had to be certified by three Justices of the Peace living where the property lay, and then presented to the mayor, who had to enroll it in the corporation records. This property qualification was probably intended to ensure that the boy would have the means to set up for himself when he became free. In small towns the apprentice might come from another town within the county, and in such cases his parent had to have an estate of sixty shillings a year. Many other trades, including the following, were under no conditions: bricklayers, brickmakers, burners of ores and wood ashes, carpenters, coopers, earthen potters, fullers, limeburners, linenweavers, millers, millwrights, plasterers, ploughwrights, rough masons, sawyers, shinglers, slaters, smiths, tilemakers, wheelwrights, and woollen weavers of household cloth.

By a statute of 2 & 3 Anne (her REGNAL YEARS), a boy of 7 or more could be apprenticed to a shipowner, a fisherman, a ship's gunner or a shipwright, for ten years or less. In 1710 a stamp duty was levied on bindings, and this caused the establishment of a central register which is now among the Inland Revenue records at the Public Record Office, Kew (IR 1, and Index IR 17). The register gives the name of the apprentice and his father (or mother, if she was widowed), the name and trade of the master, and the abodes of them all. After 1760 the information is not so full and often omits the father's name. If the indenture fee was less than one shilling, no stamp duty was charged, and so no record exists. Such cases were usually of boys bound to relatives. In many trades there were regulations as to how many apprentices one master might have, and as to his apprentice/journeyman ratio. In 1766-7 the maximum age for an apprentice was reduced from 24 to 21. Compulsory binding to the specified trades was abolished in 1814.

Records The indentures were held by the master and the father, and so are usually lost; but register books are available, kept by the Corporation (from 1681) and livery companies of the City of London (from the sixteenth century) and by some corporate boroughs. An index of the Inland Revenue records, 1710-74, is available at the Society of Genealogists and the Guildhall Library, London. The Society also has a collection of original indentures with an index, but there is as yet no index to the Inland Revenue Apprentice records after 1774.

If the search is for a London apprentice and his company is not known, one can write to the Clerk of the Chamberlain's Court, The Guildhall, London EC2P 2EJ who has a register of all London freemen from 1981. He will allow a search or have a search made through five years of the register for a small fee, and if the name is found will give more details for a further small fee. The Corporation of London Record Office has a card index of freedom entries in the Repertories (Court of Aldermen proceedings) between 1495 and 1649.

Poor Apprentices

Parish officials also put out apprentices under the Statute of 1563, but most of their activities were governed by the *Poor Law Act* of 1601. Churchwardens and Overseers of the Poor, with the consent of two justices, were empowered to apprentice to a trade or husbandry any child under 16 whose parents they judged not able to maintain him, until the age of 24 in the case of a boy, and 21 or marriage in the case of a girl. Masters failing to provide for the apprentice or carry out the conditions of the indenture could be fined by Justices of the Peace, with appeal to Quarter Sessions. The master of every ship of 30-50 tons was obliged to take an apprentice over 10 years of age, one more for the next 50 tons and one more for every additional 100 tons.

Poor Apprenticeships were exempt from stamp duty. Until 1757 apprenticeship was by indenture; after that by any properly stamped deed. Both before and after that date it was often done merely by agreement and entered in the vestry minute book.

In the eighteenth century, apprenticeship to someone in another parish was often no more than a convenient way of getting rid of a pauper child, because apprenticeship conferred settlement after 40 days. Instead of a trade, a boy learned 'husbandry', and a girl 'housewifery'. In other words, they were just servants. Anyone taking an apprentice in husbandry had to be a householder and have, and use, half a ploughland in tillage. In the Overseers' and child's own parish the master chosen was compelled to receive the child. He was often picked in rotation, or 'house row', and could be fined for refusal. In some parishes he could pay to be excused. Sometimes the children were drawn for in a lottery. If the pauper's parent disagreed with the Overseers' decision, he might find his relief docked. In the Industrial Revolution, pauper children were often apprenticed by the waggon-load to a mill-owner in another town.

Records Documentary evidence of Poor Apprenticeships is to be found in the records and accounts of the Overseers of the Poor, and in the vestry minutes of the parishes concerned. A free leaflet, No. 44 *Apprenticeship Records* is available at the Public Record Office.

Approvement An early form of enclosure of common land, especially unredeemed waste, by a lord of the manor under the statutes of *Merton* (1235) and *Westminster II* (1285).

Approver A hired false witness.

Appurtenances The rights and duties attached to the holding of manorial land. The most important were submission to the manor court, grazing rights and the payment of various fines to the lord of the manor. A pew, or part of a pew, in church was often an 'appurtenance' of a specific house in the parish.

Archbishop The bishop in charge of an ecclesiastical province. He also exercises episcopal authority in his own diocese. In England there are two Church of England provinces: York covers Northumberland, Cumberland, Westmorland, Durham, Lancashire, Yorkshire, Cheshire, Nottinghamshire and the Isle of Man. Canterbury covers the remaining part of England and Wales until recently when Wales became a separate Archbishopric. The Archbishop of York is Primate of England; the Archbishop of Canterbury is Primate of All England and has precedence.

Archdeacon The ecclesiastical dignitary next under a bishop of the Church of England, having jurisdiction over either the whole or part of a diocese. It is his duty to visit the parishes of the archdeaconry from time to time to see that the churches are in good repair, that parish affairs are being carried out according to Canon Law, and to hear reports from churchwardens on any public scandal. All the larger dioceses have more than one archdeaconry. Archdeaconries were sub-divided into rural deaneries.

The most important archdeaconry records for genealogists are those of the probates granted in their courts, but the judicial records of the archdeaconry courts (*see* ECCLESIASTICAL COURTS) and the records of the archdeacons' visitation (*see* ECCLESIASTICAL VISITATIONS) can also supply valuable information.

Arches, Court of The Provincial Court of Appeal of the Archbishop of Canterbury. In the late Middle Ages it was held in Bow Church, the church of 'Blessed Mary of the Arches', which was exempt from the jurisdiction of the Bishop of London. The judge, appointed by the archbishop, was known as the Dean of the Arches. Appeals from the decisions of the court had to be made to the king in chancery. The court records are in the Lambeth Palace Library.

The Court dates from the thirteenth century, but few medieval or sixteenth-century records survive. The series now extant starts in 1660, but many documents are in a bad state, having at one time been stored in a well in St Paul's Churchyard. Until 1733 some are in Latin. There are over 10,000 cases, of which more than half deal with disputes over Prerogative Court of Canterbury wills and Letters of Administration, and with matrimonial troubles including applications for nullity and separation, which continue till the *Court of Probate* and *Matrimonial Causes* Acts of 1857. Other cases concern defamation, the morals and church duties of clergy and laity, liability for tithes, and the structure of churches.

Cases in the Court of Arches, 1660–1913, published by the British Record Society, is an index and calendar to all the cases.

Arches, Deanery of the *see* **London**

Architects Details of the careers of early architects are to be found in two works: *English Mediaeval Architects, a Biographical Dictionary down to 1550*, by John Harvey, and *A Biographical Dictionary of English Architects, 1660–1840*, by H.M. Colvin.

For the sixteenth to eighteenth centuries, the archives of the Masons', Carpenters', Joiners' and Bricklayers' companies (*see* LIVERY COMPANIES) are useful for ancestors in the building trades. Researchers should also consult the publications of the Wren Society.

In 1985, *Edwardian Architecture* — a biographical dictionary by A. Stuart Gray — was published, giving details of the career and often the ancestry of architects and sculptors who flourished in the first decade of the twentieth century.

For architects of more recent times, reference should be made to the Royal Institute of British Architects, 66 Portland Place, London W1N 4AD.

Archive Class *see* Class, Archive

Archives Documents that were originally drawn up, with no thought of posterity in mind, in the course of administrative or executive transactions. Having passed out of current use, they were preserved by the transactors and their legitimate successors for reference purposes. For instance, the archives in a county record office are the multifarious official records of the County Council and its predecessor, the Court of Quarter Sessions. Other records deposited there are more properly designated 'Collections' of various kinds. There are two professional associations of their guardians. The Society of Archivists and the Association of County Archivists.

Ark A chest, often found mentioned in the inventories of the possessions of deceased persons.

Armiger An armiger is someone entitled to bear arms.

Arminians Arminian dissenters held Calvanistic views; some of their thinking contributed towards Wesleyan Methodism and General Baptists. *See also* BAPTISTS.

Armory Either a book which records the arms of individuals and families or the branch of heraldry which deals with armorial insignia.

Arms, Coat of To find out whether your ancestors bore a coat of arms, first inspect their original wills, many of which until the mid nineteenth century were not only signed but also sealed with a signet. Inspecting them is not always possible. Some probate courts (*see* WILL), after copying a will brought to them by an executor, handed the original back to him, in which case it is almost certainly now lost. Other courts made two copies, one in their Register Book and another for the executor, and they kept the original. The probate court in which the wills of England's most prosperous testators (who were also the most likely to be armigerous) had their wills proved, was the Prerogative Court of Canterbury.

RIGHT Among other APPURTENANCES of a manorial tenancy were the grazing rights for the tenant's animals. The extent of these depended upon the number of acres of arable land in the common fields that went with his holding. These seventeenth-century manorial 'Orders' put on record the grazing rights of the tenants of Uphoe Manor, Buckinghamshire. Part of the document is transcribed as follows:

Orders

Wee order that every acker of Greene sward Grown may keeape upon the Common three sheeape, and every tow ackers of areable Land one sheepe and no more, upon payne for every defalt to forfitt to the Lord of the maner [£0-1-0

Wee order that every six acres of Land may keepe upon the Common one Cow & no more, upon payne [etc.]

Wee order that every 12 acres of Land may keepe upon the Common one horse & no more, [etc.]

Wee order that the sheepe shall not come upon the lean stuble untill St Luke [18 October], upon pain [etc.]

Wee order that the Cowes shall not come upon the barly stuble untill three dayes after all the barly be att home, [etc.]

Wee order that every inhabitant shall keepe for every two cowes Common one hogg & no more, [etc.]

Courtesy of Buckinghamshire Archaeological Society

This court retained original wills, many of which survive at the Public Record Office (PRO) repository at Hayes, Middlesex. They must be ordered at the PRO, Chancery Lane, London, Class PROB 10. Delivery to the Long Room there takes about a week.

Not all wills, even those of armorial persons, were sealed with heraldic signets. Some show non-heraldic devices from signets probably handed to the testator for the purpose, by the lawyer who drew up the will or the scrivener who wrote it out. When the device is heraldic it may be that of a crest or a coat of arms, or both, and sometimes shows the ancestor's arms impaling those of his wife's family, a useful additional piece of information. The tinctures of course are not shown; for these, see Papworth's *Ordinary of British Armorials* or Burke's *General Armory*, both mentioned later in this article.

The fact that an ancestor used an heraldic signet is no guarantee that he was genuinely entitled to arms, but the discovery that he made an armorial seal makes it more worthwhile to engage in the process of checking with the College of Arms, the only authoritative source of such information.

Orders.

Wee ordor that every acker of Groene Sward Ground
may keepe upon the Common three sheepe and every tow
ackers of areable Land ont sheepe and nomore upon payne
for every defult to forfitt to the Lord of the manor — 0 — 1 — 0

Wee order yt every 10 acres of Land may keepe upon ye Common
and Cow & no more upon payent for every defalt to forfeit } 0 — 1 — 0
to ye Ld of ye manor

Wee order yt for every 12 acres of Land may keepe upon ye Common
and hors & no more upon payn for every defalt to forfeit to ye Ld } 0 — 1 — 0
of ye manor

Wee order yt ye sheepe shall not runn upon ye bean stubble
untill yt Linke upon pain for every default to forfeit to ye Ld of } 0 — 1 — 0
ye manor.

                                                    barly
Wee order yt ye Cowes shall not come upon ye stubble untill three
dayes after all ye barly be att hand upon paine to forfeit to ye } 0 — 5 — 0
Ld for ~~the first offence~~ — 0 — 1 — 0 & for every offence after

Wee order yt every inhabitant shall keepe for every two yards Common
and hogg & no more upon paine to forfeit for every Hogg. } 0 — 1 — 0

Wee order yt no horse mare, Colt, or Cow shall be kept or staked in ye
follow field upon pain to forfeit to ye Lord of ye manor } 0 — 1 — 0

Wee order yt no mare ~~and~~ or Colt shall be staked in ye barly field after ye
Colt be a month old upon payn for every offence to forfeit to ye Ld } 0 — 1 — 0

Wee order yt ye sheepe shall not ~~runn~~ upon ye barly stubble untill six
dayes after al ye barly be at home upon pain to forfeit to ye Lord } 0 — 1 — 0

Wee order yt no beanes shall be gleaned but upon every ones
land upon pain to forfeit ~~to every~~ to ye Ld of ye manor } 0 — 3 — 4

Wee order yt no man shall let any Comon to any Inhabitant in
any new erected Cottage upon payn to forfeit to ye Ld of ye manor } 0 — 1 — 0

Wee order yt no man shall cutt any bushes or willowes yt are not
in his owne ground upon pain to forfeit to ye Ld of ye manor } 0 — 1 — 0

Wee order yt no horse mare or Colt shall lye a loose in
ye meadow in ye night till harvist be home upon pain to
forfeit to ye Ld of ye manor } 0 — 1 — 0

Wee order yt no person shall fish in ye Lds waters wthout his
licence upon pain to forfeit to ye Ld of ye manor } 0 — 1 — 0

Wee order yt no Hogs shall goe unrninged from St Michael mas
untill yt George upon pain to forfeit to ye Ld of ye Manor } 0 — 0 — 6

Wee order yt no Colles shall goe loose

Crest

Torse

Helm

Mantling

Motto

Shield with Arms

The armorial achievement of the Fenton family. The blazon of the arms in heraldic terminology is: 'azure, on a chevron between three secretary birds' heads erased argent as many fleur de lis of the field'; which means that the background (field) is blue, the chevron and birds' heads silver (in practice, white), and the fleur de lis the same as the background. 'Erased' means that the head looks as though it had been forcibly pulled off. *Drawing by Peter Haillay*

To be entitled to arms by inheritance, a family of today needs to prove a direct legitimate male line descent from an ancestor who is on the official record of the College as being entitled to the same arms. Modern firms which advertise shields of arms 'associated with your surname' are using a vague phrase to sell armorial insignia to people not entitled to them, and, in doing so, cause future confusion.

Armorial bearings were originally marks of identification for knights in armour, whether in war or at tournaments. The earliest known are those of Geoffrey of Anjou, father of Henry II, described in a chronicle of 1127. Heraldic devices probably came into England in the reign of Stephen (1135–54).

The personal identifying device of those days, the equivalent of our signature, was the engraved seal. On this a knight or lord was usually depicted fully armed and on horseback; so, once armorial bearings came into widespread use they were soon visible on the seal's shield and/or lance flag. Because they were more readily identifiable than the mounted figure they soon came to form the whole of a seal's device, at least on one side. The earliest known English seal showing arms is of 1136–8. Later in the century part of a knight's bearings also came to be displayed on his helmet, and this gave rise to the crest, of which the earliest known example is of 1198, that of the Black Prince.

In the thirteenth century the application of armorial bearings spread to horse-trappings and surcoats, from which came the name 'coat of arms'. The supporters that later became the privilege of peers were at first merely decorative additions on the larger seals used by magnates.

Like surnames at this time, arms gradually became hereditary and therefore spread among the male-line descendants of knights. Thus they became a symbol of social status. By the year 1300, about 1500 families were armigerous and so some regulation of armorial bearings was required to prevent duplication. This responsibility was laid upon the heralds — the officers whose work, at tournaments and in the armies, already entailed a professional knowledge of such matters (hence the name 'Heraldry' for the science and art of armorial display). The earliest extant English grant of arms is of 1389. It was also about this time that the hereditary nature of arms led to the quartering of an 'heiress's' coat by her descendants when her father's blood and name became extinct in the male line.

In the fifteenth century, the senior heralds (called Kings of Arms), were given the right to grant arms; and in March 1483, or 1484, the College of Arms was incorporated by Richard III. Coats of arms were to be granted to 'men of virtue and repute, worthy to be received among noble gentlemen', and also to guilds and other corporate bodies. Crests were not automatically included in such grants. The heralds began to compile registers both of the arms they granted and of those already in approved use.

The sixteenth century saw the establishment of minimum property requirements (land worth £100 per annum or movables worth £360) before grants of arms would be approved; and at the same time a drive was made to tighten controls on the use of arms and ensure the proper registration of those already justifiably borne. The Kings of Arms made tours (visitations) of the country from 1530 onward to examine gentlemen's claims. They took consideration of personal knowledge, family muniments, family traditions and the records of previous visitations, and finally either confirmed or disallowed the claim. This gave rise to a large number of written family trees of varying reliability.

The heralds' visitations continued until 1686. During the seventeenth century, crests first became an automatic feature in grants of arms. The Harleian Society has printed copies of visitation pedigrees, but some of these contain unauthorised additions to the originals at the College.

Arms and quarterings should, ideally, assist the genealogist in one of his problems, that of distinguishing armigerous families of the same surname from one another. Unfortunately many people in the past used arms to which they had no real right. This practice was even condoned by some heralds, though sometimes the latter salved their consciences by adding marks of difference. If a researcher can establish a descent from a person who rightly bore arms, he may be able to obtain considerable information about previous generations from the College of Arms.

Women's use of arms An unmarried woman bears her father's arms upon a diamond-shaped 'lozenge' instead of a shield. A widow bears her late husband's arms on a lozenge 'impaled' with her father's, or with the latter on an escutcheon of pretence if she is an heiress. (For an explanation of this, *see* HATCHMENT.) It is inferred from hatchments that a married woman may, during the life of her husband, use a shield of his arms, but suspended from a ribbon and without a helmet, mantling, crest or motto. The last four items are never used by women, who traditionally did not go to war or take part in tournaments, except in the case of Royal arms. (*See also* ACHIEVEMENT.)

To obtain a grant of arms a 'petition' or 'memorial' must be addressed to the Earl Marshal, which will be drawn up for the petitioner by one of the heralds. He will be asked for personal details to ensure that he has the standing of a Gentleman. If he has served in the regular armed forces, he will be expected to have been an officer. If the College is satisfied with the replies, the petitioner will then be asked if he has formed any opinion as to the bearings he would like to have on his shield. If he has not, he will be asked what his, or his family's, interests or occupations have been, so that appropriate charges may be chosen. He will also be asked to choose a motto. An artist employed by the College will prepare a coloured sketch of the proposed arms, which is submitted to the petitioner for his approval and initialling. In due course, Letters Patent granting the arms will be issued to him. The arms are granted to a person and his male-line descendants; so the petitioner needs to register details of his family at the College. If he applies in his own name, he need only give particulars of himself, his wife, children and grandchildren, and he need not offer documentary evidence. If he applies in the name of his father (who must be living), he must also give details of his father, mother, siblings, sisters- and brothers-in-law, nephews and nieces. This latter type of petition enables the arms to be borne by his brothers and sisters and his brothers' descendants.

The Harleian Society has also printed lists of numerous persons who received grants of arms between 1687 and 1898. The descents of many armigerous families appear in the issues of Burke's *Peerage, Baronetage and Knightage* and *Landed Gentry*. The British Library MSS department, at the British Museum, has a collection of MS pedigrees compiled at the times of the Visitations and sometimes added to later.

A classified list of arms arranged under blazons is contained in the *Ordinary of British Armorials* by J.W. Papworth and A.W. Morant (1961 reprint of 1874 edition). It refers to arms listed in Burke's *General Armory*, which gives an alphabetical list of families, with blazons of the arms they use, with or without authority, and is very inaccurate. Crests are listed in Fairbairn's *Book of Crests* (1905), and mottoes in Elvin's *Handbook of Mottoes* (1860). Their accuracy cannot be relied upon. For further reading, see *A Complete Guide to Heraldry* by A.C. Fox-Davies, revised by J.C. Brook-Little (1969). The Society of Genealogists has published a leaflet on *The Right to Arms*. *See also* ARMS, COLLEGE OF; HERALDRY.

Arms, College of

Arms, College of   This is the corporation of heralds responsible for controlling, granting and confirming arms in England under the general supervision of the Duke of Norfolk in his capacity of Earl Marshal. It was incorporated by Richard III in March 1483, or 1484. Its activities and those of the heralds are described under ARMS, COAT OF. The Officers of arms are:

Kings of Arms

Garter (the Senior)
Clarenceux   Norroy and Ulster

Heralds

Somerset   York   Lancaster
Chester   Windsor   Richmond

Pursuivants

Bluemantle   Rouge Croix
Rouge Dragon   Portcullis

Occasionally the Earl Marshall appoints additional heralds, known as extraordinaries, and generally given titles relating to the Duke of Norfolk's family, such as Arundel or Beaumont.

The College, in Queen Victoria Street, London EC4V 4BT is open daily from 10a.m.–4p.m., with an Officer of Arms always in attendance to deal with enquiries.

The Official Registers of the College include the armorial bearings granted or confirmed to English and Welsh families from the fifteenth century until today, and family trees of thousands of families of English and Welsh origin. See *The Records and Collections of the College of Arms*, A.R. Wagner (1952).

Army

Army   Although there had been MILITIA of various types prior to its formation, there was no standing army in England before the Civil War of 1642–9. During that war Cromwell raised his New Model Army. This was disbanded in 1660 on the Restoration of the Monarchy and the first standing army was raised on the instructions of Charles II. Although centralised under

a Secretary at War, the army consisted of regiments organised and run by their commanding officers from whom they usually took their name. Over time the control, and records, became more centralised but the regiments remained the basis of the army and its record keeping. As a result genealogical information may be obtained from a variety of sources and even the records created by central government were filed by regiment. In addition divisions of responsibility within what became the War Office (WO) created further divisions of records.

The army consists of the Arms, comprising the cavalry, infantry and artillery, and the Services, a term which covers the Royal Engineers and a variety of corps. Most of the corps date to the post-Crimean War period. The cavalry and the infantry were the responsibility of the Commander in Chief, whilst the Royal Artillery (RA and RHA) and Royal Engineers (RE) came under the BOARD OF ORDNANCE. As a result there are two basic groups of records. There is a further division of the records according to whether the person being researched was an Officer or an Other Rank. This last term refers to all Warrant Officers, Non-Commissioned Officers and Private Soldiers. The majority of records relating to the army are in the PRO at Kew.

Records of Officers   For the pre-1660 period Peacock (1865) or Firth and Davies (1940) are valuable guides. Additional material may be found in State Papers (especially SP 28), the records of the Exchequer (E 101, E 403) and the Audit Office (AO).

The outline of an officer's career may be traced from the *Army List*. This list of army officers has been published at least annually since 1754. It is indexed from 1766. Officers of RA and RE are not included until 1803. Details of promotions and regiment are given as well as some notifications of deaths. The Army List includes officers retired on full or half pay. Between 1839 and 1915 an unofficial version, *Hart's Army List*, was published which contains more detail, including records of war service and awards. Information on officers prior to 1754 may be found in Dalton (1892–1904 and 1910–12) and in manuscript lists at the PRO, Kew (WO64) the *Army List* for 1740 has been published by the Society for Army Historical Research (1931). Lists of officers of the artillery, engineers and medical services have been published and details will be found in Watts and Watts (1992). Many regimental histories contain biographical details of officers who have served with the regiment (White 1988) and some have published lists of officers.

Before 1871 Officers purchased their commissions. Records relating to the purchase of a commission may include personal and family details (WO 31, WO 25/209–229, WO 43 and WO 74). From time to time the War Office compiled returns of officers service, some of which contain much useful genealogical material (WO 25, WO 54 and WO 76 which are partially indexed at the PRO, Kew). Returns of service are particularly good for 1828 and 1871.

Until 1871 there was no pension system for officers. They could choose to sell their commission or to retire on full or half pay. Records of officers who retired on full or half pay may be found in PMG 3–4 and WO 23–25. Half Pay Ledgers (PMG 4) normally include an officer's address and the date of his death. Returns of service for officers who had retired on full and half pay were compiled in the same way as for serving officers and will also be found in WO 25. Pensions were sometimes awarded to officers wounded on active service (WO 23 and PMG 9). It was rare for wives or dependents to be awarded any form of pension by the War Office unless the officer had been killed on active service or there were very good compassionate grounds for so doing. Fifteen Drouly Annuities were payable under the will of Colonel John Drouly. Records of pensions, annuities and payments from Compassionate Funds are in PMG 10–11 and WO 23–25.

Additional records relating to officers include reports of marriages (WO 25) and details of attendance at the Royal Military Academy (WO 149–150).

Records of Other Ranks In order to trace the records of an Other Rank it is necessary to know in which regiment he served. Advice on this is given in Watts and Watts (1992), Fowler (1992) and Holding (1991). Prior to 1871. Other Ranks listed for 21 years and served until they were no longer fit. After 1871 enlistment was for a fixed term.

The best source of information on Other Ranks is the Soliders' Documents (WO 97). These are usually discharge papers which include records of service and personal details. Attestation papers are often attached. The records cover the period 1760 to 1913. Until 1882 they only pertain to soldiers who were discharged to pension through the Royal Hospital at Chelsea. From 1760 until 1872 they are filed alphabetically by regiment whilst from 1873 until 1882 they are alphabetically by branch of service e.g. cavalry. For the period 1883–1913 the documents cover all soldiers who left the service but not those

who died whilst in service. This last series are filed alphabetically for the whole of army. There are no Soldiers' Documents for those men who deserted and records of soldiers who served from 1914 onwards are still held by the Ministry of Defence. An index to Soldiers' Documents (WO 97) is in the process of being compiled at the PRO, Kew. Certificates of service for Other Ranks awarded pensions by the Royal Hospital Kilmainham between 1783 and 1822 will also be found at the PRO, Kew (WO 119 with WO 118). Other sources of discharge papers will be found in WO 121, WO 122 and WO 131.

Returns of Service for Other Ranks only survive for the period of the Napoleonic Wars. They were compiled as at 24th June 1806 (WO 25). Description Books give personal details of Other Ranks as well as their physical description. Although they cover the period 1749 to 1908 their survival is extremely patchy. Some regiments have no surviving Description Books. (WO 25, WO 54, WO 67 and WO 69).

The entire career of a soldier may be followed using the Pay Lists and Muster Rolls (WO 10–12, WO 14–16). These were compiled by regiments monthly and record the whereabouts and pay of every soldier. For most regiments the period covered is from 1760 to 1878, but records do survive for some regiments as early as 1708 and as late as 1898. It should prove possible to trace a soldier from enlistment, usually recorded in the Depot lists, through his army life (Service Troops) to his discharge. Depot Pay Lists may also provide details of where a soldier intended to live after leaving the service as well as family details. Pay Lists and Muster Rolls for regiments serving abroad are less detailed than those on Home Service. Forms at the back of the musters often contain useful information e.g. details of deaths, marriage roll and transfers in and out of the battalion.

Details of deserters, together with their physical description, may be found in Registers of Deserters 1811–1852 (WO 25). Similar details are often given in two police publications, *Hue and Cry* and *Police Gazette*. Bounty certificates for deserters exist between 1716 and 1830 (E 182, partially indexed at PRO, Kew). Yvonne Fitzmaurice has published a list of British Army deserters in Australia, *Army Deserters from HM Service* (Victoria, 1988).

Two Royal Hospitals were built at CHELSEA and KILMAINHAM to house wounded and disabled soldiers, who became known as 'in-pensioners'. Demand for places in the hospitals soon resulted in a system of 'out-pensioners' being established for non-resident soldiers. Pensions of both types were initially granted only for disability or infirmity arising from service in the army. After 1750 length of service became an additional criterion. Three main sets of pension records exist for pensioners of Chelsea. These are Admission Books (WO 116–117 and WO 23), Regimental Registers (WO 120 and WO 23) and Pension Returns (WO 22 and PMG 8). Whereas the first two of these relate to the award of pensions, the last details payment of pensions by district for the whole of the British Isles, 1842–62, and gives details of the death of the pensioner. Muster Rolls for 'in-pensioners' will be found in WO 23. For Kilmainham, Admission Books cover all pensions awarded between 1704 and 1922 and there is a list of 'in-pensioners' 1839–1922 (WO 118). There are separate pension records for RA and RE personnel in WO 54. Some pension records have been indexed (eg. Beckett index of Chelsea Pensioners discharged 1806–1838).

Other Records Other army records of use to genealogists include Casualty Returns (WO 25, WO 32, WO 108 and published indexes to some campaigns), Courts Martial (WO 71, WO 86–93 and WO 213), and the papers of the Duke of York's Royal Military School and the Royal Hibernian Military School (WO 143). In addition the whereabouts of regiments may be obtained from Monthly Returns (WO 17 and WO 73).

Records available for both Officers and Other Ranks for the twentieth century are limited. Personal records are still held by the Ministry of Defence and can only be obtained by next-of-kin. Application should be made to the Ministry of Defence, CS (R) 2b, Bourne Avenue, Hayes, Middlesex UB3 1RF. War Diaries for World War I (WO 95 and WO 154) and World War II (WO 166–175, WO 215 and WO 218) provide general details of events and mention names of officers but references to Other Ranks are rare. War Diaries for other twentieth century campaigns will be found in WO 191, WO 281 and WO 288. The Women's Army Auxiliary Corps was formed in 1917 and records of this, and also Queen Alexandra's Imperial Military Nursing Service, may be found in WO 162. Information about soldiers who died in World War I is given in 81 published volumes. Details of those who were killed in World War II are in WO 304. The COMMONWEALTH WAR GRAVES COMMISSION can supply details about the graves and memorials to those killed in wars during the twentieth century. They may also be able to supply photographs. Details of pensions paid for disability will be found in PMG 42–47.

Regimental museums hold significant collec-

tions of records which are of use to genealogists. These include both published works and manuscripts. Particularly useful are regimental histories (often with biographies of officers), enlistment books, records of service and regimental journals, which are of particular value for information on army personnel in the twentieth century. Wise (1991) contains details of regimental museums. The National Army Museum and Imperial War Museum hold useful collections at a national level.

The following registers of births, baptisms, marriages and deaths are available for army personnel.

At GRO, St Catherine's House:
Regimental Registers (1761–1924) of births, baptisms, marriages, deaths and burials at home and abroad.
Chaplains' Returns (1796–1880) of births, baptisms, marriages and deaths abroad.
Army Returns of births (1881–1955), marriages (1881–1965) and deaths (1881–1950) abroad.
War Deaths of Natal and African Field Forces (1899–1902)
War Deaths of Army Officers (1914–1921)
War Deaths of Army Other Ranks (1914–1921)
War Deaths of Army Officers (1939–1945)
War Deaths of Army Other Ranks (1939–1948)

In addition the PRO holds some regimental and garrison registers at Kew (WO 68, WO 69, WO 156, WO 256) and Chancery Lane (RG4/4330–1, 4387).

For the Indian Army *see* EAST INDIA COMPANY.

See also CHELSEA, ROYAL HOSPITAL; IMPERIAL WAR MUSEUM; KILMAINHAM, ROYAL HOSPITAL; MEDALS; MILITIA; NATIONAL ARMY MUSEUM; WAR GRAVES COMMISSION, COMMONWEALTH.

For further reading see, David Ascoli, *A Companion to the British Army 1660–1983* (Harrap, 1983); Anthony Bruce, *A Bibliography of the British Army 1660–1914* (Saur, 1985); Arthur S. White, *A Bibliography of Regimental Histories of the British Army* (London Stamp Exchange, 1988); Simon Fowler, *Army Records for the Family Historian* (PRO, 1992); Michael J. & Christopher T. Watts, *My Ancestor was in the British Army* (SOG, 1992); Terence Wise, *A Guide to Military Museums* (Athena, 1991)

For finding aids see, Charles Dalton, *English Army Lists and Commission Registers, 1661–1714* (6 vols, London, 1892–1904); Charles Dalton, *George the First's Army 1714–1727* (2 vols, London, 1910–12); Charles H. Firth and Godfrey Davies, *The Regimental History of Cromwell's Army* (Oxford, 1940); Edward Peacock, *The Army List of Roundheads and Cavaliers* (London, 1865); Norman

Holding, *The Location of British Army Records 1914–1918* (FFHS, 1991); Norman Holding, *World War I Army Ancestry* (FFHS, 1991); Norman Holding, *More Sources of World War I Army Ancestry* (FFHS 1991), *Officers who died in the Great War, 1914–1919* and *Soldiers who died in the Great War, 1914–1919* (both published by J. B. Hayward & Son).

A number of societies exist which specialise in research into the army and its campaigns. The two major national societies are the Army Records Society and the Society of Army Historical Research. Details of these and other societies may be obtained from the National Army Museum.

Array, Commission of *see* Militia

Arrentation The commutation of manorial services for rent.

Artillery A term covering all types of military missile weapons. An Artillery Ground was an area set aside for practising marksmanship in archery and hand firearms. The word is also used to refer to the Royal Artillery.

Ascent A term, unfortunately little used, to describe an ancestral line when thought of as running back into the past; the reverse concept to a descent, which applies to the same line when considered as leading down from the past to the present. In researching a family tree one is, in practice, tracing an ascent, i.e. working backwards from later generations to those earlier.

Assart A piece of land recently brought under cultivation after woodland clearance. The field name and family name Newlands usually derive from such a development.

Assignation Books These are act books of the contested causes in the Prerogative Court of Canterbury seen in PRO class PROB 43 *Assignations*. The actions they record are the assignment of a title to a legacy or a claim, to be transferred to someone else.

Assize From the thirteenth century onward an Assize was the periodic regulation and examination of the quality, weights, measures and prices of certain products offered for sale, notably ale, bread and cloth.

The term originally applied to the jury appointed to deliver verdicts, hence the derivation of the name of the later Courts of Assize (*see* ASSIZE, COURTS OF).

Assize, Courts of Since Plantagenet times, a county court presided over by the king's judges on circuit, administering the Common Law. The judges held commissions of OYER AND TERMINER, GAOL DELIVERY and NISI PRIUS.

Freeholders could buy royal writs that obliged persons with whom they were in dispute to come to court. The name of the writ in question was often added to that of the court that tried the case, e.g. an Assize of Darrein Presentment. In Tudor and Stuart times the most important function of the Courts of Assize, which worked in seven circuits (see county entries for circuit groupings) with two judges at each, was the control of local justice, as the judges were more susceptible to royal authority than the county Justices of the Peace sitting in Quarter Sessions. The judges also reported back on political feeling in the provinces. No hard and fast rule distinguished the types of case heard by the Assize courts, but after about 1590 the prestige of the judges led to the more serious felonies being sent to the Assizes in addition to those involving any finer points of law. As they represented the king, the judges were able to arbitrate between local magnates and decide on inter-jurisdictional disputes. The trials, however, were often hurried through, and the penalties were severe, so much so that juries often returned verdicts of 'not guilty' in order to save the neck of those charged with minor offences. However, they could be fined if they refused to return a verdict as the judges directed. The records are at the Public Record Office, Chancery Lane, London, under Groups JUST and ASSI 1–76, except those for London (which are at the Corporation of London Record Office), the printed Old Bailey Sessions Papers (at the Guildhall Library), and those of Middlesex (which are at the Greater London Record Office). The most useful are the Minute Books and Indictments. Those of some counties have been calendared and printed. The official records are laconic, but those of the nineteenth century can often be supplemented by reports in local newspapers. The Gaol Calendars attached to the Indictments give the names, ages, occupations and abodes of prisoners awaiting trial, accompanied sometimes by lists of gentry eligible for grand and petty juries.
See also PRISONERS.

Association at County Archivists *see* Archives

Association Oath Rolls The *Act of Association*, 1695/6, in consequence of a Jacobite plot against the life of King William III, required all

office holders to take a Solemn Oath of Association vowing to combine with others for the better preservation of His Majesty's royal person and government. Actually, most men of any standing took the oath. The rolls containing the names of the oath-takers, mainly under parish headings, are now at the Public Record Office, Chancery Lane, London, in class C 213. A list of the surviving ones is given in *The Genealogists' Magazine* of December, 1983. There are separate lists for the livery companies of the City of London, but under the same reference.

Association of Genealogists and Record Agents

In 1968 a few of the leading professional genealogists in England came together to form the Association (known as AGRA), with the objects of upholding the standards of professional genealogy and record research and of protecting the interests of those requiring such services. A distinction is made between genealogists and record agents. The former class of members are recognised as qualified to direct genealogical research on behalf of clients, and the latter to carry out searches in records specified by clients in any field of enquiry. The membership of the Association is now around one hundred. Management is by an elected Council. A list of members' names and addresses are obtainable from The Secretary, 29 Badgers Close, Horsham, W. Sussex RH12 5RU.

There is also an association of records agents in Scotland called Association of Scottish Genealogists and Record Agents (ASGRA) P.O. Box 174, Edinburgh, EH3 5QZ and another in Ireland, the Association of Professional Genealogists in Ireland (APGI), 2 Kildare Street, Dublin 2, Eire.

Asylum

An asylum is a place of refuge, generally a church, where a fleeing criminal cannot be apprehended. Alternatively it is an institution which gives help to the poor or those with disabilities. Some such organisations were self supporting and consequently were quite large establishments.

Attach

To place under constraint pending attendance at a court, by virtue of a writ or precept. It differs from an arrest in that the latter lies only against the body of a person, whereas an attachment may alternatively lie against a person's goods.

Attainder

A declaration of Attainder, by Act of Parliament, was made after judgement of death or judgement of outlawry on a capital charge. The consequences were forfeiture and 'corruption of blood' (see below). From 1539, Attainder Acts were used in lieu of trials.

In a case of treason, lands and any rights in them were forteited to the Crown for life, or for a term of years. For murder, the forfeiture to the Crown was of the profits of any freehold land, or, if the lands were held in fee simple (see FEE), of the lands themselves, for a year and a day. In both cases goods and chattels were also forfeited. In the case of lands, the forfeiture was backdated to the date of the crime in order to obviate sales in the meantime, but in the case of goods and chattels is dated only from the conviction.

'Corruption of blood' meant that the attainted person could neither inherit nor transmit lands; they would escheat (revert) to the superior lord, subject to the Crown's rights of forfeiture. Attainder was ended by the *Forfeiture Act* of 1870.

The verb 'to attaint' could mean no more than just to convict.

See also ACTS OF PARLIAMENT.

Attestation

Attestation is the giving of evidence or proof.

Attorney

An Attorney-at-Law practised in the courts of Common Law representing suitors who did not appear in person. He was known as a Solicitor in Equity courts. It was not until 1875 that the word attorney was dropped and anyone who represented another person in court was called a solicitor. Letters of Attorney or Power or Attorney were formal witnessed instruments that empowered someone to act on another's behalf.

Augmentation, Court of

A branch of the Exchequer formed in 1535 to carry out the dissolution of the monasteries and to administer their lands, properties and revenues about to accrue to the Crown. Its records contain a number of cases between owners and/or claimants of such lands. In 1547 it was combined with the Court of General Surveyors. The Proceedings are at the Public Record Office, Chancery Lane, London, under references E 315 and 321. Some of them have been calendared by the List and Index Society. The Court was abolished in 1554 as a separate section of the Exchequer.

Aulnager

An official responsible for inspecting and measuring woollen cloth and seeing that it was sold in correct widths and lengths. Approved cloth bore his stamp.

Australian Ancestry

The northwest coast of Australia was discovered as early as the sixteenth century and its west coast was explored in the seventeenth century. No attempt was made to colonise the newly found land even when Captain Cook discovered the east coast of Australia in 1770. Soon after this, England, unable to use her American colonies for the transportation of criminals after the War of Independence, decided to set up a penal colony in New South Wales in 1788. It was not until 1793 that the first free settlers arrived. Land grants were given to immigrants and freed convicts but settlement was limited to certain areas in New South Wales. Squatters, vagrants and ex-convicts, illegally settled land away from the penal settlements. From 1836, however, it was possible to purchase a licence to squat and after a particular length of time, a squatter could purchase the land so settled for a preferred price. In the 1820s coal mining began, supplementing the sheep farming already established. More convict settlements were established in other colonies – Van Dieman's Land, Moreton Bay and Swan River and free settlers in Port Phillip and Adelaide. Convicts continued to be transported to Western Australia until 1868. In 1851 gold was discovered at Ballarat, Victoria, bringing the usual fortune seekers. Immigration was assisted by the English government, the Church, landowners and businessmen.

Records of Civil Registration began as early as 1838 in Tasmania and as late as 1930 in the Australian Capital Territory when it became a separate administrative area. (New South Wales covered the geographic area of the Australian Capital Territory prior to 1 January, 1930). Before this church records were available for each Colony. There is no central repository for these records and their information can only be accessed by application to the appropriate State Registry. Most State Registries have published indexes on microfiche and CD-ROM covering various time periods and these are readily available. Application for a specific certificate can be made to the appropriate Registry and these provide excellent details. A death certificate, for example, gives age, place of birth, names of both parents, when, where and to whom the deceased married, issue of the marriage, their names and ages, cause of death, age and place of burial, and length of time in the Colony or State. Census records do not survive in Australia as they do in the UK but some do exist relating mostly to the pre 1841 period in New South Wales and outlying settlements. Most have been published and are also available at the Public Record Office, Kew in HO 10/21–27.

Church records survive from 1788 for New South Wales and separate records for other States commence at later dates. Unfortunately, some have not survived. Some of the earlier registers are only available upon application to the appropriate church archive.

Wills are found in the appropriate Probate Registry in each State and many have been indexed.

Each State Archives Office has passenger arrival records which can be consulted if the port of arrival is known. Many libraries, both genealogical and public, have indexes of some of these arrival records. Indexing is ongoing. Better records survive of those who had assisted passages or were convicts than those who paid their own way.

As well as each State having their own Archives Office, the Australian Archives has its main office in Canberra, Australian Capital Territory and Regional Offices in each State. Some research services are supplied by these archive offices. For large research projects you will need to make a personal visit or arrange for a record agent to do the search for you.

The Society of Australian Genealogists was founded in 1932 and is based in Sydney, NSW. There are many family history societies in Australia and these usually have extensive library collections and most can offer a research service for a small fee (*see* GENEALOGICAL RESEARCH DIRECTORY). The Australasian Federation of Family History Organisations can provide a list of societies on receipt of a self addressed stamped envelope or three International Reply Coupons. (The Australian Institute of Genealogical Studies, Victoria, is just another Family History Society like any of the others. It is no different from the Genealogical Society of Victoria).

Records at the Public Record Office, Kew   For settler emigrants to New South Wales, *Original Correspondence* (CO 201) has lists for 1801–21. Correspondence for 1823–33 has been indexed. CO 384 contains many letters from settlers or intending settlers, from 1817 onward, and Entry Books (CO 385) start in 1814. Also useful are Land and Emigration Commission Papers, 1833 –94 (CO 386), Colonies General, Original Correspondence (CO 323) and Entry Books (CO 324 and 381). (*See also* TRANSPORTED CONVICTS). Dr M Watts, of 77 Church Lane, Lowton, Warrington, Lancashire, is compiling an index of emigrants to Australia and New Zealand.

Emigrants to Tasmania Free immigrants from Britain have been calendared in *Records Relating to Free Immigration* (Tasmanian Archives Office).

Through the Australian Joint Copying Project

Australian researchers have immediate access to British Public Record Office records. Microfilming of vital records relating to Australian history began in 1948 and participation by various Australasian libraries has fluctuated over the years. There are many guides to these records, which have been produced by the National Library of Australia and the State Library of New South Wales. The project is currently in abeyance due to lack of funding.

Further reading: There are several books on sources in each State but for more general reading try *Tracing Your Family History in Australia, a guide to sources,* by Nick Vine Hall, Rigby, 1985 (now out of print). *Compiling your Family History,* by Nancy Gray, 19th edn. ABC books, 1993.

Avon A county formed in 1974 out of parts of Gloucestershire and Somerset. For the Bristol and Avon Family History Society, *see* GLOUCESTERSHIRE.

Avowry A protector or guardian, such as the lord of a manor in relation to the manor's tenants. Also such a guardianship. A stranger outside any tithing could purchase a lord's avowry by paying a fine. The word has other legal meanings.

Axholme, Isle of, Family History Society *see* **Lincolnshire**

B

Badge (i) An heraldic device, not part of an ACHIEVEMENT, used to mark property or allegiance. In modern times, it is recommended by the College of Arms as a convenient property mark for anciently armorial families having no crest.

(ii) A military cap badge is a useful clue for discovering the regiment in which a soldier served.

(iii) Badge and maintenance see LIVERY and MAINTENANCE.

Badge-Man By an Act of 1697 the poor in receipt of parish relief were obliged to wear badges bearing the letter 'P', and were forbidden to beg. However, at certain hours they could beg broken victuals from their neighbours, who were pledged to give none to unbadged applicants.

Badger In Tudor times a licensed begger: later also meaning an itinerant pedlar, chapman or other type of dealer.

Bailiff A manorial lord's local manager, appointed from outside the tenantry. He watched his lord's interests, superintended his demesne land and conducted relations with the tenants of the manor through their representative, the reeve. He was responsible to the lord or his steward for the efficient carrying out of his duties.

Bait To break a journey for food or refreshment, for either travellers or horses. In farming, a baiting-place was where the cattle were gathered for feeding.

Balk An unploughed length of turf between the FURLONGS in the open fields, not those between the strips. Those running parallel to the SELIONS were 'sidebalks'; those at right-angles to them, 'waybalks' or 'headlands'.

Bankrupts Bankruptcy is a legal declaration of a debtor's insolvency. The courts that had jurisdiction in such matters consisted, until 1831, of commissioners appointed by the Lord Chancellor. Later, two judges of the Chancery division dealt with them in the London area, and county court judges in the rest of the country. Notice of every adjudication was, and is, published in the Government's official paper, the *London Gazette,* and advertised in a local paper. The winding-up proceedings before 1710 are among the records of the Court of the King's Bench at the Public Record Office (PRO), Chancery Lane, London. After 1710 they are among the records of the Court of Bankruptcy, also held at the PRO, under class B 3 and indexed. They are available for search after 75 years. Insolvents of the period 1820–43 are listed in *The Bankrupt Directory, 1820–43* by George Elwick (1843).

Banneret, Knight Once a military rank. The banneret was a small square banner distinguishing the knight banneret from the knight bachelor. On promotion to this rank, the man-at-arms might have his 'banner' created by cutting the points off the forked pennant of his former rank. Such promotion might be conferred on the field of battle. The knight banneret had command of a group of men-at-arms and was superior to a knight bachelor.

Banns of Marriage A proclamation of intended marriage, repeated three times at weekly intervals in the parish churches of the bride and bridegroom, was order by the Lateran Council in 1215. To dispense with banns required the obtaining of a marriage licence.

In 1653, under Cromwell's Protectorate, marriage was made a civil contract performed by a Justice of the Peace, and banns had to be published either on three consecutive Sundays after 'the Morning Exercise' or on three market days in three consecutive weeks in the market place. The Banns were then recorded, sometimes in a separate book and sometimes in the marriage register, either as a full entry or by adding the letter M (for Market) after the marriage entry. At the Restoration of the monarchy, marriage once more became a sacrament of the Church.

On 25 March 1754, Lord Hardwicke's *Marriage Act* brought Banns Registers into regular keeping, sometimes in separate books and sometimes in the parish marriage registers. Separate Banns Books tended to be discarded after they were filled, so only a comparatively small number survive today. The requirement to register banns continued until 1812.

A typical wording is: 'Banns published between John Smith, bachelor of this parish, and Jane Brown, of the parish of Aldford, spinster. 7th June 1806, 14th June, 21st June'.

Banns Registers may still be found in a few church vestries, but where marriage registers have been deposited at the county record office any surviving Banns Books have usually gone with them. They offer a substitute for a missing marriage register and provide a cross-reference from the parish of one party to that of the other. Where the corresponding marriage entry still exists, the banns entry may supply additional information. However, a banns record by itself is no guarantee that a marriage actually took place. *See also* PARISH REGISTERS.

Baptismal Register *see* Parish Registers

Baptists In 1611 the English Baptist movement was founded in Amsterdam by John Smith, an English Puritan in exile. In 1612 one of his followers, Thomas Helwys, came to London and formed the first Baptist church in England in Newgate Street (one authority says, in Spitalfields). This was the origin of the General Baptist denomination. They repudiated infant baptism and Calvinistic predestination, and affirmed the Arminian view of individual responsibility for the salvation of one's soul.

1633 A church of Independents broke away and founded the first Calvinistic or Particular Baptist Church in Southwark. They, too, rejected infant baptism.

1640 The first local Baptist Association was founded at Bristol.

1644 A Confession of Faith was published by the Particular Baptists. This was a theological agreement, but not an organisational conjunction, between the General and Particular churches. They adopted baptism by immersion, and most Baptist churches admitted only those who had been so baptized. The Bedfordshire and Hertfordshire churches, influenced by John Bunyan, were the chief exceptions to this rule.

1660 At the Restoration, persecution of the Baptist and other nonconformist churches began. In the following year, the *Corporations Act* restricted membership of corporations to those who took the sacrament according to the rites of the Church of England.

1673 The *Test Act* intensified the restrictions on opportunities for nonconformists, by requiring holders of civil or military office to produce SACRAMENT CERTIFICATES and take an oath recognising the king as supreme head of the church.

1689 Under William III the *Act of Toleration* ended the persecution. Dissent increased, especially in manufacturing districts. The Particular Baptists became more numerous than their General Baptist brethren. Applications for the registration of new chapels came in to both the diocesan and archidiaconal registrars and also to the county Clerk of the Peace. These are now to be found at county record offices.

In the eighteenth century a Baptist theological academy was founded in Bristol. Many General Baptist churches became Unitarian in theology. Before 1754, marriages were sometimes performed in meeting-houses, the fact of a public contract making it lawful.

1754–1837 Baptists could only marry lawfully in a licensed Church of England church or chapel, so the records of the ceremonies must be sought in parish registers.

1770 The General Baptists founded the General Baptist New Connection, and since then the Old Connection has gradually merged with the Unitarians. In 1800, the New Connection had 40 churches and 3,400 members.

1828 The *Corporation* and *Test Acts* were repealed.

1837–40 Nearly all Baptist registers were deposited with the Registrar General, and are now at the Public Record Office, Chancery Lane, London, under references RG 4 and 8. Some certificates housed at Dr Williams's Library are indexed in RG 4 and are to be found in RG 5. New registers were started from 1837, after the old ones had been sent in for inspection.

1891 The General and Particular Baptists united in the Baptist Union of Great Britain and Ireland.

Minutes of congregations, committees and associations are at the Baptist Union Library (at the Angus Library, Regent's Park College, 1 Pusey Street, Oxford, OX1 2LB) which incorporates the Baptist Historical Society Library. Other archives are at Baptist Church House, Southampton Row, and at Dr Williams's Library, Gordon Square, London WC1H OAG, and with the church secretaries and trustees' secretary. The Secretary of the Baptist Historical Society is the Reverend Roger Hayden, 15 Fenshurst Gardens, Long Ashton, Bristol BS18 9AU. The Society publishes the *Baptist Quarterly*, formerly entitled its *Transactions (see also* WILLIAMS'S LIBRARY, DR).

The Baptist College, Rusholme, Manchester 14, has records of the college only. Bristol Baptist College, Woodland Road, Bristol 8, has archives of the college, of the Western Baptist Association and of Dr John Rylands (1753–1835). It also has the MSS of William Prynne, Puritan pamphleteer (1600–99). Baptist Missionary Society Archives are at Baptist House, 129 Broadway, PO Box 49, Didcot, Oxon OX11 8XA.

Further reading: *My Ancestors were Baptists*, G.R. Breed; D.J. Steel. *Sources for Non-Conformist Genealogy and Family History*, vol. II of the National Index of Parish Registers, SOG (1973).

Barbers The Company of Barbers was first incorporated in 1461, but under Henry VIII it was united with the Company of Surgeons. Apart from shaving and the cutting of hair and beards, the barbers were only allowed to undertake such minor 'surgery' as blood-letting and toothdrawing, while the surgeons were barred from 'barbery and shaving'. In 1745 the companies were again separated as the surgeons strove for higher professional status. The barbers' sign was a spirally striped pole with a basin hung from the end. The white stripe signified the filet or bandage used in blood-letting,

and the basin was the receptacle for the blood. Barbers' shops were popular places of resort for news and chat. Stringed musical instruments were often kept for the use of waiting customers. The records of the Barbers' Company are held at the Guildhall Library, London.

Bargain Formerly meant any contract, not necessarily advantageous.

Bargain and Sale A procedure for the private and secret conveyance of property, devised to take advantage of a loophole in the *Statute of Uses* of 1535–6. When property was transferred, the Statute made possession pass at once to the person who was to have the use of the land, instead of to any trustee who was the nominal purchaser. By Bargain and Sale procedure, the vendor bargained and sold a property to a purchaser and so found himself holding it to the purchaser's use, but, according to the Statute, ownership had passed at once to the user, so there was no need to enrol any conveyance documents and so make the sale public. However, the *Statute of Enrolments* was quickly passed, enforcing enrolment of such transfers either at one of the central courts or before a Justice of the Peace. This regulation made the procedure less popular and it was gradually replaced in favour by that of LEASE AND RELEASE. *See also* ENFEOFFMENT TO USE.

Barkerites The Barkerites are Unitarians who split away from the Methodist New Connexion. They are otherwise known as Christian Brethren.

Barnado's Homes, Dr The archives of these homes for orphans and foundlings now belong to the University of Liverpool. The records are closed for one hundred years after they are made, but there is provision for bona fide academic researchers to apply to consult within the closed period. Records more than one hundred years old are available for research; enquiries

RIGHT This Banns Book of 1824 shows the marital status of contracting parties, their parish(es) of residence, the dates of the three Sundays on which their banns were called, and the names of the clergymen who read them. In cases where only the groom's parish is known and there is no record of his having been married there, a banns book can lead the searcher to the bride's parish and the approximate date of the marriage there – provided, of course, there was no last-minute hitch. *Chertsey Parish Church*

BANNS published in the Parish Church of _Chertsey_ in the County of _Southampton_ in the Year 1824

NAMES.	Residence.	Publication.	When	By whom.
William Skeet Bachelor & Sarah Paice Spinster	both of the Parish of Chertsey	1 2 3	Sepr 26th Octr 3d Octr 10th	Thos Chas May V C. Pembroke cur C. Pembroke cur
James Dolby Bachelor and Mary Pullen Spinster	both of the Parish of Chertsey	1 2 3	Sepr 26th Octr 3d Octr 10th	Thos Chas May V C. Pembroke cur C. Pembroke cur
William Stephen Bachelor and Harriett Ellis Spinster	both of the Parish of Chertsey	1 2 3	Octr 10th Octr 17th Octr 24th	C. Pembroke cur C. Pembroke cur C. Pembroke cur
Benjamin Moxam Bachelor, and Ann Snelling, Spinster	both of the Parish of Chertsey	1 2 3	Octr 17th Octr 24th Octr 31st	C. Pembroke cur C. Pembroke cur C. Pembroke cur
Richard Heasley Bachelor and Ann Warner Spinster	both of the Parish of Chertsey	1 2 3	Octr 17th Octr 24th Octr 31st	C. Pembroke cur C. Pembroke cur C. Pembroke cur
John Watt, Bachelor Martha Stent Widow	both of the Parish of Chertsey	1 2 3	Octr 24th Octr 31st Novr 7	C. Pembroke cur C. Pembroke cur James H Le

should be addressed to the Dr Barnardo's After-Care Dept, Tanners' Lane, Barkingside, Ilford, Essex.

Barnsley Family History Society *see* **Yorkshire**

Baron   The lowest and second oldest of the five ranks of the peerage. Originally a 'baro' was the king's, or a great magnate's, 'man' who held the land of him, having done homage for it, as distinct from the 'homo' of lesser magnates. The barons became differentiated into greater and lesser barons. The former were summoned by writ directly to the king's council, the latter through the county sheriffs. Barons as peers of the realm are the successors of the greater barons. The earliest writs now considered to have created hereditary peerages are those of Edward I. The limits of the inheritance of a hereditary baronage are defined by the Letters Patent creating the barony. Today a baron is styled 'Lord' both in conversation and also, unlike other ranks of the peerage, in formal written address. His wife is styled 'Lady', his children 'The Honourable' in formal written address, and 'Mr', 'Mrs' or 'Miss' in conversation.

Baron and Feme   (i) A man and his wife legally considered as one person.
(ii) In heraldry, the situation in which the arms of a man and his wife (not being an heiress) are borne side by side on a shield.
See also ARMS, COAT OF; HATCHMENT.

Baronet   The lowest hereditary dignity and not of peerage rank, it takes precedence above that of knight and below that of baron, and carries the title of 'Sir'. The rank, the latest to be created, was instituted by James I in 1611 to raise money for the maintenance of troops in Ulster, the fee payable by the new baronet being £1,095. It was at first limited to those who held land worth £1,000 per year and whose paternal grandfather had borne heraldic arms. Separate baronetcies of Ireland and Nova Scotia were created. Those of Nova Scotia were descendable to heirs collateral of the original grantee, as well as to his descendants.

1616 As an inducement to potential applicants, the eldest sons of baronets became entitled to claim knighthood on coming of age.

1634 Englishmen and Welshmen became eligible for Nova Scotia baronetcies, originally instituted in 1625 for Scotsmen, to provide for settlement in that transatlantic colony.

1783 During the eighteenth century a number of baronetcies were illegally assumed, owing mainly to the large numbers of collateral descents from Nova Scotia baronets; so new grantees became obliged to register their arms and descents at the College of Arms.

1827 The right of eldest sons to claim knighthood was rescinded.

1898 The Honourable Society of the Baronetage was formed to maintain the privilege of the rank. Its name was later changed to the Study Council of the Baronetage.

1910 To prevent the continued illegal assumption of baronetcies, an official roll of the rank was established by royal warrant.

In conversation and correspondence, baronets are styled 'Sir' followed by their forename alone. Their formal title — on an envelope, for instance — is 'Sir' followed by both forename and surname and 'Bart', to distinguish them from knights. Their wives are styled 'Lady' (formerly 'Dame'), and their children 'Mr', 'Mrs' or 'Miss'. The arms of baronets are distinguished by the Red Hand of Ulster either on a canton or on an inescutcheon, except for those of Nova Scotia titles, which display a saltire badge.
For families in which there is, or was, a baronetcy, *see* Burke's *Peerage and Baronetage*, and Burke's *Extinct and Dormant Baronetage* (1844). Also *Index of Baronetage Creations* by C.J. Parry.

Barons of the Exchequer   Four judges, usually not peers, appointed to deal with causes between the king and his subjects on matters of revenue.

Barristers   A Barrister is a lawyer who has been called to the Bar. In Scotland he can practise as an advocate in the superior courts of law.

Barrowists   Barrowists were an Elizabethan dissenting sect who believed that the Church should be separate from the State and be free to elect its own ministers, as did the Congregationalists.

Barton   (i) The home farm of the lord of a manor. (ii) A monastic farm. (iii) A barley farm.
A 'bartoner' was the supervisor of a monastic barton or grange.

Bastardy   The state of being begotten and born out of lawful wedlock. In the Middle Ages, the term 'bastard' referred only to the baseborn child of a father of gentle or noble birth, but later applied to any illegitimate child. The Common Law descent of land was to legitimate heirs only, but land could be passed to a bastard by enfeoffment to trustees, combined with a last will.

Bastardy is a circumstance which presents problems for a genealogist tracing a male line of ascent. The baptismal entry in a parish register for an illegitimate child will normally mention the fact of bastardy and omit the name of the father, which was also usually omitted from birth certificates issued by registrars from 1837 onward. However, arriving back at an ancestor who was illegitimate is not necessarily the end of the road. Bastardy was a condition liable to give rise to a number of documents. Sometimes the father and mother of the child would marry later, and this is a possibility that should be explored first, though it may not always be possible to be sure that the husband was the same man as the father. The Christian name given to the child is sometimes an indication.

If no marriage took place and the mother seemed likely to 'fall on the parish', she would be questioned on oath by the Overseer of the Poor and the churchwarden, as to the father's identity. The answer would be recorded among the records of either the vestry or the Overseer. The putative father would then be required to enter into a bond to pay for the woman's lying-in and to support the child. Such a bond is known as a Bastardy Bond or Indemnity Bond, and may survive among the parochial records. Alternatively, a parent of either the father or mother could give an Indemnity Bond to the same effect.

If no bond was forthcoming, the churchwardens would apply to the Quarter Sessions for a court order obliging the father to do his duty. This document was a *Maintenance Order* or *Filiation Order*, and a copy will be in the Quarter Sessions records. If the father ignored it, he would be brought before the court by the issue of a summons. Sometimes the desired result could be reached without fuss by the father agreeing verbally to pay the Overseer his paternal dues, and this may be discovered from entries of moneys received and disbursed in the Overseers' Accounts. The regulations with regard to the illegitimate children of the poor varied from time to time.

Bastardy appears to have increased considerably from the sixteenth to the nineteenth century, although all children born more than a month after marriage were considered legitimate. The following parliamentary Acts were passed on the subject:

1575–6 Justices were empowered to charge either the mother or the putative father with the cost of the child's upkeep, either directly or by reimbursing the parish. The father often discharged himself by payment of a lump sum, until, in the eighteenth century, this was made illegal. The *Application Order* made by the justices gives the mother's name and sometimes the names of both parents. It remained the basis of the law until 1834.

1597–8 Pauper children were to be apprenticed.

1609–10 Any mother of a bastard who became chargeable to the parish might be sent to the county House of Correction for one year. On a second offence, she had to be. The murder of bastards therefore increased. At this period the whipping of both mother and father was a common sentence at Quarter Sessions.

1662 If the mother and father of a bastard ran away, the overseers might, on the order of two justices, seize their goods.

1732–3 A woman pregnant of a bastard was required to declare herself and name the father.

1733 Any man convicted of being the father of a bastard was to be gaoled until he gave security to indemnify the parish from its expense.

1743–4 A bastard was to have the settlement of his or her mother, wherever he/she was born. The mother was to be publicly whipped. Previously a bastard had had settlement where he/she was born.

After 1750, illegitimacy rose sharply. If the father married the mother during pregnancy, the child had its paternal settlement. This might lead to the deportation of the family to the father's parish. Applications for this can be found in the Quarter Sessions records. The vast majority of bastard births have no record except in the baptismal registers.

The above documents and other mentions may be found among the parish registers, in vestry minutes, and in churchwardens', constables' and overseers' accounts, which may have been deposited at the county record office, and also in Quarter Sessions records at the CRO. If paternity was not contested, Justices of the Peace normally issued maintenance orders in Petty Sessions, and of these virtually no records remain.

Settlement Examinations may also contain evidence of illegitimate children (*see* SETTLEMENT).

Other sources of information about bastards are the records of the ECCLESIASTICAL COURTS, in which the churchwardens of the parish are likely to have presented the mother and, in many cases, named the father. The mother will then have been sentenced to do penance in the church. *See also* FOUNDLINGS.

Bawdy Court The popular name for the ecclesiastical courts, so called because they were so often concerned with cases of divorce and immorality. *See also* ECCLESIASTICAL COURTS.

Beadle (i) A minor official with disciplinary duties. In some parishes another term for constable. (ii) A law court messenger.

Beast Gate The right to pasture one animal on the manorial common.

Beasts, Great These, in connection with tithes, were equine animals (horses, mules, donkeys) and bovine animals (oxen, bullocks, cows). The latter were also known as rother beasts.

Bederepe A special reaping service carried out for the lord of the manor by his tenants, originally as boonwork, but later compulsory.

Bederoll The list of a church's benefactors, for whose souls the faithful were asked to pray. It was read out from the pulpit each Sunday, and at Christmas and Michaelmas.

Bedesman (i) A person paid, endowed or voluntarily vowed to pray for others.

(ii) Any person obliged to pray for the benefactors of an institution of which he is a member.

(iii) A polite self-description — 'your bedesman' — acknowledging obligation; used, for example, in a letter applying for a favour.

Bedfordshire The county falls within the province of Canterbury and the diocese of Lincoln. It has 127 ancient parishes of which a great many copies of registers are held by the SOG library; nearly all registers have been deposited at the CRO though records for Whipsnade are at the Hertfordshire Record Office. Pallots marriage index covers forty-five of its parishes from 1790 –1812.

The Hundreds of Barford, Biggleswade, Clifton, Flitt, Manshead, Redbornestoke, Stodden, Willey, Wixamtree and Bedford Borough lie within its boundaries. It has Bedford, Biggleswade, Ampthill, Woburn, Leighton Buzzard and Luton RDs/PLUs. It falls within the Norfolk Assize circuit. The local FHS is Bedfordshire Family History Society who publish a quarterly journal and meet in Bedford.

There are two record offices in Bedford, at the County Hall and the Town Hall. The Family History Centre at Luton has now been moved to Hitchin in Hertfordshire.

Wills before 1858 were proved at either the Archdeaconry Court of Bedford or the Peculiar Courts of Biggleswade and Leighton Buzzard. Wills could also be proved in the Consistory Court of Lincoln and the Prerogative Court of Canterbury. For those wills proved in the Commissary Court of London and the Archdeaconry Court of Huntingdon see HUNTINGDON. Herald's Visitations have been printed for 1566, 1582 and 1634.

The Bedfordshire Historical Record Society has published many volumes of the county's records since 1913, including the Hearth Tax Returns. *Genealogia Bedfordiensis* is a well known printed source of transcripts, but experience has shown that it has a 28 per cent discrepancy from the originals, so all information from it should be checked.

See *Guide to the Bedfordshire Record Office* (1957) with *Supplement* (1962) and its *How to trace the history of a family tree in Bedfordshire*. See also *National Index of Parish Registers*, vol. 9, Part 1 (1991).

Benefice Properly, the established income from an ecclesiastical office, derived from land appertaining to it, but popularly used for the office itself, which could be held for life. A Donative Benefice was one to which a parson could be appointed without any presentation to a bishop.

Beneficiary A beneficiary is one who receives a benefit especially someone who inherits property from a will.

Benefit of Clergy A product of the conflict between the claims of Common and Canon Law. As a compromise, the Common Law courts abandoned the death penalty for some less serious capital crimes when the person convicted was a clericus (clerk), and a secondary punishment was inflicted. As a result, offences came to be classed as 'clergyable' and 'unclergyable'. The term 'clerk' had always included a large number of people in minor orders, but in 1305 it was extended to apply to secular clerks able to read and understand Latin. The test text was the first verse of the Fiftieth Psalm in the *Vulgate* (the Latin version of the Bible), popularly known as the 'Neck Verse'. In English it reads, 'Have mercy upon me, O God, according to thy loving kindness; according unto the multitude of thy tender mercies, blot out my transgressions'. This requirement degenerated into the ability to read the same verse — which in the Authorised Version became the first verse of the Fifty-first Psalm — in English. If a convicted prisoner on a capital charge read this successfully, he was merely branded on his thumb. The device had become a legal fiction to modify the severity of the English criminal law for first offenders. Even the test was abandoned in 1705, but it was not until 1827 that Benefit of Clergy itself was abolished.

Berkshire   In 1974 the northern part of the county was transferred to Oxfordshire. The county falls within the province of Canterbury and the diocese of Salisbury. There are transcripts of forty of its parish registers at the SOG library. Nearly all registers have been deposited at the CRO but Hinskey South is at the Bodleian Library and Oxford and Coombe is at the Hampshire Record Office, Winchester. Pallots marriage index covers 13 of the parishes mostly from 1800–1837.

The Hundreds of Beynhurst, Bray, Charlton, Compton, Cookham, Faircross, Farringdon, Ganfield, Hormer, Kintbury Eagle, Lambourn, Moreton, Ock, Reading, Ripplesmere, Shrivenham, Sonning, Theale, Wantage, Wargrave and the Boroughs of Abingdon, Newbury Town, Reading, Wallingford and New Windsor Town lie within its boundaries.

It has Newbury, Hungerford, Faringdon, Abingdon, Wantage, Wallingford, Bradfield, Reading, Wokingham, Cookham, East Hampstead and Windsor RDs/PLUs. It falls within the Oxford Assize circuit.

The local FHS is the Berkshire Family History Society who publish the *Berkshire Family Historian* quarterly and have branches at Bracknell, Newbury, Reading and Slough. There are two record offices in Reading at the Shire Hall and the Central Public Library and the archives at St George's Chapel, Windsor Castle. There is also a Family History Centre in Reading.

Wills before 1858 were proved at the Archdeaconry Court of Berkshire or the peculiar courts of Great Farringdon, the Dean and Canons of Windsor in Wantage (held for 1582–1668 at the Bodleian Library and 1669 onwards at Wiltshire Record Office) and the Dean of Salisbury (held at the Wiltshire Record office). Herald's Visitations have been printed for 1532, 1566, 1623 and 1665/6.

Berkshire Record Office publishes *Finding your family: sources for genealogy in the Berkshire Record*
Office. See also *Guide to the Berkshire Records Office* by F. Hull (1952) and *National Index of Parish Registers*, vol. 8, Part 1 (1989).

Bernau Index   This is the only nominal index to Chancery and other court proceedings, held by the Public Record Office, that exists. It is not complete and does not give full PRO references but it is very useful when trying to find your way around such a large mass of records. It was compiled by the late C.A. Bernau and sold after his death to the Genealogical Society of Utah and later to Mr Malcolm Pinhorn. It also includes some Exchequer depositions, the proceedings of the Courts of Requests and Star Chamber, Inquisitions Post Mortem, Ancient Correspondence, Naturalization Certificates, Prerogative Court of Canterbury Wills, Male Servants Tax, Quaker Sufferings, Close Rolls, Life Annuities, Association Oath Rolls and Poll Books for Kent and Essex. The entries give Christian name, surname, date or period, the location (usually a county), sometimes the age and/or occupation, a partial PRO class reference and the page number within the document where you will find the entry you seek. It is available at the Society of Genealogists. For a more detailed explanation of its contents see the article by Mark H. Hughes in vol. 18, page 129 of the *Genealogists Magazine* for September, 1975.

Betrothal   From the twelfth century, a betrothal followed by a pregnancy, or even simply by consummation, was considered a valid marriage, though a formal declaration of matrimony before witnesses was expected. An entry in a sixteenth or early seventeenth century parish register of a baptism shortly after, or even before, the marriage of the parents may be due to an official betrothal. Espousal Books, recording such contracts, survive for a handful of parishes. Betrothals gradually declined to the freely breakable status of engagements.

Bible Christians   (O'Bryanites) seceded from Wesleyans and later joined the Methodist New Connexion and United Methodist Free Church which became the United Methodist Church.

Bibliographies (of Genealogy)   The following are recommended:

Gatfield, George *Guide to Printed Books & MSS Relating to English and Foreign Heraldry and Genealogy* (1892)

Harrison, H.G. *Select Bibliography of English Genealogy* (1937)

Humphery-Smith, Cecil R. *A Genealogist's Bibliography* (Phillimore, 1985)

Kaminkow, M.J. *A New Bibliography of British Genealogy* (Magna Charta, 1965)

Raymond, S.A. and J.S.W. Gibson *English Genealogy: An Introductory Bibliography* (1991)

Raymond, S.A. and J.S.W. Gibson *Occupational Sources for Genealogists: A Bibliography* (1992).

Raymond, S.A. and J.S.W. Gibson *County Bibliographies* (1991–1993). Volumes published so far are for Dorset, Somerset, Gloucestershire and Bristol, Suffolk, Oxfordshire, Cumberland and Westmorland, Wiltshire, Buckinghamshire and Norfolk. Further volumes in this series will be published with London and Middlesex soon to appear.

Steel, D.J. *National Index of Parish Registers* Vol. 1. (Society of Genealogists, 1968)

Bid Ale   A social function organised by the churchwardens of a parish to raise money for those in need or temporary distress.

Bigamy   (i) In ecclesiastical law, a second marriage or a marriage with a widow or widower.
(ii) Having two wives or husbands at once.

Big R   The Big R stands for the Big Register of members' interests that is being compiled by the Federation of Family History Societies. It differs from other interest listings in that it sorts the surnames by the county from where the people came, so that the chance of contacting someone with a similar interest is improved.

Bill   (i) A document acknowledging an obligation to pay money.
(ii) In law, a declaration in writing, e.g. a Bill of Complaint, expressing a wrong alleged to have been suffered, thus initiating a law suit.

Bill of Exchange   A written request or order from one person (the drawer) to another (the drawee) to pay a stated sum of money to a third person (the payee) at a certain date. If the drawee accepts the bill — normally by an arrangement made in advance — he thereby becomes the acceptor. Such bills were sometimes discounted at an earlier date by a money-lender. Eventually the drawer has to repay the drawee. Bills of exchange were much in use before bank cheques became the normal method of payment.

Birmingham and Midland Society for Genealogy and Heraldry   *see* **Warwickshire**

Birth Brief *see* **Ancestry Chart**

Birth Certificate *see* **General Register of Births, Deaths and Marriages**

Births at Sea *see* **Sea, Births and Deaths at**

Bishop   A priest consecrated for the spiritual direction of a diocese. A Coadjutor Bishop or Suffragan Bishop is an assistant to a Diocesan Bishop. Bishoprics were abolished in 1645 but restored on the Restoration of the monarchy. Bishops have the right to confer holy orders, administer confirmation, and consecrate churches. Since the Reformation the appointment of bishops has been vested in the Crown, but the form of election by the cathedral chapter is retained. Their consecration is carried out by an archbishop. A bishop can dispense with the proclamation of banns by issuing a marriage licence. As spiritual peers all bishops once had seats in the House of Lords, but these are now limited to 25, of which five are always occupied by the two English archbishops and the bishops of London, Winchester and Durham.

Bishops' and Archbishops' Registers

The Registers, extant from the early thirteenth century, record matters dealt with in an official capacity by the archbishop, his suffragan and his vicar-general, and by the bishop and his chancellor, including always the institution of parochial incumbents. The patrons of benefices are mentioned and also any special conditions attached to the institution. The building or repair of a church gives rise to entries, as do legal disputes, tithes, the endowment of chantries and the relations between vicar and rector and any neighbouring religious houses.

For further reading, see *Guide to Bishops' Registers of England and Wales*, ed. D.M. Smith (Royal Hist. Soc., 1981).

Bishops' Transcript   A copy of one year's entries in a parish register, sent by the incumbent to his bishop, usually at Easter. This practice was made general in 1598 in accordance with an archiepiscopal order of the previous year, but in some dioceses it had been the custom from about the beginning of Queen Elizabeth I's reign.

In almost any series of Transcripts there are annual gaps and also errors and omissions owing to insufficient care in copying. However, they sometimes contain entries and valuable details omitted from the original registers. This stems from the practice by some incumbents of making notes of all baptisms, etc., on loose sheets or in rough notebooks and copying them into the register book at the end of the year, at the same time as making another copy for the bishop. During the Commonwealth, very few transcripts were made. From 1813 all Transcripts had to be sent to the Diocesan Registrar. Incumbents of peculiars sent their Transcripts to their ecclesiastical superior instead of to their bishop, but from 1813 they were obliged to conform to the general practice. Bishops' Transcripts should not be treated as a source alternative to registers, but as a check on them and as a substitute when the registers are missing or contain gaps or omissions. The spelling of personal names, often differs from that in the parish register, which may be a help in identification.

The Federation of Family History Societies has published a useful guide to the location and indexes of the Transcripts, entitled *Bishops' Transcripts and Marriage Licences*, by J.S.W. Gibson.

Bishops' Visitations *see* Ecclesiastical Visitations

Black Death *see* Plague

Blazonry *see* Heraldry

Blodwite A fine paid as compensation for bloodshed. Also called Angwite.

Blood Descent *see* Ancestry Chart

Blue Coat Boy Many lower orders such as servants or almoners, bedesmen, beadles, soldiers or sailors, wore blue clothing. Charity children were known as Blue Coat Boys because of their prescribed dress.

Board of Guardians *see* Guardians of the Poor

Bona Notabilia These words (Considerable Goods) appear as a note in probate records to indicate that the estate was of the value of £5 or over. Sometimes they also implied that it came under more than one probate jurisdiction. The phrase 'having etc' in an Act Book entry refers to *bona notabilia*.

Bond A binding engagement with a penalty for non-performance. A bond deed is in two parts, the *Obligation* and the *Condition*. Before 1733 the *Obligation*, which records the penalty, was written in Latin. The *Condition* describes what the bonded person has undertaken to do, or otherwise committed himself to (e.g. the truth of a statement), and was always in English.

Bonded Servants *see* Indentured Servants

Bondland Bondland was an early form of copyhold tenure where a man received land in return for the performance of particular duties.

Bookland Land held by rights granted by a written 'book' or title deed. It was transferable by the holder.

Boonmaster One of the many local names for the parochial official who was the Surveyor of the Highways.

Boonwork Major seasonal labour services on a medieval manor, such as ploughing, haymaking or reaping. Originally done as a favour to the lord, but later compulsory. The tasks had to be performed at certain times during the year, for example at the spring and autumn ploughing and at harvest. These were, of course particularly inconvenient to the tenant.

Bordar A small-holder, usually on the outskirts of the village. It has been suggested that the word derives from the French *borde*, meaning 'a hut'. Bordar is a term occurring frequently in the *Domesday Book. See also* COTTAR.

Border Marriages The practice by English couples of contracting marriage at villages just over the Scottish border became common as a result of Lord Hardwicke's *Marriage Act*, which came into force in 1754. As that Act made marriages in England legal only if performed in a building licensed for that purpose, it became necessary for runaway couples to cross into Scotland, where marriage by mere consent, given before witnesses and followed by cohabitation, was legally valid. As even the presence of a minister was unnecessary, a number of men set themselves up in business in Scottish border villages solely to perform such marriages. Gretna Green has become the best known of these places, but the 'ceremony' was also available at Springfield, Halidon Hill, Coldstream, Sark Toll Bar, Lambton Toll Bar and Alison's Toll Bar. In 1825 one of the ministers turned Old Gretna Hall into a marriage centre and hotel, thus offering facilities for both ceremony and consummation.

The various ministers kept their registers in their own custody, for which reason many of them no longer exist. However, the following are still extant at the places shown, see table on page 56.

Place of Marriage	Period	No. of Entries	Minister	Present-Day Location
Allison's Toll Bar	1843–1864	6000+	John Murray & daughter	Messrs. Wright Brown & Strong, Solicitors, 7 & 9 Bank St. Carlise CA3 8HQ
Coldstream Marriage House	1793–1797			Museums Officer Berwickshire District Council, 8 Newton St., Duns, TD11 3DT
Gretna Hall	1829–1855	1134	John Linton	Ewart Library Catherine St. Dumfries DG1 1JB
Lamberton Toll	1833–1848		Henry Collins	SOG, 14 Charterhouse Buildings, Goswell Road, London EC1M 7BA
Sark Toll Bar	1832–1845	342	George McQueen	Ewart Library Catherine St. Dumfries DG1 1JB
Springfield	1783–1895	4 vols	David, Simon & Wm. Lang	Messrs. Robert Mickle, Son & Hall, 12 New Bridge St., Newcastle on Tyne NE1 8AS
Springfield	1811–1838	25 Notebooks	Robert Elliot	Mrs Pearson 51 St. Nicholas Street, Carlise
Springfield	1825–1840	600	John Linton	J. Armstrong Dumfries
Springfield	1843–1862	910	John Douglas	Gretna Registration Office, Central Avenue, Gretna CA6 5AQ

Border Marriage Registers

There are photocopies of the Springfield register (1843–1862) at the Ewart Library, Dumfries, of the Lamberton Toll at the General Register Office, New Register House, Edinburgh EH1 3YT and of the Coldstream Marriage House at the Northumberland Record Office, Berwick and at Borders Regional Archives, Selkirk.

In 1856 Lord Brougham's *Marriage Act* made it illegal to be married, except by licence, where neither of the partners had been resident during the preceding twenty-one days. From 1878, marriages in Scotland had to be performed in buildings licensed for that purpose.

Borough English A custom of inheritance in certain ancient boroughs and manors in southern England, where the youngest son, and not the eldest, was considered the heir to his father's burgage or copyhold tenement. The custom died out with the ending of copyhold tenure.

Borough Records In the Middle Ages a large number of towns and villages were granted royal charters giving them powers of local government. Their records, therefore, are those of bodies carrying out the same administrative and judicial functions as those of the counties, plus a number dealing with specifically urban problems. Not all ancient borough archives have been carefully preserved, but some extend back into the Middle Ages. For the genealogist, the most important are the Minute Books and the Orders and Decrees of the Common Council, which may be supplemented by Depositions and Books of Examination covering preliminary enquiries. Also useful are the account books of the chamberlain, steward and treasurer, and the records of municipal properties and their tenants. For judicial purposes, several courts would be operating within a borough, such as a manorial Court Leet, the Mayor's Court, Court of Orphans, of Conscience and Requests, and of Pie-powder (*see* PIEPOUDRÉ, COURT OF), as well as those of Gaol Delivery and Sessions of the Peace. There are also separate records of the borough's manifold responsibilities, such as Watch and Ward, Street-lighting, Paving, Turnpike Trusts and Schools. Those of the merchant and craft guilds may also be there. The names of the burgesses were enrolled on their being appointed, as also are those of apprentices. Political information may be gleaned from any correspondence between the Common Council and their elected Members of Parliament. By the *Municipal Corporation Act*, 1835, the minutes and proceedings of borough councils had to be printed and available to the public on request.

A borough's archives may be found at the town hall, often without any full-time archivist in charge of them, but in many cases they have now been deposited at the county record office or county library.

For further reading, see J.West *Town Records*, Phillimore (1983).

Borsholder   A local name, especially in Kent, for the parish constable.

Borthwick Institute of Historical Research   Based at St Anthony's Hall, York, this department of the University of York has as its main purpose the furtherance of research into ecclesiastical history, particularly that of the Province of York. However, in addition to the diocesan archives, it houses parish registers, bishops' transcripts and other parochial records; also Poor law records, the probate records of the Prerogative, Consistory, Chancery and Exchequer courts and a number of Peculiars, marriage licence allegations and bonds, manor court rolls and tithe awards. Searchers wishing to visit the Institute should make an appointment. A charge is made for searches by genealogists in 'parish register transcripts'. The Institute has published a very useful *Guide to Genealogical Sources in the Borthwick Institute of Historical Research*.

Bote   The right, common to all tenants of a manor, to take timber from the waste for the repairing of hedges, fences or houses, or for firewood, tools, and so on. Often more specifically called haybote (for hedges), housebote, firebote, ploughbote.

Bottom   A low-lying meadow, as distinct from an upland or dry one.

Bovate   One eighth of a ploughland. Also called an oxgang.

Bow   The six-foot longbow came into its own during the Hundred Years' War, especially after its success at Crécy. As its use called for a high degree of skill, an Act of Edward IV compelled every Englishman between the ages of 16 and 60 to own a bow of his own height, and every township to set up its own butts on Artillery Grounds, where shooting practice was compulsory on Sundays and feast days. Games that might draw men away from archery, such as football, were designated 'unlawful sports'.

Though firearms came into use in the fifteenth century, the bow was still valued for its mobility, its speed of fire, which was six times that of the musket, and also for its cheapness. Every local militia was expected to include bowmen. The longbow played an important role in battle in the reign of Elizabeth I, but archery was still officially encouraged for Londoners under Charles I. In early Victorian times it experienced a popular revival as a sport among the upper classes.

The cross-bow was used mainly by the French, who placed their faith in men-at-arms, the cavalry arm. Henry VIII forbade the use of the cross-bow in England, regarding it as an inferior weapon.

Bower Hold   Land held in customary tenure.

Boyd's Marriage Index   This index of marriages covers, in varying degrees of completeness, the marriage registers of sixteen counties from their beginnings until the year 1837. It was compiled by Percival Boyd mainly from printed register copies, and is available to searchers at the Society of Genealogists and the Guildhall Library, London. Each of the counties listed below is indexed in a separate series of volumes. Others are grouped together in two miscellaneous series, containing additional parishes of the named counties. Each volume, except the first and last, covers 25 years. The Society has published a *List of Parishes in Boyd's Marriage Index*.

The counties included, and the number of parishes covered, or partly covered, in each, excluding the miscellaneous series, are:

Cambridgeshire	169	London &	
Cornwall	202	Middlesex	160
Cumberland	34	Norfolk	146
Derbyshire	80	Northumberland	84
Devon	169	Shropshire	125
County Durham	72	Somerset	120
Essex	374	Suffolk	489
Gloucestershire	121	Yorkshire	174
Lancashire	101		

See also MARRIAGE INDEX.

Bradford Family History Society   *see* **Yorkshire**

Breach   The removal of dead hedges after the corn or hay harvest.

Bread, Assize of   In 1266 the principle was established that the price of a loaf of bread should remain fixed, but that its weight might vary according to the price of wheat. The Assize was the inspection and weighing of loaves, one of the functions of an offical of the manorial Court Leet.

Break *or* **Breck** A temporary enclosure, especially from forest land. It often became permanent. A type of ASSART.

Brewster Sessions Victuallers had to renew their licenses annually which were issued at these sessions. Their records barely survive.

Bride Ale A function organised in the parish by the churchwardens, to raise money to help a young married couple to set up house.

Bridewell At first a workplace for vagabonds and beggars, but, by the 1750s, used as a county gaol or House of Correction.

Bridgewardens' Accounts During Tudor and Stuart times the transportation of goods by road was increasing, and could not be allowed to be held up by broken bridges for which no one would assume responsibility. In 1531 the *Statute of Bridges* authorised Justices of the Peace 'to enquire, hear, determine in the King's General Sessions of the Peace all manner of annoyances of bridges broken in the highways'. The responsibility was placed upon the city, borough or parish in which the bridge was situated. Sometimes a guild undertook the upkeep of a bridge as a pious duty. Many people also left legacies for this purpose.

Boroughs appointed bridgewardens to collect rents from lands donated for the upkeep of the bridge. The earliest bridgewardens' accounts date from 1526. Such accounts usually mention by name men paid to work on the bridge, and people from whom materials were bought. The records will now usually be at the county, city or borough record office.

The Bridge House records of Old London Bridge are at the Corporation of London Record Office at the Guildhall. In addition to the usual details of maintenance, they contain the names of the leaseholders of the houses and shops on the bridge, which in most cases were not those of the actual inhabitants.

Brief A royal mandate for a collection towards some deserving object. It was addressed to the parish incumbent and churchwardens, and was read from the pulpit. At the end of the service the clerk took the collection at the church door.

The funds were handed to an authorised travelling collector, and the brief was returned with an endorsement of the amount raised. The sum was also entered in the parish records, often in the parish registers. The mandate was sometimes called a Church Brief, or King's Brief.

Bristol and Avon Family History Society *see* **Gloucestershire** *and* **Somerset**

British Association for Local History *see* **Local History**

British Genealogical Record Users Committee In 1986 a committee was set up to discuss matters of general interest to family historians. It does not sit regularly but only when there are particular matters that need addressing. The organisations represented are the Society of Genealogists, the Federation of Family History Societies, the Institute of Heraldic and Genealogical Studies, the Genealogical Society of Utah, the Society of Archivists, the Association of County Archivists, the British Association for Local History, Local Population Studies, CAMPOP, the Association of Genealogists and Record Agents, the Guild of One-name Studies, the Scottish Association of Family History Societies and the Public Record Office.

British Library The Reference Division's Department of Printed Books is situated in the British Museum in Great Russell Street, London WC1, and was formerly known as the British Museum Library. A reader's ticket is required for access to the Reading Room, and this has to be applied for personally at the library.

Under the *Copyright Acts*, the British Library is given a copy of every book printed in the country, so almost any book required by the genealogist will be found here, and some of those most commonly consulted are immediately available on the open shelves — including the *Annual Register*, *Calendars of State Papers*, *Gentleman's Magazine*, *Historical MSS Commission Reports*, *Notes and Queries*, the *Rolls* series, *The Times* index, and the *Victoria County Histories*.

London newspapers before 1801 are also here, but later ones are at the British Library's Newspaper Library, for which *see* NEWSPAPERS. A guide to the use of the catalogues is available.

The Reading Room is open from 9 a.m. and closes at 9 p.m. on Tuesday, Wednesday and Thursday, and at 5 p.m. on Monday, Friday and Saturday. There is also a Map Library in the King Edward Building on the north side of the British Museum, open from 9.30 a.m. to 4.30 p.m.,

Monday to Saturday. Also in the British Museum, the British Library has a Department of Manuscripts containing deposited collections from numerous sources. These are all well catalogued. Printed indexes to the Library's manuscripts can be found in some of the larger public libraries.

British Newspaper Library *see* **Newspapers**

British Record Society Formerly the Index Society (founded 1888) it publishes the Index Library, consisting of indexes of important groups of historical records, nearly all of assistance to genealogists. The records include wills, marriage licences, Chancery proceedings and Inquisitions Post Mortem. There is particular emphasis on indexes to probate records pre-1750, though many continue until later. Their Secretary is Patric Dickinson, College of Arms, London EC4V 4BT.

British Records Association Founded in 1932, the Association's main purpose is to advise and to give assistance on all matters which relate to the preservation of records. To the Association's influence has been largely due the establishment of the National Register of Archives, the setting up of county record offices and the professional status of archivists. The Association's address is: 18 Padbury Court, London E2 7EH. For a more detailed account of the Association see *Family Tree* December 1988 pp. 5–6.

Brother A term often used to mean a brother-in-law. Sometimes, to make clear which is meant, a real brother is referred to as 'my own brother'.

Brothers Keeper A SHAREWARE genealogical programme for recording family history data and producing charts.

Brownists An alternative name for the Separatists, the earliest sect of Puritan dissenters. They were led by Robert Browne (*c*. 1550–*c*. 1633), a schoolmaster. His following, suppressed in England, fled to Middelburg and Amsterdam and in time gave rise to the Independent (Congregationalist) and Baptist denominations.

Buckinghamshire The county falls within the province of Canterbury and the diocese of Lincoln. It has 266 ancient parishes of which 104 register copies are held by the SOG library.

Pallots marriage index covers seventy-two parishes from 1790–1812.

The Hundreds of Ashendon, Aylesbury, Buckingham, Burnham, Cottesloe, Desborough, Newport, Stoke and Alyesbury and Buckingham Boroughs lie within its boundaries.

It has Amersham, Eton, Wycombe, Aylesbury, Winslow, Newport Pagnell and Buckingham RDs/PLUs.

It fell within the Norfolk Assize Circuit from 1558–1876 and then the South Eastern Assize circuit.

The local FHSs are The Buckingham Family History Society (who have branches at Aylesbury and Milton Keynes) and the Buckingham Genealogical Society who publish *Origins* and *Bucks Ancestor* respectively. There are two record offices in Aylesbury at the County Hall and the County Reference Library.

Wills before 1858 were proved at the Archdeaconry of Buckingham and the peculiar courts of the Archbishop of Canterbury, the Prebend of Aylesbury, the Prebend of Buckingham, Monks Risborough and Thame (all these are held at the CRO). The wills proved at the Peculiar Court of the Provost of Eton are at 'Penzance', Eton College, the Hertfordshire CRO has those of the Archdeaconry Court of St Albans and the Bodleian Library has those of the Peculiar Court of Bierton.

Herald's Visitations have been printed for 1566 and 1634. The Buckinghamshire Record Society has published local material since 1937.

Buckinghamshire Record Office publishes notes for the guidance of genealogists. See also *National Index of Parish Registers*, vol. 9, Part 3 (1992) and *Buckinghamshire: a genealogical bibliography*, by S. Raymond (FFHS, 1993).

Bulletin Board A computer accessible using dialled telephone lines from other computers. The remote user can send messages to it, read messages left by others and copy program and information files.

Burebrige A breach of surety.

Burgage A small-holding in a town, rented by a free burgess under burgess tenure.

Burgess A person holding some of the privileges conferred by a municipal corporation. Also a person elected to Parliament to represent a borough.
Finding Aid: *Electoral Registers, 1832 and Burgess Rolls*, by Jeremy Gibson and Colin Rogers.

Burgess Tenure   A form of tenure peculiar to boroughs. The tenant had the free disposal of his land or property in accordance with the custom of the borough, and paid only a nominal rent (called a land-gable) which made him quit of all other services to his feudal superior. If the lord was the king, the tenant held in chief.

Burial Register *see* **Parish Register**

Burial Grounds *see* **Cemeteries**

Buried, Partly   An expression meaning that the heart of the deceased was buried separately from the rest of the body, usually in conformance with a will or dying wish.

Burke's Peerage *see* **Peerage**

Burleyman   Another name for the manorial beadle or constable, probably a corruption of 'bylawman'.

Business Records *see* **Company Records**

Butt   (i) A land (or selion) in a common field abutting more or less at right angles upon another selion.
(ii) A land which, because of the irregular shape of the field falls short of the full length.
(iii) A mark to be shot at.

Buttery   A room or area where beer was brewed.

Byblow   An illegitimate child.

C

Cadet   A member of a subsidiary branch of a family.

Cadency, Marks of *see* **Heraldry**

Calderdale Family History Society *see* **Yorkshire**

Calendar   (i) A catalogue of documents that gives the essential data contained in them, and the names of all persons and places mentioned.
(ii) The system fixing the civil year's beginning, length and sub-divisions. In the Middle Ages, dates were usually indicated (for years) by the REGNAL YEAR of the reigning monarch, and (for days) by the number of days before or after the nearest church festival or fast. When *Anno Domini* years were shown, there was no regularity as to the day on which the year was considered to have begun. To the writer of the document, New Year's Day might have been 1 January, 25 March or 25 December. At the Reformation it was laid down in the *Book of Common Prayer* that 'the Supputation [reckoning] of the year of our Lord in the Church of England beginneth the Five and twentieth day of March, the same day supposed to be the first day upon which the world was created and the day when Christ was conceived in the womb of the Virgin Mary'. In the 1662 version, that date for New Year's Day was retained but the reason for it was omitted.

In 1752 two changes were made in the English calendar. The first was from the Julian to the more accurate Gregorian system that had been introduced in Catholic countries by Pope Gregory XIII in March 1582. A difference of eleven days had accumulated between the systems, so the change necessitated England's 'losing' that number of days. To bring that about, the day following 2 September 1752 was renumbered 14.

The second change, of far greater importance to genealogists, was that the commencement of that year was brought forward from 25 March to the preceding 1 January. This changed January, February and most of March from being the last months of the Old Year to the first of the New. As the new system had already been put into use by some people in advance of its official introduction, care has to be taken when transcribing documents of the pre-1752 period dated between 1 January and 24 March. The correct transcription procedure is to use both Old and New Style for example, by copying '5th February 1626' as '5th February 1626/7'.

The months of September, October, November and December, which used to be the seventh to tenth months of the year, are sometimes found abbreviated to the '7ber, 8ber, 9ber and 10ber' respectively, and must not be mistaken for the present seventh to tenth months, July to October.

The festivals and fasts often used to date events are too numerous to list here *in toto*, but the following are the fixed ones most often found, plus some of the dates observed as 'solemn days'. In most parishes the day of the saint to whom the local church is dedicated may also be found used for dating purposes.

January	1 Circumcision
	6 Epiphany. Twelfth Day
	13 St Hilary the Bishop
	30 Death of Charles, King and Martyr (solemn day)
February	2 Purification of the Blessed Virgin Mary (Candlemas)
	24 St Matthias*
March	25 Annunciation of the Blessed Virgin Mary* (Lady Day, a quarter day)
April	23 St George
May	1 St Philip and St James the Less (May Day)
	29 Restoration of Charles II (solemn day)
June	24 Nativity of St John the Baptist* (Midsummer Day, a quarter day)
	29 St Peter the Apostle*
July	25 St James the Apostle*
August	24 St Bartholomew the Apostle*
September	21 St Matthew the Apostle*
	29 St Michael and All Angels (Michaelmas, a quarter day)
October	25 St Crispin, anniversary of Agincourt
	28 St Simon and St Jude the Apostles*
November	1 All Saints (Allhallows)*
	2 All Souls
	5 Gunpowder Plot (solemn day)
	30 St Andrew the Apostle*
December	6 St Nicholas
	21 St Thomas the Apostle*
	25 Christmas Day* (a quarter day)
	26 St Stephen
	28 Holy Innocents

*The eve of the festivals marked thus was kept as a fast, but when the festival fell on a Monday, the fast was kept on the previous Saturday.

The most important movable feast is Easter, for which see the table overleaf. The dates of the other movable feasts are governed by that of Easter, as follows:

Septuagesima ⎫
Sexagesima ⎪
Quinquagesima ⎬ Sunday is
Quadragesima ⎭

nine ⎫
eight ⎪
seven ⎬
six ⎭

weeks ⎫
before ⎪
Easter ⎬
Day ⎭

Ash Wednesday is six and a half weeks before Easter Day.

Rogation Sunday ⎫
Ascension Day ⎪
Whitsunday ⎬ is
Trinity Sunday ⎭

five weeks ⎫
forty days ⎪
seven weeks ⎬
eight weeks ⎭

after Easter Day

Advent Sunday is the nearest to the feast of St Andrew the Apostle, whether before or after.

For further reading, see *A Handbook of British Chronology* by Sir Maurice Powicke and D. & E.B. Fryde, and *A Handbook of Dates* by C.R. Cheney. See also PERPETUAL CALENDAR; LAW TERMS.

Calvinists Calvinists believed in predestination which means that some have been chosen for salvation and some have not. They also believe that God is supreme in Church and State.

Cambellites Scottish Baptists were called Cambellites. They were founded by Alexander Campbell, son of a Secessionist Presbyterian Minister with Arminian views.

Cambridgeshire Since the boundary changes of 1974, Cambridgeshire has included not only the Isle of Ely but also the ancient county of Huntingdon and the Soke of Peterborough.

The county falls within the province of Canterbury and the diocese of Ely. Transcripts of nearly all its parish registers are held by the SOG library. Pallots marriage index covers forty-four parishes from 1790–1837. Boyds marriage index covers nearly all of the parishes.

The Hundreds of Armingford, Chesterton, Cheveley, Chilford, Flendish, Longstow, Northstow, Papworth, Radfield, Staine, Staploe, Thriplow, Wetherley, Whittlesford, the Isle of Ely, Wisbech, Witchford, North and South, and Cambridge Borough lie within its boundaries.

It has Caxton, Chesterton, Cambridge, Linton, Newmarket, Ely, North Witchford, Whittlesey and Wisbech RDs/PLUs.

It fell within the Norfolk Assize circuit until 1876 and then the South Eastern Assize Circuit.

The local FHS is the Cambridgeshire Family History Society who publish a quarterly journal and meet at Cambridge.

There are record offices at the Shire Hall, Cambridge and at Cambridge University Library. There is a Family History Centre at Cambridge.

Wills before 1858 were proved at the Court of the Chancellor or Vice Chancellor of the University, records of which are held at the University

Easter Day

Year			Year			Year			Year			Year			Year			Year		
1500	A	19	1556	A	5	1612	A	12	1668	M	22	1724	A	5	1778	A	19	1834	M	30
1	A	11	7	A	18	3	A	4	9	A	11	5	M	28	9	A	4	5	A	19
2	M	27	8	A	10	4	A	24	1670	A	3	6	A	10	1780	M	26	6	A	3
3	A	16	9	M	26	5	A	9	1	A	23	7	A	2	1	A	15	7	M	26
4	A	7	1560	A	14	6	M	31	2	A	7	8	A	21	2	M	31	8	A	15
5	M	23	1	A	6	7	A	20	3	M	30	9	A	6	3	A	20	9	M	31
6	A	12	2	M	29	8	A	5	4	A	19	1730	M	29	4	A	11	1840	A	19
7	A	4	3	A	11	9	M	28	5	A	4	1	A	18	5	M	27	1	A	11
8	A	23	4	A	2	1620	A	16	6	M	26	2	A	9	6	A	16	2	M	27
9	A	8	5	A	22	1	A	1	7	A	15	3	M	25	7	A	8	3	A	16
1510	M	31	6	A	14	2	A	21	8	M	31	4	A	14	8	M	23	4	A	7
1	A	20	7	M	30	3	A	13	9	A	20	5	A	6	9	A	12	5	M	23
2	A	11	8	A	18	4	M	28	1680	A	11	6	A	25	1790	A	4	6	A	12
3	M	27	9	A	10	5	A	17	1	A	3	7	A	10	1	A	24	7	A	4
4	A	16	1570	M	26	6	A	9	2	A	16	8	A	2	2	A	8	8	A	23
5	A	8	1	A	15	7	M	25	3	A	8	9	A	22	3	M	31	9	A	8
6	M	23	2	A	6	8	A	13	4	M	30	1740	A	6	4	A	20	1850	M	31
7	A	12	3	M	22	9	A	5	5	A	19	1	M	29	5	A	5	1	A	20
8	A	4	4	A	11	1630	M	28	6	A	4	2	A	18	6	M	27	2	A	11
9	A	24	5	A	3	1	A	10	7	M	27	3	A	3	7	A	16	3	M	27
1520	A	8	6	A	22	2	A	1	8	A	15	4	M	25	8	A	8	4	A	16
1	M	31	7	A	7	3	A	21	9	M	31	5	A	14	9	M	24	5	A	8
2	A	20	8	M	30	4	A	6	1690	A	20	6	M	30	1800	A	13	6	M	23
3	A	5	9	A	19	5	M	29	1	A	12	7	A	19	1	A	5	7	A	12
4	M	27	1580	A	3	6	A	17	2	M	27	8	A	10	2	A	18	8	A	4
5	A	16	1	M	26	7	A	9	3	A	16	9	M	26	3	A	10	9	A	24
6	A	1	2	A	15	8	M	25	4	A	8	1750	A	15	4	A	1	1860	A	8
7	A	21	3	M	31	9	A	14	5	M	24	1	A	2	5	A	14	1	M	31
8	A	12	4	A	19	1640	A	5	6	A	12	New style			6	A	6	2	A	20
9	M	28	5	A	11	1	A	25	7	A	4	2	A	2	7	M	29	3	A	5
1530	A	17	6	A	3	2	A	10	8	A	24	3	A	22	8	A	17	4	M	27
1	A	9	7	A	16	3	A	2	9	A	9	4	A	14	9	A	2	5	A	16
2	M	31	8	A	7	4	A	21	1700	M	31	5	M	30	1810	A	22	6	A	1
3	A	13	9	M	30	5	A	6	1	A	20	6	A	18	1	A	14	7	A	21
4	A	5	1590	A	19	6	M	29	2	A	5	7	A	10	2	M	29	8	A	12
5	M	28	1	A	4	7	A	18	3	M	28	8	M	26	3	A	18	9	M	28
6	A	16	2	M	26	8	A	2	4	A	16	9	A	15	4	A	10	1870	A	17
7	A	1	3	A	15	9	M	25	5	A	8	1760	A	6	5	M	26	1	A	9
8	A	21	4	M	31	1650	A	14	6	M	24	1	M	22	6	A	14	2	M	31
9	A	6	5	A	20	1	M	30	7	A	13	2	A	11	7	A	6	3	A	13
1540	M	28	6	A	11	2	A	18	8	A	4	3	A	3	8	M	22	4	A	5
1	A	17	7	M	27	3	A	10	9	A	24	4	A	22	9	A	11	5	M	28
2	A	9	8	A	16	4	M	26	1710	A	9	5	A	7	1820	A	2	6	A	16
3	M	25	9	A	8	5	A	15	1	A	1	6	M	30	1	A	22	7	A	1
4	A	13	1600	M	23	6	A	6	2	A	20	7	A	19	2	A	7	8	A	21
5	A	5	1	A	12	7	M	29	3	A	5	8	A	3	3	M	30	9	A	13
6	A	25	2	A	4	8	A	11	4	M	28	9	M	26	4	A	18	1880	M	28
7	A	10	3	A	24	9	A	3	5	A	17	1770	A	15	5	A	3	1	A	17
8	A	1	4	A	8	1660	A	22	6	A	1	1	M	31	6	M	26	2	A	9
9	A	21	5	M	31	1	A	14	7	A	21	2	A	19	7	A	15	3	M	25
1550	A	6	6	A	20	2	M	30	8	A	13	3	A	11	8	A	6	4	A	13
1	M	29	7	A	5	3	A	19	9	M	29	4	A	3	9	A	19	5	A	5
2	A	17	8	M	27	4	A	10	1720	A	17	5	A	16	1830	A	11	6	A	25
3	A	2	9	A	16	5	M	26	1	A	9	6	A	7	1	A	3	7	A	10
4	M	25	1610	A	8	6	A	15	2	M	25	7	M	30	2	A	22	8	A	1
5	A	14	1	M	24	7	A	7	3	A	14				3	A	7	9	A	21

M = March   A = April

Library, the Archdeaconry Court of Ely, Consistory Court of Ely and the Peculiar Court of Thorney, held at the CRO, the Peculiar Court of Kings College, held at that college in Cambridge, and the Archdeaconry of Sudbury and the Peculiar Court of the Bishop of Rochester (for Isleham and for Freckenham in Suffolk), held at the Suffolk Record Office. The Archdeaconry of Ely had jurisdiction only in the 52 parishes of the deaneries of Bourn, Cambridge and Shingay, and the parishes of Haddenham and Wilburton in the Isle of Ely. Thirteen parishes near Newmarket lay in the deanery of Fordham and the diocese of Norwich. Wills for these could be proved in the Archdeaconry Court of Sudbury or in the Consistory Court of Norwich.

Herald's Visitations have been printed for 1575 and 1619. The Cambridge Antiquarian Records Society has published local material since 1974.

Cambridge County Record Office publishes *Genealogical sources in Cambridgeshire*. See also *National Index of Parish Registers*, vol. 7 (1983).

Camden Society *see* **Royal Historical Society**

Cameronians Cameronians were reformed Scottish Presbyterians.

Campipars Rent of land in the form of a proportion of the crop.

CAMPOP Is the Cambridge Group for the History of Population and Social Structure. Formed in 1964, the group specialises in research projects based on population studies. *See also* DEMOGRAPHY, HISTORICAL.

Canadian Ancestry Canada was French until the end of the eighteenth century when the Treaty of Paris caused the French to hand over their possessions on the mainland of North America and cede them to the British. Fish, furs and the prospect of a passage to China drew many explorers and traders to the northernmost part of the Americas from the sixteenth century onwards. Early settlements were established on the eastern seaboard and along the St Lawrence river by the French and immigrants from New England. The British did not arrive in Canada in any great numbers until after France had ceded their northern territories to England by the Treaty of Paris in 1763. After the American Revolution those who had remained loyal to the Crown chose to settle in Canada rather than remain in the States and they went in the main to New Brunswick. Most British immigrants

settled in Canada from the second decade of the nineteenth century. In 1791 the Canada Act divided Upper Canada (mainly Ontario) from Lower Canada (mainly Quebec). It was not until 1867 that the Dominion of Canada was formed from these four provinces. In 1870 Manitoba, 1871 British Columbia, and in 1873 Prince Edward Island, joined the Dominion. The Yukon Territory joined in 1897, Saskatchewan and Alberta in 1905 and finally Newfoundland and Labrador in 1949, the Northwest Territories having been purchased from the Hudson's Bay Company in 1869. Canada was, therefore, not united in the way we know it today. This means that although the National Archives are in Ottawa, many records needed for genealogical research are only to be found in provincial archives. Since the administration of the provinces was not part of a national administration, therefore, the survival and coverage of records differs from province to province and in Quebec are based on the original French civil code.

The Provincial Archives are held in Newfoundland at St John's; in Nova Scotia at Halifax; in Prince Edward Island at Charlottetown; in New Brunswick at Fredericton; in Quebec at Sainte Foy but the Birth, Marriage and Death registration records and local records are at nine regional offices; in Ontario at Toronto; in Manitoba at Winnipeg; in Saskatchewan at Regina and Saskatoon; in Alberta at Edmonton; in British Columbia at Victoria; in Yukon Territory at Whitehorse and in the Northwest Territories at Yellowknife.

Since there is no established church in Canada, church records are either with the incumbent, at a denominational archive or at the provincial archives who may hold transcripts of those they don't hold in the original. The registration of births, marriages and deaths was begun in the late nineteenth century but starting dates differ from province to province. In Quebec civil registration was not started until after 1926. There are some early censuses but many only give the names of heads of households. It is not until after 1851 that nominal censuses were taken for each province then in the Union. Probate records are held in provincial probate courts. Records of land titles are held in provincial archives since the province took responsibility for Crown lands. Land petitions from 1764–1841 are in the National Archive but are also widely available on microfilm.

There is a Canadian Federation of Genealogical and Family History Societies based in Winnipeg, a United Empire Loyalists Association and a Huguenot Society of Canada, both based in

Toronto. Local family history societies exist in every province and territory.

Further reading: *Tracing Your Ancestors in Canada from the National Archives of Canada*, 1991; *In Search of Your Canadian Roots*, Angus Baxter, Toronto, Macmillan of Canada, 1989; *Genealogists's Handbook for Atlantic Canada Research*, ed. Terrence M. Punch, Boston New England Historic Genealogical Society, 1989; Ontario – *Genealogy in Ontario*, by Brenda Dougall Merriman, Toronto, Ontario Genealogical Society, 1988; *Manitoba and the Prairies – Handbook for Genealogists*, by Elizabeth Briggs, Winnipeg, Manitoba Genealogical Society, 1990; Alberta – *Tracing Your Ancestors in Alberta*, by Victoria Lemieux and David Leonard, Edmonton, Lemieux-Leonard Research Associates, 1992.

Candlemas   The 2nd of February; the Feast of the Purification of the Blessed Virgin Mary. The stock of candles required for use in the church during the ensuing year was consecrated on this day.

Canon   (i) A law of the Church. All clerics were subject to Canon Law.

(ii) A cleric in a group observing a definite rule of life, for example an Augustinian Canon.

(iii) A cleric possessing a prebend for his support in a cathedral or collegiate church.

Cantref   The name given to some fiefs on the Wales-Cheshire border. Though they came under the jurisdiction of the justices of Chester, they were also partly subject to Welsh customary law.

Cap Money   To promote the wool trade, a statute of 1571, repealed in 1597–8, laid down that all persons of common degree should wear a cap of English wool on Sundays and holy days. Cap money was the fine paid for non-observance — three shillings and four pence.

Capias   A warrant for an arrest.

Capite, Tenant in   One holding his land by feudal tenure direct from the king. This Latin term is often used in English documents instead of Tenant-in-Chief.

Caption, Letters of   A letter from an ecclesiastical dignitary invoking the aid of the secular government against an obdurate excommunicate.

Cards, Genealogical Record   Printed cards, 6 × 4 inches, with spaces allotted for card number, name of person, dates and places of birth, baptism, marriage, death, burial and probate of will; also names of father, mother, spouses and children. A useful aid for rapid reference and the reconstitution of families. Available from the Society of Genealogists.

Cartulary   A register of the estates and liberties granted to owners (e.g. monasteries and manorial estates) by charter, together with the charters themselves. The term is also used to include additional classes of record such as rentals. Surviving cartularies are listed in *Medieval Cartularies of Great Britain*, by G.R.C. Davies. Those held at the Public Record Office, Chancery Lane, London, can be found in classes E 36, 132, 135, 164 and 315, LR 2 and DL 42.

Carucate   In the Danelaw, an area of ploughland assessed for taxation. As much land as an eight-ox plough team could maintain in cultivation, which varied between 160 and 180 acres, according to the soil and lie of the land. About the same area as a hide. By 1086 it had come to mean a unit of taxation.
See also HIDE; PLOUGH TEAM; VIRGATE.

Cathedral   The chief church of a diocese, where the bishop's throne (*cathedra*) was located. Often referred to as the 'mother church'.

Catholic Apostolic Church *see* **Irvingites**

Catholic Record Society *see* **Roman Catholics**

Cause   A legal suit, or case, of one party in civil proceedings at law in equity.

Caveat   A caution.

CD-ROM   Compact Disc–Read Only Memory disc, the same size as an audio compact disc. CD-ROM discs each hold about 250,000 pages of information, which can be accessed through a computer with a CD-ROM drive.

Cemeteries   Burial grounds not appertaining to any church or chapel were first made available as private ventures, but in 1852 for London and in 1853 for the rest of the country, an Act of Parliament enabled local authorities to purchase and use land for that purpose, and many cemeteries came into existence shortly afterwards. The superintendent normally has a small office near the entrance to the ground, where burial registers are housed and grave-lots listed as a guide for visitors looking for a particular grave.

PLACE	Uninhabited or Building	Inhabited	NAMES of each Person who abode therein the preceding Night.	Males	Females	PROFESSION, TRADE, EMPLOYMENT, or of INDEPENDENT MEANS.	Whether Born in same County	Whether Born in Scotland, Ireland, or Foreign Parts.
Mill Gate		1	John Hammond	50		Ind	yes	
			Isabella Varley		65	F. S	y	
do		1	John Grime	40		Bankers Col	y	
			Mary Ellwood		50	F. S	y	
do		1	Matthew Spence	45		Shoemaker	y	
			Mary do		50		y	
			John do	15			y	
			William do	13			y	
			Alice do		7		y	
			William Lye	20		Shoem Ap	y	
			William Graham	15		Shoem Ap	y	
			James Lumbley	15		Shoem Ap	y	
			William Lumbly	25		Shoem Jour	y	
			John Bolton	25		do	y	
			Jane Milner		15	F. S	y	
			John Depple	55		Ag Lab	y	
do		1	James Metcalfe	40		Plumber and Glazier	y	
			Caroline do		40		y	
			Mary do		12		y	
			Maria do		10		y	
			George do	8			y	
			Henry do	6			y	
			Margaret do		2		y	
do		1	Peter Dobson	33		Plumber & Glazier	y	
			Thomas Sanderson	25			y	

A page from the Census Record of 1841. HO 107/1254, *Crown copyright: reproduced with permission of the Controller of Her Majesty's Stationery Office.*

The registers of cemeteries in existence before 1837 are now at the Public Record Office, Chancery Lane, London. One of the earliest non-parochial cemeteries was that of Bunhill Fields, London. It was open to the deceased of all denominations, but in fact was mostly used for nonconformist burials.

For further reading, see *Greater London Cemeteries and Crematoria and their Registers* SOG (1994).

Census Returns

A census of the population of England and Wales, the Isle of Man and the Channel Isles, was first taken in 1801. This was followed by others every ten years, except for 1941 when the country was at war. The original purpose of the census was to provide population statistics, so the existing records (with a handful of exceptions) do not show the names of individual people until the Returns of 1841. From then onward the records show the names of each person at the address at which he or she spent the night of the census date.

The Returns become available for public inspection on the first working day of the year following the year in which they become one hundred years old. They are an invaluable aid to the genealogist in enabling him to discover where his ancestors were born in the early nineteenth and late eighteenth centuries, and in revealing the existence of unsuspected members of the family.

The Census of 1841 was taken on Sunday, 6/7 June, 1841, not only of every person in each house that night, but also of night workers who would return to the house in the morning. The Returns were compiled in civil parishes, and the families are shown in the order in which their houses were visited by the enumerators. The Registration Districts were the same as for the General Register. Each was sub-divided into Enumeration Districts of not less than 24, and not more than 200, inhabited houses. The forms were distributed to householders and collected and checked by the enumerators. At hotels, hospitals, ships and other institutions, the forms were filled in by the official in charge. The enumerators were volunteer schoolmasters, clergymen, businessmen and other persons of some education. The Returns were then copied, in pencil, into printed books of blank forms. These books are now available for searching on microfilm. Each one is prefaced with a description of the boundaries of the enumerator's district.

The forms show the street in which each house stood, and sometimes the number of the house or its name. The questions asked on the forms are: names of persons in the house, their ages, occupations, whether born in the same county, and whether born in Scotland, Ireland or Foreign Parts.

Names Only the surname and first Christian names are given.

Ages Exact ages in years are given for children up to the age of 14 inclusive. For persons of 15 and older, ages are given in five-year groups indicated by the youngest year of the group; that is ages from 15 to 19 inclusive are shown as 15, from 20 to 24 as 20, and so on. People, however, did not always state their ages correctly.

Occupations Often abbreviated: for example, Ag.Lab. for agricultural labourer; F.S. for female servant; F.W.K., framework knitter; Ind., of independent means; J, Journeyman; M.S., male servant; N.K., not known.

Born (County) This question is only answered by 'Yes' or 'No', abbreviated to 'Y' or 'N', depending on whether or not the person was born in the county in which he was residing on census night.

Born (Country) This is answered by 'S', 'I' or 'F', for Scotland, Ireland or Foreign Parts.

No relationships between members of the household are given, but the head of the house usually heads the list. Children may be nephews and nieces. A single stroke in the margin marks the end of a family; a double stroke, the end of a household.

The Returns may be seen at the Public Record Office (PRO) Chancery Lane, under the Class HO 107. Place name indexes are available. Large towns have separate index volumes showing each street separately. The number shown after the piece number is that of the book in the bundle, followed by the folio number of the page where the street occurs.

The Census of 1851 was taken on 31 March for the night of 30/31 March, using methods similar to those of 1841. However, the questions asked

RIGHT A page from the 1851 Census Return for Chertsey, Surrey HO 107/1593. Most of the information in the 'Where Born' column shows the genealogist what parish register to search next, but the first, third and fourth entires are annoyingly vague in this respect. *Crown copyright: reproduced with the permission of the Controller of Her Majesty's Stationery Office.*

No. of House	Name and Surname of each Person who abode in the house on the Night of the 30th March, 1851	Relation to Head of Family	Condition	Age of Males	Age of Females	Rank, Profession, or Occupation	Where Born	Whether Blind, or Deaf-and-Dumb
	William Challis	Head	Mar	62		Labourer	Berkshire	
	Sarah do	Wife	Mar		59		Surrey Chertsey	
	Eliza do	Gr Daur					London	
	William Latham	Lodger	U	57		E.F. Company Drover	Yorkshire	
	William Latham	Head	Mar	33		Butcher	Surrey Chertsey	
	Hannah do	Wife	Mar		28		do Chertsey	
	Emma Anne do	Daur			4		do Chertsey	
	Ann Harris	Niece	U			Cook	Berks Brayton	
	Esther Taylor	Cousin			3		Middx Piccadilly	
	Walter do	Son					Essex Temple	
	Charles Woolvett	Head	Unm			Sawyer	Surrey Chertsey	
	John Butt	Lodger	U		27	Labourer	do	
	Hannah Stone	Wife	Mar	64		Charwoman	Berks Chobham	
	Charles do	Son		12		Silver	Surrey Chertsey	
	James do	Gr Son		5		Silver	do	
	Eleanor do	Daur					do	
	Mary do	Gr Daur					do	
	George Beed	Wife	Mar	25		Coachman	Wilts Corsham	
	Rebecca do	Wife	Mar				Gloster Purton	
	Mary do	Daur				Scholar	Middx Westminster	
					Total of Persons...		9	11	

B

make this census considerably more useful than the earlier one.

Names Christian and surname. Sometimes a second Christian name or an initial is given.

Relationship to head of family Essential genealogical information, but beware of assuming that a person's relationship to the head of family is the same as the relationship to his wife. The man may have married twice, in which case his wife may be stepmother to some or all of his children.

Condition Married, Unmarried, Widower or Widow.

Age Shown in two columns, one for males, the other for females. Verbal returns were sometimes misheard. Again, ages were not always correctly stated.

Occupation As for 1841. Children being educated were shown as 'scholars'.

Where born Parish and county if in England or Wales, but the country only if in Scotland or Ireland or if abroad. Verbal returns by illiterates were sometimes misheard.

Whether blind, deaf-and-dumb, imbecile or lunatic.

Deposited, as for the 1841 census, at the PRO, the returns are mostly written in ink on blue paper. They are in books grouped into folders, with the parishes arranged in the same sub-districts and districts as the General Register. Each house has a schedule number which should not be mistaken for its house number, and is shown in the order in which it was visited by the enumerator. The reference is HO 107. The page numbers of the books are printed in the centre of the page at the top. Because these are repeated frequently throughout a piece number, the pieces are foliated by a machine at the top right hand corner of every other page. This numeration can be used to locate an entry precisely as it is consecutive right through the piece number. To find the right microfilm, consult first the place name index then the class list which is arranged by registration district number. There are also street indexes available for those towns with a population of over 40,000.

The Census of 1861 was taken on 8 April for the night of 7/8 April. The information given on the Returns is the same as at the census of 1851. From 1861 the page numbers of the enumerators' books are in the top outside corner of each page and not in the middle as they are in 1841 and 1851. The class reference is RG 9.

The Censuses of 1871, 1881 and 1891 were taken for the night of 2/3 April, 3/4 April and 5/6 April respectively. The references are RG 10, 11 and 12. The information is as for 1851 and 1861. Additionally in 1891 the census enumeration in Wales included a question on the language spoken. From 1891 women were allowed to apply for the job of enumerator and many took up the challenge.

In order to find the entry for a family living in a town it is necessary to find out in advance their exact address. This can be done either from a local directory or an electoral register, or by obtaining a birth or death certification of a member of the household who was born or who died at a date as close as possible to a census night.

Censuses after 1891 are still in the custody of the Registrar General. Returns are not open to the public sooner, because people still alive may be included in them, and the original information was obtained under a pledge of secrecy. However, an extract covering members of a family in one household may be obtained on application to the Registrar General for 1901 only, by, or with the written authorisation of, a descendant of the family concerned. The application must mention the exact address in the census, because no searches can be undertaken. An undertaking must be given that the information will not be used for the purposes of litigation. A fee is charged. Apply to The Registrar General, General Register Office, St Catherine's House, Kingsway, London WC2B 6JP.

Most CROs have microfilm copies of census returns for their area.

The Federation of Family History Societies has published three useful booklets, *Census Indexes and Indexing, Local Census Listings* by J. Gibson and M. Medlycott FFHS 2nd Edn. (1994) and *Marriage, Census and other Indexes for Family Historians*. They have also published a beginner's guide called *Introduction to . . . the Census Returns*. There is a PRO Readers Guide. No. 1 called *Making Use of the Census*. For a detailed study of how the census was taken read E.J. Higgs *Making Sense of the Census* HMSO, 1989.

Cess   A parochial rate, tax or assessment.

Champion   Open-field land as distinguished from land held in SEVERALTY.

Chanceling   An illegitimate child.

Chancery, Court of   The court and the office of Chancellor date from the reign of Edward the Confessor. The Chancellor was then a sort of Secretary of State for all departments. The surviving records of his Chancery date from 1199, when important letters from the king began to be enrolled in Charter Rolls, Patent Rolls and Close Rolls. The earliest are in Latin, but during the Commonwealth and after 1733, records are in English. Charter Rolls contain grants and confirmations more formal than those in Letters Patent. Fine Rolls record moneys received by the king for grants and privileges accorded, and the Parliament Rolls record transactions in Parliament down to 1886.

Chancery as a court of law dates from about 1348. It was a court of equity to deal with cases for which the Common Law made no provision, and later with cases remediable under Common Law but in which the plaintiff would have found himself under a legal disadvantage. It was absorbed into the Supreme Court of Judicature in 1875. Any propertied family is almost sure to have been concerned at some time in a Chancery suit. It is the court with more surviving records than any other. The Bills and Answers down to the year 1875 amount to 19,000 bundles, each containing on average 70 cases, making more than a million in all. Early proceedings have been briefly listed: later ones only have the title of the suit given in the list. Evidence was received in writing, and the Depositions make up a further 4000 bundles: unfortunately the list of Depositions is not helpful. These records, exceptionally rich in information for the family historian, are housed at the Public Record Office, Chancery Lane, London, and are of three main kinds:

(a) *Proceedings*

(1) Bill of Complaint by the plaintiff (or of Information by the Crown) addressed to the Lord Chancellor or the Lord Keeper of the Great Seal.

(2) Writ of Subpoena, ordering the defendant to appear. Few of these survive.

(3) Answer by the defendant, of a Plea to reject the Bill on legal grounds.

(4) Replication, or Exception, by the plaintiff.

(5) Rejoinder by the defendant.

(6) Rebuttal by the plaintiff (sometimes).

(7) Surebuttal by the defendant (sometimes).

(8) Interrogatories — lists of questions drawn up by counsels for both parties — to be put to witnesses.

(9) Depositions by witnesses, whose names, abodes, ages and occupations are shown.

(10) A Bill of Revival became necessary if one of the parties died before the case was heard.

(b) *Registers*

(1) Orders and Decrees — injunctions (for example, to appear in court or to produce papers or witnesses) and decisions of the court.

(2) Awards and Agreements, which were decisions by arbitration.

(3) Masters' Reports: reports by Masters, officials of the court, to the Chancellor commenting on the quality of the evidence, the probity of deponents, etc.

Decrees   In addition to the Register note of the court's decision, a document was issued recording it in full. (PRO class C 78).

Overleaf is a table of the classes of documents to the above-mentioned records.

(c) *Exhibits* (C103–115)

Relevant (and often irrelevant) documents were lodged with the Masters: those not reclaimed are in the classes of Chancery Masters Exhibits:

Master Blunt's Exhibits	C103	c.1250 – 1859
Master Tinney's Exhibits	C104	c.1250 – 1850
Master Lynch's Exhibits	C105	1466 – 1835

Of the above, only the Bridges Division of the Chancery Proceedings (C 5) and the Decree Rolls (C 78), provide a full index of litigants. The rest, including the Depositions, merely list the cases under the initial letters of the first plaintiff. Plaintiffs can change during a case so causes may not always be listed under the name of the original first plaintiff. Some do not show more than his single name. Where defendants are shown, and there are more than one, only one may be given and that not always the same in every listing of the case. The BERNAU INDEX, which is at the Society of Genealogists, lists all litigants, but for the 1613–1713 period, covers only the Bridges Division. The Society's Great Card Index covers all the divisions in that period but fails to give the divisions' names, so the bundle and piece numbers still have to be searched for at the PRO before the number can be found. Also, when indexing the defendants the compiler reversed the order of the names of the disputants, thus converting the defendant into the plaintiff and vice versa. This needs to be kept in mind when searching the PRO lists for the reference.

Class Title	Reference	Covering Dates	Class Title	Reference	Covering Dates
Chancery Proceedings			*Town Depositions*	C24	1534 – 1853
Early		Richard II –	*Interrogatories*	C25	1598 – 1852
	C1	Philip and Mary	*Entry Books of Decrees &*	C33	1544 – 1875
Series I		Elizabeth I –	*Orders*		(Then J 15)
	C2	Charles I	*Reports and Certificates*	C38	1544 – 1875
Series II		Elizabeth I – the	*Supplementary Reports*	C39	1580 – 1892
	C3	Commonwealth	*Chancery and Supreme*		
Supplementary Six Clerks			*Court of Judicature,*		
Series	C4	no date	*Chancery Division:*		
			Six Clerks Office	C78	1534 – 1903
Before 1714			*Chancery and Supreme*	C79	1534 – 1903
Bridges	C5	James I – 1714	*Court of Judicature, &*		
Collins	C6	James I – 1714	*Successors, Decree*		
Hamilton	C7	James I – 1714	*Rolls*		
Mitford	C8	James I – 1714			
Reynardson	C9	James I – 1714	*Supreme Court of Judicature*		
Whittington	C10	James I – 1714	*Chancery Division,*		
			Entry Books of	J15	1876 – 1955
Various Six Clerks			*Decrees and Orders*		(previously
Series I	C11	1714 – 1758			C33)
Series II	C12	1758 – 1800	*Master Chandler's*	J46	1850 – 1890
Series III	C13	1800 – 1842	*Papers*		
			Master Mosse's Papers	J63	1852 – 1917
Country Depositions			*Master Hawkins*	J64	1849 – 1925
Series I		Elizabeth I –	*Pedigrees*		
	C21	Charles I	*Master Hulbert's*	J66	1849 – 1926
Series II	C22	1649 – 1714	*Pedigrees*		
Unpublished Depositions		Elizabeth I –	*Master Newman's*	J67	1893 – 1931
	C23	Victoria	*Papers*		

The document classes for Proceedings and Registers.

Until the time of the Commonwealth, suits brought in the Court of Chancery can only be dated, and that approximately, from the name of the Lord High Chancellor or Lord Keeper of the Great Seal to whom the Bill of Complaint is addressed. A list of the Lord Chancellors can be found in the *Handbook of British Chronology* by Powicke and Fryde (Eds.) (2nd Edn. 1961) which can be seen in the PRO Reading Rooms.

The Court of Chancery's *Guardianship Orders*, creating Wards in Chancery, do not survive unless there was litigation on the subject. For 'Money in Chancery' see DORMANT FUNDS.

Litigants often sued variants of the same case in the other equity courts as well as the Chancery: so, at different times, a case may have occurred in different courts. See EXCHEQUER, COURT OF; REQUESTS, COURT OF; STAR CHAMBER, COURT OF.

Further reading: The PRO issues an information leaflet No. 30 *Chancery Proceedings (Equity Suits)*. A useful booklet *Chancery and other Legal Proceedings* by R.E.F. Garrett, has been published by Pinhorns. A PRO guide to Chancery and an SOG guide to legal records are in preparation.

Change of Name It has always been legally possible to change one's surname. A sixteenth- or seventeenth-century change is sometimes discernible when a person is found mentioned in a record as 'Smith alias Brown' (*see* ALIAS). By the seventeenth century, the convenience of having a record of the change was recognised, and wealthier people would resort to a private Act of Parliament. The last time this was done was in 1907. Another method, in use since the seventeenth century, was by Royal Licence. After 1783, applications for this were referred to the College of Arms, but nowadays this is necessary only when arms also have to be changed. The issue of a Royal Licence was normally advertised in the *London Gazette*. A third, and now the most common, method is by Deed Poll, accompanied by enrolment in the Close Rolls of Chancery (until 1903) and later in the Enrolment Books of the Supreme Court. The earliest enrolment was in 1851. The indexes of the Close Rolls at the Public Record Office, Chancery Lane, London, show the name used by the person concerned in making his declaration, usually his old name. From 1905 until 1941, both names are indexed. A fourth method of making a change is simply by advertisement in the press. A fifth, by making a Statutory Declaration before a Justice of the Peace, or Commissioner for Oaths.

By an Act of 1916, enemy aliens – and by another of 1919, all aliens – are allowed to change their names only by Royal Licence or special permission from the Home Secretary. Such changes are advertised in the *London Gazette*.

To find a recorded change, the first step is to consult *An Index to Change of Name, 1760–1901*, edited by W.P.W. Phillimore and E.A. Fry (London, 1905), available at the Society of Genealogists. Further information can be traced as indicated there. Omitted from it are only those changes by Royal Licence not advertised in the *London Gazette*, and those by Deed Pool not advertised in *The Times* from 1861. From the late nineteenth century, deeds pool enrolled can be found at the Public Record Office (PRO), Chancery Lane, London, in classes C 54 and J 18; and from 1914 they were published in the *London Gazette*. A free leaflet, *Change of Name* No. 38, is available at the PRO.

Channel Islands   Guernsey, Jersey, Alderney and Sark are included in the Census for England and Wales, occurring at the end of the classes of records that cover the census. There is a Channel Islands Family History Society and La Societé Guernesiaise has a family history section, both of whom publish journals. See *How to Trace Your Ancestors in Guernsey* by D.W. Le Poidevin, Taunton, (1978). The Societé Jersiase has published local records since 1876. See *Family History in Jersey* by M.L. Backhurst (1991).

Chantry   In its most modest form, a chantry was the provision of church services of intercession for the dead, usually parents, ancestors or benefactors, performed in a parish church by a cleric who was usually paid from the proceeds of land granted for that purpose. More elaborately it might be, for the same purpose, an altar or chapel in a church or even a separate building, to which the name became attached. Chantries were abolished in 1547.

Chapel   (i) A small Church of England church without parochial status or rights of sepulture (burial), etc., usually dependent on a parish church. Widespread parishes consisting of several hamlets, very common in the north of England, often contained chapelries served by chapels, some of which kept independent registers and were, after 1754, licensed for the performance of marriages.

(ii) An enclosure for a side altar in a large church.

(iii) The religious meeting-house of a nonconformist sect.

Chaplain   (i) An unbeneficed priest, living on a stipend from an employer.

(ii) The priest in charge of a chapel.

Chapman   A buyer or seller of various goods, often both and sometimes itinerant.

Chapman County Codes   Colin Chapman devised a set of county codes which are now used universally by family historians when they need to indicate counties briefly in indexes. They conform to BSI 6879:1987 with one or two minor exceptions.

Chapter   (i) The governing body of a cathedral or secular collegiate church, consisting of a dean, archdeacon, precentor, chancellor, treasurer and canons.

(ii) The periodic assembly of a religious community, originally so called from the custom of reading a chapter from the Rule of the Order (e.g. of St Benedict) in such assembly.

Charities   Records of charities can be found in Quarter Session records (held in County Record Offices), in vestry minutes and in printed histories. From the late eighteenth century Clerks of the Peace were required to collect copies of accounts for charitable organizations within their jurisdiction. These were then presented to Parliament. In 1853 this was taken over by the Charity Commissioners.

Charter   Properly a document granting lands or privileges, but also loosely used to cover related documents. The Charter Rolls record royal grants of land or rights to boroughs, churches and families, by enrolment of copies of the originals from 1199 to 1537.

Chartered Companies   Companies of merchants incorporated by Royal or Parliamentary charters, and engaged in foreign trade to areas of the world for which they were granted monopolies. Among the most famous and successful were the Merchant Adventurers (to the Netherlands and Hamburg), the East India Company (to southern Asia), the Levant Company (to the Turkish Empire), the Royal African Company (to West Africa), the Hudson's Bay Company (to what is now Canada), the Virginia Company (to the new American colonies of the sixteenth century), the Russia Company (to Muscovy), the Eastland Company (to the Baltic), and the South Sea Company (to South America).

The records of some of these great companies survive and provide historians with a wealth of biographical material.

Chase   A hunting area presented to a subject by the king, as distinct from a forest which was exclusively for the king's use. Offences committed in a Chase were not usually dealt with under forest law.

Chatham Chest   This is the popular name for a fund set up in the late sixteenth century to provide relief for wounded sailors. It was collected by deductions from pay and was administered by the Navy Board from offices at Chatham, hence its name. The administration of the fund was transferred in 1803 to the Royal Hospital at Greenwich.

Chattel   Any kind of property except a freehold and things appertaining to it. A more extensive term than 'goods' or 'effects'. In old wills it is sometimes written 'cattel', causing some doubt as to its true meaning. Both 'cattel' (beasts) and 'chattel' come from the Old English and Old French words meaning 'property', and the Latin *catallum* served both meanings.

Cheat   Second-quality wheaten bread. *See also* MANCHET.

Chelsea, Royal Hospital   The Royal Hospital at Chelsea was founded by Charles II in 1681 to provide for wounded and disabled soldiers. Only a small percentage of such soldiers could be housed within its walls. These became known as 'in-pensioners'. The vast majority of those eligible became 'out-pensioners' and received money to live elsewhere. The majority of records of the Royal Hospital relate to the granting and payment of such pensions. Registers of baptisms (1691–1812), marriage (1691–1765) and burial (1692–1856) for the hospital are held at the PRO Chancery Lane (RG 4/4330–4331, 4387). *See also* ARMY.

Cheminage   A toll charged on roads in royal forests during the month when hinds were dropping their calves.

Cheshire   The county now includes the southern border of Lancashire. It now falls within the diocese of Chester and the Province of York but prior to 1541 it was in the diocese of Lichfield and therefore the Province of Canterbury. Nearly all its parish registers have been deposited at the CRO and the Society of Genealogists has copies of a number of them.

The Hundreds of Broxton (Higher and Lower Divisions), Bucklow, Eddisbury (First and Second Divisions), Macclesfield, Nantwich, Northwich, Wirral (Higher and Lower Division), Chester City and Stockport Borough lie within its boundaries.

It has Stockport, Macclesfield, Altrincham, Runcorn, Northwich, Congleton, Nantwich, Great Boughton and Wirral (later Birkenhead) RDs/PLUs. It falls within the North and South Wales Assize Circuit.

Pallot's Marriage Index covers nine parishes, mostly 1790–1812. The Bishops' Transcripts are at the CRO.

The Family History Society of Cheshire publishes its journal quarterly and has branches at Altrincham, Birkenhead, Chester, Congleton, Daresbury, Macclesfield, Nantwich, Northwich, Runcorn, Wallasey and Wirral. The North Cheshire Family History Society publishes the *North Cheshire Family Historian* quarterly and has branches at Hazel Grove, Sale and Wilmslow. The South Cheshire Family History Society publishes a quarterly journal called the *Cheshire Genealogist* and meets at Crewe.

There are two record offices in Chester, one the Cheshire Record Office and one the Chester City Record Office. There is also a Family History Centre in Chester.

Wills prior to 1858 are at the CRO but were proved at the Consistory Court of Lichfield and the Prerogative Court of Canterbury prior to 1541 and after that at either the Prerogative Court of York or Canterbury. Indexes of wills, 1545–1837 have been printed by the Lancashire and Cheshire Record Society.

Transcripts of records are published by the Chetham Society, since 1844, and the Lancashire and Cheshire Record Society, since 1879. Heralds' Visitation Pedigrees have been published for 1533, 1566, 1580 and 1613.

Cheshire Record Office publishes a *Record Office guide*. See also *Archives and records of the City of Chester* by A.M. Kennett (1985), *Genealogy in Stockport* (Stockport Archive Service) and *A guide to sources for family historians* (Wirral Archives Service).

Chevage (i) A payment made by a villein to his lord for permission to live away from the manor.

(ii) A payment to the lord by an outsider for permission to live within the manor.

Chirograph A document written more than once on the same sheet of parchment, for example in an indenture.

Chirugeon A SURGEON.

Chivalry, High Court of *see* **College of Arms**

Cholera This disease was widespread in England in 1831–2 and 1849, causing great anxiety and a large number of deaths. Places with high mortality rates can be identified from parish registers and local newspapers.

Chrism A mixture of oil and balsam, consecrated by the bishop on Maundy Thursday and used throughout the succeeding year in baptism, confirmation and extreme unction, being kept in a chrismatory. When brought out it was covered with a silk cloth called a chrism cloth, which is not to be confused with a CHRISOM cloth.

Chrisom A Chrisom cloth was the white shawl, provided by a baby's parents and put upon the child by the minister during the baptismal ceremony. The child continued to wear it until its mother was 'churched', at which time the cloth was presented to the church for use in ablutions. If the child died before its mother's churching, the cloth became its shroud. Such a child would be entered in the burial registers as a Chrisom Child, Chrisomer, or Innocent. In some parts of the country this term was applied to children dying before they could be baptized. *See also* CHURCHING OF WOMEN.

Christian Names (Given Names) Within two or three generations after the Norman Conquest, Anglo-Saxon names had disappeared from among the upper classes, though they lingered on among the peasantry until the end of the thirteenth century. The few pre-Conquest names that survived were those of saints and kings, notably Alfred, Edmund, Edward, Hilda and Mildred. The most popular Norman men's names were William, Robert, Richard, Ralph, Eudes, Hugh, Walter and Alan. In a few cases Anglo-Saxon names became changed to more Norman-French forms, such as Ethelward becoming Aylward, and Regenwald, Reynold.

In the Plantagenet period, under church influence, saint's names grew in popularity, particularly Matthew, Mark, Luke, John, Philip, Simon and Michael, and, from the Mystery plays, Adam, Daniel, Isaac, Joseph and Noah. Biblical women's names were even more popular, especially Mary, Anne and Elizabeth, and also those of post-biblical saints such as Agnes, Catherine and Margaret and the Mystery play characters, Eve, Sarah and Anna. However, during this period the range of Christian names in use progressively lessened until, in the fourteenth century, the five men's names of William, Richard, Harry, Robert and John comprised nearly two-thirds of all those recorded. For long after that time the restricted choice of Christian names poses problems for genealogists in distinguishing one person of the same surname from another. In documents, Christian names were latinised, and the Latin versions often gained favour; the English name Harry became less popular than Henry (from Harry's Latin version *Henricus*), and Piers less popular than Peter (from *Petrus*). The popularity of a Christian name under the Plantagenets can be estimated from the extent to which it gave rise to patronymic surnames; compare Harrison with Henryson, and Pearson with Peterson.

Women were often given men's names, such as Philip, Alexander, Nicholas and James, but the confusing effect is minimised by the Latin versions, which were always of feminine gender; for example, Philippa and Alexandra, which have become the modern forms. Nicholas, however, was retained as a girl's name as late as the eighteenth century.

Before the Reformation it was a grave offence under Canon Law to change a name that had been given at baptism, and anyone guilty of such a change was obliged to perform a penance. Surnames, on the other hand, could be changed at will. However, pet names and nicknames were countenanced, such as Will, Sim, Wat, Dick and Hodge (Roger), and Bess, Betty and Molly; and this was necessary when parents gave more than one of their living children the same name. One reason suggested for this is that it was to preserve intact a 'lease for three lives' in which the leaseholders-to-be had to be named.

After the reformation, post-biblical saints' names fell into disrepute as being papistical. Biblical names, on the other hand, increased in popularity because of the Puritan emphasis on the Bible as the sole authority for truth. In the seventeenth century the religious influence on Christian names reached heights now considered absurd, with children being named Praise-God, Much Mercy, Repentance, Sin-deny and Livewell. Twins might be called Moses and Aaron, Esau and Jacob, Joseph and Mary. The influence of an extreme Puritan parish minister was often behind such excesses, and foundlings were, of course, particularly vulnerable. Names such as Flee-Fornication and Misericordia-Adulterina tell their own story.

The genealogist may encounter difficulties from the fact that some women's names were interchangeable. The most common are Elizabeth and Isobel, Anne and Agnes, Gillian and Julian, Anne and Hannah, Hester and Esther, Phyllis and Felice, Marion and Mary Ann, Joan and Jane.

The Renaissance period saw the beginning of the use of surnames as Christian names. One of the first to be so christened was Lord Guildford Dudley, the husband of Lady Jane Grey, whose mother's maiden name was Guildford. Often the surname was that of a godparent. Sometimes a godfather conferred his surname on his god-daughter. A married woman who has what appear to be two Christian names, of which the second is a surname, may turn out to be a Scot, conforming to the custom north of the border of retaining her surname in addition to that of her husband.

Before the Stuart period it was very rare for a man to have two Christian names, but the practice became more noticeable in the seventeenth century, though still not common. King James I had two names, Charles James; and so had his eldest son, Henry Frederick, who died before his father. But for men, two names only became really common from the end of the eighteenth century. After the Revolution of 1688 appeared the female pair-names Mary Anne, Mary Jane, Sarah Jane and Anne Maria, which were treated as one and went out of fashion only after they had dropped in social status in the mid nineteenth century.

The early part of the Georgian period was classical in mood, and a fashion developed for the classical forms of women's names, such as Anna, Maria, Sophia, Olivia, Evelina, Amelia, Cecilia and Juliana, and also for Latin names that had no English equivalent, such as Lavinia.

At the end of the Georgian period, England, indeed Europe, was dominated by the Romantic movement stressing the beauty of strangeness. This made people look back to early times, because they were little known. So Anglo-Saxon names came in again. Edward had never gone out entirely, but new favourites were Edgar, Edwin, Alfred, Emma, Ethel, Matilda, Arthur and Wilfred.

In the Victorian period, the Tractarian Movement, reinforcing the Romantic trend, revived the names of long-neglected saints such as Aidan, Augustine, Theodore, Benedict and Bernard. The pre-Raphaelites and Tennyson increased the taste for medievalism and revived such names as Lancelot, Hugh, Walter, Aylmer, Roger, Ralph, Ella, Alice, Mabel, Edith and Gillian. The influence of royalty made Albert a popular name.

The following are the Latin versions of a number of common Christian names. They will sometimes be found under variant spellings; for example, ae for e, and au for al. Men's names that are virtually identical with the English, except for the suffix -us, -ius or -dus, have been omitted, as have women's names ending in -a and -ia.

Agenta	Agnes
Aluredus	Alfred
Alienora	Eleanor
Aloysius	Lewis
Amabilia	Mabel
Amia	Amy
Amicius	Amyas
Andreas	Andrew
Caius	Kay
Carolus	Charles
Coleta	Nicholas (f)
Constantia	Constance
Dionisia	Denise
Dionisius	Dennis
Egidius	Giles
Emelina	Emily
Francisca	Frances
Galfridus	Geoffrey
Godefridus	Godfrey
Gratia	Grace
Gualterus	Walter
Guido	Guy
Gulielmus	William
Hamo	Hamon
Helena	Ellen, Helen, Eleanor
Henricus	Henry, Harry
Horatius	Horace
Hugo	Hugh
Isabella	Isabel, Elizabeth
Jacobus	James, Jacob
Jocosa	Joyce
Johanna	Joan, Jane
Johannes	John
Joscia	Joyce
Juetta	Jowet, Ivote

Lucas	Luke
Marcus	Mark
Marta	Martha
Milo	Miles
Paganus	Payn
Petronilla	Parnell
Petrus	Piers, Peter
Radulfus	Ralph
Ro(h)esia	Rose
Tedbaldus	Theobald
Villefridus	Wilfred
Willelmus	William

Latin names are often abbreviated to the first syllable, followed by the declension ending, e.g. Willus (William), Rici (of Richard). A special case is Xpoferus (Christopher), in which the first two letters are not really X and p but the Greek letters X (Ch) and p (r). Xp was the customary abbreviation for Christ. In 'Xmas' the second letter has been dropped. *See also* DIMINUITIVES.

Chronicle   A bare record of events in order of time without comment or analysis. The term is used in a derogatory sense for an historical work which lacks depth. Family histories are often little more than chronicles for want of sufficient data. Among the best known chronicles are those called the *Anglo-Saxon Chronicles* which were compiled, often well after the events, by monastic chroniclers. They form the basis for much of the early history of England.

Church Ale   Periodic festival gathering for the purpose of raising money for the parish church. The ale for the occasion was brewed in the church house from malt either bought or begged by the churchwardens. In 1603 it was forbidden to hold such functions within churches, chapels or churchyards, but the ban was not always effective.

Church Hay   Another term for a churchyard.

Churching of Women   A purification ceremony performed for a mother shortly after the birth of each child.
See also CHRISOM.

Church of England *see* **Anglican Church**

Churchwardens   Men acting as the chief lay officers of a parish. The office has been in existence at least since 1127. There were commonly two wardens, the Rector's (or Vicar's) Warden and the People's Warden, but in the north-west and in populous towns it was common to have

more. The method of selection varied with the custom of the parish. A 'tied' churchwarden was one who served by rota by virtue of his occupation of a certain house or certain land. During the fifteenth and early sixteenth centuries, as the parish took the place of the manor as the effective unit of local government, many civil duties were placed upon the wardens. They were *ex officio* the senior members of the parish vestry. Levying church and other rates was among their responsibilities, and their books of accounts are an important source of parish, and often of family, history. In some places they were known as churchmen or church reeves.

Citation Mandates *see* **Ecclesiastical Visitation**

Civil Registration *See* **General Register of Births, Deaths and Marriages**

Clandestine Marriages   Before 1754 it was the rule that the clergy could perform marriage ceremonies only for people who either had banns called, or had obtained a marriage licence, but the breaking of this rule did not invalidate the marriage. The bride and bridegroom were liable merely to be censured, and even the penalties inflicted on the parson did not involve his permanently losing his benefice or going to prison. This laxity led to a large number of clandestine marriages, and certain churches became known for providing the facility.

In addition to some of the churches, prison chapels were especially liable to be used for clandestine marriages. The most notorious of these was the Fleet Chapel in London, but the prison chaplains soon began to perform marriages outside the prison, in rooms in taverns fitted up as pseudo-chapels. On the day before Lord Hardwicke's *Marriage Act* came into force (25 March 1754), 217 Fleet marriages were performed. About 300 registers recording clandestine marriages are now at the Public Record Office, Chancery Lane, London, under reference RG 7. Some selective surname indexes to them have been compiled.
Further reading: T. Benton, *Irregular Marriage in London Before 1754*, SOG (1993).

Class, Archive   The technical term indicating the coverage of a single type of record, intermediary between a group and a piece. For example, the Public Record Office reference for the microfilm of the 1871 Census Return of Cleator in Cumberland is RG 10/5261. RG are the Group letters, showing that it came from the

April ye 7th 1760

Officers Chosen for this Ensuing year are
as follows
Mr Farindon   } Church
William Laker   } wardens

Francis Killick.
Robert Head   } Overseers
Richard Agate
Charles Kember

The Account of the Legacy given by the last will
and testament of William Saxeby Gent to the Parish
of Lingfield for Ever and was Disposed of by
Ellis Bostock Esqr and Anthony Farindon Esqr
Church Wardens for the year 1759

John Long a Coat and ——————————— 00 = 01 = 00
Thos: Everest a Coat and ——————————— 00 = 01 = 00
Willm White a Coat and ——————————— 00 = 01 = 00
Willm Bongs a Coat and ——————————— 00 = 01 = 00
John Brown a Coat and ——————————— 00 = 01 = 00
Robt Webb, wife a Gown and ——————— 00 = 01 = 00
Thos: Jupp, wife a Gown and ———————— 00 = 01 = 00
Peter Everist wife a Gown and ————— 00 = 01 = 00
Robt Dennis wife a Gown and ————— 00 = 01 = 00
Widow Robt Lock a Gown and ————— 00 = 01 = 00

Churchwardens' Accounts of Lingfield, Surrey, 1760, showing the names of the men and women in the parish who received coats and gowns from a charitable bequest. *Courtesy the Vicar and Parochial Church Council, Lingfield*

Registrar General's Office; 10 is the Class number of the 1871 Census; and 5261 is the Piece number of the enumerator's folder covering the parish of Cleator. Now seen on microfilm.

Class, Social Nowadays the differences between social classes are very much smaller than they used to be, yet not so long ago they were immediately apparent — in speech, dress, manner and education. People recognised who were their 'betters' and who their 'inferiors', and accepted their own state of life as being that (in the words of the Catechism) to which it had pleased God to call them. The main classes were the aristocracy, the gentry, the middle class, lower middle class and working class, though those are modern terms for them. The following brief generalisations, on constantly changing conditions, have most relevance to the early nineteenth century.

The *aristocracy* consisted of titled families and their relatives. Their wealth came mainly from large landed estates. From one generation to another, the head of the family lived in the same stately home; at his death his personal papers tended not to be destroyed, but to be removed to capacious attics or cellars, and so great family archives accumulated. The pedigrees of the aristocracy have been published in the recurrent volumes of Burke's *Peerage*.

The *gentry* had much in common with the aristocracy, but on a smaller scale. They were armigerous, had private incomes and were educated at public schools and universities. The heads of county families inherited manor houses, and younger sons became officers in the navy and army, or barristers, clergy and bankers. The pedigrees of many gentry families have been published from time to time in Burke's *Landed Gentry*.

The *middle class* made their living as master tradesmen and businessmen, as physicians, surgeons, solicitors and yeoman farmers, and their sons attended grammar schools.

The *lower middle class* consisted of small master craftsmen, keepers of small shops and ale-houses, and husbandmen cultivating their own small plots of land. Many were unable to read or write, but in the early nineteenth century their children were the first to attend the new schools being opened by church bodies.

The *working class* was made up of journeymen, agricultural labourers and servants, working for wages and liable in times of misfortune, to become 'paupers' dependent on a parish relief. Some were able to attend charity or church schools, but only a minority was literate. Of the whole population, agricultural labourers formed the largest occupational group for men, and domestic servants for women.

In England, the dividing lines between classes have never been impassable. Men of ability have risen in the world, while the less able, the younger sons of large families, and the wastrels, have correspondingly sunk. Neighbouring classes have intermarried, and this, too, has led to class mobility. The industrial revolution gave all social classes a big shake-up, as agriculture ceased to be the largest sector of the economy. The professions moved up in the world because of the intellectual attainments that became increasingly necessary in their practitioners.

See also peerage titles, and BARONET; KNIGHT; ESQUIRE; FRANKLIN; GENTLEMAN; GOODMAN; HUSBANDMAN; MR; VILLEIN; YEOMAN.

Clergy, Anglican (See table on page 78)
For the records of Anglican Clergy see ANGLICAN CHURCH.

Clerical Subsidy Whenever lay subsidies were levied by Parliament, religious bodies also paid taxes, which were assessed and voted upon in the councils of the two archiepiscopal provinces. At the Public Record Office, Chancery Lane, London, the records are under the same class as Lay Subsidies, E 179.

Clerk (i) A man or boy who had been ceremonially tonsured by the bishop, whether he subsequently took holy orders or not.

(ii) A clergyman, in which case the term is an abbreviation for 'clerk in holy orders'.

(iii) A man skilled in writing work; but a clerk in the modern sense of one engaged in office work was called a Writer.

(iv) The Clerk of the Peace was the principal legal officer of the Quarter Sessions. He was a trained attorney who guided the court proceedings and superintended all county business in the intervals between sessions.

(v) The Parish Clerk was often responsible for entering up the registers of baptisms, marriages and burials, and might keep a draft register from which the official register book was posted up at intervals. Today, if a clergyman is asked to make a search in his parish register for genealogical purposes, he is liable to pass the job on to his parish clerk, a fact worth bearing in mind.

Cleveland A county formed in 1974 out of parts of Durham and Yorkshire. For the Cleveland Family History Society, *see* YORKSHIRE. Cleveland County Archives publishes a leaflet

Sources for Genealogical study in the Cleveland County Archives Department.

Close   A piece of land enclosed within hedges, fences or walls.

Close Rolls   These contain the registered copies of Letters Close issued by, and private deeds enrolled in, the royal Court of Chancery. Many of the private deeds are conveyances. The copies were written on parchment sheets, or membranes, which were then stitched together and rolled into one or more rolls for each year of the king's reign. They are housed at the Public Record Office, Chancery Lane, London, in class C 54 with annual calendars. The original Letters derive their name from the fact that they were folded before being sealed, and so could only be read after first breaking the seal. They issued orders to royal officers and writs of summons to Parliament.

Codicil   An addition to a will (sometimes a will will have several codicils attached) to record changes in the original will.

Cognate   A term meaning related on the mother's side.
See also AGNATE.

Colindale *see* **British Newspaper Library**

Collectioner   A pauper in receipt of parish relief.

Collector of the Poor   An early name for the Overseer of the Poor, because of his duty to collect the Poor Rate.

College   A body of people, living together in the same endowed foundation, such as the members of a collegiate church, school or university. Also the buildings for such a body.

College of Arms *see* **Arms, College of**

Colonial Records Index *see* **Currer-Briggs Colonial Records Index**

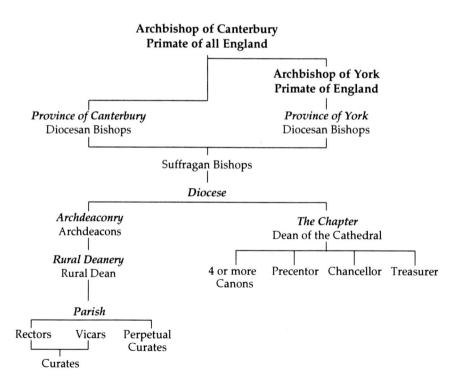

The organisational structure of the Church of England.

Commissary One to whom is committed some charge, duty or office by a superior power; a commissioner. In the Church of England, he was an officer of the diocesan bishop, empowered to exercise ecclesiastical jurisdiction on his behalf over an area at some distance from the bishop's residence — by presiding over a Commissary Court. A Commissary General was a general assistant to a bishop, empowered to perform a number of functions on his behalf.

Commissary Court Commissary and Consistory courts acted on behalf of the bishop. The difference between them was that the Commissary court acted for one Archdeaconry only whereas the Consistory court acted for them all.

Common Law The law of the king's courts, as distinct from that of the local courts, because it was common over the whole country. It was also distinct from Statute Law and equity. The records start with the Curia Regis (King's Court) Rolls down to 56 Henry III (*see* REGNAL YEARS), containing pleas heard in the courts both of King's Bench and Common Pleas, but from the reign of Edward I these were separated.

Common Pleas, Court of Henry II appointed five justices to sit permanently in his Curia Regis (King's Court) to cope with the increasing number of pleas being brought by his subjects, one against another. The court was usually held at Westminster, but did sometimes follow the king from place to place as a section of his Curia (Court). This mobility was raised by the barons as one of their grievances against King John, and *Magna Carta* laid down that the Court of Common Pleas should stay in one place which, eventually, became a certain spot in the vast Westminster Hall.

From 1272 the court was granted its own Chief Justice, and so its separation from the Curia Regis became complete. In 1875 its jurisdiction was transferred to the King's Bench Division of the High Court of Justice. The early rolls of the Court of Common Pleas are called De Banco Rolls, after the bench of judges, and the later ones Common Rolls. At the Public Record Office, Chancery Lane, London, the records are located in Group CP.

Common, Rights of These were the rights enjoyed by householders living within the manorial system in virtue of the MESSUAGE they held.

The rights were of many kinds, agricultural, beast-owning and miscellaneous. Common of Stock was the right to graze a certain number of cattle and sheep (according to the tenement held) upon the ploughland left fallow that year, and the land from which the crop had been reaped. Common of Turbary was the right to cut turf and other fuel within the manor. Common in Gross was a right detached from house or land, unlike the more usual Common Appendant (or Appurtenent) — rights that went with a holding. *See also* APPURTANCES; WASTE.

Commonable Land Manorial land held in SEVERALTY, but subject to common rights for part of the year; specifically, after the hay crop from the meadow and the harvesting of the arable. *See also* LAMMAS.

Commoners, History of the Four volumes of this work by John Burke appeared between 1836 and 1838. They contain narrative pedigrees of county families of that period. The series was continued under the title of the *Landed Gentry*.

Commonwealth War Graves Commission *see* **War Graves, Commission of**

Company Records There are three types of company. For very large concerns Chartered Companies were set up but they were in the minority. A charter was granted by the Crown for a particular enterprise such as the great trading companies that helped to create the Colonies. Then there were Regulated Companies also for trading purposes rather like an association with each member trading in his own right but having a liability to the company's debts. Joint Stock Companies are the third kind, where members joined into a single company and their liability was limited with regard to the company's debts. There was still a need to provide for much smaller businesses and from the seventeenth to the nineteenth centuries there were many unincorporated companies. Some obtained Letters Patent but most were not backed by any kind of legal document. To regulate matters the Board of Trade set up a Register of Companies in 1844. In 1856 this act was repealed and a new system of registration began with many amendments at later dates to form what we call Company Law. From the 420 registered companies in 1868 the business of registration has grown; 69,000 companies having been registered by the early 1980s.

Two types of company are registered until 1981, one the Private Limited Liability Company and the other the Public Limited Liability Company. Files on the business of both kinds of company were sent to the Registrar to be available for public inspection. The information contained therein does not provide personal details of investors but does provide a background to your ancestor's involvement and day to day concerns. The main advantage of registration to family historians is that a company must, by law, file annually a list of shareholders and directors. This list gives the name, address, aliases, if any, occupation until 1948 and, latterly, nationality, of those shareholders. If you know of an ancestor involved in a company you may then use the register as you would a directory and trace his connection with the company year by year.

Not all records handed to the Registrar of Companies survive since they have been weeded from time to time. Those that do survive are at the Public Record Office, Kew, in BT 41 and class BT 31 holds Files of Dissolved Companies for companies registered post 1856 and still in existence after 1860. PRO Information Leaflet No.48 tells you more about the documents available at the PRO. If a company is still operating or has been dissolved in the last twenty years then the file will still be at the Companies Registration Office, Companies House, 55–71 City Road, London EC1Y 1BB, where there are indexes to current companies and companies dissolved prior to 1976. The public search rooms open from 10.00–4.00 Monday to Friday. Copies of the files for current companies can be obtained for a modest fee by post. *See also* CHARTERED COMPANIES.

Comperta Literally 'Things discovered', and written up for a bishop or archdeacon after his visitation of a parish. Together with detecta — things of which people had been accused (or, in the language of the courts, for which they had been 'presented') — they formed the basis of the bishop's or archdeacon's injunctions. *See also* PRESENTMENT.

Compotus Rolls These are estate accounts by royal and seignorial officials, of which there are about 1200 bundles at the Public Record Office, Chancery Lane, London, under the title *Special Collection No. 6, Ministers' Accounts.* Many of them are the records of the royal escheators. *See also* ESCHEAT.

Compters The common gaols of London and elsewhere, used for debtors. Also written 'Counters'.

Compton Census In 1676 each parish had to furnish a list of all parishioners (sometimes simply by numbers and not names) and indicate which ones did not attend church regularly. This does not survive for the whole of the country but where it does it can be found in local record offices.

Compurgator One who swore to the truth of a statement made in court by another.

Computers The contribution of computing to Genealogy and Family History has become increasingly important in recent years. Not only are more genealogists using computers at home, but the machines now available to the individual have greater power and versatility than most business computers of just a few years ago. The computers currently used include the standard desk-top models and a range of smaller portables, from the 'handheld', through the 'laptop', to a computer the size of a small suitcase. The smaller portables are being used in libraries and record offices to enter information from record sources directly into the computer.

A large number of commercially written programs are available. *Wordprocessor* programs are the most frequently used. They are a sophisticated substitute for a typewriter, allowing the editing and rearrangement of text while preparing letters and reports or transcribing documents of all kinds. Many wordprocessors now include spelling checks and can sort and index material automatically. *Database* programs are used to store information from record sources and sort and process these in various ways in order to discover connections which are not otherwise apparent. *Genealogical* programs allow the particulars of individuals to be recorded, including the relationship between husbands, wives and children. In this way ancestral lines can be constructed over several generations. These programs will print out BIRTH BRIEF style ancestor charts. They will also print out the descendants of a given individual in an indented form, where the details of the individual of each generation are indented from those of the previous generation. A few of these programs can also save many hours of work by printing full drop-line FAMILY TREES.

Two factors have made the transfer of material between different computers and programs easier than in the past: many genealogists now use the standard computers and programs used by businesses; programs are now available which will read information stored on the most common disk formats and convert it for use on computers using other disk formats. This has helped Family History Societies and other bodies to expand the indexing of census returns and other source material as group projects. Indexes of substantial size can now be prepared by several people each entering part of the information on their own computer at home. The information is then transferred to one computer where it is combined to produce the final index, which is often published on microfiche.

The largest collection of genealogical information held on computer is stored by the Church of Jesus Christ of Latter Day Saints on their large mainframe computers in Utah, U.S.A. (*See* LATTER DAY SAINTS). They are most well known for producing the INTERNATIONAL GENEALOGICAL INDEX (IGI). But it is also possible for an individual's ancestral lines, entered on his/her own computer, to be incorporated in the 'Ancestral File' at Salt Lake City and merged with related families whose details have already been stored in this databank. They are also pioneering the publication of genealogical material such as the IGI on Compact Disk Read-Only Memory (CD-ROM).

The Society of Genealogists in London has a Computer Committee and a Computer Interest Group which holds lunch time and evening meetings (open to non-members) at Charterhouse Buildings, London EC1. Occasional day and half-day conferences are also held, at which there are demonstrations of genealogical programs, using different types of computers. Since 1982, the Society has published a quarterly magazine, *Computers in Genealogy*, in which different computers and programs for ancestry research are discussed and problems aired. *Family Tree Computer Magazine*, a similar commercial magazine has been published since 1992.

Any genealogist thinking of buying a computer for his hobby, without previous experience of using one, is recommended to consult a fellow genealogist already using a computer. Information on local computer users can be found through Family History Societies, many of which now have Computer Groups holding regular meetings.

For further reading, see *Computers for Family History*, by David Hawgood (4th Edition, 1992) and *Genealogy Computer Packages*, by David Hawgood (1st Edition, 1993).

Concorde *see* **Feet of Fines and Warranty**

Condition *see* **Bond**

Confirmation *see* **Chancery**

Congregationalists This nonconformist denomination began as a movement within the Church of England, founded by Robert Browne.

Its followers were at first called Separatists or Brownists because they believed that religion should be separate from the State and that the congregation is independent and has the right to choose its own ministers. They were later known as Independents, and still later as Congregationalists. They were firmly suppressed, and in 1608 Browne's followers emigrated for a time to Amsterdam to escape persecution. But some returned, and in 1620 the church provided the London contingent of the passengers of the *Mayflower* when she sailed for America.

During the Commonwealth, Cromwell and several of his closest associates were Independents, though the official doctrine of the established church was then Presbyterian. When the monarchy was restored, the 1662 *Act of Uniformity* placed legal disabilities upon the sect, as it did upon other nonconformists. Although the persecution was ended under William and Mary, by the 1689 *Act of Toleration*, meeting-places were still subject to the granting of licences by either the county justices, the bishop or the archdeacon.

In 1742/3 a register of births for the Three Denominations (Congregationalists, Presbyterians and Baptists) was started at Dr William's Library (*see* WILLIAM'S LIBRARY, DR).

1832 saw the Union of Congregationalist Churches inaugurated, and five years later, on the commencement of civil registration, marriages were allowed to be performed by Congregationalist ministers before a registrar.

In 1837, nearly all known registers were sent to the Registrar General for authentication, and in 1840 the records were deposited with that office on a permanent basis. Registers discovered later were added in 1858. The Births Register of the Three Denominations was also deposited. All are now held at the Public Record Office, Chancery Lane, London, under references RG 4,5 and 8. Some of the undeposited registers have since been published. The earliest registers of baptisms and burials began in 1644, but comparatively few are extant earlier than the late eighteenth century. They often give more information than parish registers. The churches also kept Minute Books and Rolls of Church Members, but most of them have been lost.

Miscellaneous records and histories of individual churches are kept at DR WILLIAMS'S LIBRARY. Others are kept at the New College Library, Hampstead, North London.

The London Missionary Society archives are in the library of the School of Oriental & African Studies, University of London, Malet Street, London WC1.

County record offices have Quarter Sessions records that contain presentments of persons for not attending parish churches as required by the *Act of Uniformity*, and for holding conventicles contrary to the Clarendon Code.

The Congregational Historical Society, founded 1899, publishes its *Transactions*, which are indexed, and the Society has also published C.E. Surman's *Bibliography of Local Congregational History* (1947).

For further reading, see *Sources for Nonconformist Genealogy and Family History*, by D.J. Steel, vol II of the National Index of Parish Registers, SOG, *My Ancestors Were Congregationalists*, by D. J. H. Clifford, SOG (1992).

See also BROWNISTS; NON-PAROCHIAL REGISTERS.

Coniger   A Rabbit warren.

Consistory   A solemn assembly or council. In the Church of England, a Consistory Court was normally the spiritual court of a diocesan bishop held before his Official or Chancellor in his cathedral church or other convenient place. The term consistory is occasionally used by other courts, such as that of a dean.
See also COMMISSARY.

Constable   (i) The High Constable was the official of the hundred to whom petty (i.e. parish) constables were responsible for some of their duties. He was an assistant to the Lieutenant of his county in carrying out his military functions. When a muster was ordered by the Crown, the Lieutenant passed the word to his High Constables, giving each one the quota of men required of him. Each High Constable then passed the order and individual quotas on to the constables of the parishes in his hundred. The office was abolished in 1872.

(ii) The Petty Constable was one of the most ancient of the offices of the manor and later of the parish. In the Middle Ages he was chosen by the manor, but served for the township.

He had to report, and take action on, a great many matters, among them: felonies committed, escaped prisoners, riots and unlawful assemblies, non-attendance at church, oppression by other officers, commercial irregularities, licensing of ale houses, compiling Jurors' Lists, drunkenness, his assistants, unauthorised building of additional cottages and dovecotes, vagabonds, intruders, militia Muster Rolls, taking lewd women before the Justice of the Peace, and detaining refractory fathers of bastards.

The appointment of the constable was taken over from the manor court by the parish vestry in the early seventeenth century. The position was an honorary one and required no property qualification until 1842, when anyone taking the appointment had to occupy lands or tenements assessed to poor rate or county rate at £4 or more per year. Constables' account books often throw interesting light on family history. Many of them have now been deposited by parish incumbents at county record offices.

Consul   It was not until 1825 that consuls abroad became members of the Civil Service. Before that, the title was conferred on a prominent member of an English business community abroad, chosen by them to represent and lead them in negotiations affecting their status and safety with the authorities of the country in which they were residing. Even today, in smaller towns abroad, the British 'Consul' is often not a career official, or even British, but a trusted resident and citizen of the country of residence.

Consular Returns *see* **General Register Office**

Contumacy   (i) A refusal, after a threefold citation, to appear before an ecclesiastical court.
(ii) Refusal by an excommunicate to submit to ecclesiastical authority.

Convent   A community of monks, friars or nuns living in a single house. The popular restriction of its meaning to nunneries is late, as also is its application to the community's building.

Conventicle   An assembly for the exercise of religion, otherwise than as sanctioned by law. The term was commonly used in the seventeenth century for meetings of non-conformists.

Conveyance *see* **Title Deed**

Cookites   The Cookites split away from the Wesleyan Methodists to form the Wesleyan Unitarian movement.

Copyhold   A form of tenure for land held of a lord of a manor in return, originally, for agricultural services but, since Tudor times, for money payments. On the admission of a new tenant, a payment (fine) to the lord was required, and on the death of the tenant a HERIOT. Tenure of such land could be transferred only by its surrender to the lord, and by admission by him of the new tenant, who might be the heir of the old one.

Each admission was recorded in the Court Rolls and a copy of the entry given to the new tenant, for whom it fulfilled the function of a title deed; hence the name Copyhold.

This form of tenure was made commutable to freehold by an Act of 1841, but it was an Act of 1853–4 that brought about a general commutation, although copyhold tenure was not finally abolished until 1 January, 1926. Copyhold is also known as customary tenure, since its conditions were governed by the custom of the manor.

Cordwainer Pronounced 'cordner'. A worker or trader in leather goods. The name derives from Cordovan, a resident of the Spanish town famous for its fine leather. In general its use means a shoemaker or cobbler.

Corndealers Men of this trade had to be licensed annually by the Quarter Sessions. The licence records are at the county record offices.

Cornet The lowest commissioned rank in a cavalry regiment, equivalent to the present 2nd Lieutenant. The equivalent rank in the infantry was that of ENSIGN. Like the latter, he carried the regiment's colours. *See also* ENSIGN.

Cornwall The county falls within the diocese of Exeter and the Province of Canterbury. The library of the SOG holds 200 transcripts of its parish registers. Boyd's Marriage Index covers 202 parishes up to 1812 and Pallot's Marriage Index covers 153 parishes.

The Hundreds of East (Middle, North and South Divisions), Kerrier, Lesnewth, Penwith, Powder (East and West Divisions), Pyder, Stratton, Trigg, West and the Scilly Islands lie within its jurisdiction.

It has Stratton, Camelford, Launceston, St. Germans, Liskeard, Bodmin, St. Colum, St. Austell, Truro, Falmouth, Helston, Redruth, Penzance and Scilly Isles RDs/PLUs.

It falls within the Western Assize Circuit.

The Cornwall Family History Society publishes a quarterly journal and meets at Truro. There is a Family History Centre at Helston.

There are the Cornwall County Record Office and the Royal Institution of Cornwall at Truro.

The Bishops' Transcripts for 1670–1736 and 1741–72 are at the CRO but those for 1737–1812 are at the Devon Record Office in Exeter as are the Marriage Licence Records. Wills were proved at the Consistory court of Exeter, the Episcopal Principal Registry of Exeter and the Prerogative Court of Canterbury. Pre 1858 Wills proved at the following courts are located as follows. Those

for the Archdeaconry of Cornwall and the Royal Peculiar Court of the Deanery of St. Bunyan are at the CRO but those held at Exeter were destroyed by bombing, a few of which have survived, see *Wills and Their Whereabouts*, by A.J. Camp. The wills held at Exeter were for the Peculiar Courts of the Bishop of Exeter and the Dean and Chapter of Exeter plus the Archdeaconry of Totnes.

The Devon and Cornwall Record Society have transcribed and published a number of records, including many parish registers, since 1906. The Heralds' Visitation Pedigrees have been printed for 1530, 1573 and 1620.

See also *Sources for Cornish family history* (Cornwall Record Office, 1991), *Guide to the parish and non-parochial registers of Devon and Cornwall 1538–1837*, by H. Peskett (1979) and *Cornwall: a genealogical bibliography*, by S. Raymond (FFHS, 1989).

Coroner The office originated in 1194 as Keeper of the Pleas of the Crown, when four keepers were appointed for each county, three of whom were knights and the remaining one a clerk. By the early thirteenth century they had been reduced to two, both knights, each assisted by a clerk. They were elected by the knights and freeholders of the county, and the office was unpaid. From 1200 some boroughs had coroners of their own.

The duties of the office included holding inquests on the dead, hearing Abjurations of the Realm appeals and confessions (*see* SANCTUARY), and carrying out the confiscations that arose from declarations of outlawry. The coroners had to keep records and present them at the Eyre court, after which they were usually destroyed. However, from 1337 the records handed in to Superior Eyres were preserved, and these are at the Public Record Office (PRO) under *Justices Itinerant* (JUST).

The office was radically revised, first by the *Coroners Act*, 1887, and then by the *Coroners Admendment Act*, 1926. A coroner is now either a barrister, a solicitor, or a qualified medical practitioner, and may have deputies and assistant deputies. Some records are not available for public perusal. In the period immediately prior to the Acts, coroners regarded their records as their private property. Accounts of the proceedings of their courts are best discovered through reports in the local press (*see* NEWSPAPERS), as there is a 70 year closure rule.

Finding Aid: *Coroners' Records in England and Wales*, by Jeremy Gibson and Colin Rogers, FFHS.

Corporal Oath   An oath taken with one hand on a sacred object, usually a volume of the Gospels.

Corporation of London Records Office
Holds the records of the Corporation of London from the early medieval period to the present day including Admissions to the Freedom of the City of London. The Corporation is the local authority to the 'square mile' of London City.

Correction, House of   A type of county gaol, especially one founded in accordance with Acts of 1575–6 and 1603–4, for rogues, vagrants, unmarried mothers and parents who had left their children chargeable to the parish.

From 1697, paupers who refused to be badged (*see* BADGE-MAN) could be sent to a House of Correction for whipping and three weeks' hard labour. The records are at the county record office.

Corrody   Originally the right of free accommodation to be provided by a vassal to his lord when on his circuit; later the term came to apply to the boarding provisions made by monasteries to their living benefactors.

Corruption of Blood *see* **Attainder**

Cote   (i) An enclosure for sheep or cattle.
(ii) A cottage.

Cottar   The tenant of a cottage, with or without a small piece of land. After villeins, the largest class of people in the Domesday record (*see* DOMESDAY BOOK). A cottar's land was probably insufficient to support him, so he would also work on the land of others.
See also BORDAR.

Counters *see* **Compters**

Countess of Huntingdon's Connexion *see* **Huntingdon's Connexion**

Country   A word often used, until the nineteenth century, in the modern sense of 'county', or, even more loosely, as 'neighbourhood'.

County   The counties of England are of Anglo-Saxon origin and are divided into hundreds. At the Conquest, the leaders of the county organisation were the earldorman (an Anglo-Saxon term soon changed to the Danish earl) and the sheriff. As earldoms under the Normans became very large, it was left to the sheriff to carry out the

county's administrative duties, and in time an earldom ceased to be an office and became merely a title. Important towns were entitled to elect their own sheriff; London, Bristol, Canterbury, Exeter, Gloucester, Poole and Southampton.

In the sixteenth century the sheriff's military functions were handed over to a lieutenant, later known as the Lord Lieutenant, who in time also took over a number of the sheriff's other duties.

The county was administered through the holding of Quarter Sessions until, by the *Local Government Act of* 1888, elective county councils were established. At the same time, the Isle of Ely, parts of Lincolnshire, London, the Soke of Peterborough, East and West Suffolk, East and West Sussex, the Isle of Wight and the Ridings of Yorkshire, all became separate administrative counties. In earlier centuries certain cities and boroughs had been made corporate counties, and many of them became county boroughs under the 1888 Act.

As from 1 April 1974, the boundaries of a number of counties were adjusted. Some counties disappeared; for example, Cumberland and Westmorland were combined, along with an area of northern Lancashire, to become Cumbria, while Yorkshire was divided into North, West and South Yorkshire and the new counties mentioned below. Huntingdonshire was absorbed into Cambridgeshire, Rutland into Leicestershire. Several new counties and metropolitan counties were formed; i.e. Tyne and Wear (from SE Northumberland and NE Durham), Cleveland (from SE Durham and NE Yorkshire), Humberside (from SE Yorkshire and N Lincolnshire), Greater Manchester (from the area around that city), Merseyside (from SW Lancashire and the north Wirral), West Midlands (from the areas around Birmingham), Avon (from S Gloucestershire and N Somerset), and Herefordshire and Worcestershire were combined under their joint name. About one third of the area of Berkshire was transferred to Oxfordshire. The above metropolitan counties and Greater London are under threat of abolition, and it is not known what will replace them.

Under the entries for the pre 1974 historical counties are listed the administrative boundaries that affect genealogical research. Also listed are the names of the FHS that operate within that county whose address or addresses can be found on the cover of the latest edition of Family History News and Digest. Because their mailing addresses change when new secretaries are appointed it is best to send any communication to an individual society c/o The Administrator,

The Federation of Family History Societies, The Benson Room, Birmingham and Midland Institute, Margaret St, Birmingham B3 3BS. Liaison with or membership of the Local Record and History societies in the county can provide useful background information so that your family is put into its context. There may be occasion for cooperative transcription, indexing projects and seminars. For other county addresses see the appropriate Gibson Guide, such as *Marriage, Census and other indexes for Family Historians*, 4th edn by Jeremy Gibson and Elizabeth Hampson, FFHS (1992) and *Record Offices: How to find them* 6th edn FFHS.

County Record Office (CRO) Before the Second World War only six counties had record offices, but today all English counties have one or more. They house the archives of the County Councils, Courts of Quarter Sessions, Boards of Guardians, Lords Lieutenant, Sheriffs, etc., and have attracted deposits of many other archives and collections of value to genealogists, such as parish registers, wills, marriage licence records manor court rolls, as well as documents privately owned and those of solicitors, businesses and semi-public bodies. In most cases the CRO and the Diocesan Registry are now combined.

The record offices have the duty not only of housing records in conditions suitable for their preservation, but also of maintaining them by fumigation, repair and reprographic copying, and of making them available for research by listing, calendaring, indexing and rapid production. The present popularity of genealogy is due in large part to the facilities provided by CROs. For their location, *see* the relevant counties. The Federation of Family History Societies has published a useful booklet with town plans, entitled *Record Offices: How to find them*.

Some county record offices operate a Combined Readers Ticket scheme. On a first visit to a participating office, a researcher will be required to obtain such a ticket by completing a form and giving proof of identity such as a driving licence, NHS medical card, etc. which can be used in any of the CROs in the scheme.

County Families, Walford's Volumes issued annually from 1860 to 1920, giving details not of families but of individuals considered to be members of county families.
See also LANDED GENTRY.

Court Baron A term distinguishing one aspect of the work of a manorial court.
See also MANOR.

Court Leet A term distinguishing one aspect of the work of a manorial court.
See also MANOR.

Court Deal Demesne lands arrented; also called Boardland.
See also ARRENTATION.

Courtesy of England, Estate by the A widower's right to hold for life his deceased wife's dower land held in Fee Simple (*see* FEE) or Estate Tail (*see* ENTAIL). He had this right only if he had had, by her, a child, who was thus the wife's heir or would have been so had it lived.

Cousin A term formerly loosely used, and often meaning a nephew or niece. A cousin german is a first cousin, i.e. the child of an uncle or aunt. A cousin once removed expresses the relationship between a person and his cousin's child or parent, the 'once removed' referring to a difference of one generation: hence, 'twice removed' indicates a difference of two generations, and so on. People who are 'second cousins' to each other are the children of first cousins.

Creature A baptismal name bestowed, according to some opinions, when the sex of the child was not known at the hurried baptism of a weak new-born baby, but more likely, perhaps, when a name had not yet been chosen and the baby seemed unlikely to survive to need one. It is an anglicisation and abbreviation of the Latin *Creatura Christi*, which was sometimes the wording of the register entry.

Crenellation The technical term for the fortification of a house, for which a royal licence was required. Many of the records are to be found in the Patent Rolls from Henry III onwards. To surround a house by a moat also required a licence. Most of the licences issued were to religious houses or the palaces of bishops. (*See* the article 'Licences for Crenellation' by J.H. Parker in *Gentleman's Magazine* for 1856.)

Crest An heraldic device depicted in an ACHIEVEMENT as mounted upon the helmet. It seems to have originated in decorative representations painted upon the body of the helmet itself, or upon a protective fan-shaped ridge or crest that surmounted it. The earliest known example of a crest in its present form is one of 1198. Thereafter the choice of device seems to have remained personal long after arms had become hereditary, and crests were more usually worn in tournaments than in battle. In the later years of Queen Elizabeth I's reign it became a common practice to issue grants of crests to men already bearing ancient arms; and during the seventeenth century most new grants of arms included crests. The practice was invariable by the eighteenth century, but today many older arms are still without crests.

See also ARMS, COAT OF; ARMS, COLLEGE OF; HERALDRY.

Crockford's Directory   First published in 1858, this directory has been produced at intervals ever since. Now it is published by the Church Commissioners and the Central Board of Finance of the Church of England. The directory lists all clergy who hold current appointments in the Church or who have retired recently from them. It also includes an index of churches and other places of worship in the Church of England with the benefice to which they relate and an index to benefices in England, Wales and Ireland together with Scottish incumbencies and their assistant clergy. Before 1982 it was a directory of all the clergy of the Anglican Communion with the exception of the episcopal church in the USA.

Croft   Land adjoining a house, often enclosed.

Cucking-stool   Equipment for ducking a female scold.

Cumberland   The ancient county is now absorbed in Cumbria. Cumberland falls within the diocese of Carlisle and the Province of York. Some of its parish registers have been deposited at the CRO and there are transcripts of some in the library of the SOG. Boyd's Marriage Index covers 34 parishes but only for the seventeenth century. Pallot's Marriage Index covers 17 parishes, mostly 1790–1812. The CRO has another marriage index and the Bishops' Transcripts.

The Wards of Allerdale (above and below Derwent), Cumberland, Eskdale, Leath, Whitehaven Town and Carlisle City lie within its boundaries.

It has Alston, Penrith, Brampton, Longtown, Carlisle, Wigton, Cockermouth, Whitehaven and Bootle RDs/PLUs.

It falls within the Northern Assize Circuit.

The Cumbria Family History Society publishes a quarterly newsletter and has a branch that meets in London at the SOG.

There are Cumbria Record Offices at Carlisle and Barrow-in-Furness and the Cathedral Lib-

rary at Carlisle. There is also a Family History Centre in Carlisle.

The original Marriage Licence records no longer exist but there is a calendar of those for the Diocese of Carlisle at the CRO. Those for the Archdeaconry of Richmond are at the Lancashire Record Office. Pre 1858 wills proved in the following courts are located as follows; Consistory Courts of Carlisle and Durham (for Over Denton before 1703 and Alston) are at the CRO; those for the Archdeaconry Court of Richmond are at the Lancashire Record Office. As the Archdeaconry of Richmond lay in the Diocese of Chester, wills could be proved in the Consistory Court of Chester. They could also be proved at the Prerogative Courts of York and Canterbury. The SOG has a microfilm index of Carlisle Consistory Court wills.

Heralds' Visitation Pedigrees have been printed for 1530 and 1615. The Cumberland and Westmorland Antiquarian and Archaeological Society has published much local material since 1877.

Cumbria Record Office publishes *Cumbrian ancestors* and an *Introduction to house history/family history*. See also *Cumberland and Westmorland: a genealogical bibliography*, by S. Raymond (FFHS, 1993).

Cumbria   A county formed in 1974 from Cumberland, Westmorland and part of Lancashire. For the Cumbria Family History Society *see* CUMBERLAND AND WESTMORLAND.

Curate   Until the seventeenth century the term 'curate' was often synonymous with 'incumbent', but latterly it has applied almost exclusively to an assistant parish priest, paid a salary or stipend and removable by the incumbent or bishop. A Perpetual Curate is one in charge of a parish church where the tithes have been impropriated and there is no endowed vicarage.

See also CHURCH OF ENGLAND HIERARCHY.

Curation   Curation is the guardianship of orphans under 21 but over 14 years of age. Guardians were appointed when not provided for in a will.

Curia Regis   The King's Court. Originally the permanent royal judicial tribunal, but during the thirteenth century it gradually became divided into the separate courts of Common Pleas, King's Bench and Exchequer. At the Public Record Office, Chancery Lane, London, the records from the fifth year of Richard I to the fifty-sixty of Henry III are under reference KB 26. In order to establish their right as free subjects to plead, plaintiffs often submitted their pedigrees to the court.

Currer-Briggs Colonial Records Index

An index of emigrants to the southern colonies of America during the period 1560–1690. Compiled from unpublished sources in England and Virginia, it contains the names of almost 50,000 persons. Enquiries should be addressed to N. Currer-Briggs MA FSG, 3 High Street, Sutton in the Isles, Cambs. CB6 2RB

Cursitor The cursitor (also called a Clerk of Course) made out all original writs and processes returnable in the twenty-four courts of King's Bench and elsewhere. This function was performed by the Petty Bag Office after 1835.

Curtilage A plot of land near a house, usually a vegetable garden.

Customary Tenure *see* Copyhold

Customs and Excise Customs are duties imposed on certain imported goods whereas excise duties were levied on some products produced in England and Wales. If your ancestor was employed in either service you should look at the records which are held at PRO Kew in the group CUST. See Information Leaflet no. 106 *Customs and Excise Records as Sources for Biography and Family History*.

Custumal One of the records of a manorial or monastic estate. Drawn up at fairly long intervals, it lists the customs guiding administrative procedures, and the rents payable.

D

Dame A form of address once customarily applied to the wives of baronets, knights and untitled gentlemen in positions of some authority, but sometimes to any elderly woman.

Danegeld A tax raised in the tenth and eleventh centuries to buy peace from Viking raids. It continued to be levied by Anglo-Norman kings as a method of financing military and naval services.

Danelaw The name given to the eastern and northern parts of England which were occupied and settled by Vikings in the ninth and tenth centuries. The Danelaw divides Wessex and Mercia from Leicestershire, Rutland, Derby, Nottinghamshire, Lincolnshire, Lancashire, Yorkshire, E. Anglia and Cumbria. Cumbria and York combined formed Bernicia. The border ran along the Thames, up the river Lea, across to Bedford, along the river Ouse and then followed Watling Street. Scandinavian place-names are very common in the Danelaw and Scandinavian laws and customs lasted there for some time after the demise of the Vikings.

Dates *see* **Calendar** *and* **Regnal Years**

Daughter-in-law In old records this term is liable to mean what is now called a stepdaughter. Also, a daughter-in-law is often referred to as 'daughter'.

Deacon A clerk in holy orders, but one below the status of priest. He was not qualified to perform marriages but could officiate as a private chaplain, as curate to a beneficed clergyman, or as lecturer to a parish church; and he could administer the wine to communicants.

Dean The senior dignitary of a cathedral or collegiate church, such as Westminster or Windsor.
See also CHAPTER.

Death Certificate *see* General Register of Births, Deaths and Marriages

Death Duty Registers *see* Estate Duty

Debrett *see* Peerage

Decimation A 10 per cent tax on income from land, imposed on Royalists in 1655.

Decree The judgement of a court of equity. It differed from an order in that decree could refer to a procedural command whereas an order either was the final judgement or a temporary one (interlocutory) to allow for further consideration. Alternatively referred to as a sentence.

Deed A deed differs from an indenture in that it was made by one person or a group of people with the same purpose unlike an indenture which involved two or more parties.

Deed Poll   A deed by one person, or by several having exactly the same interest, as distinct from one in which the interested persons are of the first and second (and more) parts. A deed poll would, for example, be used to change a surname.

The word 'poll' here means 'cut smooth', distinguishing this type of deed from that which needed to be indented.
See also INDENTURE.

Defaulter   In a Manor Court Roll, an absentee from the court without excuse. Such a person would be fined.

Deforciant   Defendant who deforces another or prevents him from inheriting an estate.

Delegates, High Court of   The ecclesiastical court of appeal from sentences pronounced by the Prerogative Courts of Canterbury and York.
See also WILL.

Demesne   Those parts of the land and rights of a manor that the lord retained for himself, as distinct from those used by his tenants. What might now be called the 'home-farm'. Ancient Demesne was a manor that had been in the king's hands at the death of Edward the Confessor.

Demise   To convey by will or lease an estate either in Fee Simple (*see* FEE) or Fee Tail (*see* ENTAIL), or for a term of life or years. When applied to the crown of England it signifies its transmission to the next heir on the death of the sovereign. *See also* DEVISE.

Democracy   Government by the common people. Until well into the nineteenth century, this word had the meaning of 'mob-rule'.

Demography, Historical   The statistical study of population, population growth and movement, and the factors involved in them. The researches of historical demographers, especially the Cambridge Group for the History of Population and Social Structure (CAMPOP) founded in 1964; using parish registers and employing advanced techniques of analysis and interpretation, are beginning to throw fresh light on the ways of life of our forebears.

Denization   The granting to an alien of some of the privileges of naturalization. The grant was made by Letters Patent instead of by a Private Act of Parliament, which was necessary for full citizenship.

A 'denizen' was allowed to buy and devise (grant by will) land, which was forbidden to aliens, but he could not inherit land and nor could any of his children born before denization; nor could he hold any office of trust or receive grants of land from the Crown. The records are at the Public Record Office, Chancery Lane, London (C 66, 67 and 54, and HO 1), and are open for inspection once they are one hundred years old. They usually show the immigrant's place of origin.
See also IMMIGRANTS.

Deodand   A legal term for the instrument, animate or inanimate, that brought about a person's death.

Deponent   One who makes a statement on oath in a court of law, or a written statement on oath (deposition), in connection with a legal case.

Deposition   A deposition was a statement made on oath, especially a written statement in lieu of the production of a witness.

Derbyshire   The county falls within the diocese of Lichfield and the Province of Canterbury. Most of its parish registers have been deposited at the county record office and many transcripts of them are in the library of the SOG. Boyd's Marriage Index covers nearly a third of the parishes and Pallot's Marriage Index covers 75, from 1790–1812 or 1837. The Bishops' Transcripts are at Lichfield joint Record Office.

The hundreds of Appletree, High Peake, Morlestone and Litchurch, Repton and Gresley, Scarsdale, Wirksworth and Derby Borough lie within its boundaries.

It has Shardlow, Derby, Belper, Ashbourne, Chesterfield, Bakewell, Chapel-en-le-Frith and Hayfield RDs/PLUs.

It falls within the Midland Assize Circuit.

Derbyshire Family History Society publishes a quarterly journal called *Branch News* and meets at Alfreton, Derby and Glossop. Chesterfield and District FHS publishes a quarterly newsletter and meets in Brampton.

Derbyshire Record Office is at Matlock and there are more records at Chesterfield Public Library.

Pre 1858 Wills are proved in the following courts and the records are located as follows; The Consistory Court of Lichfield, the Peculiar Courts of the Dean and Chapter of Lichfield,

Hartington, Peak Forest and Dawley are at the Staffordshire and Lichfield Joint Record office in Lichfield; the Manorial Court of Dale Abbey is at Nottinghamshire Record Office; wills could also be proved at the Prerogative Court of Canterbury.

The Derbyshire Archaeological Society has published a *Record Series* since 1966 and the Derbyshire Record Society has published annual volumes since 1977. Heralds' Visitation Pedigrees have been printed for 1530 and 1615.

Descend In connection with real property, this word meant 'to pass at death to the common law heir or heirs'.

Detecta Things of which people had been accused, or, in the language of the courts, for which they had been presented at an Ecclesiastical Visitation.
See also COMPERTA; PRESENTMENT.

Detinue, Writ of A writ issued for the recovery of a specific chattel, such as a plough or horse, wrongfully detained.

Devise To leave, by will, land as distinct from personal property. In the latter case, the term 'bequeath' is used.
See also DEMISE.

Devon The county falls within the diocese of Exeter and the Province of Canterbury. Nearly all the ancient parishes have deposited their registers at either the CRO, Exeter City Library or West Devon Area Record Office. There are over 100 transcripts of them in the library at the SOG. Boyd's Marriage Index covers 169 Parishes and Pallot's Marriage Index covers 26 parishes, from 1790–1812 or 1837. The Bishops' Transcripts are at the CRO, West Devon Library in Plymouth and the North Devon Library in Barnstaple. The Marriage Licence records are at the CRO.

The Hundreds of Axminster, Bampton, Braunton, East and West Budleigh, Cliston, Coleridge, Colyton, Crediton, Ermington, Exminster, Fremington, Halberton, Hartland, Hayridge, Haytor, Hemyock, Lifton, South Molton, St. Mary Ottery, Plympton, Roborough, Shebbear, Sherwill, Stanborough, Tavistock, North Taunton with Winkleigh, Teignbridge, Tiverton, Black Torrington, Witheridge, Wonford, Exeter City and Plymouth and Devonpoort Boroughs lie within its boundaries.

It has Axminster, Honiton, St. Thomas, Exter, Newton Abbot, Totnes, Kingsbridge, Plympton St. Mary, Plymouth, East Stonehouse, Stoke Damerel, Tavistock, Okehampton, Crediton, Tiverton, South Molton, Barnstaple, Torrington, Bideford and Holsworthy RDs/PLUs.

It falls within the Western Assize Circuit.

The Devon Family History Society publishes the *Devon Family Historian* quarterly and meets at Exeter, Barnstaple, Plymouth and Torbay.

The Devon Record Office, the West Country Studies Library, the Devon County Library, Exeter City Library and the Exeter Cathedral Library are in Exeter. West Devon Area Record office is in Plymouth and the North Devon Record Office is in Barnstaple. There is a Family History Centre at Plymouth and Exeter.

Pre 1858 Wills, once deposited at the Probate Registry, Exeter, were destroyed by bombing in 1942 but some collections of abstracts have been copied and are available at the CRO, The Devon County Library and Exeter City Library. Some wills relating to tenements in the City of Exeter are at the Exeter City Library.

Devon and Cornwall Record Society has made a number of historical records available in print, including many parish registers, since 1906. Heralds' Visitation Pedigrees have been printed for 1531, 1564 and 1620.

See also *Guide to the parish and non-parochial registers of Devon and Cornwall 1538–1837*, by H. Peskett (1979) and *Devon: a genealogical bibliography: vol. 1, Sources; vol. 2, Families*, by S. Raymond (FFHS, 1990).

Dexter The right-hand side of a shield in heraldry when held from behind.

Diary A number of diaries dating from the sixteenth century onward have been published, and are often to be found in the main public library of the county in which the diarist lived. They can reveal social conditions, local happenings and weather conditions useful to the family historian.
See also W. Matthews *British Diaries: an annotated bibliography 1442–1942* (1950) and J.S. Batts *British Manuscript Diaries of the 19th Century: an annotated listing* (1976).

Diem Clausit Extremum The Latin name for a writ ordering an inquiry into the lands held by a tenant-in-chief on the day he died.

Diminutives Many short forms of Christian names do not immediately indicate the name they represent. The most usually found diminutives of this nature are: Bart for Bartholomew, Bill or Billy for William, Dick for Richard, Eddie

Map showing pre 1836 dioceses (bounded by dotted lines and named in bold), and their relationship with the pre 1974 county boundaries (double lines). *Drawing by Whitney Lumas.*

for Edward, Edmund, Edwin and Edgar, Hal or Harry for Henry, Jack for John, Jake for Jacob, Jenkin a Welsh Variant of John, Joe for Joseph, Kit for Christopher, Larry for Lawrence, Ned, Ted or Teddie for Edward, and for girls: Bess, Bessie, Beth, Betsy and Bettina for Elizabeth, Binnie for Benedicta, Cherry for Charity, Cissie for Cecilia or Cynthia, Dot for Dorothy, Elise for Elizabeth, Etta and Ettie for Henrietta or Harriet, Fanny for Frances, Florrie and Flossie for Florence, Greta for Margaret, Hattie for Henrietta, Lisa or Liza for Elizabeth, Lottie for Charlotte, Madge, Maggie, Maidie, Maida, Margot, Marjorie and Meg for Margaret, Mamie and Molly for Mary, Mattie for Martha, Nan, Nancy or Nanette for Anne, Nana for Hannah, Nessa and Nessie for Agnes, Netta for Henrietta, Nora for Eleanora, Honora and Leonora, Ottilie for Odelia, Patsy for Patricia, Peg and Peggy for Margaret, Penny for Penelope, Polly for Mary, Prissie for Priscilla, Rena for Catherine, Sadie, Sal and Sally for Sarah, Sandra for Alexandra, Thea for Althea, Theda for Theodora, Tilly for Matilda, Vilma, Willa and Wilma for Wilhelmina, Winnie for Winifred. Sometimes parents named their children by the diminutives and sometimes names were recorded in different records by either the diminutive or the full name.

Diocese The area of a bishop's jurisdiction. Before 1541–2 there were fourteen English dioceses, and thereafter, until the nineteenth century, eighteen, plus four for Wales. For administrative purposes a diocese might be divided into several archdeaconries (*see* ARCHDEACON), many of them having much the same boundaries as the counties within the diocese. Every diocese has a registry for its records. In many cases the registry and the county record office are now combined.

Diplomatic The science of documentary criticism involving, among other things, a knowledge of formally laid down procedure and forms of words.

Directories, Local The first local directories were published in the latter half of the seventeenth century, and were intended for business purposes. One that appeared in 1677 was called *A Collection of the Names of the Merchants living in and about the City of London: Very Useful and Necessary*. During the eighteenth century the number of directories increased, but nearly all listed only commercial concerns. It was not until the early nineteenth century that private persons were regularly included. From that time onward

they may provide the quickest means for finding out where a family lived, but not, unfortunately, in the case of all families.

Directories were compiled and issued at frequent intervals by private publishing concerns, sometimes by several in competition. The most famous are those by the firms of Pigot and Kelly, the latter being still in business today. The area covered by any particular volume varies greatly, from the whole of England and Wales to a single town. Most of them cover either a single county or a group of three or four contiguous counties. In these, each town and rural parish is dealt with in alphabetical order, with hamlets usually included under their parochial heading. There is normally a prefatory chapter on the history and geography of the area, and a list of people holding official positions. In a volume for a single city the inhabitants and businesses will then be listed in two sections — a Court Directory and a Commercial Directory — and sometimes also a Trades Directory and a Street Directory. The first gives names and private addresses of the gentry and more prosperous middle-class householders, the second gives the business addresses of professional and commercial people and firms. The Trades Directory groups these people under occupational headings, such as Bakers, Attorneys, etc., and the Street Directory includes private and business names under street headings. Thus the whole directory is liable to mention the same persons three or even four times. As the information supplied about any given person may not be the same in each section, it is worth searching them all.

Directories do not cover every household. Labourers were never included and only a small proportion of craftsmen — those usually in rural villages. Self-employed tradesmen appear in large numbers but are not necessarily all covered. In a town, the central shopping streets seem to be favoured at the expense of outlying areas, but the directory is not always to be relied on for the relative importance of the town's businesses. In villages, the squire, parson, farmers, graziers, innkeepers and blacksmiths are regularly included. It should be remembered that a directory is at least six months out of date on the day it is published.

The largest collections of old directories are those in London in the Guildhall Library, the Victoria and Albert Museum, and at the Society of Genealogists. A catalogue of the latter has been published. Another useful source of directory information is the firm of KELLY'S DIRECTORIES, which still publishes telephone directories and manufacturers' guides.

For further reading, see *A Guide to the National and Provincial Directories of England and Wales before 1856*, edited by Jane E. Norton (Royal Historical Society), *A Bibliography of Trade Directories of the British Isles in the Victoria and Albert Museum*, by M.E. Keen (1979), and *British Directories, 1850–1950*, by Gareth Shaw and Alison Tipper.

Disseisin   Forcible eviction. Novel Disseisin was a claim in a court of law that the plaintiff had been recently dispossessed.

Dissenters *see* **Nonconformists**

Dissolution of the Monasteries   In March 1536 all monasteries with an annual income of less than £200 were dissolved by Act of Parliament, their inmates pensioned off, and their buildings and estates confiscated by the Crown. During the following four years the remaining larger, monasteries and friaries were also dissolved. Many of their properties eventually passed into private hands.

Further reading: *Alienated Tithes* by H. Grove.

Distressed Protestants in Ireland, Collection for   Towards the end of 1641 the Catholic Irish rose against the Protestant English immigrants who had been imposed upon them. The English settlers fled in conditions of destitution. The winter was hard and probably destroyed more of the refugees than were killed by the Irish, but atrocity stories spread throughout England and in March 1641/2 King Charles approved an Act for raising, from every parish in the country, a total of £400,000 for their relief. The returns of the collections, arranged under parish headings, can be found at the Public Record Office (PRO), Chancery Lane, London, under references SP 28 and E 179. The contributors are all listed by name, with the sums they gave, and include many women, who are of course not named in the contemporaneous Protestation Oath Returns. As the latter do not survive for every parish, the records of the Collection supply a valuable supplementary location record for the period. A list of all surviving returns and their PRO class numbers has been published by the West Surrey Family History Society.

Distributor   A name sometimes applied to the Overseer of the Poor or his assistant. It originated from his duty of giving out the proceeds of the Poor Rate for the support of the parish paupers. *See also* COLLECTOR OF THE POOR.

Ditchsilver   A payment by tenants towards the cost of clearing the ditches of the manor.

Divorce   Separation of husband and wife *a mensa et toro* (from board and bed) could be granted by ecclesiastical courts, but from 1668 until 1857 full divorce *a vinculo matrimonii* (from the bands of matrimony) could only be effected by a Private Act of Parliament. It was therefore available only to those of ample means.

From 1669 onwards the records of Divorce Bills are in the House of Lords Record Office, indexed in Part XIII of *The Index to Local and Personal Acts*, and accounts of the proceedings can be found in the published *Journals* of the House. The original records may also include those of any prior relevant proceedings in an ecclesiastical or civil court. Records of later divorces are kept at the Divorce Registry of the Family Division of the High Court, at Somerset House, Strand, London. Application may be made by post or in person at Room G.44. Details, if known, of the husband, wife, co-respondent and approximate date must be given on a form supplied, and a search fee paid. The search is made by the Registry staff during the next few days. If successful, the enquirer receives, for a further fee, a 'Certificate of Making Decree Nisi Absolute (Divorce)'. For postal applications, the address is: Divorce Registry, Somerset House, Strand, London WC2R 1LP. The decree once obtained will verify the names of both parties, the date of the decree absolute and the date and place of the marriage.

Petitions for divorce, once they are one hundred years old, can be found at the Public Record Office, Chancery Lane, London, among the records of the Supreme Court of Judicature in class J 77. See Information Leaflet No. 127, *Divorce Records in the Public Record Office*.

See also ARCHES, COURT OF.

Doctors' Commons   Doctors' Commons was the popular name for the College of Advocates (the doctors of civil and canon law). It had a common hall, library, dining hall and the chambers of the judges and advocates. It also served

RIGHT A document relating to the Collection for Distressed Protestants in Ireland, made in the spring of 1641/2. The parochial lists of this collection tend to reveal more than the Lay Subsidy and Protestation Oath Lists of the same period, because the names of many married women are shown on them. SP 24/194 (pt II) f. 193, *Crown copyright: reproduced with the permission of the Controller of Her Majesty's Stationery Office.*

Monies contributed and collected out of the parish
of St Margarits in Norwich, towards the releife
of our afflicted brethrin in Ireland:

Mr Samuel Dobson:	ten shillings	
Mres Newson	ten shillings	
Mr Tho Bigg	fiue shillings	
Mres Bigg	three shillings	
Will Hardingam sen:	seuen shillings	
Will: Brooks	ten shillings	
Joseph Brooke	sixe shillings	
Daniel Winter	sixe shillings	
Edward Boote	foure shillings	
The wiffe of Edward Boote	One shillinge	
Richard Howse	seuen shillings	
Ambrose Norris	fiue shillings	
Edward Beuis	fiue shillings	
Edmund Newman	fiue shillings	
William Lawes	foure shillings	
Nic: Swetman	three shillings	
Goodwife Swetman	One shilling	
John Goodings	three shillings	
Will: Hardingham iun:	two shillings	
Anne Dubery	two shillings	Six pence
William Shetringe	two shillings	Six pence
John Nobbs	One shillinge	
Edm: Turner	One shillinge	
Will: Linstead	One shillinge	
Rich Lathe	One shillinge	
Tobit Holfer	One shillinge	Six pence
Will: Hargraue	One shillinge	
Mathew Guiton	One shillings	
John Danny	One shillinge	
Jane Danny		Sixe pence
John Eckleston	One shillingo	Sixt pence
Jeremiah Brooke	One shillinge	
Hen: Blanch	One shillinge	
John Webster		Seuen pence
Peter Ransome		Sixt pence
Robt: Browne		Six pence
Edward Caruer		Six pence
Rachel Burman		Six pence
Will: Curtisse		Six pence
Simond Coe		Six pence
John Lampkin		Six pence
William Horne		Six pence
Henry Palmer		Six pence
will Lane		Six pence

as the principal London probate registry. In the hall sat the Prerogative Court of Canterbury, the Court of Arches, the Court of the Bishop of London and the High Court of Admiralty amongst others. They handled cases concerned with all matters of ecclesiastical law, prosecutions for heresy, divorce, marriage licences and testamentary affairs. Wills said to have been proved at Doctors' Commons are usually found to have been proved in the Prerogative Court of Canterbury.

Doctors, Medical In the sixteenth century, licences to practise medicine were granted by diocesan bishops and can be traced in the records of their courts. Then and much later, no professional qualifications were required.

In 1518 the London College of Physicians, now the Royal College of Physicians of London, was founded by Thomas Linacre and granted the power to supervise the practice of 'physic' within seven miles of the capital. Its members were freed from social obligations that might interfere with their work, such as serving on juries, acting as constables, keeping watch (*see* WATCH AND WARD), and militia duties.

Later many medical men became graduates in medicine and can be found in the registers of the universities of Oxford and Cambridge. In 1845 the unofficial *Medical Directory* began to appear, and the official *Medical Register* has been published since 1858. Besides giving details of the living, the former also provides obituaries of doctors recently deceased. Biographies of the Fellows of the Royal College since 1518 have been compiled by Dr William Munk in four volumes, the last posthumously, under the title *Munk's Roll of Physicians*. Some Vestry Minute Books give the names of doctors contracted to attend the parish poor.

Further reading: *18th Century Medics* by P.J. Wallis.

See also APOTHECARIES; PHYSICIANS; SURGEONS.

Doctor William's Library *see* **William's Library, Dr**

Doe, John *see* **Roe, Richard**

Dole (i) A charitable donation.

(ii) A share in the common arable fields and/or meadow, distributed afresh periodically in some manors, either by lot or rotation. Also called Lot-meadow.

Domesday Book A report of a survey of land holdings made in 1086 at the order of William the Conqueror. Three volumes deal with Essex,

Norfolk and Suffolk, and the two others with the rest of England except for Northumberland, Durham, Cumberland, northern Westmorland, Winchester and London which are omitted because the land was laid waste. The information was compiled by Royal Commission, and every hundred court appointed four Norman and four English Members to co-operate by giving sworn answers to their inquiries. The result was later checked by a second commission.

The report is arranged county by county, and under the headings of the tenants-in-chief in each county. These tenants and their sub-tenants, both at the time of the survey and those at the Conquest, are the only persons named, the rest of the householders merely being numbered class by class, as villeins, cottars, slaves, freemen and sokemen; and in spite of an impression cherished by many families, the only buildings mentioned are churches and mills. The bulk of the report is taken up by the extents of arable, meadow, pasture and woodland, and the number of plough-teams estimated as necessary and actually in use. The value of each land holding is given, at the time of Edward the Confessor, at the time of the Conquest and at the time of the survey. The first volume of the *Victoria County History* for each county deals with the Domesday returns, and separate Domesday volumes for each county are now being published.

Donative Benefice *see* **Benefice**

Doncaster Society for Family History *see* **Yorkshire**

Doom A judgement delivered by a court.

Doomsman A member of the jury of a manorial court, who were also known collectively as the Homage.

Dormant Funds This term is applied to sums of money usually belonging either to people who died intestate and for whom no next-of-kin could be found, or to testators whose legatees could not be traced after advertisement in the national press had produced no claimants, and which have since lain undealt with for fifteen years. The funds are now in the custody of the Supreme Court of England and Wales.

Until 1938, lists of sums of £50 or more were published every five years as supplements to the *London Gazette*. A complete list of all funds held was published in 1911; there is a copy at the Society of Genealogists. Since 1954, lists have been published annually. All such lists can be perused, free of charge, in Room 60, Court Funds Office, Eastern Corridor, Ground Floor, at the Royal Courts of Justice in the Strand, London, and for the period since 1893, at the Public Record Office, Chancery Lane, London. Information about the sums shown may be supplied by the Accountant General in response to a written request from a person believed to be beneficially interested, after advance payment of the fee laid down. Such applications, enclosing evidence of the beneficial interest, but not original documents, should be addressed to The Principal, Court Funds Office, Royal Courts of Justice, The Strand, London WC2A 2LL. The majority of such sums is of less than £150, and so not worth the expense of claiming.

Dormant Peerage One for which, on the death of the holder, no heir can be traced, although it is likely that a potential claimant is living. Not to be confused with a peerage in ABEYANCE.

Dorse The reverse side of a sheet of paper or parchment. Anything written on it was called an Endorsement.

Dorset Since 1974 the Bournemouth area has been included in the county. The county fell within the diocese of Salisbury until 1542 and in the diocese of Bristol until 1836 and then returned to the diocese of Salisbury. It is in the Province of Canterbury. Most parish registers are now at the CRO and there are transcripts to some of them at the library of the SOG. Boyd's Marriage Index includes a number of parishes in its Miscellaneous Series. Pallot's Marriage Index covers 74 parishes, 1790–1812. The Bishop's Transcripts from 1731 are in the Wiltshire Record Office. Marriage Licence records are at the County Record Office.

The Hundreds of Coombs Ditch, Pimperne, Rushmoor, Dewlish Liberty, Corfe-Castle, Bere-Regis, Hundredsbarrow, Hasilor, Rowbarrow, Winfrith, Bindon, Owermoigne and Stoborough Liberties, Beaminster-Forum and Redhone, Eggerton, Godderthorne, Whitchurch-Canonicorum, Broadwinsor and Frampton Liberties, Lothers and Bothenhampton Liberty, Poorstock Liberty, Buckland-Newton, Cerne, Totcombe and Modbury, Whiteway, Alton-Pancras, Piddletrenthide and Sydling, St. Nicholas Liberties, Culliford-Tree, George, Piddletown, Totterford, Uggscombe, Fordington and Isle of Portland Liberties, Piddlehinton, Sutton Poyntz and Wabyhouse Liberties, Wyke-Regis and Elwell Liberty, Badbury, Cogdean, Cranbourne, Knowlton, Loosebarrow, Monckton-up-Wimborne, Sixpenny-Handley, Wimborne St. Giles, Alcester and Gillingham Liberties, Yetminster, Halstock and Ryme Intrinsica Liberties, Brownshall, Redland, Sturminster-Newton, Castle, Stower, Provost, Blandford Town, Bridport and Dorchester Boroughs, Lyme Regis and Shaftesbury (Shaston) Boroughs, Sherborne Town, Wareham and Weymouth and Melcombe-Regis Boroughs, Poole Town and County lie within its boundaries.

It has Shaftesbury, Sturminster, Blandford, Wimborne, Poole, Wareham, Weymouth, Dorchester, Sherborne, Beaminster and Bridport RDs/PLUs.

It falls within the Western Assize Circuit.

Somerset and Dorset Family History Society publish a quarterly journal called the *Greenwood Tree* and meets in Stalbridge, Street, Taunton, Yeovil, Broadstone, Weymouth, and Beaminster. Dorset Family History Society has its own quarterly journal and meets in Poole.

The County Record Office is in Dorchester and there is a Family History Centre at Poole.

Pre 1858 Wills proved in the Consistory Court of Bristol (Dorset Division), the Archdeaconry Court of Dorset, the Manor and Liberty Court of Frampton and the Peculiar Courts of Great Canford and Poole, Milton Abbas, Sturminster Marshall and Wimborne Minster are held at the CRO. Those for the Prebendal Courts of Fordington and Writhlington, Lyme Regis and Halstock, Netherbury in Ecclesia, Preston and Sutton Poynta and Tetminster and Grimston, the Royal Peculiar Court of Gillingham, and the Peculiar Courts of the Dean of Sarum and the Dean and Chapter of Sarum are at the Wiltshire CRO. The Dorset Record Society has published local material since 1964. The Heralds' Visitation Pedigrees have been printed for 1531, 1565, 1623 and 1677.

Dorset Record Office publishes *Tracing Dorset ancestors*. See also *Dorset: a genealogical bibliography*, by S. Raymond (FFHS, 1991).

Dower The portion to which a widow was entitled of the estate of her late husband for her sustenance and the education of their children. By Common Law it was fixed at one-third, but this could be over-ruled by the customary law of the manor (or other area) to one-quarter or one-half, or his whole estate. In connection with copyhold property, the last-mentioned right was called Freebench. Dower is also used of a daughter's portion of inheritance.

Dower (Latin *donarium*) is not to be confused with DOWRY.

Dowry was the property in land or money that a wife brought to her husband at their marriage. This may have been given her by her father, or it may have been property already in her possession by inheritance.

Dowry (Latin *maritagium*) is not to be confused with DOWER.

Dozener (i) A borough official elected by the householders of a ward or street to make presentments at the Court Leet or Wardmote.

(ii) A juryman.

Drop-line Pedigree *see* Family Tree

Duke The first English dukedom was that of Cornwall, created in 1337 by Edward III for his son, the Black Prince. It took precedence over all earldoms, hitherto the highest rank of English nobility. Before that date, the kings of England alone had been dukes, but even then only of their possessions in France, i.e. of Normandy and Aquitaine. The first non-royal duke was Robert de Vere, Earl of Oxford, created Duke of Ireland in 1386.

The wife of a duke is a duchess. Their eldest son normally takes, by courtesy, his father's second title (usually either Marquess or Earl), and the younger sons and daughters are styled, also by courtesy, Lord and Lady before their Christian names.

Durham The southeast corner of the county is now in the county of Cleveland and the northwest in Tyne and Wear. The county falls within the diocese of Durham and the Province of York. Nearly all its parish registers have been deposited at the CRO and transcripts of many of them are in the library of the SOG. Boyd's Marriage Index covers 72 parishes. Pallot's Marriage Index covers 21, from 1790–1812. The Bishops' Transcripts are at the Department of Palaeography and Diplomatic, University of Durham, as are the Marriage Licence records.

The wards of Chester (East, Middle and West Divisions), Darlington (South-East, South-West and North-West Divisions), Easington (North and South Divisions), Stockton (North-East and South-West Divisions) Islandshire, Norhamshire, Sunderland Town and Durham City lie within its boundaries.

It has Darlington, Stockton (later Hartlepool), Auckland, Teesdale, Weardale (later Lanchester), Durham, Easington, Houghton-le-Spring, Chester-le-Street, Sunderland, South Shields and Gateshead RDs/PLUs.

It fell within the Northern Assize Circuit until 1876 and then the North Eastern Assize Circuit.

The Northumberland and Durham Family History Society publishes a quarterly journal and meets at Gateshead, Durham, Blyth, South Shields, Monkwearmouth and has a London branch which meets at the SOG.

Record Repositories: Durham CRO, Priors Kitchen and the Department of Palaeography and Diplomatic both at the College, Durham Cathedral and Durham University libraries are all in Durham and Gateshead Central Library in Gateshead. There are Family History Centres in Billingham and Sunderland.

Pre 1858 Wills proved in the following courts are located as follows: The Palatine and Consistory Court of Durham and the Episcopal and Chancery Courts of York are at the Department of Palaeography and Diplomatic; wills could also be proved at either the Prerogative Courts of York or Canterbury.

The Durham and Northumberland Parish Register Society has published a number of registers. The Surtees Society has published the Protestation Oath Returns and other records since 1835. Heralds' Visitation Pedigrees have been printed for 1575, 1615 and 1666.

North Eastern Ancestors is a guide to sources in the Tyne and Wear Archives Service and in the Northumberland and Durham Record Offices. See also *National Index of Parish Registers*, vol. 11, Part 1 (1984) and *Indexes for the Northumberland and Durham family historian*, by A.H. Chicken and S. Bourne (1993).

E

Earl Under the first pre-Conquest kings, earls were the highest rank of nobility and also the king's officials over wide provinces. They presided over the shire courts and commanded the FYRD. As the rank became hereditary and the work increased, the authority in each county passed to the sheriff, and an earldom became merely a title. After the Conquest, the titles first of Duke and later of Marquess were introduced as ranks taking precedence over that of Earl. The wife of an earl is a Countess, and, except for formal purposes, an earl and countess are referred to as Lord and Lady (So-and-so). Their eldest son takes, by courtesy, his father's second title (usually that of Viscount or Baron). The younger sons are styled Honourable (Mr, in conversation), and the daughters Lady before their Christian name.

Eastbourne Family History Society *see* **Sussex**

East India Company The East India Company was incorporated by Queen Elizabeth I on 31 December, 1600. It became a joint stock company and established a number of factories (trading stations) on the mainland of India, in the Spice Islands and elsewhere in the East. The Company's earliest major factory was at Surat in northwest India, followed soon after by one at Madras, called Fort St George. When Charles II married a Portuguese princess in 1662, she brought him the Portuguese-occupied island of Bombay as part of her dowry, and he leased it to the Company. In the latter part of the seventeenth century, the stockholders and, indeed, the factors became so wealthy that their monopoly was resented by English merchants, and after an appeal to the House of Commons the formation of a second company was allowed. However, rivalry between the two sets of factors in the East did both organisations so much harm that they were glad to amalgamate, in 1708, as The United Company of Merchants of England Trading to the East Indies.

During the period of rivalry, the Old Company had acquired by treaty a site on the Hooghly River on which they built Fort William, close to the village of Calcutta. The United Company's territories became organised in three 'presidencies': Bengal (administered from Fort William), Madras (Fort St George), and Bombay, each headquarters having authority over a number of satellite factories. For a time, Bencoolen (Fort Marlborough) in Sumatra was the headquarters of a separate presidency.

In the mid eighteenth century, the Company established a permanent factory at Canton in China, in order to engage in the growing tea trade, and this station became one of the most lucrative. By this time, the French were the Company's chief rivals in India. Both enlisted the influence of Indian rulers and this led to open warfare between them, in which the British were finally successful.

The safeguarding of their interests led the Company to acquire more and more Indian territory, in spite of protests from their directors in London. This led, in 1773, to the intervention of the British Government. The Company's Bengal Governor was appointed Governor-General of all its Indian lands, with succession confined to Government-approved nominees. In 1784 William Pitt created a Board of Control to supervise the Company. In 1857 came the sepoy rising, known as the Indian Mutiny, and on its suppression the Company was taken over by the Crown. India was thenceforward ruled by a British Viceroy in conjunction with the newly created India Office in London.

Many middle-class families have had members in the East India Company, and probably more than one, because service with 'John Company' was considered the high-road to a fortune, and entry depended largely on inside influence. Many families served the Company for three or four generations.

The Company's records are a uniquely rich source of biographical material. They comprise those created by the London Head Office, those of the factories in Asia, those of the Company's armed forces, and the log-books and other records of the Company's merchant ships. The records include returns of baptisms, marriages and burials in India from the end of the seventeenth century; and there are also, from 1803, annual printed *India Lists* giving names of all Company servants. These records now constitute the India Office Library and Records, and are housed at Orbit House, Blackfriars Bridge Road, London SE1 8NG, where they are open to public inspection. The Office has issued a useful 53-page *Brief Guide to Biographical Sources*, by Ian A. Baxter. *See also* INDIA OFFICE LIBRARY AND RECORDS.

East of London Family History Society *see* **London and Middlesex**

Ecclesiastical Census The Public Record Office holds the returns of an ecclesiastical census taken in 1851 which records the details and size of congregation of all places of worship, both Church of England and dissenting. The reference is HO 129. PRO information Leaflet No.51 *The Ecclesiastical Census 1851*.

Ecclesiastical Courts Under the Norman kings, separate courts were created for the hearing of judicial cases under Canon Law. They were on two levels — the Bishops' Courts and the Archdeacons' Courts — and their records survive from the fifteenth century. They dealt with such matters as heresy (bishops only), attendance at church, behaviour in church and in the churchyard, the conduct of the parson and church officials, the state of the church building and its furniture, payment of parish dues, betrothal, marriage, immorality, slander, wills, parish boundaries, usury and perjury. So many of the cases were about fornication and adultery that the court became known in some places as the 'Bawdy Court'. The cases arose very largely from presentments made at the Archdeacon's or Bishop's Visitations (*see* ECCLESIASTICAL VISITATIONS).

Archdeacons' Courts were held at about three-weekly intervals in some central or important town; more frequently if necessary. The court often occupied the west end of one of the aisles of the church. Either the Archdeacon himself or his Official Principal presided as judge. There was no jury.

An Apparitor served a citation on the accused to appear at the court. The case might be of two kinds, either an Office Cause or a Cause of Instance. The former was brought by the Office of the Judge against the defendant, but the Office might be prompted thereto by another party. The latter type was brought by one private person against another.

Many of the Office Causes could be dealt with simply. If the accused pleaded 'Guilty' the judge proceeded at once to sentence, if 'Not Guilty' the accused was examined under oath and witnesses made their depositions. The judge then ordered the accused to purge himself, which meant that he was given the chance to find a certain number of neighbours (usually about six) to be his compurgators and swear to his innocence. If he did this, the case was dismissed. If not, the judge sentenced the accused. The punishment of the guilty was normally by penance, which up to the sixteenth century might be accompanied by castigation and fines, although sometimes penance was commuted to a fine. Penances could be private (i.e. performed before only the parson and churchwardens), or public. Serious offences could be punished by excommunication, as could failure to appear in answer to a citation (this offence was 'Contumacy'). Excommunication was performed by sending a Letter of Excommunication to the accused's parish, to be read aloud in service at church.

Causes of Instance always involved a more formal procedure, beginning with the appointment of Proctors by both sides to represent them in court. The following documents record the successive stages of the cause, always carried on under oath: *Libel of Articles*, the case for the prosecution; *Responsions*, the reply made by the defence (the 'respondent'); *Attestations* (or Depositions), the witnesses for the prosecution; and *Interrogatories*, the questioning of the witnesses by the defence. In the next stage, the defence normally made its case and the same four stages were proceeded with by the opposite side. Sometimes, however, instead of making a case for itself, the defence attacked the credibility of the prosecution witnesses in *Articles of Exception*,

which could give rise to another series of *Responsions*, and so on. In the end the judge gave his sentence, and also a Bill of Taxed Costs.

After the close of the court, often considerably later, the judge's registrar wrote a description of the case in his Act Book (or Court Book). Except for the names of the parties, these contain little of interest, sometimes not even the charge against the defendant. Of Office Causes, the record is often in a separate Corrections Book but sometimes the two types of case are in the same volume. Non-judicial administrative business of the court is entered in separate volumes, such as those for faculties, marriage licences, probate records and inventories. Though in all the above-mentioned records the narrative is in Latin, any words spoken are given in English.

For genealogists the most valuable of these records are the *Attestations* (Depositions). Each begins with an account of the witness himself, his name, sex, condition, occupation, age, length of abode in the place about which he is giving evidence, where he now lives if different, and where he lived previously, right back to his birthplace. It has been reckoned that about 7 per cent of the population were deponents at one time or another.

The records are kept in the Diocesan Registries, which today may be incorporated in the county record office. Where the records are indexed, it is usually only under the names of the parties. Many Act Books are highly abbreviated notes in a technical scribble. The clerks would enter the headings of the cases first, allowing four entries to a page, and then fill in the business at a later date. For some entries the space is not enough, leading to cramped writing and sometimes even to the finishing of an entry in some blank space several folios away, accompanied by cross-reference marks. The reduced volume of business during the Civil War ended this practice.

For further reading, see *Shakespeare and the Bawdy Court of Stratford*, by E.R.C. Brinkworth, *Ecclesiastical Courts, Their Officials and Their Records* by Colin R. Chapman, Lochin Publishing (1992).

Ecclesiastical Visitations

Archdeacons were supposed to visit their archdeaconries once a year, and bishops their dioceses every three years. The Visitor would send out a Citation Mandate to all incumbents, who read it out in church, calling upon them and the church officials to appear before him at a date and place named. The latter would be a church either in a central position or in the most important town. At about the same time he would issue his Visitation Articles, listing the subjects into which he wished to enquire. These would include the church, the living, the clergy, hospitals, the parish, the parishioners and the ecclesiastical officers. All those people summoned would be required to obtain a copy of the Articles beforehand.

The Archdeacon arrived with his Register, bringing his Call Book and Fees Book to record attendances, absences and fees collected. The visited included the clergy, churchwardens, parish clerks, schoolmasters, surgeons and midwives, unless excused. The clergy brought their Letters of Orders proving their right to their cures (spiritual charges), with dispensations when they held more than one living. The parish clerks, schoolmasters, surgeons and midwives brought their licences. The clergy and churchwardens had certain fees to pay.

The clergy and churchwardens then handed in their presentments, reporting on the conduct of their parishioners since the last Visitation and answering the points in the Visitation Articles. Executors and administrators of people who had lately died were also required to come and prove the wills, or take administration, a function that at other times was performed at the relevant ecclesiastical court. The presentments were discussed and some verdicts given on the spot; the Visitation ended with the Archdeacon's Charge, an address delivered during a service in the church.

After the visitation, the Archdeacon issued, through his Registrar's office, a number of Injunctions setting out in detail, in numbered paragraphs, his orders for the amendment of any faults revealed. Among these were penances imposed, together with a certificate to be signed by the incumbent and a churchwarden that the penance had been performed. After the mid sixteenth century, the penance was normally just a Declaration Penance, which was a confession to be read publicly, usually in church, reciting the offence and expressing penitence. Sometimes the incumbent or churchwardens would give a certificate that the offender was of a sufficiently good general character — or perhaps social standing — to be allowed to perform his penance privately.

Other documents kept by the Registrar for permanent reference included the DETECTA and COMPERTA volumes, containing copies of all the presentments with a few brief additional notes; copies of Citation Mandates, summoning the more serious offenders to appear before the Archdeacon's Court; and the Act Book, recording the action taken against them there. This last overlaps the records of the court. *Exhibitions* list the licences and other documents produced in court.

Though visitations began in the tenth century, the records are only numerous from the reign of Elizabeth I. Bishops' three-yearly visitations are similar to those of Archdeacons, but less numerous: The presentments are usually written in English and the originals sometimes survive on single sheets of paper. They are full of human interest, naming and reporting on the most important parish functionaries. People who neglected or refused to receive Holy Communion (Recusants) were presented; they might be Protestant noncomformists or Roman Catholics. The state of the church might also be given in some detail, mentioning any 'popish monuments of superstition' such as candlesticks, a crucifix, handbells or banner cloths. Rogationtide perambulations of the parish are sometimes mentioned, with the boundaries described. Non payment of tithe is always mentioned. The morals of the parishioners form the largest subject of the presentments. Not even the parson was exempt from presentment.

Education *see* **Schools**

Eftsoons A second time.

Electioner A person qualified for election to a parochial office by virtue of his holding in the parish.

Electoral Registers The *Reform Act* of 1832 greatly enlarged the county franchise. As a consequence, it required the parochial registration of every person qualified to vote, and the publication of such registers. The entries show the name and abode of each elector, the property (owned or leased) that qualified him to vote, and its name and situation in the locality. Later volumes give the voters' addresses in fuller detail, including the house names or numbers. County Electoral Registers are to be found at county record offices.

Finding Aid: *Electoral Registers since 1832*, by Jeremy Gibson and Colin Rogers, FFHS, third edition in preparation.

Emigrants Emigration proper, the permanent settling of British men and women in communities overseas, began in the sixteenth century and has continued ever since. The causes have always been various: religion, politics, transportation for crime, service indenture, escape from poverty, and enterprise in search of prosperity. The chief destinations of large-scale emigration were, in roughly chronological order of their commencement, North America, the West Indies, Australia, South Africa, New Zealand and East and Central Africa. This excludes consideration of those who went abroad, for example to India, in pursuit of a career but with the intention of returning to the mother country on retirement.

See also AUSTRALIAN; CANADIAN; NEW ZEALAND; SOUTH AFRICAN; UNITED STATES ANCESTRY.

A free leaflet, No. 71 *Emigrants: Documents in the Public Record Office*, is available at the PRO.

Enclosures In the Middle Ages the typical method of agriculture was by what is now called the Open Field System. Householders in the manor held strips of land scattered among larger open fields, and they also held haymaking and grazing rights in the meadowland and pasture in proportion to the number of strips they held in the arable. The fields are called 'open' because there were no hedges or fences between the various strips.

In time it became apparent that it was more efficient for a man to hold one substantial block of land, rather than these scattered strips, so first the lord of the manor tended to withdraw his strips into one group and to take in land from the waste. These became part of his demesne. The same process was later followed by others, but affected mainly the pasture land because individuals were primarily concerned to increase their sheep-grazing capacity. However, arable land was also affected. The legal process is often spelt 'Inclosure', and the physical process of partition 'Enclosure'.

In 1517–18 the *Domesday of Inclosure* was drawn up, showing what land had been inclosed in six or seven counties. However, in 1533–4, as a result of numerous protests against inclosure, an Act was passed against the process, though it was widely ignored.

In the seventeenth century the process gathered speed, and tended to be brought about by people bringing suits in Chancery or other courts of equity, probably mostly collusive. The resulting decisions were recorded in the rolls of the court. Some enclosures were arranged within the locality, either by the Court Leet or the Vestry.

In the eighteenth century, agriculture became more scientific. This again hastened the process of inclosure — which now tended to be brought about by private Acts of Parliament, some of which merely confirmed what had already been agreed in the manor.

In 1836, a *General Inclosure Act* enabled enclosure to proceed without the cumbersome preliminary of a private Act of Parliament, provided it had the consent of a majority of the people concerned; and a further Act of 1845 set up a board of Inclosure Commissioners, in London, to supervise all inclosures. The bulk of all inclosures took place between 1750 and 1850.

The rolls of the Court of Chancery, and other equity courts contain accounts of sixteenth, seventeenth and eighteenth centuries' enclosures, in class C 54. Enclosures enrolled on the Common Pleas rolls are in class CP 43. Under private inclosure Acts the original Award documents were given to the parish concerned, with a copy to the Clerk of the Peace of the Quarter Sessions. A list of these has been printed by the House of Commons. Under the *General Inclosure Act* of 1836, one copy of the Award document was the property of the enclosed parish and another was deposited with the Clerk of the Peace for the Quarter Sessions. Most of the latter are now at the county record offices, but some are at the Public Record Office (PRO), Chancery Lane, London, and a few among parish records. They consist of a list of owners, descriptions of the enclosed land portions and a map showing their situations. In places where tithes have been commuted mainly under inclosure Acts, the Enclosure Award maps give a wider survey than those of the Tithe Awards. Awards made under the Act of 1845 are at the PRO, Kew, in class MAF 1.

The Minute Books of Commissioners, where they exist, have been listed, and the list printed in the *Bulletin of the Institute of Historical Research*, vol. XXI, 1946–8. The parish copy of an Agreement and Award can sometimes be found still in the custody of the incumbent.

For further reading, see *A Domesday of English Enclosure Acts*, by W.E. Tate, University of Reading, (1978).

Enfeoffment to Use In the Middle Ages a man who did not wish his land, or, at least, not all of it, to pass to his eldest son by primogeniture under the Common Law, could make it over during his lifetime to trustees by a written legal deed. The trustees then held it, but to the 'use' of the original owner. The latter then executed a 'last will' — not a testament — expressing his wish regarding who should be the user of the land after his death. This practice deprived the king and other lords of their escheats and fines, avoided forfeiture in cases of felony, and

defeated the provisions of the Statutes of Mortmain, so a *Statute of Uses* was passed in 1535–6 to make it illegal. However, by the *Statute of Wills*, 1540, land was allowed to be legally devised on the death of its holder, and so Last Wills came to be customarily executed in the same document as Testaments.
See also JOINT ENFEOFFMENT; WILL.

Englishry From the Conquest to the mid fourteenth century, it was necessary to establish whether a murdered person was Norman or English by descent; the penalties for killing a Norman were much the more severe. All doubtful cases were considered to be Norman. Unless the accused person could successfully plead 'Englishry' (i.e. that the deceased was English and not Norman), he would face severe penalties and a fine would be imposed on the hundred in which the crime was committed.

Engrossing (i) The gathering into single ownership, or tenancy, of lands and houses formerly supporting two or more families.
(ii) The writing out in formal script of a legal deed, a procedure that required calligraphic skill.

Enrolled Deeds In order to ensure the survival of an authentic copy of a conveyance or title, it was open to any party concerned to have it registered in some official roll or record, i.e. to 'enroll' it. This was not obligatory, but the *Statute of Inrollment*, 1535, was intended to encourage the practice. Many deeds are to be found in the Close Rolls of the Court of Chancery, the Plea Rolls of the Courts of Common Law, the Memoranda Rolls of the Court of Exchequer, and among the records of various local courts. Deeds of Bargain and Sale could be enrolled with the Clerk of the Peace among his county archives. These archives will be found at county record offices, and those of the central courts at the Public Record Office, Chancery Lane, London. Some of the latter have been calendared and printed. From the early eighteenth century, statutory registers were in existence in Middlesex (1708) and the Ridings of Yorkshire, for the recording of deeds relating to those areas. These registers are indexed under vendors.
See also the Registry of Deeds and other records relating to the archives of the Bedford Level Corporation, at the Cambridge Record Office, Shire Hall, Cambridge CB3 0AP.
See also LAND REGISTRY; TITLE DEED.

Ensign The lowest commissioned rank in an infantry regiment, named after his duty of carrying the flag. The term for the rank was changed to 2nd Lieutenant in 1871. Also written as 'Ancient'.
See also CORNET.

Entail was originated by the *Statute De Donis Conditionalibus* of Edward I. An owner of lands in Fee Simple could, by a grant of land to a person 'and heirs of his body', tie up that land in one family. Such land was called Estate Tail, and the mode of tenure 'Fee Tail'. Each successor would enjoy only a life interest in it, but it would pass to his heirs on the principle of primogeniture. If ever the direct issue of the original grantee died out, the land reverted to the grantor or his heirs.
Leases of entailed land became void on the death of a landlord who was a tenant in tail. Debts were not chargeable on such land. Heirs could be disinherited. In cases of treason (until Henry VII) or other offences, such land could not be forfeited to the Crown for longer than the tenant's life, though it did escheat to the lord. In 1833 any tenant in tail was allowed to break the entail by a deed enrolled in the Court of Chancery.
See also FEE *and* RECOVERY.

Entertain To employ.

Equity In the Middle Ages, people who did not, or could not, obtain justice at law were entitled to appeal to the king. Edward I directed his Chancellor to deal with the more important petitions, and his justices with the lesser ones. When, under Edward III, the Chancellor ceased to follow the king on his peregrinations of the kingdom, his Chancery office became a court of jurisdiction. It dealt with civil cases and administered a system of law known as Equity. It did not rely on juries, but could summon witnesses or have depositions taken in the provinces by local commissioners. Both plaintiff and defendant were placed on oath and were not allowed to remain silent. Where the Common Law courts would fine, Chancery could imprison or impose forfeiture of property, but it could not inflict capital punishment, or mutilation such as hand-amputation. Petitions were addressed to the Lord Chancellor or, in periods of vacancy in that office, to the Lord Keeper of the Great Seal. At first precedents were not required, but when, in the seventeenth century, decisions began to be recorded, lawyers took to quoting them and equity settled into as much a set of principles as had the Common Law.

Escheat   To revert to the superior lord. When a tenant of land died and there was no Common Law heir, or if the heir had forfeited his right on account of a felony, the land escheated to the immediate lord. Escheators were the royal officials who, with their deputies, usually held jurisdiction over one or more counties, and were responsible for effecting escheats of land held of the king. On the death of a tenant-in-chief, the escheator called an enquiry entitled Inquisition Post Mortem, with a local jury, to ascertain what lands the deceased had held and who was the heir. He was also responsible for wardship and the administration of Crown lands in his area.

Escutcheon   An escutcheon is the shield on which a coat of arms is placed.

Espousal   Until the early seventeenth century an espousal, or betrothal, was considered to have almost the validity of marriage, and may sometimes, at that period, account for a first child being born less than nine months after the wedding. Only a few parishes have surviving Espousal Books, which are now probably all at county record offices.

Esquire   In the Middle Ages a squire (escutifer) carried the shield and other armour of the lord or knight he served, but this duty passed later to pages. Squires in this sense were of gentle family. By the sixteenth century, Esquire was a title acquired by holding an office under the Crown, and so was not necessarily superior to 'gentleman', but in practice such office-holding carried distinction. Esquires proper held Crown commissions as Justices of the Peace, army officers, Royal Navy commanders (but not junior naval officers), the common hangman, etc. The modern courtesy use of the style became common in the nineteenth century. The squire in a country parish was the colloquial designation for the lord of the manor, or chief landowner.

Essex   The county falls within the diocese of London in the Province of Canterbury. Most of the 410 ancient parishes have deposited their registers at the CRO. Boyd's Marriage Index covers 374 parishes. Pallot's Marriage Index covers 22 parishes, from 1790–1812 or 1837. A few Bishops' Transcripts are at the Guildhall Library in London. Marriage Licence records are at the CRO.

The Hundreds of Barstable, Becontree, Chafford, Chelmsford, Clavering, Dengie, Dunmow, Freshwell, Harlow, Havering-atte-Bower Liberty, Hinckford, Lexden (Colchester and Witham Divisions), Ongar, Rochford, Tendring, Thurstable, Uttlesford, Waltham, Winstree, Witham, Colchester, Harwich and Maldon Boroughs and Saffron Walden Town lie within its boundaries.

It has West Ham, Epping, Ongar, Romford, Orsett, Billericay, Chelmsford, Rochford, Maldon, Tendring, Colchester, Lexden (later including Witham) Halstead, Braintree, Dunmow, Saffron Waldon and Witham RDs/PLUs.

It fell within the Home Assize Circuit until 1876 and then the South Eastern Assize Circuit.

The Essex Society for Family History meets at Chelmsford, Colchester, Old Harlow, Saffron Walden and Westcliff-on-Sea and publishes a quarterly journal called the *Essex Family Historian*. The Waltham Forest Family History Society publishes a quarterly journal called *Roots in the Forest* and meets at Walthamstow. The East of London Family History Society covers the boroughs of Redbridge, Newham, Barking and Dagenham and Havering and has branches at Barking, Upminster, Wanstead and the City of London. It publishes a quarterly journal called the *Cockney Ancestor*.

The Essex CRO is in Chelmsford with branches in Southend and Colchester. There is a Family History Centre at Hornchurch.

Pre 1858 Wills are located at the CRO and were proved at either the Prerogative Court of Canterbury, the Commissary Court of London for Essex and Hertfordshire, or the Consistory Court of London. The Essex Archaeological Society published the *Feet of Fines for Essex 1182–1547* in four volumes (1899–1964). Heralds' Visitation Pedigrees have been printed for 1552, 1558, 1570, 1612 and 1668.

Essex Record Office publishes *Essex family history; a genealogist's guide to the Essex Record Office* (1993) and *Guide to the Essex Record Office* (1969). See also *National Index of Parish Registers*, vol. 9, Part 4 (1993).

Essoin   An excuse for absence from attendance at a manor court for a good accepted reason, and with someone present at the court to answer for the absentee and pay his fine of 2 pence.

RIGHT A Sussex squire's estate accounts in the reign of Queen Anne throws light on the livelihood not only of the landowner, but also of the local farm labourers and craftsmen. This page of 'Moneys disbursed' records payments to 'Comer the taylor for making a coat, John Henley for curing my cow, Mr Edwards for reading prayers, Henry Barrett for looking after my clocks for one year'.

140 7/8

		d	s	

Febuary ye 7th

To Goodman Tuley for four quarters of Peas — — — 05 — 12 — 00
for Shirts and Handkerchiefs — — — — 05 — 13 — 06
To Mr Garland ten pounds — — — — 10 — 00 — 00
To Goodman Knight for ordering my fruit trees at Street — 00 — 11 — 09
To Lones ye Taylor for making a Coat — — — — 00 — 09 — 00
for one dozen of Teal — — — — 00 — 06 — 00
for pockett money — — — — 00 — 05 — 00
for token my Billetto — — — — 00 — 02 — 06
Given to Mr Clarke — — — — 04 — 01 — 06
To Thos Parker for Letters and other things — — 04 — 01 — 06
To Mr Challener ye Taylor — — — — 20 — 00 — 00

March ye 5t

To Will: Boys Collector for ye first and second quarterly payments for ye Queens Tax for my Woodlands lying in Arlington due att Michaelmas last past — te — — 01 — 16 — 04 : 1/2
To John Henley for curing my Cow — — — — 00 — 08 — 06
for pockett money — — — — 00 — 10 — 00
My Expences with Mr Medleys — — — — 02 — 00 — 00
for one years poor Tax to ye Parish of Willington — — 00 — 12 — 06
for birds seed — — — — 00 — 02 — 06
given to Goodman Fidniss — — — — 00 — 07 — 06
given to Mr Edwards for reading prayers — — — 04 — 06 — 00
for one years Water Scots for my land lying in Willington due att July last past — — 01 — 02 — 00
To Franckfield of Wilmington for 12 Bushells of horse Beans := 02 — 02 — 00
To Herrell for Looking after my Clock for one year due att Lady day next — — 00 — 07 — 06
To Thos Fidniss for Cleaning the Arms — — — 01 — 03 — 00
To Goodman Baucomb for eight days work a setting wood — 00 — 08 — 00
To Will: Obin for one years Wages due on Lady dky — 05 — 15 — 00
To Peter Merchant for altering my Wigg — — 02 — 10 — 00
To Mr Coppard for in full for Candles — — — 08 — 02 — 09

April ye 5t

To Philip Rutland for Coal — — — — 01 — 10 — 00
To Philip Rutland for looking after my Woodlands all Street — 01 — 10 — 00
for one years poor Tax for my land lying in Jevington due att Lady day last past collected by Thos Plan att ye rate of one shilling p pound — 00 — 15 — 00
To him likewise for one years Church Tax for ye same parish — 00 — 05 — 00
To Nathaniel Harrison for a Couch poale — — — 00 — 05 — 06
for one years Poor Tax for ye Parish of Falkington all te per pd — 03 — 07 — 00
A Bill to my Gardener for things he bought for me — 00 — 15 — 00
for Pockett money — — — — 00 — 10 — 00
To John Waller for two short Wiggs — — — 06 — 10 — 00
To Goody Beck for weeding in ye Garden — — 00 — 08 — 06
To Will: Whimish for seven young hogs — — 01 — 16 — 00
To Mrs Snath and Mrs Beckham for half one years Interest for two 2so due on ye 22d December last past — 06 — 05 — 00
To Philip Rutland for looking after my Rise and Garden all Street — 13 — 00 — 00
To Goodman Tranquay for twenty two days wage — 01 — 02 — 00
for one years Looking after Burrells Wish — — 00 — 08 — 00
for Pockett money — — — — 01 — 10 — 00
To Will: Rose Sadler a Bill of — — — 03 — 08 — 06
for pockett money — — — — 01 — 00 — 00
for heding att my woods — — — — 00 — 05 — 00
ta Mathew — — — — 00 — 07 — 00
Given to Goody Wyder — — — — 00 — 10 — 00
To George Glynch — — — — 01 — 00 — 00
for two payments of ye Queens Tax for my wood lands lying in Hailsham due att Lady day last past — 00 — 12 — 09

Estate Archives   The account books, terriers, surveys, extents and rent books of a landowner's estate. These throw light on many more people than the landowning family themselves. In a country parish, the squire was normally the chief employer of labour. The account books of his estate name the people paid, the amount of their wages, and the type of service rendered. The surveys or extents of the estate describe the copyhold tenements and name their occupants. Maps of the village may be attached, showing each building and field with acreages, arable, meadow or pasture, and cultivators. Many of these records, originally with the owners or their solicitors, have now been deposited at county record offices.

Estate Duty   From 1796 a tax was imposed on particular legacies and residues of estates. A series of statutes increased the coverage of the tax. By 1811 all estates except those that were very small attracted this tax. The indexes to the registers IR 26 can be useful in that they tell you in which court a will was proved and the registers tell you what someone actually left rather than what he intended to leave, as indicated in a will. The registers record the names of the legatees, in the case of an administration, and the relationship of the legatees to the deceased. The indexes and registers cover the period 1796–1903 and cover the whole of England and Wales. They fall into two groups: those for 1796–1811, and those for 1812–1903. The first group is divided into three sections, the *PCC Will Index* (IR 27/1–16), *PCC Admon. Index* (IR 27/17–20) and the *County Court Indexes* (IR 27/67–93). From 1812 onward, the sections are: *Will Indexes* (IR 27/140–323), and *Admon. Indexes* subdivided into *PCC* (IR 27/21–26) and *County Courts* (IR 27/94–139).

Estate Tail *see* **Entail**

Estreat   An extract from, or a copy of, a list of monetary penalties to be collected by the sheriff on behalf of the king, imposed by a court and delivered to the Exchequer. Filed among the Exchequer records at the Public Record Office, Chancery Lane, London.

Eugenics   Eugenics is the study of racial progress as affected by hereditary and environment. There are people who research family history solely for the purpose of discovering the progress of hereditary diseases and there is a Eugenics Society.

Evidence   The evidence upon which a family tree or history can be compiled is of two kinds — primary and secondary — with a grey area between them.

Primary evidence should always be sought, as being the most reliable. It is provided by documents or other artefacts, created at the time, or nearly so, of the events they record, and with no thought of historiography or genealogy in mind. Primary evidence requires effort not only to discover but also to interpret, since it calls for some understanding of the type of record itself. Nearly all such records have been caused in consequence of some law, the exceptions being private correspondence, accounts, etc.

Secondary evidence is that which has been brought into existence at a later period, such as histories and family trees. Every family tree and family history should be made referable to an accompanying list of the sources upon which it is based. Otherwise, generations hence, some conscientious genealogist of the family will treat it as secondary evidence which he will need to check by research all over again.

In the grey area are such contemporary records as newspaper reports, autobiographies and histories of the writers' own times, in which experience or research have been subjectively predigested.

Examinations   An examination is another word for a deposition.

Exception   An exception is an objection, especially on the grounds of insufficiency, to a pleading in court.

Exchequer, Court of   One of the three courts that evolved from the Curia Regis (King's Court), the others being those of Common Pleas and King's Bench. The name originated from the chequered cloth that covered its table for the purposes of calculation. It was an administrative body for collecting the royal revenue, and its judicial business arose out of that function. In time this side of its activities developed into an ordinary court of justice for suits between subject and subject. The Exchequer was a court of equity until 1841. Few records survive from before 1558. The best finding-aids are the Bill Books, which are arranged under counties. The evidence of witnesses was taken in writing and often contains interesting biographical material. The records are at the Public Record Office, Chancery Lane, London. Bills and Answers are in class E 112, Depositions in E 133 and 134, and Decrees and Orders in E 123–7. The Bernau Index, kept at the Society of Genealogists, lists county depositions taken on commission between 1559 and 1800. Some depositions in E 178 are calendared in PRO *Lists and Indexes, Vol. 37.*

The records of the Upper Exchequer, or Exchequer of Audit, are divided into those of the Treasurer's Remembrancer's Office and the King's Remembrancer's Office. The former includes the Pipe Rolls, Foreign Rolls, Originalia Rolls (extracts from Chancery Rolls) and Memoranda Rolls. Those of the King's Remembrancer's Office are of most use to family historians, since they include the Court's judicial cases. Among the Lower Exchequer records are suits involving Jews, and the archives of the Court of Augmentations. The Exchequer's most famous record, older than the department itself, is the *Domesday Book* E 31. PRO Information leaflet No. 75

For further reading, the proceedings are described in PRO Information Leaflet No. 96 *Equity Proceedings in the Court of Exchequer.*

Excise Excise is the duty imposed on the manufacture or sale of certain goods within the country.

Excommunication Exclusion from the communion of the Church; a penalty imposed by an ecclesiastical court in cases of heresy, simony, adultery, non-attendance at public worship, contumacious words, non-payment of fees or costs, etc. In pre-Reformation days, the greater excommunication deprived the condemned not only of the sacraments and the benefits of divine offices, but also of the society and conversation of the faithful, and even Christian burial. In the cases of sovereigns excommunicated by the Pope, their subjects were absolved from their allegiance. Both King John and King Henry VIII suffered excommunication. The excommunication of a whole country was called an Interdict.
See also ECCLESIASTICAL COURTS.

Executor An executor is the person named in a will to administer the estate and seek the grant of probate.

Exigend A writ issued when a person indicted of a felony did not appear in court and could not be found. It rendered him liable to forfeiture of his goods and, in earlier days, to outlawry.

Ex Officio Suit *see* **Office Suit**

Extent A detailed survey and valuation of manorial or other estates. Useful to genealogists because the names of the tenants were mentioned.

Extinct Title An hereditary title became extinct when the holder died leaving no heir eligible to inherit it.
See also ABEYANCE; DORMANT PEERAGE.

Extra-parochial This term applied to land uninhabited in Anglo-Saxon times, and so outside the bounds of any parish civil or ecclesiastical; this meant that it was exempt church and poor rates and sometimes tithes, though such places were generally supposed to pay tithes to the Crown. People living in such areas would be baptized, etc., at the nearest convenient church. Extra-parochial areas were made civil parishes in 1894.

Eyre The word derives from the Latin *Iter*, meaning a journey, and in law means the court of itinerant royal justices. Hence the expression 'Justices in Eyre'. In the Middle Ages they were competent to hear all kinds of cases, and administered the Common Law as a check on the local courts. Representatives of each hundred and township, and all freeholders, were required to be present at court. To initiate a suit, the plaintiff had to purchase a writ from the king, and this soon became an important source of royal revenue.

The Eyre courts became progressively more unpopular and eventually, by a statue of 1284–5, were replaced by Assizes.

F

Factory Originally the work-place of a company's factors, i.e. a trading station. A term employed by chartered companies for their branches abroad. The modern sense of the word did not come into use until the mid nineteenth century. Before that, production work-places were called 'manufactories'.

Faculty Office The office of the master of Faculties of the Archbishop of Canterbury. Applications for marriage licences had to be addressed to him if the contracting parties lived in different provinces of the Church of England. Records of the common and special licences issued by this office survive from 1660, the earlier ones having been destroyed in the Great Fire of

John Berry born Sept. 17th 1843

Mary Berry do Jany 23rd 1845

Alexander Berry do Feb 21st 1846

died Augt 3rd 1866

Frederick Berry do Aug 1st 1847

Annette Berry do Dec 29th 1848

Henrietta Berry do Oct 15th 1851

Georgianna Berry do May 29th 1853

Peter Berry do Sept 3rd 1854

Emily Berry do Sept 14th 1856

died March 6/57

Herbert Berry born Dec 13 1857

Nelson Berry born Dec 13th 1859

Kate Amelia Maude Dec 9th 1863.

Died March 7th 1895

John Berry & Amelia Mary Barnum

Married Decr 28th 1863

Annette Berry & Archibald George Buttafield

Married Decr 31st 1874

Henrietta Berry & Wm Farbow married

Sept 25th 1877

LEFT The flyleaf of Katherine Berry's Bible, a wedding present to her in August 1842. It typically records useful genealogical details about a victorian family. Photo John Tennell.

London. They are now housed in Lambeth Palace Library, London.
See also: MARRIAGE LICENCE RECORDS.

Fair The right of a market town to hold a fair was granted by Letters Patent from the Crown. Fairs were usually held annually or half-annually, and were extra-large markets accompanied by facilities for participating in shows and games. The date of such a function might be fixed to coincide with the festival of the patron saint of the parish church, starting on the eve of the feast and ending on its morrow. Traders and customers of all kinds were attracted from considerable distances. Many fairs were specific to a certain type of merchandise — horses, sheep, cheese, and so on.
See also HIRING FAIRS; PIEPOUDRÉ, COURT OF.

Falling sickness Epilepsy or convulsionary hysteria. Prior to the late nineteenth century, illnesses were commonly named after their symptoms, since their causes were unknown.

Fallow That part of the arable land of a manor that was left untilled every second or third year to allow the soil to recover and to provide weeds and grass for grazing cattle, who would at the same time manure it.

Family Until the seventeenth century the term 'family' signified a household, including any servants and apprentices. In genealogical usage the term includes all people of the same name and blood descended from a common male-line ancestor, as distinct from its colloquial use to include close relatives on both father's and mother's sides, and grandchildren by both sons and daughters.

Family Bible A popular publication in the nineteenth century; usually a large edition of the Bible, in which several of the preliminary pages were either left blank or ruled with lines, to allow the owner to record the dates and places of such, family events as births, baptisms, marriages, deaths and burials. Frequently these are found to be supplemented by earlier ones referring to events that occurred before the birth of the owner. For some of the later of these, the infor-

mation may have come from parents or other elderly relatives then living, and can therefore be assumed to be reliable, but others may hark back to much earlier generations and so, unless documented elsewhere, must be open to doubt. Such entries, not made from personal knowledge, should be treated merely as a guide to the research needed to confirm them.
See also EVIDENCE.

Family Division, Principal Registry of the This registry houses all wills proved in England and Wales since 1858 inclusive, the year in which probate jurisdiction was taken out of ecclesiastical hands. Annual index volumes identify both testator and executor(s). Having found the index entry, the searcher can arrange to see the will and make brief pencilled notes, for which service a charge is made. Also, a photocopy of the will can be ordered. Letters of Administration are also indexed. Until 1870 they are shown in separate annual volumes; after that date, in the same volumes as the will. If the searcher is confident that a will was proved or Letters of Administration granted, the indexes may be used as a quicker method of finding a date of death than by a search of the civil registration Death Registers. The Registry is situated at Somerset House, Strand, London WC2R 1LP.

Family History (i) Until recently this term was used as a synonym for genealogy, but now, in ancestor-tracing circles, it applies specifically to biographical research into one's forebears with the object of compiling a narrative history of the family; and the term 'genealogy' is reserved for the tracing of an ascent and the compilation of a Family Tree or Ancestry Chart. A family history should place the members of the family in their historical, geographical, social and occupational contexts, and describe their activities and the lives they lived.
(ii) A journal published by the Institute of Heraldic and Genealogical Studies.

Family History Centres Run by volunteers from the Geneaological Society of Utah, these family history centres make available documents on film borrowed from their extensive collection in Salt Lake City. The centres are open to all denominations not just to members of The Church of Jesus Christ of the Latter-day Saints. Once you have located the record you want to consult from their finding aids, they will order it for you. They will notify you when the film arrives and they will keep it for up to three months until you have had a chance to look at it. The service they offer is of great assistance to those who would otherwise not be able to access records out of the area in which they live. The computer system FamilySearch can usually be accessed at Family History Centres. In addition patrons not owning a personal computer may make use of the personal computer at the centre to install their own family history research files using the Personal Ancestral File software. The data are not kept on the hard disk, but on a floppy diskette which patrons keep with them.

Family History News and Digest

This is the journal of the FEDERATION OF FAMILY HISTORY SOCIETIES which is published twice a year in April and September. Besides giving reports from the officers of the organisation and from its member societies, the journal has an extensive subject index to articles recently published in the journals of member societies. The latest names and addresses of member societies are available on its back cover.

Family History Societies

The SOCIETY OF GENEALOGISTS, founded in 1911, held the field alone in England except for one university society, until in the 1960s similar societies began to appear in the provinces. In the 1970s these proliferated, until nearly every county had one, and some more than one. These provincial societies hold conferences, seminars and monthly meetings addressed by knowledgeable speakers, issue newsletters and journals (normally quarterly) with articles contributed by members, and also are involved in many indexing projects. Monumental inscriptions, marriages, census returns, settlement certificates and wills are all types of records that are indexed and either searched on behalf of correspondents or published on microfiche or in booklets.

The emergence of societies in nearly all areas has radically changed ancestry research from being a hobby pursued in isolation, to one that is as sociable as any other spare-time pursuit. Their journals, which tend to be less scholarly than the organ of the Society of Genealogists, exhibit genealogy quite as much in its aspect of a leisure activity as in that of a branch of study. It is now common practice for a genealogist to be a member not only of his local society, for the sake of the lectures and discussion of problems with fellow members, but also of the society or societies in counties where his ancestors lived, for the benefit of what can be learnt from their journals and indexes, and arrangements for exchanged research.

For the names of these societies, *see* under their county headings: postal enquiries should be sent c/o The Federation of Family History Societies, Benson Room, Birmingham & Midland Institute, Margaret Street, Birmingham B3 3BS, marked 'Please forward' and enclosing a stamped self-addressed envelope. This federation promotes and co-ordinates the activities of the member societies.

Family Registry

An index of INTERESTS issued periodically on microfiche by the Genealogical Society of Utah and available at FAMILY HISTORY CENTRES.

Family Roots

A genealogical computer program for recording family history data and producing charts.

FamilySearch

The computer system at FAMILY HISTORY CENTRES of the Genealogical Society of Utah which enables users to access the IGI and Ancestral File on CD-ROM. You may copy records either by printout or onto floppy disks for use in your own computer. You may submit information for inclusion in Ancestral File or Submit updates to Salt Lake City. You may also register a research interest for any deceased person in the file. FamilySearch includes the IGI, the USA Social Security Death Index, USA Military Index and Ancestral File. Later it will also include the 1881 census indexes for England, Scotland and Wales.

Family Tree

A summary, in chart form, of what is known about a male-line descent from a common ancestor; also called a tabular or dropline pedigree. Early forms were designed like a tree, with the earliest ancestor at the trunk or root, and his descendants shown in the branches and twigs above, but it has long been the practice in the United Kingdom to set out the tree in reverse order, with the earliest known ancestor at the top and his descendants extending below him (*see* example on facing page). Sometimes, especially in America and Australia, trees are laid out horizontally with the generations proceeding chronologically from left to right.

A marriage is indicated by an = sign, then vertical line drops from the marriage to the issue, who are linked to each other by a horizontal line, then with short drop-lines to each child's name, the eldest child being on the left and the youngest on the right. Illegitimate issue are indicated by a wavy drop-line, and probably but unconfirmed connections by broken lines. Beneath each name is shown, where known, the dates and places of birth/baptism, marriage and death/

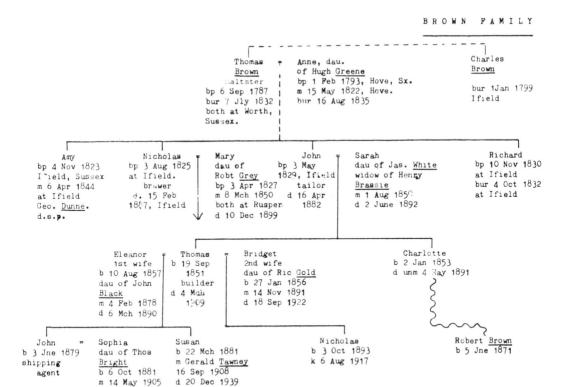

BROWN FAMILY

Thomas Brown, maltster, bp 6 Sep 1787, bur 7 July 1832, both at Worth, Sussex.

= Anne, dau. of Hugh Greene bp 1 Feb 1793, Hove, Sx. m 15 May 1822, Hove. bur 16 Aug 1835

Charles Brown, bur 1 Jan 1799 Ifield

Amy bp 4 Nov 1823 Ifield, Sussex m 6 Apr 1844 at Ifield Geo. Dunne. d.s.p.

Nicholas bp 3 Aug 1825 at Ifield. brewer d. 15 Feb 1867, Ifield

= Mary dau of Robt Grey bp 3 Apr 1827 m 8 Mch 1850 both at Rusper d 10 Dec 1899

John bp 3 May 1829, Ifield tailor d 16 Apr 1882

= Sarah dau of Jas. White widow of Henry Brassie m 1 Aug 1850 d 2 June 1892

Richard bp 10 Nov 1830 at Ifield bur 4 Oct 1832 at Ifield

Eleanor 1st wife b 10 Aug 1857 dau of John Black m 4 Feb 1878 d 6 Mch 1890

= Thomas b 19 Sep 1851 builder d 4 Mch 1909

= Bridget 2nd wife dau of Ric Gold b 27 Jan 1856 m 14 Nov 1891 d 18 Sep 1922

Charlotte b 2 Jan 1853 d unm 4 May 1891

John b 3 Jne 1879 shipping agent

= Sophia dau of Thos Bright b 6 Oct 1881 m 14 May 1905

Susan b 22 Mch 1881 m Gerald Tawney 16 Sep 1908 d 20 Dec 1939

Nicholas b 3 Oct 1893 k 6 Aug 1917

Robert Brown b 5 Jne 1871

A typical, but fictitious, family tree.

burial, employing the abbreviations b, bp, m, d and bur respectively, with c for *circa* (about) where the exact date is not known. Adopted children should have the fact noted, but should otherwise be shown as ordinary members of the family. The marriage details are usually shown under the wife's name, to leave room under the husband's for his occupation. The names of the wife's parents should also be shown. Because a family tree is a male-line descent, and space is usually limited, the spouse of a female member is usually entered below her name, together with the date and place of marriage, instead of beside her. Where space allows, other biographical details can be shown.

A tree can be embellished by the Arms, if any, of the family, and by those of any armigerous spouses. An alternative and appropriate decoration is an attractively drawn map of the family's ancestral area. Also, small photographs can be placed beside the person's names. In a working tree it is useful to underline all surnames, or write them in capitals. This prevents confusion with Christian names and occupations.

An Extended Family Tree is one that shows the descendants from all sons to collateral branches. Such a tree can take up so much space that it will require to be rolled up or folded, and the names of brothers and sisters may have to be entered several feet apart. A more convenient and visually satisfying format is that of the 'stabledoor' family tree, in which the most junior branch is charted on one sheet, from the earliest common ancestor of the family to the latest generation. Each more senior line is charted on a separate sheet of a shorter length, so that it can be laid on top of the other in such a way that descent from the common ancestor is seen to be continuous. As many sheets of appropriate length are then used as the branches of the family make necessary, and finally they can all be bound together along their left-hand edge in handy book form.

As mentioned above, abbreviations will be needed on a family tree for the ever-recurring words, born, baptized, married, died, buried, will made, probate granted, and *circa*. The abbreviations listed at the front of this dictionary should be used. It is very unwise to invent ones own abbreviations.

It must be emphasised that a family tree is only a summary, useful as a visual aid; it is valueless unless confirmable by reference to the original documentary evidence on which it is based. Reference letters shown beside each statement take up too much room and are unnecessary if the transcripts of supporting evidence are kept in a loose-leaf binder in chronological order, thus making reference possible directly through the dates themselves.

For other methods of charting ancestry, *see* PEDIGREE: ANCESTRY CHART.

Family Tree Magazine   An independently produced journal for ancestry researchers, founded in November, 1984, and now appearing monthly. It is popular in style and plentifully illustrated. Besides articles on genealogical sources, it provides news of activities among family history societies and of new developments in the genealogical world. The magazine is published by Michael and Mary Armstrong, 61 Great Whyte, Stocking Fen Road, Ramsey, Huntingdon, Cambs. PE17 1HL.

Family Trees and Histories   Several lists of family histories already in print have been compiled and updated from time to time. The first of these was *The Genealogist's Guide*, by George W. Marshall, a work usually referred to by his name. It catalogues printed pedigrees of three or more generations. First published in 1879, it went through four editions by 1903 and was reprinted in 1967. In 1953 appeared *A Genealogist's Guide*, by J.B. Whitmore, who brought the list down to that date and filled in gaps in the earlier one. Another book entitled *The Genealogist's Guide*, by G.B. Barrow, was published in 1977, and *A Catalogue of British Family Histories*, by T.R. Thomson, contains an Appendix bringing the list down to the date of the latest edition (1980).

A large number of family histories, in print, typescript and manuscript, can be consulted in the library of the Society of Genealogists, which also has a great collection of birth briefs and family trees.

For research currently being carried out by other people, it is best to consult the family history society of the relevant county or area. Many of them issue lists of Members' Interests.

Farm   (i) To work land.

(ii) To let out a process or task (e.g. the collection of a tax) for a fixed payment, leaving the 'farmer' to make what profit he can.

(iii) The rent or service paid for landholding. Also written as Ferm.

See also FARMER.

Farmer   (i) One who rents and cultivates a farm.

(ii) One who collected taxes for a taxing authority in return for a fixed sum or rate per cent.

Farthing   Originally the quarter of anything, but in time applied exclusively to a quarter-penny. Farthing land was a quarter of a yardland, which was an area of about thirty acres.

Father-in-law   This expression was often used to mean what is now called a stepfather, i.e. a mother's second husband. The same also applies to mother-in-law, etc. On the other hand, a father-in-law, is often found referred to as 'Father'.

Fealty   The oral oath of allegiance to the king, required under the feudal system from every new tenant on his entry into occupation of land, and given at the same time as his homage to his immediately superior lord. The requirement continued longer for copyholders than for freeholders. When land was held by fealty alone, i.e. not in combination with homage, no service to the lord was involved.

Federation of Family History Societies
This organisation was formed in 1974 to co-ordinate and assist the work of the growing number of family history societies in Britain and overseas. Its members are societies, specialising in family history, heraldry and associated disciplines, constituted in the British Isles; and associate membership is open to similar overseas societies and to those in the British Isles where the main interest is neither family history nor heraldry. The federation issues *Family History News and Digest* twice a year, containing news of member societies and abstracts of articles (mostly from members' journals), and publishes and stocks a wide range of booklet guides to the location of records useful to genealogists and family historians. Assistance is given in the formation of new groups in areas not already adequately covered, and national conferences are organised. The Federation advises members, commissions publications, makes representations to offical bodies and maintains a regular liaison with a number of interest-related organisations. Enquiries to the Administrator, The Benson Room, Birmingham & Midland Institute, Margaret Street, Birmingham B3 3BS, should be

accompanied by a stamped self-addressed envelope. A letter to a member society of the Federation, if its address is not known, should be sent c/o the Federation and marked 'Please forward'. Member societies are shown on the back cover of Family History News and Digest under their county and country headings.

Fee The expression 'in fee' means 'hereditarily', and 'in fee male' means 'through male descent'. A Fee Simple was a freehold estate in land which passed at death to the common law heir. For Fee Tail, *see* ENTAIL. Fee Farm was a fixed annual rent charge payable to the king by chartered boroughs.

Feet of Fines The word 'fine' is derived from the Latin *finis*, meaning 'an end'. It came to mean a judgement or Final Concord regarding a title to land after a form of legal action, nearly always collusive, and intended to provide a record of title, often after a purchase. It was written out three times in the same words on the same side of a single sheet of parchment, two copies being written vertically and back-to-back, and the third along the foot of the sheet. The word 'Cyrographum' was sometimes written in large letters above the foot copy and between the other two, and the three copies were then cut apart along wavy lines and through the cyrograph. The back-to-back parts were given to the two parties, and the Foot was filed among the rolls of the Court of Common Pleas, now at the Public Record Office, Chancery Lane, London, under references CP 25 and 27. This procedure made forgery virtually impossible, and it was only abolished as late as 1834.

Until 1733 (except under the Commonwealth) the records were in Latin. The rolls, from 1182 to 1638, are arranged under counties. The date shown is that on which the writ summoning the parties to appear was due to be returned into court, and so gives only an approximate idea of the date of the actual agreement. The person whose right (*jus*) is admitted is the purchaser or recognised title-holder. A fine often contains a 'clause of warranty', in which certain persons, often relatives of the vendor or person of whom the land is held, warrant against him, i.e. pledge themselves to stand by the agreement if the title to the holding is questioned later. Other persons may be named as co-deforciants, but this is merely to bar any right they might claim in the future. Contemporary calendars are available for the period 1509–1798. For several counties the Feet of Fines have been printed. In many cases there also exist Notes of Fines, an additional record, and Concords, which are duplicates of the Fines.

Felixstowe Family History Society *see* **Suffolk**

Felony The word originally meant 'forfeiture', but was already, in feudal times, attached to any act for which forfeiture was the penalty. Later it came to mean offences for which the punishment included forfeiture of land and/or goods and chattels. The chief Common Law felonies were homicide, rape, larceny (i.e. stealing), robbery (i.e. theft with violence), burglary and similar offences. Other classes of crime were treason (the most serious), misdemeanour, and summary offence. Counterfeiting, once classed as treason, was later made a felony.

Female Line Any line of ascent that runs through ancestresses. In an ancestry chart, or birth brief, all lines but one — that of the father's father's father, etc. — will be female lines.

Feme A woman. A Feme Covert was a married woman whose husband was alive. A Feme Sole was a spinster, widow or divorced wife.

Fencibles Volunteer Militia regiments liable for home service only. They were discontinued in 1801 as being of limited value and a drain on potential resources for the regular army at the time of the Napoleonic Wars. Pay lists and Muster Rolls survive for some Fencible regiments at the PRO, Kew (WO 13). Other records may exist in County Record Offices. *See also* MILITIA.

Feodary (i) A survey of the obligations of Crown tenants, i.e. the number of knights to be supplied, and so on.

(ii) The official responsible for enforcing such obligations. One feodary would normally cover several counties.

(iii) A person holding land on condition of fealty and service.

Feoffment The oldest form of the alienation (transfer) of land from one person to another. It was effected partly in writing and partly by a public act called Livery of Seisin. The existing owner took the owner-to-be on to the land, handed him a twig, a blade of grass, a clod or a piece of turf as a token, and stated the terms on which he handed over the land, e.g. in Fee Simple (*see* FEE). The new owner then turned everyone else off the land, thus asserting his rights as owner. The terms were put in writing in an Indenture of Feoffment, signed and/or sealed by both parties. It was endorsed on the back with a statement that the Livery of Seisin (the symbolic hand-over) had been carried out before witnesses, and without this endorsement the deed was worthless.

Feudalism   The political and social system that developed as a result of the breakdown of government at the end of the Roman Empire. Its basis was the holding of land from a powerful local patron (vassalage), who afforded protection (known as benefice) in return. Under the Carolingians on the continent, the vassal relationship became extended to include the large landed proprietors and the king. In this form the institution was introduced into England by William the Conqueror. All the land of England was owned by the king alone. His nobles held their land of him in return for military service (*see* KNIGHT SERVICE), and lesser men held in turn from them on similar terms. The system in its pure form broke down from the need of King Edward I for an efficient military organisation. Money payments (*see* SCUTAGE) became general, and indentured fighting men took the place of tenants doing temporary service. Because of this, the system from the fourteenth century until the late fifteenth is known as 'bastard feudalism'.

Feudal Levy   The troops raised for the king by his tenants-in-chief in accordance with their feudal obligations. Edward I found them inadequate in number for his Scottish and Welsh campaigns, and so took to recruiting men by means of indentures. The success of this method put an end to the feudal levy in practice, though the king's right to raise it remained in force.

Feudal Tenure *see* **Knight Service**

Fief   The same as a fee held by military service. If its holder failed to perform the service, the fief reverted to the overlord. It could not be broken up without the overlord's consent.

Field   (i) Arable land, as distinct from meadow and pasture.
(ii) A division of a building made by a low wall.
(iii) An heraldic term for the background of a coat of arms.

Finding Aids   Finding aids are the lists which enable you to select one document from a class of records. Some lists also need an index because of the way records are arranged. These indexes are known as 'additional finding aids', or 'supplementary finding aids', and can be nominal or topographical. They are compiled by the holders of the records or by readers who have a particular interest in a set of records. There are also 'contemporary indexes' meaning those indexes which were compiled when the documents were still in daily use. These are frequently not in strict alphabetical order since, as papers accumulated before the advent of word processors, all a clerk could do was to enter a name in an index to a register on the next available line that was free. The clerks did, however, enter new names under the appropriate letters of the alphabet.

Fine   (i) *See* FEET OF FINES.
(ii) The term 'fine' was also used for the sum of money paid, at the conclusion of an agreement, by the person favoured.

Fine Rolls   These contain lists of payments made to the Crown for charters, writs, privileges and pardons. They also record the appointment of royal officials, and quote the orders sent to sheriffs, escheators and exchequer officers. The Record Commission has published the rolls of King John's reign, and extracts from those of Henry III's. Since then the Public Record Office has published many calendars covering the subsequent period.

Fire Insurance Companies   In the early eighteenth century, several companies set up in the business of fire insurance. Their clients were, at first, London property owners, but provincial householders and businessmen soon followed suit. To each building insured, the company affixed a metal plaque bearing its trade mark, so that it could be identified as its liability. Some of these can still be seen *in situ*. The fire companies possessed their own fire engines, with which they endeavoured to keep their losses to a minimum.

The registers of several firms have been deposited at the Guildhall Library, London. These include the Sun Fire Office and the Hand in Hand, from 1710; the London Assurance, from 1720; and the Royal Exchange Assurance, founded in the same year but with surviving records only from 1773. For each property insured, the registers record the address and the owner's name and occupation. The passing of ownership on death to another member of the family is mentioned, and the exact location of the building is often made clear by reference to neighbouring properties.

First Fruits and Tenths *see* Annates

Five Mile Act A statute of 1665 forbidding all clergymen ejected from their benefices under the *Act of Uniformity* to live within five miles of a corporate town. This was because nonconformity had been particularly strong in urban areas.

Flat Another term for furlong.

Fleet Marriage Registers *see* Clandestine Marriages

Fleet Prison This was a prison for debtors and those in contempt of common law. It was discontinued in 1842 when its inmates were transferred to the Queen's Prison.

Flesher A butcher.

Fletcher A person who feathered arrows; commonly a maker of bows and arrows. The Fletchers' Company, one of the London Gilds, was founded in 1371.

Folio A sheet of parchment or paper which, in the making of a book, is folded to form several pages, which may be any number from four to sixteen.

Folkestone and District Family History Society *see* Kent

Foreigner This term was customarily applied by townspeople to those, of English stock, who were not freemen of their city or borough.

Forest The word originally had nothing to do with woods. It designated an area, which would almost certainly be partly wooded, over which the king had rights of hunting and preserving game. The inhabitants of the area were subject to forest law, which restricted a number of what, elsewhere, were normal rights.
See also VERT AND VENISON.

Forthfare The passing-bell tolled in the parish church tower on the death of a local resident.

Fother An irregularly shaped piece of land in an open arable field.

Foundlings Sometimes called 'dropt children', these infants were usually left on the steps of a church, or in the porch or some other frequented spot, where they were fairly certain to be found. Some might have a note pinned to them, asking that they might be called by a particular Christian name. In most cases, such children were illegitimate.

The child had to be christened and given a surname by the church authorities, or whoever adopted it. Some were named after the spot in which they were found, e.g. Church, Porch, Churchstile, Bridge, or the name of the street. Some, especially in London, were given, either as Christian or surname, the name of the nearest saint's day or the name of the saint to whom the church was dedicated. The Christian name Moses was popular for those found in a basket, because the prophet Moses was found among the rushes. During the Puritan period, a girl foundling at Baltonsborough, Somerset, was given the names Misericordia Adulterina — an extreme example of the type of Christian names bestowed at that period.

In 1745 Captain Thomas Coram (c. 1668–1751) opened his famous Foundling Hospital in Guildford Street, London, in accordance with a charter he had obtained in 1739. Outside the door was a basket suspended by a rope attached to a bell. When a child was placed in the basket, the bell rang and the gatekeeper came and collected it. At first the Hospital admitted any child who seemed to be under two months old and free from certain specified diseases. No questions were asked, and no attempt was made to trace the parents.

From 1756 the Hospital was given an annual grant by the government, and thereafter had to take in all children under one year in any state of health. The result was that in the following year, 3727 children were taken in and branches had to be opened at Ackworth in Yorkshire, Shrewsbury, Westerham in Kent, Aylesbury and Barnet. Poor parents brought dying children, in order to have them buried at the expense of the Hospital; thus of 14,934 children received in three years and ten months, only about 4400 lived to be apprenticed to trades. People in the provinces even set up a service of carrying illegitimate children to the Hospital in London at so much per head.

From 1760, indiscriminate intake was abandoned, and the government ended its grants in 1771, after which time the Hospital had to depend on charity. Later, children were taken in only if brought by their mothers, and the mothers had to show that they had been previously of good character and had been let down by the fathers. In Victorian times, foundling hospitals were thought to encourage immorality.

On admittance, the Foundling Hospital gave the child a number and a name. This name would be chosen by the hospital authorities regardless of any name left with the child. Infants requiring a wet-nurse were sent to one outside London for the benefit of their health, and were placed under the supervision of a doctor in the same locality. When weaned, the child would go into one of the branch hospitals, and would sometimes be transferred from one to another, perhaps because of age grouping. At about the age of eight, they would be apprenticed to husbandry at the expense of the Hospital (*see* APPRENTICES). Sometimes the parent who left the child attached a 'token' to identify it, in the hope that he or she might later be able to maintain it and would be able to claim it.

The parish records of the Overseer of the Poor and of the Constable contain mentions of what was done with the foundlings picked up and dealt with locally. The records of the Foundling Hospital are located at the Greater London Record Office.

See GENERAL REGISTER OF BIRTHS.

Franchise   (i) In the Middle Ages a franchise was an exemption from ordinary jurisdiction, such as that of a hundred court, accompanied by the privilege of a private jurisdiction or liberty (*see also* QUO WARRANTO).

(ii) Parliamentary franchise. The House of Commons was made up of county members, called knights of the shire; of town members, called burgesses; and of representatives of the universities, elected by university members.

From 1430 until the *Reform Act* of 1832, the franchise for electing county members was limited to those who held freehold estates to the value of 40 shillings per year or more; thus, while quite modest freeholders had the vote, large tenant farmers with no freehold did not. Also, owing to inflation, the number of 40 shilling freeholders in the counties increased greatly over the years. The Act of 1832 required anyone holding only a life interest in his freehold to be its actual occupant in order to be eligible for the vote, unless it had come to him by marriage or settlement, or was attached to an office; but those in possession of life freeholds at the time of the Act were allowed to retain their franchise.

However, the main function of the Act was not to restrict, but greatly to widen, the right to vote, which it extended to cover (a) those owning land worth £10 per year by any title, including copyhold and leases for sixty years; (b) those holding land worth £50 per year on leases for twenty years; and (c) tenants and other occupants paying rents of £50 per year. In 1867 the franchise was further extended and again in 1884 (rural voters), 1885 and 1918. In the last-mentioned year, women aged thirty and over were included, and in 1928 women were at last placed on the same footing as men. Until 1872, it is possible to ascertain the way in which many electors cast their votes (*see* POLL BOOKS.)

In boroughs, the early system was quite different from the county franchise and much less uniform. The extent of each town's franchise depended sometimes on its charter of incorporation, and sometimes on custom, and as time went by the tendency was to reduce the number of freemen voters by charging ever higher sums for the privilege of freedom of the borough. Very often the number of voters would be no more than a dozen. Over the centuries many boroughs decayed, and some disappeared altogether, but were still represented in Parliament. Other towns grew to a considerable size but were unrepresented. This inequitable distribution of the franchise was greatly reduced by the Act of 1832. Genealogists have also to thank that Act for a useful new set of location records — the Electoral Registers that listed all those entitled to vote.

Frankalmoign   or Free Alms. In the Middle Ages, when land was granted in frankalmoign the only service required to be paid (apart from the TRINODAS NECESSITAS) was regular prayer for the souls of the donor, his family and descendants. Most of the medieval religious houses held their lands by this type of tenure. When military tenures were abolished in 1660, frankalmoign was expressly excepted and is the tenure by which the parish clergy and many church and charitable foundations still hold their land.

Franking of Letters   A privilege claimed by Members of the House of Commons from 1660, and by the clerks of the Post Office. It was greatly abused until regularised by an Act of Parliament in 1764. Each peer and Member of Parliament was then allowed to send, each day, ten free letters not exceeding one ounce in weight, by signing his name in the corner of the outside of the folded letter (envelopes came later). Each Member could also receive fifteen letters per day. These privileged persons often signed letters for their friends, but in 1837 an attempt was made to restrict this practice. The franker was obliged not only to sign his name, but also to inscribe his address and post town, and the day of the month; and the letter had to be posted on the same or following day in a post town not more than twenty miles from the franker's home. In 1840, franking was abolished with the introduction of the penny post.

Franklin A substantial free tenant farmer in the Middle Ages. By the fifteenth century he was known by the term 'Yeoman'.
See also CLASS, SOCIAL.

Frankpledge The system by which every man was obliged to be a member of a group of ten or twelve, also called a Tithing, who were held corporately responsible for the good behaviour of one another. If a member of a frankpledge was accused of an offence and failed to appear to answer the charge, the members of his frankpledge were fined. A manorial View of Frankpledge was held periodically to ensure that all eligible men and growing boys were involved in such a group. Those in the household of some great man, who would be responsible for them, were exempted. By the fifteenth century the system was breaking down, but the name remained, signifying the Court Leet, of which it had previously been merely one function.
See also MANOR; TITHING.

Free Alms *see* **Frankalmoign**

Freebench The right of a copyholder's widow to the whole of her late husband's land, either for life or until remarriage — the custom varied from one manor to another.
See also DOWER.

Freehold Originally land held on nonservile tenure, either for life or in Fee Simple or Fee Tail. It could be held either by knight service or in socage. Freeholders enjoyed security of tenure in perpetuity under the Common Law. At the Conquest, such tenure was particularly widespread in the former Danelaw.

Freeholders' Lists Also called Jurors' Lists. From 1696, rural vestries and urban corporations had to send to the Clerk of the Peace for their county, lists of the people within their jurisdictions who were eligible for jury service. These were men between the ages of 21 and 70 who owned freeholds worth at least 40 shillings per year. They were listed under the parishes in which they lived, but if their qualifying property was in another parish this was sometimes also

stated. The annual value of their freeholds might be noted too, together with the owner's rank or occupation.

In 1825 the upper age of eligibility was reduced to 60, and the qualification revised to freeholds worth £10 per year, leaseholds for 21 years or more worth £20, rateability as householder at £20 (£30 in Middlesex), or occupation of a house with fifteen or more windows. At the same time the list of exempt occupations was extended. From 1832, freeholders' addresses were given on the lists, and the qualifying property specified.

The freeholders' lists provide a very useful location record for tracing the whereabouts of a family, and to some extent for establishing its economic status. The records are housed among the Quarter Sessions papers at the county record offices.

In 1873 a *Return of Owners of Land* was published, covering the whole country.

Freemasons The origins of freemasonry are obscured in legend, but there is documentary evidence for the existence of masonic lodges in England in the Middle Ages. As with all other medieval guilds of free craftsmen, the early membership consisted of 'operatives' (masons by trade) and 'speculatives' (noblemen, gentry and members of other trades), who were 'accepted' as honorary members. In the course of time the lodges ceased to have any connection with the trade that gave them their name, and benevolence and fellowship became their main characteristic, with the acknowledgement of God as the Great Architect of the Universe. Meetings of members are carried out with an elaborate system of symbolic ritual. The lodges in various parts of the country were originally independent of one another, but in 1717 began to recognise the governance of a national Grand Lodge. In the same century the society spread, and lodges were formed on the Continent and in Asia and America. Since then, in some countries (notably France), the society has shed its religious character and become largely political. In England, members of the royal family have been freemasons, and some have been Grand Masters. If an ancestor is thought to have been a member, details of his date of entry and the name of his lodge can be obtained from the Secretary, The United Grand Lodge of England, Freemasons Hall, Great Queen Street, London WC2. But from 1798 the names and addresses of freemasons had to be given to the Clerk of the Peace of their county, and so may be obtainable at the CRO.

The Manor of Ebbisham in the County of Surry }

The Court Leet or View of Frank Pledge of Ricarda Parkhurst Widow Lady of the said Manor holden for the same on Monday the 26th Day of Oct.r in the 8th year of the Reign of our Sovereign Lord Geo: the 3.d by the Grace of God of Great Brit.n France & Ireland King Defender of the Faith &c & in the year of our Lord 1767 &c Before Peter Prevost Gent Steward there.

Essoigns to wit None at this Court

Constable of Ebbisham — Thomas Butcher appears & Nothing presents

Constable of Woodcote — John Wheatley appears & Nothing presents

Headborough of Ebbisham — Wm Lang appears & nothing presents & pays 3.d accord.g to anc.t Custom

Headborough of Woodcote — Rob.t Steer Jun.r appears & Nothing presents & pays 3.d according to anc.t Custom

Aletasters — Francis Peake & Peter Kempsall — Nothing present

Common Drivers — Geo. Fox & William Adams — Nothing present

The Inquest for our Sovereign Lord the King
John Eastland first sworn

Rob.t Wrench	Wm Holland	John Yalden
Henry Reeve	Jn.o Lewis Jaquet	Henry Harris
Rich.d Hubbard	John Hopkins	Jas Greenhouse
John Winchester	John Aslewell	Benj.a Furness
sworn — sworn — sworn

The Election of Officers.

Constable of Ebbisham — James Buggs is duly elected Constable of Ebbisham for the year ensuing

Constable of Woodcote — Geo. Peters is duly elected Constable of Woodcote for the year ensuing & is sworn.

Headborough of Ebbisham — John Loveland is duly elected Headborough of Ebbisham for the year ensuing & is sworn

Headborough of Woodcote — Tho.s Davis is duly elected Headborough of Woodcote for the year ensuing & is sworn.

Aletasters — Joseph Philips & Wm Mansell are duly elected Aletasters for the year ensuing & Wm Mansell is sworn

Common Drivers — Edward Stone and Jas Griffin are duly elected Common Drivers for the year ensuing & Edw.d Stone is sworn.

The first page of the record of the Court Leet or (more usually, 'and') View of Frankpledge of the Manor of Ebbisham, Surrey, held on 26 October, 1767, showing the names of the jurors and out-going and newly elected officers of the manor. *Surrey Record Office.*

The Manor of Ebbisham in the County of Surry} to wit

The Court Baron of Ricarda Parkhurst Widow Lady of the said Manor holden in & for the same on Monday the 26th Day of Octr in the 8th Year of the Reign of our Sovereign Lord George the 3. by the Grace of God of Great Britain France & Ireland King Defender of the Faith &c and in the year of our Lord 1767 By Peter Prevoost Gentleman Steward there.

Plaintes to wit   None at this Court

Homage to wit —   John Eastland Foreman Sworn
Robt Wrench
Wm Woollard   } sworn
John Yelden
John Hopkins

Satisfactn from Joseph Shaw Esqr to John Eastland

At this Court it is attested and inrolled by the Steward there that on the 1st day of July 1760 Joseph Shaw of Ebbisham in the County of Surry Esqr Admor of the Goods & Chattels Rights & Credits of his Father Joseph Shaw late of Ebbisham afsd Esqr deced Did acknowledge to have had & received of & from John Eastland of Ebbisham aforesd Barber the Sum of £400. in full payment & satisfaction of & for all principal & Int. Monies due to him as Admor of his sd Father upon or by Virtue of a certain Condl Surrender bearing date the 3 day of June 1729 & made by the sd John Eastland of certain Copyhold Messes Tenemts & Heredits held of this Manor To the Use of the sd Joseph Shaw deced & his heirs for securing the payment of £150. & Int. at the Times & in manner therein mentd and also upon or by Virtue of a further Charge made at a Court Baron holden in & for this Manor on the 21st day of Octr 1729. whereby the sd Premes were charged by the sd Jno Eastland with the paymt to the said Joseph Shaw deced of the further Sum of £50. & Int. And also upon or by Virtue of a certain other Condl Surrender bearing Date the 8th day of May 1732 and made by the said John Eastland of a certain piece or parcel of Copyhold Ground held of this Manor To the Use of the said —

Freemen   There are three meanings to this word: a man who was free of trade taxes and who shared in the profits of the borough in which he lived and traded, a tenant who was free of feudal service and a man who had served his apprenticeship and who could then work at his trade in his own right. In the city of London nearly all freemen became so by virtue of being freemen of a City Guild (see LIVERY COMPANIES). On attaining company freedom, a man would automatically apply for the freedom of the City. He was then entitled to call himself 'Citizen' and, (for example), 'Tallow Chandler'. A few distinguished persons have been granted honorary freedom in recognition of their achievements. Records of admission to the Freedom before 1916 are at the Corporation of London Record Office, Guildhall, Gresham Street, London EC2P 2EJ. Those before 1681 are incomplete owing to a fire at Guildhall in 1786. Records from 1916 are in the custody of the Chamberlain's Court at Guildhall. Enquiries concerning the latter should be addressed to the Clerk of the Court.

French Measles   The illness now called German measles.

Friendly Societies   Friendly Societies were established in the second half of the eighteenth century and provided help to their members when they fell sick or to their dependents when they died. They met, generally in a public house, to collect subscriptions and hold annual dinners. During the Napoleonic wars such working class gatherings were banned, except for the Friendly Societies which came under government control. By the turn of the eighteenth century there were as many as seven thousand in England and Wales. Their records can be seen at the PRO, Kew in the group FS. Further reading: P.H.J.H. Gosden *The Friendly Societies in England 1815–1875* (1961).

Friends, Religious Society of (Quakers)

In 1647, George Fox (1624–91), the founder of the Society of Friends, began preaching in the north of England and soon established a large following, mainly in Westmorland, north Lancashire and northwest Yorkshire. However, the Society incurred the hostility of many of the older sects from among whom their conversions were made.

The following key dates will be found useful in historical research.

1650   An Act of Parliament made the Friends liable to charges of blasphemy. A magistrate bestowed on them the nickname 'Quakers'.

1654   The earliest records of meetings began.

1650s   The London Friends began the keeping of central records, particularly of 'sufferings', but also of committees.

1656   The first missionaries went to America.

1661   More than 4000 Friends were released from prison in a temporary relaxation of regulations, following the end of the Commonwealth regime.

1662   The *Quaker Act* enabled conventicles (unlicensed meetings) to be broken up.

1664   The first *Conventicle Act* strengthened the Act of two years before.

1666   The Society's system of organisation was established.

1668   The first Yearly Meeting was held in London.

1670   The second *Conventicle Act* made Quakers the prey of informers.

1672   The first *Test Act* required an oath of supremacy from all holders of public office. Quakers would not take any oath at all.

1673   The Society's Library was founded, which included MS records.

1675   The permanent standing committee of the Society was established; called the Meeting for Sufferings, and still so called.

1682   William Penn founded Pennsylvania as a Quaker state.

1689   The *Toleration Act* ended persecution for non-attendance at church; but Quakers still suffered for non-payment of tithes.

18th   Century: Preparative Meetings were instituted for the management of local business. There were separate Men's and Women's Meetings.

1753   Quakers were exempted from Lord Hardwicke's *Marriage Act*, which restricted marriages to churches licensed for that purpose.

1794   A record repository was founded at Devonshire House, Bishopsgate, London.

1828–9 The repeal of the *Test Acts* allowed Quakers to affirm, and gave them freedom to hold public office.

1837 All known registers up to this date, some dating from the 1650s, were copied into Digests; and in 1840 the originals were deposited at the General Register Office.

1857 Registers discovered since 1840 were also deposited with the Registrar General. They are now all at the Public Record Office, Chancery Lane, London, in class RG 6.

1926 The central records were moved to their present location at Friends' House, Euston Road, London NW1 2BJ.

Some understanding of Quaker organisation is necessary for research. Each local congregation is called a Particular Meeting; it also has a meeting of discipline to manage its affairs, called a Preparative Meeting. All the Preparative Meetings in one district send representatives to make up a Monthly Meeting, an executive body for the area, in which all lands, meeting-houses, etc., are vested. The Monthly Meetings in turn send representatives to a Quarterly Meeting. At first the jurisdiction of these covered one county, but now some counties have merged. In spring, the Quarterly Meetings send representatives to the London Yearly Meeting, which is the executive body for the whole country.

Documentary records at Friends' House comprise the minutes of regular meetings, special meetings and committees, 'Suffering Books', correspondence, registers of births, marriages and deaths or burials, admission lists, collection lists, disownments, removal certificates, accounts, deeds and property records. The minutes, especially of Preparative and Monthly Meetings, cover a number of aspects of members' lives, including care of the poor, education, apprenticeships, discipline and, most important for genealogists, marriage. Permission to marry had to be obtained from the Monthly Meetings, which checked that both parties were free to marry and had their parents' consent. A bride or bridegroom from another district had to produce a certificate from his or her own Meeting, showing that they knew of no hindrance to the marriage. The ceremony itself was by the declaration of both parties in open meeting, and a certificate was signed by all adults present. Some Quakers who could not get permission 'married out', i.e. they married by the normal ceremony in a parish church.

Researchers should be aware that the Society uses its own dating system. The names of months and of days of the week are replaced by numbers. Before 1752, March is called First Month; April, Second Month; May, Third Month, and so on: after 1752, January is First Month. Sunday is First Day; Monday, Second Day, and so on through the week.

County records are in the custody of the Meeting that produced them, and in the care of a Custodian. The annual *Book of Meetings*, published by Friends' House, gives the names and addresses of all local Clerks, who will arrange contacts. Some county records have been deposited at Friends' House, and some at the county record offices.

The Library at Friends' House has a Digest copy of all the ancient registers, and each meeting has a Digest copy of its own. The central Digest is arranged geographically in Quarterly Meeting areas. Each register is divided into decennial sections, and in each section the entries are in alphabetical order of initial letters and in chronological order within each letter. Each entry carries a reference to the volume and page where it can be found in the original register. The Digests do not contain the names of witnesses. Removal Certificates were testimonials given on Friends' emigration to Pennsylvania. *Collection of the Sufferings* by J. Besse (1753) is indexed.

The Friends' Historical Society publishes a journal issued from their headquarters at Friends' House.

For further reading, see D.J. Steel *Sources for Non-conformist Genealogy and Family History* vol. II of the National Index of Parish Registers, SOG (1973), and *My Ancestors were Quakers. How can I find out more about them?* (Society of Genealogists).

Funds in Chancery *see* **Dormant Funds**

Furlong A piece of land formed by several parallel strips (selions), 220 yards long, lying in the open arable fields of a manor. Also, in some places, called a Shot or a Flat.

Fyrd The fyrd was a local Militia in Anglo-Saxon times. It was raised by each shire on the basis of land-holding. It was called out only in times of emergency and it was unusual for the fyrd to serve outside the borders of its shire.

G

Gafol   A rent, either in money or in service.

Gang Week   A lay term for Rogationtide, immediately before Ascension Day, so called from the custom of 'ganging' round the parish to perform the perambulation of its bounds.

Gaol, Common   Either a county gaol under the High Sheriff, or a city gaol under the corporation, or a church gaol.

Gaol Delivery   A judicial hearing of the charges against all prisoners awaiting trial in the area prisons. By a Commission of Gaol Delivery, the king appointed certain persons justices and empowered them to deliver his gaols at certain places of the prisoners held within them. This commission was at first issued to Justices in Eyre, but later to Justices of Assize and of Gaol Delivery. It ordered them to meet at a certain place and at a time which they themselves could appoint, when the sheriff of the county would bring all the prisoners of the area before them. The records are at the Public Record Office, Chancery Lane, London, in class JUST 3 and PL 25.

Gate   (i) Leas or pasture. As a suffix after cow-horse, ox-, sheep-, etc., it means the common right of pasture for that beast. A 'gated pasture' was one on which only a certain number of beasts was allowed to graze. (*See* also WASTE.)

   (ii) A road or way; an element often found in the names of ancient streets.

Gavelkind   Derived from two Anglo-Saxon words meaning 'holding of a family', this term originally denoted a whole mode of tenure, but in time it became applied solely to one characteristic markedly different from the law of tenure over most of the country. This peculiarity was a local survival of a pre-feudal custom, by which a man's land was divided between all his sons instead of passing to his eldest son (as it did by the later feudal law). If he had no sons, it was divided between all his daughters; but not between both sons and daughters. However, if one of the man's sons predeceased him, having himself had only a daughter or daughters, then on the old man's death his land would be divided between his sons, and the deceased son's portion would go to his daughters, being his heirs.

This law survived in Wales, in Kent, and in pockets of the country elsewhere. In Wales it was abolished under Henry VIII, but in other places it continued until 1925. In Kent, gavelkind became the Common Law mode of land inheritance, and all lands held in socage were presumed to be partible unless proved to the contrary. Elsewhere in England, primogeniture was the Common Law, and if a claim of partibility was made it had to be proved to be customary since 'Time Immemorial' (i.e. prior to the accession of Richard I in 1189).

The following list, not necessarily complete, of places outside Kent where gavelkind was the custom, was given by P.M. Thomas in *Genealogist's Magazine* Vol. 15, No.2: Oswaldbeck Soke, Nottinghamshre, until 32 Henry VIII (his thirty-second regnal year); the fee of Pickering, Norfolk; the Soke of Rothelay, Leicestershire; the port of Rye and elsewhere in Sussex; several places in Shropshire; the manors of Monmouth, Usk and Trelleg, Monmouthshire; the two hundreds in Archinfeld, Herefordshire; Wareham, Dorset; Taunton Dean, Somerset; Kentish Town, northwest London.

GEDCOM   GEnealogical Data COMmunication, a standard developed by the Genealogical Society of Utah for transferring genealogical data between different computers and different genealogical database programs.

Genealogical Research Directory   An annual publication which lists the research interests of individual international subscribers. It also includes a list of family history societies world-wide together with maps of many countries showing their administrative divisions.

Genealogical Society of Utah *see* **Latter-day Saints**

Genealogist's Guide, The *see* **Family Trees and Histories**

Genealogists' Magazine   The journal of the Society of Genealogists.

Genealogists, Professional *see* **Association of Genealogists and Record Agents**

Genealogists, Society of   The society was founded in 1911 by a small group of genealogists, mostly professionals, and at that time occupied one room in Fleet Street. However, it grew and moved to more spacious premises in Bloomsbury, and then in 1931 to occupy a whole floor at Chaucer House, Malet Street, London WC1. It is a limited company, classified as an 'Association not for profit'. By 1952 there were one thousand members. Again it outgrew its premises, and moved to a large house in Harrington Gardens, London SW3; and in 1984 it moved to still larger premises at 14 Charterhouse Buildings, London EC1M 7BA.

The President of the Society is HRH Prince Michael of Kent. The work of the Society is administered by an elected Executive Committee, and it employs full-time, a Director, a Finance Officer, a Librarian and eleven other staff, and from a thousand members of 1954 it has grown to over 12,000 members, many of them resident overseas.

The main advantages of membership are: (i) access to the Society's magnificent genealogical library, which is still growing steadily, and to its card indexes, which contain about three million names; (ii) free subscription to the *Genealogists' Magazine*, which is published quarterly and contains useful articles on research, a list of the latest accessions to the library, and news of events likely to affect genealogists.

The most valuable research aids in the library are the copies of parish registers, some printed, some typescript and some in manuscript. Of the 11,000 ancient parishes of England there are now copies in the library of the registers — or of part of the registers — of over 8,000. More marriage registers have been copied than those of baptisms and burials. Next in importance comes Boyd's Marriage Index, compiled by Percival Boyd. It covers about 2600 registers or part registers, and contain between six and seven million names. The library also contains indexes of eighteenth-century apprenticeships, of the wills of many probate courts, and of marriage licence records. There are numbers of local directories, professional directories, poll books, transcripts of memorial inscriptions and publications of county historical societies. Where applicable, these are arranged under county headings. There are also school and university registers, works on palaeography, heraldry and surname origins and narrative family histories. Copies of most of the reference books mentioned in this dictionary are on the library shelves. There is a Document Collection kept in box files, and a Great Index containing over three million references extracted from parish registers, memorial inscriptions, will indexes, Chancery suits and other records. The Society also has the International Genealogical Index microfiches for the whole world.

The Society's library is open from Tuesday to Saturday during the following hours: Tue., Fri. and Sat. 10 a.m.–6 p.m., Wed. and Thurs. 10 a.m.–8 p.m.

For subscription purposes, members are divided into Town Members and Country and Overseas Members. There is a common entrance fee for all members.

Non-members can use the library for either one hour, four hours, or a whole day on payment of the appropriate search fee. An outline guide *Using the Library of the Society of Genealogists* is available and should be read in advance by all visitors.

The Society offers a rich programme of lectures, courses and seminars and holds an annual one-day conference. It also holds a May Fair inviting exhibitors and family history societies to sell their wares.

Besides its quarterly journal and a number of specialist guides (mentioned under their subject headings), the Society publishes aids for the genealogist in the shape of charts, record cards and birth briefs. The Society has a bookshop with a wide range of genealogical and related books which is also worth visiting.

See also BOYD'S MARRIAGE INDEX.

Genealogy The study of the descents of families and persons from an ancestor or ancestors. Genealogy takes several forms, but there are three main avenues of research. Firstly, the tracing of a male-line descent, leading to the compilation of a Family Tree showing male-line ancestors and ancestresses, and the ancestors' brothers and sisters. Secondly, the tracing of all male-line descendants of a common ancestor, leading to the compilation of an Extended Family Tree showing all collateral branches of a family. Thirdly, the tracing of all ancestors of a given person through male *and* female lines, leading to the compilation of an Ancestry Chart.

Descents are traced from evidence provided by documents contemporaneous with the family events recorded in them (Primary Evidence). The techniques have been well developed, and most of the necessary records have now become readily available. Any lack of success is usually due to faulty record-keeping in the past, destruction or loss of records, movements of families from place to place, or the number of unrelated families of the same surname. Indexes of baptisms and marriages now in course of compilation will, when complete, greatly reduce the difficulty caused by family mobility. For the methods of genealogical research, see the Guide to Ancestry Research at the beginning of this book.

Genealogy has recently become a popular leisure pursuit, and has given rise to the formation of family history societies all over the country.

See also FAMILY HISTORY.

General Register of Births, Deaths and Marriages

By the *Births and Deaths Registration Act* and the *Marriage Act*, both of 1836, civil registration of births, deaths and marriage was begun on 1 July, 1837. For the first time, these events were entered in a single register for everyone in England and Wales.

The country was divided into 27 numbered regions, which were themselves divided into registration districts under the control of Superintendent Registrars, and sub-divided into sub-districts under Registrars. In 1851 there were 623 registration districts. Registration was compulsory, but at first there was no penalty for non-observance. Some parents failed (and some still do) to register their children's births, and some children have actually been registered twice under different forenames; but for deaths and marriages, registration is complete apart from occasional human error. The clergy have duplicate registration books for marriages, and no burial is permitted without a death certificate. When a duplicate marriage register book is full the clergyman has to pass it to his local registrar, but the latter also visits his local churches each quarter and makes copies of all marriage entries up to date. He maintains an index and, at the end of each quarter, the Superintendent Registrar of the district passes the duplicates to the office of the Registrar General in London. There they are all bound into volumes, and a separate quarterly index is compiled for each type of event. Marriages are indexed under the names of both parties. If the bride is a widow or divorcee, she is entered under the surname of her former husband. Copies of these indexes are now widely available on microfiche. There is a set for 1837–1920 at the Society of Genealogists.

The following dates are useful to bear in mind:

1852 Regional areas were altered and the number of them increased to 34 (*see* list below).

1866 The index of deaths began to show the age of the deceased. Also, all indexes from this date are printed or typed.

1874 Penalties came into force for failure to register births.

1911 From September of this year the mother's maiden name is shown in the index of births.

1912 The index of marriages shows the name of the spouse beside the one indexed.

1974 The General Register Office, which had been housed at Somerset House in the Strand, London, was moved to St Catherine's House on the east corner of Kingsway and Aldwych, where it is a section of the Office of Population Censuses and Surveys. The entrance is in Aldwych.

iii

MARRIAGES REGISTERED IN OCTOBER, NOVEMBER AND DECEMBER 1912.

ROU-ROW

Names of persons married.	District.	Vol.	Page.
Rout, Emmeline	Tuck	Willesden	3 a	550
— Frederick G.	Bales	Bethnal G.	1 c	318
— Hannah	Mason	Stockton	10 a	154
— James W.	Smith	Boulcoates	9 d	361
— Walter H.	Bonds	Poplar	1 c	1032
— William H.	Wolfe	Blything	4 a	2530
Routcliffe, Bertie J.	Gardner	Kingsbridge	5 b	484
Routen, Ernest	Seal	Melton M.	7 a	699
Routh, Charles	Sidebottom	Burnley	8 e	542
— Harold	Ray	Wakefield	9 c	14
— William H.	Turner	Steyning	2 b	599
— Willie	Tunnington	Leeds	9 b	827
Routledge, Ada M.	Owens	Conway	11 b	881
— Albert A.	Hollis	Brighton	2 b	563
— Elizabeth	Kershaw	W. Derby	8 b	990
— Ernest	Taylor	Rochdale	8 e	146
— Florence H.	Dipple	Camberwell	1 d	1665
— Frederick C.	Hucklebridge	Kensington	1 a	311
— Herbert W.	Wright	Stockton	10 a	109
— Jane A.	Nicholson	Leeds	9 b	753
— Mary C.	Grey	Gateshead	10 a	1714
— Mary E.	Marschall	W. Derby	8 b	963
— Robert	Wilson	Carlisle	10 b	976
— Thirza	Hipkin	Prestwich	8 d	527
Routley, Henry	Rowe	Williton	5 c	593
— John	Vaughan	Williton	5 c	622
— Maud E.	Charlton	Birmingham	6 d	325
— Stanley H.	Annesley	Wandsworth	1 d	1137
— Walter R.	Folwell	Atherstone	6 d	952
Rover, Ethel M.	Burton	W. Ham	4 a	306
Row, Edith F.R.	Quarman	Pancras	1 b	264
— Ellen L.	Rutherford	Newcastle T.	10 b	112
— Henry C.	Mountjoy	Lancaster	8 e	1430
— Jane W.	Jameson	Sunderland	10 a	1174
— John W.	Mitchell	Paddington	1 a	4
— Lucy L.T.	Stephens	Bodmin	5 c	147
— Mary A.	Jefferies	Bristol	6 a	474
Rowan, Ada	Booth	Ecclesall B.	9 c	902
— Arthur	Sprague	Islington	1 b	516
— Catherine	Donovan	Salford	8 d	223
— Francis M.	Musk	Wandsworth	1 d	1292
— George	Lindsay	Liverpool	8 b	152
— Jessie	Beaumont	Staines	3 a	57
— Joseph	Nolan	Liverpool	8 b	154
— Lily	Oates	Ecclesall B.	9 c	785
— Sarah	Cromwell	Ormskirk	8 b	1441
— William	Hymns	Southwark	1 d	220
— William H.	Buckley	Ecclesall B.	9 c	700
Rowberry, Charles	Twigg	Stourbridge	6 c	312
— Frank	Willis	Ledbury	6 a	1067
— Laurie B.	Pearn	Swindon	5 a	23
Rowbotham, Alice L.	Hewson	Horncastle	7 a	1315
— Andrew	Lucas	Devonport	5 b	786
— Arthur H.	Salt	Stoke T.	6 b	443
— Fred	Haley	Salford	8 d	4
— Fred V.	Frost	Hayfield	7 b	1923
— Harry	Furney	W. Bromwich	6 b	1665
— John	Ellison	Stockport	8 a	86
— Sarah	Hall	Aston	6 d	640
Rowbottom, Alice M.	Pizzey	Pontefract	9 c	223
— Annie	Gregory	Worksop	7 b	119
— Ethel	Heap	Glossop	7 b	1901
— Harry B.	Hill	Huddersfield	9 a	796
— Henry	Dougall	Swansea	11 a	2225
— Hetty	Heath	Atherstone	6 d	959
— Jane	Ashworth	Salford	8 d	80
— John W.	Davidson	Sculcoates	9 d	552
— Joseph	Taylor	W. Derby	8 b	920
— Mary C.	Smales	Wakefield	9 c	66
— Mary E.	Hudson	Nottingham	7 b	849
— Richard T.	Lowe	Wigan	8 c	93
— Thomas L.	Walker	Birkenhead	8 a	1135
Rowbury, Beatrix M.	Meek	Hereford	6 a	1187
Rowcliffe, Alice M.	Parsons	Edmonton	3 a	1012
Rowcroft, James H.	Haylett	St. Clave	1 d	521

Names of persons married.	District.	Vol.	Page.
Rowcroft, John	Nightingale	Preston	8 e	1058
Rowden, Arthur	Stoneman	Totnes	5 b	245
— Charles	Mortimer	Yarnham	2 a	256
— Edith	Pitts	Totnes	5 b	261
— Emma	German	Tiverton	5 b	962
— Frederick B.	Douglas	Medway	2 a	1697
— Mary	Lowden	Lewisham	1 d	2231
Rowdon, Ernest J.	Clark	Wandsworth	1 d	960
Rowe, Albert A.A.	Cross	W. Ham	4 a	536
— Albert J.	Palmer	Holborn	1 b	1495
— Albert J.	Beckett	Alverstoke	2 b	1291
— Albert J.	Miles	Cardiff	11 a	931
— Alice	Bourne	Devonport	5 b	811
— Alice L.M.	Ward	Medway	2 a	1484
— Alice M.E.	Cole	Liskeard	5 c	111
— Annie A.T.	Wilmott	Chorlton	8 c	1192
— Annie F.	Luff	Edmonton	3 a	854
— Annie H.	Routley	Williton	5 c	593
— Annie M.	Burgess	Aston	6 d	416
— Annie V.	Pochin	Newton A.	5 b	262
— Augustus L.G.	Eldridge	Samford	4 a	2254
— Betsy	Whitear	St. Geo. East	1 c	549
— Catherine	Renfrey	Todmorden	9 a	545
— Cecil	Weeden	Strood	2 a	1435
— Charles	Nock	St. Geo. H. Sq.	1 a	1092
— Charles W.	Anthoney	Derby	7 b	1356
— Clara V.	Smith	Plymouth	5 b	660
— Dolly	Young	Willesden	3 a	599
— Edith	Moore	Southwark	1 d	321
— Edith	Patey	Plymouth	5 b	551
— Edith	Alexander	Newcastle T.	10 b	286
— Edith D.E.	Simons	Wandsworth	1 d	1356
— Edward	Pearson	Guisbro	9 d	1165
— Edward A.	Giles	Southwark	1 d	325
— Eliza	Plant	Barnsley	9 c	475
— Eliza H.	Rowe	Bethnal G.	1 c	390
— Elizabeth A.	Andrew	E. Preston	2 b	765
— Elizabeth C.	Sweeney	Lambeth	1 d	724
— Elizabeth J.	Shire	Axbridge	5 c	1154
— Ellen	Burton	Walsingham	4 b	825
— Emily	Broadbent	Haslingden	8 e	362
— Emily M.	Retallick	Falmouth	5 c	547
— Ethel	Woods	Ipswich	4 a	2375
— Ethel E.M.	Smart	Warminster	5 a	345
— Florence	Allen	Birmingham	6 d	164
— Florence M.	Davidson	Chorlton	8 c	1391
— Florence F.	Skellam	Wolstanton	6 b	185
— Frances B.	Wright	W. Derby	8 b	1025
— Frank H.	Purse	Hackney	1 b	878
— Fred C.	Allen	Chelmsford	4 a	1245
— Frederick	Rowe	Bethnal G.	1 c	390
— Frederick	Wilson	Alverstoke	2 b	1265
— Frederick	Balls	Pancras	1 b	79
— Frederick A.J.	Ferns	Salford	8 d	13
— Frederick B.	Gibbs	Blything	4 a	2575
— Frederick C.	Allen	Chelmsford	4 a	1245
— Frederick H.	Durrant	Erpingham	4 b	171
— Frederick J.	Cope	Aston	6 d	788
— Frederick T.	Harries	Haverfordwest	11a	2708
— George	Keeble	Swansea	11 a	2188
— George	Trewartha	Redruth	5 c	409
— George H.	Tyler	Bedwellty	11 a	157
— Gwladys	Griffiths	Llanelly	11 a	2361
— Harold T.	Bear	H. Hempstead	3 a	1695
— Henry	Sadler	King's N.	6 c	998
— Henry E.	Ridge	Wolstanton	6 b	221
— Herbert	Matthews	W. Ham	4 a	32
— Herbert	Whitaker	Leeds	9 b	973
— Ida	Paul	Lincoln	7 a	1271
— Isaac C.	Hutchings	Bridport	5 a	939
— Isaac J.	Dean	Devonport	5 b	728
— James	Dexter	Brentford	3 a	307
— James	Figures	King's N.	6 c	816
— James H.	Holman	Redruth	5 c	457
— Janie	Frey	Pancras	1 b	193

The photograph TOP LEFT shows family historians searching the index volumes at the General Register Office.

ABOVE A page of the General Register Marriage Index for the last quarter of 1912. In earlier years, there was no helpful second column to show the name of the spouse. *Both illustrations: Crown Copyright.*

Search Procedure The information supplied by the General Register Office is solely in the form of a certified copy of the original certificate. This can be applied for either by calling at the Office, searching the indexes and completing an application form, or by letter, giving sufficient information for the registration entry to be identified, and paying for it in advance, but indexes on microfilm are now available at some record offices and libraries.

Double-barrelled names are indexed in alphabetical order of the complete name, ignoring the hyphen; for example, the name Stone-Mogg will be found under S and after Stoneman. A guide leaflet (PSR.2) is available at St Catherine's House and can be studied before a search.

Inside the entrance of the Office are racks containing application forms printed in red for births, and green for marriages. The searcher fills in the appropriate form with any particulars already known to him. He then proceeds further into the Office, where he will find rows of bookshelves containing quarterly indexes of births and deaths. Marriages, all forces and the British overseas registration are in a room to the rear of the first search room along a short passageway. The spine of each volume shows the year and quarter of the events indexed, and the initial letters of the surnames covered. The quarter is indicated by the name of its last month, so the volume for the first quarter of the year will show 'March' on its spine, and so on. If the researcher knows the exact date of the event he is looking for, he looks up the name in the relevant volume. Against it he will find a reference consisting of the name of the registration district, a volume number which is also the number of the region in which the registration district lies, and a page number. The name of the registration district will not necessarily be the same as that of the town or village in which the event took place. Usually it is the name of a large town in the district, but sometimes of the hundred or other area. If the district name is not familiar to the searcher, and so does not tell him in what part of the country it is, he can identify the region from the volume number by referring to the list at the end of this article. When there is more than one person of the same name in the index, the volume (region) number can help the searcher to decide which is the one he is looking for.

Copies of nineteenth-century birth certificates. In the lower one, the absence of a father's name and occupation shows that the mother was unmarried. *The design of the marriage and death certificates is Crown copyright and is reproduced with the permission of the Controller of HMSO.*

CERTIFIED COPY OF AN ENTRY OF BIRTH

CERTIFIED to be a true copy of an entry in the certi
Given at the GENERAL REGISTER OFFICE, LONDON, und

CERTIFIED COPY OF AN ENTRY OF BIRTH

The fee for this certificate is 40p.
When application is made by post a
handling fee is payable in addition.

GIVEN AT THE GENERAL REGISTER OFFICE, LONDON

Application Number........*6724B*............

DISTRICT	*Wisbech*				
Walpole St Peters in the *County* of *Norfolk*					

5 Name, surname and maiden surname of mother	6 Occupation of father	7 Signature, description and residence of informant	8 When registered	9 Signature of registrar	10* Name entered after registration
Mary Wyat formerly Baker	*Labourer*	*John Wyat the Father Marsh Walpole St Peters*	*December 12th*	*John Bridgman Reg.*	

...f a Register of Births in the District above mentioned.
of the said Office, the *28th* day of *February* 1980

GIVEN AT THE GENERAL REGISTER OFFICE,
SOMERSET HOUSE, LONDON

Application Number....*AW 98383/72*

DISTRICT	*Sheffield*				
Nth Sheffield in the *County of York*					

5 Name, surname and maiden surname of mother	6 Occupation of father	7 Signature, description and residence of informant	8 When registered	9 Signature of registrar	10* Name entered after registration
Mary Ann Bennett	—	*X The mark of Mary Ann Bennett Mother Union Workhouse Sheffield*	*Twentyfourth March 1844*	*W Hardcastle Registrar*	

CERTIFIED COPY OF AN ENTRY OF MARRIAGE

Give

Registration District___*Wisbech*___

1850__. Marriage solemnized at___*The Parish Church*___
in the *Parish* of_____*West Walton*_____ in the ___*Count*

No.	When married	Name and Surname	Age	Condition	Rank or profession
91	May 14th	Edward Ulyat	Full age	Bachelor	Farmer
		Mary Anne Fisher	Full age	Spinster	—

Married in the *Parish Church*_____ according to the *rites and Ceremonies* of the_____

This marriage was solemnized between us, { Edward Ulyat   Mary Ann Fisher } in the presence of us, { Jno Thos Macdo...   Louisa Fis...

CERTIFIED to be a true copy of an entry in the certified copy of a Register of Marriages in the Distri

Given at the GENERAL REGISTER OFFICE, LONDON, under the Seal of the said Office, the   2...

CERTIFIED COPY OF AN ENTRY OF DEATH

Gi

	REGISTRATION DISTRICT				*Wisbech*	

1866. DEATH in the Sub-district of ___*Walpole Saint Peter*___ in

Columns :—	1	2	3	4	5	6
No.	When and where died	Name and surname	Sex	Age	Occupation	Cause of death
182	Third August 1866 West Walton	John Ulyatt	male	77 years	Agricultural labourer	General De... Certifi...

CERTIFIED to be a true copy of an entry in the certified copy of a Register of Deaths in the District

Given at the GENERAL REGISTER OFFICE, LONDON, under the Seal of the said Office, the   24th   day o

GENERAL REGISTER OFFICE, LONDON

Application Number ....4.7.3.9...𝒟.................

Norfolk

6	7	8
the time of marriage	Father's name and surname	Rank or profession of father
le st Peter	Abraham ulyat	Farmer
walton	William Fisher	Farmer

lished Church by Licence by me
D.P. Calliphronas

entioned.

ay of   January   19**7**8

GENERAL REGISTER OFFICE, LONDON.

Application Number.....5.1.7.1...4.................

County of Norfolk

7	8	9
gnature, description, and residence of informant	When registered	Signature of registrar
The mark of John Watson resent at death West Walton	Fifth August 1866	William Winterton Registrar

ned.

19 **80**

If the exact date of the event is not known, the researcher will have to search the volumes, of several quarters or years around the most probable one. If he finds more than one person of the same name, he should note the references against them all and decide which is the most likely. He then enters its whole reference on the application form and indicates whether the certificate, when it is ready, is to be sent or called for. On the back of the form he can also enter details about the person sought. These are called checking points. If the certificate does not correspond with them the researcher will not receive a certificate, but will be refunded part of his payment. It is therefore very important that any such details given should be known to be absolutely correct.

If the searcher finds more than one index entry that could be the one he wants, he should fill in an application form for one of them in the usual way, with checking points on the back, and ask the cashier for a Reference Checking Sheet on which to enter the others. A charge will be made for each extra entry. A certificate will be issued for the first entry that corresponds with all the checking points. Fuller details about this multiple checking will be supplied by the cashier on form PSR.11.

The difficulty most likely to be encountered in searching the index is in the spelling of the surname, which may well differ from the one expected. Before making the search it is a good plan to think of as many variant spellings as possible. The most misleading variants are those that alter the first letter of the name. The letter H is liable to be dropped, or added, and the addition or omission of a final S or E is also common.

Another difficulty arises when there has been a change of forename after registration, or when a person has been commonly known by his or her second forename or a pet name. Unfortunately, too, the indexing is not faultless; events that have been duly registered may have been

---

LEFT Marriage certificate of Edward Ulyat and Mary Anne Fisher. The entry 'Full age' is frustrating, but all too common. BELOW Death certificate of John Ulyatt. Note the difference in spelling the family name here and on his relative's marriage certificate above, a difference that can safely be ignored. *Both documents: the design of the marriage and death certificates is Crown copyright and is reproduced with the permission of the Controller of HMSO.*

omitted from the index, or one party to a marriage may have been indexed and not the other.

When the application form has been handed in and the fee paid, the applicant has to wait a few days before receipt of the certificate, either by calling for it at the General Register Office or by having it sent by post.

Birth Certificates A birth certificate supplies the date and place of birth, the name and sex of the child, the name and occupation of the father, the name and previous surname or surnames of the mother, and the name, description and address of the informant.

If the certificate shows not only the date but also the time of day of the birth, a multiple birth is indicated. The name or names of the other child or children can therefore be looked for in the same index volume, and will be recognised by having the same reference to district, volume and page.

Parents are allowed forty-two days in which to register a birth, so the registration of a child born at the end of March, June, September or December may appear in the index of the quarter following the birth.

Sometimes the child had not been named at the time of registration, in which case only 'Male' or 'Female' will appear in the index at the end of the list of named children of the same surname.

Sometimes the parent of a newborn child will have omitted to inform the registrar that the mother had been married before, so only one of her previous names will be shown on the birth certificate. If this is her maiden name, difficulty may be caused in finding the marriage certificate of the child's parents.

If the child was born out of wedlock, the father's name was usually omitted, but after 1875 a father who accompanied the mother to the registrar's office and admitted paternity could have his name entered on the certificate, in which case the birth would be indexed under both surnames.

Several children of exactly the same names may be registered in the same district in the same quarter. Even the father's name may match that shown on the child's eventual marriage certificate. So check against any other information that is known, e.g. the father's occupation, his address or the name of the mother. If none of these is conclusive, turn to the known brothers and sisters of the child and apply for their birth certificates in order to find a set with common parents — but consider the possibility of a second wife. In any case, it is wise, though expensive, to obtain birth certificates of all brothers and sisters.

They may show changes of the parents' residence and the father's occupation.

The recent Family Law Reform Act enacts that where a wife has a child by Artificial Insemination by Donor (AID) with the consent of her husband, that husband will be shown on the birth certificate as the father of the child, thus falsifying its ancestry.

Foundlings are listed after Z in the index.

Marriage Certificates A marriage certificate supplies the date, place and rites of the marriage, both parties' names, ages (sometimes), marital status, occupations and addresses, the names and occupations of their fathers, and the names of the witnesses.

If the rites by which the marriage was celebrated were not those of the Church of England, eventual searches for the baptisms of the parties will probably have to be conducted in non-parochial registers.

When starting to search the marriage index, it saves time to note in advance the date of birth of the eldest child of the marriage, so that the search backwards can start from there. If the surnames of both parties are known, it pays to search for the more uncommon one. When it is found, the name of the spouse should then be looked up in the volume for the same quarter. There it must, of course, be accompanied by the same reference details. From 1911 onward, this checking of the spouse is unnecessary, as his or her name will be shown against the name you have found.

A divorced person is described as 'single person'.

Always treat any ages shown on a marriage certificate with caution. Often no exact age is given, just 'of full age', meaning 21 or over. The same information is sometimes more misleadingly stated just by the figure 21. Also, the residence at the time of marriage, especially that of the bridegroom, may be only a temporary one. The occupation of the bridegroom, may be different from that in which he is known to have been engaged later in life. On some marriage certificates the father's name is omitted. This may mean that he was dead, or that he did not marry the mother. In other cases his name is given but not his occupation, and this usually means that he was dead.

Death Certificates A death certificate indicates the date, place and cause of death, the deceased's name, sex, age and rank or profession, and the name, description and address of the informant.

The main reasons for obtaining a death certificate are: (i) to ascertain the place and date of death for their own sake; (ii) to find out the deceased person's age as a clue to the year of his birth; (iii) to obtain his address in preparation for a search of the Census Returns; (iv) to find out the cause of death.

From 1866 onward, the age of the deceased person is shown in the index. It is wise not to enter any known occupation on the application form, as this may have changed at some time. If the deceased died later than 1857, and is thought likely to have left a will, the date of death may be more quickly found by searching the Index of Grants of Probate at the Principal Registry of the Family Division (*see* FAMILY DIVISION).

The person's place of death may not be his or her home address. Also, when the informant is not a member of the deceased's family, the age shown may be a mere guess. In any case, ages on death certificates should be treated with caution. If the informant is a coroner, the local newspaper should be searched for the report of an inquest.

Applications by post for certificates, including those for deaths, should be made to the General Register Office, Postal Applications Section, Smedley Hydro, Trafalgar Road, Birkdale, Southport PR8 2HH with any *definitely known* information about the person. However, it is safest not to give an exact age or occupation — the former may be mis-stated on the certificate, and the latter may have changed since the time of your evidence. If any particular you supply does not match that on the certificate, you will be told the person cannot be found. If the exact date of the event (birth, marriage or death) is not known, the staff will make a search through five years. Fees for searches and certificates have to be paid at the time of application. The charge for an application made by post is much higher (but it is not quite so high if the index references can be provided) than for one made in person, even if it is sent on the official form after a personal search.

Index searching can be carried out at the local register office in the district where the event is thought to have taken place.

For the registration of the births, marriages and deaths of British persons abroad, *see* GENERAL REGISTER OFFICE *and* ABROAD, BRITONS.

General Registration Regions: 1837–51

I	West London
II	East London
III	Middlesex
IV	Surrey
V	Kent
VI	Bedfordshire, Berkshire (part of), Buckinghamsire, Hertfordshire
VII	Hampshire (part of), Sussex
VIII	Dorset, Hampshire (part of), Wiltshire
IX	Cornwall, Scilly Isles, Devon (part of)
X	Devon (part of), Somerset (part of)
XI	Gloucestershire (part of), Somerset (part of)
XII	Essex, Suffolk (part of)
XIII	Norfolk, Suffolk (part of)
XIV	Cambridgeshire, Huntingdonshire, Lincolnshire
XV	Leicestershire, Northamptonshire, Nottinghamshire, Rutland
XVI	Berkshire (part of), Oxfordshire, Staffordshire (part of), Warwickshire (part of)
XVII	Staffordshire (part of)
XVIII	Gloucestershire (part of), Shropshire, Staffordshire (part of), Warwickshire (part of), Worcestershire
XIX	Cheshire, Derbyshire, Flintshire (part of)
XX	Lancashire (part of)
XXI	Lancashire (part of), Yorkshire (part of)
XXII	West Riding (part of), East Riding (part of)
XXIII	West Riding (part of), East Riding (part of)
XXIV	County Durham, North Riding
XXV	Cumberland, Lancashire (part of), Northumberland, Westmorland
XXVI	South Wales, Herefordshire
XXVII	North Wales, Anglesey

General Registration Regions: 1852–1946 (August)

1a–1d	Greater London
2a	Surrey, Kent
2b–2c	Sussex, Hampshire (part of)
2d	Berkshire, Hampshire (part of)
3a	Middlesex, Hertfordshire, Oxfordshire, Buckinghamshire
3b	Bedfordshire, Cambridgeshire, Huntingdonshire, Northamptonshire
4a	Essex, Suffolk
4b	Norfolk
5a	Wiltshire, Dorset
5b	Devon
5c	Cornwall, Scilly Isles, Somerset
6a	Gloucestershire, Herefordshire, Shropshire

6b	Staffordshire, Warwickshire (part of), Worcestershire (part of)
6c	Warwickshire (part of), Worcestershire (part of)
6d	Warwickshire (part of)
7a	Leicestershire, Lincolnshire, Rutland
7b	Derbyshire, Nottinghamshire
8a	Cheshire
8b–8e	Lancashire
9a–9d	Yorkshire
10a	County Durham
10b	Cumberland, Northumberland, Westmorland
11a	South Coast of Wales
11b	North Wales, Anglesey

The further changes to the list of districts for 1946 onward are not included, as they have little direct importance for most family history researchers.

General Register Office

This section of the Office of Population Censuses and Surveys is situated at the junction of Kingsway (east side) and Aldwych, London, and is entered by the Aldwych doorway. It houses the General Register of Births, Deaths and Marriages, and also the following miscellaneous registers.

Marine Register Books Births and deaths of people of British nationality at sea since 1 July, 1837. (*See also* MERCHANT SEAMEN; SEA, BIRTHS AND DEATHS AT.)

Air Register Books Births and deaths in UK-registered aircraft since 1949.

Army Chaplains' Returns Births, marriages and deaths of servicemen abroad, 1796–1880.

Army Returns of Births, Marriages and Deaths 1881–1955, abroad, but excluding the two World Wars (for which see below).

Army Regimental Registers Births, marriages and deaths abroad, 1761–1924.

Royal Air Force Returns Similar registers since 1920.

Consular Returns Information on births, marriages and deaths of British subjects in foreign countries since 1849, provided they were notified to Consular Officers.

Natal and South Africa Field Forces Deaths during the Boer War, 1899–1902.

Deaths abroad of Officers and Men in the Three Services (separate volumes) during the two World Wars.

Also, registers of deaths abroad in quite recent years.

The office is open from Monday–Friday, 8.30 a.m–4.30 p.m.

See also OVERSEAS, THE BRITISH for miscellaneous registers of births, marriages and deaths abroad, transferred from the General Register Office to the Public Record Office, Chancery Lane, London. *See also* LOCAL REGISTER OFFICES.

Generation

Reckonings of what is meant by a generation in terms of years (i.e. the period between the births of one male-line ancestor and the next) have varied in the past from twenty-five to thirty-three years, but all these appear to be underestimates. Thirty-five would appear to be a good working figure.

Gentleman

In the Middle Ages the word 'gentil' meant 'noble', but 'gentleman' came into use in the fifteenth century to signify a condition between baron and yeoman, or sometimes between knight and yeoman, after a statute of 1412 had laid down that in certain legal documents the 'estate, degree or mystery' of the defendent must be stated. In 1429 the term *les gentils* was used in an Act of Parliament, of men having freehold property worth 40 shillings per year or more.

From the sixteenth century onward, the distinction between gentlemen and yeomen lay more in their way of life than in their relative prosperity. A gentlemen did not work with his hands, so his household included personal servants; whereas the servants of a yeoman were his assistants on the land and in the dairy. A gentleman's son was often described as a yeoman while he was working his holding, pending inheritance of his father's lands. Members of the professions, i.e. army and naval officers and barristers, were regarded as gentlemen, some of them being entitled to the description 'Esquire'. For apprenticing a son to a London citizen a property qualification was required, so many gentlemen's sons entered the more profitable trades of the City. When a man, who during his working life was designated by his occupation (for example, tailor), retired, he would often then describe himself as 'Gentleman' as he was no longer gainfully employed.
See also CLASS, SOCIAL.

Gentleman's Magazine This magazine, known also as the *Monthly Intelligencer*, began publication in January, 1731. Its contents, modified comparatively little over the years, were then: A View of the Weekly Disputes and Essays in this Month (intellectual and literary), Poetical Essays, the Monthly Intelligencer (news day-by-day), Deaths, Casualties, Promotions, Ecclesiastical Preferments, Marriages, Bankrupts and Accidents, Observations in Gardening, Foreign Affairs, Stocks, Prices of Grain and Goods, and Books Published.

General Indexes have been published for 1731–86 and 1786–1810 (two volumes); indexes of marriages for 1731–68; indexes of obituaries and biographies for 1731–80. Each volume also has its own index, but for names of persons they are reliable only for deaths and marriages. The obituaries section contains information of value to the family historian, and the Monthly Intelligencer and Foreign Affairs sections provide interesting background material. Announcements of deaths and marriages were usually culled from newspapers, which often contain more detailed information. There is a complete typescript index of names 1731–1868 in the Family History Library in Salt Lake City.

The magazine ceased to publish births, marriages and deaths in 1868. Complete series of the volumes can be found on the open shelves of the British Library and the Public Record Office, and the library of the Society of Genealogists has a set, though one with many gaps.

German A cousin german is a first cousin, i.e. the issue of an uncle or aunt. Brothers or sisters german are those having both parents in common. *See also* SIBLINGS.

German, Anglo-German FHS *see* **Anglo-German**

Gersum *see* **Gressom**

Gibson Guides The popular name for a very useful set of guides to the whereabouts of records, written by J.S.W. Gibson and published by the Federation of Family History Societies.

Gilbert Union The administration of the poor law was the responsibility of the parish but changing needs made it necessary to increase the size of the administrative units. In 1783 'Gilbert's Act' made it possible for some parishes to group together to form larger units for poor law administration exclusively.

Glassites Glassites are Scottish SANDEMAN-IAN dissenters.

Glebe The land held by a beneficed clergyman. Glebe Terriers describe the boundaries of such land, and mention the holders of lands adjoining. These are now usually to be found in county record officers.

Gloucester Since 1974 the southern parishes of the ancient county have been in the newly formed county of Avon. It falls within the diocese of Gloucester and the Province of Canterbury. Many of the 347 Parishes have deposited their registers at the CRO and there are many transcripts of them in the library of the SOG. Boyd's Marriage Index covers 194 registers, plus extracts from some others. Pallot's Marriage Index covers 126, mainly from 1790–1812. The Bishops' Transcripts and Marriage Licence records are at the CRO.

The Hundreds of Berkeley (Lower and Upper Divisions), Bisley, Bledisloe, Botloe, Bradley, Brightwells-Barrow, Cheltenham, Cleeve (Bishop's), Crowthorne and Minty, Deerhurst (Lower and Upper Divisions), Dudstone and King's Barton (Lower, Middle and Upper Divisions), Cirencester, Tewkesbury Borough, Grumbalds-Ash (Lower and Upper Divisions), Henbury (Lower and Upper Divisions), Kiftsgate (Lower and Upper Divisions), Duchy of Lancaster, Langley and Swinehead (Lower and Upper Divisions), Longtree, Puckle-Church, Rapsgate, St Briavells, Slaughter (Lower and Upper Divisions), Tewkesbury (Upper and Lower Divisions), Thornbury (Lower and Upper Divisions), Tibaldstone, Westbury, Westminster (Lower and Upper Divisions), Whitstone (Lower and Upper Divisions), Barton Regis, and Bristol and Gloucester Cities lie within its boundaries.

It has Bristol, Clifton (later Barton Regis), Chipping Sodbury, Thornbury, Dursley, Westbury-on-Seven, Newent, Gloucester, Wheatenhurst, Stroud, Tetbury, Cirencester, Northleach, Stow-on-the-Wold, Winchcombe, Cheltenham and Tewkesbury RDs/PLUs.

It falls within the Oxford Assize Circuit.

The Gloucestershire Family History Society and the Bristol and Avon Family History Society publish quarterly journals. The Gloucestershire society meets at Gloucester, Cirencester and Lydney and the Bristol and Avon Society meets at Bristol, Bath and Yate.

Record Offices: the Gloucestershire CRO and the Cathedral Library are in Gloucester, the Bristol Archives office is in Bristol and the Gloucestershire and Cheltenham District Library is in

Cheltenham. There is a Family History Centre in Bristol and others at Cheltenham, Colesford and Yate.

Pre 1858 Wills are at the CRO. Before 1541, Gloucestershire comprised the archdeaconries of Worcester and Hereford, so a few early wills can be found proved in Consistory Courts of those dioceses. Bristol before 1542 was in the Diocese of Worcester, from 1542–1836 in that of Bristol and from 1836–1897 in the Diocese of Gloucester and Bristol, so that many wills can be found at the Bristol Archives Office. Wills could also be proved at the Prerogative Court of Canterbury.

The Bristol Record Society has published much local material since 1930. The Bristol and Gloucestershire Archaeological Society started a Records Branch in 1952. Heralds' Visitation Pedigrees have been printed for 1569, 1582, 1623 and 1682.

Bristol Archives Office publishes *Guide to the Bristol Archives Office* and *Information leaflet: sources for the family historian*. Gloucestershire Record Office publishes *Gloucestershire family history*. See also *Handlist of the contents of the Gloucestershire Record Office* (1990), *National Index of Parish Registers*, vol. 5 (1966) and *Gloucestershire and Bristol: a genealogical bibliography*, by S. Raymond (FFHS, 1992).

Goad   A land measure of five and a half yards. Another term for a rod, pole or perch.

Godparents   The practice of giving a child three godparents (two of its own sex and one of the other) dates back to pre-Reformation times and was confirmed by the restoration of Anglican rites in 1661. In medieval England a spiritual relationship, or affinity, was held to exist between godparents on the one hand and godchildren and their parents on the other, so that marriage between them was forbidden. Godparents are almost certainly the second most powerful influence in the choice of a child's Christian name, which may be one reason why, in the sixteenth century, more than one child of a family is often found bearing the same name, though both were living. Their names are rarely recorded in Anglican registers except in the reign of Queen Mary.

Goodman   The male counterpart of Goodwife. In the sixteenth and seventeenth centuries, husbandmen and those of similar status were styled, for example, Goodman Smith, and addressed as 'Goodman'.
See also CLASS, SOCIAL.

Goodwife   The female equivalent of Goodman. A woman below the status of those normally called 'Mrs', for example the wife of a husband.

Goons *see* **One-Name Studies**

Gore   A triangular piece of arable land.

Gossip   (i) A godparent (a corruption of 'Goodsib').
(ii) A friend.
(iii) A disseminator of personal news, or a rumour-monger.
(iv) The talk of a gossip — rumour.

Graduates *see* **Alumni**

Grange   (i) A centre of land cultivation belonging, until the Dissolution, to a monastery, but too far distant from it to be worked by the monks.
(ii) Later, a barn.

Grant *see* **Chancery**

Gravestones *see* **Memorial Inscriptions**

Great Britain   The term Great Britain only applies to England, Scotland and Wales as opposed to the term United Kingdom which includes Northern Ireland.

Green-sickness   Anaemia

Greenwich Hospital   Established in 1694 as a Royal Navy Hospital for sick seamen and marines, it housed in-pensioners until 1869.

Gressom (Gersum)   The fine paid to a feudal superior upon entry into a holding.

Gretna Green Marriage *see* **Border Marriages**

Group, Archive *see* **Class, Archive**

Guardians of the Poor   In 1834 the care of the poor was transferred from the parish to the Boards of Guardians newly constituted by the merging of parishes (for Poor Law purposes) into 585 Unions. Each Union was under the control of its own Board, consisting of parish representatives elected by the major ratepayers. The outrelief formerly given to the poor was restricted to cases of most serious need; for others, a spell in the Union's workhouse was substituted. Any previously existing workhouses in the area were disposed of. Workhouse inmates were segregated into seven groups, according to age and sex.

The records of the Unions include the following: *Minutes* of the Meetings of Guardians; *Rate Books* of the Overseers of the Poor of the parishes, who still had the Poor Rate to collect; the *Account Book of Workhouse Expenditure*; the Relieving Officers' *Accounts of Out-Relief*; the *Reports of Medical Officers* and *Reports of Undertakers*. Some Boards arranged for the emigration of their younger paupers. These records are at county or borough record offices. For the whereabouts of the records see the four volumes of *Poor Law Union Records* by J.S.W. Gibson, Colin Rogers, Frederic Youngs, Jr and Cliff Webb. FFHS (1993), *An Introduction to Poor Law Documents Before 1834*, by Anne Cole FFHS (1994).

Guide Books The publication of local guide books increased steadily from the middle of the eighteenth century, and by the end of that century some writers were specialising in that type of work, particularly for those resorts favoured by the gentry. In the nineteenth century, publishers followed suit by issuing uniform series of guide books, for example those of Black, Muirhead and Nelson. These supply useful information and background material for the family historian.

Guild, Craft In most of the older English towns, the master craftsmen were organised in craft guilds — associations of bakers, carpenters, mercers, shoemakers and others, whose origins date from the Middle Ages. The aims of such fellowships were to protect their members' interests, maintain prices, and exclude competition from non-members. The surviving records, to be found mainly in city record offices, are of the sixteenth to eighteenth centuries and consist of the following: *Minutes* of the meetings of the craft elders; *Ordinances*, which were the regulations laid down from time to time; *Accounts*, though it is seldom that all these are extant. For genealogists, the Accounts are the most useful, as the receipts include sums paid for admissions of apprentices and freemen (the names of masters are often mentioned), and amounts received for funeral obsequies at the burial of members deceased. They also supply, as do the Minutes and Ordinances, a wealth of background material about contemporary urban life.

Guild, Merchant A body of merchants whose members were drawn from a variety of occupations, authorised to regulate trade in their town. Their royal charter usually empowered them to hold their own courts, exempted them from the obligation to plead outside the borough, and acquitted them of toll on their goods when they traded elsewhere. Where merchant guilds existed, their records will be in the appropriate town archives.

Guildhall Library Located in Aldermanbury, London EC2P 2EJ, this library is one of the richest in genealogical material in the country, and comprises three sections: Printed Books, Prints and Maps, Manuscripts. The collections in the latter section should not, however, be confused with the archives of the Corporation of the City of London, which are also housed at the Guildhall — not in the Library, but in the Records Office.

Printed Books During the Second World War, much of the Library's storage facilities, and up to 25,000 volumes, were destroyed by bombing. Now, however, in the new extension of the Guildhall the genealogist is able to enjoy comfort and service and a wide range of works of interest to him, including Phillimore's printed marriage registers and some exceptional collections of local directories, poll books and local histories. Also available are professional directories, school and university registers, the publications of the Historical MSS Commission and the Public Record Office, and many works of the record-publishing societies, including the Harleian Society's *Heralds' Visitations*.

Prints and Maps This department holds illustrations of sites in the City of London and its vicinity, maps of London and ephemera, including playbills.

Manuscript Collections This department includes a large number of city parochial records, such as vestry minutes, churchwardens' accounts, rate books and parish registers. Deposits from the City Companies are their apprenticeship books, freemen's books, minute books, ordinances and charters. The ward rate books are there, back to 1771, plus many earlier ones in separate collections. Also available is M.A. Jewer's *Guide to the Monumental Inscriptions of the City Churches*.

The Guildhall Library also has typed transcripts of a number of useful records, including many parish registers of London and elsewhere; Boyd's *Marriage Index* and *Index of Apprentices*; the *1695 Inhabitants of the City* by M.P.E. Jones, and

17-Century London Inhabitants by the Reverend T.C. Dale. There are also CMB (Christenings, Marriages, Burials) registers of British congregations in Europe and overseas, including marriage registers of chaplains licensed by the Bishops of London, 1816–1924.

The Library also has the International Genealogical Index for the whole country.

A booklet, *Guide to Genealogical Sources in Guildhall Library*, has been published by the Corporation of London.

Guild of One-Name Studies *see* One-Name Studies

H

Hair Powder   An Act of 1795 required all persons, male and female, using hair powder to buy a permit. Registers of these permits sometimes survive in county record offices, usually giving the address of the purchaser. Such permits would be obtained by 'persons of quality' for themselves and their menservants.

Half-baptized   A colloquial term meaning 'christened privately', i.e. not in church. The clergy were, and still are, instructed to warn parents 'that without . . . great cause and necessity they procure not their children to be baptized at home in their houses. But when need shall compel them to do so, then . . . ' a very brief form of private baptism was laid down. The necessity was the weak state of a baby which might cause it to die before it could safely be taken to church, in which case the parson was hurriedly sent for and would come to the house. 'Let them [the parents] not doubt but that the child so baptized is lawfully and sufficiently baptized and ought not to be baptized again.' However, if the child unexpectedly regained health it was required then to be 'received into the Church' at a church ceremony in the presence of its godparents and congregation.

Occasionally both ceremonies were entered in the register as baptisms. It seems likely, however, that private baptisms were one cause of the baptismal registers being the worst kept. In cases of extreme urgency the midwife used to perform the baptism.

Halfpenny   A coin dating, like the penny, from Anglo-Saxon times. When sums of money are recorded in sixteenth- and seventeenth-century documents, using the symbols £-s-d (pounds, shillings, pence), a halfpenny may be shown as '½' or as 'ob' (the abbreviation for *obolus* or *obulus*, the Latin term for the coin).

Hall   Until the late seventeenth century, 'hall' meant the main living-room of a house. Often part of its ceiling would be the roof of the building. A fireplace and chimney might be in the middle of the hall, the space behind them being for cooking; and above the kitchen-space would be the bedchamber or chambers, with stairs leading up to them. A house built in this way is now known as a hall-house. Any small private living-room leading off the hall was called a parlour. In the inventory of a yeoman's house of 1596, the contents of his hall were listed as: 1 table, 3 chairs, 7 stools, 1 bench, 1 long saddle (settle), 2 pewter candlesticks, 4 brass ditto, 18 platters, 3 salts, 7 kettles, 8 pans, 12 pothooks, irons, gallowtree (on which to hang a cauldron) and tongs.

Hallmoot   Another name for a manor court.

Hamlet   A small group of houses, separate from the main village of a parish but nevertheless part of the parish. A hamlet did not rank as a township, and so had no constable of its own.

Hampshire   Formerly called the county of Southampton. Until 1974 it included the Isle of Wight, now a separate county. The Bournemouth area is now in Dorset. It falls within the diocese of Winchester and the Province of Canterbury. The registers of most of the 307 ancient parishes are in the appropriate record office. The SOG has transcripts of about 200. Pallot's Marriage Index covers 119, from 1790–1812. The Isle of Wight Record Office holds an index to baptisms, marriages and burials for all the island's parish and non-parochial registers. The Bishops' Transcripts from 1780 are at the CRO as are the Marriage Licence records on which indexes have been published.

The hundreds of Arlesford and Alton Towns, Alton, Bishop's Sutton, Selborne, Andover, Barton Stacey, Pastrow, Wherwell, Thorngate, Basingstoke, Bermondspit, Holdshott, Bishop's Waltham, Hambledon, Meon-Stoke, Alverstoke and Gosport Liberties, Bosmere, Fareham, Havant Liberty, Portsdown, Titchfield, Chuteley, Evingar, Kingsclere, Overton, Pastrow, Christchurch, Lymington Borough, New

Forest, Bentley Liberty, Crondall, Holdshott, Odiham and Odiham Town, East Meon, Finch-Dean, Breamore Liberty Christchurch and Christchurch Borough, Fordingbridge, Ringwood, Westover Liberty, King's Sombourne, Redbridge, Romsey Town, Thorngate, Beaulieu and Dibden Liberties, Mainsbridge, Bountisborough, Buddlesgate, Fawley, Mitcheldever, Mainsborough, Soke, East and West, Liberty, Isle of Wight Division, East and West Medina Liberties, Winchester Soke and City, Soke East and West Liberties, Andover and Portsmouth Boroughs and Southampton Town and County of Southampton lie within its boundaries.

It has Havant, Portsea Island, Alverstoke, Fareham, Isle of Wight, Lymington, Christchurch, Ringwood, Fordingbridge, New Forest, Southampton, South Stoneham, Romsey, Stockbridge, Winchester, Droxford, Catherington, Petersfield, Alresford, Alton, Hartley Wintney, Basingstoke, Whitchurch, Andover and Kingsclere RDs/PLUs.

It falls within the Western Assize Circuit.

The Hampshire Genealogical Society publishes the Hampshire Family Historian quarterly and meets at Alton, Andover, Barton-on-Sea, Basingstoke, Fair Oak, Fareham, Gosport, Brockenhurst, Aldershot, Portsmouth, Ringwood, Southampton and Winchester. Isle of Wight Family History Society publishes a quarterly journal.

There are record offices at Winchester, the Isle of Wight, Southampton, Portsmouth and at Winchester Cathedral Library. There are Family History Centres at Newport, Isle of Wight, and Portsmouth.

Pre 1858 Wills were proved in the Consistory and Archdeaconry Courts of Winchester and numerous Peculiar Courts and can be found at the CRO in Winchester. Wills could also be proved at the Prerogative Court of Canterbury.

The Hampshire Record Society and the Southampton Record Society have published local material since 1889 and 1905 respectively. The Hampshire Genealogical Society has published *A Guide to Genealogical Sources for Hampshire* and the Heralds' Visitation Pedigrees have been printed for 1530, 1575, 1622, 1634 and 1686.

Hampshire Record Office publishes *Sources for genealogy*, Portsmouth City Records Office publishes *Tracing your ancestors* and Southampton City Record Office publishes *Guide to official records*. See also *Parish Registers of Hampshire and the Isle of Wight* by A. McGowan and *Resources for family historians in the New Forest area*, by J. Collins (1991).

Hamsoken The offence of assaulting a man in his own dwelling.

Hanaper The department of Chancery to which fees were paid for the sealing and enrolment of charters.

Handwriting In Anglo-Saxon times, Latin documents were written in 'Caroline Minuscule', which derived its name from Charlemagne, in whose reign it appeared. Vernacular documents were written in a native script. After the Conquest most records were written in Latin, and many words were written in abbreviated form in conjunction with a system of explanatory signs above or below the line. In writing English, the same abbreviations and signs were used, as far as possible. The most common types of handwriting used from the twelfth to the sixteenth century are called Court Hands, or, less usually, Charter Hands. They were a cursive development of miniscule used in the law courts of Chancery, Exchequer, King's Bench and Common Pleas, and in each court the script had its own characteristics. However, the term Court Hand is used to cover the basic handwriting in which all records of this period were written.

There was another development from Caroline Miniscule, called Book Hand. It was not cursive and was reserved for the copying of liturgical manuscripts and literary works.

By the late fifteenth century, although abbreviation continued, most of the associated signs had degenerated into meaningless flourishes. However, they were not entirely discarded even after the reformation of handwriting in the mid sixteenth century.

This reformation took place partly owing to the more general use of paper, and partly to the secularisation of literacy. From 1570 onward, writing-masters published copybooks. These appeared in two scripts: Secretary Hand, which was based on Court Hand, and Italic or Italian Hand, which was an import from Italy. Not unnaturally — the less innovatory Secretary Hand proved the more popular, and it continued in use until late in the seventeenth century. Punctuation was little used until the eighteenth century.

From 1650 to 1660 Latin was abolished as the language of legal documents, but it was restored with the Restoration of the monarchy.

In the late seventeenth century, the Italic Hand was being more widely taught in schools, and by 1670 its use predominated. In this hand all abbreviations disappeared except superior letters (e.g. 12th), and the full stop (e.g. Nov.), which

A general Alphabet of the Old Law Hands.

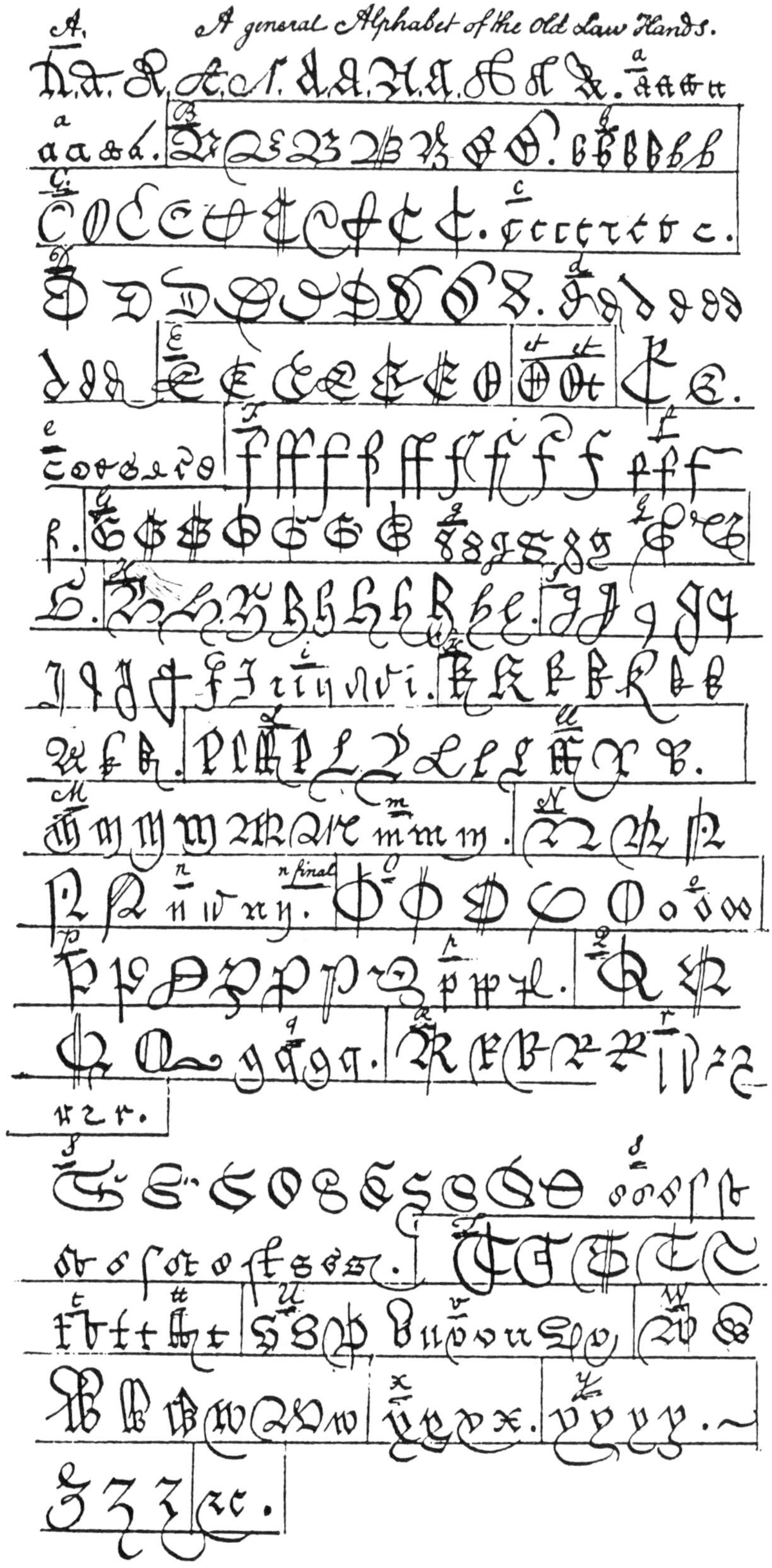

LEFT The Court Hand alphabet, from A. Wright's *Court Hand Restored*, based mainly on sixteenth- and seventeenth-century legal and chancery examples.

---

was introduced in 1703. In fact, Italic Hand is substantially the same as the one we use today. Secretary Hand is discussed under its own heading. Anyone familiar with it will have little difficulty in reading English in Court Hand.

For further study, see *Examples of Handwriting, 1550–1650*, by W.S.B. Buck and *The Handwriting of English Documents*, by L.C. Hector.

See also SECRETARY HAND.

Hardwicke's Marriage Act *see* **Lord Hardwicke**

Harkye The harvest supper. It derives from the first words, 'Hark ye', of the parson's announcement in church of the official end of the harvest. Also used in the form 'Harkey'.

Harleian Society A record-publishing society founded in 1869. It is best known for its numerous volumes of pedigrees of Heralds' Visitations of the English counties in the sixteenth and seventeenth centuries, but it has also published a great many parish registers, mostly of London, and six volumes of Musgrave's *Obituary prior to 1800*, culled from the *Scots Magazine*, the *European Magazine* and the annual and historical registers.

The address of the Honorary Secretary is the College of Arms, Queen Victoria St, London EC4V 4BT.

Hastings and Rother Family History Society *see* **Sussex**

Hatchment The word is derived from the heraldic term, Achievement. It denotes a display of the arms and other heraldic insignia of a person on the occasion of his or her death. Originally this consisted of a man's actual helmet, shield and other accoutrements, but later it was confined to a pictorial representation of the achievement on a lozenge-shaped canvas, or wooden board. The custom was to hang the hatchment on the housefront of the deceased for a period of mourning, which might be as long as a year, and then transfer it to the interior of the parish church. Sometimes two were made, one for the housefront and the other for the church. The custom, which may have been imported from the Netherlands, was in vogue from the early

seventeenth century to the mid nineteenth, and had not entirely died out in the 1920s. Many hatchments that used to hang in churches have now disappeared, owing to decay and church restorations.

The arms of an unmarried or widowed person were painted against a black background to denote mourning, but those of a married couple (i.e. with the arms of the husband 'impaling' those of his wife, or with his wife's arms on an escutcheon of pretence) had a particoloured background to indicate which party had died. If it was the husband who had died, the background behind the dexter side of the shield would be black; if the wife had died, the black would be on the sinister side. In each case the other side of the background would be white. (Dexter and sinister are the right and left sides of a shield respectively, as regarded by a person holding the shield from behind.)

When a hatchment was needed it was wanted at once, and heraldic artists often painted the arms of the local gentry on hatchments during their lifetime, so that when death came they had only to fill in the background.

For further reading, see the series *Hatchments in Britain*, edited by Peter Summers FSA.

Haybote The manorial right of tenants to cut wood for fences.

Hayward An official of the manor responsible for the maintenance of hedges and enclosures.

Headborough Originally the head of a tithing or frankpledge, but later the constable or deputy constable, according to the usage of the area, manor or parish.

Headland The space left at the end of a selion for the plough to turn on.

Health and Social Security, Department of This government department will forward letters to the last address in their records of any person sufficiently identified by their full name, any known address, date of birth or approximate age, and last known marital status. Enquiries should be addressed to Special Section A Records Branch, Room 101B, Department of Health and Social Security, Longbenton, Newcastle-upon-Tyne NE98 1YX. The service offers the best method of tracing relatives with whom one has lost contact but they do not forward letters regarding genealogy.

See also MISSING PERSONS.

were every Stranger Member of the vestry doe indeavour to obs[erve]

[...] and disorders of or in the fish and to present it at a publike mee[ting]
[...]dy

[...]ll those orders be entred in a booke and that every member of the[...]
[...]ribe his name there unto /

Cooper

	Will: Daniel	Johnsons
	Maud Vavasour	Robert Clarke
	Geo. Pearson	John Clarke
	Humfry Chapman	wm. Wadsworth
		Henry Daulton
Wil Hoskins		Robert Pearson
John Mash		Harry Amy
[...]am wouldham		Erasmus Swallin[g]
[...]tes [...]		Richard [...]
		will: Hiccok[s]
[...]illmsworth		John Taslin[g]
[...]am [...]		
[...]		
Burlace [...]		
Burton [...]		
[...] [...]tter		Geo. Heggett
[...]go [...]		wm. Longley
[...]des Carter		Thomas [...]
[...] [...]		Samuel [...]
		Charles Crayley

LEFT Ancestral autographs. In 1654, the rector and vestry men of St Olave's Southwark signed their vestry book. Only one man, George Kettle, made his mark.

Hearth Tax

Hearth Tax The first Act imposing 'Hearth Money' came into force on 19 May, 1662, and the first collection was made at the following Michaelmas. It was managed by county and county borough authorities, and only taxable hearths were listed. The tax was levied upon all houses 'which are not worth in yearly value below Twenty Shillings and are not inhabited by Almsmen', and was two shillings per annum for each hearth or stove, collected in half-yearly instalments at Michaelmas and Lady Day. Persons exempted were: those who paid neither Church nor Poor Rate; those inhabiting a house worth less than £1 per year, if they did not have any other property exceeding that value, nor an annual income of more than £10; charitable institutions, e.g. hospitals, almshouses and free schools; and industrial hearths, except for bakers' ovens and smiths' forges. The tax was payable by the occupier, not the landlord, and was assessed on the occupier's ability to pay. Attempted evasion of payment was punished by a prison sentence of up to one month.

In 1663 The *First Revising Act* of July laid down that from Michaelmas *all* hearths were to be included in the returns, including those that were exempt from the tax.

In 1664 the Ladyday assessment contains more non-chargeable hearths than those of other dates and years. By the *Second Revising Act*, of May all who had more than two chimneys had to pay the tax. Landlords with poor tenants had to pay their tax for them. If a stopped-up chimney was discovered, it was charged double. From Michaelmas 1664 until Michaelmas 1665 the collection was managed by Receivers appointed by the Treasury.

In 1666 the collection of the Lady Day assessment was made by sub-farmers acting as Receivers. From Michaelmas the tax was farmed on contract. *See also* FARMER.

1669 The Treasury Receivers took over again. Most Receivers managed two or three counties.

1674–84 The collection was farmed out again.

1684–89 Collection was managed by a Commission appointed by the Treasury.

1689 The tax was abolished by William III as 'a great oppression to the poorer sort', and also because it allowed every man's house to be entered and searched by persons unknown. Also, the tax had never raised as much revenue as had been estimated. The last collection was for Lady Day of 1689.

The Hearth Tax Records consist of: the original *Assessments*, of which very few survive; the *Payment Accounts* from the collection areas; the *Exchequer Duplicates* of the assessments, more complete and legible than the originals and the most useful source; the *Schedules of Arrears; Exemption Certificates and Miscellaneous Others*.

Some county record offices, including Devon, Kent, Essex, Lancashire, Lincolnshire (Kesteven and Lincoln only), Middlesex, Warwickshire and Westmorland, have Class 1 (Assessments), and some of the other Classes. Classes 2–6 are among the Exchequer Records at the Public Record Office, Chancery Lane, London. The payment accounts are under reference E 360 but do not contain names. The other records are under reference E 179. During the farmed periods of 1666–9 and 1674–84, and the Commission of 1684–9, no lists of names were returned to the government, so Hearth Tax lists in the PRO exist only for Michaelmas 1662 to Lady Day 1666 and Michaelmas 1669 to Lady Day 1674. Of these, the one for Lady Day 1664, is considered the fullest. The lists provide a useful location record for the whereabouts of families within a county during the region of Charles 11. Printed lists are available for Bedfordshire, Cambridgeshire, Cheshire, Dorset, Essex, Isle of Wight, Norfolk, Nottinghamshire, Oxfordshire, Shropshire, Somerset, Staffordshire, Suffolk, Surrey and Warwickshire.

Finding Aid: *The Hearth Tax, Other Later Stuart Tax Lists and The Association Oath Rolls* by Jeremy Gibson, FFHS (1990).

Heir A person who, on the death of a relative, was entitled to take over his freehold or copyhold land. Under the Common Law, the eldest son born in wedlock was the heir of his father. In the case of a copyhold, the inheritor was known as the 'customary heir', because he was so in accordance with the custom of the manor. In certain parts of southern England, different customs prevailed (*see* BOROUGH ENGLISH; GAVELKIND). If there were no sons, all the daughters were co-heirs.

Heirloom This term originally meant a chattel that had descended in a family linked to real estate but is now more popularly applied to any piece of personal property (usually of intrinsic or artistic value) that has been handed down through several generations. In some quarters, even an old photograph is now spoken of as an heirloom.

Heling   The coverlet of a bed, often mentioned in probate inventories.

Heraldic and Genealogical Studies, Institute of *see* Institute of Heraldic and Genealogical Studies

Heraldry   The science of recording genealogies and emblazoning coats of arms. One essential principle of heraldry is its hereditary character, though in its very earliest days the arms of sons often differed materially from those of their fathers. However, from the reign of Richard I onward, the bearing of arms became more frequent; they appeared on the seals of private families, and persisted unchanged in the same families from father to son. Arms are said to have been first used for purposes of identification on the shields and banners of knights, and, from the reign of Henry III, on surcoats, which gave rise to the term 'coat of arms'. The evidence of their use survives on rolls of arms and on seals showing either shields or fully armoured men.

The principles of blazonry require a volume to themselves. We may, however, comment on the genealogical aspects of heraldry. These are bound up with the hereditary character of arms, which should render their use a valuable clue in the tracing of descents of gentry families. Unfortunately it must be recognised that mistaken or unauthorised use of arms, common at all periods from the fifteenth century onward, is all too often a cause of misdirected genealogical research. Misuse often arises from the erroneous idea that all people of the same surname, living in the same district, must be related. Another, more recent cause of misuse is to be found in the activities of firms selling representations of arms by employing the phrase 'arms associated with your surname.'

Arms for subjects of the Crown in England and Wales or of English or Welsh descent, are obtainable solely by grant from the College of Arms, acting for the Earl Marshal, to an applicant and his heirs male. Scotland and Ireland have their own heraldic authorities. At the time of the grant the applicant registers the pedigree of those of his family known to him from personal experience. If he wishes to register earlier generations, the College will require to check the evidence, for which it will charge an additional fee. Thereafter, descendants of the grantee can register details of themselves for addition to the pedigree. If a genealogical researcher believes himself to be connected with an armigerous family, his best course is to apply to the College for whatever information it has about the family. As a precaution against needless expense, the researcher should first trace his line to some ancestor whom he believes to have used, rightly or wrongly, the arms in question.

Shields of arms themselves may contain genealogical clues. When an armigerous person marries the daughter of an armiger, he can display a shield with his own arms on the dexter half, 'impaling' his wife's arms on the sinister half. (Dexter and sinister relate to the right and left side, respectively, of a shield when held from behind.) If the wife is an heraldic heiress (i.e. if she has no surviving brothers or brothers' heirs) her husband can place her arms on a small shield in the centre of his own; this device is called 'in escutcheon'. For a descendant, an ancestress's arms will only appear on this shield if she was such an heiress, or became 'an heiress in her issue' owing to the subsequent extinction of her father's male line, in which case her male-line descendants are entitled to quarter her arms on the shield with their own. If he has several heiresses in his male line, or if the arms of any of them were already quartered with those of ancestresses in their (female) lines, he may well have more than four quarters to deal with. In such cases the ancestresses' arms are arranged in rows after his own, with the most recently acquired one first, followed by any quarterings it had, and then by the next most recent, with its quarterings if any, and so on.

Officially, arms should, where the rule is applicable, bear marks of 'cadency' to show whether the bearer is the eldest, second, third or fourth son of his father, but this rule is commonly ignored.

The descents of many armigerous families are to be found in the *Heralds' Visitation* volumes published by the Harleian Society, and in the many editions of Burke's two works, the *Peerage, Baronetage and Knightage* and the *Landed Gentry*; but the information shown there should be treated as secondary evidence that requires checking.

The Heraldry Society, founded under another name in 1947, has as its aims and objects to increase and extend interest in and knowledge of heraldry, armory, chivalry, genealogy and allied subjects. Its President is the Earl Marshal of England, and its Vice-Presidents and Council

include a number of Kings of Arms, Heralds and Pursuivants. Membership is open to all. Meetings are held in London throughout the winter, and often elsewhere. There are also classes in heraldic art. The Society publishes a newsletter, *The Heraldry Gazette*, and a quarterly magazine, *The Coat of Arms*. The office of the Secretary is at 44/45 Museum Street, London WC1A ILY.
See also ARMS, COAT OF; ARMS, COLLEGE OF.

For further reading: *A New Dictionary of Heraldry*, edited by Stephen Friar and *The Oxford Guide to Heraldry* by Thomas Woodcock and John Martin Robinson.

Heralds' Visitations *see* Arms, Coat of

Herd Used of a person, this meant a herdsman or shepherd.

Hereditament Property which may be inherited is termed an hereditament. If someone died intestate it was that property to which his heir was entitled.

Herefordshire The county is now joined to Worcestershire under their joint names. It falls within the diocese of Hereford and the Province of Canterbury. The registers of most of the ancient parishes have been deposited at the CRO and there are a few transcripts at the SOG library. The Bishops' Transcripts are also at the CRO. The Marriage Licence records are mainly at the CRO but those for parishes in the Archdeaconry of Brecon and the Diocese of St David's are at the National Library of Wales in Aberystwyth.

The Hundreds of Broxash, Ewyas-Lacey, Greytree, Grimsworth, Huntingdon, Radlow, Stretford, Webtree, Wigmore, Wolphy, Wormelow Upper and Lower Division and Hereford City lie within its boundaries.

It has Ledbury, Ross, Hereford, Weobley, Bromyard, Leominster and Kington RDs/PLUs. It falls within the Oxford Assize Circuit.

The Herefordshire Family History Society publishes a quarterly journal and meets at Hereford.

Record Repositories; the County of Hereford and Worcester Record Office is at Hereford as are Hereford Cathedral Library and Hereford City Library.

Pre 1858 Wills are at the CRO and were proved at the following courts: Episcopal Consistory Court of Hereford, Consistory Court of the Dean of Hereford Peculiar, the Court of the Chancellor of Little Hereford, and the Peculiar Prebendary Courts of Upper Bullinghope and Moreton Magna.

Hereford and Worcester County Record Office publishes *The Parish Registers of Herefordshire*. See also *National Index of Parish Registers*, vol. 5 (1966). Heralds' Visitation Pedigrees have been published for 1567, 1643 and 1683.

Heriot A fine payable by a villein, and later a copyholder, to his lord on inheriting copyhold land. Some freeholders, too, were liable to pay heriots. It was an early form of estate duty. In practice, it might take the form of the best beast of the new tenant.

Hertfordshire The county falls within the province of Canterbury and is divided between the dioceses of London and Lincoln. The Registers of its ancient parishes are mostly at the CRO and many transcripts of them are held by the SOG library. There is, at the CRO, the Allen Index of Marriages which is virtually complete for the county.

The Hundreds of Braughin, Broadwater, Cashio (or the liberty of St Albans), Dacorum, Edwinstree, Hertford, Hitchin and Pirton and Odsey, and the boroughs of Hertford and St Albans lie within its boundaries.

It has Ware, Bishops Stortford, Royston, Hitchin, Hertford, Hatfield, St Albans, Watford, Hemel Hempstead and Berkhamsted RDs/PLUs. It falls within the Home Assize circuit.

The local FHS are Hertfordshire Family and Population History Society who publish *Hertfordshire People* three times a year and who have branches at Watford and Hitchin, Digswell, Hoddesdon and St Albans, and Royston and District FHS who also publish their journal three times a year.

There is a CRO in Hertford and a Family History Centre in Hitchin.

Wills before 1858 were proved at the Archdeaconry Court of St Albans and the Archdeaconry Court of Huntingdon (Herts. Division) both of whose records are at the CRO; the Archdeaconry Court of Huntingdon (Hunts. Division) at Huntingdon CRO; the Archdeaconry Court of Middlesex (Essex and Herts) at the Essex CRO; the Peculiar Court of the Dean and Chapter of St Paul's at St Paul's Cathedral Library, London. Wills could also be proved in the Consistory Court of Lincoln, the Consistory and Commissary Courts (Essex and Herts) of London and the Prerogative Court of Canterbury.

Marriage Licence records can be found at the CRO for the Archdeaconries of St Albans and Huntingdon (Herts. Div.). The Essex CRO has those of the Archdeaconry of Middlesex in Essex and Hertfordshire, as well as those for the

Bishop of London's Consistory Court, which had jurisdiction in east Hertfordshire until 1730, and the same bishop's Commissary Court in Essex and Hertfordshire. The marriage licences of the Archdeaconry of Huntingdon (Huntingdon Division) are at the Huntingdon Record Office. The SOG has indexes to most surviving licences for 1584–1600/1.

Heralds' Visitations have been printed for 1572 and 1634. The Hertfordshire Record Society has published annual volumes since 1985.

Hertfordshire Record Office publishes *Genealogical sources*. See also *Guide to the Hertfordshire Record Office: Part 1: Quarter sessions and other records in the custody of the officials of the county* (1961).

Heusire

Heusire   A customary payment made by the tenant of a manor to his overlord for the right to hold a manorial court.

Hide

Hide   Originally land considered sufficient for the maintenance of one family, and therefore roughly what one eight-ox ploughteam could keep in cultivation. It would measure anything between 90 and 120 acres according to the type of soil and the lie of the land. Later, a tax-assessment unit.
See also CARUCATE; PLOUGH TEAM; VIRGATE.

High Commission, Court of

High Commission, Court of   The highest ecclesiastical court in England. At the Reformation, Thomas Cromwell appointed in 1535 a council of ecclesiastics, ministers of state and lawyers, to deal with cases of heresy, but such appointments were of a temporary nature until, in 1565, the amount of work gave the commissions a permanent tenure, and they became known five years later as the High Commission.

The penalties imposed by the court were mainly the secular ones of fine and imprisonment. The court was resented by the increasingly influential Puritans because of its enforcement of the ritual and vestments of the Anglican rites. Also, defendants could be examined on an oath imposed upon them by the judge and so be compelled to convict themselves. The court was also disliked by the Common Law judges, and those judges appointed to the Commission soon ceased to attend. This was because of its mixed ecclesiastical and temporal character, and the infliction of non-ecclesiastical penalties. The opposition became political with the Puritans powerful in Parliament, and the court was abolished in 1641. It was restored by James II in 1686, but three years later was finally ended under William and Mary by the Bill of Rights.

Of the Commission's records that have survived, the majority are at the Public Record Office, Chancery Lane, London, in group SP, and the rest are held at the Borthwick Institute of Historical Research, a department of the University of York.

High Court of Delegates *see* Delegates

Highways, Surveyor of

Highways, Surveyor of   The parish official responsible for the upkeep of the roads. The *Highways Act* of 1555 laid down that the main roads of each parish should be maintained by the unpaid labour of every householder, cottager and labourer of the parish, able to labour and being no hired servant, for four days per year (six days, after an Act of 1563).

The Act created the honorary parochial office of Surveyor of the Highways, two in each parish, to supervise the work within the parish bounds. They were selected by the Justices of the Peace from a short-list drawn up by the Vestry. They were expected to keep accounts and submit them to the Justices on the completion of their year of office, but very few accounts survive from before the *Highways Act* of 1691, which, among other improvements, authorised the raising of a Highway Rate. Farmers were often appointed Surveyors, because they had horses, carts and men available. Some Surveyors' accounts are still in the keeping of parish incumbents, but many have been deposited at county record offices. They may mention names in rate-lists and composition-lists, also names of those who were paid for working, and of those who paid because they were unable to perform their duties (defaulters). They also provide background information about parish life. In 1862, the duty of maintaining roads was passed to Highway Boards.

Hilary

Hilary   Hilary is an educational and law term starting approximately January 13th.

Hillingdon Family History Society *see* London and Middlesex

Hiring Fairs

Hiring Fairs   Such fairs were held annually, usually in market towns, and sometimes as part of a general fair. Their purpose was to enable employers to find employees, and vice versa. The latter were mainly domestics, farm labourers and other artisans. They were hired for a year, when the engagement could be either terminated or renewed.

Both masters and servants would be attracted to the fairs from places miles away, and this is one cause of the mobility of families. An employer from fifteen miles east of the market town might well engage a servant from a similar distance to the west of it. If master and man were well suited, and the man found a wife locally, he would settle down and thus accomplish a personal migration of thirty miles for no reason obvious to his twentieth-century descendant. In fact, Census Returns show servants working at considerably greater distances from their homes.

Historical MSS, Royal Commission on
This body was appointed by royal warrant in 1869 with the task of locating, and making accessible to researchers, records in the private ownership of persons, families and institutions. The owners are approached for permission to inspect and edit their records, and then reports on them are published in the form of calendars, lists and edited texts. Well over 200 volumes of these reports have now been published, dealing with the papers of prominent families and institutions, counties and boroughs, Parliament, statesmen, admirals, generals and other important personages. The series is now being replaced by *Guides to sources of British history* — volumes on cabinet ministers, scientists, diplomats, colonial governors and churchmen. A list of *Publications of the Royal Commission on Historical Manuscripts* (1985) is published by HMSO as Sectional List 17.

The Commission also co-operates with record societies in the publication of local historical documents of wide general interest. In 1945, it was given the task of directing the newly instituted NATIONAL REGISTER OF ARCHIVES. In 1958, the *Registers of Manorial Documents* (*see* MANOR) and of *Tithe Documents* (*see* TITHE) were transferred to the Commission from the Public Record Office. Since then it has been given the task of promoting and assisting the preservation of records. The principal officer of the Commission is the Secretary, and its offices are at Quality House, Quality Court, Chancery Lane, London WC2A 1HP.

The Commission published in 1982 *Guide to the location of Collections Described in the Reports and Calendars Series, 1870–1980*, showing the whereabouts of those collections in December, 1981.

Hitched Land
A part of a common field used, in its fallow year, for special crops such as beans, peas and root vegetables. Sometimes the hitched land was part of the waste. Also called Hookland, or Hitchland.

Hocktide
The second Monday and Tuesday after Easter. On Hock Monday the men, and on Hock Tuesday the women, of the parish obstructed the roadway and bound passers-by with ropes until they ransomed themselves by contributing to the church dues and other 'pious uses'. Hence the expression 'in hock' (in pawn).

Hogsleas
Pasture for pigs.

Holograph
A document hand-written by the person who signed it, or in whose name it appears.

Homage
(i) Acknowledgement by a freeholder of his feudal obligations to his overlord. A man often held land of more than one lord, and had to do homage to each of them, with his hands between the lord's, 'touching life and limb and earthly honour in what is honest and profitable, keeping his counsel to the best of his power, saving his faith to God and the king' (*see* FEALTY). But the lord of whom a man held his principal residence was his liege-lord, on whom the tenant could never sit in judgement and whom he must follow in war against everyone but the king. The liege-lord, on his side, was obliged to act as surety for his liegeman whenever necessary.

(ii) The jury of a manor court, sometimes also referred to as 'the twelve men'.

Honour
A large estate held by a single lord, usually consisting of several scattered manors. Subtenants were obliged to attend the Honour Court.

Hookland *see* Hitched Land

Hospital
(i) An institution for the temporary reception and treatment of sick persons. Before 1710 there were very few general hospitals in England, and they were intended for the poor. Although many were built in the nineteenth century, especially lying-in hospitals, the great majority of people continued until the twentieth century to be born and to die at home. London had only two general hospitals in the Middle Ages: St Bartholomew's in West Smithfield, founded in 1102 and refounded in 1547; and St Thomas's in High Street, Southwark, founded in 1213 and refounded by Edward VI. Guy's Hospital was founded by a wealthy bookseller in 1726. St George's Hospital at Hyde Park Corner (now closed) was founded in 1733. The London Hospital, founded to serve the East End was opened in 1840.

The registers of Holborn Lying-in Hospital are in the Public Record Office in class RG 4.

(ii) A permanent retreat for the elderly or infirm. Among these were the Chelsea Hospital, 1690, for. maimed and superannuated soldiers, and Greenwich Hospital for seamen, 1694.

(iii) Early specialised institutions were Bethlehem, or Bedlam, Hospital for lunatics, founded in 1247; St Luke's Hospital for the incurably insane, 1732; and the Foundling Hospital (in the sense of hostel) for abandoned children, 1745.

These hospitals normally keep their own archives, from which details may be obtained on application, not only about patients but also about the surgeons who worked there and the apprentices who trained under them. When a patient died in hospital, his 'last reputed address' is sometimes given.

Housebote The right of a manorial copyholder to take wood for the purpose of house maintenance.

House of Lords Record Office Papers presented to Parliament are kept at the House of Lords Record Office. Amongst these are the PROTESTATION RETURNS. It is advisable to make an appointment before your visit. Because the only way to obtain a divorce before 1857 was by a judicial separation through the ecclesiastical courts or by act of parliament, private divorce acts are mainly found at the House of Lords Record Office.

House-row The system in force in some parishes whereby some parish offices, such as that of constable, went annually by rotation from the occupier of one house to that of the next. Such a system was fair — some offices were unpopular — but often inefficient, since not all householders were equally suitable for the tasks to be performed.

Huddersfield and District Family History Society *see* **Yorkshire**

Hudson's Bay Company One of the great Chartered Companies, it was founded by royal charter in 1671 as 'The Governor and Company of Adventurers of England Trading into Hudson's Bay'. It was granted all the land 'within the entrance of the straits commonly called Hudson's Straits', not already granted or belonging to others, and a monopoly of the trade there, which was almost exclusively in furs. Settlements were established on the rivers of Rupert's Land, and furs were obtained chiefly by means of barter with the Indians. In the early years enormous profits were made, which attracted competition from the French, who were also in the northern territories of America. During the next century, when England and France were at war, this competition developed into military hostilities, and several of the Company's forts were captured by the enemy. However, they were restored on the return of peace and the profitability of the Company was not seriously disturbed.

When France finally ceded her Canadian lands to Britain in 1763, more serious competition arose from the founding, by British settlers, of the North-West Fur Company to exploit the ceded areas. In 1812, the Hudson's Bay Company sold land to Lord Selkirk with the aim of bringing in Scottish settlers to consolidate its rights. This led to open warfare between the companies, which was finally brought to an end by their merger in 1821. By this time the large-scale slaughter of animals and the consequent increase in the volume of trade brought about a slump in the price of furs. In 1869, the Company ceded its lands to the Canadian Government; but it still remained a trading company. Its historical records are in Canada, with microfilm copies at the Public Record Office, Kew. Requests for information should be made to Hudson's Bay Company Archives, Provincial Archives of Manitoba, 200 Vaughan Street, Winnipeg, Manitoba R3C 1T5.

Hue and Cry When a felony was committed, the victim, or a witness, had to raise the alarm by shouting — raising a hue and cry — and all within earshot had to come to his aid in securing the guilty person. However, if the latter succeeded in crossing the parish boundary, the responsibility for his capture passed to the township to which he had fled. Failure to raise the hue, or to report the offence to the tithingman (*see* TITHING), made the person so negligent liable to a fine. Anyone who raised a hue falsely was likewise fined.

Huguenots This name for French Protestants is said by one authority to be a nickname bestowed by a Catholic preacher, from the practice of the Protestants of Tours to assemble by night under the gate of King Hugues. By others, it is thought to be a corruption of the German *eidgenossen* (confederates united by oath), a league of Swiss Protestants. It was already in popular use by 1560, and has since come to cover Walloons and other Protestant refugees from Spanish persecution in the Low Countries.

The first French communities were followers of John Calvin. They increased rapidly after a synod held in 1559, and there followed the series of internal French Wars of Religion which gave rise to some Protestant emigration and culminated, during a period of apparent reconciliation, in the Massacre of St Bartholomew in 1572, which caused many Huguenots to flee to Protestant countries, including England. When Henry of Navarre came to the throne, French Protestants were granted religious and political freedom by the *Edict of Nantes*, 1598. However, the Catholic Church kept up the pressure against the Huguenots and eventually on 18 October, 1685, Louis XIV revoked the *Edict of Nantes* and caused the greatest flood of emigration by Protestants of all classes to England and elsewhere.

When a Huguenot settled in England, he would apply for either Naturalization or Denization, and become a member of one of the numerous Huguenot churches in the country. Except for the large community in Spitalfields, east of London, who retained their French character for some time, the settlers' descendants were soon absorbed into the social life of their new homeland. The earliest Huguenot ecclesiastical register is that of their church in Southampton, dating from 1567. Those of congregations in London and other large towns soon follow.

The researcher into Huguenot ancestry should turn first to the many volumes of *Proceedings, Church Registers, Returns of Aliens*, and other records published by the Huguenot Society since its foundation in 1885. Especially helpful are: vol. 10 (in 4 parts), *Returns of Aliens in London*, 1523–1603; vol. 8, *Denizations and Naturalizations of Aliens in England*, 1509–1603; vols 18, 27 and 35, *Letters of Denization and Acts of Naturalization for Aliens in England*, 1603–1800; and vol. 30, *Oaths of Naturalization* (late seventeenth century).

Many of the French surnames have become anglicized in spelling, or even translated. The registers of baptisms, marriages and burials outside London were deposited with the Registrar General in 1858, but are now at the Public Record Office, Chancery Lane, London. They have been published by the Huguenot Society.

For further research, the library of the French Protestant Church of London, in Soho Square, and the joint library of the French Hospital de la Providence and of the Huguenot Society at University College, London, contain many records, and these are listed in the *Huguenot Society Proceedings*, vols 14, 18 and 13 respectively. The Secretary of the Huguenot Society of London is Mrs Mary Bayliss, Huguenot Library, University College, Gower Street, London WC1E 6BT.

The Secretary of the Huguenot and Walloon Research Association is Mrs J. Tsushima, 'Malmaison', Church Street, Great Bedwyn, Wilts SN8 3PE. They publish a journal twice yearly called the *Huguenot and Walloon Gazette*.

Further reading: *Huguenot Ancestry*, Noel Currer-Briggs & Royston Gambier.

Humberside A county formed in 1974 out of south-east Yorkshire and north Lincolnshire. *See also* LINCOLNSHIRE; YORKSHIRE.

Hundred Until Tudor times, this was an administrative subdivision of a county, probably so named from its having originally contained either a hundred families, a hundred fighting men or a hundred hides. Jurisdiction was supposed to be vested in the county's sheriff, but many hundreds got into private hands. In either case, a bailiff, to whom the profits were sublet, held a Court Baron and Court Leet every few weeks. They dealt with minor offences such as trespass, obstruction of the highway and assizes of bread and ale.

Presentments of these offences were made by a reeve and four men from each township in the hundred. If these representatives failed to appear, their township was amerced. From the thirteenth to the fifteenth century a special court was held after Easter and Michaelmas, called the sheriff's tourn, the main object of which was to check that the system of frankpledge was being observed. Hundred courts, much decayed since Tudor times, lost almost all their functions after the *County Courts Act* of 1867. Of its few remaining duties, that of repairing damage caused by rioters was taken from them in 1886. Surviving records are to be found in county record offices.

Hunt, Hugh *see* **Recovery Rolls** *and* **Roe, Richard**

Huntingdon's Connexion, Countess of
Selina Hastings, Countess of Huntingdon (1707–91) was left a wealthy widow in 1746. Already a member of a Methodist society, she now threw herself into the Calvinist branch of that movement. In 1751 she appointed its leader, George Whitefield, her chaplain. Under his tutelage she poured money into the movement, built chapels at Bath, Brighton, Tunbridge Wells and other resorts of the upper classes, and employed chaplains, all regularly ordained Anglicans, to serve them. In 1756 she founded the Tottenham Court Chapel in London.

At this time Methodism was still a movement within the Church of England, but its followers were much divided and in 1763 a Plymouth preacher was ordained by dissenting clergy and set up an Independent church there (see CON-GREGATIONALISTS). The London chapels, too, were registered as Independent and in 1767 Lady Huntingdon founded a theological college at Trevecca in Breconshire to train young men of Calvinist persuasion for the universities and eventual ordination. Whitefield died in 1770, and in 1779 there came a general break with the established church and the founding of a movement organised nationally on the same lines as the Presbyterians. By this time the Countess's followers had become known as Lady Huntingdon's Connexion. Sixty years after her death they had upwards of one hundred chapels, and their services were still conducted according to the rites of the Church of England. Their registers are deposited at the Public Record Office, Chancery Lane, London, in groups RG 4 and 8.

Huntingdonshire The former county of Huntingdon and Peterborough was absorbed into the new Cambridgeshire in 1974. The county fell within the diocese of Lincoln until 1837 and then came under the Ely diocese both within the Province of Canterbury. Many of the parish registers are at the CRO and the SOG has transcripts of some of them. Marriage Licence records and a marriage index for 1701–1837 are at the CRO and a copy of the index at the library of the SOG. Pallot's Marriage index covers 6 parishes, mostly 1790–1837. The Bishops' Transcripts are at the CRO.

The Hundreds of Hurstingstone, Leightonstone, Norman Cross, Toseland and Huntingdon Borough lie within its boundaries.

It has Huntingdon, St Ives and St Neots RDs/PLUs.

It falls within the Norfolk Assize Circuit to 1876 and then the South Eastern Assize Circuit.

The Huntingdon Family History Society publishes *The Huntsman* twice-yearly and meets at Huntingdon.

The CRO is the Cambridge County Record Office at Huntingdon.

Pre 1856 Wills are found at the CRO and were proved in the following courts: the Commissary Court of the Bishop of Lincoln and the Archdeacon in the Archdeaconry of Huntingdon. The Peculiar Courts of Brampton and Buckden, the Prebendal Courts of Stow Longa and Leighton Bromsgrove and a few at the Consistory Courts of Lincoln or Ely and the Prerogative Court of Canterbury.

Protestation Oath Returns for 1641–2 have been printed in vol. 5 of the *Transactions of the Cambridgeshire and Huntingdonshire Archaeological Society*, pp. 289–368. Huntingdon County Record Office publishes a summary of document and library holdings. See also *National Index of Parish Registers*, vol. 9, Part 1 (1991). Heralds' Visitation Pedigrees have been published for 1613 by the Camden Society, Old Series, vol. 43, 1849.

Husbandman The term may be used in several ways. When it describes an occupation it could apply to a man of any status who was engaged or interested in husbandry (i.e. the cultivation of the land); but it was also used to designate a status, in which sense it usually aplies to a small-holder, who might also have to work on the land of larger owners to maintain himself (i.e. one below the status of a yeoman).

See also CLASS, SOCIAL; YEOMAN.

Hussites The followers of John Huss, precursors of Moravians.

Husting, Court of Derived from a Saxon word meaning 'house of trial', it was the name of courts held in London, Winchester, York and some other cities. In London it was a lay court of the Corporation of the City, and was held annually at the Guildhall before the mayor and aldermen. Its records are at the Corporation of London Record Office, Guildhall, Gresham Street, London EC2P 2EJ. Wills relating to London property could be proved there, and conveyances of real estate could be enrolled for permanent evidence. The Corporation's record office has a name index of vendors and purchasers.

See also LONDON AND MIDDLESEX.

Hutch A chest or cupboard. A term often found in inventories.

I

Illegitimacy *see* **Bastardy**

Immigrants By this term is meant foreigners settling in England since the Norman Conquest. Of these, the largest single community was made up of the French and Walloon Protestants of the seventeenth and late sixteenth centuries, who are dealt with under the separate heading of HUGUENOTS. In the nineteenth century came immigration from Ireland and Eastern Europe and in this century from the West Indies, Africa, India, Pakistan and other parts of the former British Empire.

Those immigrants who could afford to obtain Acts of Naturalization are covered by the records of those Acts in Parliament Rolls at the Public Record Office (PRO), Chancery Lane, London (C 65), and the greater number who obtained Denization are covered by Letters Patent recorded in Patent Rolls (C 66 and 67), followed by Close Rolls (C 54) for the period 1844–73. They are indexed in the printed *Index to Rolls of Parliament, Calendar of Patent Rolls* and *Letters and Papers, Henry VIII* (HMSO). For aliens entering under the Stuart kings, refer to *Calendars to the State Papers* for that period, and also the *Calendar of Treasury Papers, 1557–1728. Chancery: Original Letters Patent of Denizations, 1751–93* (C 97) are indexed in the Chancery class list on the search room shelves; and *Home Office Patents for Denization for 1804–43* (HO 4) are also enrolled on the Patent Rolls, where they were indexed.

Immigrants fleeing from the French Revolution can be found in the *Bouillon Papers* (HO 69), *Unbound Papers* (PC 1), *Foreign Office Miscellanea* (FO 95) and *War Office in Letters* (WO 1). Those who were assisted by the French Refugees Relief Committee are recorded in *Treasury Papers* (T 93). From 1793 onward, the Home Office became responsible for aliens and, from 1844, for the granting of naturalization. For these, there is an *Index to Names: Certificates of Naturalization, 1844–1900* (HMSO), with class references to the original records. For 1836–52, the certificates issued to aliens (HO 2) are arranged under ports of arrival and record arrival date, nationality, last country visited, occupation and signature. For indexes to these, see HO 5, Vols 25–32. There are also passenger lists made by the ships' masters, but these are unindexed and so should be consulted only after the immigrant has been found in the certificate records. For later periods, see the *Index to Denizations, 1801–73*, and *Index to Memorials for Denizations and Naturalization, 1835–44*, available at the PRO. From 1792, aliens had to register their names, addresses and occupations with the Quarter Sessions of their county. The registers will be found at county record offices. A free leaflet No. 70. *Immigrants, Documents in the Public Record Office*, is available at the PRO. *See also* ALIENS; DENIZATION; NATURALISATION.

Imperial War Museum A museum founded to house material relating to the wars of the twentieth century. In addition to extensive collections of objects the museum has a large library which contains manuscript diaries and letters in addition to printed books. It is situated in Lambeth Road, London SE1 6HZ.

Impertinent This expression, often found in Chancery proceedings, means 'irrelevant'. If a defendant's answer was reported for 'impertinence' it meant that it failed to answer the plaintiff's complaint.

Impropriate As a verb, this means to annex an ecclesiastical benefice to a corporation or lay person as their private property. The Great Tithe would be payable to such person, and the care of the parish would be in the hands of a vicar.

As a noun, an impropriate signifies such a benefice.

Inclosure *see* Enclosures

Incumbent The holder of a benefice; for example, the rector or vicar of a parish. In applying to a parson for a parish register search, or for permission to make a search oneself, it is generally advisable to address the envelope to 'The Incumbent', because Crockford's *Clerical Directory* (*see* CLERGY), like all directories, is inevitably partly out of date on the day it is published and the parson may well have left the parish. If the envelope has been addressed to him by name it will be forwarded to his new address and have to be forwarded back to the new incumbent at the original addressee's expense. At best, this causes delay and can even mean that the enquiry never reaches the new parson. A stamped, self-addressed envelope should be enclosed.

Indenture A deed executed between two or more parties and written out in as many copies as there were parties — all on one sheet of parchment or paper. An 'indented' or wavy line was drawn between the copies, sometimes with the word 'Chirograph' written through it, and the sheet was then cut into parts along the line. The copies could later be identified as tallies when brought together. The term is now used of any sealed agreement, and particularly for a contract of apprenticeship.

See also CHIROGRAPH; DEED POLL; FEET OF FINES.

Indented Narrative Pedigree The system of setting out a family descent in indented and numbered paragraphs. This is the system employed in Burke's *Peerage and Landed Gentry*. For showing a number of collateral lines, it is the method most economical of space, but it does not have the merit of instant clarity.

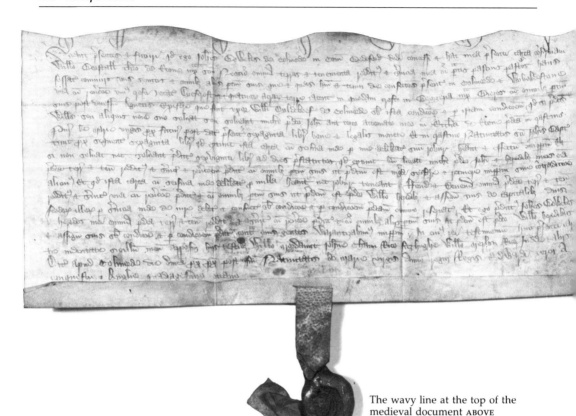

The wavy line at the top of the medieval document ABOVE identifies it as an indenture. *By permission of The British Library MSS Dept.*

Independents *see* Congregationalists

Indentured Servants
When workers were needed for England's new plantations in America many people were persuaded to emigrate by a system of indenture. Their passage to the States was paid provided they agreed to work for a set number of years before branching out on their own. They were also referred to as bonded servants. Further reading: P.W. Coldham *Bonded Passengers to America 1615–1775*.

Index
Many family historians contribute to research by creating indexes, either individually or as part of a group. As yet there is no proper guidance on how this should be done or what basic elements should be included. Much experience has been gained, however, as more and more indexes are created. If there was a standard for each type of record indexed, it would be possible to amalgamate the end results of several indexes and produce a more useful finding aid.

It is important to choose a clearly defined quantity to index that related to the arrangement of the records being worked on. It is also important to use the referencing system in which the documents are kept, rather than devise a new one for indexing purposes. This way a finished product can be intelligible to everyone.

India Office Library and Records
The archives and collections of the East India Company and the India Office, both now defunct, cover the period from 1600 to 1947. They are housed at Orbit House, Blackfriars Road, London SE1 8NG. One of the most popular collections for genealogists are the ecclesiastical returns from 1698–1969 which are copies of registers of baptisms, marriages and burials sent to London for the information of the East India Company and the India Office. The practice was begun by the chaplains of the East India Company's principal settlements and became a regular feature of the British Administration in India. The returns relate mainly to European and Eurasian Christians but do include those of a few

local converts. Apart from India and Burma there are returns for settlements elsewhere such as St Helena, Sumatra, Penang, Macao, Canton, Kuwait and Aden. Other types of records cover Aden, Afghanistan, Ascension Island, Bangladesh, Burma, Central Asia, China, Indonesia, Japan, Pakistan, Persian Gulf States, St Helena and Zanzibar. *See also* EAST INDIA COMPANY.

Infangtheof The right of a manor borough court to judge a thief caught within its area of jurisdiction.

Infant An infant was a child under the age of seven.

Infant Mortality The incidence of death among children of less than one year old. Even as late as 1842 three-hundred and fifty out of every one-thousand babies died before the age of one. There were certain obvious causes, such as deficiencies in, or absence of, plumbing and other aspects of domestic hygiene, the feeding of babies with unsuitable foods, and the lack of pre- and post-natal trained care. But some modern researchers believe that strong parental affection for babies, regarded today as almost instinctive (especially in mothers), is a social phenomenon that has evolved during the last 250 years, at different rates among different classes, and that infant deaths in the past were largely due to what would now be regarded as neglect. Country mothers were often kept busy outdoors for much of the day, leaving their babies unattended: such infants were obviously at considerable risk. And even the practice of stopping a baby's crying by violent shaking survived among European peasant communities into the age of scientific observation. Middle-class people often put their newly born babies out to nurse for two years. The christening of weakly infants as 'creature', and the baptizing of later children with the same names as earlier ones who had predeceased them, are practices quoted as evidence of lack of parental feeling.

In earlier times, the term 'infant' designated a child under eight years of age.

Ing A common meadow in manorial land.

Inghamites A small nonconformist sect founded by Benjamin Ingham (1712–72), whose wife was Lady Margaret Hastings, sister-in-law of Lady Huntingdon (*see* HUNTINGDON'S CONNEXION, COUNTESS OF). Ingham's group was founded in 1754 when he and his followers broke away from the Moravians. A year later they had

a large number of followers, mostly in Yorkshire and Lancashire, and broke away from the Church of England, within which they, like the Moravians, had previously been internal societies. Ingham became influenced by the ideas of the Scotish Sandeman sect, and this caused the break-up of his own group in 1763; some becoming Methodist, where Ingham himself had begun, some Sandemanian, and some Baptist. However, a few societies remained loyal. In 1814 they amalgamated with the Daleites of Scotland, and the church still survives today in Yorkshire, Lancashire and Cumbria. In 1840, eight Inghamite baptismal and burial registers were deposited at the General Record Office, and these are now at the Public Record Office, Chancery Lane, London, in class RG 4.

For further reading, see D. J. Steel, *Sources for Non-conformist Genealogy and Family History*, vol. II of the National Index of Parish Registers, SOG (1973).

Injunction An injunction is an order to terminate a wrong.

Ink The medium in which virtually all of the genealogist's information is made available to him. It used to consist of oak-galls, sulphate of iron, gum-arabic and water, often made up at home from private recipes of varying value. Such ink was liable to turn yellow and fade in the course of time, through decay of the vegetable matter, leaving only rust and peroxide of iron, though it could be restored by 'the careful application of an infusion of galls'. On the other hand, the fading of a manuscript may also be due to the paper on which it was written having been made from inferior rags and with an excess of chlorine in the bleach. Faded writing can be more easily read under ultra-violet light, and lamps of this kind are often available at record repositories. On the introduction of steel nibs in the nineteenth century, the composition of ink had to be changed to eliminate acid constituents.

Inn A house that provided overnight accommodation, as distinct from a tavern or alehouse, though all these would offer beer for sale, drawn by 'tapsters'. The bedroom accommodation in a large inn was looked after by an employee called a 'chamberlain'. Records of inns and innkeepers can be found among Quarter Sessions papers because the keepers had to be licensed by Justices of the Peace and to give recognizances for the proper running of their houses. Title deeds, where extant, will give the names of previous owners. The names of many inns have been changed from time to time, and signs for the King's Head are not always repainted with a portrait of the same king.

Innage Enclosed cultivation of portions of manorial arable land during its fallow year.
See also HITCHED LAND.

Innocent A CHRISOM child.

Inns of Court The Inns of Court are collegiate houses of law societies existing in order to exclude all but their members from being called to the Bar. There are now four, Gray's, Lincoln, Inner and Middle Temple. Earlier inns were taken over by the surviving four: Middle Temple took over New, Gray's Inn took over Staple and Barnards, Lincoln's Inn took over Furnivals and Thavies and the Inner Temple took over Clements, Cliffords and Lyons. Sergeants and Barnards Inns no longer exist.

Inquisition Post Mortem In 1235, Henry III created regional officials called Escheators, who, on the death of any tenant-in-chief in their area holding lands in fee, were to take possession of the deceased's lands and summon juries of free local men in the neighbourhood, to give details, on oath, about the lands and their value, the services by which they were held, the date of the deceased owner's death, and the identity and age of the heir. The escheator then sent his report to the royal Court of Chancery, with a copy to the Exchequer. After 1540, in relevant instances, another copy went to the Court of Wards and Liveries.

If the heir was a minor, the king became his guardian and disposed of him in marriage, meanwhile taking the revenues of his lands. If he was, or when he became, of age, the lands were delivered to him on payment of a relief. This procedure continued to operate until Knight Service, which was its basis, fell into disuse and was finally abolished in 1662.

The documents created by this procedure were as follows:

The *Writ of Diem Clausit Extremum* ('he has closed his last day') from the Court of Chancery to the escheator, instructing him to make the inquisition. Sometimes the escheator acted without a writ.

The *Inquisition Post Mortem*, the escheator's report to the Court.

A *Writ of Mandamus* issued when there was a delay between the death and the first writ, to discover who had been taking the revenues of the lands in the meantime.

A *Writ ad Melius Inquirendum* issued to amend a first report, if thought desirable.

A *Writ Que Plura* issued if it was found that some lands had been omitted from the return.

A *Writ of Devenerunt* issued if the heir died while a minor.

A *Writ De Dote Assignanda* issued when the return showed that a widow could claim dower.

There are separate series of records for the Palatine Counties, as they had their own chanceries.

The action subsequently taken is reported in a *Writ of Livery*, filed with the Close and Fine Rolls at the Public Record Office (PRO).

All these documents are in Latin. The Chancery series is less legible than those of the other two courts. The records enable a link to be established between two or more generations or brothers, and also provide the date of the tenant's death and the age of the heir.

The records are at the PRO, Chancery Lane, London, and calendars of Inquisitions Post Mortem (IPM) have been published covering the period Henry III to Edward III, and for Henry VII, with indexes for later reigns. For the missing period, there is a *Calendarium* (Record Commissioners), giving tenants and their lands. Some local record societies have published more detailed calendars for their areas. The PRO references are C 133–142 for the Chancery records, and E 149 and 150 for those of the Exchequer.

Inquisition Quo Warranto *see* **Quo Warranto**

Inquisitor A person appointed to report on any shortcomings of parishioners so that they could be 'presented' at the next Archdeacon's Court.

Instance Suit *see* **Ecclesiastical Court**

Institute of Heraldic and Genealogical Studies The Institute was founded in 1961 to make provision for training, study and research in family history. It maintains a School of Family History as well as organising other courses, both by lectures and correspondence, in genealogy. Its library, of many thousands of books, is open to visitors. *Family History*, the journal of the Institute, appears quarterly, containing articles on

#	Name	Father, Mother or Spouse	Sex	Type	Date	Town, Parish
1	ULYAT	JOHN ULYAT/ELIZABETH	F	C	12JAN1760	TIMBERLAND
2	ULLIOT, ABRAHAM	ROBERT ULLIOT/MARY	M	C	05NOV1749	WADDINGTON
3	ULYAT, ABRAHAM	JOHN ULYAT/ELIZ.	M	C	12DEC1762	TIMBERLAND
4	ULYAT, ABRAHAM	JOHN ULYAT/ELIZ.	M	C	05MAY1765	TIMBERLAND
5	ULLYAT, ABRAHAM	ABRAHAM ULLYAT/LEVINA	M	C	23SEP1807	HOLBEACH
6	ULYAT, ABRAHAM	ABRAHAM ULYAT/MARY	M	C	12DEC1813	KYME
7	ULYATT, ABRAHAM	REBECCA GREEN	H	M	22MAY1832	HOLBEACH
8	ULLIOT, ALICE	JOHN MIDLETON	W	M	03MAY1671	MABLETHORPE, SAINT MARY
9	ULLYET, AN	CHRISTOFER ULLYET/AGNIS	F	C	15FEB1629	HOLBEACH
10	ULLIATE, ANN	JOH ULLIATE/ANN	F	C	06OCT1686	BILLINGHAY
11	ULLYET, ANN	JOHN ULLYET/DEBORAH	F	C	04APR1736	ORBY
12	ULLYATT, ANN	JOHN ULLYATT/MARY	F	C	08JUL1749	GRANTHAM
13	ULYATT, ANN	WILLIAM WATSON	W	M	11FEB1782	SURFLEET
14	ULYEAT, ANN	JOHN ULYEAT/ANN	F	C	05JUN1785	ANCASTER
15	ULITT, ANN	SAMUEL TURNBULL	W	M	21OCT1799	MOULTON NEAR SPALDING
16	ULYATT, ANN	ABRAHAM ULYATT/MARY	F	C	16JUL1809	KYME
17	ULYATT, ANN	EDWARD ULYATT/SARAH ANN	F	C	11JUL1830	KIRTON IN HOLLAND
18	ULLYATTE, ANNE	WILLIAM FENWICKE	W	M	08DEC1597	ADDLETHORPE
19	ULLYET, ANNE	JOHN ULLYET/ANNE	F	C	18JAN1699	ORBY
20	ULLYETT, ANNE	JOHN ULLYETT/JANE	F	C	23MAY1730	ORBY
21	ULYAT, ANNE	JOHN ULYAT/ELIZ.	F	C	01NOV1754	TIMBERLAND
22	ULYATE, CALAMANA	ROBERT BRIGGS	W	M	12AUG1788	GRANTHAM
23	ULLYETT, CATHARINE	JOHN ULLYET/DEBORAH	F	C	15AUG1732	ORBY
24	ULYATT, CATHARINE	WILLIAM BONNER	W	M	06MAY1832	BOSTON
25	ULYETT, CATHERINE	THOMAS ULYETT/CATHERINE	F	C	02SEP1821	KYME
26	ULLYATT, CHARLES	ABRAHAM ULLYATT/SARAH	M	C	17JUN1798	HOLBEACH
27	ULYATT, CHRISTOPHER	JOHN ULYATT/SARAH	M	C	22JUN1817	KYME
28	ULLIAT, COLLIMANA	WM ULLIAT/COLL.	F	C	25JAN1764	GRANTHAM
29	ULIOTT, CONSTANCE	WILLIAM ULIOTT/CONSTANCE	F	C	05JUL1733	GRANTHAM
30	ULLYET, DEBORAH	JNO. ULLYET/DEBORAH	F	C	18DEC1737	ORBY
31	ULLYET, DOBSON	JOHN ULLYET/DEBORAH	M	C	09JAN1739	ORBY
32	ULLYET, DOBSON	JOHN ULLYET/DEBORAH	M	C	07NOV1740	ORBY
33	ULLYETT, DOBSON	WILLIAM ULLYETT/FRANCES	M	C	27JUL1813	HOGSTHORPE
34	VLYET, EDWARD	WILLM VLYET/	M	C	14JAN1590	TATHWELL
35	ULLIOT, EDWARD	ROBT. ULLIOT/	M	C	01JAN1630	GRANTHAM
36	ULLIOT, EDWARD	THO. ULLIOT/SARAH	M	C	22JAN1681	GRANTHAM
37	ULLIOT, EDWARD	JOHN ULLIOT/JANE	M	C	01JUN1707	GRANTHAM
38	ULLIOTT, EDWARD	JOHN ULLIOTT/ELIZABETH	M	C	26DEC1712	SOUTH ORMSBY
39	ULYATT, EDWARD	ABRAHAM ULYATT/MARY	M	C	16JUN1809	KYME
40	ULLYAT, EDWARD	ABRAHAM ULYAT/LEVINA	M	C	17JAN1810	HOLBEACH
41	ULYATT, EDWARD	THOMAS ULYATT/CATHERINE	M	C	20JUN1826	KYME
42	ULLYETT, EDWARD BRADSHAW	/MARY ULLYETT	M	C	13JUN1817	HOGSTHORPE
43	ULYATT, EDWARD WOODS	THOMAS ULYATT/JANE	M	C	11FEB1827	SWINESHEAD
44	ULYAT, EDWD.	JANE PEARS	H	M	16JAN1753	BOSTON
45	ULLIOT, ELIZ.	WM ULLIOT/MARY	F	C	17SEP1699	GRANTHAM
46	ULITT, ELIZ.	JOHN ULITT/MARY	F	C	13NOV1727	GRANTHAM
47	ULYET, ELIZ.	JOHN ULYET/CATHARIEN	F	C	29MAY1731	BOSTON
48	ULLYETT, ELIZ.	DOBSON ULLYETT/MARTHA	F	C	01FEB1788	ORBY
49	ULLIAT, ELIZABETH	JOHN ULLIAT/	F	C	06JAN1651	GRANTHAM
50	ULLYETT, ELIZABETH	THOMAS ULLYETT/ELIZABETH	F	C	27AUG1703	ORBY-IN-THE-MARSH
51	ULLIOT, ELIZABETH	ABRA. ULLIOT/ELIZ	F	B	05AUG1725	WADDINGTON
52	ULIOTT, ELIZABETH	WILLIAM ULIOTT/CONSTANCE	F	C	12MAR1733	GRANTHAM
53	ULLIOTT, ELIZABETH	JOHN ULLIOTT/ELIZABETH	F	C	06DEC1734	SOUTH ORMSBY
54	ULLYET, ELIZABETH	HENRY ULLYET/MARY	F	C	06MAY1739	ORBY
55	ULLIAT, ELIZABETH	ROBERT ULLIAT/MARY	F	C	08JUL1744	WADDINGTON
56	ULYAT, ELIZABETH	JOHN ULYAT/ANN	F	C	01MAY1745	BICKER
57	ULYAT, ELIZABETH	JOHN ULYAT/ELIZABETH	F	C	11OCT1752	TIMBERLAND
58	ULYAT, ELIZABETH	RICHARD GOULDING	W	M	26NOV1761	KYME
59	ULYAT, ELIZABETH	ABRAHAM ULYAT/LIDIA	F	C	18OCT1796	SUTTON SAINT EDMUND

Column 1 gives the names of the person. Col.2. the parents of a person baptized, or the spouse of a person married. Col.3. the sex, abbreviated to M=male, F=female, H=husband, W=wife. Col.4. the type of record, abbreviated to B=birth, C=christening, M=marriage. Col.5. the date of baptism or marriage, but not of birth. Col.6. the name of the parish of record. *Courtesy of The Church of Jesus Christ of Latter-day Saints* heraldry, genealogy, family history and related subjects. The Institute is also the publisher of a valuable series of maps of English and Welsh counties for genealogists, showing parochial boundaries, commencement dates of extant parish registers, and areas of probate jurisdiction. Other useful publications are maps showing the census and registration regions and districts for 1837–51 and 1852–1947, a bibliography, and numerous leaflets. The address of the Institute is Northgate, Canterbury, Kent CT1 1BA.

Intercommon   Pasture land shared by adjoining parishes.

Interests *see* **Family Registry, Genealogical Research Directory, Big R and Members' Interests**

Interlocutory   Interlocutory is a temporary or provisional order which allows for further consideration.

International Genealogical Index   IGI, This Index contains over 187 million baptismal and marriage entries from parish and non-parochial registers all over the world, including about 80 million from the British Isles. These have been compiled and computerised by the Genealogical Department of The Church of Jesus Christ of Latter-day Saints, situated at Salt Lake City, Utah, USA and is re-issued approximately every four years with new additions.

The index is arranged under counties, and the entries are listed in alphabetical order of surnames, which are grouped under spellings decided on by the compilers, but the orginal spellings are cross-referenced. The surnames themselves are arranged in alphabetical order of forenames, and, where several forenames are the same, in chronological order. The forenames are arranged in alphabetical order of their original spelling or abbreviation. Marriages are indexed under the names of both parties. The coverage of any given parish is not necessarily complete, and in many cases consists only of extracts.

The illustration on page 151 shows the first six columns on a microfiche frame of the International Genealogical Index (IGI). The last five columns give further information on the use of the extracted items. *Columns 7, 8 and 9* are dates on which Mormon ceremonies were carried out following the discovery of the names, with code letters for the temples concerned. The word 'Cleared' means that the entry is in the process

of being checked. 'Infant' means that the burial records have been checked and the child died before the age of eight. Illegitimate children who died as infants are not included in the index. *Columns 10 and 11*, headed 'Batch' and 'Serial Sheet', give coded references to further information available at Salt Lake City. If the third digit from the front is less than 4, the whole register has not been indexed.

The IGI is the most helpful of all finding aids because of its wide range, although, in all counties, many parishes have yet to be included. If a name corresponding to the one sought is found in the file, the same should then be looked up in the original parish register both to check its correctness and to obtain any additional information given there, such as occupations and names of witnesses. The index is published on microfiche, of which new sets with additional entries are issued from time to time. Many county record offices, public libraries and family history societies have the microfiche and the equipment for viewing them.

The recent distribution of this index on CD-ROM, enabling country-wide searches to be made in a few seconds, is rapidly revolutionizing research. *See* FAMILYSEARCH.

International Society for British Genealogy and Family History   This society was established in the United States for anyone who has British ancestry. It now has an international membership and aims to help those who need to research in a country other than the one where they now live. It has formed many British Interest Groups in the USA. Enquiries to P.O. Box 3115, Salt Lake City, Utah 84110–3115, USA.

OPPOSITE AND OVERLEAF An inventory of the goods and chattels of William Thetcher, yeoman, of Chertsey, Surrey, who died in 1625. After mentioning the value of his wearing apparel and the money in his purse, all his household possessions are listed room by room: the hall (the main living-room), the chamber over the parlour, the cheeseloft, the chamber over the hall, the garret, the kitchen, the bolting house (where flour was sifted), the milk house, and the loft over the kitchen; then his pewter and linen; and finally the farm equipment and animals. Only the parlour seems to have been overlooked. The value put upon his belongings came in all to £247.16.4d. *Crown copyright reproduced with the permission of the Controller of Her Majesty's Stationery Office.*

An Inventary of all the goods Cattell
and Chattells of Mr William Thatcher late
of Ockleybone in the pish of Shortockley in the
Countie of Surrey yeoman deceased praised
by Edward Voysey Thelder John Mpilott &
Henry Cole the second day of June 1625
in manner & forme followinge viz

Imprimis the wearinge apparrell   iiij li
of the deceased and money in his house

In the Hall

Item one table & a payne of trestells
one Cubberd, one fourme, fourme, ioyned &   xviij s
stooles and a Cradle

In the Chamber over the parler

Item one ioyned bedd steddle one fetherbed
two ffether boulsters, two pillowes, two
blanketts, one Coverlett, one payre of sheets   liij s iiij d
three Chests & one wooden chaire

In the Cheeseloftt

Item one olde Chipp Chest & one other
one table
Chest thirteene Cheeses, twelve yarde of
wollen Cloth, eighteene yarde of lynen   ... li
yarne, one Javelin w.th other small thinges

In the Chamber over the hall

Item one ioyned bedd stedd one fetherbed
one fether boulster, one strawbedd, two
blanketts one Coverlett & one payre of   ... li
sheets, one trundle bedd stedd, one flockbedd
two fether boulsters, one blankett one Coverlett
one payre of sheets and three Chests

In the Garrett

Item one sack of wooll and one   vj s
lynnen wheele

In the Kitchen

Item two brasse potts, one brasse
posnett, one Chafer, one skillett two brasse   ... li
Kettells, one Cauldron, three spytts and one
frynate

And one yron dripping pann, one tridyron,
two paire of potthokes, two paire of potthangers,
one fryenge pann, one roastinge yron, &c.
one morter & pestle, two paire of childrens'
and one trevett ___

In the boultinge house

Item one fledtrough, one saltrough,
one boultinge hytch, one chesepresse, one
olde Cubbord, one little table, wth other lumber

In the milke house

Item fower cheesmoate & followers'
eight boules, one tubbe, seven firkins, w^th
other wooden vessells & lumber ___

In the lofte over the kitchen

Item of Rye & wheate, fifteene bushells,
and two bushells of Malte ___

Pewter

Item five & twenty platters & pewter
dishes, one Bason, five sawcers, fowre
saltsellers, three pottingers', one dozen of
spoones, two candlestickes, one chamberpott

Lynen

Item five paire of shete, fowre table
clothes, one dozen of napkins & five hand
towells ___

Item one Longe cart, one muck carte,
one plough, one paire of harrowes' wth other
implementes of husbandry ___

Item five kyne, one steere & one weaninge calfe

Item three olde horses ___

Item seven & forty sheepe & tenn Lambs

Item five hogge & shote & her weaninge pigg

Item one goose & a gander, five ducks,
five hennes and a cocke ___

Item corne upon the ground ___

Item one crope of a close of land ___

Item two stalles of bees ___

Debtes sperat and desp' ___

**Sum tota'
of ye Invent'**

Interred   An expression sometimes meaning 'buried without Christian rites'; used, for example, of excommunicates or unbaptized persons.

Interregnum   The period between the reigns of Charles I and Charles II, 1649–1660.

Interrogatories   An interrogatory was a written question put to witnesses out of court. Their answer was a deposition.

Intestate   A person was intestate when he died without having made a will. Unless his estate was small, and the inheritance undisputed, the next-of-kin would need to apply for Letters of Administration to administer it.

Inventories   Among probate records, the inventory is a list of the movable effects of a deceased person, sometimes expressly called for by the Probate Court, especially in the case of intestate persons whose next-of-kin were applying for Letters of Administration. The list had to be drawn up and signed by two reputable neighbours of the deceased. Such inventories, almost all required during the period 1529–1750, give a fascinating glimpse into a person's lifestyle. His household goods were listed, often under the headings of each named room (i.e. the hall, parlours, chambers, shops (workshops), etc.), and include furnishings, plates and drinking vessels, bedclothes, personal clothes, tools and stock in trade, as well as anything stored in the barn, animals and growing crops, with the estimated value of each item. Debts, credits and leases were also listed, but the law on what should be included differed from time to time. The tools and stock in trade often give a truer indication of how the deceased earned his livelihood than the description he gave of himself in his will; e.g. gentleman, yeoman, husbandman, etc. Larger pieces of equipment might be regarded as fixtures and therefore omitted. His wife's property would be excluded from the list, even when she had predeceased him. Because inventories were usually compiled by unscholarly neighbours, and the spelling was apt to follow the phonetics of the local dialect, they are often difficult to read.

Many records are held at county record offices, and at the Borthwick Institute at the University of York. Those for the Prerogative Court of Canterbury are at the Public Record Office, Chancery Lane, London, under PROB 2–5 and 31 (PROB 4 is only partly indexed). Inventories are occasionally found among Chancery proceedings and other records.

For further reading, see *Probate Inventories — a glossary of Household, Farming and Trade Terms* (Derbyshire Record Society).

Irish Ancestry   Ireland was formerly divided into four provinces: Ulster, Connaught, Leinster and Munster, but these divisions were only occasionally used for official surveys. The county is the principal unit of local government. There are 26 in the Republic and six in Northern Ireland. Each county is divided into baronies; there are about seven to ten in each. There are 331 baronies; a few occupy parts of two counties. Next come some 2508 civil parishes, often breaking both barony and county boundaries. The ecclesiastical parishes of the Church of Ireland tend to coincide with the civil parishes but the boundaries of the more recently formed Catholic parishes differ widely. The townland is the smallest administrative division. There are 60,462 of these, many with the same name and varying in size but having an average of about 350 acres. Many changes took place over the years. See *General alphabetical index to the townlands and towns, parishes and baronies of Ireland 1851* (reprinted 1984) and *A new genealogical atlas of Ireland* by B. Mitchell (1986).

The valuable *Census of Ireland for the year 1851, showing the area, population and number of houses by townland and electoral divisions* (Irish University Press, 1968) shows the exact numbers of people and houses in each townland in both 1841 and 1851, immediately before and after the famine.

Ireland was united as one country within the United Kingdom until 1921 when the whole of the island apart from six counties (now called Northern Ireland) in the Province of Ulster seceded to become in time the Republic of Ireland. Although all Ireland had been part of the United Kingdom until 1921 the majority of the administrative records remained in Dublin where many local records were also centralised. The national archives there were destroyed by fire in 1922.

The Public Record Office of Northern Ireland (closed the last week in November and the first week in December) is at 66 Balmoral Avenue, Belfast BT9 6NY. In the Republic are the National Archives, Bishop Street, Dublin 8 (closed in November), and the National Library, Kildare Street, Dublin 2.

Registration   The registration of non-Catholic marriages began in 1845 but the general registration of births, marriages and deaths did not start until 1 January 1864, centralised indexes covering the whole of Ireland are being compiled. The records are at the General Register Office, 8–11 Lombard Street East, Dublin 2. The indexes have been microfilmed by the Genealogical Society of Utah 1864–1921 and summaries of the birth certificates 1864–1867 are included in the INTERNATIONAL GENEALOGICAL INDEX. From 1921 the entries for Northern Ireland are at the General Register Office, 49–55 Chichester Street, Belfast BT1 4HL. A report listing every surname for which five or more births were registered in 1890 which gives a useful key to the distribution of most names in Ireland is reprinted in Begley, pp. 199–232.

Census Returns   These are available for the whole of Ireland for 1901 and 1911, arranged by townland and not indexed by surname. There are copies at Dublin and Belfast and both have been microfilmed by the Genealogical Society of Utah. The census returns 1861–1891 were competely destroyed. Surviving fragments of pre-1851 census returns and some valuable census substitutes are listed in Begley, pp. 63–74.

A general valuation of Ireland was taken and printed between 1846 and 1865. It lists landowners and tenants by county, barony, civil parish and townland and is known as Griffith's Valuation after its compiler. An index to the names was compiled by the National Library of Ireland and is widely available on microfiche. This index is also an index to the Tithe Applotment Books which record taxes paid by occupiers of agricultural land to the Church of Ireland 1823–1827. G or T by a name in the index tells you whether the index entry relates to Griffiths valuation or the Tithe survey.

Parish Registers   Many Church of Ireland parish registers had been deposited at Dublin and were destroyed in 1922. Copies of some had been retained locally and others printed. A fair number have been deposited with the Representative Church Body Library and at the National Archives; others remain with the incumbents. Those now available in Dublin are listed in Grenham, pp. 251–270.

The majority of Roman Catholic registers had remained with the clergy. Few, except in the towns, begin before the end of the eighteenth century and in the poorer areas they may not commence until the mid-nineteenth. Microfilms of most up to 1880 are available at the National Library of Ireland but permission to consult them may need to be obtained from the parish priest.

See *A guide to Irish parish registers*, by B. Mitchell (Baltimore, 1988) and for the other denominations *Irish church records: their history, availability and use*, by J.G. Ryan (1992).

Heritage Centres, sponsored by the Irish Government, have been established to transcribe and index parish registers and other material. One or more exists in every county with the exception of Louth which is covered by its neighbour, Co. Meath. For details of this 'Irish Genealogical Project' see Grenham, pp. 272–8.

Wills   Irish wills were proved in ecclesiastical courts prior to 1858. Their records were practically all destroyed in 1922 but most indexes, large numbers of abstracts and some substitute material survives. From 1858 detailed calendars survive together with the will books from the district probate registries. There are card indexes at Dublin and Belfast. See Begley, pp. 157–180.

Many other sources have importance in Irish research. These include the Registry of Deeds established in Dublin in 1708, newspapers, workhouse records from 1840, gravestone inscriptions (see *A guide to Irish churches and graveyards*, by B. Mitchell, Baltimore, 1990) and estate records. Details of many will be found in the works by Begley and Grenham mentioned below.

Emigration   100,000 Irish were transported by Cromwell to the American colonies. In the 17th and 18th centuries they were followed by indentured servants, including many Presbyterian farmers from Ulster. At the end of the Napoleonic wars many more were transported to Australia whilst others fled to the continent, where they served in foreign armies. From 1820 to 1840 about 225,000 more went to North America including some who travelled in empty merchant ships after they had brought timber to the United Kingdom from Canada. Many who went to Canada moved into the United States. The potato famine caused a further exodus in the 1840s when many left for England hoping to reach the United States but who never got further than England, migrating from Liverpool, their point of entry, to other parts of the country. After 1776 when transportation to America was no longer possible, New South Wales became the recipient of convicts including in 1791 the first ship directly from Ireland. From the late 1840s to the late 1860s the shipment of poor Irish orphan girls to Australia resulted in about 4,000 of them leaving home. For the records of Irish overseas see *Aspects of Irish genealogy* (Irish Genealogical Congress, 1993).

The Irish Genealogical Research Society in London was established in 1937. For details of family history societies in Ireland see the GENEALOGICAL RESEARCH DIRECTORY. A quarterly commercial magazine, *Irish Roots*, has been published by Belgrave Publications, Belgrave Avenue, Cork, Ireland, since 1992.

Further reading: *Irish genealogy: a record finder*, by D.F. Begley (Dublin, 1981), *Tracing your Irish ancestors*, by J. Grenham (Dublin, 1992), *An introduction to Irish research*, by B. Davis (FFHS, 1992) and *Irish records: sources for family and local history* by J.G. Ryan (Salt Lake City, 1988).

Irvingites   The popular, but not accepted, cognomen of the Catholic Apostolic Church in which Edward Irving (1792–1834) played a prominent role. He was ordained by Presbytery at Annan, Scotland, in 1822, and became minister of the Caledonian Church, Hatton Garden, London. His sermons attracted influential supporters but his theology was viewed with suspicion by the London presbytery, and when his followers began to claim the gifts of tongues and prophecy, they excluded him. In 1833 he was deposed by the Presbytery of Annan but re-ordained by his new Catholic Apostolic Church, which was led by twelve 'apostles' and six 'prophets'. Churches were founded in London, and elsewhere in England, the increase in followers being helped by their not having to separate themselves from the churches of their former allegiance. The rites of their ceremonies were very different from the plain services of other nonconformist bodies, being based on those of the Greek Orthodox and Roman Catholic Churches, and in time even the presence of a statue of Buddha was not considered inappropriate. The registers of nine churches (five from London) were deposited with the Registrar General in 1840, and are now at the Public Record Office in group RG 4.

For further reading, see D. J. Steel, *Sources for Nonconformist Genealogy and Family History*, vol. II of the National Index of Parish Registers, SOG (1973).

Isle of Man   The Isle of Man is treated like the Channel Islands and listed in the census returns as a separate island at the end of the collection. The Isle of Man Family History Society publishes a journal called *Fraueyn As Banglaneyn*. The Manx Society has published local records since 1859. See *The Manx Family Tree (a Beginners Guide to records in the Isle of Man)* by J. Narasimham (1986).

Isle of Wight   A county formed in 1974. Formerly in HAMPSHIRE. There is an Isle of Wight Family History Society. *See also* HAMPSHIRE.

Italic Hand *see* **Handwriting**

J

Jewish Ancestry   Jewish communities may have existed in Britain during the Roman occupation and individuals may have visited the Saxon Kingdoms, but the earliest documentary proof of settlement postdates the Norman Conquest. From this time all the money and effects of the Jews in England belonged to the king, and he could resume them at any time. Jews were not allowed to engage in agriculture or wholesale or retail trade, but were encouraged in money-lending because usury was forbidden to Christians by the Church. From time to time royal tallages of enormous sums were levied on the Jewish community, which had to be paid from among its members. Their numbers probably varied between 3000 and 10,000, but at one time the taxation of the Jews produced about one-seventh of the total revenue of the Crown. From time to time, massacres of Jews took place, especially when a crusade was being prepared or after some unexplained child murder. The smaller barons, who were the chief debtor of the Jews, would organise riots with the aim of killing their creditors and destroying their IOUs.

By 1290, tallages had finally impoverished the Jews to a point at which they were of no further use to the king, so Edward I expelled them from England (the first national expulsion of its kind) and later from his Norman possessions. No line of descent has been traced back to any of this community's members, or from the small number of apostates permitted to remain. For the next 350 years, virtually the only persons of known Jewish origin permitted to enter England were converts to Christianity. Some were scholars employed to teach Hebrew to theologians, more existed on Royal charity as inmates of the Domus Conversorum, erected on the site of the Public Record Office in Chancery Lane.

Following the mass expulsions and conversions effected in Spain and Portugal at the end of the fifteenth century, secret congregations of crypto-Jews (Marranos) existed from time to time in England during the sixteenth and early seventeenth centuries. They were largely importers and exporters, wholesalers, ship's chandlers and ship owners, some of them wealthy and armigerous. Their presence tended to be evanescent: threats of denunciation and wars with the Catholic powers led in every instance to their members dispersal and often hurried flight abroad.

Re-establishment of an overt Jewish presence dates from the Commonwealth, after a small number of merchants settled in London were informally permitted by the Lord Protector to meet privately for prayer. Following the Restoration of the Stuarts, the small congregation successfully fought off all challenges to their presence, thus laying the foundation for the present community, currently estimated as being in the region of 300,000. In 1760 the Board of Deputies of British Jews was formed to undertake political, social and administrative tasks on behalf of Jews. The *Jewish Chronicle* began weekly publication in London in 1841. The early issues have been subject-indexed. In 1870 the Ango-Jewish Association was formed. Membership was, and is, by invitation to prominent Jews. Its functions tend to duplicate those of the Board of Deputies.

Today's population is principally composed of the descendants of those who left the Russian Empire during the period 1881–1914 and refugees from Germany and territories incorporated into the Third Reich who arrived between 1933 and 1939. Their numerical predominance has tended to obscure the presence of smaller national groups. The original settlers, former residents of Spain, Portugal and the Netherlands, were followed during the eighteenth century by Italians and Moroccans. Nineteenth century Central Europeans, Levantines and West Indians have, in turn, been augmented by late twentieth century Egyptians, Iraquis, Adenis and Iranians. Many of these immigrants have preferred to set up their own institutions rather than be absorbed into existing structures, thus adding greatly to the diversity of present day communal life.

There are about 375 synagogues in England. Sixty-one per cent of British Jews belong to a synagogue, but a much smaller proportion is in regular attendance. The synagogues are grouped in various denominations. The United Synagogue consists of 81 London synagogues and is in the central Jewish tradition. The Federation of Synagogues comprises 42 synagogues in London and is right-wing. The Union of Orthodox Hebrew Congregations has 42 small London synagogues and is extreme right-wing. The Liberal Synagogues and the Reform Synagogues are recently formed left-wing groups, numbering about 45 congregations over the whole country. The names and addresses of the synagogues, and of the cemeteries maintained by some of them, are listed in the *Jewish Year Book*, published by the Jewish Chronicle Ltd. It also lists most other Jewish organisations.

Extensive information about the development of the Anglo-Jewish community is to be found in the English language *Jewish Encyclopaedia*, New York (1901–1906) and the *Encyclopaedia Judaica*, Jerusalem (1971–1972). A comprehensive contemporary guide to every kind of communal institution and organisation is the *Jewish Year Book*, issued annually since 1896, except during the Second World War. The current edition, which contains a detailed section on libraries and archives of Jewish interest, is available from Jewish Chronicle Publications, 25 Furnival Street, London EC4A 1JT and from bookshops specialising in Judaica.

Throughout the past century the Jewish Historical Society of England (JHSE) has published a wealth of material relating to Anglo-Jewish history, including the following bibliographies:

Cecil Roth, *Magna Bibliotheca Anglo-Judaica: a bibliographical guide to Anglo-Jewish History*, London (1937)

Ruth P. Lehmann, *Nova Bibliotheca Anglo-Judaica: a bibliographical guide to Anglo-Jewish History*, London (1961)

Ruth P. Lehmann, *Anglo-Jewish Bibliography, 1937–1970*, London (1973)

Ruth P. Lehmann-Goldschmidt-Lehmann, Stephen W. Massil and Peter S. Salinger, *Anglo-Jewish Bibliography, 1971–1990*, London 1992.

A consolidated index to the first 25 volumes of the Society's *Transactions* and volumes 1–7, 9 and 10 of its *Miscellanies* appeared in 1986. The office of the Society at 33, Seymour Place, London WC1H 5AP is merely that of the administrator: its book collection is housed at the Jewish Studies Library, University College London, Gower Street, London WC1E 6BT.

A committee called Anglo-Jewish Archives was formed in 1962, under the joint auspices of University College, London, and the Jewish Historical Society of England, to record collect and preserve archives. Their records were transferred to the University of Southampton in 1990. The collections, which include a number of manuscript pedigrees and records created by extinct communities are catalogued in C.M. Woolgar and K. Robson, *A Guide to the Archive and Manuscript Collections of the Hartley Library*, University of Southampton Library Occasional Paper No. 11 (1992).

The Society of Genealogists possesses substantial collections of Anglo-Jewish interest, principally those compiled by Sir Thomas Colyer-Fergusson, Bart., Alber M. Hyamson, Ronald J. D'Arcy Hart and Isobel Mordy. Pedigrees in both the Colyer-Fergusson and Hyamson collections are fully listed in David S. Zubatrsky and Irwin M. Berent, *Jewish Genealogy: a Sourcebook of Family Histories and Genealogies*, Garland, New York (1984).

No survey of archives in communal custody has been compiled, though it is known that substantial losses have occurred, especially among those held by educational, charitable and refugee organisations and societies. Few records survive from the older provincial congregations, many of which no longer exist. The principal series of records of value to genealogists are those held by the major London-based institutions created during the nineteenth century and can briefly be described as follows:

Office of the Chief Rabbi, Adler House, Tavistock Square, London WC1H 9HP.
Marriage authorisitions (c.240,000) July 1845 onwards. The partie's place(s) of birth are provided from February 1880.
London Beth Din (Court of the Chief Rabbi), Adler House, London WC1H 9HP.
Proceedings Books, 1876–1938, 1940 onwards. Divorce papers 1917 onwards (incomplete to c. 1945). Case files: adoptions, conversions, proof of Jewish and marital status 1945 onwards. Certificates of Evidence 1922–1966 providing the dates and place of birth and/or marriage abroad for those wishing to obtain Old Age Pensions and passports, applying to friendly and benefit societies etc.

None of the records held at Adler House are open to public inspection, but the Research Unit of the London Beth Din will conduct paid enquiries on behalf of those considered to have a bona fide legal or historical interest. The registers of the oldest Ashkenazic congregations formerly located in the City of London are in the custody of the United Synagogue, Woburn House, Tavistock Square, London WC1H OEZ. Partly microfilmed by the GSU the original registers can be viewed by arrangement with the Research Unit of the London Beth Din. A consultation fee is charged.

Virtually all the records of historical value belonging to the Western and Maiden Lane Synagogues, the first to exist in the Westminster area, were destroyed by bombing during World War II.

Sometimes Jews can be found among the baptismal, marriage and burial entries of Church of England parishes, especially, in London, those of St Dionis Backchurch, St Katherine Cree and St Helen's Bishopsgate.

All enquiries connected with the holdings of the Spanish and Portuguese Jews' Congregation of London should be addressed to the Hon. Archivist, Communal Offices, 2, Ashworth Road, London W9 1JY. Transcripts of most of the earlier vital records have now been published; the original documents are not open to public inspection.

Further reading: Wilfred S. Samuel, *Sources of Anglo-Jewish Genealogy*, Jewish Museum Publication No. 2, London, 1933. Edgar R. Samuel *Jewish Births, Marriages and Deaths*, in *National Index of Parish Registers* Vol. 3 pp. 961–975, ed. Don J. Steel, Phillimore, Chichester (1974). Dan Rottenburg, *Finding Our Fathers: a Guidebook to Jewish Genealogy*, Random House, New York (1977). Arthur Kurzweil, *From Generation to Generation*, Schocken Books, New York (1981). Michael Gandy, *My Ancestor was Jewish: How Do I Find Out More About Him*, Society of Genealogists, London (1982). *Proceedings of the Second International Seminar on Jewish Genealogy, London 5–10 July 1987*, IJGR (UK), Birmingham (1987). Carol Clapsaddle, *Tracing Your Jewish Roots in London: a Personal Experience*. Society for the Jewish Family Heritage, Tel Aviv, Jerusalem (1988).

Jewish Genealogical Society of Great Britain Formed in 1992, this society holds eight meetings a year, either in London or in the various regions of its sphere. It holds workshops under the auspices of the Sternberg Centre and a Library has been started. It publishes a journal called *Shemot*. Enquiries to the Membership Secretary, 32 Tavistock Street, London WC2E 7PD.

Joint Enfeoffment The settlement of a property on a husband and wife jointly. Such an arrangement made it possible to avoid the lord's rights of relief and wardship, if the husband predeceased his wife.

Jointure A fixed yearly sum payable to a widow out of her husband's freehold, either for life or until she remarried. She had a right to this payment, if she wished, instead of a dower.

Journeyman A day labourer who had served his apprenticeship. The *Statute of Artificers* of 1563 laid down the journeyman's hours of work as being, in summer, from, at or before 5 a.m. until between 7 and 8 p.m., with not more than 2½ hours off for breakfast, dinner and drinking; and in winter from dawn till dusk. Unlike apprentices and employees engaged on a longer-term basis, most journeymen lived away from their work. The term has no connection with travelling. In London, journeymen employed under licence by freemen had themselves to be freemen until 1750. Indexed licence books for 1750–1845 are at the Corporation's Record Office, Guildhall, Gresham Street, London EC2P 2EJ, showing names of journeymen and masters.

Judicature, Supreme Court of Set up in 1875 this court was divided into the Court of Appeal and the High Court of Justice. The latter now consists of Chancery, Queen's Bench and Admiralty, Probate and Divorce Divisions. When it was created it also covered the work of the Common Pleas and the Exchequer Divisions separately, which, in 1880, were merged into the Queen's Bench Division. This was the end of the distinction between the doctors of Civil Law and the Common Law Lawyers. In 1970 the Probate, Divorce and Admiralty Division became the Family Division.

Jurors' Lists *see* **Freeholders' Lists**

Jury of Presentment By an ancient custom confirmed at the Assize of Clarendon in 1166, twelve respectable men of the hundred and four similar men from each vill were liable for bringing suspected offenders before the justices and sheriff of the county in the hundred court.

Justices of the Peace Originally called Keepers of the Peace, these magistrates were appointed by a commission under the Great Seal, to keep the peace within a stated jurisdiction. The justices first acquired their name, and the power to try major offences, under a statute of 1361. On appointment they gave their services without pay. In order to exclude men too poor to be suitable, a statute of 18 Henry VI (his eighteenth regnal year) required that each justice should hold lands to the value of £20 per annum. This amount was raised to £100 clear of all deductions, in 1744. Parish constables and other parochial officials were responsible to Justices of the Peace for the satisfactory performance of their duties. The justices enforced the law in their county and tried cases before a jury at Quarter Sessions. Between sessions, justices could meet together in Petty Sessions to settle very small matters. They are named in the Quarter Session rolls, but not all the justices named in the commission were obliged to be present at every court.

K

Keighley and District Family History Society *see* **Yorkshire**

Kelly's Directories This series of local directories started in 1799 with a volume for London, and has since covered all the counties and large cities of England, outlasting all their competitors. New editions of the county volumes appeared roughly every eight years until 1939, and city volumes were published rather more frequently. Their contents in the nineteenth century expanded in line with those of other local directories. The earliest contained the names and addresses of commercial concerns, then those of the more prosperous private householders were included, and finally of all householders. In the 1930s and 40s, as more and more private people owned telephones and so had their names and addresses in the free Post Office Telephone Directories, Kelly's sales were seriously affected. However, the firm now publishes British Telecom's directories and manufacturers' guides; enquiries to Kelly's Directory, Windsor Court, East Grinstead House, East Grinstead, West Sussex RH19 1XA. A copy of each publication since the beginning is kept at the Guildhall Library in London. Many of the volumes can also be seen at county libraries and at the Society of Genealogists.

Kent The county lies within the dioceses of Canterbury and Rochester within the Province of Canterbury. The registers of most of the 400 ancient parishes have been mainly deposited at the CRO but some are at other repositories within the county. About half the parishes have transcripts in the library of the SOG. The Bishops' Transcripts and Marriage Licences for the Rochester Diocese are at the CRO Maidstone and those for the Canterbury Diocese at the Cathedral Archives. Bishops' Transcripts and Marriage Licences for the Peculiar of the Arches, Shoreham (Kent) are at Lambeth Palace Library. The House of Lords Record Office has Bishops'

Transcripts of 98 parishes for 1640–2 with modern copies at the Institute of Heraldic and Genealogical Studies in Canterbury.

The Lathes of Sutton-at-Hone (including Axton, Dartford and Wilmington, Blackheath, Codsheath, Bromley and Beckenham, Lessness, Ruxley, Somerden and Westerham, Canterbury City and Borough, Chatham Town, Rochester City, Deptford Town, Greenwich Town, Dover (Town and Port) Maidstone Borough, Sandwich (Town and Port) and Woolwich (Town), St Augustine (including Bewsborough, Bleangate, Bridge and Petham, Cornilo, Downhamford, Eastry, Kinghamford, Preston, Ringslow or Isle of Thanet, Westgate, Whitstable and Wingham), Aylesford (including Brenchley and Horsemonden, Chatham and Gillingham, Eyhorne, Hoo, Larkfield, Littlefield, Maidstone, Shamwell, Toltingtrough, Tonbridge Lowey, Twyford, Washlingstone and Wrotham), Scray (including Barnfield East, Berkeley, Blackbourne, Boughton-under-Blean, Calehill, Chart and Longbridge, Cranbrooke, Faversham, Felborough, Marden, Milton, Rolvenden, Selbrittenden, Isle of Sheppey Liberty, Tenterden, Teynham and Wye), Shepway (including Aloesbridge, Bircholt Franchise and Barony, Folkestone, Ham, Hayne, Hythe, Langport, Loningborough, St Martin Ivychurch, or Pountney, Newchurch, Oxney, Romney Cinque Port, Stouting, Street, Worth and Romney Marsh Liberty) lie within its boundaries.

It has Bromley, Dartford, Gravesend, Strood, Hoo, Medway, Malling, Sevenoaks, Tonbridge, Maidstone, Hollingbourne, Cranbrook, Tenterden, West Ashford, East Ashford, Bridge, Canterbury, Blean, Faversham, Milton, Sheppey, Thanet, Eastry, Dover, Elham and Romney Marsh RDs/PLUs.

It fell within the Home Assizes Circuit until 1876 and then the South Eastern Assizes Circuit.

Kent Family History Society meet at Canterbury, Maidstone and Margate and publish a quarterly journal. North West Kent Family History Society meet at Bromley, Dartford and Sevenoaks and publish a quarterly journal. Folkestone and District Family History Society meet at Folkestone and publish *Kentish Connection* quarterly. Tunbridge Wells Family History Society publish a twice-yearly journal and Woolwich and District Family History Society meet in London SE18 and publish a quarterly journal.

Record Repositories: Kent County Archives Office is at Maidstone and has a branch at Folkestone Central Library, Cathedral Archives and Library, the Diocesan Registry and the City Record Office in Canterbury, Greenwich Town Clerk's Department, London SE18, Greenwich Borough Archives at Blackheath, Archives and Local History Department at Lewisham Library, Gravesend Public Library and the Institute of Heraldic and Genealogical Studies in Canterbury. There is a Family History Centre at Maidstone.

Pre 1858 Wills at the CRO were proved at the following courts: Consistory Courts of Canterbury and Rochester, Peculiar Courts and the Archdeaconry Courts of Canterbury and Rochester. After 1846, wills for the extreme northwest corner of the county were proved in the Consistory Court of London. Wills could also be proved at the Prerogative Court of Canterbury. The SOG has indexes to the Consistory and Archdeaconry Courts of Canterbury.

Kent Archaeological Society has transcribed and published a number of records of the county since 1912. Heralds' Visitation Pedigrees have been published for 1530, 1574, 1592, 1619–21 and 1663–8.

See *Guide to the Kent County Archives Office*, by F. Hull (1958) and its *Supplements* (1971, 1983), *National Index of Parish Registers*, vol. 4 (1980), *West Kent sources* (North West Kent FHS, 1989) and *East Kent parishes*, by D. Wright (1991).

Kilmainham, Royal Hospital The Royal Hospital at Kilmainham, near Dublin, was founded in 1679 to provide for wounded and disabled soldiers. Like the Royal Hospital at Chelsea it catered for both 'in-pensioners' and 'out-pensioners'. It continued to house the former until its closure in 1929, but 'out-pensioners' were transferred to the care of Chelsea in 1822. Kilmainham dealt with pensioners who were stationed in Ireland at the time of their discharge, not merely with those in Irish regiments. *See also* ARMY.

King's Bench, Court of One of the three courts that evolved from the Curia Regis (King's Court) of the Norman and early Plantagenet kings, the others being the Courts of Common Pleas and Exchequer. It had become separate by the reign of Edward I, with the function of trying cases affecting the king himself and magnates privileged to be tried only before the king (Coram Regis) or, in his absence abroad, by his Council. It also corrected the errors of other courts. After the civil wars of Henry III it tried criminal cases (the Crown Side), but in time came to deal also with civil suits (the Plea Side). The records are at the Public Record Office, Chancery Lane, London; of the Crown Side under references KB 1–4, 6–13, 18–19, 30–32; 35; of the Plea

Side, KB 20–29, 33, 36. The Placita Coram Rege Rolls (KB 27), 1272–1701 contain entries of all proceedings in the Court of King's Bench. The Judgement Rolls record suits between private persons.

King's Evil Scrofula; a disease of the lymphatic glands, once thought to be curable by a touch from the king's hand. Accounts of the origin of this idea in England differ widely; W.E. Tate ascribing it to the time of Saint Edward the Confessor (and others to Edward III) inheriting the power from Saint Louis IX of France. Originally the king used to wash the diseased parts and present the sufferer with a penny, but Henry VII and his successor did no more than touch the afflicted persons during the course of a special church service, after which they were presented with the 'touch-piece', which by then was a gold angel pierced for hanging round the neck. Charles II gave a gold medal worth ten shillings. The last monarch to touch for the King's Evil was Queen Anne.

Each applicant for the royal touch had to bring a certificate from the incumbent and church-wardens of his or her parish, that the suffering was genuine and the touch had not been administered before. The issue of such certificates was usually noted in the parish records. Most of the touchings were performed in London, for which afflicted people came from all over the country, but when the king was on a visit to a subject he sometimes touched sufferers in his host's parish.

Kitchen Until the sixteenth century, the kitchen of a house was almost always a building separate from the dwelling house itself, because of the fire risk; but when brick chimneys were introduced, it was brought indoors and became the area at the back of the chimney base, which stood fairly centrally placed in the hall on the ground floor. See also HALL.

Knight Knights were the fighting men, fully equipped, who followed the Conqueror into England and were rewarded by grants of land (knights' fees) which they held either directly from the king or, more often, from his barons, in return for Knight Service. The knight's male descendants served as squires (esquires) in their teens, and were dubbed when they came of age. However, in the course of a few generations, actual military Knight Service became separated from the holding of land, by the practice of division and sub-infeuding of knights' fees between smaller land-holders. This led to the commutation of service by a money payment, called Scu-

tage (shield-money), with which funds the king was able to employ paid fighting-men. In 1224, at a time when more than half the holders of knights' fees were paying for exemption from service, Henry III issued them a summons either to take up knighthood or be fined for refusal, which was probably a device for bringing in additional funds. The holder of a knight's fee who did not take up knighthood remained an esquire all his life, and so the style of (e)squire became permanently attached to the social class of gentry, and especially land holding gentry, in spite of efforts to give it a more limited technical connotation later on (see ESQUIRE).

Bereft of all hereditary connection, knighthood became a purely personal honour, the reward at first for military, and later, for any other kind of service. The knight was, and is, styled 'Sir', followed by his forename.

It was only the abolition of feudal tenure in 1646, confirmed in 1662, that ended the obligation (since 1306) of a landholder worth £40 per annum to take up the privilege of knighthood, though it had long been a dead letter, but Charles I tried to extract fines from all such men who would not accept knighthood. Lists of the men involved in this Distraint of Knighthood are at the Public Record Office, Chancery Lane, London, under reference E 178/7154, grouped under counties.

From the early crusades onward, special orders of international knighthood were instituted, including the Knights Hospitallers of the Order of St John of Jerusalem, the Knights Templar, and others in Europe. The earliest English order was that of the Garter, founded in 1343 by Edward III, an enthusiast for the principles of chivalry. It was followed at the end of the same century by that of the Bath, and in course of time by a number of others. An ordinary knight who had not achieved the rank of knight banneret (see BANNERET, KNIGHT) was called a knight bachelor and was entitled to a forked pennant.

A register of knights has been maintained at the College of Arms since 1622. New knighthoods are reported in the *London Gazette*, and living knights are listed in the volumes, issued from time to time, of both Burke's and Debrett's *Peerage, Baronetage and Knightage*. W.A. Shaw's *The Knights of England* (1906) lists knights from 1257 onward.

Knighthood, Distraint of: To raise money for his royal Exchequer, King Charles I revived a neglected device called Distraint of Knighthood originally employed by Henry III. Any gentleman possessing freehold land worth £10 per annum was, ostensibly, considered worthy of knighthood. The Sheriff of each county was ordered to issue personal summonses to all such gentry within his jurisdiction and to send a list of them to the Chancery. From there it was passed to the Exchequer, the office responsible for administering the royal revenues. The option to accept knighthood or pay the fine was widely resented and rejected, so County Commissioners were appointed to collect the dues. The first summons was sent out in January 1626, but was largely ineffective. Between 1629 and 1635, £173,000 was collected in fines from 9,280 gentlemen.

The lists of these assessments, arranged by counties, are among the Exchequer records at the PRO, Chancery Lane, under reference E 178/7154. They show the men's names and parishes and whether they compounded and paid the fine or claimed exemption or were simply in default. In some cases, correspondence on the matter is included.

A list of the names of those fined for failure to appear at Charles I's Coronation and to take up knighthood, with the amount of composition paid, from 1630 to 1632, appears in Class E 407/35 at the PRO, Chancery Lane, London.

Knight Service The military tenure by which freehold land was held under the feudal system of the Middle Ages. From the Conquest, all the land of England was owned by the king and he enfeoffed all of it, except his own royal demesnes, to earls, barons and lesser men in return for their liability for military service. The service required was based upon the 'constabularia' of ten knights. An important tenant-in-chief might be expected to provide one or more of these units, and lesser men, half of one. To obtain such knights for the king's service, the tenants-in-chief sub-infeuded some of their manors to gentlemen in return for the necessary obligation. The sub-infeuding process then continued downwards to a lord of a single manor, representing only a fraction of a knight's fee, which was therefore paid in money (*see* SCUTAGE). The total number of knights' fees was between five and six thousand.

Knight Service consisted of active military service in the field, if called upon, for forty days per year, bringing arms, armour and horse as laid down. It also involved castle ward (guard duties) at his immediate lord's chief castle for a fixed number of days per year. Certain other obligations were also involved, including (i) a relief paid on succeeding to his land) (ii) wardship, the liability of an heir who was a minor

to become a ward of his lord (*see* WARDS AND LIVERIES); (iii) marriage (unless bought off), the liability of an heir (if a minor) to be given in marriage by his lord, the same also applying to an heiress or a widow.

The principle of knight service remained until 1662. *See also* MANUEL RENTE.

Knight of the Shire A Member of Parliament elected on the county vote; not necessarily, indeed seldom, a knight in rank. The term was a survival into the nineteenth century from the medieval early days of Parliament, when knights were selected to represent the smaller gentry of the countryside.

Knobstick Wedding The wedding of a pregnant single woman to the putative father-to-be, under pressure from the parish vestry. The churchwardens attended to see that the ceremony was performed, and the name is derived from their staves of office which had a knob on the end.

Knocknobbler A parishioner given the responsibility for driving dogs out of church, if they were a nuisance. Also called a dog-whipper.

Kymnell A wooden trough or tub, used in kneading dough and in home brewing, a utensil often listed in inventories.

L

Lady Day Lady Day, the 25th March and the feast of the Annunciation of the Virgin Mary, was New Year's Day until 1752 when it was moved to January 1st. Lady Day is also a quarter day.

Lairstall A grave inside a church.

Lambeth Palace Library Founded in 1610 by Archbishop Bancroft as a public library, it is now administered by the Church Commissioners. For single searches, application should be made in advance, in writing, to the Librarian at the address given below.

The records most generally useful to genealogists are the marriage licence records of the Faculty Office and Vicar General's Office, and the probate records of the Court of Arches and of the Peculiars of the Archbishop of Canterbury in the Peculiar Deaneries of the Arches (London), and — to a lesser degree, because all the records are not here — of Shoreham (Kent) and Croydon (Surrey). There are also a great number of documents originated by the spiritual and temporal functions of the Archiepiscopate.

The address is Lambeth Palace Library, Lambeth Palace, London SE1 7JU. The separate library entrance is by a door in the long wall in Lambeth Palace Road.

Lambrequin *see* **Mantling**

Lammas Commonly said to be the festival of the wheat harvest, celebrated, before the 1752 change in the calendar, on the first of August and afterwards on the thirteenth. The name is often said to originate from loaf-mass. However, Dr Johnson, in his dictionary, derived it from Lattermath (a second mowing), which would appear to have agricultural practice in its favour, since all the hay should be in by Lammas while it would still be too early for all the wheat. Lammas land was land enclosed and held in severalty until Lammas, and then thrown open to the beasts of the manor for grazing. There was once an old saying, 'at latter Lammas', meaning 'never'.

Lancashire Since 1974 the ancient county has been divided into Lancashire, Greater Manchester and Merseyside, Furness has been transferred to Cumbria and the county's southern border to Cheshire. It lies in the diocese of Chester and the Province of York. Of the ancient counties nearly all the parish registers have been deposited at the appropriate record office. There are more than 100 transcripts of them at the library of the SOG. The Bishop's Transcripts are nearly all at the CRO but those for the Peculiar of the Dean and Chapter of York are at the Borthwick Institute and the University of York. Marriage Licence records are either at the Cheshire Record office if they pertain to the Archdeaconry of Chester (south of the River Ribble), at the CRO if they pertain to the Archdeaconry of Richmond or at the Borthwick Institute if they pertain to the Peculiar Court of the Dean and Chapter of York.

The Hundreds of Amounderness, Blackburn (Lower and Higher Divisions), West Derby, Salford, Leyland, Lonsdale (North of the Sands and South of the Sands) and Liverpool and Manchester Boroughs lie within its boundaries.

It has Liverpool (later Toxteth Park as well), West Derby, Prescot, Ormskirk, Wigan, Warrington, Leigh, Bolton, Bury, Barton-upon-Irwell, Chorlton, Salford, Manchester (later Prestwich as well), Ashton-under-Lyne, Oldham, Rochdale, Haslingden, Burnley, Clitheroe, Blackburn, Chorley, Preston, Fylde, Garstang, Lancaster (later Lunesdale as well) and Ulverston (later Barrow-in-Furness as well) RDs/PLUs.

The Lancashire Family History and Heraldry Society publishes *Lancashire* quarterly and meets at Blackburn, Bury, Chorley, Bury, Blackpool, Preston, Morecombe, Colne, Clitheroe, Rochdale, Rawtenstall and has a London and South Branch which meets at the Society of Genealogists. Liverpool and South West Lancashire Family History Society publishes *The Liverpool Family Historian* quarterly and meets at Leigh, Liverpool, Upholland, Southport, St Helens, Warrington and has an Anglo-Irish branch. The Manchester and Lancashire Family History Society publishes *Manchester Genealogist* quarterly and meets at Manchester and Bolton and has an Anglo-Scots group. The North Meols Family History Society meets at Churchtown and publishes a quarterly newsletter and the Ormskirk and District Family History Society publishes a journal twice-yearly and meets in Ormskirk.

Record Repositories: Lancashire Record Office is at Preston; Greater Manchester County Record Office, Manchester Central Library Archives Department, John Ryland's University Library, Chetham's Library and Salford Archives Centre are all in Manchester; Liverpool Record Office and Merseyside County Archives are in Liverpool; Rochdale Public Library in Rochdale. There are Family History Centres at Blackpool, Rochdale, Chorley, Liverpool, Manchester and Rossendale.

Pre 1858 Wills proved in the following courts are at the CRO: Episcopal Consistory Court of Chester, the Consistory Court of the Commissary of the Archdeacon of Richmond (Western Deaneries) and the Manor Courts of Halton, Nether Kellet, Slyne with Hest and Skerton. Those proved at the following courts are at the Borthwick Institute: Peculiar Court of the Dean and Chapter of York, Exchequer Court of York and the Chancery Court of York. There are also abstracts of 2400 wills and letters of administration at Rochdale Public Library from 1553–1810 which relate to local people. Wills could also be proved in the Prerogative Courts of York and Canterbury.

The Lancashire and Cheshire Record Society have printed indexes of wills for 1545–1837 and published many local records, wills and marriage licences, since 1879. The Lancashire Parish Record Society and the Chetham Society (since 1844) also transcribe and publish records pertaining to Lancashire. Heralds' Visitation Pedigrees have been published for 1533, 1567, 1613 and 1664–5.

See *Handlist of genealogical sources* (1986) and *Guide to the Record Office* (1985) published by Lancashire Record Office, and *Manchester & Lancashire Family History Society handbook: a guide to genealogical sources* (1993).

See also *Tracing your ancestors in Bolton* (Bolton Archive Service), *Routes: a guide to family history in the Bury area* (Bury Library Service), *Guide to Greater Manchester Record Office*, by V. McKernan and J. Hodkinson (1992), *Some genealogical sources in the Merseyside Record Office* (Merseyside Record Office), *Brief Guide for family historians* (Liverpool City Libraries), *Genealogical sources for the City of Salford* (Salford Archive Service), *Tracing your family tree* (Tameside Archive Service) and *Guide to genealogical sources* (Wigan Archive Services).

Lance (i) A long spear for use by a horse soldier.

(ii) A medieval army unit consisting of a knight or man-at-arms, two archers, a swordsman and two pages armed with daggers. The term 'Lance Corporal' derives from this body.

Land Another name for a selion; i.e. a strip of ploughland within a furlong in the open arable field of a manor.

Landed Gentry, Burke's This series of volumes, the last of which appeared in 1972, began as Burke's *History of the Commoners*, but changed its title with the volume of 1846 to *A Genealogical and Heraldic Dictionary of the Landed Gentry*. The volumes contained constantly updated paragraph pedigrees of the landed and county families of Great Britain, accompanied by representations of their arms. In the course of time many families sold their estates, but continued to be included in Burke as 'formerly of . . .' In each volume the main pedigrees section is preceded by essays of genealogical interest.

Landgable A nominal rent payable to their lord by borough tenants on burgess tenure.

Land Registry Although the statutory registration of the buying and selling of land in England and Wales started in the nineteenth century not all land is yet registered. The Land Registry has information on about 13 million of the estimated 22 million property titles in England and Wales and the Land Registry Public Index Map indicates which properties are registered and which are not. The register merely shows the geographical location and extent of the property with a plan, the quality of the title and details of registered mortgages or other financial burdens secured on the property. Fees are payable for searches in the Index Map and in the Register. Write to HM Land Registry, 32 Lincoln's Inn Fields, London WC2A 3PH. *See also* ENROLLED DEEDS; TITLE DEED.

Land Tax The Land Tax was first regularly imposed in 1693, on an assessment made in 1692. A quota was fixed for each county, and local assessors were left to allot appropriate amounts to each parish and, within the parishes, to each taxpayer. At first movable property and salaries were taxed too, but because of the difficulty of assessing them it was soon decided to confine assessments to real estate, some offices of profit, tithes, and some buildings. The early records of collection were defective in compilation, and very few survive. In time, anomalies arose, leaving rural areas too heavily taxed compared with the new industrial districts. In 1772 the returns were altered to incorporate a list of all the occupiers of land in each parish. From 1780, duplicates had to be lodged with the Clerk of the Peace, so that they could be used to establish the qualifications of parliamentary voters. In 1782 a further column was added to show the proprietor of each building. These deposited records are available down to 1832, after which date they become less regular.

From 1772, the tax was normally levied at the rate of four shillings in the pound, and in 1798 landowners were allowed to buy themselves out of the liability by a lump sum of fifteen years' purchase, but until 1832 the names of 'exonerated' owners continue in the lists. By the end of 1815 about one-third of the land had been thus redeemed.

After 5 April, 1816, the tax lapsed but was levied again from 1842.

Documents consist of *Assessments and Returns*. The former show the assessed value of the land; the Returns, the amounts actually collected. Sometimes the columns are unheaded, and this can be misleading because some clerks reversed the columns for proprietors and tenants. Comparison should be made with previous or subsequent years. The property shown does not necessarily indicate the tenant's abode, much less the proprietor's. Most of the returns were drawn up annually, but some quarterly, and in the latter case the tax shown is a quarter of the annual rate. 'Exonerated holdings', from 1798 until about 1815, were usually listed at the end of the parish return.

The records from 1780 are in county record offices, usually in annual volumes or 'bundles', with the parishes grouped in Hundreds. Not all start from the same date, and there are often gaps. Some assessments and minutes of commissioners' meetings are to be found among parish records.

The tax records are a useful aid in finding the whereabouts of a householder, once his county is known. The researcher who cannot find his family among the Land Tax records of a given county should refer to a series of volumes at the Public Record Office, Kew, under reference IR 23. These contain a copy of the Land Tax assessments for the whole country for the year 1798, and show proprietors, occupiers and sums assessed but no details of the properties, nor are sub-tenants or sharing tenants shown. The volumes are arranged by counties, Hundreds and parishes, with sub-divisions for boroughs and hamlets, and so provide an excellent location record for people needing to find their family's whereabouts at the turn of the century.

The Federation of Family History Societies has published a booklet guide, *Land and Window Tax Assessments*, FFHS (1993), by Jeremy Gibson, Mervyn Medlycott and Dennis Mills, FFHS (1993).

Lanspesado   A rank in the militia, equivalent to lance-corporal.

Larceny   Stealing. Grand larceny (a felony) was the theft of goods above the value of twelve pence from the owner's house; not from the person, or by night. It was a capital crime. Petty larceny was the theft of goods to the value of twelve pence or less, and the punishment was imprisonment or whipping. The distinction between grand and petty larceny was removed in 1827.

Lathe   A sub-division of the county of Kent.

Latin, Medieval   Before 1733, except for the period 1651–60, Latin was the compulsory language of legal documents and often, by the writer's choice, of other records. It is therefore, a stumbling block for researchers who have not studied classical Latin at any level, and even to some extent for those who have, because texts of the Middle Ages and the sixteenth and seventeenth centuries employ Latin words for things and ideas that did not exist in classical times. Furthermore, they were written in a system of abbreviations that require practice to read. Fortunately, certain aids are available, the most impor-

tant of which is Eileen A. Gooder's *Latin for Local History*, a textbook of grammar for beginners, using, as examples, words and phrases helpful to local historians and genealogists, and giving translations of frequently consulted records. It is intended to be used in conjunction with B.H. Kennedy's *Shorter Latin Primer*, but is very effective on its own.

A second aid is R.E. Latham's *Revised Mediaeval Latin Word-List* (Oxford, 1965), listing non-classical meanings occurring in English and Irish documents between the fifth and sixteenth centuries. A third is C.T. Martin's *The Record Interpreter* (Kohler & Coombes, 1979). This contains a medieval Latin word-list, lists of abbreviations and of the Latin names of places, bishoprics, surnames and Christian names. The vocabulary at the end of Eileen Gooder's book contains only a tiny portion of the words in the two other word-lists, but is helpful because they are specially selected.

Because genealogical research involves only a comparatively small number of Latin records, the vocabulary required is not large; the same words and phrases are met with again and again. Parish registers, the records most frequently consulted, were often written in Latin until about 1625, or even later, so a vocabulary of the words and phrases likely to be found in them is given under the entry PARISH REGISTERS. Translations are also supplied under ACTS OF ADMINISTRATION, CHRISTIAN NAMES, MANOR AND PROBATE.

Further reading: *A Latin Glossary for Family and Local Historians*, by Janet Maris, *Latin word list for Family Historians* compiled by Elizabeth Simpson FFHS (1985).

Latten   An alloy of copper and zinc, yellow in colour, used for a variety of household plates, dishes and vessels, and for monumental brasses in churches.

Latter-day Saints   The members of The Church of Jesus Christ of Latter-day Saints are commonly known as Mormons, from the Book of Mormon, one of the books of scripture used in the Church upon which the beliefs of the Church are based. One of its tenets encourages its followers to discover the names of their ancestors. The assistance given to their researchers by the Church's Family History Department, with headquarters in Salt Lake City, Utah, USA, in microform historical records, indexing and computerisation, has been of enormous assistance to all British genealogists. The most notable of their aids has been the creation of a consolidated INTERNATIONAL GENEALOGICAL INDEX (IGI) which

Landlords	Land & Houses	Occupiers	Rents	Rents	Taxes
			£	£	£ s d
Mr Larkin	Bro.t forward		52		
Do	House How Lane	Wm Hugley	4		
Do	Do Do	Jno Chamberlain	4		
Do	Do Do	Jno Smith	4	64	3 4 -
Marg.t Toms	Late ye 3 Compasses Ale house	Matt. Dakers	12		
Do	House hill Abot	Bn Denham	5	17	17 -
Mr Pechell	House, Garden Gro and Stables	Counte Worenzow	80		
Do	House Do	Jno Willis	5		
Do	Do adjoining Do	Do	3		
Do	1 Acre of Land Earl Bancroft	Wm Fuller	3	91	4 11
Benj.n Fox	Ground under hill	late Pechell	To be let pat		
Do	House	Jno Hosier Esq.r	40		
Do	Do	Do Mrs Rider	40		
Do	Do	Do Countess of Darby	120	200	10 - -
Josh Jebb Esq.r	House on ye Hill	Leon Davell Esq.r	110	110	5 10
Fran Watkins	The Ivy house and Land on ye hill	Himself	27	27	1 7
Tho.s Skinner	House & Garden on the Common	Lady Eglinton	23		
Do	Land adjoining Do	Jno Wizard	10	33	1 13 -
Late Mr Sowle	House & Garden	P. Turie Esq.r	55		
Do	Land near Do	The Cope	8	43	2 3 -
The Trustees of the Marshalsea Prison	Two houses, Coach house & Stables on the Hill	Drake Esq.r	47	47	2 7 -
Dan.l Grose	House on ye Hill	Himself	40		
Do	Coach house, and Stables on ye Common	Do	5	25	1 5 -
				32 17 ~	

ABOVE A page from a Land Tax record, showing the owners and occupiers of properties in a parish. The order of the columns is not necessarily the same in all records, and sometimes the headings are omitted, creating uncertainty as to who are owners and who occupiers, but generally the most numerous 'ditto' entries appear in the owners (or landlords) column. *Courtesy the Surrey Record Office* includes a large number of baptismal registers, and some marriages, for all parts of the British Isles. Copies of the IGI on microfiche are now available to the public at most county record offices, many public libraries, the Public Record Office and a number of family history societies. They also initiated a national indexing project for the 1881 census which is being produced in total transcript and with various indexes to each county. Eventually when the whole country is covered it will be available in a national sort on FAMILYSEARCH the Church's genealogical computer system. The Church's family history centres are open to all worldwide. The Genealogical Society of Utah also has an ongoing filming programme to preserve and make available an ever increasing number of records in microform.

In the Family History Library at Salt Lake City, further data are available to local searchers. A list of these searchers can be obtained from the Family History Department, The Church of Jesus Christ of Latter-day Saints, 35 North West Temple Street, Salt Lake City, Utah 84150, USA.

Law Day The day on which a manor Court Leet, or view of frankpledge, was held. Often used to refer to the court itself.

Law Merchant Commercial law administered in borough courts. In detail it varied from town to town.

Law Reports They are published reports of Case Law as opposed to Enacted Law covered by Statutes or Acts of Parliament, which are used as precedents to back up arguments in present day cases. There are over eight hundred series of law reports covering all Courts of Law, dating from 1066 to the present day, the current series of official Law Reports starting in 1865. There is a separate series of Law Reports in 176 volumes plus indexes to plaintiffs covering many cases tried before 1865. They can be seen on microfilm at the London Borough of Camden Public Library, 32 Theobalds Road, London WC1X 8PA (tel: 071 405 2705) where there is also a specialist Law Section. *See* Sweet and Maxwell's *Guide to Law Reports and Statutes.*

Law Terms There are four law terms, Michaelmas (from late September until the end of November), Hilary (from mid January until mid February), Easter (from Easter until mid April or May – Easter was a moveable feast) and Trinity (from mid May until 24th June depending on when Easter had been). These definitions are approximate, not only because the date of Easter varied but also due to changes over the centuries and that some sittings could take place outside the terms as well.

Lawyers As is the case with other professions, details of the careers of lawyers, both barristers and solicitors, are to be found in an annual printed publication, the *Law List*, which has appeared since 1775. For barristers there are also the printed registers of the four Inns of Court, namely Lincoln's Inn, the Middle Temple, the Inner Temple and Gray's Inn. The Inner Temple's register covers only admissions of an early period, but information can be obtained from the Librarian, Inner Temple, London EC4Y 7DA.

The Inns of Court were founded as schools of common lawyers in the fourteenth century. By the sixteenth century they were attracting not only men intending to practise law, but also the sons of the nobility and gentry, who attended them as an alternative to the two Universities, since a knowledge of law was useful in the management of their estates and also in any political ambitions they might have.

There were also Inns of Chancery, Staple Inn and Barnard's Inn (affiliated to Gray's Inn), Clifford's Inn and Clement's Inn (affiliated to the Inner Temple), New Inn (affiliated to the Middle Temple), and Thavie's Inn and Furnival's Inn (affiliated to Lincoln's Inn). These were originally preparatory colleges for younger students, who might later go on to an Inn of Court, but who often ended their studies there and became either solicitors acting for clients in the equity court of Chancery, attorneys licensed in the Common Law courts, or proctors in the ecclesiastical and admiralty courts. Inns of Chancery no longer exist. Details of articles of clerkship, and admissions of both types of lawyers from 1729, are to be found at the Public Record Office, Chancery Lane, London, in the records of the Court in which they practised. These are indexed. They include the names and addresses of fathers and of the lawyers to whom the clerks were articled.

For further reading, see *Tracing Your Ancestors in the PRO*, by Amanda Bevan and Andrea Duncan (HMSO, 1990).

Further reading: *Petty Foggers and Vipers of the Commonwealth*, by C.W. Brooks, for the early history of solicitors.

Lay Subsidy By the end of the thirteenth century, land was no longer the only indication of a person's wealth, so a new tax, called Lay Subsidy, was levied on movables. Assessors were appointed for each district and they appointed local collectors. Not every householder's name is to be found in the returns, because some were too poor to be taxed and clerical properties were assessed and taxed separately; hence the name Lay Subsidy (*see* CLERICAL SUBSIDY). Certain items of property necessary to a person's livelihood were exempted; e.g. a knight's armour and riding horses, and a merchant's investment capital. So it is not possible to deduce with any certainty a taxpayer's relative prosperity.

At the head of each roll, the rate of tax is mentioned. This may be a tenth, twelfth, fifteenth or twentieth, depending upon the need of the Crown at the time. Sometimes two rates are indicated, in which case the larger fraction applies to urban populations and those who lived on the ancient demesnes of the Crown, and the smaller one to country folk. The two categories are usually listed separately on the roll.

From 1334, for two centuries, the rolls of personal names cease and only place names are listed, but in course of time the relative economic conditions of localities changed, so the Great Subsidy of 1542–5 lists all people over 16 years of age with income from land or with taxable goods worth £2 per annum, or with annual wages of £1 or more. Later subsidies, which continued to the end of the seventeenth century, give less detail.

The original Lay Subsidy Rolls are at the Public Record Office, Chancery Lane, London, in class E 179, and are catalogued in the List and Index Society series. Many county lists have been printed by record publishing societies. These are accompanied by explanatory articles.

League This measure of distance cannot be relied on to be either the medieval 1½ miles, or the present 3 miles. It differed from one part of the country to another.

Leas Meadowland. Also called 'lease'.

Lease and Release A procedure for transferring land from one party to another without the necessity of enrolment. The intending new owner first took a lease of the property for one year, which could be done by a deed that did not need to be enrolled. Then, a day later, the vendor conveyed the reversion of the lease to the purchaser, which, being only a right, could be transferred without livery of seisin or enrolment on a court roll, since possession did not pass as a result. This method of conveyance remained popular until the *Statute of Uses* was

repealed in 1845. The records (*see* TITLE DEED) consist of two documents, the Lease and the Release.

See also BARGAIN AND SALE; ENROLLED DEEDS.

Leasehold Tenure Such tenure could be for a term of years, for life, for up to three lives, or at the will of the landlord. Land available for such leases was mainly either demesne land or land reclaimed from the waste, or a copyholder's holding that had reverted to the lord through the extinction of his family. In leases for three lives (not necessarily of three generations) the names of the three persons had to be recorded, and it has been suggested that this is one reason why a man would christen more than one of his sons with the same name.

Lecturer A clergyman without a benefice, employed to preach. Not all beneficed clergy were able or licensed to preach. Instead, they used to read from *The Book of Homilies*, but by the beginning of the seventeenth century congregations were not satisfied with this practice and so subscribed funds to employ a lecturer, usually on an annual basis.

Legacy Goods bequeathed to someone (the legatee) in a will.

Leicestershire Since 1974 Rutland has been a part of Leicestershire. The county falls within the diocese of Lincoln in the Province of Canterbury. Nearly all parish registers have been deposited at the CRO and the SOG has copies of nearly 200 of them. Pallot's Marriage Index covers 107 parishes for 1790–1837. The CRO holds a marriage index for 1801–1837. The Marriage Licence records and Bishops' Transcripts are at the CRO. The SOG holds several indexes to Leicestershire Marriage Licences to 1748.

The Hundreds of Framland, Gartree, East and West Goscote, Guthlaxton, Sparkenhoe and Leicester Borough lie within its boundaries.

It has Lutterworth, Market Harborough, Billesdon, Blaby, Hinckley, Market Bosworth, Ashby-de-la-Zouch, Loughborough, Barrow on Soar, Leicester and Melton Mowbray RDs/PLUs.

It falls within the Midland Assize Circuit until 1863, then the Norfolk Circuit until 1876 and it reverts to the Midland Assize Circuit again in 1876.

The Leicestershire and Rutland Family History Society meets at Leicester, Loughborough and Market Harborough and publishes a quarterly newsletter.

Leicester Record Office, the County Library

and the Museum are all in Leicester. There is a Family History Centre at Loughborough.

Pre 1858 Wills proved at the following courts are in the CRO: Bishop's Commissary Court and Archdeaconry Court, Prebendal Court of St Margaret and Chapelry of Knighton and the Commissary Courts of the Manor of Rothley, the Manor of Evington and Groby. Wills could also be proved at the Consistory Court of Lincoln and the Prerogative Court of Canterbury.

Heralds' Visitation Pedigrees have been published for 1563, 1619 and 1683.

See *Family forbears: a guide to tracing your family tree in the Leicestershire Records Office*, by J. Farrell (1987) and *The descent of dissent: a guide to the nonconformist records at the Leicestershire Record Office* (1989).

Letters Close *see* **Close Rolls**

Letters of Administration *see* **Administration**

Letters of Attorney *see* **Attorney**

Letters Patent *see* **Patent Rolls**

Levant Company The Worshipful Company of Merchants of England Trading to the Levant Seas was founded in 1581, though it acquired its name a little later. It became, however, commonly known as the Turkey Company as the lands it traded with were then parts of the Ottoman Empire. In 1606, the Company was granted a virtual monopoly of that trade in the shape of considerable reduction in excise duty. Unlike the East India Company, it did not trade as one organisation; its members, who had to be Freemen of the City of London, operated as independent merchants but under rules laid down by themselves corporately. By the Turkish Government it was seen as the commercial and diplomatic agent of the English Crown, and was granted a commercial treaty known as the capitulations; but, unknown to the Turks, the British Ambassador's salary and expenses were paid by the Company, not by the Crown. The Company had factories (trading stations manned by factors) at Aleppo (the largest), Constantinople, Smyrna, Cairo, Iskanderun (Alexandretta), Larnaca in Cyprus, Angola, Tripoli and Acre. In each, one of the factors was appointed Consul to represent its interests with the local authorities. In 1753, agitation in London against the Company's monopoly was successful in throwing membership open to anyone who would pay an entrance fee of £20. However, British trade with the Levant was already in decline and the Seven Years War, 1756–63, made conditions still more difficult. The Company's monopoly trade with the Levant was finally ended in 1825. The records are at the Public Record Office, Chancery Lane, London, in class SP 105.

Lewd Contemptible, profligate; but it can also mean 'lay', as in 'layman'.

Lewis's Topographical Dictionary A *Topographical Dictionary of England* (1831, 1833 and 1849) and *A Topographical Dictionary of Wales* (1833, 1849), both by Samuel Lewis, describe in a number of volumes every town and village in the country, giving brief historical details of each. Its great value to genealogists is that it states whether a place is a parish in its own right, or, if not, in which parish it lies.

The England editions of 1831 and 1833, and the Wales edition of 1833, also show in what ecclesiastical probate jurisdiction a place is situated. References to 'townships' means civil parishes.

All information of genealogical value has been extracted from these volumes and published separately as *A Genealogical Gazetteer of England* (compiler, Frank Smith) by the Genealogical Publishing Company of Baltimore, USA. Lewis compiled similar gazeteers for Ireland in 1837 and for Scotland in 1846.

Lex An entry, made in the margin of the minutes of a legal suit, indicating that either the defendant or the plaintiff was to go to 'wager of law'; i.e. his statements were to be vouched for by a number of neighbours or friends.

Leywrite A fine due from a medieval villein to the lord of his manor, if his unmarried daughter became pregnant. It was to compensate for the depreciation of her manorial value.

Libel The written case of a plaintiff in an ecclesiastical court.

Libertate Probanda, Writ of de If a villein absconded from his manor but was caught and reclaimed by his lord on a *Writ of de Nativo Habendo*, he himself was entitled to a *Writ of de Libertate Probanda* allowing him to remain free until his lord had succeeded in proving his claim in a royal court.

Liberty A manor, or group of manors, or other area lying outside the jurisdiction of the sheriff, and having a separate Commission of the Peace. Also called a 'soke' or a 'lordship'.

Licence to Pass Beyond the Seas This was an early form of passport issued between the late years of Elizabeth I and 1677. The records consist of registers of soldiers taking the oath of allegiance, before serving in the Low Countries, 1613–24; people going abroad, mainly to Holland, in the period 1624–37; and passengers to New England, Barbados and other colonies, 1634–9 and 1677. The last class has been printed in J.C. Hotten's *Original Lists of Persons Emigrating to America, 1600–1700*. The original records are at the Public Record Office, Chancery Lane, London, in class E 157.

Liege *see* **Homage**

Linch *or* **Linchet** The strips of grassy turf between two pieces of arable land in a common field.

Lincolnshire The north of the ancient county is now in Humberside. It fell within the diocese of Lincoln and the Province of Canterbury. Most of the 627 ancient parishes have deposited their registers at the CRO. The SOG has transcripts of over one hundred. Pallot's Marriage Index covers 72 parishes from 1790–1837. The Marriage Licence records and the Bishops' Transcripts are at the CRO.

The county is divided into the following Wapentakes: Parts of Holland includes Elloe, Kirton, Skirbeck and Boston Borough; Parts of Kesteven includes Aswardhurn, Aveland, Beltisloe, Boothby-Graffo (Higher and Lower Divisions), Flaxwell, Langoe (1st and 2nd Divisions), Loveden, Ness, Winnibriggs and Threo and Grantham and Stamford Boroughs; Parts of Lindsey includes Aslacoe (East and West), Bolingbroke East and West Soke, Bradley Haverstoe, Calceworth (Marsh and Wold Divisions) Hundreds, Candleshoe (Marsh and Wold Divisions), Gartree North and South, Corringham, Hill Hundred, Walshcroft (North and South Divisions), Well and Wraggoe (East and West Divisions), Yarborough (South, East and North Divisions); also Horncastle Soke, Lawress, Ludborough and Manley (Eastern, Northern and Western) Wapentakes and Louth-Eske Hundred (Marsh and Wold Divisions), Lincoln City, County and Liberty.

It has Stamford, Bourne, Spalding, Holbeach, Boston, Sleaford, Grantham, Lincoln, Horncastle, Spilsby, Louth, Caistor, Glanford Brigg and Gainsborough RDs/PLUs.

It falls within the Midland Assize Circuit.

The Lincolnshire Family History Society meets at Boston, Bourne, Grantham, Grimsby, Horncastle, Lincoln, Louth and Scunthorpe and publishes a quarterly journal and the Isle of Axholme Family History Society meets at Epworth and publishes *The Islonian* quarterly.

Record Repositories: Lincolnshire Archives Office and the Lincoln Central Library both at Lincoln. There is a Family History Centre at Grimsby.

Pre 1858 Wills are at the CRO and were proved in the following courts; Consistory Court of Lincoln, the Archdeaconry Court of Stow, the Court of the Dean and Chapter of Lincoln, the Manorial Court of Kirkstead and the Peculiar Courts of Caistor, Corringham, Heydown, Kirton in Lindsey, Louth, Bishops Norton, Sleaford and Stow in Lindsey. Wills could also be proved at the Prerogative Court of Canterbury.

The Lincolnshire Record Society has published many local records since 1911. Heralds' Visitation Pedigrees have been published for 1563–4, 1592, 1634 and 1666.

See *Genealogical sources in Lincolnshire* (Lincolnshire FHS, 1990). Lincolnshire Archives Office publishes *Your family history in Lincolnshire's archives* and *Deposited parish registers and non-parochial registers*.

List and Index Society A society formed to print lists and indexes of records in the Public Record Office. They are not to be confused with the volumes of the Index Library, published by the British Record Society.

Literacy Reading and writing were already being taught in the Middle Ages to boys attending Grammar and English Schools; and Professor F.R.H. Du Boulay has reckoned that in the fifteenth century about 30 per cent of the population, taking both sexes into account, could read but not necessarily write — a proportion increasing to about 40 per cent by 1530. In the middle of the sixteenth century, literacy was increased by the publication of copybooks both in Secretary and Italic hands (*see* HANDWRITING).

From 1754 onward, the proportion of the population that was literate has been calculated mainly from the number of people who subscribed their signatures to their marriage entries in parish registers, instead of 'making their mark'. In the year 1857, all except 28 per cent of bridegrooms signed their certificates and all except 39 per cent of women. However, it has been found from other sources that some of those who authenticated their certificate with a mark certainly could write. Perhaps their mark had become their customary 'sign manual'. Conversely, a written signature at that period did not necessarily indicate that the signatory could write anything else.

Liverpool and South West Lancashire Family History Society *see* Lancashire

Livery (i) The giving and taking of possession; called 'livery of seisin'. A manorial copyholder who was alienating his holding would deliver a rod or wand to the lord of the manor or his steward as a sign of surrender of the tenement, and the lord or steward would deliver the rod to the new tenant, both actions taking place in the presence of other tenants called upon to witness the 'act of livery'. In the case of freeholders, the delivery was made with a piece of turf or a clod of earth, or the ring of the door, direct to the new owner. By the *Real Property Act*, 1845, such transactions could be carried out by deed alone, without livery.

(ii) Release from wardship.

(iii) A uniform worn in the Middle Ages by squires and pages as a sign of allegiance to their knight or nobleman. It usually bore upon the left sleeve the patron's heraldic badge (*see* MAINTENANCE). From Henry VII to the beginning of Charles II's reign, the keeping by magnates of retainers in livery was made subject to royal licence, which had to be paid for. By the eighteenth century, livery in the sense of a special dress had become a prerequisite provided by a private employer to certain of his servants, such as footmen and coachmen, and usually took the form of an out-dated and colourful costume. Those menials who wore it were addressed by their Christian names, but the more senior servants, such as the butlers and ladies' maids, who wore an approved form of contemporary dress, were spoken to by their surnames.

(iv) For the liveries worn by members of London Guilds, *see* LIVERY COMPANIES.

Livery Companies The Guilds of the City of London, the earliest of which were in existence in the twelfth century. From the reign of Edward III they were incorporated by royal charter, and they became known as livery companies from their assumption of a distinctive dress or livery.

An ordinance of Edward II required all Freemen of the City to be members of one or other of the guilds, and it became the practice for all guild freemen to become freemen of the City. The original function of the guilds was to regulate trade and traders in their particular mystery (a word originating in 'mistery' from the Old French *metier*, an occupation), but by the end of the sixteenth century London trades and crafts had outgrown their old form of organisation, and new trades had been introduced. The companies were becoming wealthy charitable institutions whose members were not necessarily connected with the occupations indicated by the guild name. A linen-draper might, for instance, be a member of the Fishmongers' Company, and it was possible for a man to be described in one document as 'William Brown, hosier', and, equally correctly, in another as 'William Brown, Citizen and Merchant Taylor', the latter description indicating that he was a freeman of the company named and of the City of London, but saying nothing about how he earned his livelihood. The guilds continued for some time, however, to be closely linked with the constitution of the City's government, and the restrictions of trade in the City to freemen lasted until the end of the eighteenth century.

Freedom of a company could be obtained by one of three methods: (i) by servitude, after apprenticeship to a freeman of the company (*see* APPRENTICES; (ii) by patrimony, being a child of a freeman of the company; (iii) by redemption, i.e. by buying the freedom of a company. On gaining his company's freedom, the new member immediately applied for, and obtained, the freedom of the City (*see* FREEMEN OF THE CITY OF LONDON). From a company's freemen were recruited the liverymen, a privileged middle rank from whose numbers the Court of Assistants, the governing body of the company, was elected. This, in turn, elected the Master, Wardens and Renter Wardens for the ensuing year. Liverymen were enfranchised to vote for the Lord Mayor and for Members of Parliament for the City of London. A man could be a freeman of more than one company, or change from one to another. The charitable work of the City companies can be seen in the schools that owe to them their foundation and support. The list opposite is of the ancient Livery Companies and associated organisations.

The records of those listed opposite, or microfiche of them, are deposited at the Guildhall Library, except those marked*. Those marked** have deposited part of their records. The Pinmakers' records are in the Egerton series of the MS Department of the British Library. The records of the Linen Drapers' Company have disappeared. The Guildhall Library has a number of published histories of the London Livery Companies, and has itself published a *Guide to the Archives of the Livery Companies and related Organisations in Guildhall Library*.

Apothecaries
Armourers and
   Brasiers
Bakers
Barbers
Basketmakers
Blacksmiths
Bowyers
Brewers
Broderers
Brown-Bakers
Butchers
Carmen
Carpenters
Clockmakers
Clothworkers*
Coachmakers
Combmakers
Cooks
Coopers
Cordwainers
Curriers
Cutlers
Distillers
Drapers*
Dyers
Fanmakers
Farriers
Fellowship Porters
Feltmakers
Fishmongers
Fletchers
Founders
Framework Knitters
Fruiterers
Gardeners
Girdlers
Glass-Sellers
Glaziers
Glovers
Gold and Silver
   Wyre Drawers
Goldsmiths**
Grocers

Gunmakers
Haberdashers
Horners
Innholders
Ironmongers
Joiners
Leathersellers*
Loriners
Masons
Mercers*
Merchant Taylors
Musicians
Needle Makers
Painter Stainers
Parish Clerks
Patternmakers
Paviors
Pewterers
Plaisterers
Playing Card Makers
Plumbers
Poulters
Saddlers
Salters*
Scriveners
Shipwrights
Silk Throwsters
Skinners*
Spectacle Makers
Stationers*
Tallow Chandlers
Tin Plate Workers
Tobacco Pipe Makers
Turners
Tylers and
   Bricklayers
Upholders
Vintners
Watermen
Waxchandlers
Weavers
Wheelwrights
Woodmongers
Woolmen

Local Historian, The   A journal founded as *The Amateur Historian* in 1952 to publish articles on documentary sources and related subjects, for spare-time researchers into local, family and institutional history and archaeology. In 1961 it was presented, by its proprietor, to the Standing Conference for Local History as its offical organ. In 1968 its name was changed to *The Local Historian*. Over the years, the articles, originally addressed to amateurs, have become increas-

ingly scholarly, reflecting the growth in interest in local history taken by universities since the 1950s.

Local History   (i) An ancestor's home town or village as it was in his lifetime is one context into which the family historian needs to set him. The history of the counties and smaller districts of England has been an object of study since the sixteenth century, and since then local histories have been published in increasing numbers and are available in public reference libraries in their own areas. In 1899, work on *The Victoria History of the Counties of England* was begun and has been progressing, with set-backs caused by two wars, ever since.

The destruction of ancient buildings in England caused by bombing in the Second World War, gave rise to a great surge of interest in local history in the late 1940s and the 1950s, and many local history societies came into existence at that time. In 1948 the Standing Conference for Local History was formed, with members representing one hundred historical bodies, including the Society of Genealogists. In 1961 it adopted the quarterly journal, *The Amateur Historian*, as its official organ and, in 1968, changed its title to *The Local Historian*. The Standing Conference has now been reconstituted as the British Association for Local History, and today most local history societies are members.

The Association issues a number of pamphlets for the guidance of local historians. Information about societies researching in any particular area can be obtained through the British Association for Local History, Shopwyke Manor Barn, Chichester, PO20 6BG.

(ii) The name of a national subscription magazine whose address is 3 Devonshire Promenade, Nottingham NG7 2DS.

Local Population Studies   Founded in 1974 to promote the study of local historical demography and the social structure of past societies. It exists to enable discussion between local historians, demographers, geographers, family historians and all those with an interest in population history at all levels of expertise. The Society also encourages the educational use of local population studies in schools, colleges and other

OVERLEAF London in 1832. Seventy years before Kingsway, the present mecca of genealogists, came into existence.

institutions. It publishes a journal in the spring and autumn of each year and a newsletter twice a year. Address enquiries to Sir David Cooke, 8 Royal Crescent, Harrogate, North Yorkshire HG2 8AB.

Local Record Offices In the United Kingdom national archives are not all kept in one repository. National records are housed in the Public Record Office but locally created records are held by local record offices, at borough or county level. *See also* COUNTY RECORD OFFICE.

Local Register Offices These are the offices of the local Superintendent Registrars of Births, Marriages and Deaths. Searching in local register offices may be more economical when several ancestors exist in one area. Access is at the discretion of the local registrar. The current fee is £15 for six consecutive hours general search on any one day, by appointment. You may look at the indexes but may also be allowed limited access to the registers for the purpose of verification for which there is a fee of £2.50. The fees are reviewed annually, so check before you go.

London and Middlesex London City is a county in itself and is subdivided into Wards whose boundaries do not coincide with those of the parishes in the City. In 1889 the Administrative County of London was formed from the City of London and parts of Middlesex, Kent and Surrey and was divided into boroughs. In 1963 this county was replaced by Greater London which also took in the rest of Middlesex and parts of Essex and Herts as well as some county boroughs. New London Boroughs were then formed.

The London parts of Surrey and Kent are in the dioceses of Winchester and Rochester respectively, the rest of London is in its own diocese and all are in the Province of Canterbury. Nearly all parish registers have been deposited either at the Greater London Record Office or the Guildhall Library but there are some at local libraries. The Society of Genealogists has copies of about 200. Boyd's Marriage Index covers 163 parishes and institutions, some only extracts. Pallot's Marriage Index covers 235 registers mostly from 1800–1812 or 1837. The SOG has the City of London Burial Index. The Bishops' Transcripts, mainly from 1800 are at the Guildhall Library. Marriage Licence records of the London Diocese are at the GLRO which also has marriage licence records for the Royal Peculiar of St Katherine by the Tower and the Peculiar of the Dean and Chapter of St Paul's. The records

of the Faculty Office and the Vicar General's Office are at Lambeth Palace Library as are those of the Peculiar Deanery of Croydon and the Peculiar of the Dean and Chapter of Westminster.

The Hundreds of Edmonton, Elthorne, Gore, Isleworth, Ossulstone (Finsbury, Holborn, Kensington and Tower Divisions), Spelthorne, London within and without the Walls, the Inns of Court and Chancery, and Westminster City and Liberty lie within the boundaries of London and Middlesex.

Middlesex has Staines, Uxbridge, Brentford, Hendon, Barnet and Edmonton RDs/PLUs. Metropolitan London had Paddington, Kensington, Fulham, Chelsea, St George Hanover Square, Westminster, St Martin-in-the-Fields, St James Westminster, Marylebone, Hampstead, Pancras, Islington, Hackney, St Giles, Strand, Holborn, Clerkenwell, St Luke, London City, Shoreditch, Bethnal Green, Whitechapel, St George-in-the-East, Stepney, Mile End Old Town, Poplar, St Saviour and St Olave Southwark, Bermondsey, St George Southwark, Newington, Lambeth, Wandsworth, Camberwell, Rotherhithe, Greenwich, Lewisham and Woolwich RDs/PLUs.

Local Family History Societies: West Middlesex (meets at Hounslow) and Hillingdon (meets at Ickenham) who both publish quarterly journals, Westminster and Central Middlesex (has branches at Harrow and Wembley) who publish *Greentrees* twice-yearly, London and North Middlesex (has branches at Barnet, Enfield, Islington and the City of London) who publish *Metropolitan* quarterly, the East of London (meet at Barking, City of London, Upminster and Wanstead) who publish *Cockney Ancestor* quarterly, and the North West Kent (meet at Bromley, Dartford and Sevenoaks), East Surrey (meet at Caterham, Croydon, Richmond, Southwark, Sutton and Wandsworth) and Woolwich and District (meet at Shooters Hill) societies who all publish quarterly journals.

Record Offices and Local History Libraries: The Public Record Office, the Greater London Record Office, the Guildhall Library, the Corporation of London Record Office, General Register Office, Lambeth Palace Library, House of Lords Record Office, Principal Registry of the Family Division, British Library, British Museum, British Newspaper Library, St Paul's Cathedral, the Library of the Society of Genealogists, Westminster Library (to be amalgamated on one site in 1994 from the Victoria and Marylebone Libraries), Minet Library, Shepherd's Bush Library, Lewisham Public Library, Shoreditch Library, Dr

William's Library, Southwark Local Studies Library, Friends' House, India Office Records and Library, Historical Manuscripts Commission and National Register of Archives. For their whereabouts consult E. Silverthorne *London Local Archives: a directory of local authority record offices and libraries,* 2nd edn., Guildhall Library and the Greater London Archives Network (1989), R. Harvey *Guide to genealogical sources in Guildhall Library* (1988) and S. Bourne *Ten London repositories* (1992). Several borough archives have published guides to family history sources in their collections.

There are Family History Centres at Staines, Balham and South Kensington.

Pre 1858 Wills are found at the following repositories: the GLRO for those provided at the Consistory Court of London, the Commissary Court of Surrey and the Archdeaconry Courts of Middlesex (Middlesex Division) and Surrey; The Guildhall Library for those proved at the Commissary Court of London (London Division), the Archdeaconry Court of London, the Peculiar Court of the Dean and Chapter of St Paul's and the Royal Peculiar of St Katherine by the Tower; the Corporation of London Record Office for those proved at the Court of Hustings; at Lambeth Palace Library for the Peculiar Courts of the Deaneries of the Arches and of Croydon; and at Westminster Library for the Royal Peculiar of the Dean and Chapter of Westminster. Wills were also proved at the Consistory of Winchester and at the Prerogative Court of Canterbury.

Memorial Inscriptions: Many from City churchyards have been published in P. Rushden *The Churchyard Inscriptions of the City of London* (1910) and M.A. Jewer *Guide to the Monumental Inscriptions of the City Churches.*

Heralds' Visitation Pedigrees have been published for London for 1568, 1633–34, 1664 and 1687; and for Middlesex, for 1634 and 1633.

Record Publishing Societies: London Record Society has been publishing annual volumes since 1965; London and Middlesex Archaeological Society, London Topographical Society.

Further Reading: M.P.E. Jones *The 1695 Inhabitants of the City* and T.C. Dale, *17th Century London Inhabitants*, both from the Guildhall Library. Boyd's *Index of London Citizens,* at the SOG Library. J.S.W. Gibson and H. Creaton, *Lists of Londoners,* FFHS (1992). Cliff Webb's *London Middlesex and Surrey Workhouse Records, Middlesex Parish Documents, Genealogical Research in Edwardian London* and *Genealogical Research in Victorian London,* all available from the West Surrey FHS (1990–1992).

London Gazette This official publication first appeared under that name on Monday, 5 February, 1665/6, and for a long time was issued each Tuesday and Friday but now appears daily. It publishes official church, civil, naval, military and legal appointments and promotions, including those of the militia, and advertisements relating to the formation and dissolution of business companies and partnerships; settlements of estates and claims, and other financial and legal matters appertaining to private persons and corporate bodies, including bankruptcies, changes of name, the naturalization of aliens and insolvent debtors. In 1787 half-yearly indexes were commenced, one relating to official government news such as State Intelligence and appointments and promotions, and the other to the remaining matters mentioned. The Guildhall Library, London, has a complete set of the *Gazette,* though some of the early indexes are missing. The set in the British Library is indexed only from the year 1803.

For further reading, see *A History of the London Gazette, 1665–1965,* by P.M. Handover.

Lord Hardwicke's Marriage Act In 1754 this Act made it illegal to marry without the publishing of Banns. This effectively put a stop to the quickie marriages which proliferated in the marriage shops which had sprung up to enable people to marry with the least amount of fuss.

Lord Lieutenant In 1551, the control of the militia forces of the country was placed in the hands of newly created officials known as the king's lieutenants. As these officials were almost always noblemen, they came to be known as 'lords lieutenant'. At first the lieutenant was commissioned only for some special occasion, such as a threat of invasion or rebellion, but in time tended to be appointed until notice to the contrary, and so the post became nearly permanent, in some counties even hereditary, until in 1662 the *Militia Act* established it as personal and permanent.

The lieutenant was responsible for musters and beacons, and was allowed to appoint deputies as well as a provost marshal and muster master. After a reorganisation of the office in 1757, minute books were kept by a Clerk to the Lieutenancy, some of which are extant. From 1797, the danger of invasion by the French threw many responsibilities upon the Lord Lieutenant, calling for the keeping of detailed minutes and returns. These include nominal lists of militiamen, their available implements for constructing makeshift defences, supplies of flour, emergency baking facilities and available transport. The Lieutenancy records are kept at the county record office.

Lord of the Manor *see* Manor

Lorimer *or* **Loriner** A word, and surname, derived from the Old French *lormier* (the rein of a bridle). A maker of bits, spurs and metal mountings for bridles and saddles; hence, a saddler.

Lot A church rate.
See also SCOT.

Lot-Meadow A portion of the manorial meadow that was held in severalty, but subject to annual re-allotment.

Lozenge An heraldic term meaning diamond shaped.

Lug A land measure of five and a half yards; another term for a rod, pole or perch.

Lutherans Followers of Luther who sought to rectify the behaviour of the clergy. Because he attacked the church he was seen to attack the church's role in salvation. Reform movements had been in existence before he came on the scene but it was his actions that made the Reformation an accepted fact.

M

Magistrate A civil officer responsible for the administration of the law.

Mainpast The surety of good behaviour from the head of a household for those in it, as part of the security system of tithing.

Mainport A due payable, in some parishes, to the rector by poorer householders in lieu of certain tithes. It usually consisted of loaves of bread.

Mainprise The commital of a person, who might otherwise be imprisoned into the friendly custody of someone (his 'mainpernor') who had given security that he would be forthcoming at a certain time and place. Unlike bail, of which it is a special obsolete form, mainprise forbade the mainpernor to put the person under physical constraint.

Maintenance The keeping by a landed magnate, mainly in the fourteenth to sixteenth centuries, of a retinue of followers, usually in a badged livery. From Henry VII's time, such a privilege was allowed only under royal licence. In the fourteenth century some of these bands of men were little better than gangs, robbing their patron's smaller neighbours, seizing their lands and giving false witness against them in law suits. In return, the lord supported his followers in legal disputes, by force if necessary. The system was known as Badge and Maintenance.

Manchester, Greater A metropolitan county formed in 1974 out of a part of LANCASHIRE.

Manchet Best quality wheaten bread.

Mandamus, Writ of An order to a public officer to carry out his duty, from the Latin, 'we command'.

Manor For 500 years after the Conquest the manor was the unit of estate administration. Its head was the Lord of the manor (literally a landlord, not necessarily a titled person), who held the estate from the king either directly or through one or more mesne lords. Typically the inhabitants of the early manor included villeins, bound to the land, cottagers, and one or more freeholding franklins. Over a large part of England the typical manor contained a village with a church, and agricultural land consisting of two, or more, usually three, large arable fields in which the inhabitants held scattered strips. The lord's own demesne might be in scattered strips or in a consolidated block, tending more to the latter as time went by. The land near the local stream was the meadow, where grass was grown for hay, and the less lush grassland was the permanent pasture for the beasts of the manor. There would usually also be some woodland. Each villein's tenement (his holding) entitled him to a certain number of strips of arable land, and grazing for a certain number of cattle and sheep.

An important part of manorial administration was the manor court, a periodic meeting of the tenantry, presided over by the lord of the manor or his steward. In many places the courts met regularly, at intervals laid down by the custom of the manor that might be anything between six weeks and six months. The procedure was judicial, but the matters dealt with were both judicial and administrative. Every manorial court was a Court Baron, which administered the agriculture of the manor, the lord's and tenants' rights and duties, changes of occupancy, and disputes between tenants; some manorial courts were also a Court Leet, also called the View of Frankpledge, which covered the election of constables, alctasters and some other officials, and what would now be called police matters (for example, maintenance of the lock-up, disturbances of the peace, and so on).

Customs which vary from manor to manor, governed everything and checked the rights and duties of both the lord and the tenants. The principle was 'Justice shall be done by the lord's court, not by the lord'. The steward (*seneschallus*) who might be a neighbour of some substance and legal training and similarly responsible for several manors in the district, convened the court and usually presided over it. All tenants were bound to attend and the opening procedure (recorded in Latin) included:

Election of the jury (*juratores*) or homage (*homagium*) and their swearing in. Anyone who refused to serve was fined.

Consideration of excuses for absence, called essoins (*essonia*) and absences without a valid excuse (*defalte*). These defaulters were punished by a fine.

Local officials for the ensuing year might be elected in the manorial court. They might include the lord's local manager, the reeve (*prepositus*); the hayward (*heiwardus*); the beadle (*bedellus*); the constable (*constabulus*); and the aletaster. Also elected were two affeerors (*afferatores*) whose job was to assess the amount of each penalty imposed by the court. If the culprit was amerced (*in misericordia*), the amount to be paid was laid down by the affeerors, having regard to the custom of the manor.

Transfers of property (*alienationes*) and other matters were raised and dealt with, and orders (*precepta*) issued. There was often an adjournment for a midday meal. By the eighteenth century there was usually only one aspect of the court, the Court Leet having lost its functions to the parish Vestry and the Justices of the Peace.

Besides the regular courts there came, by the sixteenth century, to be two special ones, held when the lordship of the manor changed hands, either by sale or inheritance. The first was a Court of Recognition, or *Curia Prima*, at which the new lord became formally 'seized' of the services of the tenants and received their recognition as the new lord. They made him a symbolic money payment and all renewed the

oaths of fealty that they had first taken when entering into their tenancies. Secondly, a Court of Survey was summoned either just before or just after a change of lordship. Its purpose was to list all the lands of the manor and the customary dues by which the copyhold tenants held their lands.

The origins of the manorial court are lost in antiquity, but treatises on procedure were being written as early as the thirteenth century. Usually a majority of tenants held land by villein (unfree) tenure, but there were usually freeholders too, whose tenure was protected by the royal courts. In the course of the later middle ages the constraints on villeins declined, but this so-called customary tenure continued under the sole jurisdiction of the manorial court. It was only in the sixteenth century that royal courts began to protect customary tenure, known as copyhold, because on entry into the holding the tenant was given a copy of the court's record of the fact as a title deed. The early court rolls were written in Latin, but under the Commonwealth, English was introduced. However, after the Restoration, Latin became again the language of the rolls, persisting in many manors until 1733.

During the nineteenth century the holding of manor courts gradually came to an end, and in 1925, copyhold tenure formally ended in accordance with the *Law of Property Acts*, 1922 and 1924.

The records of a manorial estate included:

The Court Rolls The record of the court's proceedings written by the steward's clerk and kept by the steward or the lord himself. For the genealogists, these are the most useful.

The Valor A record of financial values.

The Rental Details of rents due and paid.

The Custumal Intended for permanent reference, a description of the customary rights and duties of the lord and tenants.

The Terrier A description of the whereabouts and size of the lord's and each tenant's lands within the manor.

The Extent A custumal with every item valued.

The court rolls record changes of occupancy of villein or copyhold lands, and, in some manors, of freehold land, giving the names of the late and new owners. As these were often father and son, it is sometimes possible to trace several generations of a family from court rolls. When the new occupant came from outside the manor, his place of origin was usually given. Dates of death can also be established. When a tenant died, his will, or an extract from it, might be quoted in the court roll. Sometimes this is the only surviving record of the will. Even a new freehold tenant had to pay the lord a relief, a small sum of money

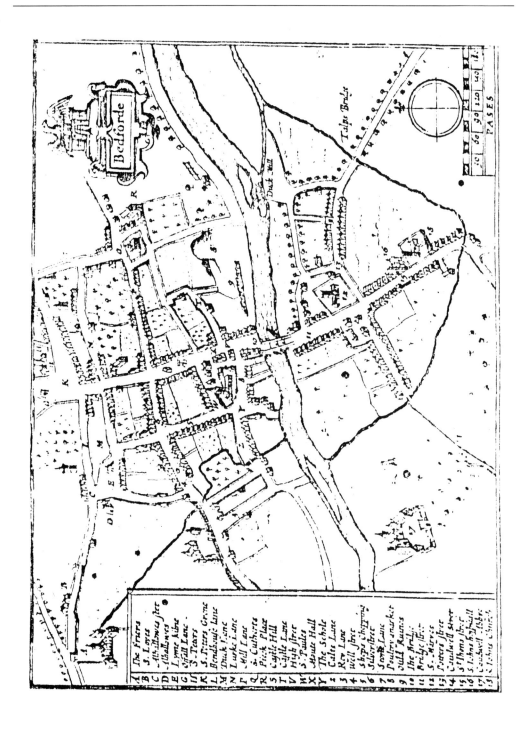

Changes in urban street names can make an ancestral house hard to locate. This plan of Bedford by John Speed, 1600, supplies all the names of that period.

for taking up his tenancy; so there is some record of freeholders, too. The villein or copyholder paid an entry fine and swore fealty, i.e. to pay the customary dues and observe the ancient rules of the holding with regard to his animals, etc. Disputes between tenants often reveal the names of members of a family hitherto unknown, or serve to confirm or disprove hypotheses based on parish registers.

Since 1926, all manorial records have had to be reported to the Master of the Rolls on request as also any changes in their ownership and custody. The Historical Manuscripts Commission maintains a *Manorial Documents Register*, which takes the form of two series. The first, arranged under parishes, shows the names of the manor or manors in each parish; the second, arranged under manors, shows the last-known whereabouts of the manorial records. In a great many instances the solicitors of manorial families are still the custodians of the rolls, but many have been deposited at CROs. The Public Record Office and the British Library have considerable deposits, but the majority of manorial records have failed to survive.

For further reading, see *Manorial Records*, by P.D.A. Harvey (British Record Association 1984), 'Manorial Documents', by A. Travers, in *Genealogists' Magazine*, vol. 21, No.1 and *My Ancestors were Manorial Tenants*, by P.B. Park (Society of Genealogists, 1994).

Mansfield and District Family History Society *see* Nottinghamshire

Mantling A short cape, depicted in a heraldic achievement as held on the helmet by a wreath of twisted silk (the torse), and flowing around the shield of arms. Its edges are usually slashed for decorative purposes. The outside and the lining are normally depicted in the two main tinctures of the arms. The purpose of the cape was to protect the metal helmet from becoming over-hot in the sun of Palestine. It was also deadening to a sword-cut, and could entangle an opponent's sword. Also called a lambrequin.

Manuel Rente The money paid for a commuted feudal service.

Manumission The act of a feudal lord that gave a villein his freedom.

Maps It can sometimes be important to know the lie of the land around an ancestor's home. The nearest neighbouring town or village as the crow flew may not have been the quickest to reach. Hills might intervene, or bridges over the local river might be few and far between. Contacts between neighbours would be governed by such considerations, and also by the whereabouts of the market town, where people needed to gather at regular intervals to buy and sell. The market town was not always the obvious one, because charters were often ancient and a town's importance could alter with the centuries. Where a bride and bridegroom were of different parishes not very close together, the local market may have been the cause of their meeting: 'Where are you going to, my pretty maid?' 'I'm going to market, sir,' she said. The study of old maps may provide possible explanations for family migrations. Many town street plans exist from the seventeenth century, and a careful comparison of one with the local rate assessments may make it possible to pinpoint an ancestral home. The maps that form part of a parish's Tithe Redemption Award, *see* TITHE, and Enclosure Award, *see* ENCLOSURES, are an absolute must for identifying a family's home site in the mid nineteenth century. Ordnance Survey maps, which began to appear from 1805, can be found at county record offices. The old directories and guide books that can be found in some libraries often contain county maps. David & Charles Publishers have reprinted early nineteenth century Ordnance Survey maps, but with the later railways inserted.

A useful series of Victorian Ordnance Survey Maps has been reprinted by Alan Godfrey in Gateshead. They do not cover the whole country but are published whenever one becomes available for reproduction. Their scale is approximately 15 in. to the mile.

Estate maps can be found in the deposited records of landed estates, and sometimes, in church terriers and the records of the Ecclesiastical Commissioners. Estate maps of lands held by the Crown are in the Public Record Office. An estimated six million maps, depicting areas in all parts of the world, are held there.

A valuable modern aid is provided by the *Phillimore Atlas and Index of Parish Registers*, ed. C.R. Humphrey-Smith (1984) published by the Institute of Heraldic and Genealogical Studies. They show the position and shape of each pre 1832 parish, the date from which its registers survive, whether deposited, IGI index, whereabouts of copies and the ecclesiastical probate jurisdictions in which it lay.

For further reading, see *County Atlases of the British Isles published after 1703*, vol. 1 by D. Hodson (Tewin, 1984). PRO Information Leaflet No. 91. *Maps in the Public Record Office.*

Maritagium A gift to a daughter on her marriage.
See also DOWRY.

Mark A monetary unit of account worth 13 shillings and 4 pence, but never minted as a coin.

Market A gathering of vendors of goods and services for sale. The right of a town or village to hold a weekly market was granted by the sovereign and had to be paid for. Originally, markets were held on Sundays but were moved to weekdays in the thirteenth century. In the sixteenth century many village markets closed down, unable to compete with more popular ones in nearby towns, or with those in villages more favourably placed. Market day attracted people from surrounding villages, some to sell their goods, some to buy, and some for social gatherings. When an entry in a marriage register shows that the partners came from different parishes, the district's market may well have been the means of bringing them together.

Marque, Letters of In time of war, the Lord High Admiral received a special commission from the sovereign to grant letters of marque. Issued to a private ship-owner or commander, letters of marque empowered him to fit out an armed vessel or vessels for the purpose of harassing the enemy. Such ships, called privateers, were usually employed to capture the enemy's merchant ships.

Marquess The peerage title next in dignity after a duke, and before an earl. The first English marquess was Robert de Vere, Earl of Oxford, created Marquess of Dublin by Richard II in 1385. The function of lords marchers, or margraves, on the continent was to guard the borders of a kingdom; and the lords of the marches of Scotland and Wales were termed marchiones from early times; but that authority, by then already a dead letter, was formally abolished by Henry VIII. The title is often spelt in the French way, marquis. The wife of a marquess is a marchioness.

On the creation of a dukedom, a marquisate has sometimes been granted at the same time, to provide a second title to be borne by courtesy during the duke's lifetime, by his heir. Except for formal purposes, a marquess and marchioness are referred to as Lord and Lady (So-and-so), and their children are termed Lord and Lady before their Christian names.

Marriage Certificate *see* **General Register of Births, Deaths and Marriages**

Marriage Horizon The term coined by demographers to express the radius within which a certain percentage of extra-parochial marriage partners lived; e.g. 90 per cent of partners from outside the parish came from within a radius of fifteen miles — the marriage horizon.

Marriage Index An index, compiled for genealogical purposes, of marriages in a certain area, usually a county, using information culled from parish registers, bishops' transcripts and marriage licence records. It is one of the most valuable of location records, providing a short cut to finding the whereabouts of a family at a given period. The first index to be compiled was PALLOT's Marriage Index, mainly of London and Middlesex marriages. This was followed by BOYD's Marriage Index of sixteen counties and two miscellaneous series. Neither of these covers every parish nor, in many cases, the whole period of a register. During recent years many family history societies have been indexing the marriages of their counties, and some are already complete. Information from most of them is open to non-members of the societies. Some counties are indexed under the names of both parties; others of bridgegrooms only. Each entry shows the name of the spouse, the parish of marriage and the date, or at least the year, of marriage. If present progress is maintained it should not be many years before all recorded marriages in England are indexed. When information is sought, attention should not be confined to one particular marriage; those of people of the same surname should be extracted, unless the name is very common. Regarded as clues to a family's whereabouts, the marriages of women are more helpful than those of men, because there has always been a tendency for weddings to be held in the bride's parish. Any marriage found in an index should be looked up in the original register for additional information, such as the names of witnesses, the bridegrooms occupation and the parties' parishes of residence, also check that no indexing error has been made.

The Federation of Family History Societies has published *Marriage, Census and Other Indexes for Family Historians*, by J.S.W. Gibson and E. Hampson (4th edn 1992).

Marriage Licence Records From the early sixteenth century, people intending to marry were able to avoid the inconvenience of banns by obtaining a marriage licence. The inconveniences included delay and publicity, and besides this, well-to-do people felt it undignified to invite

The illustration ABOVE shows a marriage licence allegation of 1750, made at the office of the Dean and Chapter of St Paul's. *Courtesy Guildhall Library, Corporation of London. Photo: Godfrey New Photographics*

every Tom, Dick and Harry in the parish to object to their marriage. The result was that most people who could afford the fee married by licence. Later, dissenters objected to their banns being called in a parish church.

The licence was normally obtained from the chancellor or surrogate of the diocese in which one of the parties lived, and in which the marriage was to be celebrated; but application could be made to the Vicar-General of the Archbishop of the province. If the parties lived in different dioceses, they had to apply to the Vicar-General. If they lived in different provinces they applied to the Master of Faculties of the Archbishop of

Canterbury. In fact, the Archbishop of Canterbury could issue a licence to any couple in England. If the wedding was to be performed in a diocese other than that of either of the parties, a special licence had to be obtained, either from the Faculty Office of Canterbury or the Registry of York, or the Vicar-General of Canterbury. Licences could also be obtained from certain deans and chapters and archdeacons within their jurisdiction, and also from the Ordinary or presiding authority of certain peculars, provided both the parties lived within them.

To obtain a licence, one of the parties, normally the bridegroom, had to make a formal statement called an allegation, including an oath that there was no lawful impediment to the marriage.

If either of the parties was under age, the application had to be accompanied by the consent of his or her parent. The bridegroom brought a friend with him and they might (jointly until 1823) be required to enter into a bond to forfeit a sum of money, if the proposed marriage was found to be contrary to Canon Law. Sometimes the name of the friend was fictitious, and sometimes the bridegroom was not one of the two bondsmen.

The licence was issued to the applicant for delivery to the clergyman performing the ceremony. It cannot be taken for granted that a marriage licence always meant a marriage — there is always the possibility that the engagement was broken off or one party died. Also, the marriage did not always take place at the church, or any of the churches, named. It could be performed in any place not necessarily at church or a chapel.

Marriage licence allegations and bonds are usually to be found at diocesan registries and county record offices. The licences themselves were issued to the bridegrooms and have normally not survived. Some records include a register of licences issued, with the names of the bondsmen. Both the Canterbury Vicar-General's and the Faculty Office records are in the library at Lambeth Palace, the London residence of the Archbishop of Canterbury, and can be seen by appointment with the librarian. They have been published on microfiche. Microfilms of the calendars are available to 1837 at the Society of Genealogists. The following indexes have been printed:

Faculty Office
1543–75 in Harleian Society Volume 24.
1632–1714 in British Record Society Volume 23. Extracts 1632–1869 in Harleian Society Volume 24.

Vicar-General
1660–94 in Harleian Society Volumes 23, 30–34.
1664–1709 in typescript; 1801–3 on cards at the Society of Genealogists.

The Federation of Family History Societies has published a useful booklet, *Bishops' Transcripts and Marriage Licences. Bonds and Allegations, a Guide to their Location and Indexes*, by J.S.W. Gibson 3rd edn FFHS (1991).

The Society of Genealogists has a collection of abstracts and indexes and has published a guide to them.

Marriage Registers *see* **Parish Registers**

Marshalling The grouping together of more than one coat of arms on one shield.

Marshalsea A debtors prison in Southwark until 1842.

Matrilineal Descent a descent entirely in the female line.

Meadow An area where grass was grown for a hay crop. After Lammas, the hay having been cut, the beasts of the manor were driven into the meadow, which was then used as pasture during the ensuing autumn, winter and spring. Meadows were often on low-lying ground near a river or stream, where they might be subject to flooding, in which case they were called wet meadows or meads. A water-meadow was one that was deliberately 'floated' i.e. flooded. A dry meadow was one not liable to flooding. Lot meads or meadows were common grassland, of which the crop each year was allotted to a manorial tenant by lot.

Mechanic A journeyman engaged in one of the lower forms of handicraft.

Medals Medals have been awarded for service, participation in campaigns or gallantry. The main source of information relating to the award of medals are the medal rolls, which will be found at the PRO, Kew in the following classes:

Long Service and Good Conduct (WO 102)
Campaign Medals (WO 100)
Waterloo Medal Book (MINT 16/112)
Meritorious Service Awards (WO 101)
Distinguished Conduct Medal (WO 146)
Victoria Cross (WO 98, CAB 106/320, CAB 106/312)

Distinguished Service Order (WO 32)
Military Cross (WO 32)
Volunteer Officers' Decorations (WO 330)
Conspicuous Gallantry Medal (PMG 16)
George Cross (HO 250, AIR 2, MINT 16)

Citations for gallantry awards are published in the *London Gazette*.

Medal Rolls for World War I are held in WO 329. These cover only the general issue medals. A microfiched card index is available to these and also to Gallantry Awards for World War I. Medal Rolls for later wars are still held by the Army Medal Office, Government Buildings, Worcester Road, Droitwich, Worcestershire WR9 8AU. It will only provide information to next-of-kin.

Files with information relating to recommendations for the award of medals will be found in WO 32 and WO 108. Details of rewards and pensions awarded for gallantry are in PMG 35.

Royal Navy and Royal Marine medal rolls are in ADM 171 and those for the RAF are in AIR 1, AIR 2 and AIR 30. Awards to civilians may be found in HO 45, HO 250, PREM 2, MT 9, BT 97, BT 251, FO 83, FO 371 and FO 409.

The Public Record Office has issued three free leaflets relating to medals: *Service Medal and Award Rolls: War of 1914–1918, WO 329; First World War: Indexes to Medal Entitlement;* and *Records of Medals* (PRO Information Leaflets 101, 106 and 108).

Further reading: E.C. John, A.R. Litherland and B.T. Simpkin, *British Battles and Medals* (London, 1988); E.C. Joslin, *Spink's Catalogue of British and Associated Orders, Decorations and Medals with Valuations* (Webb & Bower, 1983).

Finding Aids: Peter Abbott, *Recipients of the Distinguished Conduct Medal, 1855–1909* (J. B. Hayward & Son, 1975); Lionel Challis, *Peninsula Roll Call* (London, 1948); Garrett Creagh and Edith Humphris, *The Victoria Cross, 1856–1920, and the Distinguished Service Order, 1886–1923* (London, 1924); K.D.N.K. Foster, *The Military General Service Medal, 1793–1814* (London, 1947); Robert Gould and Douglas Morris, *The Army of India Medal Roll, 1799–1826* (J.B. Hayward & Son, 1974).

Meer A boundary, often a bank or hedge, between fields or furlongs, but sometimes one requiring to be marked out by meer-stones. These stones were liable to require replacing each year after being disturbed by cattle grazing on the stubble. Alternative spelling, mere.

Members' Interests The publishing of members interests by a family history society enables people to get in touch with others researching the same surname. A society will list all the surnames being researched by a new member, together with the area and dates in which they are interested. Each member is assigned a number which appears by each name. This number can then be keyed with the list of members, and their addresses, supplying the information. Some societies publish these lists as a separate booklet once a year and others include a list in each issue of their journal. Alternatively you can consult the GENEALOGICAL RESEARCH DIRECTORY. The Federation of Family History Societies is also producing a research directory (called the BIG R) but it is divided up by the counties where ancestors lived, so that it will be possible to concentrate on contacting people who are researching people who lived in the same area as your ancestors.

Membrane A sheet of parchment. It was customary to sew several sheets together end to end, to form a roll. Parchment is made from the skin of an animal. The flesh-side, the inner side of the roll, was called the face and carried the main written entry; the outer, hair-side, was the back or dorse.
See also VELLUM.

Memoranda Rolls These contain notes of matters arising during the auditing of the sheriff's accounts, and in the daily course of Exchequer business. Of greater interest to genealogists are the private deeds enrolled upon them to ensure permanent record, also details of lands and goods forfeited to the Crown, enclosure awards, and offences against statutes regulating trade or industry. The rolls, of which the later ones are actually in volumes, cover the period from 2 Henry III (his second regnal year) to 1959. They are in two series, which to some extent overlap, those of the King's Remembrancer and of the Lord Treasurer's Remembrancer. Like other Exchequer records they are at the Public Record Office, Chancery Lane, London. Their class is E 159.

Mennonites A reformed sect of the Anabaptists.

Merchant Guild *see* **Guild, Merchant**

Merchant Seamen Records of men in the merchant service were kept by the Board of Trade, and are now mostly to be found at the

Public Record Office, Kew. These are particularly useful for seamen who served from the early nineteenth century onwards. For earlier periods researchers are reliant on records of trade, taxation and legal dispute.

Ships Muster Rolls From 1747, masters or owners of merchant ships were required to keep, and file, a list of crew members. Those passing into the custody of the Board of Trade are in class BT 98 at the PRO Kew. The content of these is patchy, some giving only the master's name, and none are indexed. They survive from 1747 only for Shields and other northern ports; Plymouth from 1761, Dartmouth from 1770, Liverpool from 1772 with other ports from 1800. Some copies of these have survived locally.

Agreements and Crew Lists, Series I (BT 98) From 1835 the masters of ships owned by a British subject and engaged on a foreign voyage, and of British-registered ships of 80 tons or more on coastal trade or fishery, had to carry a written agreement with every member of the crew, stating his wages, the capacity in which he was serving and the nature of the voyage. Also required was a list of all men carried. At the end of the voyage the agreements were delivered to the Registrar General of Shipping and Seamen. Since 1861 only a sample of 10 per cent of these records has been preserved, as *Series II* (BT 99).

The remaining 90 per cent of the surviving crew lists for later dates (1861–1938 and 1951–1976 are at various repositories, namely: National Maritime Museum and several county record offices, with the bulk being at the Maritime History Department, Memorial University of Newfoundland.

Agreements and Crew Lists, Series III (BT 100) are for famous ships, such as the *Titanic, Lusitania,* etc.

Agreements and Crew Lists, Series IV cover fishing vessels of less than 80 tons, but again only a 10 per cent sample has been kept. They date from an Act of 1883. A list of merchant service officers was first published in 1869.

Register of Seamen From 1835 a register was kept of all seamen. For 1835–6 it occupies five volumes, in alphabetical order, entitled *Register of Seamen, Series I* (BT 120). A *Series II* (BT 112), with an alphabetical index (BT 119), covers the period 1835–41.

Register Tickets, to be held by every seaman, were introduced in 1844. The applications for these give the man's date and place of birth, date of first going to sea, capacity in which he served then and thereafter, and any service in the Royal Navy. Tickets were abolished in 1853. The *Register of Seamen's Tickets* (BT 113) has an alphabetical index (BT 114). On the ending of tickets a new *Register of Seamen, Series III* (BT 116) was started, listing men alphabetically and giving age, place of birth, voyage, ship, and port of departure. However, this register was ended in 1856.

Master's and Mates' Records Voluntary examinations for men intending to become masters or mates were introduced in 1845, and an Act of 1850 made them compulsory for foreign-going ships. In 1850 the same was applied to home trade vessels. Registers were kept of the certificates of competency and of service issued, showing name, place and date of birth, and date and place of certificate issue. The records are: *Certificates of Competency, Masters and Mates. Foreign Trade* (BT 112); *Certificates of Service, Masters and Mates, Foreign Trade* (BT 124); *Certificates of Competency, Masters and Mates of Steamships, Foreign Trade* (BT 123); *Certificates of Competency, Masters and Mates, Home Trade* (BT 125); *Certificates of Service, Masters and Mates, Home Trade* (BT 126); *Index to the Registers* (BT 127). Records of Masters were also compiled from crew lists, in a similar manner to the registers; these are to be found for the period 1845–54 in *Alphabetical Register of Masters* BT 115.

Engineers' Records Certificates of competency and service were begun for engineers in 1862. The records are: *Certificates of Competency, Engineers* (BT 139); *Certificates of Service, Engineers* (BT 142); *Index* (BT 141).

Colonial Records Certificates issued to the above categories at colonial ports are registered in *Certificates of Competency, Masters and Mates, Colonial* (BT 128), and *Certificates of Competency, Engineers, Colonial* (BT 140). They are indexed in BT 127 and 141. It should be remembered that, for colonial certificates, records are likely to have survived in the country of issue.

Fishermen Certificates for skippers and mates of fishing vessels were introduced by an Act of 1883. For Competency the reference is BT 129; for Service, BT 130; and for the Index, BT 138.

Apprentices The Act of 1835 authorised the indenturing of apprentices. There is an *Index of Apprentices* (BT 150), and five-yearly specimens of indentures under BT 151 and, for fishing boats, BT 152.

Other records of seamen are:

Registers of Wages and Effects of Deceased Seamen (BT 153) from 1851. They show cause, date and place of death, and are indexed in *Indexes to Seamen's Names* (BT 154).

Registers of Deaths of British Nationals at Sea (BT 159) beginning in 1888. Other records relating to births and deaths at sea are to be found in special categories at the General Register Offices in London, Edinburgh, Belfast and Dublin as well as with the Registrar General of Shipping and Seamen.

For details of passengers, *see* PASSENGER LISTS.

Lloyd's Marine Collection is at the Guildhall Library, London. Among its records of vessels are the captains' registers for 1868–1947. These show their date and place of birth, certificate number, date and place of examination, vessels in which they served, and date of death. There are also voyage records of ocean-going vessels, 1740–1970.

There is a collection of Trinity House Petitions at the Society of Genealogists who have published a nominal index to them. These are appeals for relief from poverty-stricken merchant seamen and their widows, dating from 1780 to 1854. Certificates of baptism, marriage and death are often enclosed.

A free leaflet, No. 5 *Records of the Registrar General of Shipping and Seamen* is available at the Public Record Office.

For further reading, see *My Ancestor was a Merchant Seaman. How can I find out more about him?* by C.T. Watts and M.J. Watts, available from the Society of Genealogists.

Merchet The payment due to the lord of the manor from a villein, on the occasion of the marriage of the latter's son or daughter. In some places it only applied if the marriage was to someone outside the manor.

Mere (i) As an adjective, sheer, unalloyed, pure.

ii) A boundary. Within a manor, boundaries might be marked out by mere-stones or posts.

Merrybegot An illegitimate child.

Merseyside A metropolitan county formed in 1974 out of the Liverpool area of LANCASHIRE.

Mese Another term for MESSUAGE.

Mesne Lord In the feudal hierarchy, a lord in the middle; i.e. the lord of a manor who held (was the tenant) of a superior lord, but was himself the superior lord of a lord holding one or more of his manors. The pronunciation and significance of the word are as in 'meantime'. *See also* MANOR; TENANT-IN-CHIEF.

Messuage A dwelling-house with the ground around it and any outbuildings. A capital messuage was that of the lord of a manor, or of any other large residential property. Also sometimes referred to as a 'MESE'.

Methodists The Methodist movement began in 1738, when John and Charles Wesley set out to revive a sense of spirituality and inner holiness in worship. At first, they preached to church congregations and religious societies; then their followers formed themselves into 'societies' and met at members' houses. In 1739, George Whitefield, an associate of the Wesley brothers when they were at Oxford, began to preach in the open air, and the Wesleys followed his example. They accepted the nickname 'Methodist', which had been mockingly bestowed upon them at Oxford. Although they remained members of the established church, they built supplementary preaching-houses (Wesley) and tabernacles (Whitefield), and these became grouped into Circuits under a Circuit Chapel.

In 1741 the followers of Whitefield, who were Calvinists and believed in predestination to heaven or hell, separated from those of the Wesleys, who were Arminian and held that salvation was open to all true believers. During the eighteenth century both sects continued to be called Methodists. Wesley travelled the whole country and his following grew greatly. In 1778, Wesley's Chapel in City Road, London, was founded, with its own graveyard and burial register. By 1784, Methodist clergy were being barred from Anglican churches, so they invoked the *Toleration Act* and became, officially, Dissenters. From then on they took less care to arrange their meetings at times that did not conflict with Church of England services, but the baptisms of their children were still performed and registered in church.

Charles Wesley died in 1788 and John Wesley in 1791. The movement continued to grow but, in the following decades, it was subject to an almost constant state of change, as a succession of sub-denominations developed and split off from the main body. In 1797 a sect called the Methodist New Connexion was founded. It gave its laity more control over its affairs, and by 1837 it had thirty circuits, each with its own register.

In 1807, a small group called the Independent, or Quaker, Methodists left the main body, and in the following year the followers of Hugh Bourne were expelled from the Burslem Circuit and built their first chapel at Tunstall. In 1812 they adopted the name of Primitive Methodists and expanded, especially in the industrial towns of the north. Three years later, the Bible Christians (O'Bryanites) broke away in the southwestern area of England. In 1818 a Metropolitan Wesleyan Registry of Births and Baptisms was begun in London, from duplicate certificates sent in by the circuits.

The movement continued to divide. In 1827 the Protestant Methodists became a separate body, wanting more rights for ordinary members against the Annual Methodist Conference. In 1833, the Independent Methodists took the name of the United Churches of Christ, and in 1836 the Wesleyan Methodist Association was formed, with the same aim of lay members' rights.

In 1837, the Methodists obeyed the call to deposit their registers with the General Registrar. They sent 856, of which the oldest is one of 1738 in London. However, a higher proportion of Methodist registers escaped deposit than was the case with other denominations, though some have since gone to county record offices.

1932 saw the Wesleyan Methodists, Primitive Methodists and the United Methodist Church combined to form the Methodist Church.

Baptismal registers belonged to circuits and were originally stored in the circuit chapel, but circuits sometimes altered their borders, so a genealogist should be ready to search neighbouring circuits' registers. Also, the circuit boundaries of the various sects were not the same. Burial registers are rare, and membership rolls are scattered among various collections. From 1778 onward, the various sects issued magazines which contain biographies, death notices and obituaries. An index to those of 1778–1839 has been published in Volume 9 of the *Proceedings of the Wesley History Society* (founded 1897).

The largest deposits of registers are at the Public Record Office, Chancery Lane, London, under references RG 4/4677–80, RG 5/162–207, and RG 8; others are in county record offices. The Methodist Archives and Research Centre, John Rylands Library, Deansgate, Manchester M3 3EH, have much other historical material, including the *Minutes of Conference* containing biographies of ministers. The Superintendent Ministers of Circuits still have a number of registers and some eighteenth-century membership rolls, but sometimes depute local ministers to house them.

Some useful addresses for researchers are: The Archivist, Methodist Missionary Society, School of Oriental and African Studies, University of London, Malet Street, London WC1H 0XG (for records of overseas missions); the Wesley Historical Society Library, Westminster College, North Hinksey, Oxford OX2 9AT. To consult the library you need to either belong to the Society or obtain a reader's ticket from the librarian. The charge for non-members is £5; the Wesleyan Reform Union Record Office, 123 Queen Street, Sheffield, Yorkshire S1 2DU.

The Independent Methodist Resource Centre, Fleet Street, Wigan WN5 0DS, has indexed all the names recorded in obituaries in the Independent Methodist magazines from 1823 to the present date, together with other sources of information about many of the people concerned. The index has nearly 8000 names and indicates, where known, the ages and dates of death of the people listed. Almost every entry also includes the name and location of the church to which the person was linked. The index may be consulted at the centre.

Each of the thirty-one Methodist administrative areas has an archivist, and the Connexional Archivist at the Property Division of the Methodist Church, Central Buildings, Oldham Street, Manchester M1 1JQ, will supply the name and address of the Methodist archivist of any named district. If the regional records have not been found in the appropriate record office, the Methodist Archivist for the area may know where they are.

For Further reading, see *My Ancestor was Methodist: How can I find more about him?* by William Leary, Society of Genealogists (1990); *Sources for Nonconformist Genealogy and Family History*, by D.J. Steel vol. II of the *National Index of Parish Registers*, SOG (1973) and *Methodism and Politics in British Society, 1750–1850*, by David Hempton.

Michaelmas   The feast of St Michael the Archangel, celebrated on 29 September, is a quarter-day on which rents and rates became due. Many tenancies and other agreements also date from Michaelmas. It was the custom to have Michaelmas goose for dinner, as the birds were considered to be in their prime at that time of year. Michaelmas is also the name of one of the four law and college terms; it was the beginning of the year in the Chancery Courts.

Middle Ages A modern term used to designate the period between the ancient world of the Roman Empire and the modern age ushered in by the Renaissance, the Reformation, and the development of national states. As applied to England, the period may be said to have begun with the departure of the Roman army in A.D. 410, and to have ended gradually during the late fifteenth and early sixteenth centuries. At one time, the year 1485 was used as a convenience to represent its end with the death of the last Plantagenet King, but that date ignores many complex factors.

In the past, the Middle Ages were known as the Dark Ages, to signify the period between the disappearance of the classical culture of the ancient world and its revival in the fifteenth century but now that term is applied in England to the obscure period from the departure of the Romans to the beginning of documented history under the Anglo-Saxon Kings.

Middlesex *see* **London and Middlesex**

Migration The migration of families from one part of the country to another in pre-industrial England is now recognised to have been considerable. In a number of areas it has been found that about half the rural population died in a parish other than that in which it had been born, though most movement was within a ten-mile radius and almost all of it within twenty miles. However, the migrant with a large town in his mind's eye was prepared to travel further, and it may be said that the larger the town, the greater its drawing power, with London attracting people from all parts of the country.

The most mobile sections of the population were young people who moved to the type of work where they would 'live-in', notably to domestic and farm service (*see* HIRING FAIRS), and to trade apprenticeships. Conversely the least mobile were men in the senior line of farming families, both freehold and copyhold; and the larger the farm, the more settled the family. The evidence for mobility is derived from census returns, memorial inscriptions, settlement papers, wills and depositions in ecclesiastical courts. It seems to have reached a peak in the period around 1600. After declining during the seventeenth century, mobility increased again in the eighteenth, and even more in the ninteenth, as the Industrial Revolution developed.

Most families have many members who move from where they were born, some of them to the other side of the world. Why people move, for religious, economic, criminal or occupational reasons, is a fascinating study. Just tracing a family moving within one country is worthy of study. To discover why they moved from one end of the country to another or what made them decide to travel abroad, in many cases never to return, is an essential part of family history. To trace an individual's movements you need to study his or her social background and understand the political and economic situation during their lifetime. If you need to trace a person in the British Isles whose descendants are now living in North America or the Antipodes, clues can be obtained from the place names where they settled and the people they travelled with, if they can be identified. If you understand their motivation for the move, you go a long way towards finding them. A society who exists because of man's compulsion to change his place of abode is the INTERNATIONAL SOCIETY FOR BRITISH GENEALOGY AND FAMILY HISTORY. *See also* EMIGRATION and IMMIGRATION.

Further reading: *Migration and society in early modern England* by P. Clark and D. Souden (London, 1987) and *My ancestor was a migrant*, by A.J. Camp (SOG, 1987).

Mile In early times a variable distance, of which the sixteenth-century average was 2140 yards. The English standard mile of 1760 yards was laid down in the year 1593.

Militia The militia is a term generally used to refer to the entire active male population, usually between the ages of fifteen and sixty, which might be called on to muster with its weapons in the cause of national defence. In particular, the term refers to a non-professional force raised within counties. The term was first used in the *Commons Journal* of 31 January 1641.

The earliest Militia force known in Britain was the fyrd raised in Saxon and Norman times. This was re-established by Henry II in 1181 when he enacted the *Assize of Arms*. This was replaced by Edward I under the *Statute of Winchester* in 1285 by Commissions of Array. These were issued by the Crown to two or more persons of position and authority in each county to enable them to raise troops. Soldiers raised by these commissions could be used outside England as well as for home defence. This was to remain the basic system for home defence for over 350 years.

In 1549 Edward VI established the post of LORD LIEUTENANT in each county to organise and control Militia forces in lieu of Commissions of Array. The duties of both the Lords Lieutenant and the Militia were redefined by Mary in 1558.

This force was augmented by Elizabeth I in 1573 when it was decreed that a group of men be selected at the musters for training in the use of the pike and musket. These groups became known as trained bands. With the formation of a standing army in 1660 the importance of the Militia force declined. By the early eighteenth century it had virtually disappeared. Between 1742 and 1748 the Seven Years War resulted in most of the army being away from Britain and the need for a Militia force. This was regularised by the Militia Act of 1757 which introduced an element of conscription previously missing. This lasted until 1829. Thereafter volunteer enlistment was into county regiments, which were attached to their regular counterparts under the Cardwell Reforms of 1872. In 1906 Militia regiments became part of the Special Reserve.

The records produced by the Militia forces vary greatly over time. Most are in the form of MUSTER ROLLS AND CERTIFICATES. Commissions of Array are entered on the backs of Patent Rolls which may be seen at the PRO, Chancery Lane (C 66). The Association Oath Roll of officers of Trained Bands 1696 is also at Chancery Lane (C 213/163).

Records relating to Militia Officers will be found in WO 23, WO 25, WO 32, WO 68, PMG 13 and HO 50–1. From 1865 their names appear in the *Army List*. Other Ranks' records include Attestation Papers (WO 96), Description Books (WO 68) and Pension Registers (WO 23, WO 116 and WO 118). Militia Pay Lists and Muster Rolls are in WO 13 and WO 16. Records of payments to families during the Napoleonic Wars may be found at the PRO, Chancery Lane (E 182) and also in County Record Offices.

See also FYRD; LORD LIEUTENANT; MUSTER ROLLS AND CERTIFICATES. The Public Record Office has issued a free leaflet, *Militia Muster Rolls, 1522– 1640* (PRO Information Leaflet 46, 1986).

Further reading: I.F.W. Beckett, *The Amateur Military Tradition* (Manchester University Press, 1991); Lindsay Boynton, *The Elizabethan Militia, 1558–1638* (David & Charles 1971); J.R. Western, *The English Militia in the Eighteenth Century* (Routledge & Kegan Paul, 1965).

Finding Aids: Jeremy Gibson & Alan Dell, *Tudor and Stuart Muster Rolls* (FFHS, 1989); Jeremy Gibson and Mervyn Medlycott, *Militia Lists and Musters, 1757–1876* (FFHS, 1989).

Milkhouse   Another name for a dairy, which was also sometimes called a white house. An inventory of 1596 lists the following contents of a yeoman's dairy: 10 cakes of butter, 3 cheeses, 6 cheese vats, wooden bowls and a cheese press.

Ministers' Account   These records, more fully named *Bailiffs' and Ministers' Accounts*, are the accounts of revenue and expenditure in the management of crown lands, including those taken temporarily into the king's hands. Those of the latter are sometimes supplemented by earlier accounts rendered to the manorial lords but appropriated by the royal agents, or ministers, for their guidance. An understanding of these accounts calls for some knowledge of farming and handicraft techniques, and the vocabularies, often local, belonging to them. The records are at the Public Record Office, Chancery Lane, London, under *Special Collections*, and are indexed in *Lists and Indexes*, vols. 5, 8 and 34.

Ministrant   Another name for a defendant.

Minor   A minor was a child under the age of 21. If a minor wanted to marry the age of consent was, until 1929, 12 if a girl and 14 if a boy, as long as they had the consent of a parent or guardian. After that time a child, whether boy or girl, had to be sixteen to marry with consent under the full age of 21.

Misdemeanour   An offence less serious than a felony.

Misprision of Treason   Any offence akin to treason, but not so serious. Concealment of a treasonable act was a common example and came to be a synonym for it.

Miss   A style of address that only came into respectable use for unmarried women in the early eighteenth century. In the late seventeenth century it had been an abbreviation for 'mistress' (concubine), whereas all women of the status corresponding to the men known as Mr were called Mrs (Mistress), whether married or single. The marriage announcements in the *Gentleman's Magazine*, from its inception in 1731, use the style 'Miss' for spinster brides, but unmarried women of mature years were still called Mrs as a mark of respect.

Missing Persons   In 1885 the Salvation Army set up a bureau, the main purpose of which was to find relatives with whom their enquirers had lost touch. It was known at that time as Mrs Booth's Inquiry Agency. The service is still in considerable demand. However, enquiries are not pursued if it is felt that they might cause pain, and no addresses are divulged without the consent of the persons concerned. A modest fee is charged for these searches. The present full

name and address of the bureau is, The Salvation Army Missing Persons Bureau, 110 Middlesex Street, London E1 7HZ.
Further Reading Tracing Missing Persons *by C.D. Rogers (1986).*

Mistery *see* Livery Companies

Mock of the Church
The name applied to the breaking of a betrothal after the calling of banns. Often penalised by the churchwardens with a fine.

Modus
More fully known as *Modus Decimandi*, this was a commutation of tithes in kind by money payment.

Moiety
A half

Month's Mind
A memorial service for the dead, performed a month after the death. Legacies for the provision of candles for this ceremony were often mentioned in pre-Reformation wills.

Monumental Inscriptions
These inscriptions are properly called 'memorial'. The oldest surviving inscriptions are on brasses and around effigies inside churches. The majority record peers, knights, gentry and church dignitaries, but generally they provide little information. Gravestones of this period are very few and often bear no wording.

In the sixteenth century, the custom spread of burying the gentry and more prosperous merchants within the church building, and the number of memorials on the church walls and floor increased accordingly. However, an interior memorial does not necessarily mean that the deceased was buried in the church; the clergy objected to church burial, and even many distinguished clerics are interred in churchyards. Burial ground monuments are of many kinds: wooden deadboards, vertical headstones, footstones, horizontal ledger stones at ground level, table tombs, box tombs, cyclindrical bale tombs, mummy stones, oven tombs, etc. After the Reformation, crosses on memorials were considered papistical, and fell out of use.

In the seventeenth century, the oldest churchyard inscriptions, except for those of wealthy people, were probably all engraved on wooden boards supported by wooden posts. Few have survived, and most are not longer legible. The oldest headstones date from the middle of that century. As canals made transport cheaper, memorials of stone and slate came within the means of less affluent people, and so greatly increased in number; but local sources of material were always the most commonly used, and the carving was by local craftsmen. Members of a parish's most prosperous families tended to be buried in the southern, sunny side of the churchyard, and paupers and unbaptized babies on the northern, but in some places sections of the churchyard were allocated to specific areas of the parish. Excommunicates and suicides were often denied churchyard burial. The favourite gravestone ornaments of this century were skulls and bones, hour-glasses, scythes and inverted torches.

In the eighteenth century, angel's heads and urns tended to replace the more grisly symbols of death, and it was in this century that monumental inscriptions became the most informative – and the most fulsome.

The inscriptions of the nineteenth century are less wordy, and simple crosses drove out classical decoration. Down to the middle years of the century, it was customary to have the headstone inscription on the side away from the grave, but later it became usual for the wording to appear overlooking the grave.

Memorial inscriptions tend to give more information than the bald entries in the parish register, but they are more prone to error because normally a stone cannot be put in place until about a year after the death, to allow the earth to settle. Details should therefore be checked with the registers. They often indicate places and dates of birth, former places of residence, occupation, the name of a married woman's husband and that of her father. If the death was violent, the fact may be stated. Sometimes a man's occupation may be indicated by engravings of the tools of his trade. Coats of arms – if correctly used – can link the deceased with ancestors and descendants, and distinguish his family from others of the same name. Plaques in churches often commemorate members of local families who died overseas, especially officers on active service and servants of the great chartered companies. Many gravestones and tombs commemorate more than one person, and mention their relationship to each other.

Churchyard stones are best studied with the light at an angle to throw shadows into the incisions. A stiff brush may be necessary to remove surface growth. Dates are particularly liable to become difficult to read; a worn 4 can look like a 1. The whole inscription should be transcribed and any heraldic insignia copied. If a plan is made to copy all the inscriptions of a churchyard for the benefit of other people, the

ABOVE Members of the Essex Society for Family History playing their part in the nationwide project to record every memorial inscription in the country. *Photo: Martin Reed*

RIGHT A plain gravestone, with plain lettering, nevertheless gives information about three generations of the Wheeler family in the nineteenth century.

FACING PAGE Few churchyard memorials provide so much biographical material as this; and on the back are shown the name, birthplace in France, and date of death of the soldier's wife.

IN MEMORY OF
GEORGE WHEELER
WHO DIED DEC 10TH 1814
AGED 36 YEARS.
ALSO OF
SARAH, WIFE OF THE ABOVE
SHE DIED AUG 24TH 1836
AGED 75 YEARS.
ALSO OF
THOMAS WHEELER
GRANDSON OF THE ABOVE
HE DIED NOV 19TH 1845
AGED 33 YEARS.
ALSO OF
ANN WHEELER MOTHER OF THE ABOVE NAMED THOS WHEELER
SHE DIED MAY 24TH 1847
AGED 66 YEARS.
ALSO OF
THOMAS WHEELER
SON OF GEORGE AND SARAH,
HUSBAND OF ANN AND FATHER
OF THOMAS ABOVE NAMED.
HE DIED AUGT 11TH 1852.
AGED 65 YEARS.

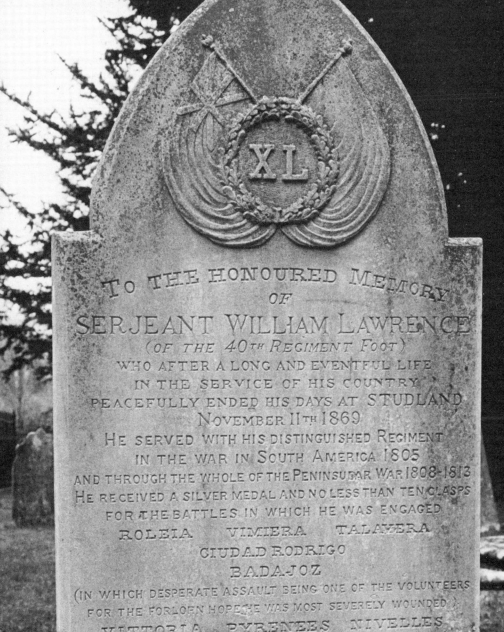

XL

TO THE HONOURED MEMORY
OF
SERJEANT WILLIAM LAWRENCE
(OF THE 40TH REGIMENT FOOT)
WHO AFTER A LONG AND EVENTFUL LIFE
IN THE SERVICE OF HIS COUNTRY
PEACEFULLY ENDED HIS DAYS AT STUDLAND
NOVEMBER 11TH 1869
HE SERVED WITH HIS DISTINGUISHED REGIMENT
IN THE WAR IN SOUTH AMERICA 1805
AND THROUGH THE WHOLE OF THE PENINSULAR WAR 1808-1813
HE RECEIVED A SILVER MEDAL AND NO LESS THAN TEN CLASPS
FOR THE BATTLES IN WHICH HE WAS ENGAGED
ROLEIA   VIMIERA   TALAVERA
CIUDAD RODRIGO
BADAJOZ
(IN WHICH DESPERATE ASSAULT BEING ONE OF THE VOLUNTEERS
FOR THE FORLORN HOPE HE WAS MOST SEVERELY WOUNDED)
VITTORIA PYRENEES NIVELLES
ORTHES   TOULOUSE
HE ALSO FOUGHT AT THE GLORIOUS VICTORY OF
WATERLOO
JUNE 18TH 1815

While still serving with his Regiment during the
Occupation of Paris by the Allied Armies
Serjeant Lawrence married Clotilde Clairet
at St Germain en Laye who died Sep.t 26th 1853
and was buried beneath this Spot

incumbent should be first consulted – the job may have been done already and, in any case, it would be discourteous not to. To prevent duplication, checks should also be made with the Society of Genealogists and the county family history society. Most of the county societies are at work transcribing the inscriptions of the burial grounds of their area, so an approach to the appropriate one may make a visit to the churchyard unnecessary. The Society of Genealogists has the largest collection of copies of inscriptions. Many transcripts are in the British Library, local reference libraries and county record offices. Some transcripts of inscriptions made at cleared burial grounds are at the Public Record Office, Chancery Lane, London, in class RG 37.

At the National Maritime Museum, Greenwich, London SE10 9NF, the Antiquities Department has a collection of inscriptions from pre-1914 monuments and gravestones of British people connected in any capacity with the sea and ships. In the British Library MSS Department is Thomas Hayward's collection of inscriptions (Add. MSS 13916–53) made in the 18th century.

For further reading, see H.L. White *Monuments and their Inscriptions: A Practical Guide* SOG (1987) and *Monumental Inscriptions in the Library of the Society of Genealogists*, 2 vols (1984–7). Also *Rayment's Notes on recording Monumental Inscriptions*, revised by P. Pattinson, 4th edn., FFHS (1992).

Moravians After the death of John Huss in 1415, some of his followers in Bohemia and Moravia (now Czechoslovakia) founded religious societies, and in 1728 three Moravian missionaries came to London and Oxford and introduced their mode of worship into England. It flourished, particularly in London, and in 1738 John and Charles Wesley joined the movement and became its leaders. However, two years later they broke away and founded their own Methodist Society.

In 1742 the Congregation of the Unity of Brethren was founded, which was the beginning of the Moravians as a separate sect in England, though they tried to keep close to the established church. They were also close in thought to the Methodists. Societies were founded in the industrial areas of Yorkshire, the villages around Bedford, and in Derbyshire, north Cheshire, south Lancashire and Wiltshire.

Moravian groups were of three types:

Societies The most numerous. Although they had their own minister and a meeting-house, the members took Communion in their parish churches. Some churches even kept special seats for the local Moravians.

Congregations These were a higher organisation, but they were few and small. In 1747, of the 1200 members in Yorkshire, only 62 were in Congregations.

Settlements A still higher order of permanent residential communities, living under austere discipline and trying to be economically self-sufficient. They had separate quarters (choirs) for married couples, bachelors, and spinsters. There were four of these Settlements: Fulneck in Yorkshire, Fairfield in Lancashire, Ockbrook in Derbyshire, and Bedford.

In 1749 the Moravians were recognised by Parliament as a Protestant Episcopal Church, but they were obliged to license their rooms as dissenters' chapels. In 1754 their first English 'bishop' was appointed, although the organisation of the movement was similar to the Presbyterian. The term 'bishop' became a mere mark of respect.

By 1800 there were about twenty-four Congregations in the British Isles, but many more Societies, mainly in London, Bristol, north Wiltshire, Berkshire and Yorkshire. As the leaders of the movement were German, the minutes of their meetings were often written in that language, or at least in German script. This tended to hold the movement back, as also did their reluctance to proselytize: they went only where they were invited. However, they were highly respected and were the first to engage in foreign missions.

In the 1830s the rise of the Oxford (high church) Movement led to the Moravians finally breaking with the Church of England.

Moravians' registers cover baptisms, burials and, at Fetter Lane, London (from 1741), Fulneck (1749/50) and Bedford (1743), marriages. After 1754, all marriages had to be performed in parish churches, but they were also recorded in the Moravian registers. The same useful duplication applies to burials, except where the Moravians had their own burial ground. Often such entries include a note of the place of birth. In the period before 1752 the dates are given in both Old Style and New Style, owing to the continental nature of the movement (*see* CALENDAR). People often travelled from far away to join a Settlement, and sometimes the entries for members of one Congregation would be made in the register of a neighbouring one. Some people are described in the registers as Non-Moravians, presumably because they were only members of a Society.

Baptismal entries normally include the date of birth and the father's occupation.

Registers are either at the Public Record Office, Chancery Lane, London, in group RG, or with the local Congregations. Those of some defunct Congregations are at the Moravian Church House, 5 Muswell Hill, London N10 3TH. Other records available to searchers are the *Congregation Book*, with valuable personal details about members; the *Congregation Diary*, recording church services, movements of members, relations with outside bodies, and obituary notices; and *Minutes of the Conference of Elders*, recording applications for membership. These are with the Congregations. The short-lived General Registry of Births, started in 1747 by the College of Arms, has entries contributed by Moravians.

For further reading, see *Sources for Nonconformist Genealogy and Family History*, by D.J. Steel (1973).

Mormons *see* Latter-day Saints

Mort d'Ancestor Cases of *mort d'ancestor* were claims to be the heir of a previous owner of a property.

Mortmain The first legislation affecting the conveyance of land to the 'dead hand' of perpetual religious bodies was incorporated in a re-issue of *Magna Carta* in 1217. In 1279, the *Statute of Mortmain*, more properly called *De Viris Religiosis*, sought to control such conveyances and to protect the rights of the king and mesne lay lords. The statute forbade alienation in mortmain without a licence, on pain of resumption of the land by the immediate lord. Before a licence was granted, an enquiry was made by the local escheator as to what lords were involved. These enquiries were called *Inquisitions ad quod damnum*. Licences to donate lands held *in capite* (direct grant from the king) were usually refused.

In 1391 a statute extended the mortmain laws to gilds, fraternities, municipal corporations and perpetual offices, and enforced the completion of conveyances by trustees. An Act of 1736 forbade the conveyance by will of land to all perpetual bodies.

Inquisitions ad quod damnum are at the Public Record Office. There is a calendar, but this gives very little of the information in the original. Patent Rolls at the Public Record Office include grants of licences (refer to the printed *Calendars of Patent Rolls*). Close Rolls at the Public Record Office give details of disputes about the legality of alienations (refer to the printed *Calendars of Close Rolls*).

Mortuary (i) A payment by a parishioner to the rector or vicar on the occasion of a death in the family; originally the family's second best animal, but commuted, under Henry VIII, to a money payment graded according to the estate of the deceased. Those under the value of ten marks were exempt.

(ii) A building to which the dead are brought, awaiting burial or identification.

Mote A meeting for discussion; as in WARDMOTE.

Mother-in-law *see* Father-in-law

Motto A sentence or phrase, usually either pious or defiant, which appears on a scroll as part of an heraldic achievement. The mottoes of English families are customarily worded in either Latin, Norman-French or English, regardless of their date of origin.

Mr An abbreviation for Master, and originally so pronounced. Harrison, in his *Description of Britain* (1577), refers to 'Master, which is the title that men give to esquires and gentlemen'. In the seventeenth century it was a courtesy title for any man of respectable status.
See also CLASS, SOCIAL; ESQUIRE; GENTLEMAN; GOODMAN.

Mrs The courtesy title for women of the status corresponding to that of men addressed as Mr, but throughout the seventeenth century applied both to married and unmarried women, and even through the eighteenth century to spinsters of mature age, as a mark of respect.
See also MISS.

Muggletonians Muggletonians rejected the doctrine of the Trinity and believed that the Father not the Son was crucified.

Muniment A title deed, or evidence of rights or privileges. A muniment chest for storing such documents is often an article of furniture in the houses of landed families.

Muster Rolls and Certificates Musters were originally assemblies of the MILITIA of the shire for the purpose of the inspection of men and equipment by the LORD LIEUTENANT. Muster rolls or certificates were produced detailing those present and the equipment which they produced. The muster rolls were returned to the secretaries of state. The earliest extant return is dated 1297 and refers to Sussex. A number of Muster Rolls survive for the Tudor and Stuart periods and will be found among Exchequer records (E 36, E 101, E 315) and State Papers (SP 1, 2, 10, 12, 14, 16, 17 and 28) at the PRO, Chancery Lane. The Lansdowne MSS at the British Library also include sixteenth century Muster Rolls. Some copies of Muster Rolls for this period survive in County Record Offices, the British and Bodleian libraries, and in private collections.

From 1757 until 1829 a number of the lists of persons eligible for service survive. These have been referred to as Militia Ballot Lists (Gibson and Medlycott 1989). They are particularly useful to genealogists as they are virtual census returns of the male population of the hundred. Similar 'Defence Lists' were produced during the Napoleonic Wars (1798 and 1803). Muster Rolls also survive from this later period. The nature of the Militia dictates that most of these later records are in County Record Offices or in private collections.

Muster Rolls for Militia, Fencible, Yeomanry and Volunteer regiments for the period 1780–1876 are among the War Office records at the PRO, Kew (WO 13). Regiments are listed under counties.

Musters were held in the regular army every month. Muster Rolls survive for most regiments from 1760 and details are given under ARMY. A useful listing of these is given in Watts and Watts (1992).

Finding Aids: Jeremy Gibson and Alan Dell, *Tudor and Stuart Muster Rolls* (FFHS, 1989); Jeremy Gibson and Mervyn Medlycott, *Militia Lists and Musters, 1757–1876* (FFHS, 1989); Michael J. and Christopher T. Watts, *My Ancestor was in the British Army* (SOG, 1992).

See also ARMY; LORD LIEUTENANT; MILITIA.

Mynge The phrase 'in mynge and undivided' in connection with arable lands in the common fields of a manor, meant 'intermingled and unenclosed'.

Mystery A handicraft or trade. A mystery play was acted by the craftsmen's gilds.

N

Nabob (i) An Indian provincial governor. A corruption of Nawab.

(ii) In the eighteenth century, an East India Company factor who had returned to England with a display of wealth, and often with one or more Indian servants. Anyone who returned with less than fifty or sixty thousand pounds was unkindly called a 'chicken nabob'.

Naked A note made in a burial register when the corpse was unshrouded and the coffin unlined. This was sometimes the case with a poor family who could not afford the expense of a woollen shroud, nor the payment of a fine for using any other type of cloth. It was caused by the *Act for Burying in Woollen*, passed in 1660 and reinforced in 1678, to support the woollen trade by making it an offence to wrap corpses or line coffins in any material other than wool. The only bodies exempt were those of people who had died of plague.

Narrative Pedigree *see* **Indented Narrative Pedigree**

National Army Museum Founded in 1960 to house the national collections of the British Army from 1485 to the present day. In addition to permanent and special displays the museum has an extensive collection of special documentary material which may be of use to family historians. This includes diaries and letters from officers and soldiers as well as regimental and campaign histories and military biographies. The Museum's collection of regimental journals is particularly good. Records of a number of disbanded regiments have been deposited with the museum. An invaluable aid to those researching officers in the service of the East India Company is the Hodson index. The museum is situated in Royal Hospital Road, Chelsea, London SW3 4HT. A readers ticket is required.

National Inventory of War Memorials *see* **War Memorials**

National Register of Archives Founded in 1945, on the proposal of the British Records Association, the National Register is a branch of the Historical Manuscripts Commission, charged with making a complete survey of all archives (except those of central government) in England,

Wales and the Channel Isles, including even those of private families and clubs.

The Register comprises over 30,000 unpublished reports on collections held by persons of note, families, estates, businesses, religious institutions, local authorities and other bodies. They are indexed by titles and by locations of the collections, also by subsidiary indexes of persons, subjects and business companies. For the register of manorial and tithe documents, see MANOR and TITHE.

The indexes and reports, as well as the manorial and tithe documents registers may be consulted in the search room of the Royal Commission on Historical Manuscripts at Quality House, Quality Court, Chancery Lane, London WC2A 1HP, between 9.30 a.m. and 5 p.m. No appointment or reader's ticket is required. Limited and specific enquiries can be answered by post, but photographic copies of reports cannot be supplied.

Nativo Habendo, Writ of de A writ that could be issued by a feudal lord demanding that a sheriff hand over a villein who had fled from his manor.
See also VILLEIN.

Naturalization Before 1844, aliens could become naturalized British subjects only by private Act of Parliament. The records of these Acts can be consulted at the House of Lords Record Office and are indexed in Part XIII of the *Index to Local and Personal Acts*. From 1844, naturalization could be granted by a certificate from the Home Secretary. The records are at the Public Record Office, Chancery Lane, London, under classes HO 1, 2, 3 and 5. Many aliens never troubled to apply for naturalization. By marrying English women and begetting children born in Britain, their families automatically acquired British nationality. *See also* IMMIGRANTS.

Neck Verse *see* **Benefit of Clergy**

Negative Proof The discovery of a baptismal entry of a person of the same name as a sought-for ancestor cannot, by itself, be assumed to have solved the problem of the ancestor's baptism or parentage. Until recent times, the range of choice for Christian names was small, so that many people in the same neighbourhood bore identical Christian names and surnames. If there is no independent evidence that the entry found refers to the person sought, then an effort must be made to find whether there is any other entry of the same name. The registers of all the parishes and non-parochial chapels within a fifteen-mile radius of the 'parish (or parishes) of indication' should be searched. The parish of indication can be any or all of the following: the parish in which the family was later living; the one stated to be the person's birthplace (e.g. in a census return); the parish of the entry already found.

In addition, an effort should be made to discover whether the person named in the entry died or married under such circumstances as to eliminate him from consideration. Only if such searches fail to throw doubt on, or disprove, the identification is it reasonably safe to conclude that the entry found is the one sought. The general principle is — if an identification is unconfirmed, try to disprove it.

Neif A female villein.

Nephew Until the end of the seventeenth century this word meant a grandson, descendant or kinsman.

Newgate Calendar The Calendar lists prisoners tried at Newgate. There are sixty volumes for 1782–1853 at the Public Record Office, reference HO 77.

New Jerusalemites The Swedenborgians' New Church was founded in London in 1788 by a group influenced by the ideas of the Swedish theologian, Emanuel Swedenborg (1668–1772). Churches were soon established in many parts of England, but especially in Lancashire. In 1837–40 their well-kept registers were deposited with the Registar General and are now at the Public Record Office in Group RG 4, but duplicates, made at the same time as the originals, are at The General Conference of the New Church, Swedenborg House, 20 Bloomsbury Way, London WC1A 2TH, with other archives of the Church.

For further reading, see D. J. Steel, *Sources for Nonconformist Genealogy and Family History*, vol. II of the *National Index of Parish Registers*, SOG (1973).

Newspapers The earliest English newspaper appeared in 1622, and the first with domestic news in November 1641 after the freeing of the press by the abolition of the Court of Star Chamber. Newspapers proliferated during the Civil Wars, but in September 1655 all were suppressed except *Mercurius Politicus* and *The Publick Intelligencer* (1655–60). The *London Gazette* actually started on 16 November, 1665, though it was called the *Oxford Gazette* until 5 February, 1666/7. It has been published ever since as the government's official organ. The *Gazette* was, for twelve years, the only newspaper permitted, but press censorship was abolished in 1693, and then several London and provincial weekly newspapers began publication. In 1702 came the first English daily newspaper, *The Daily Courant*, and *Lloyd's List* started in 1726, at first weekly then twice weekly.

In the eighteenth century the outstanding daily was the *Public Advertiser*, earlier called the *General Advertiser* (and for a time *The London Daily Post*). Other important papers were, *The Morning Chronicle* (1769–1862), *Morning Herald* (1781–1869), *Morning Post* (seventeenth to twentieth century), *The Times* (1788–today, and indexed, but founded in 1785 as *The Daily Universal Register*), *Morning Advertiser* and *Examiner*. Their main function was to report Parliamentary debates, but *Advertisers* were connected with business and carried numerous advertisements.

The first provincial newspapers were the *Worcester Postman* (1690) and *The Lincoln, Rutland and Stamford Mercury* (1693).

The first tax on newspapers, from 1712, was one penny on a whole sheet and a half-penny on a half sheet. In 1756 it was raised to 1½ pence, in 1789 to 2 pence, 1798 to 2½ pence, 1804 to 3 pence, and in 1815 to 4 pence less 20 per cent. From 1831 to 1835 hundreds of newspapers appeared without tax stamps in spite of prosecutions. They were of a sensational and revolutionary character.

At the beginning of the nineteenth century the provincial press consisted of less than one hundred journals, with a minimum of local news; but after 1836 the local press came into its own, carrying both national and local news. Thanks to Bulwer Lytton, M. Gibson and Richard Cobden, the tax on newspapers had in that year been reduced to one penny, and in 1855 it was abolished. Many newspapers began in this period, including *The Daily Telegraph*. In 1836 the circulation of newspapers rose from 39 million to 122 million. The railways, the telegraph and automatic printing machines all helped to promote their production and distribution.

The British Library has a catalogued collection of early newspapers at the British Museum. Called the Burney Collection, after Dr Charles Burney, it is arranged chronologically and not by separate newspapers. Other papers of the seventeenth and eighteenth centuries are listed in the *General Index* under their titles. The *Thomason Tracts*, also in the British Library, include newspaper items which are listed separately in the catalogue. Newspapers, national and local, since 1800 are at the British Newspaper Library in Colindale, Middlesex, but the building was bombed during the war and parts of the collection were destroyed. The card index should first be consulted to find what newspapers, for what districts and dates, are available. On the open shelves are indexes for births and marriages from certain East Anglian newspapers. Newspaper publishers themselves usually retain copies of past issues. Public libraries, too, often have files of old local newspapers. At the Public Record Office are a number of colonial newspapers in a Colonial Office series, running from the mid 1820s to the mid 1850s. The Bodleian Library, Oxford, has a collection of newspapers from 1622 to 1800.

The Times Tercentenary Handlist of English and Welsh Newspapers, 1620–1920 lists all known newspapers of the period. This can be found at county libraries. Palmer's *Index to The Times* has appeared quarterly from 1791, but the births, marriages and deaths are not included. The main reference libraries have a copy.

See also HARLEIAN SOCIETY.

Finding Aid: *Local Newspapers, 1750–1920*, by Jeremy Gibson. *An Introduction to Using Newspapers and Periodicals* by Colin R. Chapman FFHS (1993).

New Zealand Ancestry   Compared to English genealogy, New Zealand genealogy is relatively recent. Although New Zealand was discovered by Europeans in 1742, by 1800 there were only 50 Europeans living there. Whalers and missionaries came to the islands but no attempt to colonise was made until 1826 and even then most of the settlers found conditions too harsh and moved on to New South Wales, Australia. Other nationalities who came there were Danes, Norwegians and Czechs. In the 1820s and 1830s New Zealand came under the jurisdiction of New South Wales. British Sovereignty was declared in 1840 and self-government attained in 1852. Various settlements were established from then on with a marked increase in population when gold was discovered in 1852 and again in 1861. The offer of an assisted passage was accepted by many people with a large number of Scottish emigrants arriving in Dunedin in the 1850s. 31,774 assisted immigrants, mainly from Great Britain, arrived in the early 1870s and many Irish arrived in the second half of that decade.

Once self-government had been attained, six provinces were established, each with provincial government. In 1876 provincial government was abolished and the country divided into counties and boroughs. In 1902 New Zealand was made a Dominion.

Registration of births and deaths started in 1848 and marriages in 1854. Copies of the register entries were sent by the district record office to the Registrar General's Office, at Lower Hutt where a national index was compiled. Microfiche copies of the indexes pre 1921 are available at the RGO and at some public libraries and Family History Centres.

Census returns have not been retained.

Church records are either with the encumbent or have been transferred to the diocesan archives for safekeeping. Indexing and transcription of surviving registers is being carried out by the New Zealand Society of Genealogists.

Wills were proved in New South Wales, Australia, prior to 1842 and indexes to them are available on microfiche. Since 1842 wills have been proved at the High Court nearest to the deceased's place of residence. The exception being wills lodged with the Public Trustee from 1879 to the mid 1950s. These were proved at Wellington High Court. Many wills have subsequently been transferred from the High Courts to the National Archives at Auckland, Wellington or Christchurch. A national index to wills and administrations is being compiled, by members of the New Zealand Society of Genealogists in cooperation with the Department of Justice and National Archives.

Transcriptions of monumental inscriptions and some burial records are available on microfiche as part of the New Zealand Cemetery Records collection published by the New Zealand Society of Genealogists. Consult *New Zealand Cemetery Records, a List of Holdings*, by June Springer.

Newspapers are a useful aid to research. Consult the *Union List of Newspapers preserved in Libraries, Newspaper Offices, Local Authority Offices and Museums in New Zealand*, by D.R. Harvey to ascertain what is available.

Education: missionary societies started the first schools in New Zealand but the first public school system was not set up until 1871. The admission registers of some state schools have been deposited in the National Archives but many are retained by the school itself. The New Zealand Society has a continuing project to transcribe and index the surviving earlier registers.

Land records: New Zealand is divided into twelve land registration districts. Deeds and certificates of title exist and can be searched but this must be done personally or by using the services of a record agent. The names of passengers arriving from Europe are more likely to have been recorded in the newspapers of the assisted immigrants lists at National Archives than are people who arrived from Australia or other Pacific islands. It is important to establish an approximate date and place of arrival from family papers and stories if possible. Land and Deeds Division of the Department of Justice is responsible for certificates of title and other records relating to land holdings. Copies of maps showing the subdivision of land, roading and railways are also available from the Department of Survey and Land Information offices.

Shipping and Passenger arrivals: more information is available about people who arrived directly from Europe than about those who came to New Zealand from Australia. The name of the ship and date and place of arrival need to be discovered and as this is not an easy task and will have to be ascertained from family papers or from other records which happen to mention arrivals in the country. A national index to passenger shipping does not exist but there are some local indexes of people arriving who have been mentioned in local newspapers mainly pre 1900. Assisted immigrants are recorded on surviving passenger listings held at the National Archives in Wellington and are indexed to 1910.

The headquarters of the New Zealand Society of Genealogists is in Auckland but there are more than 70 branches. There are Family History Centres at many locations. The National Library of New Zealand is the Alexander Turnbull Library in Wellington. The National Archives are at Wellington, Auckland and Christchurch. The Genealogical Research Institute of New Zealand is at Lower Hutt.

The Australasian Society of Genealogists and Record Agents based in Australia, can supply news of professional researchers as does the New Zealand Society of Genealogists, based in Auckland.

For more detailed particulars of researching New Zealand ancestry read: *Tracing Family History in New Zealand* and *Tracing Family History Overseas from New Zealand*, by Anne Bromell (1992).

Niece Until the seventeenth century, this word meant a descendant, either male or female; but occasionally it was used to mean any younger relative.
See also NEPHEW.

Nisi Prius When a date was fixed for a trial at one of the central courts, the note *nisi prius* ('unless before') was often added, meaning that if the appropriate County Assizes were held first, the case should be heard there. Unless there was a good reason for the case to be tried in a central court, it was usual to fix a date falling after the next Assize.

Noble A gold coin, first minted in 1351 and valued at 6 shillings and 8 pence. On one side it bore the image of the king, Edward III, in a ship, and on the reverse a floriate cross. Edward IV added a rose to the ship (from which it was called a rose-noble) and raised its value to 10 shillings. At the same time, he introduced a new coin, the angel, valued at 6 shillings and 8 pence.

Nonconformist Non-conformists are those who did not wish to conform to the Church of England. Called Puritans or Dissenters prior to the 1662 Act of Uniformity, the term generally means Protestants, as Roman Catholics were usually called Recusants *see* under the names of the various denominations.

Nonconformist ministers The records of the clergy of many nonconformist churches for the seventeenth to nineteenth centuries were less systematically kept. The best course is to apply to the archivist of the denomination concerned. In more recent times the names of the clergy can be found in the annual directories published by the churches.
See also NON-PAROCHIAL REGISTERS; RECUSANT ROLLS; WILLIAM'S LIBRARY, DR.

Non-parochial Registers These are the records of baptisms and burials, plus a few marriages, maintained by religious bodies other than the Church of England. For details of any particular denomination, *see* under the name of that denomination, and under WILLIAMS'S LIBRARY, DR.

1837 With the founding of the General Register of Births, Deaths and Marriages, marriages in nonconformist meeting-houses were permitted from July, 1837. Existing non-parochial registers of England and Wales, including some of foreign churches, were called in by a specially appointed commission, and 3630 congregations complied, sending in about 7000 registers. The Roman Catholic bishops refused to authorise the depositing of their registers, and the Jews, College of Arms, Quakers, the non-denominational Bunhill Fields burial ground of the City of London, and the East India Company (for marriages in India) also refused. However, schedules were made of the registers of the three last-named.

1840 In accordance with the *Non-parochial Register Act* of this year, the surrendered registers were deposited in the care of the General Register Office. The denominations affected were: Baptists, Independents, Presbyterians, Scottish churches in England, the Methodists of the Wesleyan, New Connexion and Primitive persuasions, the Bible Christians, Inghamites, Moravians, Lady Huntingdon's Connexion, Calvinistic Methodists, Swedenborgians, foreign Protestant churches and some cemeteries. Some Roman Catholic registers from the north of England were deposited.

1841 The Quakers surrendered some of their registers.

1857 About 300 more registers were sent in by the above-mentioned denominations, by the Chelsea, Foundling and Greenwich Hospitals, and by Bunhill Fields burial ground, and these were authenticated and deposited in the following year.

1859 The List and Index Society published, in its Volume 42, *The General Register Office List of Non-parochial Registers, Main Series*, and the *Society of Friends Series*. It includes about 8800 registers.

1961 The deposited registers were transferred from the General Register Office to the Public Record Office, Chancery Lane, London, in classes RG 4–8.

Some non-parochial registers have come to light since 1857 and are housed either by the denominations' historical societies, or at county record offices. Most of the chapels that were in existence at the beginning of the nineteenth century no longer exist, and many of their records are lost.
For further reading, *see* D.J. Steel, *Sources for Nonconformist Genealogy and Family History*, vol. II of the *National Index of Parish Registers*, SOG (1973).

Norfolk The county is in the diocese of Norwich and the Province of Canterbury. Many of the 691 ancient parishes have deposited their registers at the CRO and there are about 22 transcripts in the SOG Library. Boyd's Marriage Index covers 146 and Pallot's Marriage Index covers 138, from 1790. The Bishops' Transcripts and Marriage Licence records are at the CRO.
The Hundreds of Blofield, Brothercross, Clackclose, Clavering, Depwade, Diss, Earsham, Erpingham (North and South) Eynsford, Flegg

(East and West), Forehoe, Freebridge-Lynn, Freebridge-Marshland, Gallow, Greenhoe (North and South), Grimshoe, Guilt-Cross, Happing, Henstead, Holt, Humbleyard, Launditch, Lodden, Mitford, Shropham, Smithdon, Taverham, Tunshead, Walsham, Wayland and King's Lynn Borough, Norwich City and County, Thetford Borough and Great Yarmouth Borough lie within its boundaries.

It has Yarmouth, Flegg, Tunstead or Smallburgh, Erpingham, Aylsham, St Faith's, Norwich, Forehoe, Henstead, Blofield, Loddon, Depwade, Guiltcross, Wayland, Mitford, Walsingham, Docking, Freebridge Lynn, King's Lynn, Downham, Swaffham and Thetford RDs/PLUs.

It falls within the Norfolk Assize Circuit until 1876 and from then on in the South Eastern Assize Circuit.

The Norfolk and Norwich Genealogical Society publishes *Norfolk Ancestor* quarterly and the society has branches at Norwich, Thoresby, Great Yarmouth and a London Branch which meets at the SOG.

The Norfolk and Norwich Record Office, the Central Library and the Muniment Room of the Dean and Chapter of the Cathedral are all at Norwich. The Borough Record Office at Great Yarmouth and the Town Hall King's Lynn also hold records. There are Family History Centres at King's Lynn and Norwich.

Pre 1858 Wills are at the CRO and were proved in the following courts: the Consistory Court of Norwich, the Archdeaconry Courts of Norwich and Norfolk, the Peculiar Courts of the Dean and Chapter of Norwich, Castle Rising and Great Cressingham, and the Court of the City of Norwich. Wills could also be proved at the Prerogative Court of Canterbury.

The Norfolk Record Society has published local material since 1931. Herald's Visitation Pedigrees have been published for 1563, 1613 and 1664.

Norfolk Record Office publishes *Guide to genealogical sources* (1985). See also *National Index of Parish Registers*, vol. 7 (1983) and *Norfolk: a genealogical bibliography*, by S. Raymond (FFHS, 1993).

Norman-French Language Brought into England at the Norman Conquest, it was maintained by schools because it was the tongue of the royal court, the upper classes and, with Latin, of literature. As late as the seventeenth century it was also the language of oral argument in the courts of law. English did not become the literary language of the country until the mid fourteenth century. The first post-Conquest king to speak English as his native tongue was Henry IV. In 1487 Anglo-Norman ceased to be the language of the operative parts of Parliamentary statutes. Only the sentence 'la Reine le veult', giving the Queen's consent, and (in theory) 'la Reine s'avisera' ('the Queen will think about it') remain today.

Northamptonshire In 1974 the Soke of Peterborough was transferred to Cambridgeshire. The County lay within the diocese of Lincoln until 1541 and then Peterborough but it was always within the Province of Canterbury. Of the 292 ancient parishes, most registers have been deposited at the CRO and the SOG has transcripts of about 50. Pallot's Marriage Index covers 20, from 1790. Marriage Licence records and the Bishops' Transcripts are at the CRO.

The Hundreds of Chipping Warden, Cleley, Corby, Fawsley, Greens-Norton, Guilsborough, Hamfordshoe, Higham-Ferrers, Huxloe, King's Sutton, Navisford, Nobottle-Grove, Orlingbury, Polebrook, Rothwell, Spelhoe, Towcester, Willybrook, Wymersley, Northampton Borough, Nassaburgh, or Peterborough Liberty, and Peterborough City lie within its boundaries.

It has Brackley, Towcester, Potterspury, Hardingstone, Northampton, Daventry, Brixworth, Wellingborough, Kettering, Thrapston, Oundle and Peterborough RDs/PLUs.

It fell within the Midland Assize Circuit until 1863, then the Norfolk until 1876 and finally the Midland again.

The Northamptonshire Family History Society meets at Kettering and Weston Favell and publishes a quarterly journal called *Footprints* and the Peterborough and District Family History Society meets at Peterborough and publishes a quarterly journal.

The Northampton Record Office and the Northampton Central Library both hold records. There are Family History Centres at Peterborough and Northampton.

Pre 1858 Wills proved at the Consistory Court of Peterborough and the Archdeaconry Court of Northampton are held at the CRO but those proved at the Peculiar Courts of Gretton with Duddington and Nassington are held at the Lincolnshire CRO as are those proved at the Consistory Court of Lincoln prior to 1541. Wills could also be proved at the Prerogative Court of Canterbury.

The Northamptonshire Record Society has published local material since 1924. Heralds' Visitation Pedigrees have been published for 1564, 1618–19 and 1681. See also *National Index of Parish Registers*, vol. 9, Part 2 (1991).

North Meols Family History Society *see* Lancashire

Northumberland Newcastle-upon-Tyne is now in the new county of Tyne and Wear. The county lies within the diocese of Durham and is in the Province of York. Of the 96 ancient parishes nearly all the registers are now at the CRO. The SOG has copies of more than half of them in its library. Boyd's Marriage Index covers 84 parishes and Pallot's Marriage Index covers fifteen, for 1790–1812. The Bishops' Transcripts and the Marriage Licence records are at the Department of Palaeography at the University of Durham.

The Wards of Bamborough (North and South Divisions), Castle (East and West Divisions), Coquetdale (East, North and West Divisions), Glendale (East and West Divisions) Morpeth (East and West Divisions), Tindale (East, North East, North West, South or Hexham and West Divisions), Berwick-upon-Tweed Town and Newcastle-upon-Tyne Town and County of the Town lie within its boundaries.

It has Newcastle-upon-Tyne, Tynemouth, Castle Ward, Hexham, Haltwhistle, Bellingham, Morpeth, Alnwick, Belford, Berwick, Glendale and Rothbury RDs/PLUs.

It fell within the Northern Assize Circuit until 1876 and then within the North Eastern Assize Circuit.

The Northumberland and Durham Family History Society publish a quarterly journal and meet at Gateshead, Durham, Blyth, South Shields, Sunderland and have a London Branch which meets at the SOG.

The records are held at Northumberland CRO, Tyne and Wear Archives Department and the City Archives Office all at Newcastle-upon-Tyne.

Pre 1858 Wills are located at The Department of Palaeography and Diplomatic at the University of Durham if proved at the Consistory Court of Durham. They are at various places (*see* YORKSHIRE) if proved at either the Consistory and Chancery Courts of York for clergy possessed of *bona notabilia*, and those for the Peculiar Court of the Archbishop of Hexhamshire, 1593–1602 are at the Borthwick Institute of Historical Research in the University of York. Wills could also be proved at the Prerogative Courts of York and Canterbury.

The Surtees Society has published many local records since 1835. The Newcastle-upon-Tyne Records Committee has published since 1920 and the Newcastle Society of Antiquaries of Newcastle-upon-Tyne has published a *Record Series* since 1968. Heralds' Visitation Pedigrees have been printed for 1615 and 1666.

North Eastern Ancestors is a guide to sources in the Tyne and Wear Archives Service and in the Northumberland and Durham Record Offices. See also *National Index of Parish Registers*, vol. 11, Part 1 (1984) and *Indexes for the Northumberland and Durham family historian*, by A.H. Chicken and S. Bourne (1993).

Notary An act of renunciation was made when an executor did not wish to undertake the task of proving a will and settling the accounts of the deceased. It was also made by a legatee who did not wish to inherit what had been bequeathed. The act had to be attested by a notary and registered in the court files. A distinctive notarial symbol was drawn at the foot of the document.

Notes and Queries A magazine described as 'a medium of intercommunication for literary men, artists, antiquaries and genealogists, etc.' It began publication in November, 1849, and is still continuing. Its volumes, a store-house of curious items of historical and genealogical information, are available in a number of public libraries and at the Society of Genealogists.

Nottinghamshire The county is in the diocese and Province of York. Of the 220 ancient parishes, virtually all the registers are at the CRO and the SOG Library has copies of about 200. Pallot's Marriage index covers 168 registers, mostly from 1790. The Bishops' Transcripts are at Southwell Minster Library and are on microfilm at the CRO. The Marriage Licence records are at the University MSS Department and the SOG has indexes to them from 1754.

The Wapentakes of Bassetlaw (Hatfield, North and South Clay Divisions), Bingham (North and South Divisions), Broxtow (North and South Divisions), Newark (North and South Divisions), Rushcliffe (North and South Divisions), Thurgaton (North, South and Southwell Divisions), the Borough of Newark-upon-Trent and the Town and County of the Town of Nottingham lie within its boundaries.

It has East Retford, Worksop, Mansfield, Basford, Radford (later part of Nottingham), Nottingham, Southwell, Newark and Bingham RDs/PLUs.

It falls within the Midland Assize Circuit.

Nottinghamshire Family History Society meets at Nottingham and publishes a quarterly journal. Mansfield and District Family History Society meet at Mansfield and publish *Roots* thrice-yearly.

The records are kept at Nottinghamshire Archives Office, Nottinghamshire County Library and the Department of MSS in the University Library in Nottingham. There is also a local studies library in Southwell Minster. There are Family History Centres at Mansfield and Nottingham.

Pre 1858 Wills are kept at the CRO and were proved at the following courts; the Archdeaconry Court of Nottingham, the Manorial Courts of Dale Abbey, Edwinstow, Gringley-on-the-Hill, Mansfield Peculiar Court of the Vicar of Knoulton and the Peculiar Court of the Chapter of the Collegiate Church of Southwell. Wills could also be proved at the Prerogative Courts of York and Canterbury and the Consistory Court of York.

The Thoroton Society has published local records since 1903. Heralds' Visitation Pedigrees have been published for 1530 and 1662–1664.

See *User's guide to the Nottinghamshire Record Office* (1980) and *National Index of Parish Registers*, vol. 6, Part 2 (1988).

Novel Disseisin, Writ of A claim of recent dispossession.

Numbered Houses Until the middle of the eighteenth century, houses in town streets were identified by overhanging signs, a custom that survives today for public houses. However, in 1708 the houses in Prescot Street on the south side of the Tenter Ground in Goodman's Fields, London, were given numbers; and in the period 1721–7, Fire Insurance Company records show that two insured houses, one in Ropemaker's Alley and one in Burr Street, had numbers, which implies that those streets were numbered. Cornhill in the City of London also had numbers early in that century.

In 1762 it was ordered that all overhanging signs in London and Westminster be removed. Even so, the local directories of the 1760s show that only about thirty houses were numbered (of which six were in Prescot Street); another seventeen in the Inns of Court and Chancery were almost certainly staircase numbers. Then an Act of Parliament of 1767 authorised the numbering of houses in the City and its liberties, and Westminster and neighbouring parishes followed suit. The directory of 1770 showed three-quarters of the capital's houses as numbered, a practice that soon spread to provincial towns. At first, many streets were numbered consecutively up one side and down the other, but the alternative practice of putting odd numbers on one side and even numbers on the other eventually prevailed. However, some streets are still numbered in the old way. In many, the numbering has been changed from time to time, making the accurate identification of properties difficult, and in country districts the house numbers can be those in the estate books, and not consecutive at all.

Numerals Until the end of the seventeenth century, figures were normally written in Roman numerals. These were shown as: j, ij, iij, iiij, v, vj, vij, viij, ix, x, l, c, d, m, etc. The j took the place of i when it was the last (i.e. right-hand) figure of the numeral; the v and x usually appeared as written in Secretary Hand (*see* HAND-WRITING).

Until the end of the first half of the sixteenth century, dates were indicated by the REGNAL YEAR of the sovereign. After about 1560, it became usual to add the year of the Christian Era, which, except when written in words, was always shown in Arabic numerals.

Nuncupative Made by word of mouth only; an expression used to designate wills that were neither written nor signed nor sealed by the deceased. They are more fully described under WILL.

Oath Ex Officio Mero A statement on oath required by an ecclesiastical court from an accused person, not because of an accusation against him but at the pleasure of the court. A great cause of discontent with ecclesiastical courts.

Oath of Allegiance *see* **Allegiance**

Obeisance In sixteenth and seventeenth-century records this word can mean Jurisdiction.

Obit A mass for a deceased person celebrated on the anniversary of his death; often mentioned in pre-Reformation wills.

Obligation *see* **Bond**

O'Bryanites *see* **Methodists** *and* **Bible Christians**

Octave An eight-day period, with the festival day (e.g. Monday to Monday). The term derives from the Latin word for eight, but it was customary, in measuring a period of time, to include the first day (or year) as well as the last. Sometimes written as *utas*.

Office Suit *or* Ex Officio Suit

An action brought against a person in an ecclesiastical court by the court itself, and not by another party.

See also ECCLESIASTICAL COURT.

Official The deputy of a diocesan bishop or archdeacon to act in judicial matters. In that capacity he would preside over the ecclesiastical court. The Official Principal was the deputy of an archbishop (*see* VICAR GENERAL). Mention of the Official by name is often made in probate acts.

One-Name Studies, Guild of Genealogists tracing families with fairly uncommon surname often note all references to persons of the name. This has led to the formation of a number of one-name societies and correspondence groups.

In 1975, under the auspices of the Federation of Family History Societies, the late Mr Frank Higenbottam started a *Register of One-Name Studies*. Its purpose was to act as a clearing house by recording the names and addresses of persons or societies specialising in research on all bearers of a single surname, so that enquirers could be referred to them. The Register covers: (i) constituted societies in the UK; (ii) family correspondence groups in the UK; (iii) individual researchers specialising in one surname; (iv) overseas groups. News of the register attracted wide interest, and resulted in the recording of a considerable volume of one-name research. Persons and societies specialising in certain names formed a Guild of One-Name Studies in 1979. The address of the Guild's Registrar is Box G, 14 Charterhouse Buildings, Goswell Road, London EC1M 7BA. They will supply an up-to-date register, and answer reply-paid enquiries on the registered names and their variants. See also *Record Keeping for a One-Name Study* by Rear-Admiral D.M. Pulvertaft.

Oral Family History The first step in genealogy — provided the start has not been left until too late — is to get elderly relatives talking about long-deceased members of the family whom they once knew personally, or heard talked of. Use a tape-recorder if one is available, provided it does not inhibit the flow of recollections. Failing that, start by drawing up, with their help and on a large sheet of paper, a family tree of the generations they knew, so that the facts revealed can be quickly noted under each name.

Try to obtain as many as possible of the items essential on every family tree, i.e. dates and places of births, marriages and deaths, occupations and spouses. Afterwards, write up your notes in narrative form under the heading 'Conversation with . . .', together with the date. Ask your informant to check it, and it will almost certainly inspire additional remembrances. Do not confine your enquiries to one relative. Each one will add something to the record, and their accounts may not agree. Ancestral legends will be repeated. 'It was always said that our family . . .' Such tales may have a core of fact within an accumulation, over the generations, of unconsciously added romance. As much of the oral information as possible should be checked against documentary evidence.

The Oral History Society, Sociology Department, University of Essex, Colchester CO4 3SQ, issues a journal, *Oral History*.

For further reading, see *Oral Evidence and the Family Historian*, by Lawrence Taylor.

Orator In legal documents a plaintiff or complainant referred to himself as 'your orator', i.e. petitioner; from a Latin word meaning to beg or plead.

Ordeal A medieval method of deciding a legal suit. For knights, ordeal was by combat ('appeal of battle'); for freemen, by fire; and for villeins, by water. In both the latter, success for the defendant was more frequent than failure. The practice fell into discredit at the end of the twelfth century, but continued to be used in criminal cases until it was abolished by papal decree in 1212.

Ordinary (i) In civil law, an official who had jurisdiction in his own right, not by deputation. In canon law, an ecclesiastical judge.

(ii) A bishop's appointee to a prison. It was he who heard condemned criminals read the Neck Verse (*see* BENEFIT OF CLERGY) and, if they failed, prepared them for death.

(iii) A public eating-house.

(iv) A collection of coats of arms classified by charges, of which the earliest was Cotgrove's *A Roll of Arms Compiled in the Reign of Edward III, 1337–40*, edited by Sir Harris Nicholas in 1829. A later one is Papworth's *Ordinary of British Armorials*.

(v) An archbishop, bishop or archdeacon; a superior.

Ordnance A term used for an artillery piece, e.g. cannon.

Ordnance, Board of A Government department, headed by the Master-General of Ordnance, established by Henry VIII. In addition to providing weapons and ammunition for the Army and Navy, it was responsible for the Royal Artillery (RA and RHA) and Royal Engineers (RE). The former was formed in 1716 and the latter in 1856, by the amalgamation of the Corps of Engineers and the Royal Corps of Sappers and Miners. The records of the Board, including documentation for military personnel serving in the RA and RE, are at the PRO, Kew (WO 44–55). The Board was officially abolished in 1855.

The Public Record Office has issued a free leaflet, *Records of the Board of Ordnance* (PRO information leaflet 67). *See also* ARMY.

Orphans Young children left orphaned by poor parents fell on the charity of their parish, and evidence of them will be found in the accounts of either the churchwardens or the Overseers of the Poor, now mostly deposited at county record offices. After 1835, Poor Law Guardians set up and administered orphanages, the records of which are also at county record offices. In due course all such children were apprenticed to trades or husbandry (see APPRENTICES). In the nineteenth century, some were shipped in parties overseas. Some institutions for homeless children were founded by wealthy benefactors, and for information on these *see* BARNADO'S HOMES, DR and FOUNDLINGS. Not all orphans were poor; in 1540 the Court of Wards was formed to appoint and supervise guardians for children whose deceased fathers had held land of the king in chief. Such minors were a source of profit to both the king and their guardians.
See also WARDS AND LIVERIES, COURT OF.

Outfangtheof The right to summon local people to court, charged with committing theft outside the court's jurisdiction.

Outlawry The punishment for anyone who either fled from justice, or refused to appear in court to answer for a transgression. The term means exclusion from all benefits and from protection of the law. From the Conquest until Tudor times an outlaw might be lawfully killed by anyone who met him, but if he was captured alive his fate was in the king's hands. To make a defendant aware of his summons to court, three Writs of Capias would be issued against him and, failing his appearance, a Writ of Exigend requiring the sheriff to call on him in five successive courts. If he still did not appear, the judgement of outlawry was pronounced. Outlawry entailed the forfeiture of goods and chattels, and the forfeiture of lands to the Crown for a year and a day, after which time they escheated to the superior lord. Women could not properly be outlawed, because they were not sworn to the law by taking the oath of allegiance in the Court Leet, so they were said to be waived.

Overseas, The British The following London repositories contain records of many births, baptisms, marriages and burials of Britons on the continent of Europe and in other overseas territories.

The General Register Office holds indexes to the Births, Marriages & Deaths of Britons overseas. See the list of registers in GENERAL REGISTER OFFICE.

The Guildhall Library, in Aldermanbury, London EC2P 2EJ holds registers of a number of congregations abroad, and of those services performed by the chaplains licensed by the Bishop of London (1816–1924), in addition to copies of memorial inscriptions.

The Library publishes *The British Overseas: a guide to records of their baptisms, births, marriages, deaths and burials available in the United Kingdom*, by Geoffrey Yeo.

The Public Record Office has, among its Foreign Office Records classes of Embassy and Consular Archives which include registers of baptisms and banns of marriage as does WO 156 in the War Office classes.

Amongst the records of the Registrar General in the PRO are births, marriages and deaths registered before British consuls in foreign countries:

Miscellanea Foreign Returns, 1831 onward (RG 32)
Foreign Registers and Returns, 1627 onward (RG 33)
Miscellaneous Foreign Marriages, 1826 onward (RG 34)
Miscellaneous Foreign Deaths, 1830 onward (RG 35)
Registers and Returns of Births, Marriages and Deaths in the Protectorates of Africa and Asia (RG 36)
RG 32–36 are indexed in RG 43

Records of births, marriages and deaths in British colonies are in the countries concerned but registration of Army families in the colonies are at St Catherine's House.

The India Office Library and Records (Orbit House, Blackfriars Road, London SE1 8NG) have *Ecclesiastical Returns of* baptisms, marriages and burials from India, Burma and St Helena from the early part of the eighteenth century. The Society of Genealogists also has printed volumes of memorial inscriptions from India.

The volumes of *Miscellanea Genealogica*, and *Notes and Queries*, also contain memorial inscriptions of Britons buried abroad.

For memorial inscriptions of Britons who died in the East, the British Association of Cemeteries of South Asia (Mr T. Wilkinson, 76½ Chartfield Avenue, London SW15 6HQ) should be contacted. Also, Miss S.M. Farringdon, 68 Tachbrook Street, London SW1, has transcripts of British memorials in Pakistani cemeteries.

For the working careers of Britons overseas, *see* CHARTERED COMPANIES.

See also EMIGRANTS; LICENCE TO PASS BEYOND THE SEAS; PASSPORTS.

Overseer of the Poor

An honorary parochial post. Before the Reformation the care of the poor was the responsibility of the Church, i.e. of the monasteries and the parish clergy. In fact, one-third of the parson's tithes were intended to be given by him to the poor. When the monasteries were dissolved, the problem of relieving poverty became acute, and the clergy were ordered to collect alms for poor people. An Act of 1572 created Alms Collectors and Supervisors of the Labour of Rogues and Vagabonds in each parish. People who would not give alms voluntarily could be compulsorily assessed. In 1597 the two offices were combined under the title of Overseer of the Poor, an official whose appointment required the approval of the Justices of the Peace.

By the great *Poor Law Act* of 1601, churchwardens became ex-officio Overseers of the Poor, together with those approved by the Justices. One of their number was appointed executive officer of the Overseers and looked after the funds raised by parochial rates. From 1691, the Overseer was obliged to keep a record of his disbursements and distribution of clothing, etc. His rate books list the sums collected from parishioners according to the value of their properties. In 1772 an Act was passed enabling parishes to buy or rent premises for workhouses, and to employ a workhouse-keeper. From 1790, such workhouses had to submit to inspection by Justices of the Peace.

In 1834, parochial responsibility for the poor was ended. Parishes were amalgamated for such purposes into Poor Law Unions, governed by elected Poor Law Guardians with a property qualification. At national level the system was controlled by Poor Law Commissioners.

See also BASTARDY; GUARDIANS OF THE POOR; RATE BOOKS; SETTLEMENT.

Oxfordshire

Since 1974 the county includes the northern part of the ancient county of Berkshire. It lies within the diocese of Oxford and the Province of Canterbury. Most parishes have deposited their registers at the Department of Western MSS in the Bodleian Library. The SOG has copies of over 200 of them. Pallot's Marriage Index covers sixteen, mostly from 1790 or 1800. The Bishops' Transcripts are at the Department of Western MSS in the Bodleian Library and the Marriage Licence records are at the CRO.

The Hundreds of Bampton, Banbury, Binfield, Bloxham, Bullingdon, Chadlington, Dorchester, Ewelme, Langtree, Lewknor, Pirton, Ploughley, Thame, Wooton and Oxford Liberty, City and University lie within its boundaries.

It has Henley, Thame, Headington, Oxford, Bicester, Woodstock, Witney, Chipping Norton and Banbury RDs/PLUs.

It falls within the Oxford Assize Circuit.

The Oxfordshire Family History Society publishes *The Oxfordshire Family Historian* thrice-yearly. They meet at Kidlington and have three house groups at Farringdon, Headington and Hook Norton.

The records are kept at Oxford County Record Office, the Bodleian Library and in Oxford Central Library.

Pre 1858 Wills are kept at the CRO and were proved at the Consistory and Archdeaconry Courts of Oxford, the Archdeaconry Court of Berkshire, the Peculiar Courts of Banbury, Dorchester, Longford, Monks Risborough, Thame, Cropredy, Harley and Harnton, the Dean and Canons of Windsor in Wantage and the Manorial Court of Sibford. Wills proved in the Court of the Chancellor of the University are in the University Archives at the Bodleian Library. Wills could also be proved at the Prerogative Court of Canterbury.

The Oxfordshire Record Society has published a *Record Series* since 1919, the Oxfordshire Historical Society has published material on the City and University since 1885, and Banbury Historical Society has published annual volumes of records since 1959. Heralds' Visitation Pedigrees have been published for 1574–5, 1634 and 1668.

See also *Oxfordshire parish registers and bishops transcripts* by C.G. Harris (1988), *National Index of Parish Registers*, vol. 5 (1966) and *Oxfordshire: a genealogical bibliography*, by S. Raymond (FFHS, 1993).

Oxgang One-eighth of a ploughland. Also called a bovate.

Oyez and Terminer, Commission of
Sometimes written 'determiner'. Originally an order 'to hear and decide' a specific case reported to King's Bench, but in the late thirteenth century, when Commissions of Eyre were being less frequently issued, the king empowered justices of the royal courts to hear all charges of felony in the provinces. By the sixteenth century, the Commission was usually combined with one of Gaol Delivery.

P

PAF *see* **Personal Ancestral File**

Palaeography The study of the rules of old handwriting, scribal practices and conventions, and the peculiarities associated with specific places and periods, resulting in the ability to identify writers and to date and place the provenance of a document from the evidence of the script. A word often misused in genealogical circles to mean merely the study of how to read old handwritings.
See also HANDWRITING; SECRETARY HAND.

Palatine Counties Counties over which Norman magnates and their successors possessed royal rights and jurisdiction, the word 'palatine' meaning 'pertaining to a palace', or 'to a high officer of a palace'. The original counties were those along the Welsh and Scottish borders, ruled by the Earls of Chester, Shrewsbury and Hereford, The Duke of Lancaster and the Prince Bishop of Durham.

In granting English manors to his chief followers, the Conqueror's policy was to scatter each earl's lands over the whole country, which had the dual effect of identifying their interests with those of the country and of preventing their acquiring undue power in any one area. However, for reasons of national defence he made exceptions along the country's borders; hence the unusual concentrations of power in the palatine counties.

Palimpsest (i) A sheet of parchment or paper that has been written upon twice, the first writing having been erased to make room for the second.

(ii) A memorial brass that has been taken up and engraved on the reverse side with another figure.

Pallot's Index of Marriages This index was begun in 1818 by a firm of record agents specialising in chancery work and intestacy cases, and was continued by their successors, among whom were Messrs Pallot & Co. It was finally purchased for the Institute of Heraldic and Genealogical Studies. The index of marriages in London's parish registers was augmented by London births and obituaries, culled from the *Gentleman's Magazine*, and by English marriages, births and deaths overseas. Unfortunately nearly all records except the London marriages were destroyed during the Second World War. What remain are the marriages of 101 of the 103 ancient parishes of the City of London, of many Middlesex parishes, and a variable number from registers of other counties. There are also about 30,000 baptisms from a small number of London and provincial registers.

A catalogue is available, listing the parishes included. Enquiries should be addressed to the Institute of Heraldic and Genealogical Studies, Northgate, Canterbury CT1 1BA.
See also under county headings.

Palmer A wandering religious votary who had visited the Holy Land, and carried a branch of palm in token thereof. Not the same as a pilgrim, since the latter was making one particular journey, whereas the palmer was a constant and homeless traveller.

Pannage (i) The right to feed pigs in the woods of a manor. In Domesday Book the size of a woodland was sometimes determined by the number of swine it would support. *See* Hereford 186 'wood for 160 swine if it bore mast'.

(ii) A payment made for that right.

Papers The term for a punishment of a convicted offender by exhibiting him, perhaps in a pillory, with papers pinned to him specifying his offence.

Parcentary A type of tenure of Norman origin, by which a younger brother held his fief of the elder of the superior lord.

Parchment *see* **Membrane** *and* **Vellum**

Parish A township or group of townships under the administration of a single priest who was originally paid by tithes on the produce of the parochial area, and who was under the supervision of a bishop. In England, parishes date back to before the Conquest, being first mentioned in AD 970, but did not appear in their full form until the second half of the fourteenth century. Any ecclesiastical parish which was in existence prior to 1597 is known as an ancient parish. The Tudor monarchs found parishes a more practical instrument of local government than the manor, and began to place civil responsibilities on them, of which the most important was the care of the poor. In the south of England, ecclesiastical parishes served adequately as civil parishes, but in the north and west the larger parishes had to be divided into two or more civil parishes, each centering on a chapel of ease.

During the seventeenth century the parish in its civil aspect gradually replaced the manor as the unit of local government. In the early nineteenth century the great increase in population, and the growth of new industrial towns, forced the sub-dividing of many ecclesiastical parishes and the building of additional churches. Some parts of parishes were known as 'detached' when they existed outside the geographical boundaries of the parish. If a bit of one parish was totally surrounded by another parish, it was termed the 'foreign parts' of the parish which included it. By 1851 the total number of churches and chapels had risen to 13,854.

Parish Registers Before the Reformation, some monasteries noted births occurring in the leading local families, but there was no standard, countrywide system for keeping such records. In 1536 an attempt was made to start parish registers, but it finally became effective only as a result of a mandate of 5 September, 1538. The registers were to be entered up weekly, and were often kept on loose sheets of paper, so it is not surprising that only about 800 registers still exist from as early as 1538. In 1555 and 1557, under Mary 1, bishops were required to see that the sponsors were named in baptismal entries, but this ceased under the next reign. In 1598, Queen Elizabeth approved an order of 25 October, 1597, that registers be kept in parchment books and that all the old register entries be copied into such volumes. The clergy were, however, given the option of starting from 1558 (the beginning of the Queen's reign), so a number of registers now start from that date. The paper originals have nearly all disappeared. In the transcription, errors naturally crept in. From 1598, copies of all entries had to be sent annually, at Easter, to the bishop's registry (*see* BISHOPS' TRANSCRIPTS).

Parish registers, once kept in church vestries, are now mostly deposited at the county record offices. Thousands of registers have been copied and can be consulted in the library of the Society of Genealogists. See *Parish register copies in the library of the Society of Genealogists* (1992). The *Phillimore atlas and index of parish registers* ed. C.R. Humphery-Smith (1984) contains for each English and Welsh parish outline details of deposited original registers, of coverage by the INTERNATIONAL GENEALOGICAL INDEX, by BOYD'S MARRIAGE INDEX and the PALLOT MARRIAGE INDEX, and of copies of the registers at the Society of Genealogists and deposited elsewhere.

The National Index of Parish Registers being published by the Society of Genealogists gives much greater detail for those counties which have been covered to date.

For the whereabouts of Welsh parish registers see *Parish Registers of Wales*, by C.J. Williams and J. Watts-Williams (London, 1986) and for the whereabouts of Irish registers see *Guide to Irish Parish Registers*, by Brian Mitchell (1989).

Parish incumbents are entitled to charge for allowing a search to be made in their registers. Fees for searches made by the incumbent are by agreement.

Baptismal Registers In some early registers, christenings, marriages and burials are all entered on the same pages, in chronological order. Usually the three were kept in the same book but in separate parts; sometimes on alternate pages. In these cases the dates shown on the cover do not necessarily apply to the christenings. Entries up to 1598 or 1603 are usually neatly written because they were deliberately copied, as mentioned above. After that the handwriting degenerates. In the sixteenth and early seventeenth centuries, entries are often in Latin (see below).

Between 1645 and 1660 many people did not have their children baptized because of their disapproval of the changed rite under the Commonwealth. This is unfortunate, because under that regime the date of birth was ordered to be entered in the christening register, and also the parents' names. On 22 September, 1653, the duty of registration was transferred by the 'Barebones Parliament' from the clergy to an official called the Parish Register (or Registrar, as we should say now), elected by the ratepayers. A fee of one shilling had to be paid, which proved another disincentive, and, to make matters worse, the registers were very laxly kept at this period. After the Anglican Restoration of 1660, many of the unchristened babies were baptized as older children or up to the age of fifteen or so.

January ye 3^d:

3   Ann ye daughter of William Hammilton baptized.

7   Elizabeth ye daughter of John May baptized.

12   Elizabeth ye daughter of Zachariah ffloodgate baptized.

28   Ann the daughter of John Biggs baptized.

Eodem   Elizabeth ye daughter of Ann Wellelove (a bastard) baptized.

Eodem   Edward the son of Edward Goddard baptized.

31   Mary the daughter of John Adams baptized.

— — — — — — — — — — —

ffebruary ye 11th

11   Ann Allenby ye daughter of Sarah Bullen (a bastard) baptized.

Eodem   Hannah the daughter of Robert Hurst baptized.

18   Sarah ye daughter of Joseph Peirson baptized.

25   William the son of William Cutt baptized.

28   William ye son of William Mitchel baptized.

— — — — — — —

March ye 2^d

2   Benjamin ye son of Benjamin Digsby baptized.

Eodem   Ann ye daughter of Nathaniel Novell baptized.

4   John the son of Thomas Huntingford baptized.

7   Mary ye daughter of John Light baptized.

8   Mary ye daughter of Thomas Ranbly baptized.

9   Jacob ye son of Jacob Sizeman baptized.

Eodem   John the son of Mr John Millest baptized.

Eodem   Joel and Isaat twins of John Goreing baptized.

10   Jane ye daughter of Daniel ffeild baptized.

11   George the son of John Tyler baptized.

Eodem   Mary ye daughter of Daniel Board baptized.

15   Richard ye son of William Edmead baptized.

22   William the son of William Atfeild baptized.

~ ~ ~ ~ ~ ~ ~ ~ ~ ~ ~ ~ ~

April ye 22^d. 1739

~ ~ ~ ~ ~ ~ ~ ~ ~ ~ ~ ~

22   John ye son of John Southy baptized.

Eodem   Jane ye daughter of John Smith baptized.

23   John y^e son of Joseph Hammilton baptized.

25   Jacob y^e son of John ffeild baptized.

29   James y^e son of John Sedgwick baptized.

Baptismal register entries of 1739

BAPTISMS solemnized in the Parish of _Chertsey_ in the County of _Surrey_ in the Year 18_31_

When Baptized.	Child's Christian Name.	Parents Name. Christian.	Surname.	Abode.	Quality, Trade, or Profession.	By whom the Ceremony was performed.
1831. Sept. 11th Born Aug. 10th No. 49.	Charles	Benjamin & Mary	Thorn	Chertsey	Carpenter	R Coulthard off. Curate
Sept. 11th Born Aug. 23d No. 50.	Eliza	Henry & Harriett	Monk	Chertsey	Labourer	R Coulthard off. Curate
Sept. 11th Born Aug. 18th No. 51.	Albert	George & Susannah	White	Chertsey	Tailor	R Coulthard off. Curate
Sept. 15th Born Aug. 29. No. 52.	Sarah	Isaac & Caroline	Hyde	Chertsey	Labourer	R Coulthard off. Curate
Sept. 16th Born Aug. 15. No. 53.	Richard	Ann Chandler Illegitimate.		Chertsey		R Coulthard off. Curate
Sept. 18th Born Aug. 21st No. 54.	Emma	Richard & Sarah Celia	Paice	Chertsey	Labourer	R Coulthard off. Curate
Sept. 25th Born Aug. 24th No. 55.	James	Richard & Sarah	West	Chertsey	Labourer	R Coulthard off. Curate
Sept. 25th Born Aug. 28th No. 56.	William	Richard Jane	Smithers	Chertsey	Labourer	R Coulthard off. Curate

Towards the end of the seventeenth century, many children were being baptized by dissenting ministers and so were not offically recorded. Because of this, in 1694 notification of birth to the Anglican incumbent was made compulsory under penalty of a fine. A tax was charged for registration, plus a fee of six pence to the incumbent, even if no baptism took place. Many clergy ignored this order, and in 1706 it was revoked.

During the late seventeenth century and all through the eighteenth, baptisms were often performed at home, and these sometimes went unregistered. However, occasionally a child's christening might be entered twice in the register — once for his or her private baptism at home, and again on public reception into the church. On the whole, christening registers have been less reliably kept than those for marriages and burials.

A later deterrent to the registration of baptisms, especially of poor children, was a tax of three pence levied between 1783 and 1794.

As a result of George Rose's Act of 1812, separate printed baptismal books were started from 1 January, 1813, and there were spaces in these for entering the names, and places of residence, of the parents, and the occupation of the father. Illegitimacy was always mentioned, and in such cases the fathers' names were given only if paternity was admitted. Foundlings were often christened with the name of the saint to whom the church was dedicated, or of the street in which they were found.

Civil registration of births began on 1 July, 1837 (*see* GENERAL REGISTER OF BIRTHS, DEATHS AND MARRIAGES). In June of that year, owing to some misunderstanding of the *Civil Registration Act*, there was, in some places, a rush of unchristened people to undergo baptism before 1 July, and many of these will have been adults. When civil registration began, no penalties were exacted for non-observance, and in consequence there are some omissions. Baptismal registers therefore continue to be of use until 1874, when fines were prescribed for non-registration.

It was a common custom for a young wife to return to her mother for her first confinement, so the baptism of the eldest child of a marriage will often be found in the register of the mother's parish.

LEFT a baptismal register page for 1831. Illegitimate children were always entered as such. *Chertsey Parish Church*

Marriage Registers Before 1929, a girl could marry at the age of 12, and a boy at 14, but a parent's consent was required. Since that date the lower age limit for both has been set at 16.

An Act of 29 September, 1654, took marriages out of the hands of the clergy and gave them as a responsibility to the Justices of the Peace. However, these civil marriages were disapproved of by many of the more devout, and such couples might get themselves married by their parish clergy, or even by ejected Anglican clergymen, in which case the ceremonies would not be registered. Also at this time, some contiguous parishes were combined for registration purposes to enable them to employ a joint Parish Register (Registrar). On the other hand, some marriages at this time, and also later, were registered in two places — the parish where they took place, and the parish of residence of one of the parties. During the Interregnum, registration was very laxly carried out, but at the Restoration in 1660 marriage and its registration by the clergy were resumed and entries became more regular. Civil marriages already contracted after marketplace banns were legalised, and the children of such marriages legitimised. Between 1698 and 1703, taxes were charged on the registration of marriages, and this led to gaps in the record for poorer families.

Until 1754, marriage by affirmation before witnesses, but without ecclesiastical rites and unregistered, was nevertheless recognised as valid by the law, but Lord Hardwicke's *Act for the Better Preventing of Clandestine Marriages*, effective from 25 March, 1754, instituted marriage register books separate from those for baptisms and burials. It also required banns books to be kept. Entries showed marital status and parishes of residence, and had to be signed by both parties and by witnesses. They follow a prescribed, usually printed, form. Also, marriages had to be performed in licensed buildings, which were always the churches and chapels of the Church of England. From this law only Quakers and Jews were exempted.

The *Stamp Act* of 1783 (effective 1 October) charged a duty of three pence on all registrations, with the same result as the earlier tax. It was repealed in 1794. Between 1795 and 1820, parochial registration is said to have virtually collapsed.

In 1813, George Rose's Act introduced new columnar forms for the registers, giving the incumbent less freedom for adding his own, often useful, pieces of information, but ensuring the recording of the bridgeroom's occupation, the marital status of both parties and their

Vicesimo nono die mensis eiusdem Sepultus fuit Thomas ...

Decimo quarto die mensis Decembris Sepulta fuit Johanna ...

... Thomas Tickner /

Decimo nono die eiusdem mensis Sepultus fuit Richardus Deane

✝2 | Secundo Anno Regni Elizabeth. |

Decimo die mensis Januarij baptizata fuit Maria filia Joh̄is Rogers

Vicesimo die eiusdem mensis baptizata fuit Johanna filia Will̄mi
Harper ij

Vicesimo secundo die mensis Februarij baptizata fuit Anna filia
Henrici Chesman /

Vicesimo quarto die eiusdem mensis baptizat̄ fuit Will̄mus filius
Richardi Cooke ij

Primo die mensis Martij baptizatus fuit Johēs filius Nicholai
Luxore /

Decimo sexto die eiusdem mensis Sepulta fuit Florentia filia ...

Vicesimo quinto die mensis eiusdem baptizata fuit Elizabeth filia
Richardi Eliott generosi /   Anno Dñi 1560

Sexto die mensis Aprilis Sepulta fuit Johanna Chenoll vidua

Octavo die eiusdem mensis Sepultus fuit Will̄mus Mergell /

Vicesima prima die mensis maij baptizaverant Will̄mus Large et
Margareta Biford /

Vicesimo tertio die mensis Maij baptizatus fuit Georgius filius
Georgij Ingilmere /

Vicesimo quinto die mensis eiusdem Sepultus fuit Richardus Coo...

Vicesima die mensis eiusdem Sepultus Thomas Stone /

Quarto decimo die eiusdem mensis baptizatus fuit Thomas filius
Joh̄is Stone /

Vicesimo nono die mensis eiusdem Sepulta fuit Anna Rogers vidua

Primo die mensis Julij Sepulta fuit Johanna Large vidua

Vicesimo primo die mensis Julij baptizata fuit Dorothea filia Walteri et
Johā

parishes of residence, with signatures of the parties and witnesses.

From 1837, when civil registration began, marriages could once more be performed in Roman Catholic and Nonconformist houses of worship, but had by law to be carried out in the presence of a registrar. Parish marriage registers are now kept in duplicate, the second copy being sent at the end of each quarter to the District Superintendent Registrar, who sends it to the Registrar General.

There has always been a tendency for marriages to take place in the parish of the bride, rather than that of the bridegroom, but sometimes in neither. In the last case, the researcher should look for a marriage licence mentioning a specific church, and, failing that, a marriage entry in the parish register of the market town nearest to the couple's homes.

Until about 1642 there were 'close seasons' of the year when few marriages took place. These were: Advent to St Hilary's Day (13 January), 41–47 days; Septuagesima to Low Sunday, 10 weeks; Rogation Sunday to Trinity Sunday, 3 weeks.

Over the years the form of the marriage entry has changed a good deal, but the researcher is likely to come across three main types: *Early* 'John Smith and Jane Brown, nupt.' (but some sixteenth-century entries made no mention of the bride); *After 1754* 'John Smith, of Mansfield, Co. Nottingham, nailer, bachelor, and Jane Brown, of Belper, Co. Derby, spinster', plus the signatures or marks of both parties and the witnesses; *From 1813* 'John Smith, nailer, of the Parish of Mansfield in the County of Nottingham, bachelor, and Jane Brown, of this Parish, spinster, were married in this church by Banns/Licence with the consent of James Brown, this fifteenth day of August in the year 1820, By me, John Austen, Rector. In the presence of Mary Smith, John Jones. Signed (by the parties and witnesses).'

Marriages after 1 July, 1837, are more easily found in the General Register, which contains copies of the register entries.

Before 1754, marriages are usually found in the same books as baptisms and burials, and can sometimes be found starting, upside down, on the last page of the book. Single entries may be mixed with those of baptisms and burials. Pages may have been bound in the wrong order, giving

a wrong impression of date at first sight. Where the registers show gaps, the Bishops' Transcripts should be consulted.

A few parishes have espousal books recording betrothals. Until the early seventeenth century a betrothal was considered to have almost the validity of a marriage and this may sometimes account for a first child being born 'rather early' after the marriage.

Before 1835, marriage with a deceased wife's sister was legal but against the canons of the Church, so some clergy would not perform the ceremony. Such marriages were 'voidable' but not 'null and void'. The 1835 *Marriage Act* recognised such marriages already contracted as legal, but from then on they were illegal until the *Deceased Wife's Sister Marriage Act* of 1907.

See also BANNS OF MARRIAGE; ESPOUSAL.

Burial Registers Entries seldom identify the deceased, but the burial of a child is sometimes indicated by implication in the addition of the father's name (e.g. 'Martha, daughter of James Smith'), though such an entry may refer to a spinster living with her father. Early burials are often to be found entered among christenings and marriages, but are sometimes in separate sections of the same volume, and sometimes in separate volumes. Some incumbents only reigstered burials by Anglican rites, which excluded suicides, excommunicates, executed criminals and unbaptized children. Burials of still-born babies were seldom recorded.

After the *Toleration Act* of 1689, Nonconformist, Roman Catholic and Jewish cemeteries were opened, so that not all burials after that will be in the parish records. In any case, relatives were free to choose any parish for their burials, and everyone had the right of sepulchre in the parish in which he died. Occasionally the social status of the deceased is shown by the title, Mr, Mrs or Dame. Acts of 1666 and 1678 encouraged the wool trade by laying down that bodies were not to be buried wrapped in anything but wool, and a relative had to make an affidavit before a justice, or, failing him, a clergyman, within eight days of the funeral, stating that the law had been complied with. In some parishes, at the conclusion of the burial service, the clergyman asked, 'Who makes the affidavit?' The making of a satisfactory reply was indicated in the register by the word Affidavit, or an abbreviation. Some parish incumbents recorded the affidavits in separate books. The Act was repealed in 1814, but by then was virtually a dead-letter.

Half of all burial entries are for infants, so that if a child is christened with the same name as

Anno Domi 1609.

Leonard Robinson were married the 25th Day of
Joan Kingam September.

John Bucher were married the 2th Day of October
Anne Harmon

Anno Dom: 1610

Edward Humphrie were married the 24th day of June, Anno Dom
Sarah Wood

Anno Domi: 1611

Anno Domini 1611 et
Regis Jacobi 9°
1. George Steere and Joane Smalpeece were married in the Parish Church of
St Saviours in Southwarke the 17th day of April, Anno Dom: 1611

2. John Bixley of Capell and Marie Jevill were married the 22th of April
3. John Weker and Elenor White were married the 28th of April
4. John Woden and Margerie Steere widdow were married the 29th of July
5. John Aunsell of Horsham & Elynour Gardiner widdow were married Octob:

Anno Dom: 1612 et
Regis Jacobi 10 °
Anno Domini: 1612.

1. Thomas Demet of Horne & Margaret Milles were Married May 11.
2. William Constable of Capell & Susan Willet were married July 27.
3. Thomas Mathew of Charlewode & Elizabeth Francis were married August 23
4. Robert Chatfeilde and Agnes Gardener were married September 29

Dom: 1613 et
Jacobi 11° °
Anno Dom: 1613.

1. Thomas Lifford and Elizabeth Elliot were married May 0.
2. Richard Taylour and Elizabeth Rossie were married Juny 13°.

Anno Dom: 1614.

Dom: 1614 &
Jacobi 12° °
1. Thomas Gemmer of Leigh and Margerie Kennington widdow were married May 30
2. James Edwardes of Reigate & Elizabeth Mischnoke widdow were married July

Anno Dom: 1615.

Dom: 1615 et
Jacobi 13° °
1. John Constable of Capell & Susan Wonham were married July 3.
2. Philip Fenell of Heild & Elizabeth Richman were married July 16.
3. Henrie Penfolde & Margaret Tipsell were married Janua: 10

An: Dom: 1616.

Dom: 1616 et
Jacobi 14° °
1. Henrie Swan of Oekley & Elizabeth Edwards widdow were married May 29.
2. Thomas Dimocke & Lydia Dudley were married September 1.
3. Thomas White & Katherine Frauncis were married Februa: 23.

Dom: 1617 et
Regis Jacobi 15
1. Edward Chitfeilde of Worth & Joane Dancis were married July 14

An: Dom: 1618.

1. William Wright & Marie Brooker were married May 17
2. John Smith & Hester Robinson were married May 26
3. Walter Longast & Margaret Nie widdow were married Juny 23

An: Dom: 1619.

1. Mathew Bishop & Sarah West were married Sept: 21°.

An: Dom: 1620.

1. Nicholas Chantler et

his father, and there is a burial entry of the same name within a year of the christening, it is probably the child, not the father, who had died (*see* CHRISOM). During the periods 1694–1706 and 1783–94, when taxes were payable on registration, burials often went unregistered, though sometimes the incumbent obtained the relevant information from the undertaker or the coffin plate and made the entry without charge. Burials are more conscientiously recorded than baptisms, but less so than marriages. Those of infants were particularly liable to be omitted.

From 1 January, 1813, in accordance with George Rose's Act of 1812, burials had to be entered in separate books, under printed headings. These required the recording of the deceased's age and abode, so making the register much more useful to genealogists.

Parochial Registers and Records Measure 1978. As from 1 January, 1979, the following are the regulations laid down regarding parish registers.

They are the property of the parochial church council of the parish concerned. Their custody is the responsibility of the incumbent, or, during a vacancy, of the churchwardens. However, parishes are required to deposit in a diocesan record office all records completed over one hundred years ago, unless they particularly wish to keep them, in which case they must conform to the following conditions: (a) the bishop must be asked for and give his consent; (b) the records shall be inspected every six years; (c) the records shall be kept in the church in a fire-proof and rust-proof cupboard, humidity and temperature of which must be checked once a week; (d) access for people wishing to see the registers is to be provided 'at all reasonable hours'; (e) fees may be charged for inspecting the registers. These fees are laid down in the Ecclesiastical Fees Order from time to time. If an incumbent is asked to make a search on an enquirer's behalf, the fee should be agreed in advance.

The clergy are bound by certain other regulations:

The incumbent must supply certificates if requested. He is not legally bound (a) to permit the photographing of records, (b) to supply certificates on postal application, though this is normally done on payment of the appropriate fee, (c) to make searches on behalf of an enquirer, though he may consent to do this for such remuneration as may be agreed.

Latin Words and Phrases found in Parish Registers

Latin	English
ambo	both
annoque predicto	of the year aforesaid
baptizatus(-a)erat *baptizabatur* Abbrev: *bapt.*	was baptized
coelebs	bachelor
copulati sunt	were married (see also below)
coram	in the presence of
creatura Christi	child of Christ (who died unnamed)
cum contione Abbrev: *cum cont.*	with a sermon
de hac parochia *de hujus parochie*	of this parish
die	on the . . . day
dominus(-a) Abbrev: *dom.*	lord or sir (lady or dame)
duxit	led (in marriage). The word is then followed by the bride's name.
ejus	his or her (of him or her)
eques	knight
ex hac eadem parochia	of this same parish
filius(-a) Abbrev: *fil.*	son (daughter) The word is then followed by the parent's name in the genitive
filius(-a) populi	bastard son
filius(-a) vulgi Abbrev: *fil. pop.*	(daughter) of a harlot
gemelli(-e)	twins (twin girls)
in comitatu Abbrev: *in com.*	in the county (of)

LEFT The marriage register of a Surrey parish for the years 1609–21. The first three entries are written in Secretary Hand, the rest in an angular form of Italic (see HANDWRITING). *Courtesy Guildford Muniment Room*

1720

Septembris 1mo Ricardus Wakeford et Jana Harrison Copulati sunt

Septembris 4to Thomas Scott et Anna Fry Copulati fuerunt

Octobris 2do Edmandus Hawkins et margaretta Cooper Copulati fuerunt

Novembris 13tio Johannes Russell et Anna Hopkins matrimonio Juncti sunt

Eodem. Edvardus Hoxmly et Anna Greenfeild Copulati sunt

Decembris 1mo Thomas Keyberd et Anna Smith Copulati sunt

29no Thomas Penn et maria Roake Copulati sunt

Eodem Jacoby Roake et jana wakeham Copulati sunt

ffebruarij 6to Johannes Yowell et maria ffeilder Copulati fuerunt

16to Robertus Wheatley et fficia Oxeford Copulati fuerunt

Eodem. Johanes Goldhawke et maria Strickland Copulati sunt

Philippo Cole vicario
John Barker Editui

Marriage register entries written in Latin, as shown ABOVE, are unusual at such a late date at 1720 By 1770, entries are recorded in a printed book RIGHT. Of the contracting parties on page 102, only Isaac Collins and Sarah Pais could write their names. *Chertsey Parish Church*

Nᵒ 105.

John Curtis   of [this] Parish
and Ann Roberts   of [the]
same   were
Married in this [Church] by [Banns]
this Fourth   Day of October   in the Year One Thousand Seven Hundred
and Seventy eight   by me   P. H. Miller   [Minister]
This Marriage was { John Curtis his Mark ✗
solemnized between Us { Ann Roberts her Mark ✗
In the { William Roberts his Mark ✗
Presence of { Wᵐ Touch.

❊❊❊❊❊❊❊❊❊❊❊❊❊❊❊❊❊❊❊❊❊❊❊❊❊❊❊❊❊❊❊❊❊❊❊❊❊❊❊

Nᵒ 106.

Thomas Fletcher   of [this] Parish
and Mary Wells   of [the]
same   were
Married in this [Church] by [Banns]
this Nineteenth   Day of October   in the Year One Thousand Seven Hundred
and Seventy eight   by me N. Herbert Potter   [Minister]
This Marriage was { Thomas Fletcher his Mark ✗
solemnized between Us { Mary Wells her Mark ✗
In the { Richard Brown
Presence of { Wᵐ Touch.

❊❊❊❊❊❊❊❊❊❊❊❊❊❊❊❊❊❊❊❊❊❊❊❊❊❊❊❊❊❊❊❊❊❊❊❊❊❊❊

Nᵒ 107.

Isaac Collins   of [this] Parish
and Sarah Pais   of [the]
same   were
Married in this [Church] by [Banns]
this 25ᵗʰ   Day of October   in the Year One Thousand Seven Hundred
and Seventy eight   by me   P. H. Miller   [Minister]
This Marriage was { Isaac Collins
solemnized between Us { Sarah Pais
In the { Mary Pais
Presence of { Wᵐ Touch

❊❊❊❊❊❊❊❊❊❊❊❊❊❊❊❊❊❊❊❊❊❊❊❊❊❊❊❊❊❊❊❊❊❊❊❊❊❊❊

Nᵒ 108.

Benjamin Adams   of [this] Parish
and Ann Farley   of [the]
same   were
Married in this [Church] by [Banns]
this 25ᵗʰ   Day of October   in the Year One Thousand Seven Hundred
and Seventy eight   by me   P. H. Miller   [Minister]
This Marriage was { Benjamin Adams his Mark ✗
solemnized between Us { Ann Farley her Mark ✗
In the { John Gray
Presence of { Wᵐ Touch.

innuba	unmarried (woman)
juxta Christi	according to Christ (i.e. in a year starting 25 March)
in matrimonia juncti sunt	were joined in matrimony
mensis	of the month
meretrix	harlot
miles	knight
nothus	bastard
nuptifuerunt Abbrev: *nupt.*	were married
obiit Abbrev: *ob.*	died
parochie Abbrev: *par.*	of the parish (of)
per bannos	by banns
per licentiam Abbrev: *lic.*	licence
puella	spinster
renatus(-a)	baptized
sepeliebatur *sepultus(-a) erat*	was buried Abbrev: *sep.*
solutus(-a)	bachelor (spinster)
stylo Angliae	in the style of England (i.e. in a year starting 25 March)
ut dictitur	as is said
ut fertur	(of a putative father)
uterque	both
uxor Abbrev: *ux.*	wife
viduus(-a) Abbrev: *vid*	widower (widow)

Examples:

Johannes Smith, coelebs, parochie
John Smith, bachelor, of the parish of

Chertsey, et Anna Wilkes, soluta, de hac
Chertsey, and Anne Wilkes, spinster, of this

parochia, nupti fuerunt per licenciam
parish, were married by licence.

Note that in baptismal entries the Latin names of the parents are in the genitive case, to mean 'of'. In the example given above, the parents Robertus et Maria Brown have their endings changed to -i and -e. Latin entries in a parish register do not mean that the persons were called by the Latin names shown. Robertus et Maria were Robert and Mary to their friends and relations.
See also CHRISTIAN NAMES.
Further reading: W.E. Tate. *The Parish Chest* Phillimore (1983).

Parliamentary Papers

Apart from the Bills and Acts of Parliament, there are four important classes of papers that constitute the records of Parliament. These are:

Command Papers Those laid before Parliament by government departments or *ad hoc* bodies such as royal commissions. They date from the reign of Charles I.

House Papers Those ordered by either House itself, dating from 1626. The best known of these are the Protestation Oath Returns of 1641/2.

Act Papers Those compulsorily laid before Parliament under the terms of an Act, dating from 1669.

Petitions These are the papers of greatest interest to family historians, since they were laid before Parliament by private individuals, groups of individuals, trade, local and other bodies, and bear the signatures or marks of at least the chief petitioners. They date from 1601. Because of the fire that destroyed much of the British parliamentary buildings in 1834, the seventeenth-, eighteenth- and early nineteenth-century papers of the Upper House are all that survive. They are available at the House of Lords Record Office in the Victoria Tower of the Houses of Parliament.
See also ACTS OF PARLIAMENT.

Parlour

A ground-floor room off the hall for day-time use, including the entertainment of guests but not for meals. Sometimes used as a room for sleeping in when necessary.

Parochyn

A parishioner

Parson

A rector rather than a vicar

Particular Baptist *see* Baptist

RIGHT An eighteenth-century Burial Register contains several items of information useful to family historians. *Courtesy Chertsey Parish Church*

October.

3... Sarah Bauldwin Bur.

5th Henry Chapman Bur.

6th Rebecca Gazumac Bur.

9th Mary Fuller Bur. (by the Parish)

23... William Barnett Bur.

26th Ann Webb (a Poor traveller's Child) Bur.

28... Thomas Bauldwin (from Workhouse) Bur.

29th Richard Hart Bur.

do. Thomas Field (an Inf.t) Bur (by the Parish)

30th Barbara Smith Bur.

November. —

4th James Carter (from Workhouse) Bur.

13... Patience Puss Bur. (by the Parish)

26th Mrs. Ann Rowe (from London) Bur.

29... Mrs. Mary Gordon Remov'd from Marybone & Bur.

30th Henry Crockford Jun.r Bur.

December.

9th John Stevens (an Inf.t) Bur.

10th Alice Freeman Bur. (by the Parish)

10th Ann Blake (an Inf.t) Bur.

19th Sarah Moore Bur.

26th William Russell (from Workhouse) Bur.

28th Mary Benham Bur.

Tho.s Till Curate.

BURIALS in the Parish of _Chertsey_

in the County of _Surrey_ in the Year 182_9_

Name.	Abode.	When buried.	Age.	By whom the Ceremony was performed.
Mary Goring No. 1089.	Chertsey	Dec.19th	67	C Pembroke Curate
Mary Gray No. 1090.	Chertsey	Dec.19th	45	C Pembroke Curate
William Thomas White No. 1091.	Chertsey	Dec.10th	3 months	C Pembroke Curate
Rebecca Baker No. 1092.	Chertsey	Dec.27th	74	C Pembroke Curate
Charlotte Smith a foundling No. 1093.	Chertsey	Dec.27th		C Pembroke Curate
Mary Moore No. 1094.	Chertsey	Dec.28th	33	C Pembroke Curate
No. 1095.				
No. 1096.				

Passenger Lists   No regular series of passenger lists of ships leaving England for any period before the early nineteenth century exists. Stray lists for odd ships and lists of persons going abroad for a particular reason (as apprentices, ministers, convicts, etc.) are, however, extant in various places. Most have been printed and the books in which they appear are listed in P.W. Filby, *Passenger and Immigration Lists Bibliography* (2nd ed. Detroit, 1988). All the names in these lists are given in P.W. Filby and N.K. Meyer, *Passenger and Immigration Lists Index* (3 vols. Detroit, 1981) and its annual *Supplements*, which together list nearly two million emigrants.

Lists of people leaving the United Kingdom by sea, other than the ships' crews, had to be supplied by commanders to the port officers. They were then sent to the Board of Trade for statistical purposes and passed finally, from 1890, to the Public Record Office, where they are to be found at Kew under BT 27, arranged under years, ports of departure and ships. They give each passenger's occupation, age and port of destination.

From 1906, there are helpful *Registers of Passenger Lists* (BT 32) showing, under each port, the names of ships and months of departure, with exact departure dates from 1920. But before 1908, registers exist only for Southampton, Bristol and Weymouth.

The earliest regular series of passenger lists of aliens to North America starts in 1820 and this, together with a few lists of aliens from 1798, is in the National Archives at Washington. It is arranged by port of entry. These records, however, do not generally show the emigrant's place of origin.

For the period 1840–70, the American Customs House copies of lists of passengers to the United States are in the Fiscal Section, General Records Division, National Archives, Washington DC. For the period after 1907, *Manifests of Aliens arriving in the USA* are in the Library of Congress, Washington DC.

Full details of passenger arrival lists and naturalization records in the United States will be found in *Guide to Genealogical Research in the National Archives* (Washington, 1982, pages 39–69). Duplicate passenger lists deposited at English ports of departure before 1890 have been destroyed.

See also EMIGRANTS.

LEFT Page from a nineteenth-century burial register. *Chertsey Parish Church*

Passports   Passports were not compulsory for travellers from the United Kingdom before the First World War. The *Register of Passports* at the Public Record Office, Kew (FO 610) begins in 1795 and is entered up in chronological order. There are *Indexes of Names* (FO 611) for the periods 1851–62 and 1874–98, when the Register ends. There is evidence that when a family or married couple travelled, the husband alone (being the applicant) was noted in the Register. Modern book passports with descriptions and photographs of the holders were introduced in 1921. For seventeenth-century travellers, *see* LICENCE TO PASS BEYOND THE SEAS.

Patent Rolls   These comprise the registered copies of Letters Patent issued by the royal court of Chancery during the period 3 John to 9 George VI (their third and ninth regnal years, respectively). They are the longest unbroken set of archives extant in the world. The original letters were issued 'open', with the Great Seal pendant from the foot. They dealt with national affairs (such as treaties); grants and confirmations of liberties, offices, privileges, lands and wardships to private persons and public bodies; charters of incorporation; licences for the election of bishops; and creations of nobility. Before the Naturalization Act of 1844 denization was recorded on the Patent Rolls. The Rolls are at the Public Record Office, Chancery Lane, London, in class C 66.

See also CHARTER, CLOSE ROLLS.

Patrimony *see* **Livery Companies**

Patronymic   A surname derived from that of a father or ancestor; e.g. Johnson, FitzWalter. *See also* SURNAMES.

Peculiar   An area within an archdeaconry but outside the jurisdiction of the archdeacon, and mostly of the bishop too. There were over two hundred such 'peculiar' areas and courts, mostly arising from properties of church dignitaries which lay within the dioceses of other bishops. They were the probate jurisdiction of either an archbishop, a bishop, a dean and chapter, dean, sub-dean, rector, vicar, or lord of a manor.

The area of a peculiar might be anything from a single township within a parish, to a parish or even a scattered group of parishes. The powers were taken from some of them by Acts of Parliament during the first four years of the reign of Queen Victoria, and in 1858 all probate powers were transferred from ecclesiastical to civil jurisdiction. Their probate records are now mostly to be found at the county record office of the county in which they were situated.

See also WILL.

Pedigree (i) A term for charts showing the descents of human beings and pure-bred horses and dogs, but not with the same meaning in each case. The pedigree of an animal shows its descent from all known sires and dams, and so corresponds to the chart for human beings known as either a Birth Brief, Ancestry Chart or Blood Descent. A pedigree of a human being shows male-line descent, and is a synonym for the more popular term Family Tree.

(ii) A genealogical computer program for recording family history and producing charts.

See also INDENTED NARRATIVE PEDIGREE

Peerage Under the Norman and early Angevin kings, all tenants-in-chief had the duty of attending the King's Court (*Curia Regis*). When a court was to be held, a general summons was issued, via the sheriffs, to the tenants-in-chief in each county. In time it became the custom to issue personal writs of summons to the larger land-holding barons and high ecclesiastics, thus distinguishing them above the rest. This arrangement was codified in Magna Carta. At first, however, the king felt no obligation to summon a baron just because he or his predecessor had been called to a previous court or Parliament, but gradually the 'greater barons' came to be summoned regularly and their heirs likewise, thus constituting an hereditary peerage.

From the reign of Richard II, any new peerage was formally conferred by Letters Patent, but writs of summons to Parliament continued to be sent out until they were abolished under Henry VIII. A patent defined the peerage and its mode of descent, mostly to direct male descendants by primogeniture, whereas the older peerages-by-writ descended to heirs general, i.e. to females in the absence of heirs male (*see* ABEYANCE).

The peerage now consists of five ranks: Duke, Marquess, Earl, Viscount and Baron, and can be either of England, Scotland, Ireland, Great Britain or the United Kingdom. Irish peers may sit in the House of Lords only if they hold a peerage other than an Irish title. Since the Peerage Act of 1963, peers of Scotland have seats in the Lords, as do peeresses in their own right.

Details of peers and their living relatives have been published periodically since 1713 in Debrett's *Peerage and Baronetage*. A later series, Burke's *Peerage, Baronetage and Knightage* (from 1826) gives pedigrees of all living peers and baronets, the information having been supplied by the persons themselves. The most reliable account of peerages, current, extinct, dormant and in abeyance, is to be found in the *Complete Peerage* (1887), edited by George Edward Cokayne. A new edition, revised and enlarged, by V. Gibbs and others, was published in 13 volumes between 1940 and 1959.

Penance A penalty that could be imposed by the Church as a punishment for faults. Before the Reformation a penance might be the repetition of certain forms of devotion (such as Paternosters or Ave Marias), the payment of a sum of money, pilgrimage, fasting or flagellation, but after the Reformation the usual penalty was the Declaration Penance. This might be imposed as a result of the fault having been presented at an ecclesiastical visitation, or before an ecclesiastical court. It took the form of the reading of a statement containing an admission of the fault, a recognition of its sinfulness, penitence, and a prayer to be forgiven and helped never to fall into the same sin again. The guilty person had to stand up in church in the presence of the congregation and read it, clad in a white sheet but bareheaded, barefoot and bare-legged, and with a white wand in his hand. The incumbent of his parish then had to send in to the Registrar's office a certificate, signed by himself and the two churchwardens, stating that the penance had been duly performed. Certificates also survive to the effect that the offender was a person of sufficiently good general character to warrant the imposition of a private penance, i.e. one carried out before the incumbent and churchwardens, instead of before the congregation.

Perambulation A procession around the parish bounds was customarily carried out by the clergy, parish officers and schoolchildren at Rogationtide (the Monday, Tuesday and Wednesday before Ascension Day), or on Ascension Day (Holy Thursday) itself. The day of the perambulation was called Gang Day. Small boys were ceremonially beaten over boundary stones to impress their location upon their memories, and so ensure that their location would be passed on to future generations.

Perpetual Calendar A calendar for ascertaining the day of the week at any date. The chart and its key cover the period 1500–1999.

The Perpetual Calendar consists of two parts, the Calendar and the Key. To find the day of the week on which a certain date fell, look up the year in the key and note the letter assigned to it. Then turn to the calendar and find that letter in the left-hand column. Look along the same horizontal line until you come to the column for the month you want. There, two days of the week are shown, one above the other. Above the calendar are shown the dates of nine 'Days of Each Month', in two rows, one above the other. The weekdays named under each month in the calendar fall on these dates; the upper ones on those in the upper row, and the lower ones on those in the lower. If the date in the month you are looking for is one of those shown, then it will fall on the corresponding weekday shown. If your date is not shown, find the date closest to it in the 'Dates of Each Month', then count one or two days forward or backward until you come to the day you seek. The following example will make the procedure clear.

Example You want to know the day of the week on which 22 July 1572 fell. In the key you find that the letter against 1572 is E-. In the calendar, run your finger horizontally along from E- to the July column, where you will find Tuesday in the upper position and Friday in the lower. Then refer to the 'Dates of Each Month' and you will see that the 22nd (the date you want) is one of those shown in the upper row; so, that date corresponds with the weekday of July in the upper position, namely Tuesday. The 22 July, 1572, fell on a Tuesday.

If you had wanted 24 July, which is not shown among the 'Dates of Each Month', you would pick the nearest date — the 25th in the lower row. As that corresponds to the day in July shown in the lower position (Friday), then the 24th would be the day before, i.e. Thursday.

Perpetual Curate A perpetual curate was licensed by the Bishop to take care of a chapel or church in an ecclesiastical district which forms part of an ancient parish but which pays its tithes to an ecclesiatical body or a lay person. Ordinarily a curate acts as an assistant to the incumbent of a parish. A perpetual curate is also called a stipendary because he is paid a stipend or salary.

Personal Ancestral File A genealogical computer program developed by the GENEALOGICAL SOCIETY OF UTAH for recording family history and producing charts.

Personalty Movable property that, on the death of the owner, did not in Common Law pass to the heir. It includes cattle, chattels, furniture, money, debts, investments and leases. It was always bequeathable by testament.

Peterborough and District Family History Society *see* **Northamptonshire**

Petitions *see* **Parliamentary Papers**

Petty Sessions Courts of summary jurisdiction held by two or more Justices of the Peace, and, later, by a stipendiary or metropolitan police magistrate, for trying lesser offences or as a preliminary enquiry in indictable offences. In 1828, Courts of Quarter Sessions were empowered to create Petty Sessions districts. Few records exist for Petty Sessions, but some Minute Books are to be found in county record offices and borough record offices.

Physicians Practitioners of physic had, like midwives, to be licensed by the ecclesiastical authorities, so mentions of their names are to be found in the records of ecclesiastical courts and visitations. By the eighteenth century the physician was usually a graduate, and so can be found in university registers. Medical degrees were not always awarded as a result of study, they could often be bought. In the capital, the Royal College of Physicians of London was founded in 1518, and its Annals contain records of the members. The College has published several volumes, known as *Munk's Roll*, on the lives of its Fellows and Licentiates, but not of ordinary members. The fourth volume, from 1826 onward, deals solely with Fellows.
See also APOTHECARIES; DOCTORS, MEDICAL; SURGEONS.

Piece, Record *see* **Class, Archive**

Piepoudré, Court of By the charter granting a market or trade fair, the grantee was obliged to hold a court to maintain order therein. The court was presided over by the lord or his steward, often with a jury of market traders. The cases dealt with were those of false measures, inferior quality of goods, pilfering and assault; felonies were usually excluded. The courts disappeared with other feudal jurisdictions. The name is thought to derive from the French, *pieds poudreux*, meaning 'dusty feet', the nickname applied to an itinerant trader.

Pightle A small, irregularly shaped piece of arable land.

Pigs On the manor, pigs had to have their noses ringed from Michaelmas until Christmas to prevent them grubbing up the soil. Owners who failed to ring them were fined by the manor

Dates of Each Month: 1 8 15 22 29
                              4 11 18 25

	Jan	Feb	Mch	Apr	May	Jun	Jul	Aug	Sep	Oct	Nov	Dec
A	Su W	W Sa	W Sa	Sa Tu	M Th	Th Su	Sa Tu	Tu F	F M	Su W	W Sa	F M
A–	Sa Tu	Tu F										
B	Sa Tu	Tu F	Tu F	F M	Su W	W Sa	F M	M Th	Th Su	Sa Tu	Tu F	Th Su
B–	F M	M Th										
C	F M	M Th	M Th	Th Su	Sa Tu	Tu F	Th Su	Su W	W Sa	F M	M Th	W Sa
C–	Th Su	Su W										
D	Th Su	Su W	Su W	W Sa	F M	M Th	W Sa	Sa Tu	Tu F	Th Su	Su W	Tu F
D–	W Sa	Sa Tu										
E	W Sa	Sa Tu	Sa Tu	Tu F	Th Su	Su W	Tu F	F M	M Th	W Sa	Sa Tu	M Th
E–	Tu F	F M										
F	Tu F	F M	F M	M Th	W Sa	Sa Tu	M Th	Th Su	Su W	Tu F	F M	Su W
F–	M Th	Th Su										
G	M Th	Th Su	Th Su	Su W	Tu F	F M	Su W	W Sa	Sa Tu	M Th	Th Su	Sa Tu
G–	Su W	W Sa										

Perpetual Calendar

1500 D-	1550 E	1600 E-	1650 F	1700 F-	1750 G	1800 E
1 C	1 D	1 D	1 E	1 E	1 F	1 D
2 B	2 B-	2 C	2 C-	2 D	2 Sp	2 C
3 A	3 A	3 B	3 B	3 C	3 G	3 B
4 F-	4 G	4 G-	4 A	4 A-	4 F	4 G-
5 E	5 F	5 F	5 G	5 G	5 E	5 F
6 D	6 D-	6 E	6 E-	6 F	6 C-	6 E
7 C	7 C	7 D	7 D	7 E	7 B	7 D
8 A-	8 B	8 B-	8 C	8 C-	8 A	8 B-
9 G	9 A	9 A	9 B	9 B	9 G	9 A
1510 F	1560 F-	1610 G	1660 G-	1710 A	1760 E-	1810 G
1 E	1 E	1 F	1 F	1 G	1 D	1 F
2 C-	2 D	2 D-	2 E	2 E-	2 C	2 D-
3 B	3 C	3 C	3 D	3 D	3 B	3 C
4 A	4 A-	4 B	4 B-	4 C	4 G-	4 B
5 G	5 G	5 A	5 A	5 B	5 F	5 A
6 E-	6 F	6 F-	6 G	6 G-	6 E	6 F-
7 D	7 E	7 E	7 F	7 F	7 D	7 E
8 C	8 C-	8 D	8 D-	8 E	8 B-	8 D
9 B	9 B	9 C	9 C	9 D	9 A	9 C
1520 G-	1570 A	1620 A-	1670 B	1720 B-	1770 G	1820 A-
1 F	1 G	1 G	1 A	1 A	1 F	1 G
2 E	2 E-	2 F	2 F-	2 G	2 D-	2 F
3 D	3 D	3 E	3 E	3 F	3 C	3 E
4 B-	4 C	4 C-	4 D	4 D-	4 B	4 C-
5 A	5 B	5 B	5 C	5 C	5 A	5 B
6 G	6 G-	6 A	6 A-	6 B	6 F-	6 A
7 F	7 F	7 G	7 G	7 A	7 E	7 G
8 D-	8 E	8 E-	8 F	8 F-	8 D	8 E-
9 C	9 D	9 D	9 E	9 E	9 C	9 D
1530 B	1580 B-	1630 C	1680 C-	1730 D	1780 A-	1830 C
1 A	1 A	1 B	1 B	1 C	1 G	1 B
2 F-	2 G	2 G-	2 A	2 A-	2 F	2 G-
3 E	3 F	3 F	3 G	3 G	3 E	3 F
4 D	4 D-	4 E	4 E-	4 F	4 C-	4 E
5 C	5 C	5 D	5 D	5 E	5 B	5 D
6 A-	6 B	6 B-	6 C	6 C-	6 A	6 B-
7 G	7 A	7 A	7 B	7 B	7 G	7 A
8 F	8 F-	8 G	8 G-	8 A	8 E-	8 G
9 E	9 E	9 F'	9 F	9· G	9 D	9 F
1540 C-	1590 D	1640 D-	1690 E	1740 E-	1790 C	1840 D-
1 B	1 C	1 C	1 D	1 D	1 B	1 C
2 A	2 A-	2 B	2 B-	2 C	2 G-	2 B
3 G	3 G	3 A	3 A	3 B	3 F	3 A
4 E-	4 F	4 F-	4 G	4 G-	4 E	4 F-
5 D	5 E	5 E	5 F	5 F	5 D	5 E
6 C	6 C-	6 D	6 D-	6 E	6 B-	6 D
7 B	7 B	7 C	7 C	7 D	7 A	7 C
8 G-	8 A	8 A-	8 B	8 B-	8 G	8 A-
9 F	9 G	9 G	9 A	9 A	9 F	9 G

Sp = a special year (1752) to which this calendar cannot apply, see CALENDAR.

1850	F	1900	G	1950	A
1	E	1	F	1	G
2	C-	2	E	2	E-
3	B	3	D	3	D
4	A	4	B-	4	C
5	G	5	A	5	B
6	E-	6	G	6	G-
7	D	7	F	7	F
8	C	8	D-	8	E
9	B	9	C	9	D
1860	G-	1910	B	1960	B-
1	F	1	A	1	A
2	E	2	F-	2	G
3	D	3	E	3	F
4	B-	4	D	4	D-
5	A	5	C	5	C
6	G	6	A-	6	B
7	F	7	G	7	A
8	D-	8	F	8	F-
9	C	9	E	9	E
1870	B	1920	C-	1970	D
1	A	1	B	1	C
2	F-	2	A	2	A-
3	E	3	G	3	G
4	D	4	E-	4	F
5	C	5	D	5	E
6	A-	6	C	6	C-
7	G	7	B	7	B
8	F	8	G-	8	A
9	E	9	F	9	G
1880	C-	1930	E	1980	E-
1	B	1	D	1	D
2	A	2	B-	2	C
3	G	3	A	3	B
4	E-	4	G	4	G-
5	D	5	F	5	F
6	C	6	D-	6	E
7	B	7	C	7	D
8	G-	8	B	8	B-
9	F	9	A	9	A
1890	E	1940	F-	1990	G
1	D	1	E	1	F
2	B-	2	D	2	D-
3	A	3	C	3	C
4	G	4	A-	4	B
5	F	5	G	5	A
6	D-	6	F	6	F-
7	C	7	E	7	E
8	B	8	C-	8	D
9	A	9	B	9	C

court. The woodland or copse of a manor was the feeding ground for the tenants' pigs. *See also* PANNAGE.

Pinder The person responsible for rounding up stray animals and confining them in the pound, or pinfold, of the manor or parish.

Pipe Rolls The annual accounts rendered to the Exchequer by the sheriffs, arising from their function as the king's agents in the shires, and entered up each Michaelmas by the Exchequer clerks. The oldest are those for 1120–30, and from 1155 they survive as a continuous series down to the 1830s. The Rolls will be found in the Public Record Office, Chancery Lane, London, in class E 372.

The farm of royal lands was removed from the accounts in 1284 and transferred to the newly constituted, Rolls of the Bodies of Counties. A number of Pipe Rolls have been published by the Pipe Roll Society. The name is derived from the fact that when the parchment membranes are rolled up they resemble pipes. The succession of tenants-in-chief can be traced from the Pipe Rolls.

Place-names The names of most English towns and villages date from the settlement of Anglo-Saxon invaders in the fifth and sixth centuries, or from that of Scandinavian invaders in the ninth and tenth; but those of Cornwall, out of reach of the invaders, are mainly Celtic in origin. Most place-names derive either from a natural physical feature of the location (e.g. Byfleet — by the stream), from the first settler or settlers (e.g. Hastings — the Hastingas tribe), or from the settlement (e.g. Hickleton — Hicela's homestead).

Place-names form one of the main sources of family surnames and can show where an ancestor once lived (*see* SURNAMES). Some place-names have had the surname of medieval local landowning families added to them, e.g. Yardley Hastings in Northants and Tarrant Gunville in Dorset. Other local landlords of the Middle Ages are indicated by such place-names as Abbots Langley, Kings Langley, Huish Episcopi (of the bishop), and the like.

RIGHT A page from the Vestry Minute Book of Lingfield, Surrey, recording, first, the decision to build a pest house for the parish, and, at the next meeting, to rent a building for it instead. A pest house was not exclusively, as is popularly supposed, a hospital for plague sufferers.

of 12th of July 1762

At a Vestry Called and held in the Vestry Room
of the Parish of Lingfield It was Unanimously
Agreed by all present to proceed Immediately
to ye Building of a House for the Reception
of Such persons who Shall at Any time be Seiz'd
with the Small pox or Other pestilential Distemper
And that the Officers do forthwith prepare Estimates
of the Charges of the Said Building to be laid
before the Parishioners at the next Monthly Meeting

At a Vestry Called and held in the vestry Room
of the parish of Lingfield the 21st of Octobr 1763
It was then Unanimously Agreed to give Robt Bristy
the Sum of Three pounds Tenn Shillings ⅌ Annm
for the house and Orchard which he now holds by
Lease on Lingfield Common During the Tearm
of his Lease for the Use of a post house,
Exempt and free from all Taxes.

Jno Stanford
William Hotton } Church Wardens

John Brister } Overseers
Abraham Hale }

Geo: Lee.
Thos Exeter
Tho. Underhill
Richd Agate

For further reading, see the county volumes of the English Place-name Society, and the *Oxford Dicitonary of Place-names* by E. Ekwall.

Plague Although the term 'plague' was once used for any killing epidemic, it is now usually confined to bubonic plague, carried by fleas on the black rat. Incidence of plague in England was frequent from the seventh century onward, but the most devastating was the Black Death, which killed about one third of the population in 1347–50. Records of plague in the provinces are rare. Epidemics can be inferred from marked increases in the number of burials registered, but other mortal diseases, such as sweating sickness, may have been responsible. In seventeenth-century London there were outbreaks of plague in 1603 (33,000 deaths), 1625 (35,417) and 1636 (10,400), and the Great Plague of 1665 (68,596). After that there were no further severe outbreaks owing to the elimination of the black rat in England by the brown.

For further reading, see *A History of Epidemics in Britain*, by C. Creighton (1891–4, reprinted 1965).

Plaintiff A plaintiff is a person who initiates a suit in a court of law.

Plea (i) An action at law between parties.

(ii) The presentation of a case, either for the prosecution or for the defence. Certain types of plea bore special names; for example, the primary plea for the prosecution was known as First Plea (in an ecclesiastical court), the Declaration (in Common Law Courts), the Bill of Complaint (in equity courts), Articles (in criminal cases), Libel (in a court of Instance), and Allegation (in testamentary cases). In all causes, subsequent pleas were called Allegations.

Plea Rolls These are records of actions brought under the Common Law. They cover actions heard in the Curia Regis (King's Court) and in the courts that grew out of it, namely the courts of Common Pleas, King's Bench and the Exchequer; also of other Common Law courts.

The records begin in the reign of Richard I and end after the *Judicature Act* of 1873. They are written on parchment membranes (rotulets) stitched together at the top, sometimes with more than 500 membranes in one 'bundle'. Many private deeds are also recorded (enrolled) on the rolls. The earliest Curia Regis rolls are being printed in full, and the Selden Society has published extracts in their *Select Pleas*. Some Eyre Rolls have been printed or calendared by local record publishing societies. (The rolls do not include actions in the court of Chancery and other courts of equity, where the procedure differed from that of the Common Law courts.) The Plea Rolls of the above mentioned courts are at the Public Record Office, Chancery Lane, London. Plea Rolls of the City of London, preserved at the Guildhall, have been calendared and published down to 1482 under the title *Calendar of Plea and Memoranda Rolls* (Cambridge University Press).

Ploughland The area of land that could be cultivated in a year, using a single oxteam.

See also CARUCATE; HIDE; PLOUGH TEAM; BOVATE; OXGANG.

Plough Monday This was the first Monday after Christmas. Since Christmas officially ended on the Epiphany, Plough Monday is the first Monday after the 6th January.

Plough Team Eight oxen constituted a plough team in East Anglia and Lincolnshire, but not always elsewhere. In Cheshire the terms 'carucate' (Latin *caruca*) and 'hide' were used interchangeably for the area of land capable of being ploughed by one team in a year (i.e. a ploughland), but in some other counties a hide could contain several carucates.

Plurality *or* **Pluralism** The simultaneous holding by a parson of more than one benefice with care of souls; a practice always officially discouraged. By a canon of 1703, dispensation for pluralism could be permitted only to a graduate M.A. who was also a public and sufficient licensed preacher. It also required that he reside a reasonable time each year in both benefices, and that they should be not more than thirty miles apart. But this rule was often either ignored, or evaded by committing the second benefice to the parson *in commendam* i.e. by committing it to his charge temporarily.

Plymouth Brethren Plymouth Brethren are a calvinistic sect, founded in Plymouth in 1830, who feel Christianity has lost its purity and man needs direct access to God. They have no ministers.

Police Until early in the second quarter of the nineteenth century, the maintenance of law and order was in the hands of parochial constables, assisted in towns by watchmen and responsible to Justices of the Peace.

In London in the early eighteenth century there was at first one police office, at Bow Street, with a magistrate in charge of the 'Bow-Street

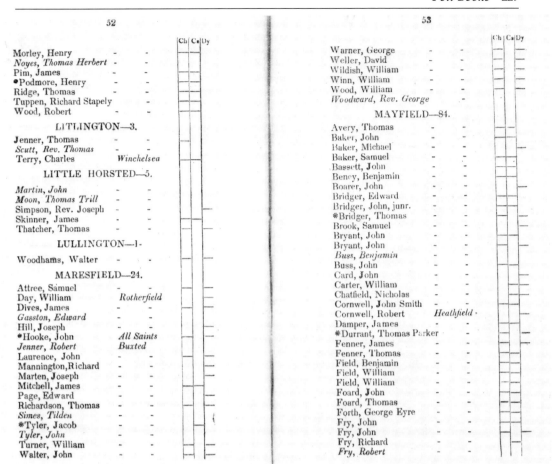

Poll Book page. The horizontal strokes in the three columns show which two candidates each freeholder voted for. *Courtesy Guildhall Library, Corporation of London*

Runners'. Henry Fielding, the novelist, was the magistrate in 1753, and his recommendations led to the setting up of more police offices, each with magistrates, clerks and a handful of constables. This was in addition to the constables of the London parishes. In 1829 Sir Robert Peel's Act for *Improving the Police in and near the Metropolis* separated the police from the magistrates and placed them under police commissioners, a step strongly opposed in many quarters as an infringement of civil liberties. Later, the City of London appointed its own commissioner and policemen. In 1829 and through the reign of William IV, 171 cities, boroughs and towns followed London's example, but in the countryside law and order was largely maintained by voluntary associations for catching and prosecuting felons, organised and supported by contributions from private persons and organisations. It was the *Rural Constabulary Act* of 1839 that empowered the appointment, by Quarter Sessions, of chief and petty constables. In 1856, county forces became compulsory. The policing of the country was the responsibility of the Home Office. The records of the Metropolitan Police are at the PRO Ruskin Avenue, Kew, Surrey. Those of the county forces are either at the appropriate county record office or remain with the local police authority. Further reading: *Police history monograph: notes for family historians* by L.A. Waters (1987) *See also* CONSTABLE.

Poll Books On 10 April, 1696, a bill intended to prevent irregularities in parliamentary elections by biased returning officers received the royal assent. One provision was that the officers should be obliged, if requested, to deliver to any member of the public a copy of the poll, showing how the electors had voted, 'at a reasonable charge for writing the same'. Soon after this, returning officers allowed Poll Books of county elections to be published as a commercial venture by local printers. Such books were usually in demand only when the result of the poll had been close. Poll Books could also be published for borough parliamentary elections, but as the members of borough electorate were often no more than a dozen or so, urban polls could often be published in local newspapers.

Poll Books continued to appear until and including the General Election of 1868. Their end was owing to the introduction of the secret ballot, which was first operated at a by-election on 17 August, 1872. Not all Poll Books are for the election of members of parliament; some have been published for elections of county coroners.

The information published in the books is not uniform. Names and votes are always given and sometimes the addresses and occupations of the voters and the nature of their qualifying freeholds. The list is usually arranged under parishes and/or hundreds. A Preface giving an account of the candidates and their opinions is sometimes included. A comparison of these with the way in which an ancestor voted can reveal his opinions on the issues of his day. From 1832, Electoral Registers are also available, but record only entitlement to vote.

The Institute of Historical Research, Senate House, University of London WC1E 7HU, has over 500 Poll Books. The British Library, London Guildhall and Bodleian Libraries also have large numbers. Smaller collections are at the Society of Genealogists, county record offices and reference libraries. County record offices may also have the original MSS of unpublished lists. The Society of Genealogists has issued a catalogue of its own Poll Books.

For further reading, see *A Handlist of British Parliamentary Poll Books*, by John Sims (University of Leicester 1984) and *Poll Books, c.1696–1872* by Jeremy Gibson and Colin Rogers. FFHS 2nd edn (1990).

Poll Tax   A tax levied on the population per head. It was imposed three times during the fourteenth century. In 1377 the rate was one groat (fourpence), but regular beggars and children under 14 were not included. In 1379 and 1381 the tax was graded socially, but after 1381 only aliens were taxed per head until another general poll tax was levied in 1513. The tax was imposed again on people over 16 in 1641, 1660, 1666, 1677, 1694 and 1698. The London returns for 1694 have been printed. The records are at the Public Record Office, Chancery Lane, London, in class E 179.

Pontage   A local tax or toll levied for the maintenance of a bridge.

Poor Law   The system of public relief of the poor laid down by Acts of Parliament since the original great *Poor Law Act* of 1601. The care of the poor was then placed in the hands of the parish, where it remained until the 'New Poor Law' replaced the 'Old Poor Law' in 1834. The responsibility was then removed to Poor Law Unions (of several parishes) administered by Boards of Guardians of the Poor. The records created by the working of the Poor Law sometimes enable the descent of a really poor family to be more easily traced than that of a more prosperous one. For the whereabouts of the records see the four volumes of *Poor Law Union Records* by Jeremy Gibson, Colin Rogers, Frederic Youngs Jr., and Cliff Webb. FFHS 1993.

For the various aspects of the Poor Law administration, *see* BADGE-MAN; BASTARDY; GUARDIANS OF THE POOR; OVERSEER OF THE POOR; SETTLEMENT; WORKHOUSES.

Population   The population of England at the time of Domesday has been accepted to be about one and a half million. Estimates of the figures for the fourteenth century, which embrace the drastic reduction caused by the Black Death, vary greatly, as indeed do all figures for the period before the first population census of 1801. The following figures, drawn from various sources, provide a rough guide. After 1200 they include Wales.

1086	1,100,000	1700	5,250,000
1345	3,800,000	1750	6,407,000
1377	2,350,000	1801	8,892,536
1400	2,100,000	1851	17,927,609
1500	2,250,000	1901	32,527,843
1600	4,500,000		

To estimate the population of a parish, a good rule of thumb is to count the householders listed in a Lay Subsidy Roll, add about one-third (some say one-quarter) of that number for poorer householders exempt from taxation, double the total to include the womenfolk, and double again to include the children. The Local Population Studies Society, 8 Royal Crescent, Harrogate, North Yorkshire HG2 8AB issues a journal, *Local Population Studies*.

For further reading, see *The Population History of England, 1541–1871*, by E.A. Wrigley and R.S. Schofield (1981).

Porail *or* **Poverail**   The poor, as a class.

Portion   The money brought by a bride to her husband.

Portraits   Portraits of ancestors are among the most treasured relics of the family past, whether they are life-size, full-length oil paintings or fading cigarette-card-size, head-and-shoulders photographs. If the sitter is known for certain, his or her name should be written on the back, so that the knowledge will be passed on with the picture. If the name is a probability deduced from evidence of provenance, vague oral tradition, costume or apparent age of the sitter, the clues should be noted alongside the probable name. All portraits should be photographed (or re-photographed) so that the copy can be filed in the same way as transcripts of documentary evidence. Original photographs should remain in any album in which they have been passed down.

Portraits can be dated from the evidence of costume and hairstyle (the latter being more reliable), and from the apparent age of the sitter; for professional photographers there is also the evidence of the photographer's name and address, which can be checked from local directories. If a painting appears to be a good one, the artist may be identifiable either by the experts at the Archive and Library of the National Portrait Gallery, The Mill, 72 Molesworth Street, Lewisham, London SE13 7EY, or by those of the auctioneers' firms, Christie and Sotheby, also in London but with regional offices throughout England. The latter two will also value them for insurance purposes. If the painter is sufficiently well known to have had his biography written and works catalogued, a reference to the catalogue, often appearing as an appendix to the biography, may lead to the identification of the sitter. Portraits are sometimes mentioned in wills, when the subject is usually named.

Posnet   A small iron pot often mentioned in inventories.

Post Office Archives   The Post Office Archives are at Freeling House, Mount Pleasant, London EC1A 1BB. They hold personal records of all employees, 1737–1940. See *A guide to the Post Office Archives*, by J. Farrugia (1987).

Pound   An enclosure, erected by local authority, for confining cattle and other beasts that were trespassing or straying. A pound overt was open overhead, and a pound covert was roofed over or entirely enclosed, like a stable or byre. Also called a pinfold.
See also PINDER.

Power of Attorney   The authority to act on someone's behalf in court.

Prebendary   A prebendary is the canon of a cathedral or collegiate church who holds a prebend (a portion of the revenues) as a stipend.

Precentor   A precentor was a member of the Cathedral chapter who was the leader of the congregational singing. Nowadays his duties are discharged by his deputy, the succentor.

Precisian   Another term for PURITAN.

Predial *see* **Tithe**

Prelatist   A mid seventeenth-century term of denigration used by Presbyterians and Independents to designate anyone, of the Anglican persuasion, who wished to preserve the episcopal hierarchy of the Church of England and the use of the *Book of Common Prayer*.

Prerogative Courts   The courts of the Archbishops of Canterbury and York, which took precedence over those of bishops. As courts of probate they had to be applied to for the proving of wills of any testator who left *bona notabilia* ('considerable goods') in more than one diocese. They could also be used for proving any will leaving property in their province, since it was always open to an executor to apply to a higher court than was necessary.

The Prerogative Court of Canterbury, being that of the Primate of All England, could prove wills of testators anywhere in England, Wales, the Isle of Man and the Channel Isles. The records of the Canterbury Court (known as PCC) are at the Public Record Office, Chancery Lane, London, and those of York (PCY) at the Borthwick Institute at the University of York.

Presbyterians   English nonconformity began as a Puritan movement, within the Church of England, to bring ritual and organisation nearer to Lutheran and Calvinistic forms by abolishing bishops, archdeacons, deans and chancellors. Most Puritans wanted parish clergy to be elected presbyters and their wider organisation to be by committees called presbyteries; but they wished to remain within the established church. The Presbyterians grew in influence and formed the majority in Charles I's early parliaments. The movement was strongest among the middle classes in towns, and it became the established church of the country in 1647, under the Commonwealth, until it was overthrown at the Restoration. In 1653, civil registration was introduced, which discouraged the starting of nonconformist registers.

On the Restoration of the monarchy, the *Act of Uniformity* required the clergy to accept the *Book of Common Prayer* and to be ordained by bishops. Presbyterian clergy who refused to conform were ejected from their livings. They retained many supporters from their congregations in conventicles. Quarter Sessions records show prosecutions. In 1664, the *Conventicle Act* forbade such assemblies, and in the following year the *Five-Mile Act* forbade dissenting clergy to come within five miles of corporate towns, which was where dissent was strongest. Bunhill (Bonehill) Fields Burial Ground was opened just outside Moorgate, London, and was used mainly by dissenters. Between 1672 and 1674 the *Declaration of Indulgence* allowed conventicles and dissenting teachers to operate if they were licensed.

In 1689 the *Toleration Act* fully recognised conventicles, and this gave rise to the building of over one thousand meeting-houses in the next twenty years. As they were not allowed to have any central or regional links, they were Independent in organisation. This brought the Presbyterians and Independents closer together, and their conventicles sometimes shared or exchanged names. The sects opened burial grounds and began keeping burial registers. Previously, deaths had been recorded in parish registers because burials had taken place in parochial churchyards.

In 1691, Presbyterians and Independent ministers in London combined under the name of the United Brethren. Sometimes one congregation would have two ministers, one of each denomination, but in 1694 the London Union broke down.

In 1695, Church of England incumbents were ordered to register the births (not baptisms) of dissenters in their parishes, either in their registers or in separate books; so the word 'born' in a parish register may be a clue to dissenting parents. As in the Church of England, the baptism of dissenters' children at home became common and lasted for one hundred years.

In 1702, 'The Three Denominations' (Presbyterians, Independents and Baptists) united under a combined General Body of Protestant Dissenting Ministers. The practice of keeping registers now became more general, though far from universal. Bunhill Fields burial register began in 1713, but was kept very negligently until 1786.

In 1719, the Three Denominations split up. Presbyterians fell under the influence of Unitarianism. Some of their ministers became Unitarians and carried their congregations with them. Sometimes they moved to other meeting-houses; sometimes the Presbyterian loyalist minority had to move. At this time the practice of dating register entries with the New Style New Year (*see* CALENDAR) became common with dissenters, ahead of the official change in 1752.

In 1742/3, a body of Protestant Dissenting Deputies set up a General Register of Births for the children of dissenters all over the country, because of the failure of so many ministers to keep registers. It was located at the library bequeathed to the movement by Dr Daniel Williams (*c.* 1643–1716), a prominent and wealthy Presbyterian minister.

Before 1754, fewer marriages were performed in Presbyterian meeting-houses than in those of the other sects. Their religious ceremony was not recognised in law, but the contracting of the two parties before witnesses was. This practice was brought to an end by Lord Hardwicke's *Marriage Act* (*see* PARISH REGISTERS). In 1768 the General Register at Dr Williams's Library began to record baptisms as well as births, but not so consistently. In the late eighteenth century, the terms Presbyterian and Unitarian were used indifferently for the same congregations, and Presbyterianism began to decline, except in Wales.

In 1837, the registers of all dissenting sects were called in to the General Register Office upon the start of civil registration. The Presbyterians obeyed, but some registers slipped through the net. Marriages were once more allowed to be performed in Presbyterian meeting-houses provided the local registrar was present.

The Public Record Office, Chancery Lane, London, has the great majority of the pre-1837 Presbyterian registers, in classes RG 4, 5 and 8. Their General Register is under the heading of London.

Presbyterian registers are far less regularly kept than parochial ones, but they sometimes give more information (for example, wives' and mothers' maiden names, or even parents' names). As ministries had no official boundaries, and ministers often travelled far to bring services to their followers, it is worth searching the registers of all meeting-houses anywhere in the neighbourhood. Also there are many 'register entries' in Minute Books and other records.

For further reading, see *Sources for Nonconformist Genealogy and Family History*, by D.J. Steel, Vol. II of the National Index of Parish Registers, SOG (1973), and *My Ancestors were English Presbyterians/Unitarians* by A. Ruston, SOG (1993).

Presently   This word used to mean 'immediately', and still does in America. Also, 'at the present time'.

Presentment   In a judicial process, the laying before the court, by a grand jury or manorial homage, of an offence, without any independent accusation having been made. *See also* CHURCHWARDENS.

Pretence, Escutcheon of   This is an heraldic device used to show a married woman's arms superimposed upon those of her husband. *See also* HATCHMENT.

Primogeniture   The right or custom whereby an estate in land, or a title of dignity, descends to a person by virtue of his being the eldest legitimate male issue. In the past, when a person died intestate, his personal property, after deduction of the widow's portion, was, under Common Law, divided equally between all his children; but all his real estate (landed property) went to his eldest son.
See also BOROUGH ENGLISH; GAVELKIND.

Priory   A religious house of monks or nuns, subordinate to an abbey. It was ruled by a prior. A priory would often be the feudal superior of a lord of a manor, the manor having been presented to the religious house by some magnate in FRANKALMOIGN. In the Middle Ages certain English priories were dependencies of French abbeys, and during wars with France such 'alien priories' were taken into the hands of the English crown, their inmates being classed as 'foreign religious, subject to the King of France and his allies'. Extents of Alien Priories can be found among the Exchequer Records at the Public Record Office, Chancery Lane, London, in class E106.

A prior might, alternatively, be the dignitary of an abbey next in authority under the abbot.

Prisoners   The records of prisoners in many gaols in the period 1770–1894 are at the Public Record Office, Kew, under Prisons, Records, Series I (PCOM); and those over one hundred years old are available for inspection. They consist of registers, photographs, Minute Books and Visitors' Books. Other particulars of prisoners can be found in Licences, Male & Female, Old Captions and Transfer Papers. Quarterly Prison Returns, September 1824 to March 1876 (HO 8, also at Kew) contain convicts' offences, date and place of conviction and period of sentence. West Middlesex Family History Society has supplied the Public Record Office with a list of prisons and hulks (dismasted ships used as prisons) covered. The records of Newgate Gaol are at Kew in class HO 10. The Corporation of London Records Office has a card index of people in London debtors' prisons from 1755 to 1820. County gaol records are at the county record offices.
Further reading: *Criminal Ancestors* by D.T. Hawkings (1992).
See also TRANSPORTATION.

Prisoners of War   The Public Record Office holds records of Prisoners of War in the Admiralty, Colonial Office, Foreign Office and War Office classes. There are lists of prisoners regarding their death, exchange and release. See Information Leaflet No. 72 *Prisoners of War: Documents in the Public Record Office.*

Prison Records *see* **Prisoners**

Privy Council   In the sixteenth and seventeenth centuries, the Privy Council was, in varying degrees, the government of England under the royal prerogative. It developed out of the inner ring of the earlier Curia Regis (King's Court). Thomas Cromwell had used its members as the instruments of his policies, but after his execution it became a body of initiative with executive functions. Minutes were kept of its meetings, which were held wherever the sovereign happened to be. The privy councillors, chosen by the sovereign, were noblemen and gentry and included the chief officers of the realm (Lord Chancellor, Lord Treasurer, etc.), and of the royal household, but most of the work was carried out by a small group of executive ministers. There were a number of *ad hoc* committees, and members of the Council had other duties, such as sitting on the bench at sessions of the courts of Star Chamber, Requests and High Commission.

The Stuart kings consulted a committee of the Privy Council nominally concerned only with foreign affairs, and took decisions to which the Council was left to give merely formal approval. The names 'cabal', 'juncto' and 'cabinet council'. were given to these committees of favoured ministers. Under Anne, a committee of the Privy

A Latin probate act (with fewer abbreviations than most) entered below the Prerogative Court of Canterbury register copy of the will of Joseph Forster (see the transcript and translation of another example under PROBATE). PROB 11, *Crown copyright: reproduced with the permission of the Controller of Her Majesty's Stationery Office*

Council met under the senior secretary of state to prepare government business, and then attended the sovereign in a meeting of her cabinet; but George I, understanding no English, never attended, so all business was done by one body, for which the name 'cabinet' survived. Its presiding officer came to be known as the Prime Minister. The records of the Privy Council Office are at the Public Record Office, Chancery Lane, London, under group PC.

Probate This term means Approval by a competent court that an instrument purporting to be the Testament of a deceased person was indeed his lawful act, together with authority to the executor(s) to carry out its terms.

From 1529 onward, no fee was charged for probate where the effects of the deceased were worth £5 or under. For larger estates, the charge was proportionate (*see* WILL).

Before 1733, the record of probate (the *Probate Act*) was written in Latin in words heavily abbreviated. The following is a typical example, unabbreviated and with punctuation inserted, and accompanied by a word-by-word translation.

Probatum fuit hujusmodi testamentum coram
Approved was this testament before

venerabile viro Ricardo Greene, artium
the worshipful [man] Richard Greene, of arts

magistro, Officiale domini Archidiaconi B——,
master, Official of the lord Archdeacon B——,

apud C——tercio die mensis Augusti
at C——on the 3rd day of the month of August

Anno Domini Millesimo quingentesimo
Anno Domini one thousand five hundred

duodecimo, juramento Willelmi Smith,
and twelve, by the oath of William Smith,

executoris in suprascripto testamento
the executor in the above-written testament

nominati. Et commissa fuit administratio
named. And committed was the administration

omnium et singularum bonorum et debitorum etc.
of all and singular the goods and debts etc.

defuncti prefato executori etc. de
of the deceased to the said executor etc. for

bene et fideliter administrando ac de pleno
well and truly administering and for a full

inventario exhibendo etc, ad sancta dei
inventory delivering etc, on the holy of God

evangelia jurato in debita de juris. Potestate
gospels sworn in due form of law. Power

reservata committendo predictam
being reserved for committing the said

administrationem Agnete Smith, vidue,
administration to Agnes Smith, widow,

relicte defuncti et alii
the relict of the deceased and the other

executrici in testamento nominate.
executrix in the testament named.

During the Civil Wars, the 300 or so probate courts became disrupted by the hostilities, except that of the Prerogative Court of the Archbishop of Canterbury (PCC); and under the Commonwealth, an Act of 8 April, 1653, abolished all ecclesiastical jurisdictions in probate matters. All wills and administrations had to be brought before 'Judges for the Proving of Wills and Craving of Letters of Administration' in London, and their records were incorporated into the PCC series. However, the old courts were restored on the Restoration of the monarchy in 1660. By an Act of the following year abolishing military tenures, all restrictions on the devising of freehold land were removed.

Before 1750, people in modest circumstances might let wills go unproved — and so unrecorded — if there was no dispute about how the estate was to be dealt with, thus saving the expense of probate. Between 1717 and 1791, the wills of all Catholics had to be enrolled either in one of the central courts or in Quarter Sessions. Before 1882, a married woman could not normally make a will without her husband's consent, because her property was considered to be her husband's; but there were occasional special circumstances, for example when she held specifically devised property from a previous husband.

As from 11 January, 1858, all ecclesiastical and peculiar jurisdictions were abolished by the *Probate Act*, and their powers were passed to the Probate Division (now the Family Division) of the High Court. England and Wales were divided into civil probate district, each with a District Probate Registry, and a Principal Probate Registry in London. All wills since that date can now be consulted at the Principal Registry of the Family Division, Somerset House, London. Indexes are also available at district probate registries and at certain record offices and libraries in the provinces. For further reading on these, see 'Printed Indexes to Probate Records after 1850' by J.S.W. Gibson, in *The Local Historian* Vol. 15, No. 4.

Probate Jurisdictions Before 1858, a testator having all his property within the area of one archdeaconry would normally have his will proved in the Archdeacon's Court, presided over by the Archdeacon's Official, though not all archdeaconries had testamentary jurisdiction. If some of the property lay outside the archdeaconry but in the same diocese, the will could be proved in one of the Bishop's Courts, i.e. either in the Consistory Court or the Commissary Court (*see* ANGLICAN CHURCH). Some bishoprics claimed probate rights over all noblemen, gentlemen-at-arms, rectors, vicars, and other clergy whose lands lay wholly within the diocese, even if they lay wholly within one archdeaconry. The indexes kept by some courts suffer from a number of omissions of wills actually proved.

Every three years or so, the bishop 'visited' his diocese, i.e. he summoned the clergy and lay officials of the diocese to him, and during this ecclesiastical visitation all lower courts were inhibited for a period of from three to six months. During a vacancy in a bishopric, the Court of the Dean and Chapter or of the Archbishop normally took over jurisdiction.

If a testator had property in more than one diocese, his will had to be proved in the Prerogative Court of the archbishop of the province, either Canterbury or York. If property was held in both provinces, then the will had to be proved in the court of Canterbury, which also had jurisdiction over people owning property in England or Wales who died in Scotland or Ireland, at sea, or in 'foreign parts'. All these regulations did not preclude persons of substance, willing to pay the higher fees, from proving a will at a Prerogative Court to gain the advantages of the highest authority, the best record keeping and privacy from local enquiries, even though their estate lay entirely in one archdeaconry. Prerogative Court wills date from 1383.

In the larger courts there were often several 'seats' dealing with different districts and keeping separate records, so their record volumes are liable to overlap one another chronologically.

In addition to the main courts described, a number of smaller courts existed. They belonged either to ecclesiastical dignitaries outside the archdeaconry, or to city corporations, colleges or lords of manors, and were known as Peculiar Courts. They could grant probate on wills of property lying wholly within their borders. Otherwise the will had to be proved in either the Bishop's Court or the archbishop's Prerogative Court. Peculiars were of many kinds. Their jurisdiction could cover a parish or parishes (not necessarily contiguous), a city, borough, township, liberty, manor, cathedral or church precinct, deanery or college precinct. Sometimes a place might lie in more than one Peculiar; indeed, one whole Peculiar is occasionally included within another. They were variously presided over by an archbishop, bishop, dean, dean and chapter, sub-dean, chancellor, precentor, succentor, vice-chancellor, prebendary, rector, vicar, lord of manor, or mayor, each, of course, able to appoint a commissary to do the actual work. Some were inhibited during visitations.

Appeals from the Bishops' Courts of the southern province lay to the Court of Arches of the Archbishop of Canterbury, so-called because it was once held at the Church of St Mary-le-Bow (*de arcubus*) in London. Appeals from that court and from both Prerogative Courts lay, after the Reformation, to the Court of Delegates of England.

Procedure and Documents The executor(s) took the will to the appropriate probate court. There it went through several procedures, each of which gave rise to a document. Many of these are still available for perusal, and are of the highest genealogical value. They are as follows:

Probate Act The Court, being satisfied that the testament was in order, passed a probate act, approving it and authorising the executors to carry out their functions, and then recorded the fact in its Probate Act Book. A note in probate calendars 'by decree' or 'by sentence' or 'int. dec.' (interlocutory decree) indicates that contested proceedings came before the grant of probate. The original will was annotated with a copy of the Probate Act and filed in a 'bundle' in the court's records. These originals bear the signature of the testator and often a seal, which may show his arms or crest (*see* ARMS, COAT OF).

A Probate Copy of the will and act was then made and given to the executors as their guide and authority. Until about 1600, it was usual to give the original will back to the executors, and file the Probate Copy. Any document given to the executors is now usually lost or hard to trace.

Testamentary Bond Some courts obliged the executors to enter into a bond to execute the will faithfully.

Registered Copy of the Will A further copy of the will and probate act was usually written into a book of registered wills, for office use and public reference. This is the copy of easiest access to the genealogist.

Unproved Wills Some courts have collections of these.

Inventory Before 1700, it was usual for the executors to be obliged to supply an inventory of the goods of the deceased, attested by the overseer or supervisor of the will named by the testator. There is often a separate file for these inventories. They are rare after 1750. A reference in the calendar of wills marked 'rpt' ('respited'), means that no inventory was demanded. These records often reveal a man's occupation, either explicitly or from his stock-in-trade of tools.

Nuncupative Wills Until 1838, these were testamentary intentions expressed by the deceased's word of mouth before 'credible witnesses', who later made sworn statements before the probate court. By the *Statute of Frauds*, 1678, there had to be at least three witnesses who had heard the deceased's wishes spoken in his own house and during his last illness. They needed to have them written down within six days, and not proved until fourteen days after the death. Since 1838, nuncupative wills can be made only by soldiers on active military service, and by seamen at sea. Freehold land could not be devised by a nuncupative will, nor could a written will be revoked by one.

Bond of Tuition, Curation or Guardianship When a minor was left fatherless, the court could appoint a guardian for him. This guardian had to give a bond, and such documents are filed either with the will or administration, or separately. Normally, tuition was for boys under 14 and girls under 12. Curation was for children older than that, but under 21.

The wills' calendar may contain some cases noted as 'Administration with Will Annexed', which usually means that the executors named in the will were not available, possibly dead; so administration was granted to the next-of-kin to act as executor. Sometimes, during a long testamentary trust, the trustees and/or beneficiaries died, which made further court action necessary. The particulars were generally entered on the margin of the register copy of the will, and are often of genealogical value.

Unsigned, Amended and Unwitnessed Wills In such cases, witnesses had to be sworn as to the handwriting or intentions of the testator. Their sworn statements are usually filed with the original will, and copied into the register book.

Caveats When someone with an interest in the estate wished to prevent probate being granted without his objection being considered, he could enter a Caveat. This was written into either a Caveat Book or the Act Book, and would give rise to a Sentence, which would be registered. Caveats sometimes reveal interesting family antagonisms.

Assignations When an executor or administrator was thought to have infringed the conditions of his bond, a person interested in the estate could summon the sureties of the bond to show why probate should not be assigned to someone else. An Assignation was an interlocutory order issued in consequence of such an application, and was copied into the Probate or Admon. Act Book. *Original wills* see ARMS, COAT OF.

Letters of Administration In a case where the deceased left no will, letters of administration were granted to the person legally entitled to administer the estate.

Apart from the wills in the archives of the probate courts (for which *see* under the relevant county heading), there are at the Public Record Office (PRO), Chancery Lane, London, a number of wills contained in other classes of record, for example among the manor court rolls. The PRO has a printed index of these.

Brief details of archdeaconry and diocesan probate records are shown under county headings, but searchers will do well to consult also one or more of the following guides: *A Simplified Guide to Probate Jurisdictions*: *Where to Look for Wills* (Federation of Family History Societies, 1989). More detailed works are, *Wills and Their Whereabouts*, by Anthony J. Camp (1974) and *Wills and Where to Find Them*, by J.S.W. Gibson (1974), both out of print but available in libraries. *Wills, Inventories and Death Duties*: *A Provisional Guide* by Jane Cox, PRO, 1988. *An Introduction to Wills Probate and Death Duty Records* by Jane Cox FFHS, 1993. Free Information leaflets, *Probate Records* No. 31 and *Death Duty Registers* No. 66, are available at the PRO. For an index to Prerogative Court of Canterbury Wills 1750–1800 see the six volumes compiled by A.J. Camp and published by the SOG. PCC Wills 1701–1749 and 1800–1858 are being indexed by the Friends of the Public Record Office.

Maps showing the boundaries of probate jurisdictions have been published by the Institute of Heraldic and Genealogical Studies, and are also shown in *Wills and Where to Find Them* and the above-mentioned *Simplified Guide*.
See also WILL *and* ESTATE DUTY.

Proctor   (i) Also called Procurator (the Latin term), an officer employed in admiralty, civil and ecclesiastical causes, corresponding to an attorney or solicitor at Common Law or equity. They were renamed Solicitors in 1875. Their appointments and admissions from 1727–1841 are recorded in class HCA 30 at the Public Record Office.

(ii) A person licensed to collect alms for hospitals and/or lepers.

Procurator *see* **Proctor**

Professional Genealogists *see* **Association of Genealogists and Record Agents**

Progenitor   Another name for a forebear.

Promotor   A promotor was the name for the prosecutor in an ecclesiastical court.

Proof of Age   Before the institution of parish registers in 1538, there was little documentary evidence to which to refer when anyone needed to prove how old he or she might be; but this need was not infrequent, especially in the case of minors. It might be necessary to show that an heir had reached the age at which his late father's estate should be made over to him, or that a girl was of an age to be given in marriage.

Proof had to be established before the sheriff of the county with the aid of a jury. At that period the jury was not a body for deciding, impartially, facts first presented to them in court, but a group of neighbours who could swear to certain facts from personal knowledge. To prove an age in question, each member of the jury would cite some incident that he remembered as having happened at, or shortly before or after, the birth of the person concerned. If one of them mentioned that the birth had been noted by someone in writing, there is no sign that the document ever had to be produced, documentary evidence not being considered at that time as having any special value. Because of the likelihood of a proof of age being required at some time in the future, a prudent father would mark his child's birth by entertaining neighbours or giving out presents.

The records of *Proofs of Age* are at the Public Record Office, Chancery Lane, London, in classes C 132–142, and calendared in print in the volumes of *Calendars of Inquisitions*. Besides the genealogical information of parentage contained in the *Proofs*, the homely incidents mentioned by the jurymen often throw interesting light on themselves and the family of the person whose age was in question.

In the period between 1538 and 1837, the evidence of baptismal registers was taken as proof of age, for instance in cases of apprenticeship and army cadetships.

When a person's age was stated in years, it was the custom, even into the early nineteenth century, to include the current year not yet completed, thus making him appear one year older than he would be considered today. However, for the Census of 1841 it was laid down that statements of age should include only completed years.

See also OCTAVE.

Prosopography

History pursued through study of the social origins, family connections and economic backgrounds of relevant individuals, together with the tensions arising from the interactions of their personal careers. In this recent development, the researches of family historians can acquire an interest and value beyond the purely domestic field.

Protestants

Those who rejected the Pope and believed in salvation by faith alone. The term is generally thought synonymous with nonconformist. However, Catholics also did not conform to the Church of England but were obviously not Protestants. In the seventeenth and eighteenth centuries they were referred to as Recusants.

Protestation Oath Returns

Following the rumours of an army plot to rescue the Earl of Strafford from the Tower, an oath 'to live and die for the true Protestant religion, the liberties and rights of subjects, and the privilege of Parliaments' was taken by members of the House of Commons on 3 May, 1641. The Protestant peers signed it the following day. A Bill imposing on all Englishmen the obligation of signing the oath was rejected by the House of Lords, but on 30 July the Commons passed a resolution that all who refused to sign were unfit to hold office in church or state.

On 4 January 1641/2, King Charles I tried to arrest five Members of Parliament; so the Protestation was printed and sent out to the sheriffs for distribution to every parish, so that every man of 18 and over should take the oath. The text was read out in the churches, and lists were made of all who signed and of all who refused to sign. Most of these lists are in the House of Lords Record Office, and some have been printed by record societies, but some survive only among parish records.

A catalogue of extant returns then known is in the *Appendix* to the *5th Report of the Historical MSS Commission* (1876), pages 120–34. The Society of Genealogists also has a list of Protestation Oath Returns, and has published a leaflet on the subject. The Returns are valuable location record for the mid seventeenth century.

Prothonotaries

A prothonotary was the chief clerk of a court.

Province

The area of jurisdiction of an archbishop. The province of the Archbishop of Canterbury was that part of England south of the River Trent, consisting until the nineteenth century of the bishoprics of Asaph, Bangor, Bath and Wells, Bristol, Canterbury, Chichester, Ely, St Davids (Exeter), Gloucester, Hereford, Lichfield and Coventry, Lincoln, Llandaff, London, Norwich, Oxford, Peterborough, Rochester, Salisbury, Winchester, and Worcester.

The province of York, to the north of the Trent, had jurisdiction over the bishoprics of Carlisle, Chester, Durham, Sodor and Man, and York. See map on page 90.

Public Record Office

(PRO). The PRO was founded in accordance with the *English Public Record Office Act* of 1838, to have the custody of all records, etc., 'of a public nature'. All collections recognised as public were brought together and placed under the control of the Master of the Rolls. In 1854, the contents of the State Paper Office were added, and after that the records of all government departments, except the India Office, were added when they were thirty years old.

The collection now falls into two main divisions — judicial and state records — plus a large collection of records not of a public nature that have been deposited from time to time. The Office has two main repositories open to the public. The older one, built in the nineteenth century, is in Chancery Lane, London the newer one, opened in 1977, in Ruskin Avenue, Kew, Surrey. Some little-used records are kept outside London, and require a week's notice for production. In 1997 the Chancery Lane building will be abandoned, even though purpose built, and all the records will be concentrated on one site at Kew where a new extension is under construction.

For regular attendance a Reader's Ticket is necessary, but it is not required for using the Census Rooms. The Offices are open from 9.30 a.m. to 5 p.m., Monday to Fridays. The Census Rooms are also open on Saturdays.

RIGHT Part of a Protestation Oath Roll of 1641/2, listing 'the names of such persons within the towneshipp of Carleton in the parishe of Rothwell [Yorkshire] which have taken the protestacion'. *House of Lords Record Office*

The names of all such persons within the townshipp of Carleton in the parish of Rothwell weh haue taken the protestation

- Mr Charles Jackson
- Robert Nalson
- George Stones
- Thomas Aberquill
- William Garrison
- Thomas Shawe
- Thomas Townend
- Thomas Cliffe
- Edward Scoter
- Richard Scoter
- William Singleton
- Robert Ward
- William Ellis
- Thomas Wright
- Robert Gamble
- John Carter
- William ffather
- William Hader
- Thomas Hop
- Anthony Williman
- William Mores
- John Jackson
- Raphe Swifte
- Richard Dobson
- William Illingworth
- William Cliffe
- Robert Robinson
- William Carter
- John Overmacher
- Thomas Berkett
- William Steade
- Abraham Butterfeild
- John Burnell
- William Corkell
- John Rayner
- Robert Smith
- Barnabas Norton
- Richard Jenkinsone
- Michaell Williman
- Henry Thompson
- William Westerman snd
- William Westerman junio
- Richard Leedes

- Richard Rawson
- William Wainewright
- Robert Swinson
- Thomas Briggs
- Valentine Berkett

The names of all such persons within the townshipp of Middleton in the parish of Rothwell as haue taken the protestation

- Sr ffardinando Lee
- Henry Gascoigne
- William Gascoigne
- Marett Puddocke
- Thomas Lee
- Robert Willson
- William Prince
- William Langfellow
- Henry Langshire
- James Saunderson
- Henry Knowles
- Henry Martin
- William Platon
- Everett Speight
- William Speight
- William Skate
- Thomas Skate
- Thomas Dodghson
- William Beaumonte
- Thomas Horne
- John Horne
- William Jackson
- Henry Jackson
- Thomas Jackson
- William Mcokeson
- Henry Mcokeson
- William Wither
- William ffather
- William Wilkeson
- Thomas Walker
- Peter Duckworth
- George Duckworth
- ffrancis Ockeram
- William Casson
- Thomas Walker
- John Moxon
- Thomas Moxon
- Raphe Moxon
- Gilbert Tallson
- Thomas Wrigglesworth

- John Mann
- Peter Husser
- John Inhards
- Joseph Ramforth
- Edmund Wood
- Thomas Jackson
- Henry Mann
- Robert Smith
- Richard Ourrer
- William Millner
- William Talbert
- John Parler
- Gilbert ffladson
- William Mann
- Henry Mann
- Gilbert Sabill
- Thomas Sabill
- George Stanforth
- Richard Damell
- John Damell
- ffrancis Luxton
- Edward Bowman
- James Jackson
- Edward Roeltmgle
- William Walker
- Thomas Walker
- John While
- Gilbert Garrett
- John William

The names of all such persons within the hamblett of Thorpe in the parish of Rothwell as haue taken the protestation

- John Gleadell
- Richard Harker
- ffrancis Holmes
- George Littlesedge
- John Dobson
- Robert Nettleton
- Henry Beaumonte
- William Beaumonte
- Thomas Nettleton
- Anthony Beaumonte
- Henry Beaumonte
- Nicholas Westerman
- William Westerman
- Thomas Westerman
- Rowland Roynton
- William Hurd
- John Carr
- Henry Casson

The PRO issues free leaflets on many subjects covered by the records and has published a guide to records of interest to family historians: *Tracing Your Ancestors in the Public Record Office*, by Amanda Bevan and Andrea Duncan, HMSO (1990) 4th Edition; Stella Colwell, *Family Roots; Discovering the Past in the Public Record Office* Weidenfeld and Nicholson (1991), *A Dictionary of Genealogical Sources in the Public Record Office* by Stella Colwell, Weidenfeld and Nicolson (1992) and *The Nation's Memory* by John Cantwell, HMSO (1991).

*Records kept at PRO, Kew***

Admiralty (ADM)
Advisory, Conciliation & Arbitration Service (CW)
Agriculture, Fisheries & Food, Ministry of (MAF)
Air Ministry (AIR)
Aviation, Ministry of (AVIA)
British Council (BW)
British Railways Board (AN)
British Transport Docks Board (BR)
British Transport Historical Records (RAIL)
Cabinet Office (CAB)
Captured Enemy Documents (GFM)
Certification Office for Trades Unions and Employers Associations (CL)
Channel Tunnel Advisory Groups (BS1)
Civil Service Commission (CSC)
Civil Service Department (BA)
Civil Service Pay Research Unit (CSPR)
Coal Industry Social Welfare Organisation (BX)
Colonial Office (CO)
Commonwealth Relations Office (DO)
Copyright Office (COPY)
Countryside Commission (COU)
Crown Agents for Overseas Governments and Administration (CAOG)
Customs & Excise, Board of (CUST)
Defence, Ministry of (DEFE)
Development Commission (D)
Distribution of Income & Wealth, Royal Commission on (BS 7)
Education & Science, Department of (ED)
Elizabeth Garrett Anderson Hospital (CF)
Environment, Department of the (AT)
Environmental Pollution, Royal Commission on (CY)
Exchequer and Audit Department (AO)
Export Credits Guarantee Department (ECG)
Financial Institutions, Committee to review the functioning of (BS 9)
Foreign Office (FO)
Forestry Commission (F)
Forfeited Estates, Commissioners of (FEC)

Friendly Societies, Registry of (FS)
Gambling, Royal Commission on (BS 3)
General Register Office (RG), except Census Returns (RG 9–12), Non-parochial Registers and Records (RG 4–8), and certain other registers and associated papers (RG 18, 19, 27, 30–7, 43)
Government Actuary's Department (ACT)
Health & Social Security, Department of (BN)
Health, Ministry of (MH)
Historical Manuscripts Commission (HMC)
Home Office (HO), except Census Returns (HO 107)
Housing & Local Government, Ministry of (HLG)
Hudson's Bay Company (BH), microfilm. Access by permission of the Company only.
Information, Central Office of (INF)
Inland Revenue, Board of (IR), except Estate Duty Registers (IR 26, 27)
Irish Sailors' & Soldiers' Land Trust (AP)
Iron and Steel Board (BE)
Labour, Ministry of (LAB)
Land Registry (LAR)
Lands Tribunal (LT)
Law Commission (BC)
Local Government Boundary Commission for England (AX)
Location of Offices Bureau (AH)
Lord Chancellor's Office (LCO)
Meteorological Office (BJ)
Metropolitan Police Force (MEPO)
Monuments, Ancient & Historic in Wales and Monmouthshire, Royal Commission of (MONW)
Monuments, Historic (England), Royal Commission on (AE)
Munitions, Ministry of (MUN)
National Assistance Board (AST)
National Coal Board (COAL)
National Debt Office (NDO)
National Dock Labour Board (BK)
National Health Service, Royal Commission on (BS6)
National Incomes Commission (NICO)
National Insurance Audit Department (NIA)
National Insurance Commissioners (CT)
National Savings, Department for (NSC)
National Service, Ministry of (NATS)
Operators' Licensing, Committee of enquiry into (BS4)
Ordnance Survey Department (OS)
Overseas Development, Ministry of (OD)
Parliamentary Boundary Commission (AF)
Parole Board (BV)
Paymaster General's Office (PMG)
Pensions & National Insurance, Ministry of (PIN)

Pensions Appeal Tribunal (BF)
Power, Ministry of (POWE)
Press, Royal Commission on the (BS2)
Price Commission (CX)
Prime Minister's Office (PREM)
Prison Commission (CX)
Public Building & Works, Ministry of (WORK)
Public Record Office (PRO) all classes, except transcripts (PRO 31) and certain classes of gifts and deposits (PRO 30)*
Public Trustee Office (PT)
Public Works Loan Board (PWLB)
Reconstruction, Ministry of (RECO)
Remploy Ltd (BM)
Research Institutes (AY)
Royal Fine Art Commission (BP)
Royal Mint (MINT)
Scientific & Industrial Research, Department of (DSIR)
Stationery Office (STAT)
Supply, Ministry of (SUPP)
Tithe Redemption Commission (TITH)
Trade, Board of (BT)
Transport, Ministry of (MT)
Treasury (T)
Tribunals, Council on (BL)
United Kingdom Atomic Energy Authority (AB)
University Grants Committee (UGC)
Value Added Tax Tribunals (CV)
Wallace Collection (AR)
War Office (WO)
Welsh Office (BD)

**Records are, in general, open to inspection when they are 30 years old

*PRO 30/1–3, 6–12, 16–17, 20, 22, 27, 29–33, 35–37, 39–40, 42–43, 45–46, 48, 51–52, 54–61, 63–79, 81–84, and PRO 31/20 are at Kew

Records kept at PRO, Chancery Lane (a)

Admiralty, High Court of (HCA)
Alienation Office (A)
Assize, Clerks of (ASSI)
Bankruptcy, Court of (B)
Central Criminal Court (CRIM)
Chancery (C)
Chester, Palatinate of (CHES)
Common Pleas, Court of (CP)
Crown Estate Commissioners (CRES)
Delegates, Court of (DEL)
Durham, Palatinate of (DURH)
Exchequer (E, LR)
General Register Office (RG). Only Census returns (RG 9–12), Non-parochial Registers and Records (RG 4–8), and certain other registers and associated papers (RG 18, 19, 27, 30–37, 43)

Home Office. Only Census Returns 1841 and 1851 (HO 107)
Inland Revenue, Board of. Only Estate Duty Registers (IR 26, 27)
Judicature, Supreme Court of (J)
Justices Itinerant (JUST)
King's Bench, Court of (KB)
King's Bench Prison (PRIS)
Lancaster, Duchy of (DL)
Lancaster, Palatinate of (PL)
Land Revenue Record Office (LRRO)
Law Officers' Department (LO)
Lord Chamberlain's Department (LC)
Lord Steward's Office (LS)
Palace Court (PALA)
Peveril, Court of the Honour of (PEV)
Prerogative Court of Canterbury (PROB)
Privy Council, Judicial Committee of the (PCAP)
Privy Council Office (PC)
Privy Purse Office (PP)
Privy Seal Office (PSO)
Public Prosecutions, Director of (DPP)
Public Record Office. Transcripts (PRO 31), and certain other classes of gifts and deposits (PRO 30) *(b)*
Queen Anne's Bounty (QAB)
Requests, Court of (REQ)
Signet Office (SO)
Special Collections (SC)
Star Chamber, Court of (STAC)
State Paper Office (SP)
Treasury Solicitor (TS)
Wales, Principality of (WALE)
Wards & Liveries, Court of (WARD)

(a) Some classes to be seen at Chancery Lane are housed at Hayes, Middlesex, and notice of several working days is required. This will no longer be the case when the records move to Kew in 1997.
(b) PRO 30/5, 18–19, 21, 23–26, 28, 34, 38, 41, 44, 47, 49, 50, 53, 80, PRO 31/20 are at Kew. PRO 30/4, 13–15, 62 are no longer held in the Public Record Office.

Puritanism Uncoordinated movements within the Church of England, beginning in the reign of Henry VIII and aiming to purify some of the aspects of its worship. Although all puritans were against the use of Catholic rites and of elaborate vestments and ornaments, and all believed in the Bible as their sole authority for belief and conduct, they interpreted it in many different ways.

Many groups held meetings of their own to expound the scriptures: these were known as 'prophesyings', and later as 'conventicles'. When Archbishop Whitgift attempted rigidly to enforce uniformity after 1583, the Puritans became united in opposition to an episcopalian form of church organisation. It was from the Puritan movements that the dissenting sects developed. Puritans were also called Precisians.

Purprestre An encroachment on land, especially on deer pasture under forest law or in other royal lands.

Putrid Fever The old name for a group of diseases that include typhus and smallpox.

Q

Quakers *see* **Friends, Religious Society of**

Quarter Days The Quarter Days are Ladyday, 25th March, Midsummer, 6th July until 1752 then 24th June, Michaelmas, 29th September and Christmas, 25th December. These were when rents were paid.

Quarter Sessions, Court of An assembly of the Justices of the Peace of any county, riding or county town, for the joint purposes of judging suits and administering the affairs of the area. A statute of 1388 laid down that 'Justices shall keep their sessions in every quarter of the year at least', from which the name of the court is derived. They were held at Easter, Trinity (Midsummer), Michaelmas and Epiphany (January), and were presided over by the sheriff or his deputy. A leading justice was appointed the permanent official and called the Custos Rotulorum, Keeper of the Rolls.

The Tudors gave to the justices the task of enforcing a wide new range of laws. In carrying out these duties, they gradually replaced the sheriff as the main organ of local administration and the Custos Rotulorum passed down his duties as permanent official to the Clerk of the Peace, who was often an attorney. Felonies were increasingly referred to the Assizes.

Owing to the increase in population in the eighteenth century, many Quarter Sessions could not be carried through within the usual time and had to be continued by adjournment. Several counties were therefore divided into two or more divisions for administrative purposes, each of which held its sessions 'by adjournment'.

The justices began acting in a more executive capacity and issued what were, in effect, by claws. During the Sessions, less administrative business was done because Standing Committees of Justices were appointed for dealing with particular problems (e.g. gaols and bridges), and new administrative offices were created: the County Treasurer, Surveyor (or Bridgemaster), Inspector of Weights and Measures, and others. In 1819 an Act of Parliament empowered justices to divide their numbers and sit in two courts simultaneously to speed up business; so the minutes may be in two series from this date.

From 1834, the scope of the justices' work was affected by the institution of a number of *ad hoc* bodies, such as the Boards of Poor Law Guardians. The *Municipal Corporation Act*, 1835, took administrative control of the towns away from the justices, and in 1888 the *Local Government Act* transferred administrative control of the counties to county councils, in more or less the form existing today.

The Records of the Court

The *Sessions Rolls*, or *Files*, comprise all the original documents used at the Sessions (including lists of the justices in the Commission, with dots against the names of those actually present), registers of officials taking oaths of allegiance, lists of licensed religious meeting-houses, indictments, recognizances and petitions.

The *Indictment* (or *Process*) *Books* deal with judicial business. They give brief particulars of defendants, offences, pleas, verdicts and, occasionally, sentences.

The *Minute* (or *Sessions*) *Books* contain either rough notes of the proceedings, or minutes fairly written out; sometimes both are extant. In the later period there are also *Minute Books* for the Meetings of Standing Committees.

The *Order Books* are the formal records of the Court, giving the justices' decisions and edicts. The earliest extant Order Book (Devon) dates from the end of the sixteenth century, but some rolls or files are in private ownership, including, for example, those for Hertfordshire, which are at Hatfield House. Most of the extant books begin in the seventeenth century, but some are later. They were compiled both for current reference and for providing precedents. Sometimes they make reference to cases dealt with by the justices 'out of Session', i.e. in Petty Sessions. The orders are entered in chronological order, with no distinction between judicial and administrative work, since the procedure for all was judicial. However, marginal notes of the names of persons and parishes are a help to searchers. Order Books also have contemporary indexes, which make them the most convenient of the Quarter Sessions records to search, but they often contain less detail than can be found in the rolls. Of the judicial proceedings, some were preliminary hearings of cases that would be sent on to the Assizes. The administrative business included recusancy, conventicles, taxation, rating, the Poor Law, vagrancy, highways, county bridges, ale houses, markets, outbreaks of disease and fire, sacrament certificates, registration of papists and their estates, oaths of allegiance, settlement orders, gaols, Houses of Correction and prisoners, weights and measures, and wages.

Bills of Indictment were first draw up by an official and submitted to a Grand Jury on the first day of the Session, who would examine witnesses and return the indictment marked either *billa vera* (true bill), or *ignoramus* (we do not know). In the former case the accused would stand his trial, though not always at the same session. Presentments were also made by constables, hundred juries, or the Grand Jury itself. In some counties the Sessions were always held in the county town; in others at several towns in rotation. There were separate Commissions of the Peace for each Riding of Yorkshire, and for each of the three parts of Lincolnshire.

Except during the Commonwealth, writs, indictments and recognizances were written in Latin until 1733.

A few rolls of pleas survive for the fourteenth and fifteenth centuries, and are at the Public Record Office, Chancery Lane, London, but the rest of the records are deposited at the county record offices, though a few may have got into private hands or have been lost or destroyed. Many have been calendared either in full or in extracts, and the county record offices have copies.

Judicial cases usually contain interesting biographical material about the persons concerned. Whenever a person is mentioned, his or her occupation is given. The long lists of persons registered under Acts requiring oaths of allegiance supply information about dissenters and Roman Catholics that may reveal an ancestor's religious convictions.

The Federation of Family History Societies has published a booklet, *Quarter Sessions Records for Family Historians*, by J.S.W. Gibson, 3rd Edn., FFHS, 1992 which gives details of county holdings.

Quarterage County rates, payable quarterly through the parish officers.

Queen Anne's Bounty This was a fund set up in 1704 to aid impoverished clergy. It was derived from the ecclesiastical revenues that had been taken over by Henry VIII and which Queen Anne diverted to this purpose. In 1948 Queen Anne's Bounty was one of the elements which formed the new Church Commission.

Questman An assistant to the churchwarden. A sidesman.

Quia Emptores A law passed in 1290 to prevent the loss of feudal obligations that occurred when a mesne lord granted a fee to a purchaser of the land, and required only a nominal service from him thenceforward, such as a pair of gloves annually or a rose at midsummer. The law allowed the mesne lord to dispose of land, but the feudal obligations attached to land-holding fell automatically upon the purchaser.

Quindene The day falling a fortnight after a church festival; i.e. fifteen days, including the festival itself. *See also* OCTAVE.

Quire Number A quire is formed from four sheets of parchment or paper folded into eight leaves which yields sixteen pages. This is not to be confused with the other meaning of quire which is 24 sheets of loose paper. Quire numbers are the numbers by which you find a registered copy will at the Public Record Office. When the will indexes, PROB 12, are consulted, you find by the side of the name of the deceased a number. This is the number of the quire in which the will has been copied. When you look at the volumes of PROB 11 on film, the quire numbers are written in the top right-hand corner of every sixteenth page in large ink figures. Do not confuse them with the stamped folio numbers which occur in the same position on every other page.

Quitclaim A quitclaim is a formal release or discharge from a claim to property.

Quit Rent A small fixed annual rent, on payment of which a manorial or burgage tenant was quit (released) from all services to his lord. A LANDGABLE was a burgage quit rent.

Quo Warranto (i) A statute pronounced at Gloucester in 1278 by Edward I, in consequence of the abuses revealed by the RAGMAN ROLLS. By this he summoned all men who held private franchises and jurisdictions to appear before the king's judges and show by what right — *quo warranto* — they held them. Anyone failing to appear forfeited his jurisdiction to the sheriff until he proved his claim. In operating the statute, the king's lawyers refused to recognise any undocumented right, however ancient it was. This caused such injustice that in 1290 the king conceded a right to anyone who could prove by a jury of neighbours that he had held it 'since time immemorial', which meant from before the accession of Richard I in 1189.

(ii) A Writ of Quo Warranto lay against anyone who usurped a franchise or liberty against the king, or intruded himself as heir into any land.

R

Ragged Schools These were schools set up to provide free education for the poor. The first one was provided by John Pounds in 1818. It was not until 1844 that Lord Shaftesbury organised an official union of Ragged Schools.

Ragman Rolls The returns made in 1275 by commissioners appointed by Edward I to enquire throughout the country into abuses and usurpations, particularly against royal rights, committed during his absence on crusade. The king's possessions and rights, and the liberties granted by his predecessors, are listed. The Rolls are at the Public Record Office, Chancery Lane, London, under reference C 47/23.

Rape A subdivision of the county of Sussex.

Rate Books A rate is a local levy for either a specific purpose or for general purposes. The earliest extant are those of parishes and the wards of corporate boroughs for the maintenance of a local church, bridge, drainage system, or fortification. A few rate books, listing the ratepayers, survive from the Middle Ages, but the *Poor Law Acts* of 1597/8 and 1601 were the first to lay down the compulsory raising of a rate in every parish, and this was followed later in the seventeenth century by rates for the maintenance of the highways and gaols, and for dealing with vagabonds and prisoners, and, later still, for sewers and the militia. In 1738/9, many of these rates were merged with the Poor Rate.

Parochial poor rates were assessed by the Overseers of the Poor, and approved by the vestry on the basis of lands and buildings. The rate books list the ratepayers by name, showing the amounts collected and, sometimes, the assessments, often with marginal notes about either the properties or their occupiers. After 1834, both occupier and owner are named. The order in which the ratepayers were listed tended to remain the same from year to year, and in towns they are shown under street headings; so a careful comparison of the lists with other sources, such as local directories, may enable an ancestral home to be located. In towns, the parish and ward boundaries did not always coincide; so with the additional aid of the street name, the area in which a house stood can often be closely narrowed down. Parochial rates, where they survive, have mostly been deposited by the incumbents at county record offices, but some still remain in parish churches. Borough and ward rate books are usually at the town's record office.

Rebuttal A rebuttal is an answer made by a defendant to a plaintiff's surrejoinder (a contradiction).

Recognizance (i) A legal document obliging a person to do something under a certain stated condition, in the same manner as a bond; the only difference being that the recognizance did not require the party's seal. The licensees of public houses were obliged to take recognizances before two Justices of the Peace.

(ii) A court's acknowledgement of deeds deposited, e.g. a conveyance, or a bond for good behaviour or appearance in court.

Record Cards, Genealogical Printed cards, 6 × 4 inches, with spaces alloted for card number, name of person, dates and places of birth, baptism, marriage, death, burial and probate of will; also names of father, mother, spouses and children. A useful aid for rapid reference and for identifying and linking persons for whom stray references have been found. Published by the Society of Genealogists.

Recorders Recorders are judges or magistrates whose jurisdiction applies to a city or borough in civil and criminal cases from 1882–1971.

Record Offices As an aid to locating the local record offices, the Federation of Family History Societies has published a booklet with sketch town plans, entitled *Record Offices, How to Find Them*, by J.S.W. Gibson and Pamela Peskett, 6th edn, FFHS (1993). *In and around record repositories in Great Britain and Ireland* by J. Cole and R. Church (1992) contains much practical information about visiting record offices, *Record repositories in Great Britain* (HMSO, 1991) gives addresses and opening hours, and *Geneaological resources in English repositories* by J.W. Moulton (1988, supplement 1992) summarises their holdings and shows which records have been transfered to microfilm. *See also* under county headings.

Record Societies   Many local record societies have been set up to transcribe and publish older records thereby making available records which some would find difficult to interpret.

Recovery Rolls   Common Recovery is a type of property conveyance first found in the fifteenth century. Like the Final Concords (*see* FINE) it took the form of a collusive legal action. The recoverer (purchaser) sued the tenant (vendor), alleging that he had no legal title because he had only come into possession after (a fictitious) Hugh Hunt had turned the recoverer out. The tenant brought a third party to court (the vouchee), who was supposed to have warranted the title to him and therefore was bound to defend the issue in his place. The recoverer then asked permission to imparl (to confer with) the vouchee. When the court reassembled, the vouchee failed to appear, so judgement was given for the recoverer. The vouchee was supposed to give land of equal value to the tenant for having misled him, but he never had any land, being often the court cryer. In later times there was usually more than one vouchee, and the procedure was recovery by double or treble voucher. The action could be heard in the Court of Common Pleas, the Court of Hustings, or a manor court. It was entered on the court rolls, and a copy of the entry, described as an exemplication, was handed to the recoverer. This procedure lasted until 1833, and the records (except those enrolled with manor court proceedings) are at the Public Record Office, Chancery Lane, London, in class CP 43. The records of the Court of Hustings are at the Corporation of London Record Office. This procedure is sometimes found to be followed by a conveyance that restored the land to the tenant, the recovery having been merely a legal device for ending his original type of tenure.

Recto   The right-hand page of an open book, the opposite of verso (the reverse, or left-hand, page).

Rector   The owner of a parish benefice, who was also the recipient, until they were commuted, of the Great Tithes. He was responsible for the upkeep of the chancel of his church as his private portion of the building.
See also INCUMBENT; VICAR.

Recusant Rolls   A recusant was one who absented himself (or herself) from the services of his parish church. Under the *Act of Uniformity*, 1559, he was fined 12 pence for each absence. In 1581, the fine was raised to £20 per lunar month, and under Acts of 28 & 29 Elizabeth I, and 3 & 4 James I (their regnal years), he was liable to forfeit all his goods and two-thirds of his real property. The Recusant Rolls list the fines and forfeitures, but are by no means full lists of recusants. The properties confiscated are described in some detail. Many recusants were Roman Catholics, but in some areas the majority were Puritan dissenters; the rolls give no indication as to the religious convictions of the person penalised. Many upper-class recusants seem to have been overlooked by the authorities and poor recusants were not prosecuted as in practice they could not be fined. The annual rolls of the county sheriffs cover the period 1592 to 1691 inclusive, but some years are missing. They are held at the Public Record Office, Chancery Lane, London, in class E 376 and E 377/1–82. The Catholic Record Society has published a number of rolls.
See also NON-CONFORMISTS; ROMAN CATHOLICS.

Redditch Family History Society *see* **Worcestershire**

Redemption *see* **Livery Companies**

Reeve   The foreman of the villeins — and, later, of the copyholders — of a manor. He was the official with whom the lord's bailiff dealt. He was elected by the tenants, but could pay to be excused his office. In small villages, the reeve might do double duty as constable.

Reference   A reference is a unique code which identifies a specific document. Each archive has its own numbering system relating to its own collections. It is essential to record the reference of any document you consult. Those that yield information you require are proof but you cannot prove something unless someone else can also read what you have seen. If you wish to prove a fact in your pedigree, therefore, you need to produce the reference to the document you have consulted. It is also advisable to record the reference to those documents you have consulted which yielded no useful information, otherwise you may return at a future date and waste time doing the same negative search all over again.

In the Public Record Office, references are three part. The first part in capital letters (the Group Code) identifies the provenance of your document (the government department or court of law where the document originated). The second part is what is called the 'Class Number'. Documents of a similar nature are grouped together in a class and there will be several classes of documents in the group of records. Within each class there are several individual items (known as 'pieces' but formerly 'bundles') each of which have a unique number which is the third element of your reference. Occasionally you also need a sub-number to the piece number or a regnal year to identify a part of that piece.

If you are citing a document you have consulted at the PRO, or elsewhere, you need to cite not only the reference but also where it is. A correct citation for a probate inventory in the PRO could read therefore, PRO PROB 5/323.

Registrar General *see* **General Register of Births, Deaths and Marriages**

Registration Districts When civil registration began in 1837 the country was divided into eleven regions which were subdivided into Superintendant Registrar's Districts, based on the old Poor Law Unions. Each Superintendant Registrar's District was divided into sub-districts. Enumeration districts for the purpose of census taking from the 1851 census onwards, were subdivisions of the sub-districts, as the same administrative structure was used to record the population both for registration of births, marriages and deaths and for the census statistics.

Regnal Years In the Middle Ages, documents were dated by the year of the monarch's reign; thus, a document of the third year of the reign of King Henry VI would be shown as such (and in modern calendars as 3 Henry VI). In later records, the *Anno Domini* year either replaced the regnal year or was given in addition to it. After the Restoration of the monarchy in 1660, all documents used by genealogists will bear the AD date, even though regnal years continue to appear, even (in the case of Acts of Parliament) into the present century.

The sovereigns' regnal years began on the dates shown on pp. 247–50, and continued until the same day twelve calendar months later. One exception is the reign of King John. He came to the throne on Ascension Day, which is a movable feast; so each of his regnal years starts on Ascension Day and not on the calendar anniversary of his accession.

Regrate To buy with the intention of selling retail.

Rejoinder A rejoinder is a defendant's answer to a plaintiff's replication.

Relationship, Degree of Degrees of relationship for purposes of inheritance follow a biological path, and advance by one with each person in that path, as follows:

one degree: parent and child.
two degrees: siblings (i.e. via the parent); grandparent and grandchild.
three degrees: uncle or aunt, and nephew or niece; great-grandparent and great-grandchild.
four degrees: first cousins; great-great-grandparent and great-great-grandchild.

Degrees of cousinship First cousins are the children of siblings; second cousins are the children of first cousins; and so on. Cousins are once, or more, removed when they are not (in the family tree sense) both of the same generation. The removal number indicates by how many generations they differ. For example: my son's child and my daughter's grandchild are first cousins once removed. Although, logically, one might also say they were second cousins once removed, in practice the relationship is always measured from the closer cousinship.

Relief A customary manorial payment due from the heir of a deceased freeholder to the lord of the manor, for the privilege of taking up the estate of his predecessor (*see* HERIOT). Also due from the purchaser of such a freehold. Payment was usually the value of one year's rent.

Relieving Officer An official who administered poor relief. *See also* POOR LAW.

Remainder (in a will) In the phrase 'with remainder to', the word indicates the right of succession to a legacy in the event of the death of the named beneficiary before the death of the testator, or before a stipulated age.

Removal Order *see* **Settlement**

Renders *see* **Serjeanty**

Renunciation, Act of A document relinquishing a right or title to something such as an executor refusing to apply for probate. It was also made by a legatee who did not wish to inherit what had been bequeathed to him. The Act had to be attested by a notary and registered in the court files.

REGNAL YEARS

William I
14 Oct.

1	1066
2	7
3	8
4	9
5	1070
6	1
7	2
8	·3
9	4
10	5
11	6
12	7
13	8
14	9
15	1080
16	1
17	2
18	3
19	4
20	5
21	1086

William II
26 Sept.

1	1087
2	8
3	9
4	1090
5	1
6	2
7	3
8	4
9	5
10	6
11	7
12	8
13	1099

Henry I
5 Aug.

1	1100
2	1
3	2
4	3
5	4
6	5
7	6
8	1107
9	8
10	9
11	1110
12	1
13	2
14	3
15	4
16	5
17	6
18	7
19	8
20	9
21	1120
22	1
23	2
24	3
25	4
26	5
27	6
28	7
29	8
30	9
31	1130
32	1
33	2
34	3
35	4
36	1135

Stephen
26 Dec.

1	1135
2	6
3	7
4	8
5	9
6	1140
7	1
8	2
9	3
10	4
11	5
12	6
13	7
14	8
15	9
16	1150
17	1
18	1152
19	3

Henry II
19 Dec.

1	1154
2	5
3	6
4	7
5	8
6	9
7	1160
8	1
9	2
10	3
11	4
12	5
13	6
14	7
15	8
16	9
17	1170
18	1
19	2
20	3
21	4
22	5
23	6
24	7
25	8
26	9
27	1180
28	1
29	2
30	3
31	4
32	5
33	6
34	7
35	1188

Richard I
3 Sept.

1	1189
2	1190
3	1
4	2
5	3
6	4
7	1195
8	6
9	7
10	8

John
Ascension

1	27.5.
	1199
2	18.5.
	1200
3	3.5.1
4	23.5.2
5	15.5.3
6	3.6.4
7	19.5.5
8	11.5.6
9	31.5.7
10	15.5.8
11	7.5.9
12	27.5.
	1210
13	12.5.1
14	3.5.2
15	23.5.3
16	8.5.4
17	28.5.5
18	19.5.1216

Henry III
28 Oct.

1	1216
2	7
3	8
4	9
5	1220
6	1
7	2
8	3
9	4
10	5
11	6
12	7
13	8
14	9
15	1230
16	1
17	2
18	3
19	1234
20	5
21	6
22	7
23	8
24	9
25	1240
26	1
27	2
28	3
29	4
30	5
31	6
32	7
33	8
34	9
35	1250
36	1
37	2
38	3
39	4
40	5
41	6
42	7
43	8
44	9
45	1260
46	1
47	2
48	3
49	4
50	5
51	6
52	7
53	8
54	9
55	1270
56	1
57	1272

Edward I
20 Nov.

1	1272
2	3
3	4
4	5
5	6
6	7
7	8

REGNAL YEARS

Edward I
20 Nov.

8	1279
9	1280
10	1
11	2
12	3
13	4
14	5
15	6
16	7
17	8
18	9
19	1290
20	1
21	2
22	3
23	4
24	5
25	6
26	7
27	8
28	9
29	1300
30	1
31	2
32	3
33	4
34	5
35	1306

Edward II
8 July

1	1307
2	8
3	9
4	1310
5	1
6	2
7	3
8	4
9	5
10	6
11	7
12	8
13	9
14	1320
15	1
16	2
17	3
18	4

19	1325
20	1326

Edward III
25 Jan

1	1326/7
2	7/8
3	8/9
4	9/0
5	1330/1
6	1/2
7	2/3
8	3/4
9	4/5
10	5/6
11	6/7
12	7/8
13	8/9
14	9/0
15	1340/1
16	1/2
17	2/3
18	3/4
19	4/5
20	5/6
21	6/7
22	7/8
23	8/9
24	9/0
25	1350/1
26	1/2
27	2/3
28	3/4
29	4/5
30	5/6
31	6/7
32	7/8
33	8/9
34	9/0
35	1360/1
36	1/2
37	2/3
38	3/4
39	4/5
40	5/6
41	6/7
42	7/8
43	8/9
44	9/0
45	1370/1
46	1/2
47	1372/3
48	3/4
49	4/5
50	5/6
51	1376/7

Richard II
22 June

1	1377
2	8
3	9
4	1380
5	1
6	2
7	3
8	4
9	5
10	6
11	7
12	8
13	9
14	1390
15	1
16	2
17	3
18	4
19	5
20	6
21	7
22	8
23	1399

Henry IV
30 Sept.

1	1399
2	1400
3	1
4	2
5	3
6	4
7	5
8	6
9	7
10	8
11	9
12	1410
13	1
14	1412

Henry V
21 Mch.

1	1412/3
2	3/4
3	4/5
4	5/6
5	6/7
6	7/8
7	8/9
8	9/0
9	1420/1
10	1421/2

Henry VI
1 Sept.

1	1422
2	3
3	4
4	5
5	6
6	7
7	8
8	9
9	1430
10	1
11	2
12	3
13	4
14	5
15	6
16	7
17	8
18	9
19	1440
20	1
21	2
22	3
23	4
24	5
25	6
26	7
27	8
28	9
29	1450
30	1
31	2
32	3
33	4
34	5
35	6
36	7
37	1458
38	9
39	1460

Restored
9 Oct.

49	1470

Edward IV
4 Mch.

1	1460/1
2	1/2
3	2/3
4	3/4
5	4/5
6	5/6
7	6/7
8	7/8
9	8/9
10	1469/0
11	1471/2
12	2/3
13	3/4
14	4/5
15	5/6
16	6/7
17	7/8
18	8/9
19	9/0
20	1480/1
21	1/2
22	1482/3

Edward V
9 Apr

1	1483

Richard III
26 June

1	1483
2	4
3	1485

Henry VII
22 Aug.

1	1485
2	6
3	7
4	8
5	9
6	1490
7	1

REGNAL YEARS

Henry VII
22 Aug.

8	1492
9	3
10	4
11	5
12	6
13	7
14	8
15	9
16	1500
17	1
18	2
19	3
20	4
21	5
22	6
23	7
24	1508

Henry VIII
22 Apr.

1	1509
2	1510
3	1
4	2
5	3
6	4
7	5
8	6
9	7
10	8
11	9
12	1520
13	1
14	2
15	3
16	4
17	5
18	6
19	7
20	8
21	9
22	1530
23	1
24	2
25	3
26	4
27	5
28	6
29	7
30	1538
31	1539
32	1540
33	1
34	2
35	3
36	4
37	5
38	1546

Edward VI
28 Jan.

1	1546/7
2	7/8
3	8/9
4	9/0
5	1550/1
6	1/2
7	2/3

Jane
6 July

1	1553

Mary I
6 July

1	1553
2	4

Philip & Mary
25 July

1/2	1554
2/3	5
3/4	6
4/5	7
5/6	1558

Elizabeth I
17 Nov.

1	1558
2	9
3	1560
4	1
5	2
6	3
7	4
8	5
9	6
10	7
11	8
12	9
13	1570
14	1
15	1572
16	3
17	4
18	5
19	6
20	7
21	8
22	9
23	1580
24	1
25	2
26	3
27	4
28	5
29	6
30	7
31	8
32	9
33	1590
34	1
35	2
36	3
37	4
38	5
39	6
40	7
41	8
42	9
43	1600
44	1
45	1602

James I
24 Mch.

1	1602/3
2	3/4
3	4/5
4	5/6
5	6/7
6	7/8
7	8/9
8	9/0
9	1610/1
10	1/2
11	2/3
12	3/4
13	4/5
14	5/6
15	6/7
16	7/8
17	8/9
18	1619/20
19	1620/1
20	1/2
21	2/3
22	3/4
23	4/5

Charles I
27 Mch.

1	1625
2	6
3	7
4	8
5	9
6	1630
7	1
8	2
9	3
10	4
11	5
12	6
13	7
14	8
15	9
16	1640
17	1
18	2
19	3
20	4
21	5
22	6
23	7
24	1648

Charles II
30 Jan.

1	1648/9
12	1659/60
13	1660/1
14	1/2
15	2/3
16	3/4
17	4/5
18	5/6
19	6/7
20	7/8
21	8/9
22	9/0
23	1670/1
24	1/2
25	2/3
26	3/4
27	4/5
28	1675/6
29	6/7
30	7/8
31	8/9
32	9/0
33	1680/1
34	1/2
35	2/3
36	3/4
37	1684/5

James II
6 Feb

1	1684/5
2	5/6
3	6/7
4	7/8
till	12.12.88

Wm. & Mary
13 Feb.

1	1688/9
2	9/0
3	1690/1
4	1/2
5	2/3
6	1693/4

William III
28 Dec.

6	1694
7	5
8	6
9	7
10	8
11	9
12	1700
13	1
14	1702

Anne
8 Mch.

1	1701/2
2	2/3
3	3/4
4	4/5
5	5/6
6	6/7
7	7/8
8	8/9
9	9/0
10	1710/1

REGNAL YEARS

Anne		George III (cont.)		George IV / William IV / Victoria		Victoria (cont.)		Later reigns	
8 Mch.		29	1755	44	1803	9	1845	61	1897
11	1711/2	30	6	45	4	10	6	62	8
12	2/3	31	7	46	5	11	7	63	9
13	3/4	32	8	47	6	12	8	64	1900
		33	9	48	7	13	9		
George I		34	1760	49	8	14	1850	**Edward VII**	
1 Aug.				50	9	15	1	*22 Jan.*	
1	1714	**George III**		51	1810	16	2	1	1901
2	5	*25 Oct.*		52	1	17	3	2	2
3	6	1	1760	53	2	18	4	3	3
4	7	2	1	54	3	19	5	4	4
5	8	3	2	55	4	20	6	5	5
6	9	4	3	56	5	21	7	6	6
7	1720	5	4	57	6	22	8	7	7
8	1	6	5	58	7	23	9	8	8
9	2	7	6	59	8	24	1860	9	9
10	3	8	7	60	1819	25	1	10	1910
11	4	9	8			26	2		
12	5	10	9	**George IV**		27	3	**George V**	
13	1726	11	1770	*29 Jan.*		28	4	*6 May*	
		12	1	1	1820	29	5	1	1910
George II		13	2	2	1	30	6	2	1
11 June		14	3	3	2	31	7	3	2
1	1727	15	4	4	3	32	8	4	3
2	8	16	5	5	4	33	9	5	4
3	9	17	6	6	5	34	1870	6	5
4	1730	18	7	7	6	35	1	7	6
5	1	19	8	8	7	36	2	8	7
6	2	20	9	9	8	37	3	9	8
7	3	21	1780	10	9	38	4	10	9
8	4	22	1	11	1830	39	5	11	1920
9	5	23	2			40	6	12	1
10	6	24	3	**William IV**		41	7	13	2
11	7	25	4	*26 June*		42	8	14	3
12	8	26	5	1	1830	43	9	15	4
13	9	27	6	2	1	44	1880	16	5
14	1740	28	7	3	2	45	1	17	6
15	1	29	8	4	3	46	2	18	7
16	2	30	9	5	4	47	3	19	8
17	3	31	1790	6	5	48	4	20	9
18	4	32	1	7	1836	49	5	21	1930
19	5	33	2			50	6	22	1
20	6	34	3	**Victoria**		51	7	23	2
21	7	35	4	*20 June*		52	8	24	3
22	8	36	5	1	1837	53	9	25	4
23	9	37	6	2	8	54	1890	26	1935
24	1750	38	7	3	9	55	1		
25	1	39	8	4	1840	56	2	**Edward VIII**	
26	2	40	9	5	1	57	3	*20 Jan.*	
27	3	41	1800	6	2	58	4	1	1936
28	4	42	1	7	3	59	5		
		43	2	8	4	60	6		

Replevin, Writ of A writ issued for the wrongful distraint of cattle.

Replication A replication is the reply of the plaintiff to the plea of the defendant or the reply to an answer. It is the third step in common pleadings.

Requests, Court of Petitions by poor persons, heard during the Middle Ages by justices in Eyre, and then by the Court of Chancery, were, in 1390, transferred to a committee of the King's Council functioning as a court of equity. In 1483, the Lord Privy Seal became its president. After having followed the king's movements for over a century, it was given a permanent seat in Whitehall in 1516, and for a time took its name from that palace. Eventually it became officially known as the Court of Requests. The Lord Privy Seal was assisted by four Privy Councillors, as Masters of Requests, sitting with professional judges and assessors. Although intended to be a poor man's court, it was much used by members of the royal household and came, in time, to hear complaints from all sorts of people. All evidence was taken in writing and often contains interesting biographical material. The Court was abolished in 1642.

The records are at the Public Record Office, Chancery Lane, London, in classes REQ 1–3, and are calendared from Henry VII to Elizabeth I in *Lists and Indexes*, Vol. 21, and indexed from Henry VIII to James I in *Supplementary Lists and Indexes 7* (4 volumes), under the names of the parties, places and subjects.

Residence, Certificate of In the sixteenth and seventeenth centuries, certificates were issued to people who had moved their abode, to show that they had made their Lay Subsidy payment in a certain place and were therefore to be excused elsewhere. A duplicate of the certificate was attached to the subsidy return. This practice began in the reign of Edward VI and continued until that of Charles II.

The certificates, now detached from the returns, are in 462 bundles among the Exchequer records at the Public Record Office, Chancery Lane, London. They are calendared, by surname only, under reference E 115. The calendars are on the shelves of the Round Room. Against each surname is shown the county of residence, but it must be remembered that this may not be the county of residence already known for that person. The certificates are a valuable aid for tracing a family move.

Respondent A respondent is someone who answers, a defendant in a law suit.

Ripon, Harrogate and District Family History Society *see* **Yorkshire**

Roe, Richard A fictitious personage introduced into many legal documents; as also John Doe and Hugh Hunt. These imaginary persons were introduced to enable the Common Law to cope with new situations and needs, while still, to outward appearance, preserving its ancient forms.

Rogationtide The Monday, Tuesday and Wednesday before Ascension Day, originally kept as a period of fast and supplication, especially for the coming harvest. In Roman Catholic England, litanies were chanted in procession, but after the Reformation the processions lost their religious significance and became simply the perambulation of the parish boundaries.

Rogue Money A payment due annually from each parish to the High Constable of the hundred, for the maintenance of prisoners in the county gaol.

Roll A roll is a document which has been written on parchment, each membrane of which has been stitched to another, top and bottom and then rolled up for safe keeping. The term can also be applied to those documents which are stacked one on top of the other and only attached at the top of the membranes and then rolled up.

Roman Catholics From 1559, the history of English Catholics became a subject separate from that of their compatriots, as a result of the Acts of *Supremacy* and *Uniformity*. The latter made non-attendance at services of the Church of England an offence, called recusancy. A fine of one shilling for each absence was collected by the churchwardens and used for the relief of the parish poor.

In 1569, many Catholic nobles took part in the 'Rising of the North' in favour of Mary Queen of Scots, which led to the active persecution of their co-religionists. However, English Catholics trained for the priesthood at the theological college at Douai in France, and, from 1574 onward, entered the country secretly to keep the faith alive against the time when Mary, the heir presumptive, should succeed her cousin, Elizabeth.

From 1581, fines were raised to £20 per lunar month for absenteeism, 100 marks plus one year's imprisonment for attending a Catholic

Mass, and 200 marks plus the same imprisonment for celebrating the Mass. Four years later it became high treason for laymen to receive the ministrations of Catholic priests.

In 1586, non-payment of fines became punishable by seizure of all one's movable goods and two-thirds of one's lands. The missionary priests were concealed by wealthy co-religionists in hiding holes in their country houses. Such priests had no geographical boundaries for their missions, and there was no question of keeping registers because these would have constituted documentary evidence against their flock. Catholics, however, were baptized and even married by their missionary priests, but they usually went through a Church of England marriage too, to avoid a fine, to obtain legal registration and to avoid any doubt about the legitimacy of their children. Burials were usually only possible in parish churches. Catholicism survived mainly in the north. In 1678, the Popish Plot invented by Titus Oates temporarily revived the persecution of Catholics, whose legal disabilities had for some years not been too strictly enforced. (For Roman Catholics of the mid seventeenth century, *see* ROYALIST COMPOSITION PAPERS.)

At the end of the seventeenth century, so many dissenters were not having their children baptized by the parish priest that they were obliged by law to inform him of the births of their children, and were fined for non-compliance. Therefore many Catholic births (not baptisms) can be found recorded in parish registers of that period.

At the turn of the century, anti-Catholic feeling grew sharper as the danger of a Catholic heir to the throne became imminent. Papists were forbidden to buy or inherit land. In 1701, the *Act of Settlement* barred Catholics from the throne of England.

After the Jacobite rebellion of 1715, an Act was passed compelling all persons over the age of 18 to take an Oath of Allegiance, in the wording of which they renounced the Catholic Church. Lists exist of people of property who refused to take this oath. Papists were compelled to register the value of their lands, whether freehold, copyhold or leasehold, with the Clerk of the Peace. On the death of a registered landowner, his heir had to register. Sometimes a copy of the will would be attached. Some papists forfeited their lands; all were liable to special taxes. There are national censuses (often with names) for 1705 and 1767. The House of Lords Record Office has lists of late seventeenth-century and eighteenth-century papists. From 1754, only marriages in Church of England churches were legal. In 1778, an Act was passed 'to relieve, upon conditions and under restrictions, persons professing the Popish religion'. This is popularly known as 'the repeal of the penal laws' (the years from the Reformation until 1778 are called by Catholics 'the penal times'). Catholics were now allowed to take an Oath of Allegiance and attend the law courts, and many Catholic registers date from this time. However, the Act provoked the Gordon Riots in London and disturbances elsewhere.

The *Catholic Relief Act* of 1791 enabled Catholics to worship at their own registered churches under registered priests, and many churches were built. Several thousand priests fled from the French Revolution to England.

In 1829, the *Emancipation Act* enabled Catholics to vote, sit in Parliament and hold property unconditionally.

In 1837, the Catholic Church, like the nonconformist churches, was asked to deposit its existing registers of baptisms and burials with the newly appointed Registrar General. Only 79 Catholic chapels agreed, mostly in Yorkshire, Durham and Northumberland. Their registers are now at the Public Record Office, Chancery Lane, London, in class RG 4; the rest are held at the Catholic churches. Reference should be made to the published yearbook, *The Catholic Directory*. For details of Catholic registers and their whereabouts see M.J. Gandy *Catholic Missions and Registers 1700–1880*, 6 vols. 1993.

In the 1840s numbers increased enormously because of Irish immigration, missionary work amongst the unchurched English and the conversion of many upper-class influential Anglicans. The establishment of Bishoprics in 1850 facilitated the establishment of many schools, orphanages, old people's homes and other charities to help the poor.

In 1904, the Catholic Record Society was founded. In addition to many registers, it has published recusant lists and other sources, and a series of monographs. It issues a journal, *Recusant History*, twice yearly. The Secretary of the Society is Miss R. Rendel, Flat 5, Lennox Gardens, London SW1X 0BQ.

An index of Catholic marriages in London postal districts north of the River Thames, 1837–70, has been compiled. Enquiries should be addressed to the Institute of Heraldic and Genealogical Studies, Canterbury.

The most useful original sources are:

Pipe Rolls 1581–91

Recusant Rolls 1592–1691 (with some gaps), containing details of lands forfeited to the Crown, and fines for non-attendance at church. However, not all the recusants listed can be assumed to be Catholics; some are Protestant nonconformists. The Rolls are among the Exchequer Records at the Public Record Office, Chancery Lane, London, in class E 377.

Assize Court Records, Quarter Sessions Records and Bishops' Visitation Books have details of the presentment of recusants, and sometimes reveal the religious beliefs of the accused.

Marriages 1754–1837. Church of England registers should be searched.

Catholic Burial Grounds Enquire of local parish priests, whose names are obtainable from the yearbook, *The Catholic Directory*.

Oath of Allegiance Records and the *Register of Roman Catholic Estates* are at the county record offices.

There is a Catholic family history society. Its address is c/o Mrs B.M. Murray, 2 Winscombe Crescent, Ealing, London W5 1AZ.

For further reading, see Michael Gandy, *Catholic Ancestors* FHND vol. 8 No 1 (April 1991). Michael Gandy, *Catholics in Your One-Name Study*, Journal of One-Name Studies vol. 3 No. 11 (July 1990). J.A. Williams, *Archives*, in Recusant History vol. 16 No. 4 (Oct. 1983). D.J. Steel *Sources for Roman Catholic and Jewish Genealogy and Family History*, National Index of Parish Registers vol. 3 (1974). Edward Norman, *Roman Catholicism in England from the Elizabethan Settlement to the Second Vatican Council*, (1986).

Rotulet A small roll of parchment, or a small membrance bound up in a roll.

Rovers The expression 'at rovers' meant 'at random'.

Royal Air Force This arm of the fighting services was formed in April, 1918. During the First World War there were two separate services, the Royal Flying Corps and the Royal Naval Air Service, under the authority of the War Office and Admiralty respectively. Their records are at the Public Record Office, Kew, among those of the Army and the Royal Navy.

Further reading: Eunice Wilson, *The Records of the Royal Air Force*, FFHS, 1991 and PRO Information leaflet no. 13 *Air Records at Sources for Biography and Family History*.

Royal Commission on Historical MSS *see* **Historical MSS, Royal Commission on**

Royal Historical Society The object of the Society is to promote the study of history by issuing publications. Founded in 1868 as the Historical Society, it attained its present title in 1887 by royal permission. In 1897 the Camden Society was amalgamated with it, and that society's *Camden Series* of texts with introductions was continued. Other publications are the Society's *Transactions*, containing the papers read before its members, and *Miscellanies*, containing several short texts. Of particular value to genealogists have been the *Handbook of British Chronology*, edited by Sir Maurice Powicke and Dr E.B. Fryde, the *Handbook of Dates*, by Professor C.R. Cheney, and *Texts and Calendars*, by E.L.C. Mullins.

Royal Marines The corps was founded in 1664 as the Duke of York and Albany's Maritime Regiment of Foot. They were disbanded by William III, but not long afterwards he raised two regiments, called the 1st and 2nd Marines, for the duration of the war with France.

On the outbreak of the War of the Spanish Succession in 1702, six Marine Regiments were formed, again for the duration. For the War of the Austrian Succession in 1755, ten regiments were raised, but this time they became a permanent body and were transferred from the Army to the Navy as the Marine Corps. In 1802, they became the Royal Marines. Two years later, companies of Royal Marine Artillery were formed, known, from their uniform, as the Blue Marines, to distinguish them from the Royal Marines, who wore red. The artillery companies were amalgamated with the Royal Marines in 1923.

The records are all at the Public Record Office, Kew. The Description Books (ADM 158) cover 1750–1888, and summarise in convenient alphabetical order the information given on the Attestation Forms, 1790–1883 (ADM 157) — i.e. the birthplace, pre-service trade, height, eyes, complexion and hair, and enlistment details of each recruit, with some details of his service and discharge. A number of Description Books are missing. From 1842 to 1905, similar details can be obtained from the *Registers of Service* (ADM 159). No records of officers' services, similar to other services, have been published.

The Royal Marines Museum is at Eastney, Portsmouth, Hants. Entry is subject to previous appointment.

For further reading, see *Tracing Your Ancestors in the PRO*, by Amanda Bevan and Andrea Duncan (HMSO, 1990) and *Britain's Sea Soldiers*, by C. Field. A free leaflet, No. 74, *Royal Marines Records in the Public Record Office*, is available at the Public Record Office.

Royal Navy Under William the Conqueror, the Cinque Ports (Dover, Sandwich, Hastings, Romney and Hythe and later on Rye & Winchelsea) were responsible for providing ships and men for the defence of the realm. By the time of Henry I, the Court of Admiralty was in existence. In Henry VIII's reign, the Navy Board was formed to take over from the Cinque Ports. The Lord High Admiral's Council was formed to assist the Lord High Admiral in carrying out the executive functions of the Navy. This later became the Admiralty Board.

Naval Accounts and Inventories were kept, and these have been published by the Navy Records Society. They include the names of some officers and officials. From the reign of Henry VIII onward, references to the Navy and some naval men can be found in the published *Calendar of State Papers*. At the Restoration (1660) the occupation of naval officer became a regular career, providing half-pay for some men on reserve, but ratings continued to be taken on only as required and mainly by pressing those men who 'used the sea', such as merchant seamen, ferrymen, etc. At this time, the personnel of the Navy was divided into Commissioned Officers, Warrant Officers and Ratings. The records of these classes differ, as follows.

For *Officers*, there are printed or typescript sources for the outlines of their careers. *Navy Lists* have been printed since 1749; they became annual in 1782 and official from 1814. There is also the *List of Sea Officers* from 1800. The *Seniority Lists* (ADM 118) are annotated lists of officers from 1717. There is also a printed list, *Commissioned Sea Officers of the Royal Navy, 1660–1815*. A number of collections of naval biographies have also been printed, including *Lives of the British Admirals* (to 1816), by J. Campbell and W. Stevenson, *Royal Naval Biography*, by J. Marshall, *Biographia Navalis, 1794–8*, by J. Charnock, and *Naval Biographical Dictionary* (1849), by W.R. O'Bryne.

Original official sources are in the Public Record Office, Kew, and include the following. *Records of Officers' Services* (ADM 196), from the last quarter of the eighteenth century; *Lieutenants' Passing Certificates* of both the Navy Board (ADM 107) and Admiralty (ADM 6 & ADM 13), covering the period 1691 to 1902 with some gaps. There is a complete cumulative typescript index for 1789–1818 of the Navy Board series. From 1789, the certificates often have baptismal certificates attached. *Returns of Officers' Services* (ADM 9) consist of two censuses, one of officers alive in 1817–22, annotated to 1828, and the other of officers living in 1846, in which their ages are mentioned. ADM 11/10 shows the ages of officers serving in 1847. ADM 6/30 covers lieutenants, mates, midshipmen and others, from 1799 to 1854, showing dates of birth and baptism, place of birth, and parents' names.

Other returns available are: *Appointments and Commissions*, 1695 onward (ADM 6 and 11); *Officers Appointed 1660–88* (ADM 10/10); *Lieutenants unfit for service, 1804–10* (ADM 6/123); *Officers who passed HMS Excellent gunnery school* (ADM 6/60).

Warrant Officers were heads of departments, e.g. boatswain, carpenter, cooper, engineer, gunner, master, sailmaker, surgeon. They are included in *Records of Officers' Services* (ADM 196), already mentioned. Other records are, *Warrant Officers' and Seamen's Services* (ADM 29), which give brief service records of warrant officers and ratings superannuated or applying for admission to Greenwich Hospital 1802–1894; the *Seniority Lists* (ADM 118); the *Commissions and Warrant Books* (ADM 6 and ADM 11); *Succession Books 1673–1903* (ADM 6, 7, 11, 29, 104, 106) are arranged by name of ship. Using informal nominal indexes it is possible to trace an officer's or warrant officer's career.

For *Engineers* see ADM 196 13/200–6 and ADM 11/48–9. *Surgeons* 1774–1886 are recorded in ADM 104/12–29, and see also ADM 11/40 and ADM 106/2952–3. Selected *Surgeons' Journals* are in ADM 101. *Masters' Qualifications* 1660–1830 (ADM 106/2908–50) include certificates of baptism, as do some *Passing Certificates* 1851–63 (ADM 13/72–4). For *Clerks' Passing Certificates* see ADM 13/75–8 and 196–9.

For *Midshipmen* see also ADM 196, and *Passing Certificates* 1857–99 in ADM 13/102 and 240–5. Those serving in 1814 are shown with their ages and birthplaces in ADM 6/182, and an index is available.

Chaplains are listed in *Chaplains of the Royal Navy, 1626–1903*, by A.G. Kealy. See also ADM 82, 24 and 30/7.

For *Ratings* enlisting before 1853 it is generally necessary to know the name of the ship in which a man served. *Ship's Musters* from 1667 onward are under ADM 36–9. The men's ages and birthplaces should be shown from 1764 and from about 1800 *Description Books* may be among them, giving ages, height, complexion, scars, tattoos, etc. Ships' *Pay Books* (ADM 31–5) survive from 1669. In 1853 Continuous Service Engagement for ratings was first introduced; *CS Engagement Books* cover the period 1853–72. *Ratings Services*, 1873–1891 (ADM 188) give full details of service for ratings enlisting between those dates. Records of service, 1892–1939 are held by the Ministry of Defence, CS(R) 2A. Room 17, Bourne Avenue, Hayes, Middlesex UB3 1RF; and after 1939 by PP1 A1, HMS Centurion, Grange Road, Gosport, Hampshire PO13 9XA. If a man is known to have been serving in a given area at a certain time, but not in which ship, the *List Books* 1673–1893 (ADM 8) show the whereabouts of vessels.

During the Napoleonic Wars, a kind of naval militia was raised called the Sea Fencibles, and the paylists of this body for 1798–1810 are under ADM 28. For officers and men killed in action or dying from wounds there are records of petitions from widows, orphans or mothers, in the *Bounty Papers* (ADM 106/3023–4) for the period 1675–1822. These include evidence of kinship and often give details of the death. Records of the estates of the deceased, including some wills, are under ADM 44, 48, 141 and 142.

For biographical details, see the *Log-books of Captains* 1669–1852 (ADM 51/1–4563), and the *Log-books of Masters* 1672–1840 (ADM 52/1–4660).

For further reading, see *Tracing Your Ancestors in the PRO*, by Amanda Bevan and Andrea Duncan (HMSO 1990) and *Naval Records for Genealogists* by N.A.M. Rodger (PRO Publications). See also the PRO Information Leaflets No. 2 *Admiralty Records as Sources for Biography and Genealogy*, Nos. 3, 49 and 43, *Operational Records of the Royal Navy 1660–1914, 1914–1919, 1939–1945*, available at the PRO. The Navy Records Society has been publishing volumes of records since 1894.

The Naval Historical Library, Ministry of Defence, Empress State Building, London SW6 1TR is open to the public by previous appointment (tel: 071 385 1244. Ext. 3246).

Royalist Composition Papers In 1643, a Parliamentary Committee was set up called the Committee for the Sequestration of Delinquents' Estates, to confiscate the lands of those who were taking the Royalist side in the Civil War. Papists and other recusants were also included, even though not taking an active military part.

When a person was accused, his estate was seized pending investigation of his case. If found guilty, his whole estate was confiscated, but one-fifth was allowed him for the maintenance of his family and another fifth of the proceeds of the estate went to the informer. In cases of mere recusancy, one-third of the estate was allowed

to the guilty party. In 1653, the war being over, the work of the Committee was taken over by the Committee for Compounding the Estates of Royalists and Delinquents. The accused were urged to confess, and if they pledged their loyalty to the Commonwealth government they were allowed to compound in proportion to their guilt. One-sixth was taken from anyone who had taken part in either the first or second civil war (i.e. before or after 1647), one-third from those who had been active in both. Delinquent Members of Parliament lost half their estates. The records of both Committees are at the Public Record Office, Chancery Lane, London, the first under reference SP 20 and the second under SP 23 in volumes G1–269. The PRO has issued a free leaflet, *Confiscations, Sales and Restoration of Crown and Royalist Lands, 1642–60*.

Rutland The county was merged with Leicestershire in 1974. It lay within the diocese of Lincoln until 1541 and then Peterborough in the Province of Canterbury. Most of the parish registers have been deposited at the Leicestershire CRO. There are a few transcripts in the library of the SOG. Pallot's Marriage Index covers 19, mostly from 1780. The Bishops' Transcripts and the Marriage Licence records are at the Northamptonshire CRO.

The Hundreds of Alstoe, East, Martinsley, Oakham-Soke and Wrangdike lie within its boundaries. It has Oakham and Uppingham RDs/PLUs.

It fell within the Midland Assize Circuit until 1863 when it came under the Norfolk Circuit and reverted to the Midland Circuit in 1876.

The Leicestershire and Rutland Family History Society publishes a quarterly newsletter and meets in Leicester.

The records are kept at Oakham Library.

Pre 1858 Wills are at the Northamptonshire CRO except for those proved at the Peculiar Courts of Caldecott and Ketton and Liddington which are at the Leicestershire CRO. Wills could also be proved at the Consistory Courts of Lincoln until 1541 and Peterborough after that and at the Prerogative Court of Canterbury.

Rutland Record Society has published the Muster Certificates 1522, Lay Subsidy Rolls 1524 –5 and has produced an annual journal *Rutland Record* since 1980. Heralds' Visitation Pedigrees have been published for 1681–2.

Royston Family History Society *see* **Hertfordshire**

Rural Dean *see* **Anglican Church**

S

Sac ad Soc The privilege of holding courts, trying causes and imposing fines, as in a MANOR.

Sacrament Certificate In 1673 the (*First*) *Test Act*, directed against Popish recusants, compelled every person holding civil or military office to take the oaths of supremacy and allegiance, accepting the king as 'the only supreme governor of this realm', and acknowledging that his authority existed 'as well in all spiritual and ecclesiastical things or causes as temporal'. It also compelled every such person to receive the sacrament of the Lord's Supper according to the usage of the Church of England, and to deliver into Quarter Sessions a certificate to that effect, signed by the minister, churchwarden and two witnesses. He also had to make a declaration against transubstantiation. These certificates frequently give the occupation of the man and of his witnesses. A register had to be kept of all persons who took the oaths. The law was not repealed until 1828, but from 1750 fewer certificates were made out.

In 1688 a new form of oath was required of all office-holders, namely:

I, [A.B.], do swear that I do from my heart abhor, detest and abjure, as impious and heretical, that damnable doctrine and position 'That Princes excommunicated or deprived by the Pope or any Authority of the See of Rome may be deposed or murdered by their Subjects or any other whatever.' And 'I do declare that no foreign prince, person, prelate, state or potentate hath, or ought to have, any jurisdiction, power, superiority, preminence, or authority, ecclesiastical or spiritual within this Realm. So help me God.'

Some Protestants were allowed to practise 'occasional conformity', i.e. taking the sacrament a certain minimum number of times.

The certificates are among the Quarter Sessions records at county record offices.

St. Catherine's House The present location of the indexes to the registration of births, marriages and deaths for the whole of England and Wales. *See* GENERAL REGISTER OFFICE.

Saints' Days *see* **Calendar**

Salt Library, William *see* **Staffordshire**

Sampler From the seventeenth to the early twentieth century it was the custom for a young girl to embroider a piece of material as an example of her skill in needlework. The embroidery of the sampler normally included a pattern, the alphabet in capitals and lower case, the numerals, a pious verse, quotation or motto, the maker's name and age, and the date on which she completed her work. These examples of the childish skill of little girls tend to be treasured and passed down the generations, long after all other material evidence of the family past has disappeared. An index of some surviving samplers is being compiled by Mrs Jenny Mukerji, 1 Elsdon Road, Goldsworth Park, Woking, Surrey GU21 3NX.

Sanctuary The privilege of safe refuge in a consecrated place. Sometimes the right of sanctuary for a fleeing criminal or refugee applied to the whole church, but more often to the chancel only. To remove a person from there within forty days of his reaching it was sacrilege. There were two kinds of sanctuary: general and peculiar. General sanctuary applied to every church, and only to felonies; peculiar sanctuary was a right granted by charter to certain churches, and covered even treason, and for life.

The procedure laid down obliged the fugitive to confess his crime in detail to one of the clergy, surrender his weapons, and pay an admission fee. Within the forty days, and in the church, he could confess his crime to the coroner and take an oath of Abjuration of the realm. He would then be convicted, suffer attainder, and forfeit his goods. To leave the realm, he would have to travel on foot, dressed in a long white robe, bare-headed and carrying a wooden cross. He had to keep to the highway, stay no more than two nights at any one place, and make straight for the coast. Sometimes his port of embarkation was laid down by the coroner.

Sanctuary for crime was abolished in 1623, but for civil processes it hung on in certain places, the best known of which was Whitefriars also known as Alsatia, between Fleet Street and the River Thames in London. These relics of sanctuary were abolished by Acts of 1697 and 1723.

Sandemanians Known as Glassites in Scotland as they were founded by John Glas, but as Sandemanians elsewhere after Robert Sandeman, one of his followers, these non-conformists held an extreme view of justification by faith and founded several churches in England, Scotland and the United States.

Sappers and Miners *see* **Ordnance, Board of**

Sasines *see* **Scottish Genealogy**

Scavenger An urban official responsible for keeping the streets clean. Under him he had 'rakers', who went around three times per week doing the actual work of clearing the night-soil and rubbish put out by householders. The scavenger sometimes combined other responsbilities with that of the cleanliness of his area.

Schools The most accessible and informative of school records are the registers that have been published by public schools, anciently endowed grammar schools, and charity schools. They usually provide the pupil's date of birth, father's name, period at the school and a few details of his later career. The Society of Genealogists has a collection of these. For some ancient schools the minutes of Governors' Meetings survive. Another numerous class of records consists of the Log Books kept by the masters or mistresses of the thousands of schools begun in the early and middle nineteenth century, and administered under the auspices of either the National Society for Promoting the Education of the Poor (Church of England) or the British and Foreign Schools Society (Nonconformist); both societies receiving government aid from 1839. An Act of 1879 set up local school boards all over England and Wales, which founded Board Schools wherever there was need. The Log Books of pupil attendance and other records, may still be in the custody of the school, parish or local education authority, but many of those that survive have found their way to the county record offices. Though they contain little genealogical information, the noted causes of absences throw light on the ways of life of the children and their families. A prospectus of the archives of the British and Foreign Schools Society may be obtained from their Archives Centre, West London Institute of Higher Education, Borough Road, Isleworth, Middlesex TW7 5DU. For further reading: *The Growth of British Education and its Records* by Colin R. Chapman, Lochin Publishing (1991)

Scot The parochial poor rate, as distinct from Lot, which was for church maintenance.

Scottish Ancestry Throughout the centuries, inhabitants of Great Britain have migrated between England and other parts of the United Kingdom, so that many a single line of descent comprises generations on both sides of a border. Despite the fact that the Crowns of both England and Scotland became vested in King James VI of Scotland and I of England in 1603, and notwithstanding the subsequent *Act of Union* of 1707, Scotland has had, and continues to have, a completely separate identity from England.

There are still many differences between the two countries (for example, Scotland continues to have quite a different legal system, her national religion is Presbyterianism and she operates the feudal system of land tenure), and they all serve to emphasise that we are dealing with a separate nation, the origin of whose people is Celtic in contrast to the rather mixed origins of their English neighbours.

Scotland's history, riddled as it is with hardship and strife, has helped to mould the Scottish character, in which devotion to the family and to the larger concept of the clan is paramount. Moreover, the comparatively small number of surnames, its relatively small population, the massive emigration, coupled with the precision of the Scottish temperament, has made Scotland notorious for its genealogical and heraldic awareness.

Insofar as research into Scottish records is concerned, we should continue to follow the same procedures and guidelines as described in the Guide to Genealogical Research, at the beginning of this book. There are many different records to search, but, fortunately, most of these are centralised and housed in Edinburgh, either at New Register House or at the Scottish Records Office.

Public Registers

(a) The General Register of Births, Deaths and Marriages for Scotland is housed at New Register House, Edinburgh, and dates from 1 January, 1855. The entries may be accessed on computer by the public and then the certificates viewed on microfiche. It is more comprehensive than the English system, and Scottish certificates give the following additional information:

Births — date of marriage of parents (except 1856–61), thus eliminating the need for much searching; qualification of informant and his residence, if out of the house at which the birth occurred.

Marriages — how married (e.g. after proclamation); exact ages of parties; the maiden surname of the mother to each party of the marriage.

Deaths — name, surname, rank or occupation of deceased's father; maiden name of deceased's mother (with a notation if they are deceased); qualification of informant and residence, if out of house in which the death occurred.

The information given in certificates in 1855 is even more extensive and the researcher is strongly advised to make the effort to find an ancestor, even if not a direct one, being born, married or dying in that year.

(b) Although there has been an official Census return every ten years since 1801, as in England, those of genealogical value started in 1841 (with the same limitations as its English equivalent), being followed in 1851 by the more comprehensive Return.

Census Returns can be consulted on microfilm at New Register House in Edinburgh and in various cities throughout Scotland.

Parochial Records

(a) All the Presbyterian Parish Registers of Scotland (usually known as the Old Parochial Registers) are in the custody of the Registrar General for Scotland, where they can be inspected, and in much the same way as in England they give details of baptisms, marriage proclamations and burials.

The records of some 900 parishes were kept by their Presbyterian ministers, and most date from about 1740 (except the Western Isles). However, no uniform method for recording baptisms, proclamations or burials was in force and therefore the details vary considerably from one parish to another, but burial registers were often not kept at all. All the baptismal and marriage entries in these registers have been indexed by county by the GSU and are widely available on microfiche.

(b) Scotland, too, was racked by religious dissention, and for non-Presbyterian or nonconformist records, the Scottish Record Office has various valuable and useful collections of records, and the Registrar General has custody of a small collection of nonconformists records, a handlist of which is available from New Register House. These by no means represent the full extent of dissent in Scotland.

Naming Customs

Although there are some variations on the theme, many families in Scotland followed a highly developed system for naming their children, whereby the eldest son is named after his paternal grandfather; the second son after

his maternal grandfather; the third son after his father; the eldest daughter is named after her maternal grandmother; the second daughter after her paternal grandmother; the third daughter after her mother.

Thus, it is important to note the names and details of any sponsors or witnesses where they occur in records, which, when examined in the light of the naming customs, can provide useful leads.

Wills

There are many printed indexes to wills (Testaments) and Letters of Administration (Testaments Dative), which have been published by the Scottish Record Society, giving details of testaments recorded in the Commissary courts, the earliest of which was in Edinburgh and dates from 1514.

There are also indexes for all Commissariots until 1800, and typescript indexes are available for the twenty years or so thereafter, until the Commissariot jurisdiction was transferred to the Sheriff courts.

Thereafter, records of testaments and their indexes formed part of the Sheriff Court Records, which are kept in the Scottish Record Office.

Unfortunately there is no national index as such, and it is necessary, therefore, to search in the regional indexes. However, a *Register of Confirmations*, giving the value of the estate, the executors and the sheriffdom in which the testament was confirmed, is available from 1876 onward, as also is a printed *Register of Defuncts* (testators) largely culled from Sheriff Court Records for part of the nineteenth century. Present-day confirmations are dealt with at Register House, whereas the older records prior to 1823 are held in the Scottish Record Office.

Monumental Inscriptions

Certain additional information as to trades or professions is sometimes incorporated on Scottish tombstones. In the eighteenth century it was common practice to put only the initials of the head of the family and his wife, and the year in which the stone was erected (often that of the first death in the family, or the date of acquisition of the lair, or grave-plot), together with certain symbols denoting trades (as listed below), as well as those denoting mortality.

Baker — baker's peel or shovel decorated with loaves

Barber — scissors and comb or razor, and occasionally a bleeding bowl

Butcher — a cleaver
Cooper — a head knife
Farmer — plough-share or coulter, or oxen yoke
Gardener — spade and rake
Hammerman — crown and hammer
Maltman — spade and broom
Mariner — ship/compass/coil of rope, nautical quadrant (like a sextant) or mariner's cross/star
Mason — mell and chisel
Merchant — a pair of scales, or the figure 4
Miller — the mill-rind (the heraldic moline)
Shoemaker or Cordiner — a crown and a circular knife
Smith — crown and hammer, with pincers and horseshoe
Tailor — scissors and tailor's 'goose' (iron)
Weaver — shuttle or stretcher

Scottish monumental inscriptions can be very informative, but beware the habit of 'revising' the tombstone, where the first entries are erased to make way for later burials. A comprehensive collection of lists giving details of monumental inscriptions is available at the Scottish Record Office, or local lists are available at local libraries.

Services of Heirs

This register is useful in that it identifies many people who died intestate, together with the jury's decree as to whom the deceased's heirs should be. The registers, which are partly indexed, span some 500 years until 1847 (when the system was superseded by decrees of sheriffs) and are housed at the Scottish Record Office.

Register of Sasines

The General Register of Sasines, which is housed in the Scottish Record Office, dates from 1617, when the Scottish Parliament decreed that General and Particular Registers should be kept. It is still in use and exceeds 50,000 volumes. The register provides fairly comprehensive registration of the ownership of all land in Scotland from then until now, except for land within the royal burghs which was recorded from 1681. Through it, it should be possible for the researcher to trace the ownership of even a small piece of land over many generations. As land usually descends within a family, details of relationships can often be gleaned. There is also an abridged printed register dating from 1781, referring to the main registers, which can reduce the amount of searching required.

Registers of Deeds

The Registers of Deeds housed in the Scottish Record Office, and exceeding 12,000 volumes, have been described as 'an inexhaustible store of information about the private life of our forefathers'. They date from 1554 and include bonds, indentures, marriage contracts, protests and writs, together with a vast array of other material with which the researcher can clothe the skeleton. Other records include the *Calendar of Deeds* from 1554 to 1595, and the *Register of Acts and Decrees*, together with the indexes from 1750 onward (except 1755 to 1770).

The Registers of Deeds are a vast repository of information. Greater detail can be obtained from *The Public Records of Scotland*, by J. Maitland Thomson (1922).

Hearth and Poll Tax Records

The Hearth Money accounts of 1690–3, giving the names of the heads of households which had hearths, and the Poll Tax records of 1694 and 1695 are kept at the Scottish Record Office.

In addition, various other tax rolls, including valuation rolls and window tax rolls, are available for the sixteenth, seventeenth and eighteenth centuries; and from 1855 the Valuation Rolls, giving details of proprietors and tenants of all properties, are also available.

Service Records

Service Records peculiar to Scotland are housed at the Scottish Record Office, and are included in the Register of the Privy Council for Scotland, 1545–1691.

The Treasury records include many muster rolls.

Prior to the Union, records become rather more specialised, and reference should be made to the bibliography of the publications mentioned in the General section below, which relate to service records.

The records of Scottish regiments in the British Army are held at the PRO, Kew, although many of them have their own museums and record offices in Scotland.

Heraldry

The Court of the Lord Lyon at New Register House is the Scottish equivalent of the College of Arms. However, in Scotland heraldry is governed by statute law, and the Lord Lyon King of Arms as a judge of the Lyon Court sits in judgement. Unlike England, he is armed with sufficient powers to command rather greater respect and obedience, and besides his role as a judge he is also a Minister of the Crown, and responsible direct to the Sovereign for all Scottish heraldic and genealogical matters, as well as for all matters relating to clans, their chiefs, tartan, badges and designations, etc. The records of his court, and particularly those dating from 1672 (which contain the *Public Register of All Arms and Bearings in Scotland* in 64 volumes, and the *Public Register of All Genealogies and Birthbrieves* in 4 volumes) form part of the public records of Scotland and can be inspected by the public on payment of a nominal fee. There are many practical differences between English and Scottish heraldry, but in simple terms only the eldest son of someone rightly entitled to arms inherits his father's arms undifferenced. All younger sons have only the right to matriculate a differenced version of their paternal arms, and this then forms the basis of the arms of that line. The system encourages cadets to update their pedigrees, and this is invaluable for the researcher and makes the Lyon Office records an exceedingly valuable source of information, especially bearing in mind that in 1707 a third of the population were deemed to have been noble. Details of all Scottish Coats of Arms from 1672 to 1973 are given in *An Ordinary of Scottish Arms, 1672 to 1902*, by Sir James Balfour Paul, with Volume 2 by David Read (of Robertland) and Vivien Wilson covering 1902 to 1973.

For further information about Scottish heraldry, see *Scots Heraldry*, by Sir Thomas Innes of Learney, revised by Malcolm Innes of Edingight.

General

In so short an article, one cannot possibly do justice to the many record repositories and sources covering many hundreds of years. There are equivalent Scottish repositories for newspapers (from 1700) and estate and family papers in abundance, many of which are catalogued in the National Register of Archives at the Scottish Record Office. For those wishing to pursue the subject in greater detail, the following general books are particularly recommended.

Hamilton-Edwards, Gerald *In Search of Scottish Ancestry* (Phillimore)

Steel, D.J., *The National Index of Parish Registers*, Vol. XII, SOG (1993)

Tracing Your Scottish Ancestry by K.B. Cory, Edinburgh (1990).

Each of these publications contains a valuable bibliography for those wishing to study a particular subject in depth. It is probable that the researcher will need to employ expert help in consulting many of these rather specialised records. Not only are the language and the handwriting very different, but many of the registers are exceedingly voluminous, which makes the services of an experienced record searcher all the more valuable. The Association of Scottish Genealogists and Record Agents has a number of members who specialise in Scottish research.

Scutage   An annual money payment to a feudal lord. The practice (which developed within a century after the Conquest) of holding land of more than one lord made Knight Service difficult to operate. Also, knights grew old and might be succeeded by daughters only; so tenants in respect of whom such conditions arose were allowed to pay in lieu of service a sum of money which the lord would use toward paying a man-at-arms. This payment was called scutage, or 'shield-money', from the Latin *scutum* (a shield). In the twelfth century it was assessed at 20 shillings per whole knight's fee, payable annually in two instalments, at Easter and Michaelmas.

Sea, Births and Deaths at   Since 1 July, 1837, ships' captains have returned a certificate of each event to the Registrar General of Shipping and Seamen, giving the name(s) of the person(s) concerned, the date and place (latitude and longitude), the sex, occupation, rank or rating, and nationality; and, in cases of death, the age, birthplace, last place of abode, and cause of death. The *Marine Register Books* recording these events are at the General Register Office. The International Genealogical Index also includes a section of events 'at sea' which should not be overlooked.

See also MERCHANT SEAMEN.

Secessionists   Presbyterians who seceded from the Church of Scotland c. 1733.

Secretary Hand   The great majority of sixteenth- and seventeenth-century records are written in this script. By the year 1700 it had given place to the italic hand which is very like our own. Two alphabets of Secretary Hand are shown here: the first consists of extracts from a sixteenth-century copybook and shows how the letters were meant to be formed; the second

A Secretary Hand alphabet extracted from a sixteenth-century copybook, showing how the letters were meant to be written. They should be compared with the examples shown on pages 262–3. (C.H. = draws attention to Court Hand letters radically different from their Secretary Hand counterparts.)

shows examples of how the letters are usually found in seventeenth-century texts written by clerks who were not calligraphers.

The first sight of a document in Secretary Hand can be daunting, but fluent reading is simply a matter of getting used to it and being aware of certain difficulties presented by it — difficulties that were almost certainly responsible for its eventual supercession. These are:

Lower case letters

a The only difficulty with this letter occurs when it is written with a diagonal ascender, which gives it a very unexpected look.

b and *l* These can look very alike if the circle of the b is small.

c and *t* These are often difficult to distinguish, and c is sometimes used where today we use a t; for example, in words ending in -ation.

d, e and *o* The e is most frequently found written without the pen having been taken off the paper, which makes it look very like an o with a small, accidental-looking circle at the top. Sometimes, too, this continuous action with the pen disconnects the smaller circle altogether from the larger one, and makes the letter look very like a d. For an example of this, compare the examples of e shown in the seventeenth-century alphabet with the second and third d.

f and *s* The f should have a short stroke across it, which is absent from the s, but sometimes it is missing. Both letters are often written with loops, both in the ascender and the descender. The s at the end of a word is written as the last two examples shown in the copybook alphabet and the second, fourth and sixth in the seventeenth-century alphabet. At that period, many words were spelt with a final e that is not used now; the plural 'es' was represented by what looks like a curly figure 9.

g, y and *th* The descender of the g tails away to the left, and that of the y to the right. The sound 'th' at the beginning of a word is often represented by the Anglo-Saxon letter called 'thorn'. It can be confused with the y, but, unlike that Secretary Hand letter, it is open at the top and its descender tails away to the left. This makes it identical with a modern y, but it should always be transcribed as it sounded, i.e. as 'th'.

h This letter is nearly always scrawled as in the last three examples shown in the seventeenth-

BELOW AND OPPOSITE Secretary Hand alphabets showing the letters as they are often found. They should be compared with the copybook alphabet on page 261, on which they are based. *Drawn by Alf Ison*

century alphabet, but it is easily recognised from having both an ascender and a descender, and the latter, unlike those of f and s, tails away to the right.

i, m and *n*, also *u* and *j* The first three are made up of minims. A minim is a single short downward stroke, which by itself represents the letter i. Two of them form an n, and three make up either m, 'in' or 'ni' (the dot is often missing).

Sample letters from the 17th century

(handwritten letter forms and examples)

= per, par

= pre, pri

= pro

- - - - indicate omission

= the

= she   = her   = his

= parish

Abbreviations

contractions

manñer — manner
commoy — common
that
Mr (Mister)
Majestie

and horizontal line developed to:

John
William
Wiltshire

signs

Ω = er   oury — every

$\wp$ = es   dayr — day
sayr — days

propertie

names

P (thorn)   ye — the
            ym — them
            yt — that

3 (yog)   Mongies   . . . . .

To make matters worse, the letter u, as generally written, is undistinguishable from n. Also, the letters i and j were largely interchangeable, so that three minims can also represent 'ju'.

j See above.

k and *t* The lower, smaller loop of the k is often difficult to make out, and the larger loop, in the ascender, fails to ascend much, so that the latter looks at first glance like a t. But any sign of a loop indicates a k. (For t, see also c and *t* above.)

l, m, n and *o* See above.

p The letter itself is fairly simple, though it can sometimes look like a carelessly written y; but with variations it can represent any one of several syllables. The sounds 'par' (as in parish) and

ABOVE A neatly written sixteenth-century example of Secretary Hand. It reads: 'In the name of God Amen. the Fyvetene daye of March In the Yere of our Lord God A thousand Fyve hundreth three score & Seventene, I,/Symond Josslyn of Felsted in the Countie of Essex, yoman, beyng of holle Mynde & in good & parfight Remenbrance, I prayse & thanke/Almightie God for yt, do make & ordayne thys my present Testament & last Wyll in Maner & forme followyng, that ys to saye/Fyrst & pryncypallye I commend my Sowle to Almightie God my Maker, savior & onlye Redemer, And my bodye to be buryed/in the Church or Churchyerd of Felsted Aforsayd. Item, I gyve & bequeth to Margarett, my wyffe, & Raffe Josslyn, my sonne,/all & every those my landes, tenementes, leazes, medowes, pastures & growndes Whych I holde by copye of Courtt Roule of the maner of/Felsted To have, hold to occupye togither from the daye of my death forthwardes duryng all the tyme & As long as she, the sayd/'. Apart from the handwriting, these lines from a will supply instructive examples of the kind of spelling and capitalisation to be expected, and the use of 'y' where we write 'i'; also the ampersand and the commonly found abbreviated syllable 'pre-' in 'present'. *Reproduced by courtesy of the Essex Record Office*

'per' are indicated by the letter p with its descender curving up to the left and turning back across itself to the right. Sometimes this appears as no more than a stroke across the descender. The syllables 'pre' and 'pri' are indicated by keeping the pen on the paper after finishing the p, and making an upward flourish to the right of the letter and curving back to the left above it. The sound 'pro' is formed by continuing the curve of the p across the descender and then down and across again to the right.

q presents no difficulty.

r A letter often difficult to recognise, because it tends to be written in different ways, even in the same document.

s and t See above.

u and v These are largely interchangeable. At the beginning of a word, u is usually written as a v. (For u, see also above.)

w This is formed as a double v.

x This letter is also used for the ampersand, '&'. With a c following it, it stands for 'et cetera'.

y See above.

z This letter is very like the modern version.

Capitals

These are more difficult than the lower case letters, partly because there is usually more than one way in which they could be written, and partly because they so often (but by no means always) begin proper names, which themselves tend to be difficult because they cannot be deduced from the sense of the text, as other words so often can. Compare the letters closely with all the examples given in these two alphabets. The capital letter F was formed by combining two lower case ones, and should be transcribed as a capital, not as two small ffs.

Abbreviations and contractions

Medieval Latin texts were written in an exact system of these, and English texts came to be treated in the same way, but to a lesser extent.

For the Latin there were various signs above the line to indicate exactly the nature of the shortening in each case, but by the sixteenth century these had degenerated into mere dashes or flourishes above the word, which did little more than indicate the use of some unspecified abbreviation or contraction. Often the writer merely kept his pen on the paper at the end of the word, and his superscribed sign became just a flourish curling up from the last letter. When a flourish of this sort (except after p) occurs in the middle of a word, it indicates the missing letters 'er'.

The contractions of syllables starting with a p have been described above. Sometimes an abbreviation is indicated by writing only one or two letters above the line. Our cardinal numbers (e.g. 1st, 2nd) are a survival of this practice.

Spelling

When trying to make out a word, remember that it may not be spelt as it is today, or even as elsewhere in the same text.

Two pieces of general advice can be given. When you first need to read a Secretary Hand text, set out to transcribe it in full. Leave a gap for any word or part of a word that you cannot read, and press on to the end. By the time you get there you will be more used to the handwriting and will be able to fill in some of the gaps. Then, read your transcript through, and the sense of the document will enable you to fill in still more. If any unsolved difficulties remain, study them carefully and search the record for other occurences of them. These, in their context, may have caused you no trouble and will now enable you to complete your transcript.

The second piece of advice is to transcribe in full the first example of each particular type of document you consult. You can then use your transcript as a guide on future occasions, because the same words and phrases will crop up in all documents of the same type, and knowing what to expect is half the battle.

At first sight, Secretary Hand may look formidable, but one does not have to be clever to read it. Every seventeenth-century schoolboy did so. It is simply a matter of practice.
See *Reading Tudor and Stuart Handwriting* by Lionel Munby (1988).
See also HANDWRITING.

Secular Clergy　Priests not in any monastic order.

Seisin　Legal possession with occupation. To disseise is to dispossess.
See also LIVERY; TERRE TENANT.

Seize Quartiers　It is said that to gain admission to the court of Louis XIV, French nobles had to be able to show that all their (sixteen) great-great-grandparents were of armigerous families. In England the term has been adopted to refer to any person's complete set of great-great-grandparents, without any armorial connotation. For young people of the late twentieth century, the identifying of all members of their great-great-grandparents' generation is often not difficult, thanks to the General Register of Births, Deaths and Marriages.

Selion　A strip of arable land in the common fields of a manor, normally about 22 yards (20 metres) in length. The team ploughing it kept going in the same direction, round and round the strip in narrowing turns, so that each furrow turned the soil inwards, eventually making a ridge along the centre of the selion. The lowest furrow round the outside acted as a drain. This practice is known as 'ridge and furrow ploughing'. Several adjacent selions made up a furlong. A selion was also called a 'land' or 'strip'.

Seneschal　Another word for steward, from the Latin *seneschallus*.

Sentence　A judgement of an ecclesiastical court regarding a disputed will. Alternatively referred to as 'decree'

Separatists *see* **Brownists**

Serf　An inhabitant of a manor whose status was even lower than that of a villein, in that even his body belonged to his lord. In England, serfdom, common at the time of Domesday, soon thereafter became extinct.

Sergeant-at-Law　In the Middle Ages, a highly qualified lawyer. He was said to be 'of the degree of the coif', from the white silk coif that he was entitled to wear. The equivalent of the modern Queen's Counsel.

Serjeanty　A type of tenure intermediate between knight service and socage. Land was held on condition of the performance of a certain individual service, other than those classed under knight service. This might be anything from service in the army of a special kind, escort service, keeping a gaol, or providing an armed man, down to rendering up some small article such as a sword or dagger each year, or even a specified flower at midsummer. These small payments were called 'renders', and tenure by virtue of them was known as petty-serjeanty. The more onerous services constituted grand-serjeanty, and the holder of such a tenure was liable to wardship if he inherited while he was under age.
See also WARDS AND LIVERIES, COURT OF.

Servitude *see* **Livery Companies**

Sessions, Special　Monthly meetings of Justices of the Peace on an informal basis. Few records survive, but some may be found at the county record office.

Settlement　A legal right to poor relief, arising out of a settled place of abode. By the *Poor Law Act* of 1601, a person was recognised as being legally a settled inhabitant of a parish after a month's abode. Parish vestries soon began to use this principle to operate an unofficial system of

RIGHT A handsome example of Secretary Hand in a parish apprenticeship from 1673. *Courtesy Berkshire Record Office*

Know all men by these presents that I Christian Bombey ... of the County of ... one of the Daughters of Thomas (Bombey) ... of Brimington in the County of ...

... John Osborne and William ... Osborne and ... Phillipps ...

Know all men by these presents ...

refusing relief to paupers who had settlement elsewhere.

The *Settlement Act* of 1662 laid the basis of the law of settlement for the next two centuries. Anyone entering a township and occupying a tenement worth less than £10 per annum might, within the next forty days, be removed by the parochial Overseers of the Poor, acting on an order from two Justices of the Peace who had examined him on oath. He would then be escorted, by the constable or by a series of constables along the route, back to the place where he was considered to be legally settled, unless he could give security for indemnity against becoming chargeable to the parish. However, if he managed to stay for forty days, he obtained settlement at his new abode.

In a family, a child's place of settlement was the same as his father's until he or she was apprenticed, which could happen at the age of seven. Then his place of apprenticeship would become his parish of settlement. Unmarried persons not apprenticed could obtain a new settlement after service in a parish for one year. At marriage, a woman took on the same settlement as her husband.

Illegitimate children were granted settlement where they were born. This led Overseers to try to get rid of women pregnant with bastards. If the child was born while the mother was actually under an order of removal, it was given the same settlement as hers.

From 1685, the forty days' removal period began from the date of delivery in writing to the Overseers of a notice of residence. This led to private compassionate arrangements between paupers and Overseers; so, in 1691, the forty days were made to begin from the publication of the notice in church. It is from this year that records of removal begin.

In 1697, an Act circumvented paupers who hired themselves to serve a master or mistress for a year but actually quitted their service after a few weeks. It also took the important step of authorising the Overseers to issue Settlement Certificates to paupers of their parish, but this issue was of grace, not of right. The document eased the pauper's temporary acceptance into another parish (e.g. for helping with the harvest), since it enabled the parish authorities there to send him back where he had come from if he even looked like becoming chargeable to them. In fact, the parish into which he moved was given the right of demanding such a certificate.

In 1795, removal by the Overseers was forbidden unless the pauper became actually chargeable to the parish, which did away with much of the injustice of the law. Though the *Settlement Act* was repealed in 1834, the principle of settlement remained substantially in force until 1876, and was finally removed from the statute book in 1948.

The main documents relating to settlement are:

(i) The *Indemnity Certificate of Settlement*, given to the pauper by his own churchwardens.

(ii) The *Examination* of the pauper by churchwardens or a magistrate, prior to the issue of a *Removal Order*. This mentions his family, recent moves, and other valuable information.

(iii) The *Removal Order*, made out in duplicate, after application by the Overseer to two Justices of the Peace; one copy was for each parish concerned.

(iv) Quarter Sessions records of appeals against removal orders, sometimes with counsel's opinion on the case.

(v) Vestry minutes and the accounts of overseers and constables.

Most of the above are to be found at county record offices, but some of the parochial records may still be kept at parish churches. In these records, 'pass' was a term meaning 'send to his/her parish of settlement'.

Severalty Land 'in severalty' was held outside the conditions of common tenure customary in a manor. 'Several' meant 'separate', and so 'private'.

Shack The right of grazing upon the common arable and meadow lands of a manor after the crop has been taken.
See also LAMMAS.

Shareware A computer program for which the user pays by sending a registration fee to the publisher after a free evaluation period. Evaluation copies are available from BULLETIN BOARDS or from a shareware distributor. After registration, the user generally receives a printed manual and, sometimes, an enhanced version of the program.

Sheffield and District Family History Society *see* **Yorkshire**

RIGHT A Settlement Examination revealing valuable biographical information. Note that the word 'Earl' has been accidentally omitted from the second line. *Courtesy Guildford Muniment Room*

Guildford Town,
IN THE COUNTY OF
Surrey.

Voluntary

The **Examination** of Dorothy Brinkwell — now residing in the Parish of the Blessed Virgin Mary —

in the said Town Poor Widow taken on Oath the seventh day of July 1820 before — John Nealds Esquire Mayor and Samuel Russell Esquire two — of his Majesty's Justices of the Peace for the said Town,

Who on her — Oath saith that upwards of forty years ago she — hired herself as a yearly Servant to the Earl of Winterton of Shillingley in the parish of Kirdford in the County of Sussex and lived with him as a yearly Servant upwards of five years and she believes — that the last forty days of her service were performed in the said parish of Kirdford — That on quitting the service of the Earl of Winterton she intermarried with John Brinkwell of the parish of the Blessed Virgin Mary in Guildford aforesaid Plumber and Glazier And that the said John Brinkwell at the time of his death which happened about twenty eight years ago he was a settled parishioner in the parish of the Blessed Virgin Mary And this Examinant further saith that she hath done no Act whatever since the decease of her said Husband whereby to gain a legal settlement either by renting a Tenement or by service or otherwise

Sworn before me,
John Nealds
Mayor

S. Russell

Dorothy Brinkwell
her × mark

Sheriff The chief official of a county. At the Conquest, the administration of the shires was placed in the hands of the earls, but as that rank became hereditary, and the work increased, the authority and duties passed to the sheriff. The office was for a time elective, but later by royal appointment through the Exchequer. Sometimes one man held the post for two adjacent counties. The sheriffs' functions were progressively reduced as many of them were passed to Commissioners of Array, coroners, Justices of the Peace, tax-collectors and, in the sixteenth century, to Lieutenants.

Ship's Passenger Lists *see* **Passenger Lists**

Shop A workshop. Not until the nineteenth century was the term used to mean a retail outlet, although in earlier times goods were quite often sold direct from the workshop in which they were made.

Shot (i) Another name for furlong, or in some places, for a selion.

(ii) A body of soldiers or militiamen armed with firearms.

Shropshire The county lies within the dioceses of Hereford, Lichfield and St Asaph and the Province of Canterbury. A large proportion of the 229 ancient parish registers are now at the CRO and copies of many of them are in the library of the SOG. Boyd's Marriage Index covers 125 and Pallot's Marriage Index covers 119, mostly from 1790. The Bishops' Transcripts and the Marriage Licence records are kept at the Lichfield Record Office for the Northern part of the county, at Hereford Record Office for the Southern part of the county and a few at the National Library of Wales for St Asaph diocese.

The Hundreds of North Albrighton, Bradford (Drayton, Wem and Whitchurch Divisions), South Bradford (Newport and Wellington Divisions), Brimstree (Bridgenorth, Hales-Owen and Shiffnall Divisions), Chirbury (Lower and Upper Divisions) Condover (Condover and Cound Divisions), Ford (Ford and Pontesbury Divisions), Munslow (Lower and Upper Divisions), Oswestry (Lower and Upper Divisions and Town and Liberties), Overs, Pimhill (Baschurch and Ellesmere Divisions), Purslow (Bishop's Castle and Stow Divisions), Clun (Clun and Mainstone Divisions), Stottesden (Chelmarsh and Cleobury Divisions), Bridgenorth Borough, Ludlow Borough, Shrewsbury Borough and Liberties and Wenlock Borough lie within its boundaries.

It has Ludlow, Clun, Church Stretton, Cleobury Mortimer, Bridgenorth, Shifnal, Madeley, Atcham, Shrewsbury, Oswestry, Ellesmere, Wem, Market Drayton, Wellington and Newport RDs/PLUs.

It falls within the Oxford Assize Circuit.

The Shropshire Family History Society meets at Shrewsbury and publishes a quarterly journal.

The records are kept at the Shropshire Record Office, the Shropshire County Library and the Shrewsbury Borough Archives.

Pre 1858 Wills are kept at Lichfield Record Office and were proved at the Royal Peculiar Court of Bridgnorth, the Peculiar Courts of Buildwas and Wombridge Abbeys, the Manorial Court of Ellesmere, the Manor Court of Longton-on-Tern and the Prebendal Court of Prees or Pipe Manor. Those for the Peculiar Court of Ashford Carnbonal are at Hereford Record Office. Wills could also be proved in the Consistory Courts of Lichfield, Hereford and St Asaph and the Prerogative Court of Canterbury.

The Shropshire Archaeological Society has published a number of county records. Heralds' Visitation Pedigrees have been published for 1623 and 1663.

See *Sources of Shropshire genealogy*, by S.C. Clifford (Shropshire FHS, 1993). See aslo *National Index of Parish Registers*, vol. 5 (1966).

Siblings Brothers and/or sisters with at least one parent in common.

Sigla A word abbreviated to a single letter, sometimes preceded and followed by a full stop; for example, .s. (*scilicet*), .f. (*folio*) and .n. (*enim*). Commonly encountered in documents written in medieval Latin.

Sign Manual A handwritten signature, especially of the sovereign.

Silly Innocent, simple.

Single A 'single person' maybe a divorced person; a 'single woman' may be one who had borne a child, though unmarried.

Sinister The left-hand side of a shield bearing a coat of arms when held from behind.

Sir (i) The title, placed before both Christian name and surname, of baronets and knights, and before the Christian name alone in the oral form of address.

(ii) Until the sixteenth century, a courtesy title for a priest who was not a university graduate; translated into Latin as *dominus*.

Sister A term often used to designate a sister-in-law. Sometimes, to make clear which is meant, a real sister is referred to as 'my own sister'.

Six Clerks Prothonotaries in the Chancery Court they recorded and filed all records in equity causes in Memoranda Books. Each had about ten underclerks (sixty clerks).

Size A kind of candle.

Slavery After a court decision of 1772, all slaves in this country became free, but this ruling did not affect those in the colonies. In 1807, an Act of Parliament abolished the slave-trade in the British dominions and this provision was strengthened by an Act of 1811, but the ownership of existing slaves remained. To check that the trade from Africa to the colonies was not continuing, slaves on the plantations had to be registered, and the lists were checked from time to time against the facts. These records, arranged under islands, parishes and plantations, are at the Public Record Office, Kew, in class T 71. They give the slaves' names, ages and occupations, 'colour' (negro, mulatto or mestee), and 'country' (African or Creole). In 1833, an Act converted all British-owned domestic slaves into apprenticed labourers as from 1 August, 1834, and they were to be made completely free in 1840. This latter date was later brought forward to August, 1838, but by then many plantations had already freed their slaves. The T 71 class of records also lists the numbers of slaves as at 1 August, 1834, giving their value and the proportional compensation to be paid for them by the British Government.

Smoke-penny One of the dues once payable at Eastertime to the incumbent of a parish by his parishioners; in this case, from the occupier of a house with a fireplace.

Socage A form of feudal tenure in which the land was held in return for a money rent. Although no knight service was required, the tenant still had to do fealty to the king.

Society of Archivists *see* **Archives**

Society of Genealogists *see* **Genealogists, Society of**

Socman An early term for a tenant who held his land in socage.

Soiled Land Land originally held freehold, but converted to villein or copyhold tenure.

Sojourner A temporary resident in a parish.

Soke District under a particular court's law.

Solemn League and Convenant On 25 September, 1643, the Members of the House of Commons took a covenant to which, in the following year, all males above the age of 18 in areas controlled by Parliament were expected to subscribe. It committed them to the reformation of religion (Protestantism), the extirpation of popery and prelacy, the preservation of the rights of Parliament and the person and authority of the king, and the exposure of all malignants (Royalists). The returns were kept locally among the parish records and only the names of refusers were sent in to Westminster. Surviving lists will now be either in church vestries or at county record offices.

Solar (i) An upper room or loft.
(ii) A room for the owner of the house, separate from the hall, which was commonly used by all the household.

Solicitor In 1875 proctors, attorneys and solicitors all became known as solicitors. Prior to that the distinction between them was that a solicitor specialised in equity matters; an attorney practised in the superior courts of common law representing suitors who did not appear in person and proctors served in the ecclesiastical courts.

Somerset The northern part of the ancient county is now in the new county of Avon. The county lies within the diocese of Bath and Wells in the Province of Canterbury. Registers of most of the ancient parishes have been deposited at the CRO and the SOG has copies of nearly 400. Boyd's Marriage Index covers 120 parishes and Pallot's Marriage Index covers 160, mostly for 1790–1812. The Bishops' Transcripts and the Marriage Licence records are at the CRO.

The Hundreds of Abdick and Bulstone, Andersfield, Bath-Forum, Bempstone, Brent with Wrington, Bruton, Cannington, Carhampton, Catsash, Chew, Chewton, Crekerne, North Curry, Frome, Glaston-Twelve-Hides, Hampton and Claverton, Hartcliffe with Bedminster, Horethorne, Houndsborough, Barwick and Coker, Huntspill and Puriton, Keynsham, Kilmersdon, East and West Kingsbury, Martock, Mells and Leigh Liberty, Milverton, Norton-Ferris, North

One hundred years separates the illustrations ABOVE and RIGHT. The engraving, published in the *Illustrated London News* of 1875, shows the Search Hall of what is now called the Principal Registry of the Family Division, Somerset House. The photograph RIGHT (*Copyright Skyline Publications Ltd*) shows how little things have changed.

and South Petherton, Pitney, Portbury, Somer-
ton, Stone, Taunton and Taunton-Deane, Tintin-
hull, Wellow, Wells-Forum, Whitstone, Whitley,
Williton and Freemanners, Winterstoke, Bath
City, Bridgewater, Bristol City and Taunton Boroughs lie within its boundaries.

It has Williton (later Dulverton), Wellington,
Taunton, Bridgewater, Langport, Chard, Yeovil,
Wincanton, Frome, Shepton Mallet, Wells,
Axbridge, Clutton, Bath, Keynsham and
Bedminster RDs/PLUs.

It falls within the Western Assize Circuit.

Somerset and Dorset Family History Society
meets at Stalbridge, Street, Taunton, Yeovil,
Broadstone, Weymouth and Beaminster and
publish the *Greenwood Tree* quarterly. The
Weston-Super-Mare Family History Society
meets at Worle Library and publishes a twice-
yearly journal.

Somerset Record Office is in Taunton, Somerset County Reference Library is in Bridgewater
and the Bath City Record Office is in Bath. There
is a Family History Centre in Yeovil.

Until 1942 the probate records of the Diocese
of Bath and Wells were held at the Probate Registry in Exeter but they were then destroyed by
bombing. However, indexes, calendars and
extracts have been collected at the CRO and
Estate Duty Office copies from 1812. Wills could
also be proved in the Prerogative Court of
Canterbury.

The SOG has transcripts of Memorial Inscriptions from about 150 churchyards.

The Somerset Record Society has published
early local records since 1837. Heralds' Visitation
Pedigrees have been printed for 1623.

See *Primary genealogical sources in the Somerset
Record Office* (1983) and *Somerset: a genealogical bibliography*, by S. Raymond (FFHS, 1991).

Somerset House   The location of the Divorce
and Probate registries from 1858.

Son-in-law   A term often used to mean 'step-
son'. The existence of a son-in-law is often concealed, when his surname is not mentioned,
under the term 'son'.

Soul-Scot   A customary payment to the
parish incumbent for a burial, paid at the open
grave.

South African Ancestry   The Cape of Good
Hope was known to early Portuguese sailors
such as Dias and de Saldanha and, indeed, Natal
was named by da Gama in 1497. Others followed, such as Sir Francis Drake and in 1620 two

British captains tried to proclaim British sovereignty in the Cape but this was not confirmed
and the opportunity was lost. It was not until
the Dutch East India Company sent van Riebeeck
and about 90 men, women and children to open
a victualling station there in 1652, that any
attempt was made to colonise the area on a permanent basis. A small community was maintained at Cape Town to provide food supplies
and water for the company's ships en route to
and from the Indies. At first the community was
not allowed to grow crops for their own profit
but later free burghers were allotted farms of
their own.

To supplement the work force on the farms
and in the settlement itself, slaves were imported
from Angola, West Africa, Madagascar, Mozam-
bique and the East. It was not until 1806 that this
slave trade was abolished by the British and not
until 1838 that all slaves in the Cape were
released. There is still an important Islamic community in the Cape which is descended from
slaves and political prisoners from the East.

A limited trade was established with indigen-
ous Khoikhoi (or Hottentot) herdsmen but it was
many years before often violent contact was
made with Bantu-speaking peoples along the
south-east coast and in the far interior. Over
the years a few trek-boers (cattlemen who led a
nomadic life) ventured further into the vast areas
beyond Cape Town in order to escape from the
Company's harsh rule and who, generation after
generation, slowly moved further afield. At this
time no organised settlement was encouraged as
was done later in the United States, Australia
and New Zealand.

Towards the end of the seventeenth century
some two hundred Huguenot refugees who had
fled to Holland to escape persecution in France,
agreed to move to the Cape. By their hard work
and perseverance they became upstanding
members of the community into which they
became fully integrated in a relatively short time,
even to the extent of dropping use of the French
language. Many Germans and Dutch also came
to the Cape as servants of the Company and
stayed.

The British arrived upon the scene in 1795
when they occupied the Cape to keep the French
out. They stayed only until 1803 when the area
was handed back to the Batavian Republic. However, in 1806 the British returned in order to
secure the route to India and from then on the
Cape remained a British Colony until the Union
of South Africa was established in 1910. Many
English, Scottish, Irish and Welsh pioneers
arrived from 1795 onwards and these included

small parties, such as the two hundred Scottish artisans brought out by Benjamin Moodie, and others. *British Residents at the Cape 1795–1819*, by Peter Philip lists biographical records of 4,800 pioneers. Then in 1820 some 4,500 British settlers arrived as assisted immigrants and were placed in the eastern Cape to provide a buffer against Bantu incursions.

Many Boer farmers became disillusioned with British rule and in 1836 the Great Trek began as a trickle of emigrant Boers which soon became a flood. Known as Voortrekkers, some 5,000 men, women and children set out in small parties into the unknown interior of the continent. Some found their way to Natal while others were instrumental in opening up and founding what were to become the Republics of the Orange Free State and the South African Republic (the Transvaal).

From 1849–1851 more than 4,000 British immigrants arrived in Natal in 57 shiploads, brought out by an enterprising Irishman named J.C. Byrne. Others came over the years independently or as assisted immigrants, including parties of juvenile and female immigrants.

The discovery of diamonds in the Cape Province in 1866 followed by gold in the Transvaal (the Witwatersrand Goldfields were proclaimed in 1886) brought many more immigrants as large numbers of fortune seekers scrambled into the country from all over the world. Then after the Anglo-Boer Wars numbers of soldiers decided to stay on in the country which was formed in 1910 by union of the colonies of Natal and the republics of the Orange Free State and the South African Republic. In 1961 the Union became a Republic.

Records are held in the national Archives Service's Depots in Cape Town, Bloemfontein, Pietermaritzburg and Pretoria (which are open to the public) and in several Intermediate Depots (which are not). Their holdings of Deceased Estate files and their computer retrieval sytem, which has some five million references, are of particular importance. The Department of Home Affairs' central registry of births, marriages and deaths is housed in Pretoria. Its records begin at various dates for each province, mainly in the late nineteenth century and at the beginning of this century, although marriage records in the Cape go back as far as 1701. Unfortunately neither these registers nor the relative indexes are open for examination by members of the public but applications for certificates may be submitted. The application for a full certificate must contain all relevant information to enable acceptable indentification to be made of the rela-

tive entry. Requests take anything up to six weeks to be processed. Certain regional registers of births, marriages and deaths are in the process of being passed by the Department of Home Affairs to the Archives Depots but these contain a minimum of information, are incomplete and bear embargoes which make examination difficult. No census returns survive.

Church records are spread around the country, with incumbents, parish or diocesan offices, libraries and universities. The best organised and preserved are the registers of the Dutch Reformed Church which maintains its own Archives in Cape Town, Bloemfontein, Pietermaritzburg and Pretoria. Many Church of the Province of Southern Africa (Anglican) records are with the University of the Witwatersrand while many Methodist records are with the Cory Library for Historical Research at Rhodes University.

Deceased Estate files are held initially by the various offices of the Master of the Supreme Court, in Cape Town, Bloemfontein, Kimberley, Grahamstown, Pietermaritzburg and Pretoria. All their older files are passed to the relative provincial archives depots. The most useful documents on these files are the Death Notices which often list three generations of persons but Wills, Liquidation and Distribution Accounts and other documents can all be of interest. Unfortunately the archives depots in Cape Town, Bloemfontein and Pietermaritzburg no longer allow photocopying of these records and it is necessary to find a local researcher prepared to visit the depot and make a written copy for you.

Among other sources of information are Deeds Registries (in Bloemfontein, Cape Town, Johannesburg, Kimberley, King William's Town, Pietermartizburg, Port Elizabeth, Pretoria and Vryburg). The Albany Museum in Grahamstown is particularly rich in material concerning the 1820 Settlers (but will no longer undertake research). The Kaffrarian Museum in King William's Town has much material regarding German settlers while French Huguenots are catered for by the Huguenot Museum in Franschhoek. There are Family History Centres, established by The Church of Jesus Christ of Latter-Day Saints in Benoni, Cape Town (Mowbray), Durban (Berea), East London, Johannesburg (Highlands), Port Elizabeth (Walmer), and Pretoria (Sunnyside): unfortunately their Centre in Bloemfontein is, at present, closed. The Human Sciences Research Council in Pretoria has a division for Biographical and Genealogical Research but holds no documents. They have produced a

Handbook for Genealogical Research in South Africa and publish family histories.

Among societies are the West Rand Family History Society, the South East Witwatersrand Family History Society and the Natal Midlands Family History Society. There is a society for the 1820 settlers, the Huguenot Society and various one name family associations. The Genealogical Society of South Africa has branches in Johannesburg, Pretoria, Durban, Pietermaritzburg, Port Elizabeth and Cape Town.

For emigrants to South Africa, 1814–25, see *Cape Colony Correspondence* CO 48 at the PRO, Kew. There are also Entry Books CO 49, and Registers CO 336 and 462.

Specialty A 'debt with specialties' was one documented under seal, for instance in a bond.

Spelling Until the mid eighteenth century, spelling was not considered a matter of great importance. In manuscripts, surnames are often spelt in various ways, even in the same document. However, the appearance of the dictionaries of Nathan Bailey (1730) and Samuel Johnson (1755) was a strong influence, both directly and through the standardisation of pronunciation, toward standardising spelling on an etymological basis. It must be remembered that in most records a surname was written not by the bearer, but by clerk who often had only the sound of the word to guide him. Thus names starting with an H may often be found written and indexed under the second letter, and vice versa for names starting with a vowel. The addition of a final s was, and still is, a common error. Many names have a number of customary spellings, for example Shephard, Shepherd, Shepard, Shepherd, Sheppard and Shepperd.

It has been well said that most of us have inherited the sounds of our names, rather than the spelling, and in the Gothic Revival of the 1820s and 1830s a number of people changed the spelling of their surnames to what they fancied was the original form. Smith became Smythe, and Fitzhugh became FitzHugh; and one or two families of names starting with F changed to a double small f, from a misunderstanding of the capital F of SECRETARY HAND. *See also* HANDWRITING.

Spiritualities The property of a monastery or church, such as its charters, communion vessels, etc.; and income from 'spiritual' sources, e.g. tithes, offerings, glebe and land held in FRANKALMOIGN. Secular assets were called temporalities.

Staffordshire The southern end of the ancient county is now in the new county of West Midlands. The county lies within the diocese of Lichfield and in the Province of Canterbury. About half the registers of the ancient parishes have been deposited, nearly all at the CRO. The SOG has transcripts of many of them. Pallot's Marriage Index covers 27 registers mostly for 1790–1812. The Bishops' Transcripts and the Marriage Licence Records are held at the Lichfield Joint Record Office.

The Hundreds of East and West Cuttlestone, North and South Offlow, North and South Pirehill, North and South Seisdon, North and South Totmonslow, Lichfield City and Borough, Newcastle-under-Lyme and Stafford Boroughs lie within its boundaries.

It has Stafford, Stone, Newcastle-under-Lyme, Wolstanton, Stoke-on-Trent, Leek, Cheadle, Uttoxeter, Burton-upon-Trent, Tamworth, Lichfield, Cannock, Wolverhampton, Walsall, West Bromwich and Dudley RDs/PLUs.

It falls within the Oxford Assize Circuit.

The Birmingham and Midland Society for Genealogy and Heraldry publishes *The Midland Ancestor* quarterly and has branches at Stoke-on-Trent, Wolverhampton and Burton-upon-Trent.

The records are kept at Staffordshire County Record Office, the William Salt Library and Staffordshire County Library in Stafford, Lichfield Joint Record Office in Lichfield, Sandwell District Library, West Bromwich, and Dudley Public Library. There are Family History Centres at Wednesfield, Lichfield and Newcastle-under-Lyme.

Pre 1858 Wills are kept at the Lichfield Joint Record Office. Wills were also proved in the Prerogative Court of Canterbury.

The Staffordshire Record Society (until 1936 the William Salt Archaeology Society) has published *Collections for a History of Staffordshire* since 1880. Heralds' Visitation Pedigrees have been published for 1583, 1614 and 1663–4.

Staffordshire Record Office publishes *History of a family*. See also *Tracing ancestors in North Staffordshire*, by H.E. Beech (1991) and *National Index of Parish Registers*, vol. 6, Part 1 (1992).

Stallage A tax levied by city and borough corporations for the priviledge of setting up a stall for a market or fair.

Stamp Duty When duties were collected on taxable items a stamp was affixed or impressed upon the item to show the tax had been paid.

Star Chamber, Court of The Court of the Lord of the Council at Westminster, popularly known as the Court of Star Chamber from its place of session, was one of the courts that grew out of the King's Council to afford justice that complainants found difficult to obtain in the ossified procedure of the courts of Common Law. It sat without a jury and its hearings were public. It was liked and respected until the reign of Charles I, when its decisions were used to favour the causes of the king and the Anglican Church, an abuse which led to its being abolished by the Long Parliament in 1641.

Records of the proceedings are at the Public Record Office, Chancery Lane, London, under group STAC, and those of Elizabeth I's reign have been indexed in *Lists and Indexes, Supplementary 4*, Vols 1–5. The Order Books showing how suits ended were destroyed during the Civil War. All evidence was taken in the form of written depositions (filed with the Bills and Answers), and these often reveal intimate information about a person's or family's circumstances and way of life.

State Papers   A collection of correspondence by royal officials, starting from early in the reign of Henry VIII. The State Paper Office was established in 1578 with two Secretaries of State, for the Northern and Southern Departments respectively. The records subsequently became separated into Domestic, Foreign and Colonial. The first and last have been calendared to the early eighteenth century, and the Foreign Papers for the reign of Elizabeth I. Forming one of the most important collections of documents in the Public Record Office, the State Papers are those of the Secretary of State to Whitehall. A keeper was appointed for them in 1610. They include policy and proclamations but also petitions from individuals and dealings in trade, military and ecclesiastical matters. They are calendared and indexed in the various classes in the SP group. After 1782 the affairs of the State Paper Office were handed over to the newly formed Home and Foreign Offices.

In 1782, the Foreign Office was created, with the Secretary of State for the Northern Department as its head. The *State Papers* series are now at the Public Record Office, Chancery Lane, London. The calendared volumes can also be found on the open shelves at the British Library, British Museum Reading Room, and contain, among much political material, items of biographical data, mainly of the gentry. The references to original documents in this series are: Edward VI's reign, SP 10; Mary, SP 11; Elizabeth, SP 12; Domestic Addenda, SP 13. The piece numbers are those of the volumes shown in the calendar, not those of the calendar volumes.

Steward   The senior administrative official of a manor, or of a monastery (for its temporal affairs); he was often a lawyer. The steward of a manor represented the lord, appointed the bailiff for the day-to-day management of the manor, and presided at manor courts unless the lord himself was present. Also termed the Seneschal. Monasteries commonly had a steward and a substeward. The latter did all the work, but the former had influence which he used in the monastery's favour.

Stewhouse   Originally a public bath-house, but the term came to apply to a brothel. A street of stewhouses was called 'the stews'.

Stint *see* **Gate** *and* **Waste**

Stipendary   A stipendary is one who receives a stipend or salary such as a salaried clergyman, magistrate or a military pensioner.

Stocks   A wooden structure for the punishment of petty offences. The delinquent sat on a bench in a public place, such as a village green, with his ankles through apertures in boards that were then locked in position. He was thus exposed to public ignominy and possible reprisals for a specified number of hours. This form of punishment dated from Anglo-Saxon times and was last used in 1865 at Rugby.

Strays   A stray is a recorded event in which a person is described in the record as being from, or connected with, a place outside the area in which they have been recorded. The Federation of Family History Societies is compiling a national index to such people. Individuals submit such entries, most frequently found in marriage and census records, to the Strays Clearing House (Mrs Thelma East, Brynroma, The Esplanade, Carmarthen, Dyfed SA31 1NQ) which publishes lists of such strays from time to time. No searches are made on behalf of enquirers.

Strip *see* **Selion**

Subinfeudation   The process by which a tenant-in-chief or his sub-tenant (a mesne lord) granted one or more of his fees to a further sub-tenant. The feudal service required of the sub-tenant might be knight service, or a portion of it, or something purely nominal such as the provision of a falcon or a rose at midsummer. In the last-mentioned case, the superior lord was giving away all his rights except those of wardship and escheat. A stop was put to this practice

by the *Statute of Quia Emptores* in 1291. A mesne lord's own feudal obligations arising from the land always passed to his sub-tenant.
See also MESNE LORD.

Subpoena, Writ of A writ of subpoena is issued to summon a witness or defendant to appear in court.

Subsidy *see* **Clerical Subsidy** *and* **Lay Subsidy**

Succentor A succentor is a deputy to a precentor and part of the cathedral chapter.

Succession, Law of In the Middle Ages the land of a deceased person could not pass by testament (*see* WILL). Under the Common Law it passed to the eldest male heir (*see* BOROUGH-ENGLISH; BURGESS TENURE; GAVELKIND; PRIMO-GENITURE). A man's movable goods were divisible at death into three parts: one for his widow, one for his children, and one that he could leave by testament as he wished. This practice gradually became obsolete. In cases of intestacy (which were the majority) the custom grew that one-third went to the widow and two-thirds to the children. If the wife had predeceased her husband, everything went to the children. If there was a widow but no children, half of the movable goods went to her and half to the deceased's next-of-kin (*see* CHATTELS). This practice was confirmed by the *Statute of Distributions* in 22 & 23 Charles II. When a will appears at first sight to give a widow less than her due, this Law of Succession should be borne in mind.

Suffragan Bishop A bishop whose function it is to offer assistance (suffrage) to an archbishop by performing certain duties in a diocese. He does not perform the full duties of that diocese.

Suit of Court The duty of attendance at the manor or hundred court. Absentees were obliged to provide excuses (essoins). Those who did not were listed as defaulters, and fined.

Suffolk The county falls within the diocese of Norwich in the Province of Canterbury. Nearly all the registers of the 504 ancient parishes have been deposited at the appropriate record office and the SOG has copies of many of them. Boyd's Marriage Index covers 489 registers. Pallot's Marriage Index covers 57, mostly from 1790–1812 or 1837. Marriage Licence records for the Archdeaconry of Sudbury are at the West Suffolk Record Office and those for the Archdeaconry of Suffolk are at the East Suffolk Record Office.

The Hundreds of Babergh, Blackbourn, Blything, Bosmere and Claydon, Carlford, Colneis, Cosford, Hartismere, Hoxne, Lackford, Loes, Mutford and Lothingland, Plomesgate, Risbridge, Samford, Stow, Thedwestry, Thingoe, Thredling, Wangford, Wilford, Bury St. Edmunds, Ipswich and Sudbury Boroughs lie within its boundaries.

It has Risbridge, Sudbury, Cosford, Thingoe, Bury St Edmunds, Mildenhall, Stow, Hartismere, Hoxne, Bosmere, Samford, Ipswich, Woodbridge, Plomesgate, Blything, Wangford and Mutford RDs/PLUs.

It fell within the Norfolk Assize Circuit until 1876 and then the South Eastern Assize Circuit.

The Suffolk Family History Society publishes *Suffolk Roots* quarterly and meets at Bury St Edmunds, Haverhill, Ipswich, Lowestoft, Saxmundham and Stowmarket. The Felixstowe Family History Society publishes *Roots and Branches* quarterly and meets in Felixstowe.

There are record repositories at Bury St Edmunds (West Suffolk) and Ipswich (East Suffolk). There is a Family History Centre at Ipswich.

Pre 1858 Wills are held at the West Suffolk Record office for the Archdeaconry of Sudbury and the Peculiar Courts of Isleham and Freckenham and at the East Suffolk Record Office for the Archdeaconry of Suffolk. Those proved at the Deanery of Bocking are in the Essex Record office. Wills could be proved in the Consistory Court of Norwich and the Prerogative Court of Canterbury.

The Suffolk Records Society has published an annual volume since 1958. Heralds' Visitation Pedigrees have been published for 1561, 1612 and 1664–8.

See *Guide to genealogical sources* (Suffolk Record Office, 1987), *Indexes for the Suffolk family historian*, by S. Bourne (1991), *National Index of Parish Registers*, vol. 7 (1983) and *Suffolk: a genealogical bibliography*, by S. Raymond (FFHS, 1992).

Suling A measure of land about twice the size of a HIDE, used in southeastern England.

Summoner The official who summoned people to appear before an ecclesiastical court. Also called an Apparitor.

Supporters Representations of creatures, real or imaginary, placed at the sides of an armorial shield in an achievement, and appearing to support it. The right to supporters is limited to peers, Knights of the Garter, Thistle and St Patrick, and Knights Grand Cross and Grand

Commanders of other Orders, though exceptions to this rule have been made. The hereditary right of peers to supporters is limited to the actual holders of the title. Some local authorities and institutions of standing have been granted supporters.

See also ARMS, COAT OF; HERALDRY.

Supreme Court of Judicature   *see* Judicature

Surebuttal   A response in Chancery proceedings from the defendant.

Surety   (i) A godparent.

(ii) A person pledged to give security for the performance of a bond, or for the proper carrying out of duties.

Surgeons   The early history of London surgeons is bound up with that of the Barber Surgeons' Company (*see* BARBERS). Elsewhere, surgeons were licensed by the church authorities (*see* ECCLESIASTICAL COURTS; ECCLESIASTICAL VISITATIONS).

In 1745, the surgeon members broke away from the barbers and formed a separate Company, which, in 1800, obtained a charter founding the College of Surgeons, now the Royal College. Even after this date, the profession of surgeon did not carry the same prestige as that of physician. The early records of the Barber Surgeons are at the Guildhall Library, London, and of the later period, at the college. New entrants to the profession were apprenticed to a surgeon, and details of their apprenticeship can be found among the records of the hospital in which they served.

Details of the College's fellows have been published in Plarr's *Lives of the Fellows of the Royal College of Surgeons*. Surgeons of the Royal Navy kept *Medical Journals*, which are at the Public Record Office, Kew, under reference ADM 101. The annual *Medical Directory* has given details of surgeons since 1845. *See also* APPRENTICES; DOCTORS; MEDICAL; PHYSICIANS.

Surnames   A surname is a name borne hereditarily by all members of a family in male-line descent. In Anglo-Saxon times people had personal names only, even when they were known by an additional 'to-name' (e.g. Edmund Ironside).

Hereditary surnames were first introduced into England by some of the leading followers of the Conqueror, and most were derived from the place-names of their estates, either in France or in England. They were usually inherited only by the eldest son. The custom of applying a man's surname to all his children began in the late twelfth century and spread slowly, with the manorial classes and the south of England leading the way. In 1267 is found the first legal recognition of an hereditary surname (de Cantebrigg). By 1400, three-quarters of the population are reckoned to have borne hereditary family names and the process was complete by about 1450. It is these names that make genealogy possible.

Surnames had five main origins: place-names, location of abode, occupations, nicknames and patronymics.

Place-name surnames, derived from towns and villages, indicated either where a person had come from (the majority), or of what place he was lord of the manor or most important resident. In early documents the names were prefaced by 'de' ('from' or 'of'). The large number of 'from' names is evidence of early family mobility.

Location-of-abode surnames were originally often prefaced by 'At' or 'Att' ('at the') — for example, Attwell — and include such names as Wood, Ford, Lane and Hill. It is not always possible to be sure to which of these two geographical groups (place-names and locations) a name belongs. A fourteenth-century person called Mayfield may have been so named because he came from the Sussex village of that name, or he may have himself lived beside a field of mayweed in any county. These two geographical groups together account for nearly half our surnames.

Occupation surnames are the second most common, and it is reckoned that most of them originated in medieval towns. Examples are Carter, Mercer, Hayward, Thatcher and Smith. Some were adopted from their form as written in Latin documents; for example, Faber (Smith). The reason for the prevalence of Smith today is that there were so many kinds of craftsmen in the Smith category — blacksmith, shoesmith, arrowsmith, swordsmith, goldsmith, silversmith, tinsmith, etc. A less immediately obvious type of occupation name is that formed from the personal name or even surname of an employer; e.g. Roberts (meaning Robert's man), or Abbot (abbot's man), or simply the employer's personal name of Luke, Thomas, etc., as mentioned under Patronymics, below.

Nicknames, the third most numerous class, arose from a custom especially prevalent among peasants, and so are thought to point to a village origin. They may be obviously descriptive (such as Short, Brown, Smart), or from a likeness to something else, often an animal (Bull, Byrd, Peacock).

Patronymics are derived from the personal name or occupation of a person's father or, more rarely, mother or other relative (e.g. Johnson, Fitzwalter, Smithson). Such personal names mentioned above as showing occupational origin may, alternatively, have originated as patronymics (e.g. the first Richards may have been either Richard's man or Richard's son).

It is never safe to draw a quick conclusion about the origin of a surname from its modern form. Corruption of sound and spelling has gone on for centuries, and is still continuing. Jerningham, which looks very like a place-name, is in fact a corruption of Jernegan, a personal name. To be reasonably sure of an origin, the line of descent of the family concerned must be traced back as far as possible, and its earliest-found spelling considered. Unrelated families of the same surnames may well trace back to different name-origin groups.

It should be remembered that all people of the same surname do not necessarily descend from a common ancestor, even when at an early date they are found inhabiting the same district.

The English Surname Survey has as its objects not merely the etymology of surnames, but their whole history from the period when hereditary names first appeared until about 1700. It publishers volumes dealing with the subject county by county, showing the differences which existed between various regions, social classes and types of surname, why some names became common while others remained rare, and how married women came to take the surname of their husbands. Volumes so far published cover West Yorkshire, Norfolk and Suffolk, Oxfordshire, Lancashire and Sussex. The Survey is under the direction of Mr R.A. McKinley, the Marc Fitch Research Fellow in English Surnames, in the Department of Local History at the University of Leicester.

For further reading, *A Dictionary of British Surnames* by P.H. Reaney (London, 1976), or *The Surnames of Scotland* by G.F. Black (New York, 1963), or *Welsh Surnames* by T.J. & P. Morgan (Cardiff, 1985), or *A Guide to Irish Surnames* by E. McLysaght (Dublin, 1964). Earlier works in this field have little value.

See CHANGE OF NAME.

Surrender A document extinguishing an owner's right in property. Conditional surrender was a mortgage of a manorial copyhold. If the copyholder failed to repay his loan, he would surrender his rights to the mortgagee, but the latter would need to apply to the lord of the manor for acceptance as his tenant.

Surrey Many of the county's northern parishes are now in the Greater London area. The county lies within the diocese of Winchester and the Province of Canterbury. Most of the registers of the 146 ancient parishes have been deposited either at the CRO at Guildford, the GLRO, the Guildhall Library or at the Minet Library. The SOG has transcripts of more than 100. Pallot's Marriage Index covers 39, mostly from 1790—1812. The Bishops' Transcripts are at the GLRO. The Marriage Licence records for the Archdeaconry of Surrey are at the GLRO but the few for the Peculiar Court of Croydon are at Lambeth Palace Library. The Minet Library has a large collection of original licences.

The Hundreds of Blackheath (First and Second Divisions), Brixton (Western and Eastern Divisions), Copthorne (First and Second Divisions), Effingham, Elmbridge (First and Second Divisions), Farnham, Godalming (First and Second Divisions), Godley, Kingston (First and Second Divisions), Reigate (First and Second Divisions), Tandridge, (First and Second Divisions), Wallington (First and Second Divisions), Woking (First and Second Divisions), Wotton, (First and Second Divisions), Guildford and Southwark Boroughs lie within its boundaries.

It has Epsom, Chertsey, Guildford, Farnham, Farnborough (later part of Hartley Wintney), Hambledon, Dorking, Reigate, Godstone, Croydon, Kingston and Richmond RDs/PLUs.

It fell within the Home Assize Circuit until 1876 and then the South Eastern Assize Circuit.

The East Surrey Family History Society publishes a quarterly journal and meets at Caterham, Croydon, Richmond, Southwark, Sutton and Wandsworth. The West Surrey Family History Society publishes *Root and Branch* quarterly and meets at Camberley, Dorking, Farnham, Guildford, Walton-on-Thames and Woking.

Surrey Record Office is at Kingston-upon-Thames as is the County Reference Library. Guildford Muniment Room and the Surrey Archaeological Society's Library are at Guildford and the Minet Library is in London SE5.

Pre 1858 Wills proved at the Archdeaconry and Commissary Courts of Surrey are at the GLRO. Those for the Peculiar Court of the Archbishop of Canterbury in the Deanery of Croydon are at Lambeth Palace Library but there is an index to them at the SOG library. Wills were also proved at the Consistory Court of Winchester and in the Prerogative Court of Canterbury. The West Surrey FHS has published an index to the Archdeaconry Court wills, 1752–1858.

The Surrey Archaeology Society and the Surrey Record Society (since 1916) have published a number of historical records. The Heralds' Visitation Pedigrees have been published for 1572, 1623 and 1662–1668.

Surrey Record Office publishes *Notes for family historians*. See also *National Index of Parish Registers*, vol. 4, Part 1 (1990).

Surrogate A deputy presiding over a court; for example, on behalf of an archdeacon.

Surveyor of Highways A local official whose responsibility it was to look after the upkeep of the roads and provide statute labour to maintain them. He was appointed from amongst the parishioners of a parish and received no wages. He was also known as a boonmaster, stonewarden, waymaster, wayman or waywarden.

Sussex The county lies within the diocese of Chichester and the Province of Canterbury. Most of the registers of the 305 ancient parishes have been deposited at the appropriate county record offices. The Guildhall Library, London has copies of all Sussex Registers and the SOG has transcripts of nearly 200. Pallot's Marriage Index covers 24, mostly from 1790–1812. The Bishops' Transcripts and the Marriage Licence records are at the West Sussex Record office.

The Rape of Arundel (Arundel, Avisford, Bury, Poling, Rotherbridge and West Easwrith hundreds), the Rape of Bramber (Brightford, Burbeach, East Easwrith, Fishergate, Patching, Singlecross, Steyning, Tarring, Tipnoak, West Grinstead, Windham and Ewhurst hundreds), the Rape of Chichester (Aldwick, Bosham, Box and Stockbridge, Dumpsford, Easebourne, Manhood, Westbourne and Singleton hundreds) the Rape of Hastings (Baldslow, Battle, Bexhill, Foxearle, Goldspur, Gostrow, Guestling, Hastings Borough and Cinque Port, Hawkesborough, Henhurst, Netherfield, Ninfield, Rye Cinque Port, Shoyswell, Staple and Winchelsea Cinque Port hundreds), the Rape of Lewes (Barcombe, Buttinghill, Dean, Fishergate, Holmstrow, Lewes, Poynings, Preston, Street, Swanborough, Whalesbone and Younsmere hundreds), the Rape of Pevensey (Alciston, Bishopstone, Burleigh Arches or Burarches, Danehill Horsted, Dill, Eastbourne, East Grinstead, Flexborough, Hartfield, Longbridge, Loxfield-Dorset or

Loxfield-Camden, Loxfield Pelham, Pevensey Lowey, Ringmer, Rotherfield, Rushmonden, Shiplake, Totnore and Willingdon hundreds) and Chichester City, Lewes Borough and Brighthelmstone or Brighton Town lie within its boundaries.

It has Rye, Hastings, Battle, Eastbourne, Ticehurst, Uckfield, East Grinstead, Cuckfield, Lewes, Brighton, Steyning, Horsham, Petworth, Thakeham, East Preston, Worthing, Westhampnett, Chichester, Midhurst and Westbourne RDs/PLUs.

It fell within the Home Assize Circuit until 1876 and then the South Eastern Assize Circuit.

The Sussex Family History Group publishes the *Sussex Family Historian* quarterly and meet at Chichester, Crawley, Hove and Worthing. The Family Roots Family History Society (Eastbourne and District) publish *Family Roots* quarterly and meet at Eastbourne. The Hastings and Rother Family History Society meet at Hastings Old Town and publish a quarterly journal.

East Sussex County Record office is at Lewes, West Sussex County Record office is at Chichester, Brighton Area Library, Hastings Area Library and Hove Area Library all hold records of the county. There is a Family History Centre at Worthing and another one at Crawley.

Pre 1858 Wills held at the West Sussex Record Office were proved at the Episcopal Consistory Court for the Archdeaconry of Chichester and the Peculiar Courts of the Dean of Chichester and the Deaneries of Pagham and Tarring. The East Sussex Record Office holds the wills proved at the Episcopal Consistory Court for the Archdeaconry of Lewes, the Peculiar Court for the Exempt Deanery of South Malling and the Exempt Jurisdiction of the Deanery of Battle. Wills could also be proved at the Prerogative Court of Canterbury.

The Sussex Record society has published many historical records of the county since 1902. The Heralds' Visitation Pedigrees have been published for 1570 and 1634.

See *How to trace the History of your family* (East Sussex Record Office, 1971) and *Genealogist's guide to the West Sussex Record Office* (1983). See also *National Index of Parish Registers*, vol. 4 (1980).

Sweating Sickness Once a common epidemic disease, swift in fatal effects. Its symptons began with cold shivers, giddiness, headache and pains in the neck and shoulders, but the cold soon turned to heat and sweating, followed by intense thirst, palpitations and delirium. Some sufferers died within three hours of its onset, but any who survived for twenty-four hours were considered safe. It was also known as the English disease.

Swedenborgians *see* New Jerusalemites

T

Table This article of furniture, when mentioned in inventories, is often simply a board laid on trestles, though the two constituents are sometimes listed separately as such. A 'joined table' was a carpentered one.

The word 'tables' was also used for the game of backgammon.

Tabular Pedigree *see* Family Tree

Tallage A medieval tax that could be levied by a feudal lord upon his villeins, by a borough upon its burgesses, and by the king upon towns and his demesne manors. As it became the practice to summon representatives of boroughs to Parliaments, which were called for the purpose of obtaining approval for subsidies to the king, the royal tallaging of towns fell out of use. Also, restrictions were laid on the freedom of lords and boroughs to levy tallage, by making it compulsory to obtain royal licences for the same.

Tallet A hay-loft over a stable.

Tally A stick notched and named to act as a record of an amount of money received. The stick was then split into two, from top to bottom; the payer received one half and the payee the other. In case of any dispute, the two halves had to 'tally'.

Tavern Originally a house in which wines could be consumed on the premises. The owner or occupant was known as a vintner, and, in London, would be a member of the Vintners' Company. However, by the seventeenth century taverns also served beer. In the same century, there was a shortage of minted coins for small change, so tavern keepers used to issue tokens to make up the deficiency, and these were accepted in payment later by the same tavern. The servers of drinks were called 'tipplers'. *See* TRADE TOKENS.

Taxation It is often thought that the man in the street will not appear in official records because he is insignificant. One place he is sure to occur is in any records to do with the collection of taxes. From the Danegeld to Income Tax the man in the street had to contribute to the Exchequer and Treasury. The records which cover these taxes are in the Public Record Office. Many of them are in Class E 179 where the names of individuals are recorded who are liable to pay some of these taxes, such as Hearth, Poll, Marriage, Window, and Land Taxes. Not all these taxes were payable at one and the same time and not all assessments list people by name.

Telephone Directories An incomplete collection of telephone directories from 1880 onward is housed at the British Telecom Archives and Historical Information Centre in Telephone House (Room G 09) 2–4 Temple Avenue, London EC4Y 0HL (tel: 071 822 1002) five minutes from Blackfriars Station. It is open to members of the public throughout the year Monday–Friday, 9.30 a.m.–4.30 p.m. The archives cover all aspects of British Telecom history from scientific advances and national events to histories of individual local exchanges and telephone pioneers. There is a search room and library facility but do make an appointment before you visit as not all items are on site. British Telecom also has a museum on Blackfriars Road.

Temporalities The income of monasteries and churches arising from purely secular sources, such as rents.
See also SPIRITUALITIES.

Tenant-in-Chief In the Middle Ages, this term denoted a person holding feudal land directly from the king. Often shown as a 'tenant in capite'. In most cases such a tenant would hold a number of manors, which he would subinfeud to subtenants (*see* SUBINFFUDATION).
See also MESNE LORD.

Tenement Originally a holding of land and buildings in manorial terms, or a fee farm held from a superior lord. Later, any holding of land and buildings. A roweless (roofless) tenement was one without any building on it.

Tenths and Fifteenths Lay Subsidies were originally levied as a certain fraction of a householder's movable goods, after allowing for a certain minimum and specified exempt goods. The fraction differed from subsidy to subsidy, but after 1294 two fractions were commonly indicated in the heading to the Subsidy Rolls from the practice of levying separate rates on urban

Casgraue

Passenham tw Denshanger

Yardley Gobion

Roade

Stoke Brewerne

ABOVE Part of a seventeenth-century Northamptonshire Lay Subsidy record shows the names of all parishioners except those too poor to be taxed; whether they were assessed on their lands (*in terris*), or on their goods (*in bonis*); the taxable value of their estate; and the tax levied. The most prosperous residents have their status mentioned, e.g. knight, esquire, gentleman. E 179/159/422, *Crown copyright, reproduced with the permission of the Controller of Her Majesty's Stationery Office.*

and rural areas, with the larger fraction bearing upon townspeople.

Tenure In feudal times, all land was held of a superior lord, in a series culminating in the king as sole absolute owner.

There were several forms of tenure: (i) Knight Service, i.e. a freeholding by military service when required, sometimes commuted to SCU-TAGE; (ii) Socage, a freeholding by payment of rent; (iii) Frankalmoign, i.e. by prayers only, a tenure for ecclesiastical bodies; (iv) Villeinage, by agricultural services rendered by untree tenants of a manor; (v) Serjeanty, by various unclassifiable services.

Knight Service was formally abolished in 1662, but already tenure by secular bodies had become either freehold, copyhold or leasehold. The first was a development from knight service and socage, the second from villeinage, and the third was by rent for a term of either years or lives. A freehold tenure passed at death either by fee tail (*see* ENTAIL) or by fee simple (*see* FEE).
See also MESNE LORD; TENANT-IN-CHIEF; TERRE TENANT.

Terre Tenant The lord of a manor or freeholder in actual occupation of the land, as distinct from his superior lord.
See also KNIGHT SERVICE.

Terrier A written description of a landed property by acreages and boundaries. Manorial estate records usually include a terrier of the estate. Glebe Terriers are those dealing with the land belonging to a parish incumbent's benefice. The boundaries are described by reference to the holders of adjacent lands.

Territorial Army (TA) The Territorial Force was formed by the amalgamation of the VOLUNTEERS and the YEOMANRY by Haldane's Reforms in 1908. Regiments of the TF played an important part in the First World War. It was renamed the Territorial Army in 1920 and again had an important role in World War II. Some records of Territorial regiments have been deposited in County Record Offices. War Diaries will be found for both World Wars in the PRO, Kew. *See also* ARMY; MILITIA.

Tertian Ague Malaria; strictly speaking, of the type in which the symptoms recurred at forty-eight hour intervals. It was formerly not uncommon in England, and before the discovery of quinine treatment in the seventeenth century it was often fatal.

Test Act This act was passed in 1672 from which time until its repeal in 1828, Roman Catholics were barred from political office. Jews were excluded until 1860.

Testament The testament originally dealt only with personal and leasehold property, not realty. *See also* WILL.

Testator The testator is the writer of a will.

Theatre *see* **Actors**

Time Immemorial A legal term meaning all time prior to the accession of Richard I in 1189. In 1291, it was laid down that a person who held a franchise without any charter of authority, but who could prove that he had possessed it from 'time whereof the memory of man runneth not the contrary' (or, more briefly, since 'time immemorial' or 'time out of mind'), could be granted a charter for that franchise.
See also QUO WARRANTO.

Tining An enclosure formed by a fencing of dead wood. A tine was a stake.

Tinker A mender of brass kettles, pans and other metalware. In country districts he was usually an itinerant worker.

Tippler A retailer or server of ale in a tavern or ale-house.

Tithe A tenth part of anything, but especially that of the profits and stock of parishioners, due, under Canon Law, to their incumbent for his support. It is in AD 747 that the tithe system in England is first mentioned, and throughout the Middle Ages every parishioner of a tithable parish was expected to contribute one-tenth of his crop, animal produce and other trade products, directly or indirectly, to the rector of the parish. Normally, the rector was the parish priest. He received the tithes directly, and stored them in his tithe barn; but sometimes the rectorship had been bestowed upon a local monastery, which received the tithe and accepted the responsibility of paying the stipend of a parish priest, who was called the vicar (i.e. *vicarius*, substitute).

An Act of 1391 obliged monastic rectors to devote part of their tithes to the poor of the parish. Tithes were of two kinds, Great and Small. The Great Tithes were those of corn, hay and wool; all others were Small. The usual custom was for a monastic rector to pass the Small

Tithes to the vicar. Tithes of produce from the ground were predial tithes; those from the profits of labour were personal tithes; those that were partly one and partly another (e.g. calves, lambs, chickens, dairy produce) were called mixed tithes.

At the Dissolution of the Monasteries in 1538, the rectorship of many parishes passed to the new lay owners of the former monastery lands.

In 1571, the bishops caused Glebe Terriers to be drawn up. These listed church lands and endowments in each parish, including tithes. New, up-to-date terriers were made from time to time, until about 1836.

In the seventeenth century, the numerous nonconformists resented having to pay tithes to Church of England clergy, and Quakers were forbidden by George Fox to pay them at all. At this time began the gradual commutation of tithes from payments in kind to cash payments, and this continued until 1836, effected by private Acts of Parliament. Also, tithes were often commuted when the lands of the parish were enclosed under *Inclosure Acts*.

The *Tithe Commutation Act*, 1836, enabled commutation to be made more easily by commissioners, in negotiation with the inhabitants of each parish, on the basis of a professional land valuation. The commissioners' decisions were called Tithe Awards. They are incorporated in schedules, arranged alphabetically under parish landowners, and show the occupiers, the acreage of each parcel of land, the annual money tithe payable, and a numerical reference to an accompanying largescale map of the parish. The map shows houses, boundaries, acreages, land-use and field names, and has cross-reference back to the schedule. These awards continued through half a century. Tithe Awards were drawn up in three copies. The one retained by the commissioners is now at the Public Record Office, Kew, in class IR 18; the one for the bishop is either at the dioceasn registry or the county record office; and the incumbent's copy may be still in the parish chest or deposited at the county record office. The *Return of all Tithes Commuted and Apportioned under the Acts for Commutation of Tithes* (British Sessional Papers, House of Commons, Vol. LXIV) lists all districts for which awards exist, and is on the shelves at the Public Record Office. Tithe Awards may be used to confirm residence or ownership of land in a parish, and to throw light on an ancestor's way of life.

For records of commutations down to 1836, *see* ACTS OF PARLIAMENT (Private). Tithe Books of the seventeenth and eighteenth centuries have been preserved in a few parishes, as also have miscel-laneous papers referring to tithe. These may be in church vestries or at the county record office. The records of ecclesiastical courts have mentions of enforcements of tithe payments. For nineteenth century Tithe Apportionments and Tithe Maps see class IR 29 and 30 at PRO, Kew. The Exchequer Court of Pleas, and other lay courts, also have cases of disputes between clergy and laity about tithes.

Further reading: *Alienated Tithes*, by H. Grove.

Tithing   (i) A group of men and boys, originally ten in number, who were held responsible to the manor court for its members' good conduct. Every male of the age of 12 and over was obliged to be in a tithing. The tithing list of the manor was checked at each View of Frankpledge, and all boys who had reached the eligible age were enrolled. The elected representative of the tithing was the Tithingman. He was responsible for presenting to the manor court all misdemeanours commited by members of families within his tithing.

(ii) Later the term came to mean a subdivision of a parish.

See also FRANKPLEDGE.

Title Deed   A legal document drawn up to transfer property and/or rights from one person to another. The vendor is always required to produce the deed by which he acquired the property, and also, until recently, the series of deeds by which the property passed through earlier hands, perhaps through hundreds of years. In 1925, the *Law of Property Act* made it unnecessary to pursue the title back further than thirty years, provided the previous transfer had taken place within that period. This Act rendered a huge number of ancient documents unnecessary for further legal use, so they flooded in to county and other record offices from owners, solicitors, bakers and mortgagees. As many properties had titles going back to the seventeenth century or earlier, the result has been that there are now several millions of these documents in local repositories. They describe the properties in varying detail, and, since 1840, include a plan. They mention vendors and purchasers, and sometimes give details of transactions carried out many years earlier, and of documents then in possession of other people. The records of the nineteenth and twentieth centuries are of three kinds: the 'abstract' of the title, which is a lawyer's summary looking back over the title position; the title deeds; and extraneous papers such as contracts for sale, auctioneers' catalogues, and so on.

The procedure by which property has changed hands has varied a number of times since the Middle Ages, so that title deeds had taken several different forms. Our present conveyance document dates from 1840.

A free leaflet, *Private Conveyances in the Public Record Office*, is available at the Public Record Office.

See also BARGAIN AND SALE; FEET OF FINES; LAND REGISTRY; LEASE AND RELEASE; RECOVERY ROLLS.

Toft   A plot of land on which a building stood, or, as the word is more often used, had formerly stood. In a manor, it had manorial Rights of Common attached to it.

Toleration Act   This Act of 1689 allowed Protestant dissenters, other than Unitarians, to engage in organised public worship as long as their meeting-places were registered and were all organisationally independent of one another. This resulted in the setting up of a large number of nonconformist congregations all over the country. Registration was carried out at the office of the diocesan or archidiaconal authority, or with Quarter Sessions. The information recorded included the name of the minister, the denomination of the group, the name of the person in whose house the meetings were held, and generally the names of several leading members as supporters or witnesses. From 1812, registration had to be effected at all three authorities. The records are at the country record offices or diocesan registries (*see* DIOCESE).

Tontine   A form of annuity in which the total amount of money to be shared each year in interest by the investors remained the same, so that as investors died each survivor received an increased amount, and the last survivor received the income from all the investments.

The first scheme was launched by the government as a means of raising money in 1693, and was repeated in 1773, 1775, 1777 and 1789. The second, third and fourth were nominally Irish schemes, but many English people invested in them. Other tontines were organised by corporate boroughs, e.g. Newcastle-upon-Tyne in 1797. It was the practice for the 'Subscriber' to invest on behalf of a small child, usually a relative (the nominee) since long-lasting membership was necessary to obtain the maximum benefit, though nominees were divided into classes according to their ages. The registers show the names and parishes of abode of the subscribers and nominees, and the ages, dates of death, and executors of the latter.

The records of the eighteenth-century government tontines are at the Public Record Office, Kew, in classes NDO 3 (for 1773, 1775 and 1777), and NDO 2 (for 1789). A printed list of the nominees of the 1693 scheme is in the British Library. Mr F.L. Leeson has issued *Guide to the Records of British State Tontines and Life Annuities of the 17th and 18th Centuries* (1968).

See also ANNUITIES.

Tory   A political epithet of abuse directed at the court party in the country and Parliament; first used in the reign of Charles II. It was derived from the Irish *toiridhe* (prounounced similarly), meaning a pursued person, a Catholic guerilla fighter against the English colonists, because the court party was then considered to be pro-Catholic. This was not true of all Tories, but all English Catholics supported the court party.

Tory is now the colloquial name for the Conservative and Unionist Party.

See also WHIG.

Tourn   A medieval court, often called the Sherriff's Tourn, held in each hundred twice a year before the sheriff or his deputy. Every freeholder in the hundred was required to be present, but certain important magnates, both lay and clerical, had exemption.

Tournament   A jousting contest between mounted men in armour. Such sporting functions were given encouragement by Edward III, and became popular social gatherings for the upper classes. Royal tournaments were arranged by the king's constable and marshal, and the proceedings included elaborate banquets. The colourful devices on the competitors' shields, surcoats and banners, and the caparisons of their horses, helped to develop the rules and art of heraldry, to disseminate knowledge of it and to popularise the bearing of arms among the gentry. The ladies present, although only spectators, played a part in the formalities as supporters of individual competitors. Provincial nobles, smaller gentry and chartered boroughs followed the king's lead in organising jousting contests. Their meetings attracted all the sideshows customary at fairs. Tournaments were the most striking manifestations of the Edwardian cult of chivalry.

Town   Down to the seventeenth century, this term was applied not only to towns but also to villages and hamlets.

Townland, The, Index *see* **Irish Genealogy**

Township A civil division of a parish for the levying of a separate Poor Rate. Each township had its own constable. An earlier term was 'Vill'.

Trade Tokens From time to time, and especially in the mid seventeenth century, a shortage of small change caused traders all over England to issue their own brass or copper tokens for small amounts, mostly farthings and half-pennies, but also some pennies. Depending upon the worth of the issuer's reputation, these would be acceptable at a number of establishments within his neighbourhood. A token usually showed, in addition to its value, the issuer's name or initials (and sometimes his wife's, too), his trade, and the street where his shop or tavern lay. A considerable list of such tokens is to be found in *Trade Tokens Issued in the 17th Century in England, Wales and Ireland*, by W. Boyne, revised by G.C. Williamson (in two volumes, 1889–92), but many other tokens have come to light since then.

Trade Tokens may sometimes be obtained through M. Barefoot, The Barn, Fore Street, Bovey Tracey, Totnes, Devon TO13 9AE.

Transcript An exact copy of the wording of an original document, not involving the imitating of its handwriting. Spelling, abbreviation, capitalisation and punctuation should be reproduced as closely as possible. During the process of transcribing, no mark should be made on the original document, no page-corner turned down, no finger run down a column of names, and no use made of the document as a pad on which to rest the paper for transcribing. The use of pencil, on which record repositories insist, requires the subsequent making of a fair copy in ink or typescript for family record purposes (*see* RECORD KEEPING), but the pencilled transcript should be kept for possible later checking. All transcripts should be headed with the name, reference number and location of the original. Any omissions should be indicated by dashes. Dots should be used only for transcribing omissions already made in published records and indicated there by dots.

Faded handwriting can often be made more legible by viewing it under ultra-violet light. Provision for this is available at many record offices.

When the transcriber is faced with a very long document of which he requires a copy in full, he can usually by-pass the pencil-copy stage by ordering a photocopy.

See also ABSTRACT.

Transportation In 1597, the *Vagrancy Act* empowered justices in Quarter Sessions to banish offenders to such parts beyond the seas as should be assigned by the Privy Council; and in 1619, 'a hundred dissolute persons' were transported to Virginia. A later Act of 1666 empowered justices to transport notorious thieves from Cumberland and Northumberland to America. From 1718 onward, many were sent to Maryland and Virginia, and some stayed as settlers when their sentences expired. For the period 1719–44 a list has been printed from the Public Record Office Treasury records.

Transportation to America was ended by the War of Independence in 1776, so an alternative place of exile had to be found. In March, 1787, nine transport ships took the 'First Fleet' from England to New South Wales. Their original destination was Botany Bay, but on arrival there the ships immediately left for Port Jackson, where Sydney now stands. Until 1813, some prisoners were also sent to Norfolk Island.

In 1822, a prison on Sarah (or Settlement) Island, Macquarie Harbour, Tasmania, was founded as a place of 'secondary' punishment for serious and regular offenders; and in 1825, the prison on Norfolk Island was re-opened for long-term convicts and 'secondary' punishment. In 1830, Port Arthur, on the Tasman Peninsula, was opened as Tasmania's main penal station, and shortly after, in 1834, Sarah Island prison was closed.

Transportation to New South Wales officially ceased in 1840 and to Tasmania in 1853. Between 1850 and 1868 convicts were transported to Western Australia. The last convict ship, *Hougoumont*, left London on the twelfth of October 1867.

Norfolk Island prison closed in 1835, and in 1871 transportation was finally abandoned. Port Arthur prison remained open for prisoners already there, but closed in 1877.

For information about the offences for which prisoners were convicted, reference should be made to the records of the Assizes and Quarter Sessions. Old Bailey Sessions papers are in the Guildhall Library and those of the Middlesex Sessions are at the Greater London Record Office. Sometimes information concerning a person convicted in the provinces will be found in the local newspaper's report of the session.

The records for transportation to America are sparse; refer to the PRO classes PC 1, PC 2, C 66, SP 35–37, SP 44, T 1 and T 53. Much more detail may be obtained for those transported to Australia. Records of criminals convicted at Quarter Sessions will be found in County Record Offices, those convicted at Assizes are in the Public Record Office, Chancery Lane. Hawkings (1987) has provided a very useful guide to these sources. Criminal Registers (HO 26 and HO 27) and Calendars of Prisoners (HO 16, HO 77, HO 130, HO 140, PCOM 2) provide details of the convict, his crime and his place of trial. The Assize proceedings will often provide indictments and depositions of evidence which may give a place of residence of the accused. (ASSI 1–73). A variety of goods exist for the convicts stay in gaol (HO 8, HO 23, HO 24, PCOM 2, E 370 and T 90) and on the prison hulks (HO 6–9, T 38, ADM 6 and PCOM 2). Details of transportation (HO 11, AO 3/291, TS 18 and PC 1/2715–8) may be supplemented by the logs of the Master and Surgeon of the transport (ADM 1, ADM 51–4, ADM 101, MT 32). Some information about a convict's life in Australia may be obtained from Convict Musters, Pardons and Tickets of Leave (HO 10) and the 1828 Census for New South Wales (HO 10/21–27) (edited and published by M.R. Sainty and K.A. Johnson). Further information may be extracted from Colonial Office papers (CO 201, CO 207, CO 386).

Further reading: Charles Bateson, *The Convict Ships, 1787–1868* (Sydney, 1988); David Hawkings, *Bound for Australia* (Phillimore, 1987); Wilfred Oldham, *Britain's Convicts to the Colonies* (Sydney, 1990).

Finding aids: Peter Coldham, *The Complete Book of Emigrants in Bondage, 1614–1775* (Baltimore, 1988); Molly Gillen, *The Founders of Australia* (Sydney, 1989); R.J. Ryan, *The Second Fleet Convicts* (Sydney, 1982); R.J. Ryan, *The Third Fleet Convicts* (Sydney, 1982).

Trespass, Writ of   A writ against a person who 'with force of arms and against the king's peace', carried off the plaintiff's goods, or did him some other injury.

Trinity House Petitions   These are petitions for pensions from Trinity House. The Brethren of Trinity House were established by Charter in 1514 to regulate pilotage and lighthouses. The petitions list the particulars of the family of the petitioner. All the original petitions (mainly 1780 –1854) are held by the Society of Genealogists which published a calendar of them in 1987.

Trinity Term   A law term beginning after Easter.

Trinodas Necessitas   Three feudal obligations attached to landholding; namely, military service, the maintenance of roads and bridges, and upkeep of castles.

Turbary   The right of manorial villein or copyholder to cut turf or other fuel.

Tyburn Ticket   A certificate issuable to a person who had captured a felon later found guilty. It gave him exemption from serving parochial office. It was transferable and often fetched a high price.

Tyne and Wear   A county formed in 1974 out of parts of NORTHUMBERLAND and DURHAM

Tything *see* **Tithing**

U

Unitarians   At the beginning of the eighteenth century, the Socinian belief in the divinity of God the Father, and in the humanity of Jesus Christ, began to permeate Presbyterian and Congregationalist assemblies. An attempt, in 1719, to make a belief in the Trinity the official Presbyterian doctrine failed to secure a majority vote, and, as a result, congregations all over the country became divided on the issue. In some, traditional Presbyterian doctrines prevailed and members holding Unitarian views had to set up new chapels; in other places it was a Unitarian majority who retained the chapel, but many such majorities still considered themselves Presbyterians. Much the same divisions occurred in Congregationalist chapels.

When nonconformist registers were deposited with the Registrar General in 1837–40 (now held at the Public Record Office, Chancery Lane, London, in classes RG 4, 5 and 8), most of the Unitarian records dating from 1762 were classed as Presbyterian. Nevertheless, in 1851 there were 229 Unitarian places of worship in England. Other records of the movement are at Unitarian Headquarters, 1, Essex Street, London WC2R 3HU. The Unitarian Historical Society publishes records, and the Secretary's address is 6 Ventnor Terrace, Edinburgh EH9 2BL.

For further reading, see D.J. Steel, *Sources for Noncomformist Genealogy and Family History*, vol. II of the *National Index of Parish Registers*, SOG (1973). *My Ancestors were English Presbyterians/ Unitarians*, Alan Ruston, SOG (1993).

United Brethren   Another term for Moravians.

Destination and date	Title	Editor
N. America 1538–1825	*A Bibliography of Ship Passenger Lists*	H. Lancour & Wolfe (1963)
America 1600–1700	*The Original Lists of Persons Emigrating to America*	J. C. Hotten (1880, 1968)
America 1607–1657	*Founders of Early American Families*	Meredith B. Colket (1975)
Plymouth 1620–3	*The English Ancestry of the Pilgrim Fathers*	C.E. Banks, (1929, 1968)
Boston & Bay Colony 1620–40	*The Planters of the Commonwealth*	C.E. Banks, (1967)
New England 1620–50	*Topographical Dictionary of 3885 English Emigrants*	C.E. Banks, (1937, 1963)
New England 1623–50	*Ancestral Roots of 60 Colonists who came to New England, 1623–50*	Weis
New England 1630	*The Winthrop Fleet*	C.E. Banks, (1930, 1968)
Maryland 1633–80	*The Early Settlers*	G. Skordas, (1968)
America 1635–7	*Two Early Passenger Lists*	E. Putnam, (1964)
New England 1637—9	*Three Registers of Passengers from Gt Yarmouth to Holland to New England*	C.B. Jewson, (1964), Norfolk Record Society 25

Destination and date	Title	Editor
America 1654–85	*Record of the First Settlers in N. America*	R. Hargreaves-Mawdsley (1929, 1931, 1967)
Pennsylvania prior to 1684	*Penn's Colony: Passengers and Ships*	W.L. Shepherd Jr. (1970)
America 1683–96	*Some Early Emigrants to America*	C.D.P. Nicholson (1965) *The Genealogists' Magazine*, Vol. 12
America 1682–92	*List of Emigrants to America*	J. Wareing, M. Ghirelli (1968)
America 1683–4	*Some Early Emigrants to America*	J. Wareing, *The Genealogists' Magazine*, Vol. 18, No. 5
America 1690–1811	*List of Emigrant Ministers*	G.G. Fothergill (1904, 1965)
New England before May 1692	*Genealogical Dictionary of the First Settlers*	J. Savage (1860–62, 1969)
America 1697–1707	*List of Emigrants to America from Liverpool*	Elizabeth French (1913, 1969)
New England 1700–75	*Immigrants to New England*	Ethel S. Bolton (1967)

Emigration to America and the West Indies:

United Empire Loyalists

The colonists who supported the Crown during the American Revolution were known as loyalists and most enlisted in military units to oppose the revolutionists. There was a general exodus from the States to Canada by 1780. About eighty per cent were from England, Ireland, Scotland and Germany and the majority of the rest from Wales, France and Holland. In 1789 the original loyalists and their descendants were awarded the title United Empire Loyalists. It is one of only two Canadian hereditary titles. Enquiries to The United Empire Loyalists Association of Canada, Dominion Headquarters, George Brown House, 50 Baldwin St, Toronto, Ontario M5T 1L4.

United Kingdom

The full term is the United Kingdom of Great Britain (England, Wales and Scotland) and Northern Ireland. To include Southern Ireland you need to use the term the British Isles.

United States Ancestry

To research ancestors in the United States you need to know when and where they arrived and, if possible, where they migrated to in America. In the sixteenth and seventeenth centuries colonists were lured to the States by trading companies and many settled to farm and produce tobacco for the European market. Many of them were sent to the States as bonded servants, or were transported there as

Destination and date	Title	Editor
America 1718–59	List of Emigrants	J. & M. Kaminkow (1964)
America & W. Indies 1727–31	Agreements to Serve in America and the West Indies	D. Galenson The Genealogists' Magazine, Vol. 19, No. 2
America before 1750	Immigrant Ancestors	F.A. Virkus (1963) Compendium of American Genealogy
Virginia in the Colonial Period	Some Emigrants	W.C. Stanard (1915, 1964)
America 1773–6	Emigrants from England	G. Fothergill (1913, 1964)
America 1773–6	Emigrants from England	P.W. Coldham (1990)
North Carolina 1774–5	Records of Emigrants from England & Scotland	A.R. Newsome (1963)
Connecticut	Catalogue of the First Puritan Settlers	R.R. Hinman (1846, 1968)
America	Early Emigrants from Liverpool	R. Sharpe France 1965, & Genealogists' Magazine 12 & 13
Georgia	List of the Early Settlers	E.M. & A.B. Saye 1949, 1967
Mass. Nantucket	Early Settlers	L.S. Hinchman (1934)
America	Bonded Passengers to America	Gen. Publ. Co.Inc. Baltimore
Mississippi, Natchez District	Early Inhabitants	N.E. Gillis (1963)
Missouri, Cape Girardeau County	A Belated Census	W.J. Gammon (1958) National Genealogical Soc. Quarterly (1967)
America 1819–20	Passenger Arrivals, Letter – from Secretary of State	
California	San Francisco Ship Passenger Lists	L.J. Rasmussen (1965)
USA & Canada 17–19th centuries	Passenger Immigration Lists Index and Supplement	P.W. Filby & M.K. Meyer (1981, 1982, 1985, 1987)
USA 19th century	Passage to America: history of emigrants from Great Britain & Ireland	Terry Coleman (1974)

the passenger lists and related records above have been published

an alternative to execution, but some decided to try the States as a refuge from religious persecution. The earliest settlers in New England (1640s) were non-conformist.

After the American War of Independence started, transportation to America was no longer possible and new venues had to be found for convicts, such as Australia. Emmigration to the States in the nineteenth century was prompted more by economic and political difficulties in the country of origin than the need to provide labour for the colonies.

The availability of basic records varies from State to State depending on when that State was settled and joined the Union. Although you can consult the census, military and passenger records at the National Archives in Washington D.C., most of your research will need to be done in State archives. Census records may also be found there and in the county courthouses or large libraries. Unless, of course, you go to the Genealogical Library in Salt Lake City where much research can be done in one place for the whole world using the International Genealogical Index and depending on whether the records you need have been filmed or not.

The records of Births and Deaths – Vital Records as they are called in the States – are not available centrally, as they are in the United Kingdom, but State Bureaux of Vital Records, in the Health Department of each State, hold them. However, they start at different times in each state – usually well after 1900. Marriage records are county records and may be found in the county courthouse. Church records may still be kept with the individual church but may also be found at the State and/or national denominational archive. Wills are found in county courthouses or in local probate offices.

Land records are another type of record often consulted by a family historian. Land grants were made to induce settlement and reward military service (bounty land). The distribution of land varied according to local legislation and conditions but records of grants can yield useful facts about an ancestor. Land was also bought from the government on credit and the resulting certificate, issued when the purchase was completed, tells you the purchaser's previous residence and what sort of property they had bought. Since most people owned land because it was readily available and inexpensive, nearly every adult male can be found in land records from early colonial settlement until well into the nineteenth century. When all land was owned by the British Crown land grants were made to the colonies from the Crown. Colonies transferred land to individuals up to the Revolutionary War. After independence both foreign powers and individual colonists (now states) transferred land to the federal government. Land transferred in this way became public domain. Land was also transferred from the federal government to individuals from 1785–1934. Federal land records are in the National Archives Land Management Bureau, Suitland, Maryland. Most useful to the genealogists, however, are the land transactions between individuals under the direction of the county or some other local government administration. These are to be found in county courthouse records.

The first census taken in the United States was in 1790 but the census does not contain full details of individuals until 1850. Not all current states were included from the beginning because they were not part of the Union at the time when the early censuses were taken. There are printed census indexes through 1860 for all states and soundex indexes to censuses 1880 onwards but these soundex indexes are not complete and it is possible to find people who are not indexed. In many states the 1870 census is not indexed yet. Almost all the 1890 census perished in a fire. The 1920 census is the latest one to be opened to the public as the closure period in the United States is 72 years.

It is essential to understand the development and settlement of the States to do research there. Areas where you suspect an ancestor lived may not have come under local jurisdiction at the time records were created and, therefore, you will not find them recorded in state and county records, but perhaps in territorial records. Relate the history of an area to the dates of an ancestor to discover what has been recorded about him.

Further reading: PRO Information Leaflet No. 23 *Records of the American and West Indian Colonies Before 1782*, No. 34 *Land Grants in America and American Loyalists' Claims*; P.W. Coldham, *Bonded Passengers to America*; P.W. Filby's numerous publications of passenger lists to the USA and Canada. Arlene Eackle and Johni Cerni, *The Source*, Ancestry Publications Inc., Salt Lake City, Utah (1984). Val Greenwood, *The Researcher's Guide to American Genealogy*, 2nd edn. Genealogical Publishing Company, Baltimore, Maryland, (1990).

The passenger lists and related records to emigration to America and the West Indies have been published, see list on pages 288–9.

Primary evidence can be obtained from the Colonial Office records at the Public Record Office (PRO), Kew. *Colonial Papers, General Series* (CO 1) relate to the period down to 1688. *Board of Trade Minutes* (CO 391) cover later years. Both are indexed in the 38 published volumes of *Calendar of State Papers; Colonial, America and West Indies*, covering 1574–1737. From then until 1782, there are the fourteen indexed volumes of the *Journals of the Commissions for Trade and Plantations*. Another Colonial Office source is *America and West Indies Original Correspondence* (CO 5), with separate classes (grouped under the names of the colonies) for *Original Correspondnce, Entry Books, Acts, Sessional Papers, Miscellanea*, etc. These are described in PRO *Lists and Indexes*, Vol. 36.

Privy Council records at the PRO contain petitions and letters of people going to America, which have been printed for the period 1613–1783, in *Acts of the Privy Council of England*, Vols 1 –5. The Exchequer records have Licences to Pass Beyond the Seas, listing those licences issued to travellers to New England, Maryland, Virginia and Barbados in the period 1634–77. Treasury Records (T 47), Vols 9–11, give details of emigrants during the period 1773–6, for which there is a card index. The information includes name, age, occupation, reason for emigration, last abode, date of departure and destination. The Poor Law Union Papers (MH 12) at the PRO list parish-assisted emigrants from 1834 onward. The Guildhall Library, London, has memoranda of indentured servants sent to the West in the period 1718–60. Mr F. Leeson, FSG, of 108 Sea

Lane, Ferring, Sussex BN12 5HB, has a name index to nearly one hundred published and unpublished sources for emigrants to America, Canada and the West Indies, 1600–1850.
See also CURRER-BRIGGS COLONIAL RECORDS INDEX *and* LICENCE TO PASS BEYOND THE SEAS.

Universalists Universalists believe that the whole of mankind will be saved. Towards the end of the eighteenth century this belief began to spread among Unitarians. Those who adopted it, called themselves Universal Dissenters which name was first adopted in Edinburgh. In the nineteenth century a few Universalist chapels were founded, one in London and the others mainly in the West country.

Universites Details of graduates of the two ancient English universites of Oxford and Cambridge, including their parentage, have been published as *Alumni Oxonienses* and *Alumni Cantabrigienses*. These, and also the annual calendars of Durham (1832), London (1836) and other universities and colleges, are available in the library of the Society of Genealogists. For the period of the Middle Ages, Dr A.B. Emden has produced biographical registers of both Oxford and Cambridge from a variety of sources, but they contain virtually no genealogical information.

Upholder (i) An undertaker.
(ii) An upholsterer.

Use In the late fifteenth century, the conveyance of land to trustees for the use of a third person, who was in fact often the transferer himself, created a 'use'. The transferer retained the right to change the user by a later deed expressing his wish, or will, in the matter; so, when he was dying he would issue his Last Will, naming the person to whom the land was to pass on his death, usually one of his younger sons, who would otherwise be excluded from it under the Common Law provision that land passed on death to the heir (i.e. the eldest son). An attempt was made to prevent the creation of uses, by the *Statute of Uses* of 1535–6, because it deprived the king and other lords of their fines and escheats, avoided forfeiture in cases of felony, and defeated the provisions of the statutes of MORT-MAIN. By the *Statute of Uses*, possession of the land passed direct to any person named as user, instead of to the trustees. However, because of the pressure of public opinion, the *Statute of Wills* of 1540 allowed land to be legally devised on the death of its holder. The joint deed known as the

Last Will and Testament came into existence as a consequence of this statute.

Utas *see* **Octave**

Uterine A uterine brother or sister is one born of the same mother but by a different father.

V

Valet In the late Middle Ages, the term for boys of the upper and middle classes who were put out to other families to learn manners and obedience. They carried out many household duties and were a kind of social apprentice. The modern use of the word for a man's personal servant derives from this custom.

Valor Ecclesiasticus In 1535, Parliament decreed an annual tax of one-tenth of the net income of all spiritual benefices. This necessitated a survey of church wealth. The resulting report has been published by the Record Commissioners in six volumes, but not all of the original report has survived. Details of Berkshire, Cambridgeshire, Essex, Hertfordshire, Northumberland, Rutland and parts of Middlesex and Yorkshire are missing, but the summaries of benefice incomes are complete. Some county record societies have published extracts translated from the original Latin.
See also SPIRITUALITIES; TEMPORALITIES.

Valuation Office Field Books Dated from 1910–1914, these books, known also as domesday books, have an entry for every property in England and Wales, arranged by civil parish within valuation districts. They describe the properties and name the owner and occupier and record the date of any recent sale. The PRO Information Leaflet No. 68 *Valuation Office Records created under the 1910 Finance Act* will tell you more about them. They are to be seen at the PRO, Kew in class IR 58.

Variant Among other uses, a term denoting an alternative spelling of a name.

Vassal A person who held land of a superior lord, and had sworn homage to him.

VCH *see* **Victoria History of the Counties of England**

Vellum The finer types of parchment, made from the younger and therefore more delicate skins of calves (the name means veal), and kids, or even of still-born or newly born calves and lambs. *See also* MEMBRANE.

Verso *see* **Recto**

Vert and Venison The forest laws (*see* FOREST) were professed to be for the protection of Vert and Venison. By 'Vert' was meant anything that bore green leaves and so afforded food and shelter for the game; 'Venison' meant all living beasts of the chase that provided food for man, and not, as today, solely the flesh of deer.

Vestry The governing body of a parish. The name was derived from the room in the church building in which its meetings were held. The assembly consisted of the incumbent (as chairman), the churchwardens and other respected householders of the parish, who were either co-opted by existing members ('close' or 'select' vestries) or elected by the parishioners ('open' vestries), according to the custom of the parish. Of these, there might be any number from a dozen in a country parish, to forty or more in a city.

During the sixteenth and seventeenth centuries, the meeting gradually took over the functions of the manor court as the basic unit of local government. In each parish the change proceeded at its own pace. The office of churchwarden was often filled by house-row, i.e. the occupiers of certain properties in turn. The vestry appointed the Constable and the Overseers of the Poor, and the Surveyor of the Highways, subject to the approval of the Justices of the Peace. Minutes were kept of all meetings, and the books containing these (where they survive) may be either still with the incumbent or deposited at the county record office or borough record office. They tell the history of the parish, the background of our ancestors' lives, and mention the names of many of the parishioners. They are supplemented by the account books of the Wardens, Overseers, Surveyor and Constable. The *Local Government Act* of 1894 transferred the civil functions of the parish to parish councils and parish meetings.

Vicar A parish incumbent. In the past he differed from the rector in that he did not receive the Great Tithes (*see* TITHE). These went to the rector, who may have been at a monastery, or even a layman, who then paid the vicar a salary. Since the commutation of tithes, the difference between a vicar and a rector has been purely historical.

Vicar General The deputy of an archbishop or bishop. He dealt mainly with administrative matters of the province or diocese, while the Official (or Official Principal) was responsible for judicial cases. The two posts could, however, be held by the same person.

Victoria History of the Counties of England Usually known as the Victoria County History, and abbreviated to VCH. This series of volumes was launched in 1899 by Mr (later Sir) Laurence Gomme and Mr Arthur Doubleday, a member of the publishing firm of Constable and Company, with a subsidy of £20,000 and a list of subscribers. Queen Victoria consented to be the first subscriber to the project.

In the first nine years, fifty volumes appeared, but the First World War put a stop to progress and in 1920 the publishing syndicate was put into liquidation. However, the second Lord Hambledon took over the burden of its finances and enabled work to continue until his death. The assets were then acquired by the editor, Dr W. Page, who in 1933 transferred them to the University of London. Since then the work has been in the charge of the Institute of Historical Research at that university. Page was succeeded as editor by Mr L.F. Salzman, and volumes continued to appear slowly. However, after the Second World War the university was able to increase the *History's* grant and enable a regular staff to continue the work. Mr P.B. Pugh became General Editor of the series. Local authorities now raise money to pay county editors to work on their individual volumes. The work, which has always been carried out through local committees, is divided into forty-five county sets, not exactly corresponding with the original county areas. Monmouthshire and Northumberland are excluded. A separate history of the latter has been published with the aid of material transferred by the VCH to the County History Committee. The current General Editor (1993) of the VCH is Mr C.R. Elrington.

Each county starts with one or more volumes devoted to general subjects, such as political, social and economic history, religious houses, archaeology and, originally, natural history. A portion is also devoted to a translation and commentary on the county's section of the *Domesday Book*. The remaining volumes are filled with the individual histories of the towns, parishes and hamlets of the county. The earliest published volumes naturally reflect the thoughts of their own period, in that they deal largely with the descent of manors and advowsons, and the edifices of the Established Church. Later volumes include accounts of nonconformity, education, the enclosure of the fields, parish government and the physical development of the towns and villages.

Though more than 150 volumes have appeared, and a number of county sets have been completed, many more volumes have yet to come. A great deal of information can be found in them on families of manorial status, often covering several generations. Unfortunately, many of the volumes are still unindexed. They are often to be found in the larger public reference libraries.

Victuallers Persons supplying food and drink to the public had to be licensed annually by the Quarter Sessions. The licence records are to be found at the county record office.

Vi et Armis Latin for 'By force and by Arms'; an expression sometimes found in legal pleading. It would be inserted in order to enable the case to be heard in a certain court; for example, the court of Star Chamber, the original jurisdication of which was over cases of violence. It was usually a complete fiction.

Vill A district or group of houses that bore a name. A parish might contain several vills. It is an early term, more or less synonymous with the later 'township' and is not used today.

Villein The term was introduced in Norman times to denote a tenant of manorial land who held by agricultural services. He was free in regard to everyone except his feudal lord, which meant that he was bound to his holding (*see* NATIVO HABENDO). Even there, he held his land hereditarily only by right of the custom of the manor. His work service was of two kinds: week work, i.e. regular agricultural work done each week; and boon work, which was extra work done at important stages in the agricultural year (e.g. harvest).

A villein could not bring a suit in the king's court, and could not marry without his lord's permission; but he had rights, even against his lord, which were protected by the manor court. His holding — a house and, usually, a garden plot — carried with it the right to a certain number of arable strips of land, the right to graze a certain number of beasts in the pasture, and the right to a certain crop of hay from the meadow. In addition to his work service, he paid

rent of assize (commutation of earlier rent in kind), which remained fixed for centuries in spite of the continuous fall in the value of money. At death, his chattels were forfeit to the lord but might be bought by his heir.

Villein status virtually died away by 1500, after which time the villeins' descendants became entirely free and held their land of the lord of the manor by copyhold.

Vintner The term was used for either a wine merchant, or the keeper of an inn or tavern who sold wine. There is a London livery company of Vintners.

Virgate Usually thirty acres of arable land scattered among the common field of a manor, but it varied from as little as ten acres to a many as eighty in some parts of the country. It was a quarter of a HIDE, and was also known as a 'yardland'. *See also* HIDE.

Viscount The title of the fourth rank in the peerage, between earl and baron. In Norman times the terms 'Viscounte', and the Latin *Vicecomes*, were applied to the sheriffs of the counties in their capacity of deputies to the earls (*Comes*), but that usage died out. The first creation of a Viscounty in the English peerage was in 1440, when John, Lord Beaumont, was made Viscount Beaumont with precedence over all barons. A viscount is spoken of as 'Lord So-and-So'.

Visitations *see* **Arms, Coat of** *and* **Ecclesiastical Visitations** *and* **under each county heading.**

Volunteer Forces The raising of volunteer regiments in the wake of popular concern was sanctioned by the government in 1859. They were linked to the new county regiments under the Cardwell Reforms of 1872 and amalgamated with the YEOMANRY to form the Territorial Force in 1908. This was renamed the TERRITORIAL ARMY in 1920. For much of their existence volunteer regiments were not paid from public funds and records of their activities are accordingly sparse. Such records as do exist will be found in County Record Offices and the PRO, Kew (WO 13, WO 44, HO 50–1, HO 88, PMG 13). *See also* MILITIA.

Wager of Law *see* **Lex**

Wales *see* **Welsh Genealogy**

Wales, National Library of   In addition to its printed books, this library, at Aberystwyth in the county of Dyfed, houses records essential to genealogists of Welsh families; e.g. wills and administrations before 1858, Bishops' Transcripts, manorial and legal documents, and some parish registers. It also contains records of the county of Herefordshire. Welsh records formerly at the Public Record Office have been transferred to Aberystwyth.

Walford's County Families *see* **County Families, Walford's**

Walloons *see* **Huguenots**

Waltham Forest Family History Society *see* **Essex**

Wapentake   A subdivision of a county in the area of the former Danelaw; a term originally used in the shires of Derby, Leicester, Lincoln, Nottingham and York, but now usually replaced by 'hundred'. The word derives from the Scandinavian for the clash of arms by which those assembled in the court of the district used to express their assent to its decisions.

Ward Money   A payment made by a medieval tenant as commutation of his service of castleguard. The money was used to pay a professional garrison.
See also SCUTAGE.

Wardmote   The assembly of citizens that administered the affairs of a city ward. Many early Wardmote Books of the City of London are kept at the Guildhall Library.
See also MOTE.

Wards   Wards are the administrative subdivisions of a borough but their boundaries do not coincide with the parishes in the borough.

Wards and Liveries, Court of   The Court for administering funds received by the king for his rights of wardship, marriage and livery. Land held of the king in chief, either by Knight Service or Grand Serjeanty, was subject to royal guardianship if it fell by inheritance to a son under 21 or a daughter under 14. The king had the right to the management and profits of it until either the minority ended or the ward was given in marriage during minority. He had also the right of choosing the spouse. In practice, the king sold his rights, usually to a near relative of the minor, and also the use of the land, not necessarily to the same person. A further payment, for livery, was due from the estate when the heir came of age. The business of wardship and marriage was transferred from Chancery to the newly instituted Court of Wards in 1540, to which liveries were added two years later.

The occurrence of a minority in a tenancy-in-chief would be revealed by the Inquisition Post Mortem, but often the family avoided the holding of any inquisition, so the Crown relied also on informers who were rewarded by being allowed a low price for the wardship, and the land to their own use. As wardship was avoided or terminated by marriage, the child of a sickly or elderly father tended to be married off as soon as possible, which could be at 12 for a girl and 14 for a boy. A ward who refused the bride or bridegroom found for him or her by the guardian, or who married someone without the guardian's consent, caused a fine to the estate. However, guardians were obliged to undertake not to 'disparage' their wards by marriage (i.e. not to marry them below their social status) and they were allowed an 'exhibition' by the Court for their maintenance and education. In the seventeenth century, Roman Catholics were excluded as guardians. Wardships often meant the ruin of a gentleman's estate, since the guardian had only a short-term interest in its exploitation. The system and the Court were abolished in 1646, and the abolition was confirmed at the Restoration in 1660. The records of the Court are at the Public Record Office, Chancery Lane, London, in classes WARDS 1–15.
See also PROOF OF AGE.

War Graves Commission, Commonwealth   The Commonwealth War Graves Commission will supply information on twentieth century grave locations, photographs of graves and memorials and copies of cemetery register entries. Enquires should be addressed to the Director-General, Commonwealth War Graves Commission, 2 Marlow Road, Maidenhead, Berkshire SL6 7DX.

War Memorials   Civic war memorials were erected by public subscription and are often to be found at a crossroads or in another prominent position. War memorials list the names of those who died in a particular war as far back as the Crimea. They are also to be found in schools, places of business, sports clubs, and inside churches and chapels, hospitals etc. A national inventory is currently being made of their whereabouts. At present names are not being indexed. All enquiries to the National Inventory of War Memorials, the Imperial War Museum, Lambeth Road, London SE1 6HZ.

Warrants A warrant is a written authority by a defendant enabling another person to represent him in court and allow judgement to be made or to suffer judgement by default.

Warranty The grantor of land to a sub-tenant by FEOFFMENT had the obligation to guarantee (warrant) his tenant's title against any possible counter-claims. So any relative with even a remote potential claim was called upon to associate himself with the grant by 'warranting' to the grantor. The same principle applied when land was transferred from one person to another by Final Concord (*see* RECOVERY ROLLS).
See also FEET OF FINES.

Warren, Right of Free The right to preserve and hunt in a stated area anything furred or feathered, except deer and boar.

Warwickshire The northwest area of the ancient county, including Birmingham and Coventry, is now in the new county of West Midlands. The county lies within Worcester and Lichfield dioceses and in the Province of Canterbury. The registers of virtually all of the 208 ancient parishes have been deposited, mostly at the CRO. The SOG has a number of copies. Pallot's Marriage Index covers 31, mostly from 1790—1812. The Bishops' Transcripts and the Marriage Licence records for Lichfield are at the Lichfield Joint Record office in Staffordshire. Those for Worcester are at the Hereford and Worcester Record Office, Herefordshire.

The Hundreds of Barlichway (Alcester, Henley, Snitterfield and Stratford Divisions), Hemlingford (Atherstone, Birmingham, Solihull and Tamworth Divisions), Kington (Brailes, Burton Dassett, Kington and Warwick Divisions), Knightlow (Kenilworth, Kirby, Rugby and Southam Divisions), and Birmingham Borough, Coventry, City and County of the City and Warwick Borough lie within its boundaries.

It has Birmingham, Aston, Meriden, Atherstone, Nuneaton, Foleshill, Coventry, Rugby, Solihull, Warwick, Stratford on Avon, Alcester,

Shipston on Stour and Southam RDs/PLUs.

It falls within the Midland Assize Circuit.

The Birmingham and Midland Society for Genealogy and Heraldry publishes *The Midland Ancestor* quarterly and has a branch at Kenilworth.

Record Repositories are at Warwickshire County Record Office in Warwick, Birmingham Reference Library, Shakespeare Birthplace Trust Record Office at Stratford-upon-Avon and Coventry City Record Office. There are Family History Centres at Coventry and Sutton Coldfield.

Pre 1858 wills held at the CRO were proved at the Manorial Courts of Barston, Knowle, Packwood, Temple Balsall and Baddesley Clinton. Those held at the Shakespeare Birthplace Trust Record Office were proved at the Peculiar Courts of Stratford-upon-Avon and Hampton Lucy. Those held at the Lichfield Joint Record Office were proved at the Dean and Chapter's Court of Lichfield and the Peculiar Courts of Bishop's Itchington, Merevale and Bishop's Tachbrook. Wills could also be proved at the Consistory Courts of Worcester and Lichfield and at the Prerogative Court of Canterbury.

The Dugdale Society has published a number of historical records of the county since 1921. The FHS has published *Tracing Your Ancestors in Warwickshire*, by F.C. Markwell. Heralds' Visitation Pedigrees have been published for 1619 and 1682–3.

Warwick County Record Office publishes *Tracing your family history*. See also *Tracing your ancestors in Warwickshire*, by F.C. Markwell (1983) and *National Index of Parish Registers*, vol. 5 (1966).

Waste The land of a manor, not devoted to arable, meadow or wood. It usually lay on the manorial boundaries and was used for pasture, and was gradually assarted (brought under cultivation) over the centuries. As the population increased during the twelfth and thirteenth centuries, some of the waste was used for new villages. In 1236, the *Statute of Merton* allowed the lord of a manor to enclose part of the waste, provided he left sufficient for the needs of his free tenants. As the waste decreased, many manors had to limit the number of beasts each tenant was allowed to graze on it. These limits were called 'stints' or 'gates'.
See also COMMON, RIGHTS OF.

Watch and Ward The patrolling of an area both by night (watch) and by day (ward), a duty to which citizens of towns were liable.

Waynage A villein's implements of work.

Waywarden Another name for the Surveyor of the Highways.

Weekwork This is the amount of work per week that was due from a tenant to a fuedal landlord without pay.

Welsh Ancestry Throughout the centuries, inhabitants of Great Britain have migrated between England and other parts of the United Kingdom, so that many a single line of descent comprises generations on both sides of a border. Wales has been administered with England since Tudor times, so that the standard modern genealogical sources are the same in both countries. However, research in Wales can be affected by some important differences.

First, many classes of records have not survived on the same scale as in England, and rarely have early starting dates. Secondly, settled surnames were not adopted in many parts of Wales until quite modern times, in some areas as late as the nineteenth century. As a result, one has to be aware of the possible survival of the patronymic naming system, whereby a man took his father's forename. For example, Dafydd ap (= son of) Morgan (eventually just David Morgan) could well have a son known as William David — and so on over successive generations. As settled surnames began to be taken, it was inevitable that many of these were based on a few popular forenames and, as a result, identifying a specific individual can often be quite difficult. Thirdly, Welsh, though not an official language until recently, has to be taken into account in the many areas where it will certainly appear in non-official documents. Finally, the greater incidence of nonconformity in Wales increases the probability that records will not be found in the Anglican parish registers, particularly of the nineteenth century.

All these factors must be borne in mind, but their significance varies greatly from area to area within Wales, so that it is important that the family historian takes background reading and local history seriously, and that Welsh ancestors are placed in their social, geographical and occupational context, not least to help distinguish them from others of the same name. Much greater emphasis has to be placed on oral and family evidence, and on sources which elsewhere may be considered minor, such as educational records, newspapers, chapel histories, etc. Some difficulties in civil registration are perhaps more likely to be resolved by application to local registrars than by using St. Catherine's House. However, access to the original registers is the only real answer to the problems of common Welsh names.

Time has to be spent in locating possible sources which will, again, vary according to area. The National Library of Wales has long been a repository for the major classes of document, but the county record offices have considerable collections in their own right, including original parish registers. As incumbents have been able to choose to deposit their records in either place, reference should be made to *Cofrestri Plwyf Cymru/The Parish Registers of Wales* as the standard work for locating parish registers. This also gives details of modern copies and the dates of bishops' transcripts. It is advisable to make enquiries, in advance, of both record offices and the National Library to establish whether their holdings meet a researcher's specific needs, and detailed guides and lists are available for this.

At the National Library of Wales, the following have particular interest for family historians: bishops' transcripts, probate records, parish and nonconformist records, tithe maps and schedules, newspapers, estate papers, legal records (including the records of the Courts of Great Sessions, unique to Wales), and printed and manuscript pedigrees. The National Library of Wales has made steady improvements in its facilities for family historians at every stage of their searches and has copies of OPCS civil registration indexes (1837–1983) on microfiche, as well as the International Genealogical Index (for England and Wales) and census returns (1841–1891) for the whole of Wales. In general, parish registers may now only be seen on microfilm at NLW.

County record offices have the same range of holdings as those of the English counties, including some of the parish registers, nonconformist records, estate papers, quarter sessions and education records.

The manuscript holdings of university libraries in Wales should not be forgotten, nor should the collections of Welsh material in the British Library and the College of Arms and Welsh records at the Public Record Office, London. Some county and borough libraries have significant genealogical collections (often including the census and the IGI) as well as valuable Local Studies Departments.

The only book that has yet been published on research into Welsh ancestry, has been produced by the Association of Family History Societies of Wales *Welsh Family History: a Guide to Research* AFHSW and FFHS, 1993. The Gibson Guides to the locations of main sources are, however, very useful in relation to Wales.

Six family history societies cover Wales: Clwyd, Dyfed, Glamorgan, Gwent, Gwynedd and Powys. Most have a number of local branches, and all meet regularly and publish journals containing articles on general Welsh sources and on sources specific to their own areas. The names and addresses of the secretaries of the Welsh societies may be obtained from the Federation of Family History Societies. Family historians who are unsure which society will best serve their interests may write for guidance to the Association of Family History Societies of Wales, c/o 18 Greenway Drive, Griffithstown, Pontypool, Gwent NP4 5AZ (postal enquiries only). When writing to either address, please enclose a stamped, self-addressed envelop or 3 IRCs.

All the Welsh family history societies have transcribing and indexing programmes, chiefly for parish registers, census and monumental inscriptions. Much progress has been made in recent years, with results deposited in record offices and libraries; some societies offer a postal research service. Monumental inscriptions are a particularly fruitful source in Wales: many will be in Welsh but the terms used are fairly standard. *Welsh Family History* provides a glossary of Welsh words and phrases used in monumental inscriptions and other family history sources.

Welsh local history societies, established long before the family history movement developed, have always reflected the traditional Welsh love of genealogy with articles on local families and their records.

The IGI for Wales is indexed both by surname and given name. It is subdivided by Welsh county (pre-1974) but Monmouthshire continues to be included with the English counties and it should not be overlooked. In the IGI, certain general assumptions have been made about the development of Welsh surnames which may mislead, and the Index suffers because its entries are rarely taken from parish registers but rely on the bishops' transcripts, which have late starting dates in a number of areas. The IGI contains all the entries from the great body of Welsh nonconformist registers which were deposited in the Public Record Office (class RG 4). However, it should be appreciated that the contents of other non-parochial registers — such as those at the National Library of Wales, in the county record offices, or still with the chapels or in private hands — are unlikely to be included in the IGI.

The Geneological Society of Utah has also produced a finding aid unique to Wales, in its micro-fiche series of *Abstracts and Indexes of Wills* proved in the Welsh consistory courts, copies of which are held by Welsh record offices and family history societies. This is an index to testators, witnesses and legatees in pre-1858 Welsh wills, but it is liable to errors both of transcription and interpretation, so that — as with the IGI — it is essential for users to check any information obtained from it against the original records.

Record Repositories:

The National Library of Wales, Aberystwyth, Dyfed SY23 3BU (tel: 0970 623816)

University College of Swansea Library, Singleton Park, Swansea SA2 8PP (tel: 0792 205678 Ext. 4044)

University College of North Wales Library, Bangor, Gwynedd LL57 2DG (tel: 0248 351151)

Clwyd (covering the pre-1974 counties of Denbighshire, and Flintshire):

Clwyd Record Office (Headquarters), The Old Rectory, Hawarden, Clwyd CH5 3NR (tel: 0244 532364)

Area Record Office, 46 Clwyd Street, Ruthin, Clwyd LL15 1HP (tel: 0824 703077)

Dyfed (Cardiganshire, Carmarthenshire, Pembrokeshire):

Carmarthenshire Record Office, County Hall, Carmarthen, Dyfed SA31 1JP (tel: 0267 233333).

Cardiganshire Record Office, Swyddfa'r Sir, Marine Terrace, Aberystwyth, Dyfed SY23 2DE (tel: 0970 617581).

Pembrokeshire Record Office, The Castle, Haverfordwest, Dyfed SA61 2EF (tel: 0437 763707).

Glamorgan

Glamorgan Archive Service, County Hall, Cathays Park, Cardiff CF1 3NE (tel: 0222 7820282).

West Glamorgan Area Record Office, County Hall, Oystermouth Road, Swansea SA1 3SN (tel: 0792 471589).

Gwent (Monmouthshire)

Gwent County Record Office, County Hall, Cwmbran, Gwent NP4 2XH (tel: 0633 832214)

Gwynedd (Anglesey, Caernarfonshire, Merionethshire)

Caernarfon Area Record Office, Victoria Dock, Caernarfon. Letters to be addressed to: County Offices, Shirehall Street, Caernarfon, Gwynedd LL55 1SH (tel: 0286 679095)

Anglesey Area Record Office, Shire Hall, Llangefni LL77 7TW (tel: 0248 750262).

Dolgellau Area Record Office, Cae Penarlâg, Dolgellau LL40 2YB (tel: 0341 422341).

Powys (Breconshire, Montgomeryshire, Radnorshire)
Archivist, County Archives Office, County Hall, Llandrindod Wells, Powys LD1 5LD (tel: 0597 826088).

Reference and Further Reading
Benwell, R.M. and G.A., *Interpreting the parish registers and Bishops' Transcripts for Anglesey and Llŷn*, and *Interpreting the census returns for rural Anglesey and Llŷn*, from *Anglesey Antiquarian Society Transactions* (1975, 1973)
The Dictionary of Welsh Biography down to 1940 (4th edn., ed. R.T. Jenkins, 1959)
McDonald, R.W., 'The Parish Registers of Wales', from *National Library of Wales Journal* (1976).
Morgan, P.J. and T.J., *Welsh Surnames* (University of Wales Press, 1985).
Morgan, P.J. and Thomas, D., *Wales: the Shaping of a Nation* (David & Charles, 1984).
Rowlands, J. et al. (ed), *Welsh Family History: A Guide to Research* (AFHSW/FFHS, 1993).
Williams, C.J. and Watts-Williams, J., *Cofrestri Plwyt Cymru/The Parish Registers of Wales* (National Library of Wales and Welsh County Archivists' Group, in association with the Society of Genealogists, 1985).
Genealogical Sources at the National Library of Wales (NLW).

Pre-parish register genealogy and pedigrees
Bartrum, P.C., *Welsh Genealogies, AD 300–1400* (1974) and *Welsh Genealogies, AD 1400–1500* (1983).
Clark, G.T. *Limbus Patriae Morganiae et Glamorganiae* (1886).
Dwnn, Lewys, *Heraldic Visitations of Wales* (ed. Meyrick, 1846).
Griffith, J.E., *Pedigrees of Anglesey and Carnarvonshire Families* (1914, reprinted as limited edition 1985).
Griffith, T.C., *Achau ac Ewyllysiau Teuluoedd De Sir Caernarfon* (1989) [Deals with pedigrees and wills of south Caernarfonshire families.]
Jones, Major Francis, 'An Approach to Welsh Genealogy', from *Transactions of the Honourable Society of Cymmrodorion* (1948).
Lloyd, J.Y.W., *History of Powys Fadog* (1881–87).
Nicholas, T., *The Annals and Antiquities of the Counties and County Families of Wales* (1872).
Siddons, M.P., *The Development of Welsh Heraldry*, vol.1 (NLW, Aberystwyth, 1991). vols.2 and 3 in preparation.
West Wales Historical Records, ed. Francis Green (14 vols. 1912–29).

Wesleyan Methodists *see* **Methodists**

West Midlands A county formed in 1974 out of parts of STAFFORDSHIRE, WARWICKSHIRE and WORCESTERSHIRE.

Westmorland Now part of the new county of Cumbria. The county lies within the dioceses of Carlisle and Chester both of which are in the Province of York. Most of the registers of the 68 ancient parishes have been deposited at the CRO, Kendal. The SOG has copies of 29. Pallot's Marriage Index covers 14, mostly from 1790–1812. The Bishops' Transcripts are at the CRO in Kendal but the Marriage Licence records are at the CRO in Carlisle.

The Wards of East, Kendal, Lonsdale and West lie within its boundaries.

It has East Ward, West Ward and Kendal RDs/PLUs.

It falls within the Northern Assize Circuit.

The Cumbria Family History Society publishes a quarterly newsletter and has a London Branch which meets at the SOG.

The Cumbria Record Office has branches at Carlisle, Barrow-in-Furness and Kendal. Records are also kept at the Kendal Public Library.

Pre 1858 Wills for the northeastern part of the county were proved in the Consistory Court of Carlise and are at the CRO in Carlisle. Those for the southwestern part of the county were proved in the Consistory Court of the Archdeaconry of Richmond (Western Deaneries) and are at the Lancashire CRO as also are the records of three Peculiar Courts. The southwestern part of the county lay in the Diocese of Chester and wills could be proved in the Consistory Court of Chester. Wills could also be proved in the Prerogative Courts of York and Canterbury.

The Cumberland and Westmorland Antiquarian and Archaeological Society has printed a number of historical records of the county since 1877. Heralds' Visitation Pedigrees have been published for 1664–5.

See also *Cumberland and Westmorland: a genealogical bibliography*, by S. Raymond (FFHS, 1993).

Weston-super-Mare Family History Society *see* **Somerset**

Wharfedale Family History Group *see* **Yorkshire**

Whig One of the great English political parties from the late seventeenth to early nineteenth century. It was the party that looked to the great landed nobles for leadership, in opposition to the Tories who looked to the king and the court.

There are several theories about the origin of the name. One is that it came from the Scottish word for whey, the favourite drink of the Scottish Covenanters, a party opposed to Charles I. Another is that it derived from the shortened form of 'Whiggamore' (a Scottish driver of horses), because in 1648 a group of drivers marched to Edinburgh to demonstrate against Charles I and the Duke of Hamilton. A third theory is that the term was one for a Scottish rustler of horses and cattle, a nickname of abuse already used for Presbyterians. Yet another version is that it was made up of the initials of 'We hope in God', the motto of the political club from which the party took its rise. As the name of the political party, the word came into use in 1679 in the heated opposition to the party's bill to exclude the Catholic Duke of York from the succession to the throne.

By the end of the Napoleonic Wars the growth of towns and industries gave rise to new radical ideas, to which those who opposed them gave the name 'Liberal', taken from revolutionary parties in France and Spain. The word, however, grew in respectability through the 1820s and was accepted to cover those views that both the more progressive Whigs and the Radicals could share, and in 1839 it became the official name of the erstwhile Whig Party.

Whip Land   Manorial land not marked out by permanent meres, but measured out before each year's ploughing by a whip's length.

Wife Selling   Until the end of the nineteenth century, it was a common misapprehension that a wife was her husband's chattel and so could be sold by him if he wished. The customary practice was to take her to a market-place, hang a halter round her neck — ones of ribbon and straw are mentioned — and put her up for auction. Recorded cases of wife sale occur from the late seventeenth century, though the custom is said to be much older. As the most usual source of evidence is the press, mentions become more numerous with the increase in the number of newspapers, but at least one parish register entry, a baptism in 1782 at Purleigh, Essex, is known to mention that the mother was a bought wife. The practice was not confined to country districts where ignorance of the law might be excused. In 1823, the French Chargé d'Affaires in London reported to his chief that the current price at Smithfield Market was 22 shillings, having recently doubled. Prices recorded from all over the country vary between 4 pence and £50. In 1891, the Lord Chancellor of the day ruled that no law gave a husband complete dominion over the pension of his wife, but further instances of wife-selling in the later 1890s are known. Further reading: *For better for worse: British marriage 1600 to the present*, by J.R. Gillis (1985).

Will   The document now properly known as a Last Will and Testament was originally two separate ones, each directing the disposal of a deceased person's property according to his wishes while living. The earliest that survive are from the Anglo-Saxon period.

The feudal system, which attained its full form after the Conquest, was based on obligations and rights arising out of the holding of land, so freehold lands and buildings, except those held in GAVELKIND and BURGESS TENURE, could not be allowed to be divided between a man's sons. They were not bequeathable, but descended by Common Law intact to a man's heir — his eldest son, if he had one. Copyhold land descended according to the custom of the manor. Only leaseholds could be bequeathed. However, the church, influenced by Roman law, made all other types of property (known as 'personalty') bequeathable, subject to one-third going to the widow and one-third to the children (*see* SUCCESSION, LAW OF).

The document describing the owner's wishes was called a Testament, and required to be granted probate by an ecclesiastical court. It was, therefore, the custom for the testator to start by bequeathing his soul to God and to give instructions as to where his body was to be buried. He then left legacies to his local church, and sometimes to the mother church (the cathedral of the diocese), and then to the poor. After this, he itemised legacies of his personal property to his family and friends. Besides appointing the executor or executors of the testament, an overseer would usually be nominated to whom the executor could refer in case of any difficulty or dispute.

In the fifteenth century, the law forbidding the devising of land was circumvented by conveying real estate, during life, to trustees known as the 'feofees to uses' ('to hold to the use of the owner's will'), and the document instructing the trustees was known as his will. This device was made illegal by the *Statute of Uses* in 1535–6; but such dissatisfaction was caused to small landowners who were thereby deprived of the means of providing adequately for their younger sons, that in 1540, by the *Statute of Wills*, owners in fee simple (*see* FEE) holding under tenure of SOCAGE were permitted to devise all, and those holding by Knight Service to devise two-thirds of their

In the Name of God Amen

I Richard Godfrey of the Inner Temple London Esquire do make this my last Will and Testament as followeth First I bequeath my Soul to my great Creator that gave it hoping through the merritts of his blessed Son my only Saviour to obtain Everlasting life my body I desire may be buryed in the same Grave with my Dear wife and Daughter in St Brides Church London frugally decently and at the discretion of my Executrix and whereas I am intitled by Law to dispose of the Guardianship of my Daughter ffranklyn Godfrey dureing her Infancy I doe hereby give and dispose thereof to my worthy good friend Thomas Bennett Esq one of the Masters in Chancery untill she arrives at the age of one and Twenty years intreating him to accept thereof

A typical religious preamble to a will of 1732. PROB 11, *Crown copyright: reproduced with the permission of the Controller of Her Majesty's Stationery Office.*

lands. This enabled the two documents to be combined under the title Last Will and testament, now popularly known as the Will. When a will does not mention, or seem to do justice to, the relict or eldest son, or devise any land, it must be remembered that they benefitted under the provisions of the Common Law. Until 1837, a will could be made by any male over the age of 14, and female over the age of 12. After that date, a testator had to be 21 or over. Until 1882, a married woman could make a will only with her husband's consent.

When a will cannot be found in the period shortly after a man's death, it is worth searching the period after the death of his widow, because if the husband left his wife a life interest in his estate, the will was sometimes not proved until after she had died. However, the neglect of an executor to prove a will — as well as other reasons — has sometimes resulted in many years elapsing between death and probate. So far the longest period known is seventy-six years.

Because wills usually mention several members of a family of two or three generations, they are one of the most valuable sources available to the genealogist. They are often the only means of establishing the truth, or otherwise, of a family tree hypothetically compiled from parish registers alone.

See also ENFEOFFMENT; PROBATE; ESTATE DUTY.

Williams's Library, Dr

Williams's Library, Dr Dr Daniel Williams (c. 1643–1716) was a Presbyterian minister of the type whose faith developed later into Unitarianism. He bequeathed his collection of books and manuscripts for public use, and in 1729 it was opened as a library in London, where it was known as 'The Dissenters' Library in Red Cross Street'. After several moves, it settled permanently in 1890 at 14 Gordon Square. It is administered by a Board of twenty-three trustees, most of whom are usually Unitarians. However, the books and records cover the history of English nonconformity generally.

All the books and pamphlets in the library, published between 1653 and 1800, have been catalogued under the title *Bibliography of Early Nonconformity*. The contents are listed under subject and author, and chronologically. There are histories of individual nonconformist churches and congregations, arranged under counties, *Transactions* of denominational historical societies, and the publications of national and other historical societies.

Collections made by other people have been donated to the library. One of the most useful genealogically is that of Roger Morrice (d.1701/2), compiled as material for a general history of Puritans which he never managed to write. It was taken over by John Evans (c.1680–1730), who added a list of dissenting congregations and ministers of the period 1715–29. It finally formed the basis of Daniel Neal's *History of the Puritans*. There is another list of congregations, with some histories, dated 1722, by Joseph Thompson, and also the Conventicle Returns of 1669, included in G. Lyon Turner's *Records of Nonconformity*.

As nonconformist ministers continued to neglect register-keeping, the Protestant Dissenting Deputies of the Three Denominations (Baptist, Presbyterian and Congregationalist) formed the General Register of Births and arranged with the trustees of Dr Williams's Library to house it, and for the librarian to act as Clerk. The Register began on 1 January, 1742/3. It was open not only to Londoners and nonconformists, but to any parents ready to sign a certificate of their child's birth and to spend 6 pence on registering a copy. Even some births abroad are included. The certificates, in addition to the usual details of parentage, gave the exact place of birth and the name of the mother's father.

Attempts were made to persuade ministers to register their baptisms, but with little success; the first volume contains only 36 entries. Another attempt to encourage use of the register was an offer to post-register without fee any birth before 1742. This brought in some from as early as 1713. However, by 1769 there were only 303 entries, so the Registry was made a repository for ministers to deposit their register books. In 1831, the original certificates were bound into books, and in 1837 the records were transferred to the Registrar General, along with most other nonconformist registers. They contain 48,975 entries of birth. Those for the final six months overlap those in the civil General Register. They have now passed from the Registrar General to the Public Record Office, Chancery Lane, London, where they are in group RG.

Dr Williams's Library has a handlist of manuscripts with an index of names; also a card index of Congregationalist ministers from *c.* 1640 until the present century. The library is open from 10 a.m. to 5 p.m. on Mondays, Wednesdays and Fridays, and from 10 a.m. to 6.30 p.m. on Tuesdays and Thursdays. Subscribers to the library can borrow books. Application to become a subscriber must be accompanied by the names of two guarantors.

Wiltshire The county lies within the Diocese of Salisbury and the Province of Canterbury. Most of the registers of the 318 ancient parishes have been deposited, nearly all at the CRO. The SOG has copies of more than 150. Pallot's Marriage Index covers 83, mostly from 1790–1812. The Bishops' Transcripts and the Marriage Licence Records are at the CRO.

The Hundreds of Alderbury, Amesbury, Bradford, Branch and Dole, Calne, Cawden and Cadworth, Chalk, Chippenham, North and South Damerham, Downton, Dunworth, Elstub and Everley, Frustfield, Hetyesbury, Highworth, Cricklade and Staple, Kingsbridge, Kinwardstone, Malmesbury, Melksham, Mere, Potterne and Cannings, Ramsbury, Selkey, Swanborough, Underditch, Warminster, Westbury, Whorwelsdown, Devizes and Marlborough Boroughs and New Sarum (Salisbury) City lie within its boundaries.

It has Highworth, Cricklade, Malmesbury, Chippenham, Calne, Marlborough, Devizes, Melksham, Bradford on Avon, Westbury, Warminster, Pewsey, Amesbury, Alderbury, Salisbury, Wilton, Tisbury and Mere RDs/PLUs.

It falls within the Western Assize Circuit.

The Wiltshire Family History Society publishes a quarterly journal and meets at Calne, Devizes, Malmesbury, Salisbury, Swindon and Trowbridge.

The County Record Office is at Trowbridge.

Pre 1858 wills proved in the Archdeaconry and Consistory Courts of Salisbury and the Archdeaconry Court of Wiltshire and a number of Peculiar Courts are nearly all at the CRO. Wills could also be proved in the Prerogative Court of Canterbury.

The Wiltshire Archaeological and Natural History Society has published local material since 1862; its record branch was founded in 1939. Heralds' Visitation Pedigrees have been printed for 1565, 1623 and 1677.

See *Sources for the history of a Wiltshire family* (Wiltshire Record Office), *Locations of documents for Wiltshire parishes*, by B.J. Carter (7 booklets), *National Index of Parish Registers*, vol. 8, Part 2 (1992) and *Wiltshire: a genealogical bibliography*, by S. Raymond (FFHS, 1993).

Window Tax In 1696, a new tax on houses replaced the Hearth Tax which had been ended a few years earlier. One of the chief objections to the latter had been that it could involve the intrusion of inspectors into private dwellings; in contrast, the window tax was assessed from outside. Nevertheless, it was objected to on the grounds that it was a tax on light and air.

The tax was imposed upon the occupiers, not the owners, and small dwellings whose occupants did not pay poor or church rate were exempt; others were charged on an increasing scale. All paid a basic 2 shillings; houses with between ten and twenty windows paid 8 shillings, and the rates for large houses were increased in 1709. Householders would reduce their totals by blocking-up non-essential windows, and for this reason (but mainly because the tax was badly administered) the total yield over the years fell instead of rising. In order to check this, the Act was repealed in 1747 and a new one passed. By this new Act, in addition to the basic tax, houses with ten to fourteen windows paid 6 pence per window; those with fifteen to nineteen paid 9 pence; and those with over twenty windows paid one shilling per window. At first the yield rose, but the blocking-up of windows was resumed, and during the 1750s and 1760s the tax was again increased. It was not until 1851 that it was abolished, although it was not strictly enforced at the end.

The records are among those of the Exchequer (E 181 for *Drafts of Receivers' Accounts*) at the Public Record Office, Chancery Lane, London. They provide the name and address of the tax payer, the number of windows in his house, and the amount paid in tax. See *Land and Window Tax Assessments*, by J.S.W. Gibson, M. Medlycott and Dennis Mills, FFHS 1993.

Witch In the Middle Ages, witchcraft was evil-doing by supernatural means, and it was only the evil act that attracted judicial punishment. If the deed or intent was not serious (such as causing the victim to break out into boils) the punishment was light, sometimes the stocks or pillory, or a penance in church. It was in the reign of Henry VIII that witchcraft — a compact with the devil to commit an evil act — first became a crime under the law; but the statute against it was repealed under Edward VI in 1547. However, an Act of 1563 made it a felony to invoke an evil spirit for any purpose, good or bad, and a spate of trials before the Assizes resulted in a number of hangings.

When James VI came to the throne, he wrote a book on Demonology, and his Act of 1604 made the penalties more severe and widened the scope of the law to include a mere convenant with an evil or wicked spirit, regardless of any deed or purpose. For evidence, the devil's mark (which might be a wart) was searched for, or the accused might be thrown, bound, into a stream to see whether she floated or sank. The 1604 Act caused a rise in the number of people put to death, after a decline since the early years of the previous statute; but thereafter numbers declined again to nothing at all, until the year 1645/6, when a failed lawyer, Matthew Hopkins, became active as a professional witch-finder and caused an epidemic of witch hysteria in the southeastern counties. After his death in 1646, the number of hangings again fell away sharply. The last person to be executed for the offence was hanged at Exeter in 1682, and in 1735 all Acts against witchcraft and sorcery were repealed. It has been estimated that about 500 people (nearly all of them women) suffered death by hanging for witchcraft in England. The evidence is to be found in the records of the Assizes.

Without that An obsolete expression meaning either 'except' or 'denying', according to the context. It was followed by a second 'that' for example, 'without that that he had ever seen . . .'. Often found in law suit depositions.

Woolwich and District Family History Society *see* **London and Middlesex**

Worcestershire The northern parishes of the ancient county are now in the county of West Midlands. The remainder is now part of the new county of Hereford and Worcester. The county lies within the dioceses of Hereford and Worcester, both of which are in the province of Canterbury. Some of the registers of the 209 ancient parishes have been deposited at the CRO. The SOG has a number of register copies. Pallot's Marriage Index covers 50, mostly from 1790–1812. The Bishops' Transcripts and the Marriage Licence Records are at the CRO.

The Hundreds of Blackenhurst (Upper and Lower Divisions), Doddingtree (Upper and Lower Divisions), Halfshire (Upper and Lower Divisions), Oswaldslow (Lower, Middle and Upper Divisions), Pershore (Lower and Upper Divisions), Droitwich, Evesham and Kidderminster Boroughs and Worcester City lie within its boundaries.

It has Stourbridge, Kidderminster, Tenbury, Martley, Worcester, Upton-on-Severn, Evesham, Pershore, Droitwich, Bromsgrove and King's Norton RDs/PLUs.

It falls within the Oxford Assizes Circuit.

The Birmingham and Midland Society for Genealogy and Heraldry publishes the *Midland Ancestor* quarterly and has branches at Worcester, Stourbridge and Bromsgrove. The Redditch Family History Society publishes a thrice-yearly journal and meets in Redditch.

There are record offices at Worcester; The Hereford and Worcester Record Office (two branches) and the City of Worcester Records at the Guildhall. There is a Family History Centre at Redditch.

Pre 1858 Wills proved in the Consistory Court of Worcester and a number of Peculiar Courts are at the CRO. Wills in the west of the county were proved in the Episcopal Consistory Court of Hereford and are at Hereford Record Office. Wills could also be proved in the Prerogative Court of Canterbury. The SOG has an index of the Consistory Court of Worcester wills.

The Worcestershire Historical Society has published local records since 1893. Heralds' Visitation Pedigrees have been published for 1533, 1569, 1634 and 1682–3.

See also the CRO's *Genealogical resources in Worcestershire* and *National Index of Parish Registers*, vol. 5 (1966).

Workhouses Some parochial 'convenient houses of dwelling' for the impotent poor were set up as a result of the *Poor Law Act* of 1601, but workhouses became numerous only in the eighteenth century. An Act of 1723 enabled parishes to set them up either singly or in combination with neighbouring parishes. Generally, they were so ill-administered that they were said to be either 'houses of terror' or 'houses of debauchery'. *Gilbert's Act*, 1782, forbade the admission of able-bodied paupers. In 1834, under the *Poor Law Amendment Act*, newly constituted Poor Law Unions took over responsibility for the poor from the parishes, and each union was obliged to set up a workhouse. Except in serious cases, relief to the poor was confined to those who would enter the workhouse.

The records of these institutions, and the Minute Books, are at the county and borough record offices.
See also GUARDIANS OF THE POOR.

Writ In law, an instrument in writing (under seal) issued by a court, commanding or forbidding the performance of some act by the person to whom it was addressed; e.g. a Writ of Mandamus, Writ of Summons. In civil cases, an 'original' writ was issued by the Court of Chancery, under the great seal, summoning the defendant to appear. This initiated the case. The term itself is thought to derive from the fact that even in early times, when proceedings at law were conducted orally, these instructions had always been in writing.

Writer Until the nineteenth century this was the term for a commercial clerk, much of whose time, before the age of the typewriter and carbon paper, was taken up in writing out and copying. The term is still used in the Royal Navy.

Writ of Capias *see* **Outlawry**

Writ of de Libertate Probanda *see* **Libertate Probanda, Writ of de**

Writ of Exigend *see* **Outlawry**

Y

Yardland An area of about thirty acres.

Yeoman In the Plantagenet period, the word meant a knight's servant or retainer. There were also Yeomen of the King's Chamber, who were minor court officials under the Chamberlain. At that period, there was a class of freemen called Franklins, and under the Tudors the name of yeoman gradually became attached to them. Broadly speaking, they constituted a stratum of cultivators of the soil, either freeholders or tenants, who differed from the minor gentry more by their way of life than by any economic category. The yeoman would put his own hand to work that the gentleman would employ servants to do, and his wife likewise; but many a young man of gentle and even armigerous family was styled yeoman, as long as he lived like one (i.e. until he inherited his father's estate).

Below the yeoman class came the equally ill-defined stratum of HUSBANDMAN, whose landholding was normally smaller.
See also CLASS, SOCIAL.

Yeomanry The yeomanry were volunteer cavalry regiments which were liable for home service only. They were amalgamated with the VOLUNTEERS in 1908 to form the Territorial Force. The name was retained in the title of a number of regiments after the amalgamation. Records of Yeomanry regiments will be found in County Record Offices and the PRO, Kew (WO 13, WO 23, WO 44, HO 50–1, HO 88, PMG 13). *See also* MILITIA.

Yorkshire The ancient county is now divided into the new counties of North, West and South Yorkshire, Cleveland and Humberside. The county is divided between the dioceses of Chester and York and both are in the Province of York. Most of the registers of the ancient county have been deposited, mainly at the record offices of the new counties. The SOG has transcripts of nearly 300. Boyd's Marriage Index covers 174. Pallot's Marriage Index covers 93, mostly from 1790–1812. The Bishops' Transcripts and Marriage Licence records are at the Borthwick Institute except for the Bishops' Transcripts for the parishes in the northwest of the county which were in the Archdeaconry of Richmond and are held at Leeds Archives Department.

The Wapentakes of the East Riding are Buckross, Dickering, Harthill (Bainton-Beacon, Holme-Beacon, Hunsley-Beacon and Wilton-Beacon Divisions), Holderness (Middle, North and South, Divisions), Howdenshire, Ouse and Derwent, Beverley Borough and Liberty and Kingston-upon-Hull Town and county of the town. The Wapentakes of the North Riding are Allertonshire, Birdforth, Bulmer, East and West

Gilling, Hallikeld, East and West Hang, Langbaurgh Liberty (East and West Divisions), Pickering-Lythe, Ryedale, Whitby Strand and Richmond and Scarborough Boroughs. The Wapentakes of the West Riding are Agbrigg (Lower and Upper Divisions), Barkstone-Ash (Lower and Upper Divisions), Claro (Lower and Upper Divisions), Morley, Osgoldcross (Lower and Upper Divisions), Skyrack (Lower and Upper Divisions), Staincliff and Ewcross (East and West Divisions), Staincross, Strafforth and Tickhill (North and South Divisions), Doncaster Borough and Soke, Leeds Borough and Town, Ripon Liberty and York City and York Ainsty.

The RDs/PLUs of the East Riding are York, Pocklington, Howden, Beverley, Sculcoates, Hull, Patrington, Skirlaugh, Driffield and Bridlington. The RDs/PLUs of the North Riding are Scarborough, Malton, Easingwold, Thirsk, Heldsley, Pickering, Whitby, Guisborough (later Middlesbrough), Stokesley, Northallerton, Bedale, Leyburn, Askrigg, Reeth and Richmond. The RDs/PLUs of the West Riding are Sedbergh, Settle, Skipton, Pateley Bridge, Ripon, Great Ouseburn, Knaresborough, Wetherby, Kirk Deighton, Otley, Wharfedale, Keighley, Todmorden, Saddleworth, Huddersfield, Halifax, Bradford, Hunslet, Holbeck, Bramley, Leeds, Dewsbury, Wakefield, Pontefract, Hemsworth, Barnsley, Wortley, Ecclesall Bierlow, Sheffield, Rotherham, Doncaster, Thorne, Goole, Selby and Tadcaster.

It falls within the Northern Assize Circuit until 1863 and then the Midland until 1876, and from 1876 the North Eastern Assize Circuit.

The local Family History Societies are: Yorkshire Archaeological Society, Family History and Population Studies Section who publish *Yorkshire Family Historian* twice-yearly and meet at Leeds, City of York and District Family History Society publishes a thrice-yearly newsletter, East Yorkshire Family History Society publish *The Banyan Tree* quarterly and meet at Beverley, Hull and Scarborough, Barnsley Family History Society publish a quarterly journal, Bradford Family History Society publish *The Bod-Kin* quarterly, Calderdale Family History Society publish *The Scrivener Newsletter* monthly, Doncaster and District Family History Society publish *Doncaster Ancestor* quarterly and meet at Doncaster, Pontefract and Snaith, Huddersfield and District Family History Society publish a quarterly journal, Keighley and District Family History Society publish a quarterly journal, Ripon, Harrogate and District Family History Society publish *The Ripon Historian* quarterly and hold meetings at

Harrogate and Ripon, Sheffield and District Family History Society publish *The Flowing Stream* quarterly and have a branch at Rotherham and Wharfdale Family History Society publish a quarterly newsletter.

Record Repositories: Borthwick Institute of Historical Research and York City Archives Department are both in York; North Yorkshire County Record Office, Northallerton; West Yorkshire and Diocese of Wakefield Record Office and Wakefield Metropolitan District Archives; South Yorkshire Record Office, Sheffield; Cleveland County Archives Department, Middlesbrough, Humberside County Record Office, Beverley, South Humberside Area Record Office, Grimsby; Kingston-upon-Hull City Record Office; Doncaster Archives Department; Calderdale Metropolitan Borough Archives in Halifax; Sheffield City Archives Department; Leeds Archives Department and Bradford Central Library Archives Department. There are Family History Centres at Huddersfield, Hull, Leeds, Sheffield and York.

Pre 1858 Wills. There were many Yorkshire probate courts. At the Borthwick Institute there is a Deanery Book listing every parish, and showing in which of the twenty-five deaneries and numerous Peculiars each one lay. The search can then be directed to the relevant repository; i.e. either the Borthwick Institute, Leeds Archives Department, The Dean and Chapter of York Library, Hull Record Office, or Bradford Record Office. Wills could also be proved in both the Prerogative Courts of York and Canterbury. The SOG has indexes to a number of Yorkshire courts.

Memorial Inscriptions. The SOG has transcripts from about 100 churches.

Heralds' Visitation Pedigrees have been published for 1530, 1584–5, 1612 and 1665–6.

The Yorkshire Archaeological Society has published a Record Series containing will indexes and other material since 1885. Its Extra Series has, since 1914, published Yorkshire charters. There is also the Bradford Historical and Antiquarian Society, and the Thoresby Society which is particularly concerned with Leeds (from 1891). See also *Guide to Genealogical Sources in the Borthwick Institute of Historical Research*, by C.C. Webb (1988) and *A Guide to Parish Records in the Borthwick Institute of Historical Research*, by C.C. Webb (1987). See also *Family History in South Yorkshire: a Guide to Sources* (South Yorkshire Libraries), *Guide to the South Humberside Area Archive Office* (1993) and *An Introduction to Sources of Genealogy . . . in Kingston upon Hull* (1985).